THE POLITICS OF THE FIRST WORLD WAR
A COURSE IN GAME THEORY AND INTERNATIONAL SECURITY

The Great War is an immense, confusing, and overwhelming historical conflict – the ideal case study for teaching game theory and international security.

Using thirteen historical puzzles, from the outbreak of the war and the stability of attrition, to unrestricted submarine warfare and American entry into the war, this book provides students with a rigorous yet accessible training in game theory. Each chapter shows, through guided exercises, how game-theoretical models can explain otherwise challenging strategic puzzles, shedding light on the role of individual leaders in world politics, cooperation between coalition partners, the effectiveness of international law, the termination of conflict, and the challenges of making peace. Its analytical history the First World War also surveys cutting-edge political science research on international relations and the causes of war.

Written by a leading game theorist known for his expertise regarding the war, this textbook includes useful student features such as chapter key terms, contemporary maps, a timeline of events, a list of key characters, and additional end-of-chapter game-theoretic exercises.

Scott Wolford is Associate Professor at The University of Texas at Austin. He published his first book, *The Politics of Military Coalitions*, in 2015, and has published articles in the *American Journal of Political Science*, *the Journal of Politics*, *International Organization*, the *Journal of Conflict Resolution*, and *International Studies Quarterly*, among others. He is a fellow of the Frank C. Irwin Chair in Government (2011–18), a recipient of the Best Paper in International Relations Award from the Midwest Political Science Association (2009), and a former associate editor for *International Studies Quarterly*.

D1528353

THE POLITICS OF

The First World War

A Course in Game Theory and International Security

Scott Wolford

The University of Texas at Austin

CAMBRIDGE
UNIVERSITY PRESS

University Printing House, Cambridge CB2 8BS, United Kingdom

One Liberty Plaza, 20th Floor, New York, NY 10006, USA

477 Williamstown Road, Port Melbourne, VIC 3207, Australia

314–321, 3rd Floor, Plot 3, Splendor Forum, Jasola District Centre, New Delhi – 110025, India

79 Anson Road, #06–04/06, Singapore 079906

Cambridge University Press is part of the University of Cambridge.

It furthers the University's mission by disseminating knowledge in the pursuit of education, learning, and research at the highest international levels of excellence.

www.cambridge.org
Information on this title: www.cambridge.org/9781108426015
DOI: 10.1017/9781108349956

© Scott Wolford 2019

First published 2019

Printed in the United Kingdom by TJ International Ltd. Padstow Cornwall 2019

A catalogue record for this publication is available from the British Library.

Library of Congress Cataloging-in-Publication Data
Names: Wolford, Scott, author.
Title: The politics of the First World War : a course in game theory and
    international security / Scott Wolford, University of Texas, Austin.
Description: Cambridge ; New York, NY : Cambridge University Press, [2019] |
    Includes bibliographical references and index.
Identifiers: LCCN 2018035966 | ISBN 9781108426015 (hardback) |
    ISBN 9781108444378 (pbk.)
Subjects: LCSH: World War, 1914–1918—Political aspects. | Game theory—Case
    studies. | Security, International–Case studies.
Classification: LCC D523 .W656 2019 | DDC 940.3/1—dc23
LC record available at https://lccn.loc.gov/2018035966

ISBN 978-1-108-42601-5 Hardback
ISBN 978-1-108-44437-8 Paperback

Brief Contents

Contents

Figures

Maps

Preface

For years, I'd been frustrated at the lack of options for teaching undergraduate international security in the way that I conduct my own research on the topic: through the construction and analysis of game-theoretic models. Students could take a game theory course, and they could take numerous courses on international security, but despite game-theoretic work's prominence in recent theoretical advances in the field, no course taught both in an integrated way. Students taking my security course, for example, got an unrepresentative look at the why and the how of social-scientific inquiry. That's especially problematic for those who go on to grad school and learn that what they consumed as an undergraduate was produced with methods that are basically alien to them. So I took advantage of the centennial of the First World War to try something new, using history to teach both international security *and* game theory. I designed a course that followed events in the war in "real time," tracking as closely as possible to the day, week, or month the events in the war one hundred years later, using the tools of game theory to understand one of the most consequential conflicts in world history. Then, I structured lectures around identifying and resolving puzzles raised by the war, beginning with a question – e.g., if strategies of attrition were so futile, why were they so stable? – and peeling back its layers analytically before settling on a simple theoretical model that can provide insight into the why and how of the outbreak, course, and end of the first truly global war. I decided that my students would encounter the historical-empirical record by focusing on a single conflict, get puzzled by it, and then learn how to resolve those puzzles in the classroom. Students, I hoped, would learn the game-theoretic analysis of politics by doing it and by seeing it done; they'd learn both game theory and the state of the art in the study of international security, all through the endlessly fascinating lens of the First World War. Engaging history in a political science course can be challenging, just like teaching game theory in a political science course; but it turns out that combining these two goals makes each task easier. After separating the wheat from the chaff (I hope), this volume collects those lectures, presenting what I believe is a unique course on the First World War, modern theories of international relations, and the development and use of game-theoretic models to analyze politics.

The "Real-Time" Approach

This book's most distinctive feature is its focus on analyzing politics in "real time." Thinking in real time means taking seriously the options and information available to the characters in our story when they acted: the possible futures they envisioned, feared, and tried to shape, free of the decades of accumulated hindsight that can blind us to the very real, contingent, often agonizing choices that defined the outbreak, course, prosecution, and termination of the First World War. Decisions that look inevitable in hindsight look very different when studied and explained in real time, when we as analysts try to see what the characters in our story saw, looking into what was for them an uncertain, often frightening future. The real-time approach also works well as an organizing device for studying the First World War in particular. This book works from a simple temporal narrative, identifying and solving puzzles about events before, during, and after the war that illustrate both important ideas in the study of international politics and the concepts of game-theoretic analysis, the second primary feature of this book's approach. Each chapter poses questions from the vantage of the early twenty-first century, but it answers them by building and analyzing models in the present tense of the early twentieth century.

Thanks to the book's treatment of a single, sprawling, yet popularly unfamiliar event, of which the First World War is an excellent example, students can make use of a shared historical context that's strikingly distant from popular (and partisan) memory. This has two benefits. First, the Great War touches on almost everything that we'd like to cover when we teach international security, and even those trappings of the contemporary world that it lacks (e.g., nuclear weapons) can be explored in the same theoretical frameworks introduced here. Second, focusing on a single historical event with common characters, dynamics, and issues throughout the book makes it easy to spend time teaching students how to use an important – if frustratingly absent from undergraduate training – tool in the study of political science: game theory. Game-theoretic models are uniquely well suited to the real-time approach, because they force us to state clearly our assumptions about the actors in our theories, their goals, the actions available to them, and how those actions add up to produce outcomes, including war and peace, alliances and alignments, cooperation and rivalry, international law, and the art of diplomacy. Game-theoretic work is often inaccessible without the requisite training, and this book resolves that dilemma by simply providing the training, combining the goal of explaining the politics of the First World War with a course in how to build, analyze, and interpret game-theoretic models with the express goal of explanation.

Each chapter, from those focused on introducing game-theoretic tools to those dedicated to specific historical events, poses a puzzle like the following:

- Why do countries use war to resolve disagreements when there are less destructive options available?
- Why did the Ottoman Empire abandon an apparently easy neutrality, entering a war that would ultimately destroy the Empire?
- Why did the Entente grant Germany an armistice after speaking for so long of the need for total victory?

After posing a puzzle and describing the relevant historical background, I develop the game-theoretic tools necessary to solve the puzzle, at some times a new game-theoretic solution concept, at others a specific strategic problem. Then, I walk the reader through the process of building an explanation in "real time," letting the characters in our story think and speak and act in the present tense, and comparing it to alternatives before situating each puzzle and the theoretical model that solves it in the broader context of the political science literature, showing how the First World War represents specific instances of more general trends in international politics. By the end of the book, students will have been exposed to the details of an important world-historical event, its place in the social-scientific understanding of international politics, *and* the process of building theories to explain politics.

Coverage and Organization

The book's historical scope begins with prewar tensions and conflicts between the great powers, including the Russo-Japanese War of 1904–1905, the Anglo-German naval race of 1906–1912, and several prewar crises from Morocco to the Balkans that saw the great powers step back from the brink of general war. It then continues through the outbreak and expansion of the war, the politics of military strategy and wartime diplomacy, and the network of peace treaties that legally, if not de facto, brought the war to an end by the early 1920s. Along the way, I use examples from the Chinese Civil War, the Korean War, the American-led wars against Iraq of the 1990s and 2000s, 1999's Kosovo War, the outbreak of the Second World War in the Pacific, and the contemporary balance of power supported by the United Nations and the American alliance network. Given the setting, the cast of characters is far from diverse. The critical decisions are made by men, often wealthy, generally European or Asian, in the name and at the expense of women and minorities in their own countries and subject peoples in their imperial domains, many of whom are drawn eventually into the war effort. Where possible, I highlight these experiences, but their absence from the story is itself instructive about how politics looked and worked in the early twentieth century and about how much has changed – and how much hasn't.

Two other courses unfold alongside this historical narrative: one in game theory and another in international security. First, the course in game theory begins with the construction and analysis of games in the strategic form, with a special emphasis on Nash Equilibrium in both pure and mixed strategies, as well as Bayesian Nash Equilibrium for strategic-form games with imperfect information. Subsequent chapters introduce games in the extensive form, as well as repeated strategic-form games, and their associated solution concepts of Subgame Perfect Equilibrium and Perfect Bayesian Equilibrium. The treatments of game-theoretic tools are rigorous but accessible, never rising above the level of basic algebra. Statements about the existence and characteristics of equilibria are formalized in propositions, which I then prove in the text with extensive descriptions of the relevant mathematics. Propositions and their proofs serve as guided exercises, but several of the more demanding tool-building chapters – those that introduce Bayes' Rule, mixed strategies, Subgame Perfect Equilibrium, and Perfect Bayesian Equilibrium – include additional exercises based on important political science questions. Students learn both the basics of game theory and the value of using it; this is hands-on research methods training, focused consistently on practical – that is, explanatory – applications.

Second, the course in international security takes advantage of the unprecedented scope and scale of the Great War to address a variety of topics central to the modern study of international security. Bargaining and war, arms races, war expansion, signaling resolve and restraint, international law and institutions, economic interdependence, differences between civil and interstate war, building and sustaining cooperation in military coalitions, reassurance, military strategy, limited and total wars, war duration and termination, deterrence, domestic politics and war, and the politics of making and sustaining peace – even nuclear weapons and the United Nations – all enter the narrative, with extensive references to the state of the art in political science. The organization of these topics is unconventional, but by virtue of emerging from a single, unifying narrative of the First World War, they're both topical and problem driven. Thus invested in resolving the puzzles that motivate each chapter, students encounter the political science literature as critical background for understanding the object of study, not merely as a collection of citations without a common explanatory thread. This unconventional organizational scheme *works*; it's even changed the ways in which I view and contribute to my own field of inquiry.

Features

This text integrates three things that no other international security textbook does:

- deep engagement with a single (and very important) historical case;
- a fully realized introductory game theory course;
- a survey of the broader literature on international security.

Other textbooks focus on game theory, international security, and sometimes both, but they lack the common, unifying theme of a single historical case. This book's focus on World War I gives students a shared empirical vocabulary to use throughout the course. Disparities in prior knowledge about the topic of the course are, in effect, smoothed out by this focus on the Great War. There's a lot of content, which makes it a challenging text, but the analytical depth afforded by this scheme is a feature, not a bug.

Instructors will find the book most useful for upper-division undergraduate courses and, in some cases, introductory graduate courses on international security and conflict processes. Facility with algebra is the most important prerequisite, but the mathematical complexity increases slowly, affording students time to reacquaint themselves with mathematical tools they might not have used in a while. The tight focus on the logic of inquiry that guides each chapter – from observation to puzzle to explanation – encourages students to think like social scientists (and prepares those headed to graduate school for what they're likely to encounter once they get there). Political scientists often like to say that we'd like our research to be puzzle focused, and this text embraces that by setting an example of good research practice. Students see puzzles addressed and answered in a transparent, logically sound fashion, which lays bare the trial and error, the educated guesses, even the creativity that goes into crafting and evaluating explanations of the political world.

As much as possible, the course follows the unfolding narrative of the war in temporal sequence, using successive events in the war to introduce new game-theoretic concepts in the same sequence they emerge in standard game theory courses. When the text builds and analyzes games to resolve key puzzles, it speaks exclusively in the present tense, emphasizing the value of thinking in real time, of taking seriously the choices and the contingencies that defined the era under study. Early chapters take care to introduce new methodological tools slowly, giving students practice with equilibrium reasoning and the methods of solving complete-information games in the strategic form. Not until Chapter 5, for example, does the text introduce imperfect information. Each subsequent chapter that introduces a new game form or solution concept (Chapters 5, 8, 11, and 12) also includes additional exercises, giving students some guided practice and deeper engagement with the tools used in the main body of the chapter. The exercises for Chapter 12, for example, explore pooling equilibria and out-of-equilibrium beliefs to round out the introduction of Perfect Bayesian Equilibrium, because the game used to solve the chapter's puzzle about war termination needed a separating equilibrium. The proofs of propositions and exercises can be skipped, however, if instructors prefer that students only engage the game-theoretic part of the course informally.

Acknowledgments

Writing this book was superfluously fun, and I'm indebted to a great many people and places for making it possible. The course on which it's based, World War I in Real Time, emerged from a happy hour conversation with Pat McDonald and Rachel Wellhausen at Austin's venerable (and now late) Dog & Duck Pub. I blurted out an idea for a course that tracked events in the First World War in real time, one hundred years removed, keeping a tight focus on what the characters in the story knew and believed when they made their fateful choices. I wasn't sure it would work, but I was locked in. And once I got this unexpectedly popular course up and running, suggestions to make a textbook out of it, from Allison Carnegie, Joe Grieco, Jack Levy, Amy Liu, and Mike Ward, started to sound doable. At Cambridge University Press, Robert Dreesen gave me the push I needed to get the project off the ground; Brianda Reyes, Lisa Pinto, and Melissa Shivers were just the managing editors that this author needed to finish the book. Along the way, numerous people read chapters and/or indulged my overshared enthusiasm. This list includes Phil Arena, Jeff Carter, Terry Chapman, Mike Findley, Hein Goemans, Marc Hutchison, Nate Jensen, Pat McDonald, Dan Morey, Bill Reed, Toby Rider, Emily Ritter, Brian Roberts, Elizabeth Saunders, Jessica Weeks, Thorin Wright, and Amy Yuen, as well as long-suffering graduate students Kevin Galambos, Josh Landry, Hans-Inge Langø, Dan McCormack, Julie Phillips, Andy Rottas, and Cathy Wu. Going back a few years, I learned game theory from Cliff Carrubba at Emory University, and without those courses, which he graciously let me TA after I took them, this book surely would never have come about. My wife, Amy, was far, far more supportive of the time I invested in this project than any reasonable person should have to be; I'm happily in her debt. I wrote Chapters 1–9 before the birth of our son George. I'm sure that the post-George chapters bear his stamp in ways I don't yet fully appreciate, but I reserve the right to blame any errors in said chapters on the attendant disruptions to my sleep schedule.

Finally, I'm a better writer outside the office than I am in it, and the following establishments provided welcoming and often inspiring work environments: Black Turtle Pub and Milagro in Belgrade; Drukarnia and Ministerstwo Browaru in Poznań; La 100 de Beri and James Joyce Pub in Bucharest; O'Rourke's Public House in South Bend; orgAsmo and Zhang Men Brewing in Taichung; José Ramon 227 in Santiago; Old Stove Brewing and Elysian Brewing in Seattle; Beer Hive Pub, Squatters Pub, and Copper Canyon in Salt Lake City; and Workhorse Bar, Gabriel's Café, Hole in the Wall, Home Slice Pizza, Crown & Anchor Pub, Dog & Duck Pub, Flying Saucer Draft Emporium, Pinthouse Pizza, Thunderbird Café and Tap Room, Spider House Café, Taco Flats, Fara Café, Ray Benson's Road House, Schoolhouse Pub, Growler USA, and Draft Pick in Austin.

Timeline of Key Events

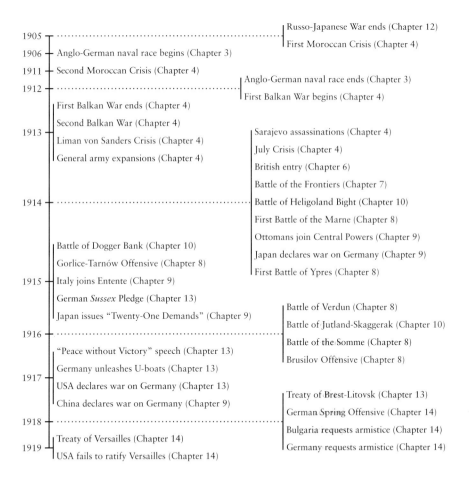

1905	Russo-Japanese War ends (Chapter 12)
	First Moroccan Crisis (Chapter 4)
1906	Anglo-German naval race begins (Chapter 3)
1911	Second Moroccan Crisis (Chapter 4)
1912	Anglo-German naval race ends (Chapter 3)
	First Balkan War begins (Chapter 4)
	First Balkan War ends (Chapter 4)
	Second Balkan War (Chapter 4)
1913	Liman von Sanders Crisis (Chapter 4)
	General army expansions (Chapter 4)
	Sarajevo assassinations (Chapter 4)
	July Crisis (Chapter 4)
	British entry (Chapter 6)
	Battle of the Frontiers (Chapter 7)
1914	Battle of Heligoland Bight (Chapter 10)
	First Battle of the Marne (Chapter 8)
	Ottomans join Central Powers (Chapter 9)
	Battle of Dogger Bank (Chapter 10)
	Japan declares war on Germany (Chapter 9)
	Gorlice-Tarnów Offensive (Chapter 8)
	First Battle of Ypres (Chapter 8)
1915	Italy joins Entente (Chapter 9)
	German *Sussex* Pledge (Chapter 13)
	Japan issues "Twenty-One Demands" (Chapter 9)
	Battle of Verdun (Chapter 8)
	Battle of Jutland-Skaggerak (Chapter 10)
1916	Battle of the Somme (Chapter 8)
	"Peace without Victory" speech (Chapter 13)
	Brusilov Offensive (Chapter 8)
	Germany unleashes U-boats (Chapter 13)
1917	USA declares war on Germany (Chapter 13)
	China declares war on Germany (Chapter 9)
	Treaty of Brest-Litovsk (Chapter 13)
	German Spring Offensive (Chapter 14)
1918	Bulgaria requests armistice (Chapter 14)
	Germany requests armistice (Chapter 14)
	Treaty of Versailles (Chapter 14)
1919	USA fails to ratify Versailles (Chapter 14)

Dramatis Personae

- **Albert I.** King of Belgium, 1909–1934. He famously rejected the German ultimatum in August 1914 and took command of the Belgian Army as it managed a fighting retreat to Antwerp and across the Yser River.
- **Asquith, Herbert Henry.** British Prime Minister, 1908–1916. He was beset by the question of Irish Home Rule, and whether it would lead to civil war, when the July Crisis erupted in 1914.
- **von Baden, Maximilian "Max."** German Chancellor, October–November 1918. He was tasked with putting his country on the path to democracy and armistice.
- **Barthas, Louis.** French Corporal, 1914–1918. Mobilized at the war's outbreak, he returned to barrel making and socialist activism at its end. His compiled diaries and letters were published posthumously in 1978.
- **Beatty, David.** British Admiral, later First Sea Lord, 1919–1927. He commanded the First Battle Cruiser Squadron in the Battles of Heligoland Bight, Dogger Bank, and Jutland-Skaggerak. Named First Sea Lord in 1919, in which role he helped negotiate the Washington Naval Treaty in 1922.
- **von Bethmann-Hollweg, Theobald.** German Chancellor, 1909–1917. Keen to observe legalities in ordering mobilization, he also promulgated the *Septemberprogramm* statement of expansive war aims. Later ousted for opposing unrestricted submarine warfare.
- **von Bismarck, Otto.** Prussian Minister-President, 1862–1890 (with a short break in 1873), and German Chancellor, 1871–1890. Responsible for overseeing Germany's unification and rise to great power status, he was sacked by Kaiser Wilhelm II, who rejected Bismarck's conservative foreign policy in favor of imperial expansion.
- **Brusilov, Aleksei.** Russian General, 1902–1917, later Commander-in-Chief, 1917. A cavalry officer best known for the 1916 offensive that

bears his name, he later appealed to former Tsarist soldiers to join the Red Army as their patriotic duty to Russia.

- **Chotek, Sophie.** Duchess of Hohenberg, assassinated with her husband Archduke Franz Ferdinand on June 28, 1914. Thanks to a birth that was noble but not dynastic, she was denied the rank of Empress Consort, and her children were legally barred from inheriting the throne slated to be their father's.

- **Churchill, Winston.** British First Lord of the Admiralty, 1911–1915, officer on the Western Front, 1915–1916, then Minister of Munitions, 1917–1919. He lost political standing after advocating the disastrous Gallipoli Campaign to force the Turkish Straits in 1915.

- **von Clausewitz, Carl.** Prussian (and briefly Russian) General, 1782–1831. A witness to Prussia's defeat in the Napoleonic Wars and to Napoleon's ultimate defeat, his magnum opus *On War*, unfinished at his death, remains a foundational text in the theory of war.

- **Conrad von Hötzendorf, Franz.** Chief of the Austro-Hungarian General Staff, 1906–1917. An ardent advocate of preventive war against Serbia, his decision to divide forces against Serbia and Russia would contribute to the rapid collapse of the Hapsburg Empire as an independent military force.

- **Crowe, Eyre.** British diplomat known for his distrust of German intentions in the prewar years and leadership in the founding of the Ministry of Blockade during the war. The son of a diplomat, he was born in Germany and even in adulthood cursed with a German accent.

- **von Falkenhayn, Erich.** Prussian Minister of War, 1913–1914, then Chief of the German General Staff, 1914–1916. Appointed to replace Moltke the Younger after the Battle of the Marne, he was later demoted after the failure of the Verdun Offensive. He went on to lead the conquest of Romania in 1916.

- **Foch, Ferdinand.** French General, then Marshal, 1914–1923, later Commander-in-Chief of Allied Forces, 1918. He commanded the French 9th Army at the First Battle of the Marne and was tasked eventually with coordinating all Entente and Associated forces on the Western Front.

- **Franz Josef I.** Hapsburg Emperor of the Dual Monarchy of Austria-Hungary, 1848–1916. He saw his empire reduced to secondary status in the Germanic world after defeat at Prussian hands in 1866, then assented to plans for a preventive war on Serbia during the July Crisis.

- **French, John.** Commander-in-Chief of the British Expeditionary Force, 1914–1916, later Commander-in-Chief, Home Forces, 1916–1918. He ended a career in the Royal Navy after discovering that he suffered from seasickness, then served in Sudan, India, and the Boer War before rising to command of the British Expeditionary Force.

- **Goschen, Edward.** British Ambassador to Germany, 1908–1914. His post was suspended at the outbreak of war in 1914, but previous postings included Washington, DC, St. Petersburg, Belgrade, Copenhagen, and Vienna.
- **Grey, Edward.** British Foreign Minister, 1905–1916. Famously cagey in 1914 about the content of the British commitment to France, he oversaw British entry into the war and, in the last year of his ministry, signed the Sykes-Picot agreement dividing former Ottoman lands in the Middle East between Britain and France.
- **Groener, Wilhelm.** German General, 1915–1919. Known for his talents as a logistician, he feuded with Ludendorff throughout the war but ended his career as Minister of Defense in the Weimar Republic.
- **Haig, Douglas.** Marshal, British Expeditionary Force, 1914–1918. Succeeding John French's command of the British Expeditionary Force, he oversaw both the costly Somme Offensive and the successful "Hundred Days" that brought Germany to heel. The creation of the Royal Army Dental Corps after the war followed his positive experiences with a Parisian dentist that treated him for a toothache.
- **von Hapsburg-Lorraine, Franz Ferdinand.** Heir-apparent to the throne of the Dual Monarchy of Austria-Hungary, his assassination on July 28, 1914, sparked the July Crisis. Loathed in Vienna and by his assassins, he was one of the few prewar advocates for peace in the Balkans.
- **von Hindenburg, Paul.** German General, Field Marshal, then Chief of the General Staff, 1916–1919. Recalled from retirement in August 1914, after victory at Tannenberg, he succeeded Moltke as Chief of Staff in 1916. Led what amounted to a military dictatorship in the waning years of the war, then appointed Adolf Hitler to the chancellorship in 1933.
- **von Holtzendorff, Henning.** German Admiral and Chief of the Admiralty Staff, 1915–1918. Like Hindenburg, he was called out of retirement by the war, though clashes with the army led him to retire a second time in August 1918.
- **House, Edward "Colonel."** Advisor, confidante, and occasional envoy for President Woodrow Wilson. A powerbroker from Texas who worked on Wilson's 1912 campaign, he turned down a cabinet appointment to be an informal advisor and diplomatic envoy.
- **Jellicoe, John.** British Admiral, 1914–1919, later First Sea Lord, 1917–1919. He commanded the Grand Fleet and made the fateful decision not to pursue German ships at Jutland-Skaggerak, then oversaw (skeptically) implementation of the convoy system as First Sea Lord in 1917.

- **Joffre, Joseph "Papa."** Commander-in-Chief, French Army, 1914–1916. He ordered the famous retreat to reorient Entente forces in the face of Germany's attempted right hook through Belgium, setting up victory at the Battle of the Marine. His star would fade as the war stalemated through 1915.
- **Jünger, Ernst.** German soldier famous for his war-glorifying memoir *In Storms of Steel*. He rejected advances from the Nazis to take advantage of his war-hero status and became, in later years, an accepted establishment thinker.
- **Kant, Immanuel.** Eighteenth-century German philosopher. He is known to political scientists as a forerunner of the democratic peace thesis.
- **Katō Takaaki.** Japanese Foreign Minister, 1914–1915 (and a few times before). He led the push for Japan's entry into the First World War and issued the infamous "Twenty-One Demands" to China.
- **Keynes, John Maynard.** English economist. After serving in Britain's delegation to the Versailles peace conference, he wrote a popular critique of the treaty and the heavy reparations imposed on Germany, *The Economic Consequences of the Peace*.
- **Kitchener, Horatio Herbert.** British Secretary of State for War, 1914–1916. He oversaw the creation of Britain's New Army, which he believed critical for a war that he predicted would last years, and made famous the recruitment poster that inspired the American "I Want You" poster featuring Uncle Sam. Died mid-war when the ship carrying him to Russia for coalition negotiations struck a German mine.
- **Lansing, Robert.** American Secretary of State, 1915–1920. He took office shortly after the sinking of the *Lusitania*, replacing the neutralist William Jennings Bryan, and backed Wilson's threats of war that secured the "*Sussex* Pledge."
- **Lenin, Vladimir Ilyich.** Russian communist revolutionary. He began the war in Swiss exile, but in 1917, with German support, made his way to Russia, where he led the Bolshevik seizure of power in the October Revolution before capitulating to Germany.
- **Liman von Sanders, Otto.** German and Ottoman General, 1913–1918. Head of the military mission to the Ottoman Empire that sparked a crisis in 1913, he organized the defense of the Gallipoli Peninsula in 1915, then led Turkish forces in the Sinai and Palestine later in the war.
- **Lloyd George, David.** British Chancellor of the Exchequer, 1908–1915, Minister of Munitions, 1915–1916, Secretary of State for War, 1916, and Prime Minister, 1916–1922. In addition to collecting cabinet appointments, he was known for his fiery rhetoric, both on the campaign trail and with regard to the threat posed by Wilhelmine Germany.

- **Ludendorff, Erich.** German General, 1914–1918, then Quartermaster-General of the General Staff, 1916–1918. He led the assault on the Belgian fortress at Liège at war's outbreak, then, as Hindenburg's chief of staff, he orchestrated the victory at Tannenberg that would make the duo's reputation. Ran for office as a Nazi in the 1920s.
- **Mehmet V.** Ottoman Sultan, 1909–1918. After overseeing the loss of European territory in the Balkan Wars, he was largely powerless after the Young Turk coup of 1913.
- **von Moltke (the Elder), Helmuth.** Chief of the German General Staff, 1871–1888. Leader of Prussian armies in the Austro-Prussian and Franco-Prussian wars, he was the uncle of Moltke the Younger, who served in the same capacity at the outbreak of the First World War.
- **von Moltke (the Younger), Helmuth.** Chief of the German General Staff, 1906–1914. Nephew of Moltke the Elder, against whom he was frequently and unfavorably compared, he succeeded Schlieffen and unleashed a modified version of his predecessor's war plan.
- **Nicholas II.** Tsar of the Russian Empire, 1894–1917. The last of the Tsars, he was sidelined for his indecision during the July Crisis. He abdicated during 1917's February Revolution, but he and his family were executed by the Bolsheviks after the October Revolution.
- **Pershing, John J.** American General and Commander of the American Expeditionary Force, 1917–1918. He led an intervention into the Mexican Civil War to chase Pancho Villa in 1916–1917, then took command of the AEF, ever cautious of "amalgamation" with French and British forces on the Western Front.
- **Potiorek, Oskar.** Austro-Hungarian General and Governor of Bosnia-Herzegovina, 1911–1914. He survived the attacks that killed Franz Ferdinand and Sophie Chotek, then took command of Austro-Hungarian forces in the Balkans. After failing to bring Serbia to heel, he was removed in December 1914.
- **Princip, Gavrilo.** Bosnian Serb nationalist. He was part of a small group that crossed into Bosnia with help from Serbian intelligence. Princip fired the shots that killed Archduke Franz Ferdinand and Sophie Chotek.
- **Riezler, Kurt.** German diplomat and personal secretary to Bethmann-Hollweg. He authored the *Septemberprogramm* for the chancellor and negotiated German subsidies to Lenin with the latter's representatives in Berlin.
- **Roosevelt, Theodore.** Former President of the United States, 1901–1909. A full-throated advocate of intervention on the side of the Entente, he was a prominent critic of Wilson's policy of neutrality in the war's early years.

- **Salandra, Antonio.** Italian Prime Minister, 1914–1916. Initially committed to neutrality at the war's outbreak, he later advocated accepting the Entente's offer of territorial gains in return for repudiating the Triple Alliance.
- **Sazonov, Sergei.** Russian Foreign Minister, 1910–1916. A veteran diplomat, he was one of the figures urging the Tsar to convert partial into full mobilization during the July Crisis.
- **Scheer, Reinhard.** German Admiral, 1916–1918, then Chief of the Admiralty Staff, 1918. He commanded the High Seas Fleet at the Battle of Jutland-Skaggerak, then ordered a last-ditch sortie in October 1918 that precipitated naval mutinies as the military situation continued to deteriorate.
- **von Schlieffen, Alfred.** German General and Chief of the General Staff, 1891–1906. Preceding Moltke the Younger in the role that made both of them famous, he drafted the war plan calling for a rapid victory over France before turning to fight Russia. His plan called for far more troops than Germany had in both 1905, when he drafted it, and 1914, when Moltke implemented it.
- **von Stürgkh, Karl.** Austrian Minister-President, 1911–1916. He refused to convene Parliament from spring 1914, allowing for rule by decree and heavy censorship once war broke out, and was assassinated in 1916 because of it.
- **von Tirpitz, Alfred.** German Admiral and State Secretary of the Naval Office, 1897–1916. A tireless advocate for turning Germany into a naval power, he found an ally in Wilhelm II for his plans to build a "risk fleet" that could contest Britain in the North Sea.
- **Tisza, István.** Hungarian Prime Minister, 1913–1917. Initially opposed to war with Serbia, which could undermine ethnic Hungarian power in the Dual Monarchy, he acceded under Vienna's threat to expand the franchise in Hungary.
- **Villa, Francisco "Pancho."** Mexican revolutionary general. He launched the raid on Columbus, New Mexico, that prompted American intervention. After nine months, when American forces withdrew to focus on Europe, Villa remained at large.
- **Wilhelm II.** Kaiser of the German Empire and King of Prussia, 1888–1918. Known for his bombast and inconsistency, he dismantled Bismarck's delicate alliance system and set Germany on the path to colonial expansion, in competition with powers like France and Britain.
- **Wilson, Henry.** British General, 1900–1918, Staff Officer for the British Expeditionary Force 1914–1915, and eventual Chief of the Imperial General Staff, 1918. An important advisor for Sir John French in the

early months of the war, rocky relations with other generals eventually led to his assignment as a liaison with the French and eventually to the Supreme War Council.

- **Wilson, Woodrow.** American President, 1913–1921. He began the war years committed to neutrality but eventually opted to join the war after the German implementation of unrestricted submarine warfare in 1917. Enjoyed global popularity for his rhetorical stance on national self-determination.
- **Zimmermann, Arthur.** German Foreign Minister, 1916–1917. The diplomatic note that bears his name proposed an alliance between Germany, Mexico, and Japan. Intercepted by the British and passed on to the Americans, it created a public sensation, though the most recent evidence suggests that it changed few minds about intervention.

1 Introduction: The Great War

It is one of those seismic disturbances in which nations leap forward or fall backward generations in a single bound.

David Lloyd George,
British Minister of Armaments
December 25, 1915

Before its sequel overshadowed it in popular memory, the First World War was simply "the Great War." Perhaps it still should be. What began in summer 1914 as a local Balkan conflict between an upstart Serbia and the wizened Dual Monarchy of Austria-Hungary became by 1918 a war that raged across the globe, involving all the great powers and ushering in a level of mass battlefield killing unimaginable just a few years earlier. The Entente coalition led by France, Britain, Russia (for a time), and (late in the war) the United States claimed victory over the Central Powers of Germany, Austria-Hungary, and the Ottoman Empire, but not before Germany knocked Russia out of the war in 1917 and sniffed victory on the Western Front in 1918. The world that emerged battered, scarred, and disillusioned from four years of unprecedented destruction, upheaval, and suffering was hardly recognizable to those who lived to see the peace.[1] Defeat shattered the German, Russian, Austrian, and Ottoman Empires, and though victory enlarged Japan's empire, it sounded the death knell of the British and French empires and moved Indian and Chinese nationalism closer to their modern forms. The world entered the new age of industrial war, during which states and empires attempted to mobilize entire populations for the conflict – and nearly succeeded in doing so – as their subjects manned trenches and produced the weapons that armies would

---

[1] The major belligerents stopped fighting in 1918, but war continued for years in the East, as Russia collapsed into a vicious civil war and the Ottoman Empire continued fighting until the early 1920s. Marking the end in 1918 isn't unreasonable, since Germany was the heart of the Central Powers, but it's also a bit misleading. On the continued fighting in defeated states, see Gerwarth (2016).

use to lay waste to the physical, social, and political face of the globe. The war killed 10 million on the battlefield alone,[2] more than twice as many as those killed in all major wars since 1790,[3] poisoning politics and class relations and straining the bonds between state and society in all belligerent countries, some of which, like the Russian, German, and Ottoman empires, succumbed to revolution and bloody civil violence.[4]

The Great War also hastened the rise to great power status of the United States, which would throw its economic and military weight behind the Entente even as it espoused an open skepticism about the nineteenth-century world order that its new partners had bled so profusely to preserve. America's wartime president, Woodrow Wilson, sought to rearrange global politics around a binding system of collective security, even as the Americans withdrew from European security politics after the war, hoping that financial might alone could do the job. The United States wasn't the only new revolutionary power; a royal abdication, crushing military defeat, the humiliating Treaty of Brest-Litovsk, a Bolshevik coup, and a subsequent civil war in Russia produced a Soviet regime that made its own rhetorical break with classical power politics, even as it pursued traditionally Russian imperial ambitions. Its military presence and political weight in Europe, diminished at war's end, would only grow in the interwar years as the result of a forcible Stalinist recovery. A nominally democratic Germany emerged from the war with its unity accepted and legitimized for the first time by the other great powers, even as it labored bitterly under the harsh peace of the Treaty of Versailles. Defeat was bitter, but victory entailed its own problems. Entente competition over former Ottoman possessions would sow the seeds for future conflicts in the Middle East, whose present fault lines echo many of the hasty decisions over borders and governance made in those early days after Germany's capitulation in 1918. On the other side of the globe, Japan scooped up German possessions in the Pacific that sat ominously astride American lines of communication its imperial possessions in Hawaii and the Philippines. Japan's disillusionment over frustrated ambitions at the peace conference, including a simple request for the recognition of racial equality opposed by the British and American delegations, strengthened a militarist faction that would, alongside Germany, play a part in igniting the Second World War barely a generation later.

Map 1.1 shows the war's reach, from its beginnings in southeastern Europe to the falling dominoes of the great powers and their colonies (like India, Canada, Australia, and New Zealand) to the eventual participation

---

[2] Prost (2014)
[3] Kershaw (2015, chapter 3).
[4] Payne (2011) and Gerwarth (2016).

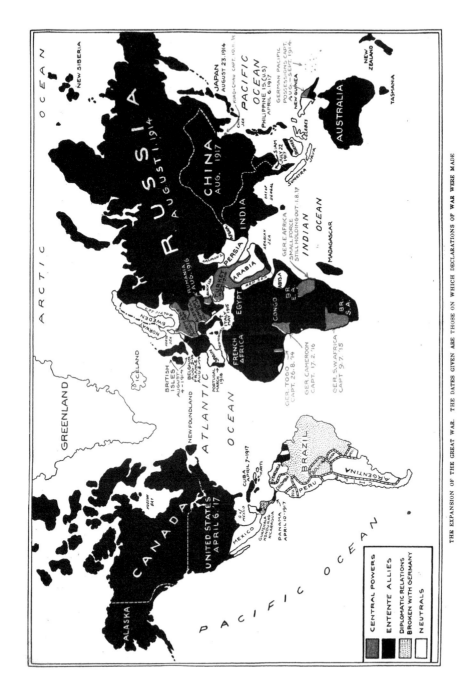

THE EXPANSION OF THE GREAT WAR. THE DATES GIVEN ARE THOSE ON WHICH DECLARATIONS OF WAR WERE MADE

Map 1.1 The global reach of the Great War. From Reynolds, Churchill, and Miller (1916).

of future great powers like the United States and China.[5] And yet, as easy as it is to see its global political footprint with a century's worth of hindsight, the Great War's participants were under no illusions that the world would again be the same. Eventual British Prime Minister David Lloyd George, addressing the public as Armaments Minister in December 1915, said

> It is the deluge, it is a convulsion of Nature … bringing unheard-of changes in the social and industrial fabric. It is a cyclone which is tearing up by the roots the ornamental plants of modern society … It is one of those seismic disturbances in which nations leap forward or fall backward generations in a single bound.[6]

That assessment, offered just under three years before the armistice of November 11, 1918, hasn't changed much in the intervening century. Modern historians call the First World War "the seminal event of modern times,"[7] an all-consuming "global revolution" that upended power relationships between and inside countries.[8] Even the ostensibly low-stakes, plodding-then-galloping July Crisis that preceded the war has been dubbed "the most complex [event] of modern times, perhaps of any time so far."[9] The First World War is one of those rare events that lives up to the historiographical hype. It gestated slowly and ominously under the shadow of the past, then burst forth violently, if not unexpectedly, to consume and change everything before it. In its destruction and dislocation, it shaped all that came afterward in global politics.

The war merits attention for its consequences alone, but it's illuminating for more than just its aftermath. Its sheer scale and complexity mean that it touches on nearly every aspect of the politics of war and peace that concern contemporary students of international relations. Its origins in great power competition, complicated by civil conflict and cross-border political violence, are eerily modern.[10] The more one looks at the Great War, the less exotic it seems, despite the intervening century, and the less comfortable one feels dismissing it as a historical curiosity, an outrageous outlier, or a pale shadow of the still more terrible world war that would follow it.[11] When that familiarity echoes the present, it offers

---

[5] However darkly shaded it is, this map is still misleading: Mexico, which preserved its neutrality, didn't remain untouched, subject as it was of a German proposal to form an alliance against the United States (see Chapter 13).

[6] Quoted in Tooze (2014, p. 3).

[7] Fromkin (2004, p. 8).

[8] Sondhaus (2011, pp. 1–2).

[9] Clark (2012, p. xxix).

[10] Clark (2012, p. xxvii).

[11] It's easy to focus on the Second World War. As David Frum (2015) notes (quoting an anonymous *Atlantic* reader), it's got "bigger explosions" and "better villains." World War II is the blockbuster, and World War I is the challenging indie film.

not answers but more questions, more puzzles in need of resolution. Why do states go to war only to draw new borders or install new foreign governments, when negotiations can (and often do) achieve the same things without wasting blood and treasure? How can small disputes involving minor powers draw in not just one of but *all* the world's great powers, especially when they stand to lose large volumes of peacetime trade and investment? When does international law shape the behavior of states, and when is it dismissed as just so many scraps of paper? Why do some military partners cooperate effectively, while others fail spectacularly to work together even as their survival hangs in the balance? Why are some countries willing to gamble everything, even their very survival, on fleeting chances of military victory? How can frugal, calculating leaders throw good money after bad, hurling citizen soldiers into an apparently futile, grinding contest of attrition? Why keep the war at sea limited while the war on land manifestly isn't? Why do wars end when and how they do, typically with both sides still standing and able in principle to continue the fight, even after years of strain, resentment, and animosity? Finally, how do states make peace after war, what makes it last, and why does it break down?

Each of these puzzles emerges from the narrative of the Great War we follow in subsequent chapters. This book introduces students to modern theories of international relations by offering answers – many old, some amended, a few new to this text – to these and many other enduring questions. We'll develop solutions to a series of puzzles using game theory, a mathematical tool that helps us build simple, elegant models of politics and strategic choice that offer pithy, useful insights into otherwise baffling, complex phenomena. Students will develop a working knowledge of (1) international war and peace, (2) building, analyzing, and learning from simple game-theoretic models of international politics, and (3) the historic and contemporary importance of an event that shaped (and continues to shape) the world in which we live. The First World War is horrifying, fascinating, challenging, and very present, and not just because international relations scholars won't (maybe can't) stop talking about it. Passing through the war's centennial, it's tempting to compare every hiccup in the international order, from nuclear weapons on the Korean peninsula to Russian attempts to regain Eastern Europe to Chinese ambitions in the South and East China Seas to American presidents questioning the value of their alliance networks, to something in the run-up to war in 1914. As such, it's fitting that we use the Great War as a starting point for understanding the challenges of a new and rapidly changing world of international politics. If it's true that everything old becomes new again, relearning the lessons of the Great War might be all the more timely precisely because of how far the Great War has receded from popular memory.

Key Terms for Chapter 1

- War
- Strategy
- International System
- Territorial State

- Anarchy
- Self-Enforcing
- Hierarchy
- Great Power

1.1   HISTORY, WAR, AND POLITICAL SCIENCE

Its focus on the past notwithstanding, this is a book not of history but of political science. We're concerned with using the tools and accumulated insights of political science to develop answers about *why* the war broke out, expanded, lasted, and ended the way it did, leveraging as much as possible our collected knowledge about other like events. We'll build explanations with models – in this case, simple mathematical constructs that represent actors, their goals, their choices, and how those choices add up to produce the outcomes we observe – that allow us to think about elements of the war as specific instances of more general political phenomena. War, diplomacy, great powers, arms races, empires, alliances, democracy, dictatorship, international law, military strategy, war finance, and peace settlements existed before the Great War, in every region of the world, and they continue to define and shape the ebb and flow of international politics. This allows us to leverage insights from modern political science to learn about the First World War, to frame its puzzles in illuminating (and sometimes new) fashion, and to understand better a war that, at first blush, appears so large, so consequential, and so unique as to defy explanation.

Key to this approach is an endeavor to explain the actions of soldiers, politicians, civilians, revolutionaries, and laborers as much as possible *in real time*. We'll explain an event – for example, the outbreak of the war itself – in terms of the goals, alternatives, and information available to the actors when they made the relevant choices, as well as how multiple choices interacted to produce the outcomes we want to explain. We'll strive to avoid relying on hindsight, which can generate puzzles but not solve them. We might be puzzled, for example, why Britain and Germany wasted six years and millions of pounds and marks on a competition in battleship construction that left both states poorer but the distribution of naval power between them unchanged. If we look at the waste of the naval race, we might be tempted to blame the leaders who made the key decisions. We might land on an apparently satisfying answer, like corrupt politicians, "bad" systems of government, or individuals that (so conveniently) lack our insight or intelligence. An answer like that isn't as illuminating as it is self-serving, an understandable but distorting attempt at self-exoneration in the face of some of the defining tragedies of political life: "dictators/capitalists/imperialists/communists/fools/devils would embark on a wasteful arms race, but, of course, no one like me." That's a polemic, not an analysis. Yet something like it is too prevalent in the way we think and talk and (sometimes) vote about war. Solving puzzles about war in the seductive and easy way blinds us to the fact that we don't need to assume that people are venal, ignorant, treacherous, or evil to explain how they might end up fighting a monstrous, bloody contest of arms – even one as calamitous as the First World War.[12]

Putting ourselves in the heads of the people whose decisions we want to explain, from Germany's Kaiser Wilhelm II to France's Marshal Ferdinand Foch to American President Woodrow Wilson, helps us see how even clever, frugal, calculating individuals can choose something that, in hindsight, looks like obvious folly. We'll work hard to avoid explaining war in ideological, superstitious, or moralizing terms. The required moral detachment may be jarring, but it's necessary. We'll explain the war, its nature, its course, and its end in *political* terms, as *political* acts with *political* goals. We'll be disquietingly silent on who's "to blame." In fact, we'll see that many of us, faced with the same choices, might act in ways surprisingly similar to the Kaiser and his generals, the Tsar and his soldiers, or the Prime Minister and his Cabinet. Confronting the political story of the First World War in real time obliges us to view its participants not as figures buried deep in the past to be vainly praised or safely condemned, but as persons to be understood. Neither excused nor pardoned, of course, but humanized and rationalized.[13] Only then, after an exercise in the analytical equivalent of empathy, can we see how Russia could have embarked with some urgency on a potentially ruinous war with Germany to protect little Serbia; how the British Empire could enter a European war in support of its erstwhile Russian rival over a so-called scrap of paper guaranteeing Belgian neutrality; how Germany could in 1917 roll the iron dice on a program of unrestricted submarine warfare that was sure to draw the last remaining uncommitted great power into the war against it; and why the United States, its rhetorical fidelity to aloofness notwithstanding, would finally choose to participate in a war to reshape the global balance of power. Stripping away the artifice of popular but bad explanations, we'll

---

[12] I know what you're thinking, and you're correct. "Seductive and easy" is basically Yoda's description of the dark side of the Force. Gird yourself, dear reader.

[13] Here, *rationalized* doesn't have its typical negative connotation. We only mean understanding the logic, the rationale, behind people's decisions.

see that the tragedy that befell the world in 1914 is not as exotic, as distant, as mysterious, or as unique as we, more than a century later, might wish it to be.

If we look back merely to cast blame, as the victors did when they sat down to make pace in 1919, we risk losing sight of the fact that many people – not just imperialists and capitalists, as Lenin had it, or autocrats and militarists, as Wilson had it – might have made similar decisions in 1914 that risked setting the world on fire. "Tragedy" won't be just a literary concept. The conscious, open-eyed decision-making of 1914 is one of the fundamental yet easily overlooked tragedies of the war. We may recoil at the idea that the characters in our story knew what they were doing, but disliking the conclusions of a line of inquiry isn't a sufficient reason to reject it. To explain politics, we need better intellectual tools than an inchoate idea of what we wish the world were like. As such, we'll leverage the tools of game theory, which helps us explain political events by forcing us to identify the relevant actors, their goals, their choices, and the ways in which their choices interact with the choices of others. By thinking hard, for example, about what the Russians and Germans most wanted in July 1914, what they would've been happy with, what they would've done anything to avoid, and how their choices could impinge on the pursuit of each other's goals, we can take personages obscured by the weight of history more seriously and, as a result, see the war's causes more clearly. We can also see the extent to which the Great War (1) fits in with broader patterns of international politics *and* (2) offers lessons for war, diplomacy, and international politics in the modern era. When we understand the First World War as a political event, we can explain its horrors in terms that are useful to us, not only as students of the war but also as citizens that must make decisions about where we stand on issues of war, peace, and global order.

Explaining complex events is difficult, all the more so when those events entail the horror, destruction, and consequence of a world war. This is especially true of the First World War, an event of such staggering complexity, upheaval, and apparent inhumanity that the mind practically rejects any explanation other than "someone unlike me must be responsible." The explanations in this book, by contrast, take the characters in our story seriously. We need not assume that they're evil, venal, naive, incompetent, vain, or cognitively limited. Avoiding these temptations is frequently difficult and often uncomfortable. It requires that we exercise what George Orwell calls the "power of facing unpleasant facts."[14] The

---

[14] For more, see Orwell's moving essay "Why I Write," originally published in the fourth (and final) issue of *Gangrel* in 1946 but more easily found in 1953's essay collection *Such, Such Were the Joys*.

clarity offered by the simple, logical tools of game theory helps us say insightful things about an otherwise messy, illogical, even irrational world. As Harrison Wagner puts it,

> Sometimes people say that politics is just "not logical." *But logic is not a property of the world, it is a property of what we say about the world.* The world is a messy and confusing place. We do not enhance our understanding of it by saying messy and confusing things about it.[15]

This standard of analysis faces few bigger challenges than the unprecedented horror and normalized madness of the First World War. To help us along, we'll leverage a body work in political science that offers a wealth of models of the workings of politics, law, diplomacy, and war. We'll draw on many of these theories in order to make sense of the Great War, to put it in the context of the international system from which it emerged and went on to reshape, and to see what lessons it offers for war, peace, and international order today.

1.2   THEORY AND SIMPLICITY

The theories we develop in each chapter will often be incredibly simple, and it may seem strange at first that we take an event like the First World War and break it down into such spare pieces. But simplification, distillation, and abstraction are the very stuff of a good theory, of a good explanation. Complication, nuance, and ornate description generally aren't.[16] A useful theory is just like a useful map. It provides only as much detail as necessary to serve its purpose, and not a single detail more. It's spare in its construction, transparent in its logic, and insightful in its implications. It is, as much as possible, the opposite of the sprawling, noisy, baffling world it seeks to explain. It simplifies the world, acting as a sharp, carefully chosen, enlightening metaphor, one that isolates and sheds light on interesting parts of the whole, all in the service of helping us make sense of the world we observe. But it doesn't – and it shouldn't – try to describe the world in anything other than the barest, most miserly possible amount of detail.[17]

As we'll see throughout this book, a good theory is hard to find – and even harder to build from scratch. It's tempting to demand things of a theory that we shouldn't, like too much descriptive accuracy. But models

---

[15] Wagner (2001, p. 4, emphasis added).
[16] If you take one thing away from this book, it should be a healthy skepticism of anyone who critiques a theory as "oversimplifying" something. More often than not, such a critique is a vacuous demand for "nuance," which is rarely useful (Healy, 2017). Let's just treat *nuance* as a four-letter word from here on out.
[17] Good theories are metaphors, not onomatopoeia.

are *supposed* to leave things out; otherwise, they wouldn't be models. The standard model of the atom, for example, does a fine job of telling us how to think about the role of protons, neutrons, and electrons in constituting the elements in the periodic table, but further description (say, at the quantum level) adds nothing more than needless complexity if all we want to do is understand what substance we get when an atom of oxygen combines with two of hydrogen. A theory's usefulness is very often inversely proportional to its complexity, or to the number of "moving parts" that it requires us to keep track of. Our goal is to build explanations that isolate the processes in which we're interested and strip away all the others, to sort the wheat from the chaff, to distill a strategic problem down to its essence. The essence of a strategic problem, though, depends not on any particular detail of the situation but on what we're interested in learning about it, on what we ask of our models. Models, therefore, are best judged against the purposes for which we design them, not any particular level of fidelity with the complex, loony, maddening world we'd like them to help us understand.[18]

Theories give us insight and explanation, but they *shouldn't* give us just a description of an event. A good theory doesn't strive for a complete characterization of an event, because the event in full – say, the First World War – is already confusing. If it weren't, we wouldn't need a theory to explain it. We need theory to strip away noise and complication, to help us focus on the essentials. Imagine, if you will, a map of Austin, Texas, that contains every detail, fully to scale. Such a map would cover the entire city, so it wouldn't do us much good if all we wanted to know was how to get from the University of Texas campus to Workhorse Bar in the North Loop neighborhood. For that, we'd need a transit map, but we certainly would't want a huge, carefully detailed map that wasted our time with extraneous information. As long as the transit map gives us routes, stop locations, and bus times, we don't even need it to be drawn to scale (or maybe even drawn at all). And yet this model would still do what we ask of it effectively and efficiently.[19] To that end, the theories in this book offer explanations for puzzling events in the political world. They don't reproduce in confusing detail the already confusing events we're seeking to understand. (That would, in the true sense of the word, be perverse.) To theorize is to simplify, to leave things out, to cut away the inessential, to make the puzzling explicable. Anything less takes us further away from

---

[18] See Clarke and Primo (2012).

[19] See Clarke and Primo (2012) for an extended treatment of the models-as-maps analogy and Wagner (2001) for a briefer discussion of the same idea.

what makes us need a theory, a map, or a metaphor in the first place.[20] This is where the spare, mathematical structure of game theory can help us make sense of the otherwise rackety, chaotic, and bewildering historical record of international war and peace.

1.3 WAR (AND WHAT IT'S GOOD FOR)

If we're to conduct a rigorous analysis of the First World War, and if we're to use it to learn about war and international security in general, we need to establish a definition of war. It's tempting to think that we know a war when we see one, but our intuition typically fails us, because the concept of war itself is politicized. It's also been stretched well beyond any common meaning in everyday conversation: we apply the term metaphorically to sports, policies aimed at curbing poverty and the drug trade, workplace politics, and even campaigns and elections.[21] But if we can establish a clear definition of war, if we can agree on what we mean when we use the term, we can know with a bit more confidence when we see it, *and* we can develop a better sense of what's important and unimportant in explaining it. A bad definition can lead to incomplete, misleading, or inaccurate explanations, but a good definition can lead to explanations that are useful, insightful, and – critical for the scientific enterprise – transparent, rigorous, and reproducible. A common vocabulary based on shared definitions (way, *way* too often dismissed as "jargon") helps us talk to each other without talking past each other. This is why scientists typically care more about agreement on a definition than whether the content of that definition happens to be perfect.[22] A good definition must be specific enough to cover the object we want to study (i.e., the First World War) but general enough to capture what our object of study has in common with other, similar objects ("war" in general), which we can use to shine a light back on the one we're studying. In other words, we have to ask of what general phenomenon the First World War is a specific instance. What *is* war?

At minimum, we can say that war is violent, organized, and competitive. That war is *violent* seems intuitive; as we think of it colloquially, war invariably involves killing and destruction. But not all violence is

---

[20] If someone doesn't (lazily) criticize your theory for being "too simplistic" or for "oversimplification," then it's probably not yet simple enough.

[21] In other words, the term had lost plenty of meaning well before John Rambo declared from a rickety boat somewhere in the Mekong Delta that "to survive a war, you gotta become war."

[22] It's also why the politicians and partisans that we study prefer not to be pinned down on what, exactly, they mean when they use certain terms. If you could ask a lab rat whether it likes being a lab rat, I'd wager that this apparently sentient rat won't say yes. (I'm indebted to my colleague Bryan Jones for this example.)

war. Riots and looting, assault and battery, or isolated instances of police brutality are violent, but these activities aren't *organized*.[23] War requires that violence be conducted by groups organized for the purpose of using force – that is, by armies. For our purposes, an "army" need not be one of the highly structured, smartly uniformed, thoroughly specialized organizations divided into service branches that we see in modern states. Armies may serve states and empires, but they also fight for rebel leaders, religious figures, monarchs, even business enterprises. They can be rigidly hierarchical or confusingly flat, highly specialized or crudely trained; our definition requires only that armies be organized for the purpose of applying violence. Unless they direct it against other armies, though, their violence isn't *competitive*. It's just one organization killing or harming members of another group not so organized, like governments dispersing demonstrators by firing on them or police departments systematically killing rather than arresting certain segments of the population. However savage, however bloody, however reprehensible, such unilaterally organized violence isn't war. War requires that at least groups organized for violence engage in combat with each other, that they "compete in killing and wounding each other or destroying things they value."[24] But this leads to a final question: why engage in combat, if all it does is destroy people and things of value? To what use can organized, competitive violence be put, and what do those uses have to do with politics?

The competitive element of war implies a goal, some end state at which the winner of the competition attains something that the putative loser doesn't. If, to take an extreme example, one group eliminates or disarms another, it can take what it wants from the vanquished. As the famous Prussian military theorist Carl von Clausewitz describes it, war is "an act of force to compel our enemy to do our will."[25] War is thus a *political* instrument, a means by which groups can impose their will on others by making refusal to bend to that will painful. War is a tool of coercion, an instrument of power, where power can be understood as the ability to get others to do things they otherwise wouldn't do.[26] Thus, we define war as *instrumental*, as a means to an end, not as an end in itself, where those ends are political. If politics is "the authoritative allocation of values,"[27] some means by which scarce goods like wealth, security, rights and privileges, land, authority, and prestige can be shared, then war itself *is*

---

[23] Not all police brutality is isolated, of course, and it's often systematic. The latter is cruel and unjust, but we'll see next that it still isn't "war."

[24] Wagner (2007, p. 105).

[25] Clausewitz (1976, p. 75).

[26] This is a more stringent version of Bertrand Russell's (1996) definition of power as "the production of intended effects" (p. 22).

[27] Easton (1985, p. 134).

politics, albeit a particularly brutal manifestation. Elections, which we can agree quite easily are politics, allocate goods by competitive voting. War simply allocates those same goods by competitive fighting. If this analogy seems strange, it's worth noting that war often substitutes for elections, when political factions opt for civil war to determine who governs their country rather than the relatively peaceful (and certainly less wasteful) process of casting votes. The outcome is the same (a new government), but the means by which it's achieved (voting versus violence) are quite a bit different in terms of lives lost and things destroyed. Therefore, the wars with which we'll be concerned in this book are violent, organized, competitive, and *political*.

DEFINITION 1.1   *War is a violent contest in which opposing groups pursue political ends at each other's expense.*

Thinking about war as a political act, we gain traction on how best to explain it. To that end, we need to look at what's constant, what's essential about its many manifestations, then focus on those essentials in constructing explanations. Many colloquial explanations of war fall short of being useful, because they work from incomplete – or nonexistent – definitions. For example, our definition of war isn't tied to any particular historical era or cultural context. As long as groups of people have armies and disagree about things, something that satisfies our definition of war can occur, but oftentimes we work from definitions with unstated historical assumptions. War predates both nationalism and imperialism, casting doubt on the usefulness of those two common (since the nineteenth century, at least) tropes about the origins of war. Religious difference doesn't get us very far, either. Groups of the same religion fight one another about as often as groups of different religions, and war predates the religions that currently command the allegiance of most of the world's religious people. Likewise, political and ideological differences – from democracy and dictatorship to communism and fascism – are preceded, straddled, created, and sometimes overcome by, yet don't cause, war. Human nature or human failings like greed, treachery, dreadful personalities, cognitive deficiencies, or simple ignorance abound as explanations for war.[28] But human nature is by definition constant, and human failings are everywhere, while war is neither constant nor omnipresent. War is in fact pretty rare, at least relative to commonly proposed causes like greed, evil, treachery, personality defects, incompetence, and ignorance. At any one time, fewer wars are happening than could be, and that's helpful in identifying

---

[28] See, e.g., Stoessinger (1993) as an example of the type.

explanations. Something else must determine when human proclivities produce war and when they don't.

One thing that *is* constant about war, regardless of when it occurs and the issues over which it's fought, is its cost. Killing and destruction make war a wasteful way of conducting politics. War destroys things (like the land, cities, or populations fought over) and expends resources (like blood, treasure, and forgone consumption) that other means of resolving disagreements, like elections and diplomacy, don't. This, as we'll see in Chapters 2, 5, 11, and 12 is the defining puzzle of war: if negotiations can lead to the same outcomes that war can, which they very often do, then why fight at all? Why fight, only to reach the very same peace settlement that could've been (and often was) proposed beforehand? Nearly all wars, even those that we tend to think of as total defeats like the Second World War, end in some kind of negotiated settlement, whether a document signaling unconditional surrender like that imposed on Germany in 1945,[29] a treaty that transfers territory from one country to another like many of the European wars of the eighteenth and nineteenth centuries,[30] or one that does little more than reaffirm the *status quo ante bellum*, like the settlement that ended the Iran-Iraq War in 1988.[31] The First World War, which ended with a collection of treaties, most notably Versailles, certainly fits the bill; it was above all else a political competition aimed at a redistribution (or reestablishment, depending on your sympathies) of rights and privileges among the great powers of the early twentieth century. But the fact that a settlement was eventually signed makes the tremendous cost of the war all the more puzzling, because nothing in principle prevented that same settlement, or even a deal that saved all the blood and treasure and kept all the original states intact, from being written down beforehand. Later chapters will bring this puzzle into starker relief, but suffice it to say that a great many settlements forgone in 1914 looked much better in hindsight than the outcome of the Great War. Armed with this definition of war, the most wasteful among many cheaper means of resolving disagreements, we'll develop a series of models that shed new light on its outbreak, expansion, conduct, duration, and end.

1.4 THE INTERNATIONAL SYSTEM

Next, it's worth asking *where* the politics of war and diplomacy takes place. Our narrative focuses on a series of puzzles that emerge from trac-

---

[29] See Plokhy (2010).
[30] See Evans (2016).
[31] See Razoux (2015).

ing the course of the First World War. Yet the politics that the narrative illuminates transcends the war itself, taking place within an international system whose basic features remain mostly fixed down to the modern era. The most important actors have changed, to be sure. Germany is no longer the military powerhouse that it was in 1914; Great Britain and France, stripped of their empires, can still project power over large parts of the globe, but they're hardly on a par with the United States; Russia possesses thousands of nuclear weapons but a medium-sized, fossil fuel-dependent economy; and China has returned to great power status after a centuries-long absence, yet its military influence doesn't yet extend far beyond its borders. One theme of this book is that today's great power actors perform on the same stage and read from a script fairly similar to the one used by the great powers of 1914. In this section, we'll characterize the international system by identifying its key elements, sketching out in the process a spare yet insightful model of international politics. The resulting theory works in the background throughout the book, and it illuminates critical parts of the story of the First World War by referencing broader features of the international systems that both preceded and succeeded it.

When we say "system," we mean a set of interconnected units.[32] Systems can entail people in a society, organs in a body, software operating a computer, firms in an economy, or the territorial states that define the contemporary world-political map. When interconnected units change, or when they interact with one another in new ways, they change other parts of the system as well, including the characteristics of other units and the modes and outcomes of their interactions. Think of a highway system. When one road falls under construction, traffic redirects to other roads, and when two highways are connected, traffic may leave other roads in favor of the new route. Interconnectedness also means that the whole of the system may be difficult to understand if we treat it only as the sum of its parts. Understanding traffic flow through the whole of a highway system, such as the locations and severity of traffic jams, is impossible if we simply look at each road without an understanding of how it connects with other roads (and how traffic is regulated on those roads), how those roads connect with others, and so on. What happens in one part of the system – say, a faulty traffic light – can have dramatic impacts in another, and understanding how requires that we understand how the system's units interact.[33] A list of individual unit characteristics, which really would just

---

[32] See Jervis (1997) and Braumoeller (2012).

[33] Another example is consciousness, which some scholars don't explain solely in terms of neurons and sensory inputs, but the relationships between them. Just like international politics emerges from the interactions of units that we can't understand in isolation, so does consciousness (see Dennett, 1991).

be the sum of the system's parts, won't do if we're to explain something like traffic patterns, which result from the interactions between, the interconnectedness of, the parts.

In this respect, the international system is similar to a complex, networked system of roads. But rather than traffic patterns and density, we're concerned with states and their interactions: war, peace, commerce, and diplomacy. And like a highway system, what happens in one part of the world can have far-reaching, often unanticipated consequences explicable only by thinking about the system's interconnections rather than isolated parts. In the 1860s, simultaneous civil wars in two of its largest markets – the United States and Imperial China – both tempted British intervention, but it could only choose one, and an American threat to make war on Canada was sufficient to ensure that China saw the British get involved in the Taiping Civil War, not the American.[34] After the stock market crash of 1929 brought on the global Great Depression the United States and other large countries tried to protect struggling domestic firms from foreign competition by placing tariffs on imported goods. But since *many* countries raised tariffs in the 1930s, trade slowed to a standstill and no single country could gain from protectionism. However politically sensible each *individual* decision might've been (they made little pure economic sense), multiple countries setting high tariffs resulted in a *collective* tragedy that worsened the Depression around the world. We'll learn in Chapters 2 and 3 how to understand the aggregation of many individual decisions into unintended, tragic, and often surprising collective outcomes by introducing the tools of game theory. And as we'll see in Chapter 4, the outbreak of World War I in 1914 can trace some of its roots to Russia's decision to modernize and expand its army after a 1905 military defeat at the hands of Japan, eight thousand miles away in Manchuria. And yet this war over growing Russian strength began in 1914 because a Bosnian Serb teenager managed to assassinate the heir apparent to the throne of the Hapsburg Empire on a June visit to Sarajevo, itself only recently annexed at the expense of an Ottoman Empire that would also soon be dragged into the global catastrophe.

Our comparison of the international system to a highway system isn't perfect, though. Roads aren't intentional. Highways and traffic lights don't make decisions, but leaders – monarchs, presidents, chancellors, general secretaries, ministers – do. This element of choice, of agency, adds a unique layer of complexity to our definition of interconnectedness. The international system is *strategically* interconnected, because the units that populate it make choices and formulate plans, or strategies, based on the likely

---

[34] See Platt (2012).

choices of other units in the system, and the outcomes we observe depend on the interaction of these strategies. States make choices about their own characteristics (e.g., their militaries, their governing institutions, or their alliances) and about their interactions with other states (e.g., whether to negotiate, go to war, or accept things as they are), shaping their ability to achieve their own goals and to interfere with others' pursuit of their own goals. International interactions are strategic, in that the outcomes we observe – say, the outbreak or avoidance of a world war – are the product of interdependent choices (often very many of them).

When states build arms, when they lower trade barriers, or when they demand territory from one another, they do so with an eye to others' likely reactions. War, for example, is the product of two choices: a decision to attack and a decision to resist. A one-sided war doesn't make sense; it would be just so much tilting at windmills. States can't sign treaties without either partners or enemies, nor can they establish their own borders without some form of acceptance from the states beyond their frontiers. In fact, there's very little that's interesting about international politics that *doesn't* depend on the aggregate choices of multiple states. This dependence on and anticipation of other's choices is what makes any given decision strategic, because states know that their ability to achieve their ends depends on whether other states choose to stand in the way, stand aside, or stand beside them in the process. As such, a **strategy** is a plan of action that stipulates what to do in response to what other states do (or plan to do).

DEFINITION 1.2   *A **strategy** is a plan that specifies what action to take in response to others' actions.*

The more states we add into the system, the more complex the strategies involved, and the more difficult it becomes to characterize a system as merely the sum of its parts. Like a road system with a traffic jam on an otherwise unobstructed road, understanding interconnections between parts of the system is crucial if we're to explain what happens in any one part of the system. The strategic interconnectedness of the international system defines its politics, and it serves as our starting point for understanding the world in which the Great War took place. We'll begin our description of the **international system** with some simple definitions, then see how we can use them to understand some more of the system's key features.

DEFINITION 1.3   *An **international system** is a set of strategically interconnected territorial states.*

We can describe an international system in terms of many features, but we'll focus on three: (1) the political *units* making it up, (2) its *ordering principles*, and (3) the *means of change* in units and ordering principles.[35] For the most part, the units with which we're concerned are **territorial states** with a nominal right to exclusive control over what goes on inside their borders (i.e., sovereignty).

DEFINITION 1.4   *A **territorial state** is a political unit with exclusive control over a defined territory.*

There's significant variation in what states look like, however, from ideal-typical national states to imperial states that control foreign populations and resources in addition to their home territory. Serbia, for example, enters our story as a nation-state, albeit a dissatisfied one with designs on expanding its own already-growing territory. At the other extreme, Great Britain is in 1914 a colossal maritime empire, controlling large swathes of Africa, the Indian subcontinent, North America, Southeast Asia, and Oceania, all from a tiny island home perched precariously off the north-western edge of Europe. Somewhere in between, we find older continental empires, like Russia and China, with no major colonies in 1914, if only because their ancient imperial holdings are already incorporated (legally, if not peacefully) into their recognized territories. However organized, the key actors in our story – the *units* making up the international system – are territorial states, some of which have empires (Great Britain, France, Germany, Japan, the United States), some of which *are* empires (Russia, China, Turkey), and many others of which fit into traditional notions of nation-states without empires (Serbia, Greece, Romania).[36]

Next, the international system has two apparently inconsistent *ordering principles*. A legal, de jure **anarchy** exists alongside an informal, de facto **hierarchy**. All states have a similar legal existence and associated set of rights and privileges; for example, they all reserve the right to self defense. Legally, they're equal. But hierarchies of wealth, power, and influence lead to significant variation in the extent to which states can (and choose to) act on their own in wielding (or carrying out) the threat of force. It's worth defining these terms before we move on, because we'll confront them often through the remainder of the book. First, when we refer to international "anarchy," we don't imply a lack of order. We don't equate it with chaos, as it's easy to do in everyday speech. Anarchy simply

---

[35] For a (deservedly) famous similar effort, see Waltz (1979).

[36] The modern "Westphalian" system of states is traditionally held to have begun in Europe before spreading around the world, but that claim is too Euro-centric. Territorial states existed in other regions of the world and at other times, including premodern East Asia (see Kang, 2010). What is notable about the post–World War II era, but less so for the first half of the twentieth century, is that virtually all political units are or strive to be territorial states; before 1945, much of the globe was made up of the imperial holdings of a few uniquely powerful territorial states.

denotes the lack of a common authority, where, from the ancient Greek, *an* means "without" and *archy* means "authority." States are formally, legally equal, and they can all resort to war if they wish, with no restraints in principle: if the leader can order an army into the field, she can threaten war in the defense or pursuit of her state's interests. Anarchy is a particular type of order that happens to involve no central authority, where formally equal actors govern themselves. It also sustains common ideas about state sovereignty, i.e., that governments are free to do what whey wish within their own borders, because there is no higher legal authority above them.

DEFINITION 1.5 *Anarchy is the absence of a common authority.*

Anarchy's main implication is that states follow rules that they make and enforce themselves, from trade agreements to the placement of borders to limitations on armaments. There is no world government to punish cheaters and secure restitution for victims. Agreements remain in force only so long as the parties are all happier inside the agreement than they would be outside of it, and the freedom to threaten war to change agreements can make self-enforcing deals difficult to create and to sustain. Therefore, de jure anarchy means that international agreements must be **self-enforcing** if they're to win states' compliance.[37] Borders are a clear example. If states can use war to take and hold territory, then disputed borders remain in place only so long as neither side thinks it'll be profitable to take the other's land; if, however, both sides have about what they expect to obtain by fighting a bloody, wasteful war, then the border doesn't require a higher authority to enforce it. That is, if both sides agree that the border won't move much after a possible war, it is *self*-enforcing. As we'll see, self-enforcing agreements are hard to reach and to sustain, because they rest on the assent of multiple parties – i.e., on strategic interaction.

DEFINITION 1.6 *An agreement is **self-enforcing** when no party expects that it can profit from trying to renegotiate the agreement.*

Legal, de jure anarchy means that states are equal. None has authority over the others, and in a strict sense that's true of the international system. In practice, however, states rank each other on a number of dimensions, sorting themselves into de facto hierarchies.

DEFINITION 1.7 *A **hierarchy** is a ranking of units along a given dimension.*

All states have the right to self-defense, but only some have the financial and material power to exercise that right effectively. In 1914, for example,

---

[37] Learn this concept. It's going to be *everywhere*.

France proved more adept at defending its territory against German attack than did its smaller neighbor, Belgium. This creates one particular hierarchy that will inform many of our subsequent discussions: the hierarchy of military power. At the top of this hierarchy are the **great powers**, those states that are rich and militarily strong, capable of projecting power beyond their own borders.[38]

DEFINITION 1.8   *A **great power** is a state whose wealth and military strength allow it to project power beyond its borders and whose status is recognized by the other great powers.*

Thanks to their significant wealth and capabilities, great powers also shape the foreign policy decisions of middle and minor powers, which fall below the great powers in the hierarchy and are often dependent on the support of more powerful patrons for their safety.[39] Great powers also recognize each other as great powers, granting each other certain rights and privileges they don't offer to other states, making membership in the great power club extremely valuable.[40] Other hierarchies exist, from prestige to moral authority. But in a system where the ultimate arbiter of who gets what is war, factors like wealth, military power, and prestige tend to track together.[41] We'll see throughout our story that positions in the global hierarchy are highly valued – and often fought over.

Finally, the international system isn't static. The geographical stage stays the same, but the script sees some occasional revision, and the actors experience fairly frequent turnover. Just compare the world of today, where the United States is a superpower set apart from its nearest competitors in terms of military capabilities, financial power, and cultural influence, to the world of 1939, where American power was substantial if primarily economic, and where its lead in military power was only potential; Great Britain, France, Germany, the Soviet Union, and Japan all wielded competitive levels of military capabilities. The world of 1914 was still more different, dominated by now-dead European colonial empires. But what drives changes in the system's units or the principles by which they're ordered? The answer is simple: war (and often merely the threat of war). Mao Tse-tung wasn't wrong when he said that political power grows out of the barrel of a gun, and nowhere is this more obvious than in international

---

[38] See Fordham (2011).
[39] See Lake (2009).
[40] Great power recognition is also a key driver in determining which secessionist groups get their own recognized states and which don't (Coggins, 2011).
[41] Pre-twentieth-century China is a great example. Thanks to its overwhelming wealth and military power, sovereign states like Korea, Japan, and Vietnam were tribute states, and the latter even allowed China to change its proposed name from "Nam Viet" to "Viet Nam." See Kang (2010).

relations. Rights, privileges, borders, the autonomy of ruling elites, and the very existence of states are the products of bargains that reflect in rough form the likely outcome of wars that are (or could be) fought to determine them. (*Could be* is an important qualifier; one hardly needs to fight if one can convince an opponent of what the outcome of the fight will be.) War destroys and creates states, hierarchies, borders, elites, alignments, and institutions; it periodically recreates the international system along new lines defined by the victors of major wars.[42] Our story will trace this process of destruction and re-creation through one specific example: the global catastrophe of the Great War.

We can use this basic framework of units, ordering principles, and agents of change to draw some conclusions about what states disagree and, sometimes, fight over. A system organized around territorial states in an anarchic (self-enforcing) legal environment will be be prone to specific types of disagreements, some of which will be resolved by resorting to armed force.[43] States tend to dispute the placement of borders and who governs particular territories, and since controlling the state is inherently valuable, the question of who governs will also provoke civil war within some states. States also fight in order to reorder their places in the hierarchy, to gain control over the behavior of other states, or to prevent, stall, or reverse the rise of others to great power status. Finally, in a strategically interconnected system, a local dispute over the assassination of a successor to the imperial throne of Austria-Hungary can lead in the span of just a few weeks to all of Europe's great powers marching to war against each other. As we'll see in Chapter 2, though, wars are not the inevitable consequence of conflicting interests or of demands for change. Much more often than not, states find diplomatic solutions to their problems without having to fight a war first. Figuring out why war sometimes precedes treaties and why states sometimes get straight to the treaties will be a challenge that follows us throughout the book.

1.5 A PLAN FOR THE BOOK

This text traces the outbreak, conduct, and end of the First World War, unfolding in a series of historical and tool-building chapters in which we introduce and practice the fundamentals of game theory as applied to politics. Some, like those focused on the modern theory of war (Chapters 2, 5, 11, and 12), are exclusively tool-focused in that they don't address puzzles specific to the Great War, but others (like Chapter 8) introduce new

---

[42] McDonald (2015).
[43] This discussion owes a debt to Wagner (2007) and McDonald (2015).

tools in the context of otherwise historical chapters. Some, like Chapter 11, include supplemental game-theoretic exercises that focus on important substantive questions, in this case the role of economic interdependence in the outbreak of war. Each chapter, whether tool-building or historical, begins by identifying a puzzle, an event or decision or pattern that seems to cut against the grain of our expectations or that runs counter to the received wisdom.[44] In Chapter 2, for example, we'll observe that wars end in peace treaties, just like most disagreements that don't need war to be resolved. Why, we'll ask, are some disagreements resolved peacefully and others violently? Then, we'll introduce the basics of game theory as a way to explore strategic problems, learning the processes of theory and explanation in political science. Finally, each chapter takes the concepts introduced in the analysis of the Great War and discusses their use in the broader political science literature on international war and peace. Returning to our example of Chapter 2, after developing one of the several explanations for war we'll encounter in the book, it explores other historical applications of the same strategic story of relative decline, credible commitments, and preventive war.

Chapters begin narrow and end wide. Some chapters (Chapters 2, 5, 11, and 12) address similar puzzles, while others address multiple puzzles, especially if they can help illustrate key concepts in the logic of explanation, the process of discovery, or the state of the art in political science. But the primary sequence of puzzles isolates several distinct events that follow the timeline of the war itself:

- **Chapter 2.** Why do states sometimes fail to reach peaceful settlements before fighting wars they know to be costly and wasteful?
- **Chapter 3.** Why couldn't Britain and Germany avoid a costly naval arms race that left their relative power unchanged?
- **Chapter 4.** Why did a local dispute between Austria and Serbia expand into a costly war between the other great powers?
- **Chapter 5.** Why do states sometimes fail to reach peaceful settlements before fighting wars they know to be costly and wasteful?[45]
- **Chapter 6.** Why was Great Britain unmoved by a German threat to *France*, but driven to intervene in the European war by a German threat to *Belgium*?
- **Chapter 7.** Why were the Entente powers able to cooperate on the Western Front, while cooperation broke down between the Central Powers in the East?

---

[44] On identifying puzzles, see Zinnes (1980).
[45] Yes, that's the same puzzle as Chapter 2.

- **Chapter 8.** What led all the belligerents to adopt conscious strategies of attrition?
- **Chapter 9.** Why did Italy abandon neutrality for the Entente, while the Ottoman Empire abandoned neutrality for the Central Powers?
- **Chapter 10.** Why did Great Britain and Germany wage a limited naval war while waging a total war on land?
- **Chapter 11.** Why do most wars end in compromise peace rather than total victory?
- **Chapter 12.** Why do most wars end in compromise peace rather than total victory?[46]
- **Chapter 13.** Why did the United States enter the Great War in 1917 after years of neutrality?
- **Chapter 14.** Why did Germany request an armistice in 1918, and why did its enemies grant it?

Chapter 15, which concludes, offers lessons for relating the international politics of the Great War to our own time but addresses no specific puzzles per se. This list makes one thing abundantly clear: the narrative of the war is necessarily incomplete. The book selects a few critical events that illustrate more general political problems, from arms races to coalition-building to war termination, then walks through their underlying strategic logics, before relating the chapter's theory to broader questions in the study of international relations. But it's manifestly not an exhaustive history of the war: key events, key experiences, key people and peoples are inevitably given short shrift or left out entirely. From the women at home allowed, if briefly, to enter the workforce, to the colonial subjects sent to the front or conscripted into labor battalions (to say nothing of the Chinese civilians that did so for their own reasons), to the Russian revolutions and subsequent civil war, to the battles that raged across Africa and the Middle East, much of the war remains outside the narrow light cast by this volume's fifteen chapters. The social-scientific tools we develop in each chapter, however, are equally applicable to the other political venues of the war that I lack the space or the expertise to cover.

Finally, the next thirteen chapters all involve mathematics, some of it intensive but none of it more demanding than basic algebra. Game-theoretic models have been at the forefront of theoretical innovation in the study of international relations for almost three decades. Game theory allows us to represent complex social phenomena in a logically coherent way, trading the slipperiness of verbal language for the logical precision and clarity of math. We'll still use sentences, of course, but not verbal ones. Verbal sentences that contain *are* and *is* become equations, and sentences

---

[46] Yes, that's the same puzzle as the previous chapter.

with *more than*, *less than*, or *preferred to* become inequalities. And what we do with those sentences isn't new: we'll just use them to build arguments. The key, though, is that translating our intuitions into equations and inequalities ensures that our logic is sound, that our arguments are valid, and that we can speak without contradiction about the how and the why of strategic interaction and international politics. The models and the associated math begin simple, then grow in complexity over the course of the book as the war itself grows in scope and scale, but we'll introduce each game-theoretic tool in simple, stark terms and walk through the math carefully and thoroughly. All chapters include guided exercises in the form of propositions and mathematical proofs, while some include supplemental exercises that offer opportunities to practice or dig deeper into important tools not used in the main body. At each point, the mathematics are worked out carefully and intuitively, allowing you to develop a facility for the tools of game-theoretic analysis that'll serve you well any time you want to learn something about the how and the why of politics, whether global, international, or local.

2 The Theory of War I: Commitment Problems

The world is a messy and confusing place. We do not enhance our under-standing of it by saying messy and confusing things about it.

R. Harrison Wagner,
"Who's Afraid of Rational Choice Theory?"

This chapter introduces the primary tool we'll use to analyze the politics of the First World War: game theory. We'll develop some basic skills, then use them to think about a question that's surprisingly difficult to answer:

> Conflicts typically end in peace settlements, so why do states sometimes fail to reach those settlements before waging wasteful wars?

Put differently, why are some peace settlements preceded by war, while most are signed (or simply upheld) without bloody, destructive fighting? Waging a war destroys lives, treasure, and sometimes the very thing being divided up, but negotiations don't. So why divide things in a wasteful way when a cheaper option is available? The answer to this question isn't straightforward, but the tools of game theory can help us reduce the clutter, identify the essentials of the problem, and gain some insight into why states sometimes fight and sometimes skip the fighting and get straight to the treaty-making. This chapter presents the first of two solutions to the puzzle of war, based on the very common – if not "quintessentially" – political problem of making credible promises. Thanks to de jure anarchy, states can't promise ahead of time to take a course of action that won't later be in their interest. In this chapter's key example, a state that expects to be more powerful in the future may be unable to promise others that it won't act in accordance with that newfound power when the chance comes along, leading others to fear that the status quo won't be self-enforcing for much longer, thus encouraging war today.

Game theory uses the language of mathematics to analyze strategic interactions, like two states bargaining over the placement of a disputed border, in a spare and logically coherent setting. Game models describe the world in terms of four basic elements: actors, preferences, strategies, and outcomes. After defining games, we'll discuss how to solve them – that is, how to figure out how goal-directed decision-makers like presidents, citizens, subjects, and generals are likely to play them – and make guesses about likely outcomes by introducing the concept of Nash Equilibrium. Therefore, in this chapter, we'll:

- introduce the components of game-theoretic models;
- demonstrate how to find a game's Nash Equilibrium;
- show how to write down a game that can resolve a puzzle about politics;
- use a simple game to provide one solution to the puzzle of war.

We close the chapter by practicing the game-theoretic skills we'll use in subsequent chapters to write down and solve our own games. We'll see that writing down the right game isn't always straightforward, that there's an art to choosing the right components for our models, but that there can be a significant payoff in terms of teaching us something new ... and in showing us just how challenging it can be to write down a useful, insightful model.

Key Terms for Chapter 2

- Strategic Interaction
- Crisis Bargaining
- Preferences
- Complete Information
- Strategy (again)
- Strategy Profile
- Nash Equilibrium
- Common Conjecture
- Profitable Deviation
- Payoff Function
- Unique Equilibrium
- Commitment Problem
- Preventive War

2.1 A BRIEF INTRODUCTION TO GAME THEORY

Game theory is a branch of mathematics developed as a way to analyze optimal choices when each of several actors' ability to get what she wants depends on others' choices. Interdependent choice is the essence of **strategic interaction**, itself one of the fundamental elements of politics (and the social world in general). Citizens voice support for political candidates, or vote for them, based on the expected reactions of their friends, family, co-partisans, and political enemies. Candidates choose to enter Congressional races based on who else they expect to compete, their chances of defeating them, and their relative abilities to raise money and get out the vote. Countries choose whether to seize territory by taking into account the reaction of the country whose land they wish to take, as well as the reaction of the target's (and their own) friends and allies. Countries also choose to join ongoing wars based on both what potential partners offer them and the punishment they expect to receive from the victors should they end up on the losing side.

DEFINITION 2.1 *The outcomes of* **strategic interaction** *depend on the aggregated, interdependent choices of multiple actors.*

It's hard to think about politics *without* thinking about strategic interaction. Game theory has been applied throughout the social sciences to gain insights into how contingency plans, or strategies, chosen by multiple actors, from presidents and diplomats to generals and soldiers to voters and protestors, can add up to frequently unexpected and often tragic social and political outcomes.[1]

Games are simple models designed to represent the essentials of strategic settings and how people, or aggregations of people, act within them. As we noted in Chapter 1, they're metaphors; they just happen to be made up of beautiful deductive structures. We'll use models to capture a few, though by no means the only, dimensions of a puzzling event or phenomenon, to distill it to a few key moving parts, to see how those moving parts interact, and to see whether these moving parts add up to something that looks enough like the real world to teach us something about it. Games are attractive for both their abstraction (or, if you prefer, simplicity) and their logical rigor. Without a reliable check on the logic of our arguments, without some kind of accounting mechanism to keep us honest, it's easy to engage in plausible but sloppy, and therefore uninsightful or misleading, thinking. We'll see that many of our intuitions, including much of the received wisdom about international politics, relies on seductive – oftentimes resonant – but ultimately incomplete or unsatisfactory arguments. We'll see that *assumption* isn't a dirty word but that *intuition* probably is.[2] Paul Krugman says it well when he identifies complex strategic settings, particularly those with economic or political components, as "the kind of situation in which words alone can create an illusion of logical coherence that dissipates when you try to do the math."[3] Our goal is to ensure that our explanations are clear, transparent, coherent, and contestable. Game theory happens to be an excellent tool for "doing the math" required to meet those goals.

---

[1] There are many accessible references on game theory available for the interested reader. I cut my teeth on textbooks by Kreps (1990), Fudenberg and Tirole (1991), and Morrow (1994). But this is only a small sample of the available options.

[2] Old Ben Kenobi would've had it right if he'd told young Luke Skywalker, "Your *intuition* can deceive you. Don't trust it." Eyes, frankly, have little to do with it.

[3] See www.nybooks.com/articles/2016/07/14/money-brave-new-uncertainty-mervyn-king/.

2.1.1   Games

A game is a setting in which at least two actors, or *players*, make choices toward the attainment of some goal and where each actor's choice affects others' ability to achieve their goals. A game can represent a parlor or casino game, snooker or chess, football or basketball, a competition for votes, passing legislation in the shadow of presidential vetoes and Supreme Court rulings, or a war in which belligerents use violence to try to force the other to capitulate to their demands. It has four elements:

1 **players** who make choices in pursuit of some goals;
2 **actions**, or courses of action, available to each player;
3 **outcomes** produced by the combination of each player's chosen action;
4 **preferences** by which each player ranks possible outcomes of the game.

Games characterize strategic interactions by defining who's involved (players), what actions they can take (strategies), the consequences of their choices (outcomes), and how players rank those outcomes against the achievement of their goals (preferences). Players can be individuals, groups of individuals, bureaucracies, voters, presidents, emperors, soldiers, sailors, generals – any entity, singly or collectively, that makes a choice in a strategic setting. Strategies are the actions available to players when they make choices: vote for candidate A or B, attack or accommodate country C, accept an alliance (or not) from country D if it offers one, raise tariffs on country E if it raises tariffs on your own country, etc. Outcomes are the endpoints of the interaction, defined by the combination of players' choices: candidate A or B wins, war or peace with country C, signing an alliance or not with country D, etc. Outcomes depend on the interaction of players' strategies, a particular combination of which we call strategy profiles (a term we'll treat in in more detail later).

Figure 2.1 shows how we can assemble players, actions, and outcomes into a game in the *strategic form*, which characterizes a matrix of strategies that combine in strategy profiles to produce outcomes.[4] Player A (the row player) wants some land currently controlled by player B (the column player). In this simple representation of an international dispute, each side chooses a strategy, which we can think of as a bargaining position specifying how much to demand or to yield in lieu of war. The interaction of our players' bargaining positions, which constitutes a strategy profile, determines whether land is transferred peacefully or whether our players end up fighting a war over that land. This situation, where countries try to resolve disagreements in the shadow of a war that imposes an agreement

---

[4] You'll also see *normal form* used as a synonym for *strategic form*, but I prefer the latter for its clarity.

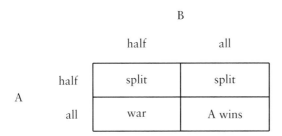

Figure 2.1 Players, actions, and outcomes.

at tremendous cost, is **crisis bargaining**. And it's become a standard the-oretical environment in which political scientists study both the outbreak and continuation of war.[5]

DEFINITION 2.2   *Crisis bargaining occurs when states negotiate over things they value in the shadow of possible war.*

Strategies, which the strategic form collapses into actions, are straight-forward in Figure 2.1. A chooses whether to demand half or all of the land under dispute, and B chooses whether it's willing to concede half or all the land. Two players with two choices each implies four possible outcomes, corresponding to four strategy profiles. Listing the row player's (A's) strategy first, we have (half; half), (half; all), (all; half), and (all; all). We can then translate strategy profiles into outcomes with a simple rule: if A demands no more than B is willing to concede, A's demands are met, but if A demands more than B is willing to concede, the two players go to war. Thus, if A demands half and B is willing to concede half, or (half; half), then they split the land. If A demands half when B is willing to concede all, or (half; all), A still only gets half, regretting of course that it didn't ask for the whole pie. Next, if A demands all but B only concedes half, or (all; half), then the two players go to war. Finally, if A demands all the land and B concedes all of it, or (all; all), then A gets all the land. Yet without some sense of how players evaluate and rank these possible outcomes – that is, without a sense of their **preferences** – we can't get a good sense of how they're likely to play the game.

DEFINITION 2.3   *A player's **preferences** rank the possible outcomes of a game.*

At minimum, a player's preferences define what it most wants, what it'll settle for if it must, and what it absolutely must avoid. In Figure 2.1, for example, A most wants to win all the land at B's expense, but it'll take half if it must, because A wants to avoid war at all costs. War may be more

---

[5] See, inter alia, Fearon (1995) and Powell (2006).

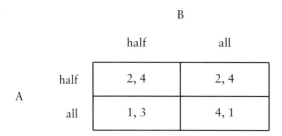

Figure 2.2 Players, actions, outcomes, and payoffs.

attractive than half the land in other settings (some of which we'll see in later chapters), but for now letting A rank war last helps demonstrate how preferences work. We use numbers to represent preferences, where larger numbers correspond to more desirable outcomes. It's important to note that the numbers we use – what game theory calls "payoffs" or "utilities" – at this point convey only *ordinal* information.[6] 2 is greater than 1, but an outcome with a payoff of 2 isn't necessarily twice as good as an outcome with a payoff of 1. All we care about for now is the rank ordering. We can thus represent A's preferences as placing 4 on "A wins," 2 on "split," and 1 on "war." (But we could also place 10 on "A wins," 2 on "split," and −7 on "war," and we would capture exactly the same set of ordinal preferences.) Next, we can posit a set of preferences for B in which it most prefers to limit concessions to a split where A only demands half (4), but B prefers war (3) to conceding all the territory (1). This version of our game, where the row player's payoffs are listed first (a convention we'll follow throughout the book), can be found in Figure 2.2. We now have a complete representation of the strategic situation: A most likes to demand and win all the land, but B would rather go to war than make a full concession.

In this and the following two chapters, we also assume that players know each of the four key elements of the games they play: players, actions, outcomes, and preferences. They know the choices available to each other, how those choices interact to produce outcomes, and how other players rank the game's possible outcomes. For our working example in Figure 2.2, A knows that B prefers war to yielding all the disputed land, and she also knows that war will result from demanding more than B chooses to concede. B, likewise, knows that A most wants to receive all the disputed territory but that A also ranks war as the worst possible outcome of the game. When players know each element of the game, we say that they have **complete information**.

[6] We'll relax the assumption of ordinality starting in Chapter 5.

DEFINITION 2.4   *In a game of **complete information**, all players know all elements of the game: players, actions, outcomes, and preferences.*

This may seem like a rather heroic assumption. Very often, players – especially states and their leaders – don't know each other's preferences. They may not be quite certain, for example, just how much their opponents will concede in lieu of war. We'll relax the assumption that players know each other's preferences in Chapter 5, but for now we'll start with complete information and see just how far we can get explaining some key features of the First World War without using any unnecessary theoretical machinery. If a theory can explain an otherwise puzzling outcome *without* reference to any extraneous theoretical constructs, that's to the theory's credit. Knowing what to leave out of the story is just as important as knowing what to keep in.

Before we continue, two brief notes about preferences are in order. First, some scholars draw a distinction between material and nonmaterial values, between factors like land and wealth on the one hand and prestige and emotional or expressive satisfaction on the other. That's not unreasonable, and our game-theoretic framework is conveniently compatible with both visions of what people value. As long as both material and nonmaterial values or goals can figure into a coherent preference ranking – and there's nothing inherent about either material or nonmaterial that says they can't be – then we don't need to worry about any such distinction: both kinds of values are consistent with our general framework.

Second, we use the language of mathematics, but we're *not* asserting that citizens, leaders, or military officers assign numerical values to or "quantify" particular outcomes. (That would be pretty strange, both for the analyst to believe about the world and for the people whose actions she hopes to explain.) As analysts, we use mathematics to *represent* players' preferences, but the math is just that: a representation, a metaphor that we can use to gain insight into the world. Preferences don't arise from payoffs; it's precisely the other way around, in that we write down payoffs to represent our players' preferences. We assign payoffs to our players in a way that we hope can usefully represent their goals, and the closer to reality our assignments of payoffs are, the deeper insight we can gain into the why and how of international politics – as long as our payoffs aren't too complicated. Remember that theories are maps, metaphors, useful abstractions from reality that help us simplify and understand an otherwise complicated, confusing reality. But their building blocks and moving parts are necessarily cruder and simpler than the real, unobservable processes playing out inside the heads of citizens, leaders, and military officers. Our goal is to write down preferences that can represent players' evaluations of outcomes reasonably well – that is, close enough to important parts of the political world for us to learn something from the models we write down and analyze.[7]

2.1.2 Nash Equilibrium

With our game specified, the next step is to figure out how A and B will play it. Faced with a particular strategic problem, what are goal-directed players likely to do? In strategic-form games, we conceive of players as choosing simultaneously, which is equivalent to (1) choosing with some uncertainty over what the other player is choosing or (2) committing to certain courses of action ahead of time. Countries work out negotiating positions, war-fighting plans, and alliance commitments by devising **strategies,** which are plans of action that specify what to do in the event that other players take a certain action. Strategies, which we define more precisely here than we did in Chapter 1, consider each possible contingency in the strategic interaction and specify what choices to make for each contingency.

DEFINITION 2.5   A *strategy is a plan of action that specifies what actions a player will take based on her beliefs about what actions other players will take.*

For the game in Figure 2.2, a strategy for player A is either "demand all" or "demand half." Either may end up being a bad strategy, but the key is that it works out a full (albeit very simple in this case) plan of action. Each of the major belligerents in the First World War worked out more complicated political and military strategies of just this type. Austria-Hungary, for example, had worked out contingencies involving different military deployments and allocations of force against Serbia, Russia, and both in the event of war, depending on which constellation of enemies it faced – and whether it had German support. When we talk about strategies, this is precisely what we mean. The plans entailed can be simple, such as "attack country D only if its allies abandon it," or incredibly complex, including contingencies that cover multiple other players over multiple interactions over arbitrarily long periods of time. The key to defining a strategy is that it specifies just such a "complete contingent" plan of action.[8] We will, however, keep the strategies we analyze as simple as possible, which makes it easier to keep track of the **strategy profiles** into which they combine to produce outcomes. For example, in Figure 2.2,

---

[7] For more on payoffs, utility, and the "rationality" of preferences, see Morrow (1994, chapter 2). Read it, think about it, and then read it again just to make sure you've got it.

[8] See Watson (2013, p. 22).

(half; half) is a strategy profile that produces a peaceful 50–50 split of the land, while (half; all) produces the same 50–50 split.

DEFINITION 2.6 *A **strategy profile** combines single strategies from each player to identify outcomes of a game.*

Next, we ask what strategies it makes sense for players to choose. To answer this question, we look for strategy profiles that exist in a **Nash Equilibrium**, named for Princeton mathematician John Nash.[9] When we say that strategies are "in equilibrium," we mean that each player in a game chooses a strategy that ensures it's doing the best it can in light of what the other players are doing. No more, no less. Suppose that we have two countries, D and E, waging war on one another, where each has the option to give up the fight by pulling its armies out of the field. Giving up while the other continues fighting amounts to defeat, while both giving up means that neither side captures the prize they're fighting over. If both choose to continue the fight, then war continues *in equilibrium* because the countries reason in this way:

- **Country D:** "Country E is continuing the fight. It's best that I also fight, because if I pull my armies out of the field while E's armies remain in the field, I'll face military defeat."
- **Country E:** "Country D is continuing the fight. It's best that I also fight, because if I pull my armies out of the field while D's armies remain in the field, I'll face military defeat."

In more technical terms, we say that strategies are in equilibrium when they are *best responses*, or *best replies*, to one another. We will also use the terms *mutual best replies* or *mutual best responses* to represent a set of strategies that are in equilibrium with each other. By definition, at a Nash Equilibrium neither player can gain or profit from choosing a different strategy.

DEFINITION 2.7 *At a **Nash Equilibrium**, each player does as well as she can, given what all the other players are doing.*

Thus, a Nash Equilibrium is self-enforcing (recall Definition 1.6): players abide by the stipulated strategies, such as honoring a mutual border or honoring the rules of international institutions, because they have no incentive to do otherwise in light of what others are doing.

---

[9] Nash worked out many of the relevant ideas in his dissertation, but they also appeared in article form in Nash (1950) and Nash (1951). It's worth noting here that the 2001 film *A Beautiful Mind* mischaracterizes Nash Equilibrium when called upon to do so. Thankfully, whether Nash Equilibrium teaches us anything about the world doesn't rely on whether people in the world know what it is or how to calculate one.

When we think about "equilibrium" colloquially, we tend to think of a state of balance, of opposing forces evenly matched. It makes us think of something peaceful, in fact. That's tempting, but it's also misleading. Equilibrium does imply a kind of balance, but only in terms of competing incentives – in terms of strategies, but *not* in terms of outcomes. A Nash Equilibrium can, for example, describe a situation in which two players fight a long, bloody war until one collapses in defeat; in this case, equilibrium means only that neither side believes that it would be better off by suing for peace. This is the essence of equilibrium – two opposing strategies matched against one another – but the example also brings home a key point about our definition of equilibrium. *Strategies* are balanced in an equilibrium, but that doesn't imply that *outcomes* have the peaceful and balanced features of our colloquial definition of the term. The chaos, dislocation, and destruction of war can emerge from strategies that are harmoniously, even elegantly, in equilibrium. When strategies are in equilibrium, we simply mean that plans, not the outcomes they produce, are in a stable balance.[10] No side has an incentive to deviate from its *plan*, given how its plan interacts with other players' plans. But this says *nothing* about whether the outcomes of equilibrium strategies, like calamitous world wars, fit any casual definition of "equilibrium" as an observable outcome.

Next, if strategies are to be in equilibrium, to be mutual best responses, then players must also have a reasonable guess about each other's strategies if they're to consider the consequences of their own choices. Therefore, Nash Equilibrium also depends on the existence of a **common conjecture**, a set of shared beliefs about what other players are likely to do under different contingencies, or what their strategies will tell them to do in response to other players' choices.

DEFINITION 2.8   *The **common conjecture** contains players' shared knowledge about features of the game and all other players' strategies.*

The common conjecture is the set of shared ideas that permeate international politics, containing definitions of war and peace, how to bargain, what terms of art in diplomacy mean peace and which mean war, who is and isn't a great power, how to tell friend from foe, and the rules of thumb and heuristics by which countries interpret international relations. The common conjecture is the very stuff of the social world, the intersubjectively constructed ideas about how the world works that facilitate and help us interpret social interactions.[11]

---

[10] There's a paper to be written about the difference between equilibrium as an outcome and as a solution concept that draws on ideas of balancing the dark and light sides of the Force, but I'm not the guy to do it, however tempting it might be.

[11] Watson's (2013) discussion of the common conjecture and its relationship to Nash Equilibrium is simple, elegant, and compelling.

Common conjectures set standards for acceptable behavior, prescribe appropriate and inappropriate responses, create anticipations about the behavior of others, allow the actors to comprehend each other's actions, and can differentiate the social roles of the actors even when they have no differences in their capabilities [or, for our purposes, power].[12]

Without some knowledge of how other players view, interpret, and respond to each other's choices, players can't choose their own strategies; they may not even know what game they're playing. The common conjecture represents the collected rules of the game of international politics. These ideas and rules can come from shared experience, readings of history, the weight of tradition, and even the content of international law, all of which are themselves the product of politics. All games have rules, but in politics the players compete in defining them. We'll talk about the sources of the common conjecture later – it'll be especially important in Chapter 6 – but for now it's worth noting that shared knowledge of each other's strategies is required for a Nash Equilibrium. This shared knowledge constitutes the social world of ideas and culture that we use to describe and understand both our actions and the actions of others; strategic interaction is inherently social, and it only makes sense that we'd take seriously the world of ideas that shape the social world when we write down and analyze games to understand it.

Finally, how do we recognize a Nash Equilibrium when we see one? The answer is pretty simple. (And it needs to be, if we're going to gain insight into otherwise complicated events.) Return to the game in Figure 2.2, where A would like to take as much of B's territory as possible without going to war over it. B, on the other hand, would like to concede as little as possible and prefers war to yielding all the disputed land. To find a Nash Equilibrium, we propose a pair of strategies (a strategy profile), which we write as (all; half), with the row player's action listed first and the column player's listed second. Then, we ask whether either player has a **profitable deviation** from the proposed strategy profile. If the answer is no, we've found a Nash Equilibrium.

DEFINITION 2.9   *A player has a **profitable deviation** when, holding all other players' strategies constant, it can do better with a different strategy than the strategy proposed for it.*

Put differently, we ask whether either player can do better than its proposed action by choosing a different action in response to the other player's action. We take two strategies, hold A's fixed and see if B can do better than the strategy we've given it, then hold B's fixed and see if A can

---

[12] Morrow (2014, p. 24).

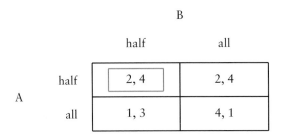

Figure 2.3 An example of a Nash Equilibrium.

do better than the strategy we've given it. If *any* player has a profitable deviation, then the proposed strategy profile can't be a Nash Equilibrium. One player might be happy with the outcome, but if the other has a better option, our candidate strategies are not in equilibrium. But if *neither* player has a better option, if neither has a profitable deviation from its strategy, then we have a Nash Equilibrium, and a sense of how the game is likely to be played.

In our candidate equilibrium of (all; half), the payoffs are (1, 3), because the players end up in a war: A demands the whole pie but B will concede only half, so a contest of arms must resolve their disagreement. Can A or B do better by choosing a different action in response to the other player's strategy? Examining the game reproduced in Figure 2.3, it's clear that B's happy to fight rather than yield the whole pie; switching to yield all the territory would yield its worst outcome of 1. A, though, *can* do better than demanding all given that B will yield only half. At the proposed equilibrium (all; half), A gets 1, but if instead it deviates to demanding half, it gets 2. Thus, A has a profitable deviation, and (all; half) can't be a Nash Equilibrium. Whether B alone is playing a best response is immaterial; all it takes to rule out a possible Nash Equilibrium is to show that one player has an incentive to do something different in response to the other's strategy. We make formal claims like this in propositions, which we can then prove by "doing the math" required to establish the claims.

Proposition 2.1 establishes a format for proofs that we'll use for the remainder of the book, where we state a set of inequalities that must be true for strategies to be in equilibrium, in that each player's payoff at the proposed equilibrium is at least as good as the payoff for deviating unilaterally to a different strategy. The inequalities include each player's **payoff function** (also called a *utility function*), labeled u_A and u_B, for the proposed equilibrium and for the best possible deviation from or alternative to that strategy profile; a utility function takes an outcome as its input, then produces a payoff as an output.

DEFINITION 2.10 *A **payoff function** translates a game's outcomes into the rank-ordered payoffs that describe a player's preferences.*

Therefore, $u_A(all; \text{half}) \geq u_A(half; \text{half})$ compares A's payoffs for (all; half) to (half; half), where it considers switching from all to half (with the choice in question italicized) given that B is playing half; and $u_B(all; half) \geq u_B(all; all)$ compares B's payoffs for (all; half) to (all; all), where it considers switching from half to all given that A is playing all.

PROPOSITION 2.1 *The strategy profile (all; half) is not a Nash Equilibrium.*

Proof For (all; half) to be a Nash Equilibrium, it must be the case that

$$u_A(all; \text{half}) \geq u_A(half; \text{half}) \quad \text{and} \quad u_B(all; half) \geq u_B(all; all).$$

But $u_A(all; \text{half}) \geq u_A(half; \text{half})$ requires $1 \geq 2$, which is untrue. At least one player has a profitable deviation, so (all; half) is not a Nash Equilibrium. □

Proposition 2.1 makes a claim – that a given strategy profile does *not* constitute a Nash Equilibrium – and we follow it with a proof of the logic supporting the claim. Demanding all when B is willing to yield half is counterproductive, given A's preferences; it would prefer taking half the land over a wasteful, risky war for the whole prize. And if one player has a profitable deviation, we can reject the proposed equilibrium. This helps us reject guesses about how a game is likely to be played, and the reason we reject this particular guess tracks with our understanding of international politics developed in Chapter 1: states generally choose freely between war and peace, and peace obtains when no side thinks war will give it a better deal than what it's got (in this case, A has no incentive to demand so much of B that they end up in war). For both Proposition 2.1 and the arguments we'll make throughout the book, proofs give readers a reason to believe what we're saying. Stripped of the ambiguity, slipperiness, and artifice of prose, our arguments can be made more transparent, more understandable, and, perhaps most importantly, more contestable.[13]

In that spirit of looking for possible equilibria, consider (half; half), where A demands half of the disputed territory and B concedes half, yielding payoffs of (2, 4). Can this be a Nash Equilibrium? To check this possibility, we again see whether A or B can do better than its proposed action, given what the other player is doing. In this case, we *do* have a Nash

---

[13] In many cases, those features of prose are valuable. But not when we're trying to build arguments. Clarity and transparency are our watchwords here.

Equilibrium; only one player gets its first best outcome, but neither has a profitable deviation from the proposed strategy profile.

PROPOSITION 2.2   *The strategy profile (half; half) is a Nash Equilibrium.*

Proof   For (half; half) to be a Nash Equilibrium, it must be the case that

$$u_A(half;\text{half}) \geq u_A(all;\text{half}) \quad \text{and} \quad u_B(\text{half};half) \geq u_A(\text{half};all).$$

The first inequality is satisfied because $2 \geq 1$, and the second is satisfied because $4 \geq 4$. No player has a profitable deviation, so (half; half) is a Nash Equilibrium.   □

Let's walk through the reasoning that supports this equilibrium. A knows that B is willing to concede half, so can A do better by switching from demanding half to demanding all? No. If A demands all, given that B is conceding only half, these incompatible bargaining postures touch off a war in which A receives 1. So A's strategy is a best reply to B's strategy. That gets us halfway there. What about player B, who must choose whether to concede half rather than all the disputed land? B receives 4 at this strategy profile, and if its bargaining posture changes to yielding all, B still only loses half, because that's all A demands. B gets 4 either way, so it's indifferent over conceding half and conceding all. And by the rules of Nash Equilibrium, this means that B doesn't have a profitable deviation. Since neither A nor B can do better against the other's strategy than they do in the proposed strategy profile, (half; half) is a Nash Equilibrium. Working through equilibrium reasoning, we can see why:

- **Player A:** "Player B is willing to concede half, so it's better that I demand only half rather than demand all and fight a costly war."
- **Player B:** "Player A is demanding half, so I can do no better than yielding exactly that much."

However disappointing the outcome for A might be (it would prefer to capture more land, after all), it can do no better in response to B's strategy than the strategy we've proposed for it. The same is true for B.[14] At this point, we know that an equilibrium of (half; half) exists, where neither side gets its first-best option. But in order to make a firm behavioral prediction, we also want to know whether the equilibrium is **unique** – that is, whether it is the only strategy profile that satisfies the definition of a Nash

[14] This is very much what Otto von Bismarck meant when he called politics "the art of the possible." In strategic settings, it's not always possible for all sides to be satisfied at once, because one's pursuit of her goals can interfere with another's pursuit of his.

Equilibrium. In Chapter 10, we'll actually hope to find multiple equilibria, but for now our goal is to find unique ones.

DEFINITION 2.11   *A Nash Equilibrium is **unique** if it is the only equilibrium that exists for a given set of preferences.*

To check for uniqueness, we must consider whether other possible strategies can exist as Nash Equilibria. We'll walk through the logic informally here, but you can easily verify these claims by writing down and proving your own propositions. Doing so is a good exercise at this point. (*Hint, hint.*) Consider (all; all), where A demands all and B is willing to concede all, producing a peaceful settlement in which A wins the whole prize. Payoffs are (4, 1), such that A gets its most preferred outcome but B gets its worst outcome – the thing B absolutely must avoid if it can. Is there a profitable deviation? Yes. If A will demand all the land, then B's better off choosing to concede only half; it would rather fight a war, netting a payoff of 3, than give up all the disputed land. Therefore, (all, all) can't be a Nash Equilibrium. We can also rule out (half; all), in which A demands half when B is willing to concede all. At the proposed equilibrium, A gets 2, but given B's willingness to yield the whole pie, A would be foolish not to demand all and secure a payoff of 4. Thus, (half; all) can't be an equilibrium either. At the end of this process, we have a single Nash Equilibrium: 1 plays "half," and 2 plays "half." A won't fight the war that would follow demanding more than B is willing to concede, and B is happy to yield as little as possible to A. Therefore, the game in Figure 2.3 has a single, *unique* Nash Equilibrium, because one and only one combination of strategies are mutual best replies.

However complicated the strategies, whatever the stakes of the interaction, we can use this simple procedure to find a Nash Equilibrium of any game that we might write down. Our first example was simple but informative. If two countries disagree over the placement of a border, as we noted in Chapter 1 that they sometimes do, both may wish to avoid the calamity of war, but one side may use the other's greater fear of that war to demand and win concessions. This redistribution of territory may be unfortunate for B at the (half; half) Nash Equilibrium, but it's also a more common outcome than war: most of the time, disputes are settled peacefully, even those between ostensibly mortal, implacable enemies. (Think about how many years, days, and months the United States and the Soviet Union avoided World War III. That's instructive.) In our example, A knows just how far it can push B without provoking war, and A does exactly that, taking as much of the desired land as possible without touching off a war that both sides will come to regret. But countries sometimes *do* go to war, whether over territory, policy, who governs territories, or rights and privileges in the global hierarchy. Our model hasn't explained war yet, but it *has* told us that the simple opportunity to do so afforded by international anarchy isn't enough to get us there, and that's informative. Anarchy alone isn't a cause of war. But thanks to the clear logical structure of our model of crisis bargaining, we can in the next section add a feature to the baseline, developing our theory in a careful and iterative way, then show how it can give us insight into the outbreak of war and the collapse of cooperation – both of which will prove critical in explaining why the great powers went to war in August 1914.

2.2   COMMITMENT PROBLEMS AND WAR

Why do countries go to war? Sending armies into the field, workers to the arms factories, bombers into the air, and battleships out to sea with the aim of imposing tremendous amounts of pain on one's enemy is only one of many ways to resolve disagreements. It's also one of the most wasteful means of doing so. At war's end, both sides can generally look at the settlement that ended the bloody, ruinous fighting and ask, "Why didn't we sign the same agreement we just signed *before* all the death and destruction?" This isn't just a rhetorical question (and not just because pens and paper were surely available beforehand). The great majority of all wars in the last two hundred years have ended with both sides still standing and able in principle to stay in the fight. Even the most crushing defeats – like those suffered by Germany and Japan in 1945 – result in treaties signed by leaderships assenting to the terms of surrender. This chapter's question follows immediately. If states will go on to sign a peace treaty whether they fight the war or not, why bother to wage war beforehand? Why not just sign a similar treaty?

PUZZLE 2.1   *Why do states sometimes fail to reach peaceful settlements before fighting wars they know to be costly and wasteful?*

Key to our story is that countries and their leaders are in general both calculating and frugal. They pursue goals that range from bare survival to the establishment of an imperium, and they do so with an eye to minimizing waste along the way. Why, after all, burn up the army's fighting strength, distort the economy, or risk the lives of the citizenry by waging a war if the same concessions can be extracted from one's enemy via negotiations? This is what James Fearon calls the "rationalist puzzle of war": if states can write down the very same agreement before and after the war, why must they fight before signing it?[15] Why, in other words, do states end

---

[15] See Fearon (1995), one of the most influential (yet oddly misunderstood) pieces of political science written in the last few decades.

up fighting wars that they *know* are more wasteful than negotiations, especially when negotiations can, in principle, produce the same treaty? (Note that when we say that war is costly, we don't mean that it's never profitable, in the sense of the benefits never outweighing the costs. We simply mean that war is *inefficient*; it requires more resources or effort than other means of achieving the same thing.) Any war in which both sides end up back where they started – say, the Korean War or the Iran-Iraq War – makes this puzzle pretty stark.

This section develops the first of our two answers to this question. This answer focuses on one specific political problem: a rising country's inability to promise not to use newfound strength in the future. We'll shorthand this particular obstacle to cooperation, which we'll also call bargaining friction, as a **commitment problem**.

DEFINITION 2.12   *A **commitment problem** exists when a player cannot credibly promise not to take a certain action if given the opportunity.*

We'll begin our discussion of commitment problems in pretty abstract terms, which helps us focus on the processes of finding Nash Equilibria and using games to answer questions about politics. When commitment problems emerge later in our narrative, the applications will be more concrete. For now, our goal is to show how the tools of game theory can shed light on why two calculating, frugal countries can end up choosing strategies that will lead to a war that they know will be costly, destructive, and wasteful. Placing ourselves inside decision-makers' heads and confronting their choices in "real time" underlies our strategy for understanding the First World War, and we'll now work at using those skills directly.

Our approach to explaining war is built on two premises that follow from our discussion of how to define war (Definition 1.1). First, war is *political*. It is a means to an end, a method of resolving disagreements over territory, governance, influence – all the things we identified as sources of conflict in Chapter 1 – but not something that countries tend to wage for its own sake.[16] War is instrumental, one policy option among many from which state leaders can choose. This leads to our second premise: war is *wasteful*. It costs blood and treasure, and it can also destroy the very things that states fight over, blighting the land, killing the populace, and wrecking the cities that belligerents wish to control. War's waste is important for us relative to other means of resolving disagreements, such as direct negotiation, which is comparatively much less wasteful. When diplomats or heads of state hash out a bargain, they need not be shooting

---

[16] This isn't to say that *all* warfare is instrumental but that the wars we're trying to explain are – at least to the people making the ultimate decisions. This definition says little about the motivations of the people who go fight these wars once the policy has been set.

If C and D negotiate   If C and D fight

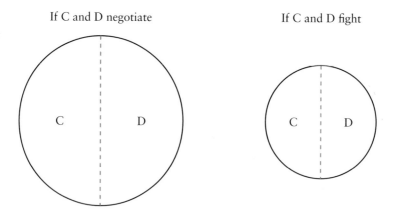

Figure 2.4 The inefficiency of war.

each other, bombing each other's cities, or stretching their economies to exhaustion in the process.

Figure 2.4 shows war's waste graphically. Suppose that countries C and D divide a patch of land down the middle. If they divide it peacefully, the land remains fertile, its citizens productive, and its infrastructure intact. The metaphorical pie to be divided is large. If, however, they fight over the land before dividing it down the middle, the destruction of war makes the land less valuable, so the circle shrinks. There's simply less to go around after a war. Calculating, frugal leaders therefore have strong incentives to avoid war if they can get a similar outcome through cheaper, less destructive means like negotiation.[17] This tells us something up front about how we should think about countries' preferences in the game-theoretic models that we specify and analyze in the remainder of this chapter: a country's first-best outcome, the thing it most wants, will rarely be war. Rather, just like A and B in Figures 2.1–2.3, it will prefer to achieve its primary goals without having to expend blood and treasure in the process. Whether a country *can* achieve its goals without ending up in war depends on what game it's playing and, in this chapter, whether a commitment problem stands in the way of reaching a settlement without having to fight for one.

Chapter 1 established that de jure anarchy in the international system means that states are free to go to (or threaten) war at any time, opting out of cooperative arrangements like borders or trade agreements or arms control treaties. This means that international agreements, if they are to work, must be self-enforcing (Definition 1.6). Agreements stick when no party prefers using war to renegotiate them, and since states can rise and fall in their military strength, they may find it difficult to promise to honor

---

[17] Even Adolf Hitler, it's worth noting, was happy to annex Austria, the Sudetenland, and then the rest of Czechoslovakia without having to fight for it. For recent histories of the period, see Tooze (2006) and Kershaw (2015).

the terms of today's agreement in perpetuity. If one side will grow stronger, it will be unable to resist the future temptation to use that newfound power to, say, expand its sphere of influence or revise a border. Fearing this, the country watching the other's rise may decide that a war today, despite its cost, will be better than a peace in which its current military position and the benefits that come with it will erode. This state might fight a wasteful war because the costs of fighting are lower than the costs of future weakness that a rising adversary will surely make it pay in the future.[18] Jack Levy notes that costs of such future weakness

> include diminishing bargaining leverage, the likelihood of escalating demands by an increasingly powerful adversary, the risk of war under worse circumstances later, and the fear of the peace that one would have to accept to avoid a future war.[19]

This is the essence of the commitment problem: a rising side will be unable to commit ahead of time not to use the strength that will so menace a declining side's position in the future.

To see this worked out in game form, suppose that countries A and B once again find themselves in disagreement over who should control a piece of land, but they must now choose strategies that look farther into the future than a single interaction in the present. Suppose that A controls the land and has the military strength to defend it. Furthermore, if A can retain control of the land peacefully, it's happy to do so. Country B, though, will grow stronger in the future if A doesn't interfere with its rise (say, by dismembering B or replacing its government). As such, we'll call B the *rising* side and A the *declining* side. If B is allowed to grow stronger, then it must choose whether it will use that strength in the future to "renege" on today's border agreement and seize some of A's land, or to continue to "honor" the agreement despite A's diminished ability to defend it. (In other words, B must choose whether or not to leave unused power on the table in the future.) For its part, A must choose between "attack" today, launching a war designed to prevent state B from rising in power, or to "pass" on that chance and hope that B doesn't renege on today's bargain from a future position of strength.

Figure 2.5 depicts this interaction in a strategic-form game that collapses each side's long-term strategy into two simple choices. A, the declining side, chooses between "pass," which means allowing B to grow stronger and dealing with the consequences down the line, and "attack," which means attacking today to limit B's ability to grow stronger (at the extreme, eliminating B). State B, the rising side, chooses between "honor,"

---

[18] This is the basic story behind many game-theoretic treatments of the commitment problem (e.g., Fearon 1995; Powell 2004b, 2006; Wolford, Reiter, and Carrubba 2011).

[19] Levy (2014, p. 139).

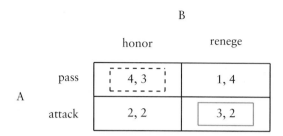

Figure 2.5 Commitment problems and war.

which entails honoring today's border into the future despite growing strength, and "renege," which entails honoring the deal today but using its future strength to renegotiate the border in the future when it gets the chance. This renegotiation can be an attack, or simply coercive demands made under pain of attack, but either would occur only *after* B has waited to grow stronger in the future and built a military advantage over state A. Our question is whether A allows this to happen when devising its own strategy.

The game has four outcomes. If A passes on war, it allows military power to shift in B's favor, which opens up two possibilities. First, if B honors the border, then A receives its best payoff (4), because it retains control of its territory despite its reduced future ability to defend it. But if A passes and B reneges, A gets its worst payoff (1), because it has allowed power to shift against it such that B can eventually force A to negotiate away valuable territory under pain of a war it can no longer successfully wage. If, however, A attacks, it fights from today's position of strength before its power can erode in the future. Even if A wins, it still pays the blood and treasure of fighting a war, so this is its second-worst outcome, yielding a payoff of 2. B's preferences are quite different. Its most desired outcome is for A to pass on war today, which allows B to rise peacefully before renegotiating the border in its favor from a position of strength (yielding a payoff of 4). B's next best option is to avoid war in the present and to honor the agreement in the future, despite its growing strength, because doing so saves the costs and destruction of war. Therefore, if B avoids war and lives with today's border into the future, it receives 3 (its second-best outcome, which is also A's first-best). Finally, B's worst outcome follows A choosing to attack, which denies B any chance to honor or renege in the future, because it is denied the chance to grow stronger *and* must pay the costs of war.

How will calculating, frugal leaders play this game? At a casual glance, our eyes are naturally drawn to the upper left strategy profile of (pass; honor), highlighted with a dashed line, where A passes and B simply honors today's border into the future. War is averted, and the total welfare of each side is maximized; A gets its most-desired outcome and B gets its second-best outcome. From the perspective of a benevolent social planner, this isn't bad. It certainly saves all the destruction and loss of war. Soldiers and civilians are alive that wouldn't be otherwise, and the land remains usable instead of bombed out, mined, irradiated, or emptied of inhabitants. But the international system has no benevolent social planner. Can the peaceful outcome of (pass; honor) be a Nash Equilibrium? First, we can see that A has no profitable deviation; attacking today is counterproductive (yielding 2) if B will honor the border (yielding 4 for state A). One player's happiness, though, isn't enough to ensure that we have an equilibrium. Continuing to check for profitable deviations from (pass; honor), it's apparent that B can't credibly promise to honor the agreement into the future: if it knows that A will pass and allow it to grow stronger, then B has every incentive to deviate from "honor" (which yields 3) to "renege" (which yields 4), keeping the peace today because it knows it can extract concessions from a position of strength in the future.

PROPOSITION 2.3 *The strategy profile (pass; honor) is not a Nash Equilibrium.*

Proof For (pass; honor) to be a Nash Equilibrium, it must be the case that

$u_A(pass; \text{honor}) \geq u_A(attack; \text{honor})$ and $u_B(\text{pass}; honor) \geq u_B(\text{pass}; renege)$.

But $u_B(\text{pass}; honor) \geq u_B(\text{pass}; renege)$ requires $3 \geq 4$, which is untrue. At least one player has a profitable deviation, so (pass; honor) cannot be a Nash Equilibrium. □

Proposition 2.3 reveals the essence of B's commitment problem: it can't promise ahead of time not to act in accordance with newfound power if given the chance. This undermines its commitment to an equilibrium honoring the current agreement into the future. As we can see in Proposition 2.4, this has implications for A's willingness to let today's military advantage pass without attacking from a position of strength.

PROPOSITION 2.4 *The strategy profile (attack; renege) is a Nash Equilibrium.*

Proof For (attack; renege) to be a Nash Equilibrium, it must be the case that

$$u_A(attack; \text{renege}) \geq u_A(pass; \text{renege})$$

and

$$u_B(\text{attack}; renege) \geq u_B(\text{attack}; honor).$$

The first inequality is satisfied because $3 \geq 1$, and the second is satisfied because $2 \geq 2$. No player has a profitable deviation, so (attack; renege) is a Nash Equilibrium.   □

Tragically, the game's only Nash Equilibrium is (attack; renege). B plays a strategy of waiting before trying to renegotiate from a future position of strength, but A attacks in the present to prevent that eventuality. The outcome can be found in the gray-highlighted cell at the bottom right of Figure 2.5, where both players are worse off than they would be at (pass; honor), receiving (3, 2) as opposed to (4, 3). Thanks to the loss, destruction, and dislocation of war, there is less to go around than there would be if the players settled on (pass; honor), which would have projected A's present military strength into the future despite B's growing power but saved the costs of war. Yet (attack; renege) is the game's only Nash Equilibrium. We can verify its existence by showing that neither player has a profitable deviation. First, knowing that B will renege on the settlement in the future if given the chance, A can only hurt itself by switching from attack to pass (because 3, 1). Second, if A will attack, B's decision is irrelevant. If it switches to "honor," it receives the same payoff that it does at "renege," because A's strategy is to attack and try to prevent a shift in power. No player can do better against the other's strategy than its proposed strategy dictates, so we have a Nash Equilibrium at (attack; renege). This equilibrium is also unique, which you can verify on your own by checking that at least one player would have an incentive to deviate from either (attack; honor) or (pass; renege).

The (attack; renege) equilibrium is also *inefficient*, because no player ends up doing as well as it would in the (pass; honor) outcome in which war would be avoided. Both can look at other possible outcomes with regret, but they can't reach those outcomes in equilibrium. The problem is that the rising side (state B) can't make a credible promise to honor an agreement in the future that it will be powerful enough to overturn. Anticipating this, A attacks from its present position of strength rather than give its rising opponent the option of exploiting newfound strength to renege in the future. The declining side imposes by force a decision to honor today's bargain on its rising opponent, possibly at tremendous cost, but of course both would be better off (relative to the outcome of this particular war) keeping today's agreement without all the bloodshed. Thanks to the de jure anarchy of the international system, nothing stands in the way of B eventually leveraging newfound power to demand revisions of the border in its favor – and this is what undermines the peaceful strategy profile of (pass; honor). A plan of peacefully sustaining today's agreement, which reflects A's present strength (not B's future strength), is simply not self-enforcing. Ensuring peace would require, for example, that B turn into a great military power *and not act in accordance with that power*. A knows full well that this is a promise B can't make. The costs of future weakness thus lead the declining side (state A) to launch a war in the present that it knows to be inefficient, imposing today's bargain at the cost of a war, because refusing to fight will allow the military advantage to pass into the hands of a rising state B.

This is our first (but not our only) solution to the inefficiency puzzle of war: a declining state may fight a costly, wasteful **preventive war** designed to reverse or arrest B's rise in power or, at the extreme, to destroy it, ensuring that A uses its military advantage over state B before that advantage disappears.

DEFINITION 2.13 *A **preventive war** aims to arrest, end, or reverse the growth of a rising side's power in order to preserve commitments to the status quo.*

A fights to keep today's otherwise fragile status quo in place, which need not even mean "victory" in the conventional sense; it simply means preventing a loss.[20] (If this sounds grim, you're not wrong. It *is* grim. And we'll go into even grimmer detail about how this plays out between great powers in Chapters 4 and 11.) As we can see by looking at the social optimum of (pass; honor), the preventive war equilibrium is inefficient; there is less to go around after war than before, because land, civilians, soldiers, and economies have all been damaged or destroyed, and each calculating, frugal side of this interaction would like to avoid the costs and waste of war. The problem, the friction in the way of a relatively efficient negotiated outcome, is that a rising state can't promise not to take advantage of its own strength if given the opportunity. In such a strategic setting, the declining state has an incentive to fight before its odds of winning grow too long.

By way of review, if we compare the preventive war equilibrium of the game in Figure 2.5 to the peaceful equilibrium in Figure 2.3, we can see precisely how commitment problems can stand in the way of efficient, peaceful bargains that both sides would in principle prefer to war. In Figure 2.3, country A can choose an option that avoids war, confident that B will both make large concessions and remain committed to them, because B

---

[20] The fear of loss that drives Anakin Skywalker to the Dark Side in *Revenge of the Sith* seems a little less hokey in this light. But only a little.

won't grow stronger (and have incentives to renege on the settlement) in the future. Therefore, the players reach a bargain that saves the costs of war; it's not the best bargain possible for B, but it's efficient in the sense of reflecting the likely outcome of a war without having to expend all the attendant blood and treasure. By contrast, for the game in Figure 2.5, peace on any terms today is dangerous for state A, because refusing to fight allows B to grow stronger and renegotiate the border from a position of newfound strength.

The idea that shifting power can lead to war predated the widespread use of game theory in political science, with some scholars even tracing the roots of the idea back to Thucydides' account of the origins of the Peloponnesian Wars, which the ancient Greek witness-to-events attributed to "the rise of Athenian power and the fear this aroused in Sparta." Early political science applications of this idea argued that war due to shifting power was most likely during power transitions, or those situations in which one great power's wealth or military strength is at parity with but risks being overtaken by a rising challenger; why, after all, would war break out unless both sides expect to have a fighting chance?[21] The logic appeared compelling – intuitive, even – and it resonated. But game-theoretic work on the commitment problem, which forced analysts to be explicit about assumptions and the logic of their arguments, soon showed that there's nothing particularly dangerous about parity when it comes to shifting power and war. As long as power will shift both far and quickly enough, then states can fight preventive wars at equal *or* unequal distributions of power, at parity *or* disparity; all that's required to make a preventive war attractive is that the costs of future weakness outweigh the present costs of war.[22] As we'll see in Chapter 4, the rational pessimism that dominates declining states' calculations can lead them to embark on preventive wars even when the distribution of power is already set against them. And without a careful accounting of players, actions, outcomes, preferences, and the strategic tensions that tie them together – without doing the math – this insight would've been harder to reach and its supporting logic even harder to verify.

---

[21] For an extensive summary of this research tradition, see Tammen et al. (2000), and for some of the original statistical evidence, see Organski and Kugler (1980). Power transition theory rests on the "why fight at disparity?" challenge, and its alternatives often rest on "why not fight at disparity?" as a rejoinder. Neither, however, takes into account the strategic dimensions of conflict; in each case, one's opponent chooses whether or not to give battle, and this simple insight has led to a major reorientation in how political scientists think about the link between the distribution of power and war (Powell 1999; Reed et al. 2008).

[22] See, most prominently, Powell (1999, 2006).

2.3   CONCLUSION

We began this chapter with a question of how two states, both of which would like to save the costs of war, nonetheless end up fighting a wasteful, destructive conflict. The solution, worked out after introducing some of the rudimentary tools of game theory, entails recognizing a central fact of international politics: states rise and fall in their military power, and those growing stronger find it difficult to convince others that they won't make use of newfound strength in the future. This *commitment problem* can drive a state that fears the other's rise into a *preventive war*, launched when the odds of success promise to decline in the future from today's (possibly very low) peak. German chancellor Otto von Bismarck famously derided preventive war as "suicide for fear of death" before the Reichstag, but his admonition aside, preventive wars are not uncommon. Japan attacked Russia in 1904 before the latter could consolidate its military influence in Manchuria,[23] it moved to seize Manchuria in 1931 when the prospects of Nationalist victory in the Chinese Civil War made its position of indirect control precarious, and it attacked Pearl Harbor in 1941 in a bid to preserve a naval advantage that it expected to erode as the United States embarked on a massive naval rearmament.[24] More recently, the United States invaded Iraq and toppled its government in order to prevent it from continuing a suspected program in pursuit of nuclear, chemical, and biological weapons.[25] After any such preventive war, both sides can look back with regret, noting that the war could've been avoided if only the rising state had been able to commit ahead of time not to use newfound power. De jure international anarchy makes such reassurances difficult if not impossible.

Game theory helped us resolve this puzzle by forcing us to think hard about the preferences of states and their leaders and how the strategic interdependence of their choices leads to inefficient outcomes, war in this case, that they generally have every incentive to avoid if they can find cheaper means of resolving disputes. We used some basic premises laid down in the first chapter, about de jure anarchy and self-enforcing bargains and the role of war in resolving international disputes, to build a simple model of bargaining in the shadow of shifting military power. Then, by thinking about explanations in terms of equilibrium, of strategies in mutual balance, we walked through the reasoning that supports the particular outcome of a game and arrive at a clear, logically sound explanation for something that is otherwise puzzling. After the fact, states always regret the

---

[23] See Connaughton (2003).
[24] See Paine (2012, chapters 2 and 7, respectively).
[25] See Keegan (2005) and Ricks (2006).

costs of war, because they can imagine a treaty that would have divided the pie the same way but didn't entail all the waste and destruction of fighting. Explaining why they'd fight a war in spite of this knowledge requires that we explain why they are unable to reach that settlement beforehand. Our simple, abstract model of shifting power and preventive war gives us one answer to this enduring puzzle. In later chapters, we'll use games for the same purposes, to look through the eyes of the actors in our story and to explain events that at first seem puzzling. However, we'll do it in the sprawling, consequential, and harrowing context of the First World War.

3 Armed Continent: The Anglo-German Naval Race

> *We are entitled to form our own conclusion as to the object for which the German navy is built up and we have and will claim every right to act accordingly.*
>
> Eyre Crowe,
> British Foreign Office
> February 11, 1908

This chapter begins our engagement with the history of the Great War, though our entry point is not 1914 but 1906, when the British and German empires embarked on a naval arms competition that allows us to pose our first puzzle:

> Why did the British and German Empires waste six years and vast wealth to compete in battleship construction, only to leave the distribution of naval power between them unchanged?

As part of its bid to secure its "place in the sun" among the other imperial powers of the early twentieth century, Germany hoped to build a modern fleet that could pose a credible threat to tie down the Royal Navy in the event of war, but Britain responded with a shipbuilding program of its own that more than made up for the German attempt to catch up.[1] With the outcome fairly predictable, why was this necessary? Put in starker terms, why do arms races occur if they're so wasteful? If neither side can outspend or outbuild the other so as to change who's stronger, and both sides *know* this, what's the point? The Anglo-German naval race is a key step on the path to the First World War, and solving this puzzle allows us to demonstrate a few things that will be useful once we begin our discussion of the war itself:

- how to specify games in order to solve empirical puzzles;
- the difference between inefficiency (or tragedy) and futility;

---

[1] See Kennedy (1980, chapter 20).

- how individually sensible decisions can add up to tragic outcomes;
- the origins of arms races and their role in international politics.

We'll show that the Anglo-German naval race, as an example of arms races in general, is a species of the strategic problem called the Prisoner's Dilemma. Each side would be better off if it could avoid an arms race that does little but waste money, but neither can make a credible promise not to build arms (ships, in this case) to gain a unilateral advantage if the other doesn't build arms. As a result, they both spend money on arming and cancel out the other's potential advantage, aiming simply to deny the other the advantage of doing so. This is clearly not the first-best option for either side – it's impossible to say that either Britain or Germany *wanted* a naval race for its own sake – but a wasteful arms race was nonetheless the best each believed it could do under the prevailing circumstances of great power rivalry. Put in terms of our initial puzzle, the Anglo-German naval race occurred *because* neither side could effectively out-spend or out-build the other in head-to-head competition. We'll show that this arms race may have been tragic and wasteful, but because each side prevented the other from seizing a unilateral advantage, we can hardly call it futile. Keep "tragedy" and "futility" in mind as we go forward; unsurprisingly, the people caught up in the maelstrom of the First World War used these words *a lot*, but they'll take on rather different meaning in light of our analysis of events. After solving the puzzle of the Anglo-German naval race, we close the chapter by reviewing what political science can teach us about arms races and arms control in international relations writ large.

Key Term for Chapter 3

- Arms Race

3.1 BRITAIN, GERMANY, AND DREADNOUGHTS

For roughly six years, from 1906 until 1912, the British and German empires competed in the production of ever greater numbers of the newest, largest, and deadliest battleships in the world. Dreadnoughts, named for the eponymous first ship in the class launched by Britain's Royal Navy in 1905, revolutionized naval warfare, outclassing virtually all other battleships then in service around the world. Boasting a larger complement of bigger, longer-ranged guns and propelled by powerful, efficient steam turbine engines, dreadnoughts were the new currency of global naval power. In a world dominated by seafaring European colonial empires, advances in naval power were as consequential as the development of long-range bombers, precision-guided munitions, or stealth aircraft in the decades that followed.[2] Countries that could field a fleet of such ships could protect lines of trade and communication – a largely physical endeavor in a predigital age – and project military power around the world, from the shores of their colonies to the ports of their enemies. Those competitors that fell behind could expect to find themselves relegated to the second rank (or worse) of naval powers, hopelessly behind a British Empire already dominant in both naval and financial might.

It's not surprising that the United Kingdom should be at the cutting edge of shipbuilding in the early twentieth century. Its navy had dominated the world's seas for over two hundred years, securing commerce and communication between far-flung elements of an empire over which the sun famously never set, supported by a sprawling global network of coaling stations. In light of preexisting British superiority, what *is* surprising is Germany's decision to respond to the launch of HMS *Dreadnought* by embarking on its own intensive program of dreadnought construction, provoking a British response and touching off a costly and high profile naval **arms race**, a competition in arming where potential enemies try to shape the outcome and cost of a potential future war.[3]

DEFINITION 3.1 *An **arms race** is a competition in which participants attempt to acquire a military advantage for potential use against one another.*

Though it was traditionally a land power, Germany attempted to undermine Britain's "Two Power Standard," a policy that aimed to sustain a number of ships greater than the next two largest navies combined, a policy that also happened to be backed by greater wealth, superior infrastructure for projecting power, and a set of military institutions that did not rely as heavily as Germany's on the maintenance of a large standing army. Nonetheless, Germany sought to build what Grand Admiral Tirpitz called a "risk fleet," one that could pose a sufficient challenge to British mastery of the North Sea in the event of war that it could keep the German coast (and shipping) safe from an overwhelming blockade in wartime.[4]

Yet it was obvious from the outset that Britain could build more ships while placing less strain on both (1) its military budget and (2) its economy as a whole. Wealth notwithstanding, it had other priorities, such as maintaining control over an increasingly restless global empire developing

---

[2] They were expensive, to be sure, but their lethality per dollar was perhaps less than the most revolutionary new armaments of the twentieth century: atomic weapons.

[3] For a recent examination of what it takes to know an arms race when we see one, see Gibler, Rider, and Hutchison (2005).

[4] More on the blockade in Chapter 10.

a taste for indigenous nationalism and increasingly targeted by Russian imperial competition (especially in Central Asia). Germany, for its part, faced a recently cemented alliance of hostile powers in France and Russia, the former looking covetously on the territories of Alsace and Lorraine lost in the Franco-Prussian War of 1871, and the latter focusing its foreign policy back on Eastern Europe after an eye-opening defeat at the hands of Imperial Japan in 1905. Russia, as we'll discuss in Chapter 4, also responded to its defeat with an ambitious "Grand Programme" of rearmament and military modernization. Alsace-Lorraine aside, France sought to contain the further growth of German power, which had occurred at an alarming rate after Prussia unified a number of smaller states as the German Empire in 1871. Russia hoped to improve its position in lands formerly controlled by the Ottoman Empire in southeastern Europe, which threatened Germany's – and its ally Austria-Hungary's – own ambitions in the region. France and Russia, an unlikely alliance of Europe's most democratic and most autocratic regimes, respectively, held a significant manpower advantage over a German army that could still boast an innovative, bold, and well-trained officer class and skilled, disciplined ground troops, even as it faced an unenviable strategic position between two large, powerful enemies keen to contain its future growth. The looming shadow of a two-front land war notwithstanding, Germany diverted substantial resources for over half a decade toward a naval race against the world's most powerful navy.

By the time Germany abandoned the naval race in favor of major increases in spending on expanded land forces (see Figure 3.1 for a timeline of events), the distribution of naval power with Great Britain was virtually unchanged. Britain remained the dominant naval power, and Germany held out only a faint hope of emerging victorious from a confrontation with the Royal Navy. Despite years of intensive effort, Germany could deploy only 17 dreadnoughts to Britain's 29 at the outbreak of war in 1914. And this mere retention of relative power came at tremendous cost to its economy. Great Britain, for its part, also poured money into dreadnought construction to counter the German program, and in hindsight the results look tragically predictable: both sides diverted large sums of money that could otherwise have gone to more productive uses over the course of six years,

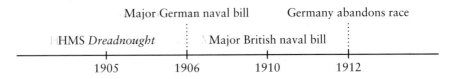

Figure 3.1 From *Dreadnought* to naval race, 1905–1912.

only to step back in 1912 to see that the naval balance remained anchored in the inescapable fact of British dominance. By almost any standard, the naval race was wasteful, with large amounts of money spent only to see each side's ability to defeat the other in a naval confrontation virtually unchanged (and Germany's credit rating damaged, with some longer-term effects we'll touch on in Chapter 4). In 1906, the Royal Navy could count on excellent odds against Germany's Imperial Navy, and by 1912, the story was largely the same; if the German fleet were to break out of the North Sea, it could only do so at tremendous cost and with dim prospects. The navies of 1912 may have been bigger than the navies of 1906, and their weapons even more terrifying, but there was no meaningful change in the naval balance.

The question for this chapter is: why? Why would Germany and the United Kingdom, two great powers with a variety of other spending priorities, embark on an expensive arms race that left neither side more able to overcome the other in a naval struggle than it was beforehand? Had they both scaled back their spending, Britain might have retained its dominance with fewer battleships, and Germany might have spent more money on its army – the sine qua non for guaranteeing its survival as a great power. Avoiding the naval race, whether or not war proved inevitable in 1914, seems ex post like a smart decision for each side. It would have saved the economic and political strain of major shipbuilding programs in both countries, to say nothing of leaving room for domestic spending to placate the domestic opposition, while each side's odds of defeating the other would have remained in practice unchanged. It is also possible that the level of antagonism that existed between Britain and Germany by 1914 would not have been so severe had the arms race been avoided.[5] Why, then, did two great powers possessed of tremendous wealth, intellectual capital, and even (the subsequent reputation of their leaders notwithstanding) strategic talent, with arguably bigger problems than their bilateral naval balance, engage in a patently wasteful naval arms race?

3.2 EXPLAINING ARMS RACES

How can we explain the long, wasteful, and apparently futile Anglo-German naval race? Why did Germany challenge British supremacy in the North Sea? Why would Britain build more dreadnoughts than necessary to maintain its naval dominance? In each country, it would be easy to find hawkish domestic factions or influential members of the political class that favored expanded shipbuilding programs for personal or institutional

---

[5] On this, see Kennedy (1980).

reasons. We might also look to rising tensions between a Britain with an established imperial position and an upstart Germany, hemmed in on the Continent but seeking overseas colonies, to explain why either might wish to increase its power at the other's expense. Both answers have the sheen of plausibility. It's probably possible to find a member of any given political class that will be willing to support any given policy, but that's not enough to explain why that policy is adopted, nor why decision-makers in *both* countries adopt it. These possible answers are also insufficient to explain the key element of the puzzle: if a naval race did little to alter the key strategic balance of naval forces, only straining the economy and distorting the allocation of military resources, why couldn't the British and Germans simply agree to avoid the arms race and put their money and effort toward less wasteful purposes?

PUZZLE 3.1   *Why couldn't Britain and Germany avoid a costly naval arms race that left their relative power unchanged?*

Following the recipe we established in Chapter 2, we begin by identifying the relevant players, goals, strategies, and possible outcomes of the interaction that puzzles us. We then use these elements to build a simple model of the strategic problem that allows us to see how each side's choices interact with the other's to produce a specific set of outcomes. Oftentimes, strategic incentives aggregate to produce an outcome – like an arms race – that we wouldn't expect of calculating, frugal players. The relevant players, for our purposes in this chapter, are the United Kingdom and Germany. Their goals, as we might expect of great powers, are to acquire as much naval power as possible while avoiding needless spending. In principle, both countries would like a massive navy, but their budgets are limited, and every Pound or Mark spent on dreadnoughts is a Pound or Mark that does not go to other spending priorities. They most want naval predominance secured by a unilateral buildup of dreadnoughts, but they'll settle for what they can achieve at a reasonable price. Each side wishes to strike a balance between ensuring that it can hold its own against the other in a naval engagement and saving resources it would like to use for the army, social policy, or personal enrichment.

Each player's actions are to build large numbers of dreadnoughts or not to build (labeled "¬build") large numbers of dreadnoughts. Building is expensive, but it increases the naval firepower that one side can bring against the other. From the standpoint of a single country, whether Great Britain or Germany, building more dreadnoughts makes sense if one can afford it; more military power is typically better than less. But translating these actions into a strategic-form game shows that even a simple set of choices can produce a range of possible outcomes. Figure 3.2 shows how

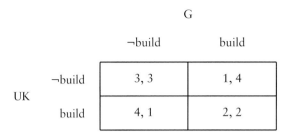

Figure 3.2 The Anglo-German naval race.

each side's choice over embarking on a large shipbuilding program or not produces four possible outcomes,

- neither builds (no arms race)
- Germany builds, United Kingdom doesn't (German naval advantage)
- United Kingdom builds, Germany doesn't (British naval advantage)
- both build (arms race),

ranging from no arms race, to one side building dreadnoughts at the other's expense, to an arms race when both sides choose to build dreadnoughts. Each player is free to build dreadnoughts, but whether it enjoys the advantages of doing so unilaterally depends on the other side's decision to build dreadnoughts. This interdependence of choice defines the problem facing rivals like Great Britain and Germany in 1906.

Figure 3.2 presents the game formally. If one side builds dreadnoughts (or does not), its ability to achieve its goals depends on the other side's choice to build dreadnoughts (or not). Recall that a player's payoffs represent a ranking over the possible outcomes from best to worst – from what a state most wants, through what it will accept if it must, on down to what it will do whatever it can to avoid. If both the United Kingdom and Germany wish to increase relative naval power at minimal cost, then the best outcome for one state is to build dreadnoughts while the other does not (4), while the worst outcome for a player is to choose not to build dreadnoughts while the other does (1), allowing an enemy to either preserve or unhinge the balance of power, ensuring that whatever rights and privileges it secures or gains come at the other's expense. If neither builds dreadnoughts, then the naval balance remains unchanged. This is less attractive than gaining a unilateral advantage over the other, but it saves resources and effort, so each side ranks it as the second best outcome (3). Finally, if both sides build dreadnoughts, neither gains the unilateral advantage of increased power at the other's expense, and both expend resources that are effectively wasted; nonetheless, blunting the other's advantage is better than allowing a unilateral enemy buildup, so each side ranks this as the third best outcome (2). Each side would like to gain a unilateral advantage over the other, but it may be thwarted by the other's attempt to gain its own advantage.

3.2.1 Solving the Puzzle

Given their complementary imperial and Continental rivalries, the game in Figure 3.2 is a plausible (if incomplete) rendering of Anglo-German strategic incentives in 1906. While each can profit from avoiding wasteful military spending, it would also like to ensure that the other can't gain a unilateral advantage, and it would like to gain its own advantage over the other if possible. If we accept these premises as roughly consistent with German and British preferences in 1914, then our next question is how the actors are likely to play the game. To answer this question, we draw again on the concept of a Nash Equilibrium (recall Definition 2.7), at which each player does the best it can with its strategy in light of what it knows about the other player's strategy. This is especially relevant in the case of potential arms races, where one rival can prevent the other from enjoying the unfettered benefits of an extensive program of unilateral dreadnought construction by embarking on a shipbuilding program of its own.

The arms race outcome associated with (build; build) in Figure 3.3, in which each side chooses to build dreadnoughts, is manifestly wasteful. The distribution of naval power is the same as it would have been if neither side built dreadnoughts, yet each side has expended national resources in the apparent pursuit of futility. And a casual glance at the payoffs suggests the attractiveness of neither side building: if only Britain and Germany can resist the temptation to build, they can secure their second-best outcome, worth 3 to each side, with a mutual avoidance of naval arming, or (¬build; ¬build). We can plausibly call this a social optimum, in that both sides are better off than they would be under the mutually worst outcome of an arms race (where each gets 2, highlighted in gray). Each side also avoids its worst outcome of not building dreadnoughts while the

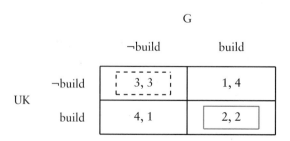

Figure 3.3 The Anglo-German naval race in equilibrium.

other does. Mutual refusals to build dreadnoughts seems like an "obvious" way to play the game: if each player can simply promise not to build weapons if the other won't, then a naval arms race can be avoided. But as is very often the case when thinking through strategic problems, our intuition isn't to be trusted.[6] As it happens, "if" is key here. International agreements, especially those involving limitations on arms, must be self-enforcing (Definition 1.6), because states can abrogate them at any time – making that "if" a big one between rivals.

Nash Equilibrium forces us to think harder about exactly what is required for mistrustful rivals, like the United Kingdom and Germany in 1906, to avoid such an arms race. Suppose that each side promises not to build dreadnoughts, implying an outcome of (¬build; ¬build). If an agreement based on these promises is self-enforcing, each side receives 3 at the social optimum. Yet Proposition 3.1 reveals an obvious – or troubling, if you prefer – problem with this line of reasoning: such an agreement is not self-enforcing, because each player has a profitable deviation in light of the other's decision not to build large numbers of dreadnoughts.

PROPOSITION 3.1 *The strategy profile (¬build; ¬build) is not a Nash Equilibrium.*

Proof For (¬build; ¬build) to be a Nash Equilibrium, it must be the case that

$$u(\neg build; \neg build) \geq u(build; \neg build)$$

for each player. But this requires $3 \geq 4$, which is untrue. At least one player has a profitable deviation, so (¬build; ¬build) cannot be a Nash Equilibrium. □

The temptation to build while the other doesn't turns out to be too great to resist. Suppose that one side, whether Germany or the United Kingdom, knows that the other will not build dreadnoughts. If it honors a hypothetical promise not to build as well, it receives 3, but if it builds dreadnoughts despite this commitment, it receives 4, gaining a unilateral advantage over its rival. Any such hypothetical bargain in which an arms race is averted requires that both sides, Britain and Germany, ignore unilateral incentives to increase naval capabilities at the other's expense. As long as at least one side has an incentive to choose otherwise, then a proposed set of strategies – even the avoidance of a mutually costly and futile naval arms race – cannot be an equilibrium.

---

[6] It rarely is. Intuition is frequently pretty misleading.

How, then, should we expect the game to be played? Suppose that one side is to build dreadnoughts while the other refrains from doing so, implying (¬build; build) or (build; ¬build). Can this be an equilibrium? The side that builds dreadnoughts unilaterally is quite happy, receiving its best payoff of 4, because it has increased its naval capabilities at the other's expense. Its dreadnoughts roam the seas nearly unchallenged, enabling it, in Britain's case, to extend its naval dominance, or, in Germany's case, to challenge British preeminence on the high seas (or, at a minimum, to make a blockade costlier to impose). Any such scheme by which one rival acquiesces in the increasing naval power of the other cannot be an equilibrium, because the side stipulated not to build dreadnoughts has every incentive to deviate from that plan, building a large fleet in order to deny the other a competitive advantage. The simple fact that one rival can't promise not to build dreadnoughts if the other won't turns out to be central to understanding why even frugal, calculating governments like those in prewar Britain and Germany could end up in a mutually costly and apparently wasteful naval race.[7]

We've established so far that the mutual avoidance of arms races can't be an equilibrium of this game, because each rival would like to build dreadnoughts if it knows the other will not. We've also shown that allowing the other to build dreadnoughts without responding in kind is unsustainable; a rival will do what it can to blunt whatever unilateral advantage the other might try to secure. So what are we left with? As indicated by the gray box in Figure 3.3, we must consider whether a naval arms race, in which both sides build dreadnoughts yet fail to gain any military advantage from doing so, might be in equilibrium.[8] Suppose that the equilibrium is (build; build). Each player receives 2, a manifestly bad outcome, keeping pace with the other side in shipbuilding, expending resources and effort on a military balance that ultimately remains the same. Consider, though, what happens if one side chooses not to build dreadnoughts knowing that the other side will. To do so would be to willfully tolerate its worst payoff of 1, even though it can secure itself a payoff of 2 by building dreadnoughts – however wastefully – in order to deny the other side the advantage of a unilateral naval buildup.

PROPOSITION 3.2   *The strategy profile (build; build) is a Nash Equilibrium.*

---

[7] It should also put you in mind of the commitment problem in Chapter 2.
[8] Sure, it's the only possibility left, so there might not be too much suspense left at this point, but bear with me; it's also going to ensure that the equilibrium we're left with is unique.

Proof   For (build; build) to be a Nash Equilibrium, it must be the case that

$$u(build; \text{build}) \geq u(\neg build; \text{build})$$

for both players. These inequalities are satisfied because $2 \geq 1$. No player has a profitable deviation, so (build; build) is a Nash Equilibrium.   □

The logic supporting Proposition 3.2 turns out to be why, despite its cost and apparent futility, the frugal, calculating rivals in our game can end up in a naval arms race. If one side, Britain or Germany, expects the other to build dreadnoughts, failing to respond courts disaster in the form of a unilateral naval buildup by one's rival. Each side receives 2 at the naval arms race equilibrium, but if it deviates – if it chooses not to build while the other does – it receives its worst possible payoff of 1, allowing itself to be taken advantage of by a rival committed to bolstering its naval capabilities. As noted in Chapter 2, this confluence of mutual best responses is what defines a Nash Equilibrium; neither side can do better than its chosen strategy, given what the other side chooses. In this Nash Equilibrium, each side embarks on a costly naval buildup not because an arms race is inherently desirable (and in this framework, it surely isn't) but because neither side can credibly commit *not* to build more dreadnoughts unilaterally if given the chance. Given their options and preferences, each side builds more dreadnoughts not in order to gain an advantage but to prevent the other side from gaining an advantage at its expense. Neither side can afford not to build dreadnoughts if the other does, nor can it refrain from building more dreadnoughts if the other refrains.

3.2.2   Was the Naval Race Futile?

This simple strategic problem, in which states fail to achieve a social optimum because they can't promise not to exploit the other, is known as a Prisoner's Dilemma. In the canonical example, two robbery suspects face interrogation in separate rooms, each caring only about minimizing jail time and knowing that the other has been offered a similar deal: to snitch in order to secure a lighter sentence. If the worst possible outcome is to stay silent while one's partner snitches, and each suspect knows that her partner will rat her out for a lighter sentence, both suspects end up snitching and each receives more jail time than she would if only both had stayed silent. Each player knows that the other will be unable to resist the temptation to secure a lighter sentence, and in the absence of some mechanism by which players can precommit not to snitch or to build dreadnoughts, they both end up confessing or engaging in a tragic, mutually costly, and apparently futile arms race.[9]

Yet it's important to emphasize, hitting a note that will stay with us throughout our analysis of the Great War, that the naval race only *appears* futile in hindsight. Yes, we can look back at the game in Figure 3.2 and see that a better outcome (the avoidance of an arms race) was at least logically possible. Ex post, that is the ostensibly missed opportunity on which the participants in the race look back with regret ... and on which later observers look with bafflement. But logical possibility is often radically different than *strategic* possibility. What we must try to understand is how the players in our game – as well as the early twentieth-century British and German governments that our players represent – were reasoning *in real time*, when they weighed their options and made these decisions. What did the leaders themselves think they were achieving? What were they *trying* to do, and how could they get in each other's way? An adequate explanation of the naval race must grapple with these questions, however appalled we might be at the waste entailed in an arms race – or at the singular horror of the war that followed on its heels two years later.

A key feature of equilibrium reasoning – and one that will come up for us time and time again throughout our narrative of the war – is that players choose their actions as best responses to their knowledge of what other players plan to do. This common conjecture (Definition 2.8) comes from an understanding of each other's motives and opportunities, which wasn't much of a mystery when it came to naval rivalries between great powers in the early twentieth century. Both Britain and Germany had a reasonable guess about how the other side's preferences were structured: each would increase its own naval capabilities unilaterally if it could, and if the other were to build dreadnoughts, then neither side could afford not to build more of the hulking battleships in response. If Germany didn't bolster its navy, the British ability to impose a painful blockade of German ports in the event of war would only increase as more dreadnoughts came into the line. For Britain's part, allowing Germany to build up sufficient naval capacity to break out of a blockade, make a run at British ports, or even to draw large numbers of ships away from their peacetime job of protecting the coaling network, was equally intolerable. Indeed, this was the essence of Tirpitz's "risk fleet" strategy. Neither side considered an arms race as an alternative to the absence of an arms race (the social optimum of neither side building dreadnoughts in Figure 3.2). Rather, the

---

[9] This should highlight why rats aren't viewed favorably in the criminal community. If your partner in crime gets caught, she needs some extra inducement – say, the threat of death or disfigurement – not to roll on you when someone offers her a deal.

alternative they avoided was allowing the other side a unilateral advantage in the high-stakes game of great power politics.

Looked at in this way, the Anglo-German naval race was certainly *tragic*: neither side appears able to have chosen other than it did, leading to an outcome that entailed regret over waste and apparent ineffectiveness at the end. But if we stop there, we lose sight of a simple fact that the Nash Equilibrium of our game makes clear. Britain and Germany did not choose an arms race because it was better to have one than not; their individual attempts to preserve their own military positions *added up to an arms race* because each individual decision to build dreadnoughts was preferable to allowing the other side to gain a unilateral advantage in building and deploying larger numbers of a new class of warship that promised to revolutionize naval power. The relevant comparison for explaining each side's actions is *not* the world before an arms race, but the world that would have existed if one side had not chosen to keep pace with its rival. In that sense, the naval race was used by each side to *avert* an anticipated future of relative naval decline. It only *appears* futile when we look at each participant in isolation, i.e., if we ignore the strategic interconnectedness of choices in the international system (recall Definition 1.3). We'll see in Chapter 10 that, had Britain not worked to keep ahead of Germany in dreadnought construction, it might not have been able to call on a sufficient number of capital ships to deter German challenges to the ultimately successful blockade it imposed and slowly tightened throughout the war.[10] The naval race was wasteful, to be sure, but it was not futile in the sense of failing to achieve its desired ends, because the ends were not in any real sense about gaining a massive naval advantage over the other, or even about improving one's position in absolute terms from time t to time $t+1$. Rather, each side sought – at great cost, to be sure – merely to prevent the distribution of power on the high seas from sliding further against it. Recalling our discussion of war in Chapter 2, arms races are certainly wasteful, and they entail ex post regret over their cost, but in rare circumstances rival states do find themselves unable to commit not to participate in them.

3.3 EQUILIBRIUM, STRATEGY, AND TRAGEDY

Our application of the Prisoner's Dilemma to the Anglo-German naval race illustrates two ideas that will be important for understanding some key elements of the war going forward. First, it highlights the importance of events that occur "out of equilibrium" – say, of roads not taken or of dogs

---

[10] Sondhaus (2014, p. 351).

that didn't bark – in explaining events that *do* occur in equilibrium. Second, it offers a clear example of inefficient, regrettable, or *tragic* outcomes, which despite being wasteful are often the best our players can do given the particulars of their strategic circumstances. This latter is often a fundamental truth of politics: when choices are strategically interdependent, states or their leaders often choose from a menu of exclusively "bad" options.[11]

First, explaining arms races, like many other costly and apparently futile political phenomena such as negative campaigning, trade wars, and shooting wars, is challenging because it is often unclear at first blush what eventualities the decision-makers of interest are trying to avoid. The equilibrium of our arms race game is a useful case in point. We do not need to assert that British and German decision-makers believed that the naval race was in their mutual interest in order to explain why it occurred.[12] In fact, both sides lamented the waste and residual hostility created by the naval race. But to infer from the acknowledgement of this waste that an arms race occurred because of perfidy, ignorance, or malicious collusion is facile and, frequently, more ideological than analytical. A simpler, more plausible story – and one that takes the preferences, incentives, and choices available to the actors in our story seriously – is that neither side could count on the other *not* to pursue a unilateral advantage in building a potentially revolutionary weapons system.

The Anglo-German naval race was not the result of both sides preferring a world with an arms race to a world without it. It occurred because neither could credibly promise not to unhinge the balance of naval power if left to its own devices from 1906 onward. Yet the cause of the arms race – one side gaining a unilateral advantage – is never observed, because each side works hard to avoid it. Part of the reason that the rule of the road ("keep right" in the United States, "keep left" in Britain and a few other locales) works so well is the consequence of getting it wrong: a head-on collision. Precisely because the rule works so well, one of the key explanations for its effectiveness (i.e., head-on collisions) is never observed.[13] The same is true of arms races; they're caused by rival states working hard to avoid an outcome that, if successfully avoided, we should never see in the historical record: one rival state building a crushing military advantage while the other inexplicably chooses not to make an effort to catch up. The fact that a major shift in the Anglo-British naval

---

[11] In many ways, political science is about explaining tragic, inefficient outcomes. If everyone's incentives encouraged the social optimum in all cases, there wouldn't be much to explain.

[12] If you're inclined toward conspiracy theorizing, though, that's *precisely* what you're likely to do. You're also likely to spend more time down the rabbit hole than learning something.

[13] As noted by Wagner (2007), the only other requirement is agreement on what the rule is. We'll return to that particular problem in Chapter 10.

balance never occurred is not sufficient to reject a potential shift in the balance of power as a cause of the naval race, however tempting it might be after the fact to attribute the event to politicians' perfidy or psychological failings.

Our explanation highlights the political nature of the problem *and* the political nature of possible solutions, which require some mechanism by which rivals can credibly (that is, believably) promise ahead of time not to increase their arms at each other's expense. This commitment problem, which manifests as an incentive to pursue a unilateral advantage if given the chance, defines the Prisoner's Dilemma. Alternative explanations for the Anglo-German naval race (or any arms race, for that matter) that rely on leaders' ignorance, psychological limitations, or venality probably overpredict arms races – these vices are fairly pervasive, after all – and they fail to offer a credible solution to the problem. Our Prisoner's Dilemma account, on the other hand, explains how two otherwise frugal, calculating governments seeking only to do as well as they can for themselves can end up in a mutually costly arms race. More importantly, it also points to how and why decision-makers can craft effective solutions around some mechanism that can make their promises not to engage in arms races credible, be it third party guarantees or, as discussed further below, the provocation of responses by multiple other states.

Second, we've referred to the Anglo-German naval race as "tragic," which is true insofar as it involves a regrettable, wasteful outcome that can be explained by forces outside the participants' immediate control. The naval race was costly, painful, and avoidable in principle, but the strategic problem of European great power competition in the early twentieth century, taken in a new direction by the German decision to pursue an overseas empire in addition to its Continental one, made any scheme designed to avoid a competitive naval buildup impracticable. The players in our game fail to avoid an arms race because of their strategic predicament. Choosing otherwise isn't desirable even if the other side will do the same, rendering the social optimum in which both sides resist temptation practically impossible. Each side accepts an outcome ranked only one spot above its worst possible outcome, yet the other side's ability to blunt any potential unilateral advantage guarantees that each takes an action that, when combined with the other's, results in a failure to achieve the socially optimal avoidance of an arms race. Both sides experience ex post regret; they can see, after the fact, that mutually renouncing an arms buildup would have left them better off, but they were trapped by their incentives into taking specific actions that look wasteful after the fact. Through the rest of our story, we'll use "tragedy" to denote the strategically unavoidable occurrence of a wasteful outcome.

3.4 ARMS RACES AND INTERNATIONAL POLITICS

The Anglo-German naval race preceded one of the most consequential wars in history, and for that it's attracted an outsized amount of scholarly attention. But it was far from the only naval race in the years before 1914, as Austria and Italy could attest, and it occurred alongside buildups in both the size and quality of Continental armies as well. Whether they involve competitive increases in the size of conscript classes, the number and quality of conventional weapons, or the degree of nuclear overkill, arms races are a frequently frightful fixture of international politics. Arms races often precede war, if only because states that don't anticipate some chance of war wouldn't engage in them, but whether and how they cause – or even discourage – war remains an open question.[14] An arms race may tempt one side into attacking the other before it falls too far behind, or it may convince a state that it can't keep up, leading it to resign from the race and acquiesce before throwing too much good money after bad.[15] As a case in point, the Anglo-German naval race ended two years before the First World War began, when Germany decided that bolstering its land power against France and Russia (themselves arming at a decent clip) was a more effective route to security. This chapter's titular arms race may be a poor candidate for a direct cause of the First World War, but the theory of arms races can teach us a great deal about international relations.

We noted in Chapter 1 that war, its realization or its threat, is the ultimate arbiter of who gets what in international politics. And arms races are nothing if not competitive attempts to shape the outcomes of potential future wars. If states bargain over the distribution of territory and influence in the shadow of potential war, then arms races are critical determinants of who gets what territory, population, influence, or rights and privileges – even when the wars that countries prepare for never occur. The arms race between the United States and the Soviet Union, for example, ended with the latter dropping out of the Cold War competition entirely once the economic gap between the Eastern and Western blocs promised to grow too large. And quick on the heels of collapsing Soviet military power came an extension of Western influence, the vanguard of the North Atlantic Treaty Organization (NATO) and European Union membership, across formerly Soviet-dominated lands in Eastern Europe. Arms races can act as a substitute for war. In the case of the Cold War, an arms race might have substituted for World War III. If arms races clarify the likely winner of a war, then they can help avert it, removing a major obstacle to

---

[14] See, inter alia, Morrow (1989), Kydd (2000), Slantchev (2005), and Rider, Findley, and Diehl (2011).

[15] See Powell (1999, chapter 2).

peace – disagreement over the likely outcome of a war – that we'll discuss in Chapter 5. However, as we will see in Chapter 4, arms races can make other obstacles to peace, such as commitment problems, loom larger. Determining when arms races convince their losers to acquiesce or to attack before they fall behind remains a primary goal of international relations research, and the next chapter will help us think about that very question.

The puzzle of arms races also highlights one of the general features of international politics that we identified in Chapter 2: the challenges of cooperation under de jure anarchy when states have incentives to seek unilateral advantages over one another. If two rival states simply said to one another, "We won't embark on an armaments program if you don't," neither would believe the other. The commitment is simply not credible, as evidenced by many countries, refusal to limit their own use of such cheap, effective, and bloody tools like cluster bombs and landmines. Such an equilibrium wouldn't be self-enforcing, because the best case scenario is ensuring that your opponent doesn't build while building unilaterally on your own. (Remember that in the Prisoner's Dilemma, your best bet is to snitch, no matter what your erstwhile partner in crime does.) If arms races occur because neither state can credibly promise not to arm unilaterally, then the analysis in this chapter tells us something about what an institution that proposes to prevent arms races must do in order to be successful: it must make mutual promises not to build new armaments credible in the face of temptations to cheat on the agreement. De jure anarchy means that international agreements work only when states have individual incentives to comply, or when agreements are self-enforcing, and the Prisoner's Dilemma shows just how hard it can be to craft effective arms control agreements.

However difficult they may be to end, arms races are rare. Most pairs of states, most of the time, are not arming competitively against each other, even when they're enemies. Furthermore, attempts to limit armaments have met with a few notable successes: the Washington Naval Treaty (WNT) addressed shipbuilding by the great powers after the First World War, and the Nuclear Nonproliferation Treaty (NPT) has governed a period during which far fewer states than are able to have actually pursued and built arsenals of nuclear weapons.[16] What makes some arms control agreements effective at discouraging unilateral arming and the arms races that would follow? One possibility, perhaps best exemplified by both the WNT and the NPT, is to introduce other interested parties into the game. Each treaty

---

[16] Nuclear weapons are, after all, the ultimate guarantee against invasion. They're virtually useless unless your back is against the wall, but that fact helps explain why countries don't tend to push nuclear states' backs to the wall. But recent research explains how the NPT has been remarkably effective (Coe and Vaynman 2015; Fuhrmann and Lupu 2016).

helps states coordinate on diplomatic, economic, and possibly military punishments for states that seek a unilateral advantage against others, rendering any attempt at a unilateral advantage unprofitable. Building a nuclear weapon in contravention of the NPT, or attempting to field a fleet beyond agreed limits of the WNT (which is no longer in effect), can be tempting in a two-state world, but if others can identify and band together to punish violations, unilateral advantages can be nullified, wiped out by the reactions of many other states adhering to the treaty. Even if third parties will take a clear side in an arms race, they can break at least one state's incentive to build unilaterally, which is enough to prevent a race from breaking out. Third parties can be brought in to make commitments against arming credible, but of course they would enter such agreements voluntarily – arms limitation treaties aren't quite jury duty – which helps explain why successful attempts at curbing arms races are so rare. We'll see in Chapter 7 why multilateral cooperation, whether in punishing states that violate agreements or even fighting a common enemy, is so difficult.

The last great power arms race involved the United States and the Soviet Union. That race ended peacefully, but the specter of potential arms races has continued to shape great power politics to the present day. For example, American alliances with Germany and Japan are designed in large part to obviate the need for these two potential great powers to arm against potential enemies – Russia and China, respectively. New arms races are possible in East Asia as China continues to recover from centuries of imperial decline, foreign exploitation, and the self-inflicted wound of a planned economy after its civil war ended in 1949, raising concerns over its territorial ambitions in the South and East China Seas. Furthermore, Russian rearmament following the fossil fuel boom of the 2000s, to say nothing of incursions into Georgia (2008) and Ukraine (2014), has also encouraged increased military spending in Central and Eastern Europe, as nations compete to position themselves favorably ahead of possible armed conflict. The Anglo-German naval race discussed in this chapter may have ended peacefully, but as we'll see in Chapter 4, not all arms races end with one side forfeiting or turning its attention elsewhere; sometimes the prospective loser of the arms race chooses war over acquiescence.

3.5 CONCLUSION

We began this chapter with the puzzle of why two states led by frugal and calculating decision-makers could find themselves engaged in an arms race whose expense and waste they'd come only to regret. Our answer was that the simmering Anglo-German rivalry created a Prisoner's Dilemma in which neither party could credibly promise not to arm unilaterally if given the opportunity. As British diplomat Eyre Crowe notes in this chapter's epigraph, rivals find it difficult to believe that each others' arms buildups aren't aimed at some kind of unilateral advantage. As a result, Britain and Germany both built dreadnoughts, not because having an arms race was better than avoiding an arms race, but because building these revolutionary new battleships was better than allowing the other to build its own fleet of them unanswered. We showed, in other words, that states can rationally engage in arms races in the full knowledge that they're wasteful and regrettable after the fact. That each side might have been better off avoiding the race may be true, but from the standpoint of explanation it's a dead end; mutual restraint isn't an equilibrium when Prisoner's Dilemma incentives are dominant. Neither side believed that a world with no arming was possible, and each country acted to prevent a future outcome (being left out of the race) that we don't observe but which directly shapes the things we do see: arms races. In the case of the Anglo-German naval race, one side being left behind in the competition for naval power is the dog that didn't bark, precisely because the actors in our game sought to make sure that it didn't bark. The fear of future consequences – like major shifts in military power – can explain costly, tragic outcomes in the present as states pay some costs today in hopes of avoiding even greater pain in the future. It also means that we have to be careful in where we look for evidence of our explanations. We'll see this tragedy made manifest in the next chapter, when war comes to Europe after decades of great power peace.

The Anglo-German naval race may not have caused the First World War, but the rivalry that produced it and its role in a still greater system of European great power politics presages the eventual expansion of war from a regional contest between Austria-Hungary and Serbia into a truly global conflagration. Germany, after six years of the naval race, eventually diverted money back into the army after 1912, as Russian recovery from the Russo-Japanese War proceeded apace and strengthened the Tsar's alliance with Germany's western enemy: France. The naval race also occurred against the backdrop of several crises between the great powers, including German protestations about French dominance in Morocco (1905, 1911), Austria-Hungary's annexation of Bosnia and Herzegovina in 1908 (about which more later), and the two Balkan Wars of 1912 and 1913 that saw a number of countries in Southeastern Europe win their independence from the Ottoman Empire in the First before turning on each other in the Second.[17] As tensions flared on the Continent, Germany began turning its eyes back to the temporarily dormant Russian threat

---

[17] For analysis of these crises and their relationship to the First World War, see Stevenson (1997).

and to what was, by 1914, its only reliable ally: the Dual Monarchy of Austria and Hungary. As Germany began to look east, toward rising (and French-financed) Russian power and an ally worried over the increasing (also French-financed) power of former Ottoman lands in the Balkans, its calculations shifted away from competing with the British in the North Sea. But the rivalry laid bare by the naval race would soon prove more enduring than Imperial Germany suspected.

4 Leaping into the Dark: Europe Goes to War

The lamps are going out all over Europe. We shall not see them lit again in our lifetime.

Sir Edward Grey,
British Foreign Minister
August 3, 1915

Our goal in this chapter is to use the skills we developed in the previous two chapters to look for a solution to a more demanding puzzle:

> How did a local dispute between Austria-Hungary and Serbia expand to include Germany and Russia?

In other words, why did the July Crisis, sparked over the assassination of the unpopular heir apparent to the throne of the doddering Hapsburg Empire, produce the First World War? Several apparently more serious crises – over French influence in Africa, Austrian expansion in the Balkans, the First and Second Balkan wars, and Germany's role in Constantinople – preceded it. But each time, the great powers walked back from the brink of a general European war. What made July 1914 different? Solving this puzzle will teach us a few things:

- the importance of getting our players' preferences right;
- how strategic interconnectedness shapes the expansion of war;
- the necessity of understanding peace if we want to explain war;
- how the Great War was neither "unintended" nor a single party's "fault."

We'll see in this chapter that the summer of 1914 presented the great powers with a Gordian knot of *three* interlocking commitment problems that pushed Austria, Russia, and Germany into nearly simultaneous and, as it happened, inseparable preventive wars. Comparing the July Crisis to earlier opportunities for a general European war, we'll look for the key causal differences that allow us to say with some confidence what made July 1914 so special in its ability to set the world ablaze. Our answer will depend on what we know about the preferences of the key players – especially Germany and Russia – which (1) tells us which games to write down and (2) helps solve the fundamental puzzle about the outbreak of general war: why, when a great power war was imminent, was each side unable to convince the other not to climb further up the ladder of escalation? The answer, just as it did in the simpler contexts of Chapters 2 and 3, lies in what we can surmise about our players' preferences, their choices, and the strategic interdependencies between them.

Key Terms for Chapter 4
- Ultimatum
- Dominant Strategy
- Deterrence

4.1 THE JULY CRISIS AND THE GREAT WAR

On June 28, 1914, the heir to the throne of the Dual Monarchy of Austria-Hungary, Archduke Franz Ferdinand, and his wife, Sophie Chotek, were felled by bullets fired from the gun of nineteen-year-old assassin Gavrilo Princip in Sarajevo, the capital of the recently acquired Hapsburg province of Bosnia-Herzegovina.[1] The Archduke wasn't particularly well liked back in Vienna – no small irony, given his desire to avoid war over the Empire's Balkan lands, which he thought might destroy the Empire – but by late July, Austria-Hungary had declared war on Serbia (the origin and quartermaster of the young assassins' plot) and set in motion plans for a punitive invasion in early August. As a consequence, Germany, Russia, and France found themselves on a collision course after a feverish, if at times halting, race to mobilize massive, heavily armed, and finely tuned industrial war machines. What we'd recognize today as a transnational "terrorist" incident, originating in the territory of an upstart minor power at the fringe of developed Europe, spawned a weeks-long crisis that would see the great powers of the early twentieth century walk to the edge of the abyss, look directly into it, then choose collectively to jump in. But why?

In the summer of 1914, it wasn't obvious that Europe would soon be at war. Few believed that a general war would be short or cheap, and the recent diplomatic record was superficially promising. The great powers had avoided war in 1905 and 1911 over French ambitions in Morocco, in

---

[1] Austria-Hungary had administered the nominally Ottoman province since 1878, but in 1908, it announced formal annexation, which didn't exactly please Russia. But more on Hapsburg-Romanov tensions later.

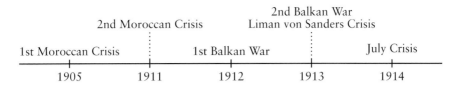

Figure 4.1 The path to war, 1905–1914.

Map 4.1 Serbian gains and Ottoman losses, 1912–1913. From Wells (1922).

1908–1909 over Austria-Hungary's annexation of Bosnia-Herzegovina, in 1912–1913 during the paroxysms of the Balkan Wars, and most recently in November 1913 over the appointment of German General Otto Liman von Sanders as military advisor to the Ottoman Empire (see Figure 4.1).[2] During the Balkan Wars, which saw Ottoman power retreat and Serbian power grow in southeastern Europe (see Map 4.1), Russia mobilized only partially, placing troops on the Austrian but *not* the German border, forcing the Dual Monarchy to back down from threats to deny Serbia its

[2] See Stevenson (1997) and Bobroff (2014).

ambitions for an Adriatic port.[3] Yet when Russia attempted a partial mobilization in July 1914, hoping to preserve Serbian independence against Austrian attack, Germany issued an **ultimatum** demanding an end to Russian war preparations under pain of war.

DEFINITION 4.1   *An **ultimatum** is a demand that, if rejected, threatens immediate consequences.*

When Russia refused to halt mobilization, Germany unleashed a war plan that saw it attack France to clear the way for a subsequent (and much longer) assault on Russia.[4] But why couldn't Russia deter the Germanic powers from a Balkan intervention when it was able to do so in previous years, over the ostensibly higher stakes of the Balkan Wars and collapsing Ottoman power in Europe?

By 1914, great power politics was defined by a Continent-wide arms race (recall Definition 3.1). Nearly all the great powers, including some of their protégés (like Serbia), were in the process of military expansion.[5] Britain and Germany, as we saw in Chapter 3, had just completed significant naval buildups. Then, after retiring from the dreadnought race, Germany instituted its largest-ever army expansion in 1913, provoking a similar increase in the size of the French army. Meanwhile, Russia had focused on political, economic, and military reform since its 1905 defeat (and near-revolution), including a French-financed modernization of its rail system and a "Grand Programme" of rearmament scheduled for completion in 1917. Russia made no bones about its desire after being shut out of East Asia to return to Europe in force, but as of July 1914 it hadn't yet arrived. Serbia, fresh off a pair of victories in the Balkan Wars that dramatically increased its size and population, had also begun buying arms on French credit.[6] The Dual Monarchy, after making official its annexation of Bosnia-Herzegovina, had overseen one of Europe's highest economic growth rates in the years leading up to 1914; its *potential* power had grown even if its actual power had not.[7] Finally, to the southeast, the Ottoman Empire had also struck deals with German firms to build parts of an

---

[3] A port that Serbia would nonetheless go on to be denied in 1913's war-ending Treaty of London. Get used to that phrase. We'll address an obscene number of declarations and treaties signed in and named after London.

[4] That's right. Germany attacked *France*, a great power in its own right, in order to clear the way for a subsequent war against *Russia*. This was the essence of German war-planning since at least 1905/1906, when outgoing Chief of the General Staff Alfred von Schlieffen outlined the difficulties inherent in breaking violently out of Germany's post-Bismarck strategic isolation. For more on the Schlieffen Plan, see Chapter 8.

[5] See Stevenson (1996) and Leonhard (2018, chapter 2).

[6] For details on these rearmament patterns, see Levy (2014, pp. 150–151).

[7] Clark (2012, chapter 2).

eventual Berlin-to-Baghdad railway, appointed German officers to advise its army and navy, and ordered two dreadnoughts from British shipyards.[8]

Yet even as the great powers armed in the years before the July Crisis, they resisted the temptations of war and became convinced that any general conflict between them, thanks to these increased armaments, would be enormously costly, potentially ruinous for European civilization – and therefore unlikely.[9] Germany was large, wealthy, and possessed the best army on the continent, and its security was nominally guaranteed by membership in the Triple Alliance with Austria-Hungary and Italy. For some in the German leadership, there was even palpable optimism that detente with Britain might be possible, if not in the short term then over the long run as London continued to compete with Moscow in Central Asia, where Russian Central Asia butted up against British India. France, expanding in Northwest Africa and not overly eager in 1914 to recover territories lost to Germany in 1871, had only recently cemented a naval understanding with its ancient British rival, yet its alliance with Russia was (finally) understood to be fully reliable – in contrast to the years immediately after Japan's very complete, very public humiliation of Russian arms in 1905. Thus, in 1914 neither France nor Germany seemed to have much to worry about.

Farther east, Vienna could rely on Berlin for security as it consolidated control over its new province of Bosnia-Herzegovina, laying the foundation for increased economic growth in the perennially troubled region that Franz Ferdinand hoped to use one day as a counterweight to Hungarian power in the Dual Monarchy. Russia's peaceful trajectory was also promising, with reforms proceeding alongside a 1907 modus vivendi with Britain over their imperial rivalry in Central Asia.[10] Russian leadership prized no higher goal than avoiding war for the foreseeable future.[11] During the Balkan War crisis of 1913, for example, Russian foreign minister Sergei Sazonov stated, "We must be content with what we shall receive, regarding it as an installment, for *the future belongs to us*" [emphasis added].[12] Why fight in 1913, when Russia would soon be able to make good temporary setbacks after completing rearmament? Finally, the Ottoman Empire had recovered from the Balkan Wars sufficiently to remove one potential spark for great power conflict, i.e., that the other great powers would circle it like carrion birds.[13] The European great powers were secured by wealth, military might, and a network of alliance

[8] McMeekin (2015, chapter 4).
[9] For the record of peace in a series of prewar crises, see Stevenson (1997).
[10] Otte (2014).
[11] Bobroff (2014, p. 240).
[12] Quoted in Fromkin (2004, p. 85).
[13] See McMeekin (2015).

relationships – some of which, like Russia-France and Germany-Austria, were more reliable during the July Crisis than they'd been in previous years.[14] None appeared in imminent danger of conquest at the hands of another – no one's back had been pressed to the wall – and the notably beautiful summer of 1914 looked as though it might continue without disruption.[15]

Even the Sarajevo murders seemed only to create a small wake. Great Britain was captivated by the question of civil war over Irish Home Rule. The French public was gripped by a scandal involving the muckracking editor of *Le Figaro*, the adulterous Minister of Finance, and the latter's vengefully murderous second wife.[16] In the days following the Sarajevo assassinations, German leaders both military and civilian left Berlin for summer vacations, and though Austria was quick to accuse Serbia of complicity in the plot to send a few students with bombs and pistols across the border to kill the Archduke, it was slow to react in any meaningful way. It issued no immediate demands for satisfaction, nor did it engage in the time-honored tradition of launching an immediate punitive raid across its border with Serbia. Only on July 24, nearly a month after the assassinations, did Austria issue an ultimatum, accusing Serbia of complicity in the assassins' plot and demanding within 48 hours an effective abdication of Serbian sovereignty by allowing Austrian officials to conduct an investigation and issue judgments against Serbian citizens on Serbian soil. If Serbia wished to retain its independence, the ultimatum was unacceptable. This fact wasn't lost on the other great powers when swirling rumors about an Austrian ultimatum designed to humiliate Serbia proved to be true. After nearly a month, any Austrian claims to be lashing out in grief were no longer credible, and Serbia's refusal to accept in full the ultimatum's terms would, within a week's time, plunge Serbia, Austria, Russia, Germany, and France into a potentially catastrophic war.

And yet the stakes of the Austro-Serbian dispute *did* seem minor. A ragtag band of Bosnian Serb nationalists pulled off an assassination whose success hardly amounted to a threat to the venerable, multinational Hapsburg state. Had Austria lashed out, occupied Belgrade, won some concessions, and withdrawn in the first couple of weeks, even Russia might have been willing to look the other way. But as the summer dragged on, it became clear that Austria was preparing not a punitive raid but a war.

---

[14] On this, in particular, see Clark (2012).

[15] See Fromkin's (2004) opening chapters for a moving account of just how temperate and peaceful that summer appeared, much like the morning of September 11, 2001, across the eastern half of the United States.

[16] Henriette Caillaux, by the way, avoided conviction, even though the facts of the case – that she walked into Gaston Calmette's office and shot him – weren't in dispute.

Austria won full German support in the now-infamous "blank check" that promised a willingness to use force against Russia – a promise also out of proportion to the stakes of an assassination scandal.[17] Likewise, Russia went from partial mobilization on July 24 to full mobilization on July 30, which meant war not just to pull Austria off Serbia but to unleash the Tsar's millions against Germany itself. France also began its own mobilization as it assured Russia of its treaty commitment to wage joint war against Germany. The war would kill millions, distort otherwise productive economies, and poison domestic politics even in winning states, and the losers would fare still worse. Why, then, embark on a war that the key decision-makers, even in Russia and Germany, *knew* would be bloody, wasteful, and potentially ruinous? Surely they could have cut a deal that left them all better off than wrecked, destitute, and – in some cases – destroyed. We'll see in the next section that solving this puzzle requires looking not at where the great powers *were* in the summer of 1914 but where they believed they *would be* after the summer of 1914 if they didn't go to war.

4.2 EXPLAINING WAR OUTBREAK AND EXPANSION

Explaining events that look like extreme outliers often appears more challenging than it needs to be, and the outbreak of the First World War, given the staggering complexity of its precipitating crisis, is no exception. The confluence of events that made the war possible was rare but hardly inexplicable. The great powers had been at peace – at least on the Continent – for decades, as Western and Central Europe had reached unprecedented levels of wealth and economic integration.[18] Yet a local crisis over a cross-border assassination in the backwater of Southeastern Europe in 1914, a region and a time in which assassinations weren't uncommon,[19] morphed in a matter of weeks into a confrontation involving the Continent's major military powers. How was it that a long, bloody war of attrition that spanned the globe and destroyed the very empires participating in it should have been the result of the July Crisis? Why was Russia, committed to the monarchical principle and working hard to recover from recent defeat by another great power, willing to cut short its convalescence over the fate of a few Bosnian Serb regicides? Why did Germany, guarded by the best army on the Continent and wealthier than many of its competitors, embark on

---

[17] For the discussions that produced the blank check, see Documents 119, 120, and 130, in Mombauer (2013, chapter 6).
[18] See Chapter 11 for more on economic interdependence and war.
[19] See Clark (2012, chapter 1).

a war in support of an unreliable Austrian ally that would pit it against Russia, France, and (unless *everything* went right) the United Kingdom?

PUZZLE 4.1   *Why did a local dispute between Austria and Serbia expand into a costly war between the other great powers?*

It's easy after the fact to look at the July Crisis and pin "blame" for the ensuing world war on nearly every party. Contemporary politicians and scholars in subsequent generations have done just that. Following a tradition associated with German historian Fritz Fischer,[20] some lay sole responsibility for the war at Germany's feet, arguing that its leaders resolved in 1912 that war – and only war – could solve problems of terminal diplomatic encirclement and fraught domestic politics.[21] Others point a finger at Russia, reading the secrecy of its initial mobilization measures as unwillingness to deter German mobilization during the height of the crisis.[22] Ferguson, predictably, blames British dithering,[23] and Clark suggests that France played its own role in encouraging Russian mobilization,[24] even as he describes a Germany that hoped to keep the Austro-Serbian war localized while looking with equanimity on the potential failure of its blank check gambit.[25] Tuchman identifies a series of misperceptions in the belligerent nations, among them the possibility of short, popular wars;[26] MacMillan links decisions to abandon peace to the shortcomings of European leadership more generally;[27] Rasler and Thompson emphasize the irreducible complexity of multiple interstate rivalries converging in what amounted to a perfect storm for global war;[28] and Vasquez reflects a popular strain of thought blaming the system of prewar alliance commitments for dragging states into the maw almost against their will.[29]

Each account captures part of the story, but not necessarily the essential parts. Germany surely saw in the July Crisis an opportunity to wage a preventive war against a rising Russia, yet as the crisis heated up, Russia seemed to believe that its *own* opportunities and privileges would decline in the near future, its wager on awaiting recovery notwithstanding. These fears don't appear compatible: how can *both* sides fear relative decline,

---

[20] Fischer (1967).
[21] See Mombauer (2001), Fromkin (2004), and Copeland (2014). But see Clark (2012) and Levy (2014) for the case that Germany didn't have a consistent policy of preventive war from 1912 until 1914.
[22] McMeekin (2013).
[23] Ferguson (1999).
[24] Clark (2012).
[25] See also Hastings (2013) and Buttar (2014).
[26] Tuchman (1962).
[27] McMillan (2014).
[28] Rasler and Thompson (2014).
[29] Vasquez (2014).

when by definition one side has to be rising if the other is declining? Faced with puzzles like this, it can be tempting to look to psychological factors, like cognitive limitations or biases,[30] but we'll show in this section that they're unnecessary; we can resolve this apparent paradox without any reference to cognitive processes. Instead, the key rests in the peculiar stakes of the Austro-Serbian July Crisis. The involvement of heavyweights like Germany, Russia, and France too often leads students of the war to dismiss the stakes of the July Crisis as secondary.[31] Far from secondary, they were central to the outbreak of general war. The July Crisis might not have determined *who* participated in the First World War, but it shaped profoundly *when* and *how* the Great War came about. Germany feared Russian resurgence, but Russia feared being shut out of the Balkans by an Austrian victory in Serbia, which itself offered Germany a preventive victory over Russia on the cheap. This explains why Germany and Russia launched preventive wars against each other in 1914, an ostensibly paradoxical outcome possible only because Austria felt compelled to bring about the fall of Russia's Balkan bulwark, Serbia. The July Crisis and its resolution threatened to unhinge the European balance of power, an opportunity for Germany and a menace for Russia that tied a Gordian Knot of commitment problems cut by conscious choices in Vienna, St. Petersburg, and Berlin to embark on a general European war.

4.2.1 Solving the Puzzle

Solving this chapter's puzzle is more demanding than the Anglo-German naval race (it's a world war, after all), but the principles are the same. First, we describe a strategic setting's players, actions, outcomes, and preferences. Then, we specify how these elements interact to identify strategies in equilibrium. But where the arms race puzzle presented us with two players, the escalation of the July Crisis into a general European war involves *four*: Serbia, Austria-Hungary, Russia, and Germany. For now, we'll assume that French participation alongside its Russian ally in a war against Austria is a foregone conclusion, nor will we be concerned yet with the question of British participation (that's for Chapter 6), about which the key players in this chapter, especially German decision-makers, were either ambivalent or dismissive.[32] Germany believed that its best chance to defeat any configuration of potential enemies was at its peak in 1914,[33] and this allows us to

---

[30] See Snyder (2014).
[31] To wit, Tuchman's (1962) famous account of the causes of the war is titled *The Guns of August*, not *The Guns of July* – which, admittedly, doesn't sound half as cool.
[32] See Lieber (2007, p. 187) and Leonhard (2018, p. 43).
[33] Hastings (2013, p. 78).

set aside calculations about French and British participation for the time being. In this section, we break the strategic complexity of the July Crisis into *three* component games, each with its own Nash Equilibrium that depends on the equilibria of the other games. If that sounds complicated, it is. But the need to embrace a little complexity will become clearer as we walk through the analysis, which confronts us with the realities of strategic interconnectedness – specifically, how an assassination in newly Hapsburg Bosnia can set off a chain of events that ends with German, Russian, and French armies on the march in seeming indifference to the original clash between Serbian nationalism and Austrian decline.

To give a brief summary, our first model isolates those states at the heart of the July Crisis, Austria-Hungary and Serbia, after the former has issued its ultimatum in the wake of Princip's successful regicide. Serbia must decide whether to honor or refuse Austria's demands, while Austria must decide whether to attack Serbia, crushing the small Balkan upstart as it's wished to for years, or to pass, which entails either backing down or engaging only in a punitive shelling, maybe occupation, of Belgrade. Critically, Austria's willingness to countenance war hinges on Germany's "blank check" offer of support. But before considering Germany's decision to honor that promise, we analyze the interaction of Russian and Austrian aims, where the former must decide whether to stand aside or to attack Austria in Serbia's defense, while Austria must decide whether or not to attack Serbia in light of Russia's potential intervention. Our third game isolates German and Russian choices over mobilizing against each other (i.e., supporting their Austrian and Serbian protégés) or backing down and opting out of an expanded war. Separating the games keeps the analysis manageable, but we can also see how the equilibrium of any one game depends on the equilibria of the others – the essence of strategic interconnectedness. This allows us to identify exactly which decisions were critical to the outbreak of the war. As we'll see, *three* preventive wars came together in the July Crisis to produce an unusually large and bloody general war involving multiple great powers. Yet solving any one of these commitment problems would be sufficient to prevent a general war in 1914.

Figure 4.2 focuses on Serbia and Austria-Hungary. Faced with an Austrian ultimatum, Serbia must decide whether to refuse or honor it, the most extreme provisions of which entail an effective abdication of sovereignty – harsh terms, indeed. Austria must decide whether to attack, in pursuit of the long-sought dismemberment of its troublesome Balkan neighbor, or to pass in the hope that Serbia complies. The structure of each side's preferences bears some similarities to the preventive war games analyzed in Chapter 2. Serbia, fresh off its extensive gains in the Balkan Wars, wants

S

	honor	refuse
pass	4, 1	1, 4
attack	2, 2	3, 3

A

Figure 4.2 The Austro-Serb crisis.

freedom to continue nationalist, irredentist agitation in pursuit of a greater Serbia, which necessarily entails trouble for Austria's attempts to consolidate its hold on Serb subjects in Bosnia-Herzegovina. The Dual Monarchy, on the other hand, fears that a growing Serbia will undermine its own tenuous grip on the "nationalities problem," which will only grow more challenging as Serbia grows in power and prestige. Austria, its great power status notwithstanding, views itself as a power in decline, running out of chances to humble Serbia before it can create even greater disruptions in, and potentially shatter, the fragile ethno-linguistic balance that sustains the Hapsburg Empire.[34]

How do these goals translate into preferences? First, acceding to Austrian demands while the Austrians pass on war yields Serbia's worst outcome (1), because it would represent the end of Serbian sovereignty without putting up a fight (for which it expects Russian assistance, without which it can't expect to fend off the Central Powers). Its best outcome entails refusing to comply while Austria passes (4), and the middling outcomes, those that Serbia will accept if it must, entail a war with Russian support.[35] If it refuses and ends up in a war, Serbia preserves some chance of surviving (3), and such defiance in the face of attack is better than acquiescence that nonetheless ends in the humiliation of war (2). Expectations of Russian support, which make war attractive at all, depend on the outcome of games between Russia, Austria, and Germany. For now, we take the equilibria of those games as given, allowing us to see how those expectations support the preventive war equilibrium that emerges in the Austro-Serbian crisis.

Austria, as we might suspect, ranks the outcomes rather differently, because its ultimatum has been drawn up with the intent of making acceptance impossible.[36] Austria's most preferred outcome is for Serbia to honor the terms of the ultimatum, effectively yielding sovereignty to the Dual

---

[34] See Clark (2012, pp. 182, 242, 282) and Herwig (2014, pp. 11–20).
[35] Again, see Levy (1990–1991).
[36] Herwig (2014, pp. 11–20).

Monarchy (4). But this is a promise that Serbia may be unable to keep. Whatever Serbia *says* it will do with respect to the regicides that killed Franz Ferdinand, it can easily continue on its path of territorial and economic growth on the one hand and its strategy of nationalist agitation on the other; any such acquiescence may be incredible. Passing up the chance to attack while Serbia refuses to comply is Austria's worst outcome (1), but war offers a unique opportunity, thanks to the German blank check. Attacking a compliant Serbia may entail some diplomatic costs for Austria of looking like a bully, *but* it may end Serbia's irredentist potential (2). Meanwhile, attacking a recalcitrant Serbia gives Austria its second-best outcome, because it appears to be attacking a defiant state that looks guilty (3). Just as it is with Serbia's willingness to countenance war against the Central Powers, Austria's willingness to attack Serbia and provoke the ire of its Russian patron depends on Germany's full support.[37] Any violent equilibrium of the Austro-Serbian game therefore depends on the equilibria of these other games involving German and Russian strategy.

PROPOSITION 4.1   *The strategy profile (attack; refuse) is a Nash Equilibrium.*

Proof   For (attack; refuse) to be a Nash Equilibrium, it must be the case that

$$u_A(attack; \text{refuse}) \geq u_A(pass; \text{refuse})$$

and

$$u_S(\text{attack}; refuse) \geq u_S(\text{attack}; honor).$$

The first inequality is satisfied because $3 \geq 1$, and the second is satisfied because $3 \geq 2$. No player has a profitable deviation, so (attack; refuse) is a Nash Equilibrium.   □

We know how this played out in the historical record, but the game – and the reasoning behind its equilibrium – sheds light on *why* war came when it did. Thinking in real time, Serbia accepts most, but not all, of Austria's demands, and Austria plays attack, making the equilibrium (attack; refuse). The Dual Monarchy declares war on July 27, desultorily shelling Belgrade across the Sava and Danube Rivers, ensuring that last-ditch attempts at third-party mediation will be too late to spare Serbia its fate. Later, with mobilization nearly complete, Austria mounts an August invasion in hopes of finally crushing its upstart neighbor. If we examine Serbia's payoffs at the equilibrium, we see that it can do no better than refusing the ultimatum, *regardless of what Austria does*. If

[37] Levy (1990–1991, p. 156).

Austria will back down (playing pass), then Serbia has every incentive
to refuse compliance ($4 \geq 1$), but if Austria will attack in any case, then
Serbia prefers to make a show of resistance rather than acquiesce in its
own destruction ($3 \geq 2$). In game-theoretic terms, we say that "refuse"
constitutes a **dominant strategy** for Serbia, just as building dreadnoughts
did for Britain and Germany in Chapter 3.

DEFINITION 4.2   *A **dominant strategy** is a best response to every strategy
another player might choose.*

Austria, for its part, chooses to attack, because Serbia is sure to flout the
ultimatum absent the threat of war (i.e., if Austria passes). If Serbia will
resist regardless of Austria's choice – that is, if Serbia won't be complicit in
its own dismemberment – then the Dual Monarchy prefers a war that can
create an acceptable outcome by force of arms. Therefore, (attack; refuse)
is the game's unique Nash Equilibrium. The incredibility of any Serbian
commitment not to continue its own growth and nationalist agitation leads
Austria to initiate a preventive war to dismember Serbia, offer its territory
to other regional powers, and end a major external threat to the resolution
of its nationalities problem.

   A simple Austrian preventive war on a neighboring minor power
might be the end of the story, but Serbia's willingness to risk war and
Austria's willingness to pursue it depend on the behavior of their patrons,
Russia and Germany. Unless Russia chooses, in an equilibrium of its own
game against Austria, to attack it in the event of an Austro-Serbian war,
Serbia's preference for refusing Austrian demands is undermined; any
chance of survival against the Central Powers depends on Russian military
support. Likewise, absent a guarantee of German military support in the
face of a Russian onslaught, Austria's willingness to fight will be severely
curtailed. If attacking Serbia without backup means facing a subsequent
Russian invasion, tolerating Serbian acquiescence becomes for the Dual
Monarchy an acceptable (if imperfect) outcome of the assassination crisis.
Therefore, to explain the outbreak of the First World War, we must link the
short-run specifics of the July Crisis to broader processes of Russo-German
antagonism. We must explain why each decision for war in this chapter
constitutes an equilibrium in its own game; if any equilibrium fails, then
the war as we know it does not break out in July–August 1914.

   To that end, the game in Figure 4.3 reveals the key to Russia's strategic
problem in the July Crisis: if Austria *can* credibly promise not to crush
Serbia, Russia is more than happy to remain at peace, biding its time as it
gains a military advantage over the other great powers. Time, as its
leaders have said for years before 1914, is on Russia's side.[38] Russia's

---

[38] For an extended discussion, see Levy and Mulligan (2017).

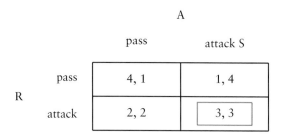

Figure 4.3 Russia and the July Crisis.

first-best outcome is to preserve and extend, peacefully, its influence in the Balkans, which it equates with retaining its status as a great power.[39] But if passing up war allows Austria to dismember Serbia, distribute the booty to grateful Serbian rivals like Bulgaria, and assert a new Hapsburg hegemony in the Balkans, Russia will lose valuable buffers on its south-western frontier *and* see its great power status under threat.[40] Long-term Russian goals entail control of Constantinople – conspicuously referred to as "Tsargrad" in St. Petersburg – and the Turkish Straits,[41] and a strength-ened Austrian presence in the Balkans poses a long-term obstacle to the achievement of that ultimate goal.[42] Indeed, Russia believes that "the bat-tle for Constantinople would be won in Berlin and Vienna."[43] Only if Austria can credibly promise not to crush Serbia can Russia feel safe in not mobilizing for the latter's defense. In July 1914, with Serbia growing in power and assertiveness, Hapsburg prestige plummeting, and Germany's blank check waiting to be cashed, the Dual Monarchy can make no such promise.

   With Russia unwilling to stand aside, the Nash Equilibrium of the Russo-Austrian game is predictable: Austria-Hungary sets in motion an attack on Serbia, which (thanks to German support) makes sense whether or not Russia intervenes, and Russia prepares to unleash the great "steam-roller" three years too early, lest its rearmament efforts go to waste while the Teutonic powers cement their hold on the European approaches to Constantinople. Figure 4.3 presents the preferences underlying this deci-sion. Russia most prefers that Austria pass, allowing it to pass as well and complete the Grand Programme (4). If Austria attacks Serbia, Russia's best hope is war (3), though it prefers attacking a peaceful Austria (2) to

[39] Bobroff (2014, pp. 240 and 246).
[40] Levy and Mulligan (2017, p. 757).
[41] See Bobroff (2014, p. 238).
[42] Generally, Russia could tolerate Ottoman control of the Straits. The only other palatable alternative was Russia itself, but St. Petersburg was under no illusions that acquiring Constantinople would require the outbreak of a general war. For more on Russian designs on Constantinople and their role in its wartime policy, see McMeekin (2015).
[43] Bobroff (2014, p. 239).

allowing a free Austrian hand to attack Serbia (1). Austria's preferences boil down to the threat of Russian intervention. Its best outcome is to attack Serbia unmolested (4), and its worst is to leave the Serbian problem unsolved by remaining at peace (1). Austria will tolerate, if it must, attacking Serbia while facing a war with Russia (3), because this is better than war against Russia after passing on Serbia, leaving its southern flank exposed to Serbian attack (2). With preferences and actions arranged this way, the equilibrium is as we'd expect: (attack; attack S).

PROPOSITION 4.2   *The strategy profile (attack; attack S) is a Nash Equilibrium.*

Proof   For (attack; attack S) to be a Nash Equilibrium, it must be the case that

$$u_R(attack; \text{attack S}) \geq u_R(pass; \text{attack S})$$

and

$$u_A(\text{attack}; attack\ S) \geq u_A(\text{attack}; pass).$$

The first inequality is satisfied because $3 \geq 1$, and the second is satisfied because $3 \geq 2$. No player has a profitable deviation, so this is a Nash Equilibrium.   □

Figure 4.3 shows that Russia can't allow Serbia to fall, given Austria's drive to attack, yet Austria can't credibly promise not to invade Serbia if Russia stands aside. The costs of war notwithstanding, each side's strategy produces a war guaranteed to result in ex post regret; if only Austria can promise not to crush Serbia and close the door on Russia's southern expansion in the process, war can be averted. Such a promise would be incredible, though, so the prospective fall of Serbia draws Russia into a war against the Central Powers – even as the Dual Monarchy almost surely would not attempt to destroy its southern neighbor without the promise of German support embodied in the "blank check." The final link in the chain, then, is explaining why Germany effectively encourages Austria-Hungary to attack Serbia, risking wider war with Russia (and its Entente partners) when St. Petersburg will almost inevitably make moves to defend Serbia from Hapsburg attack.

If Germany doesn't embolden Austria, the equilibria of the Austro-Serbian and Russo-Austrian games will be radically different – that is, peaceful. Austria will expect war to entail fighting Serbia and Russia without German help, which will either deter it from attacking in the first place or encourage a limited, punitive occupation of Belgrade that allows Russia to stay aloof, indulging a fellow monarchy's attempt to gain satisfaction after a regicide. Staying the hand of Hapsburg vengeance is only possible if Germany refuses the blank check. This would also make Austria-Hungary's commitment to limited aims credible, allowing Russia to stand aside while continuing its rearmament. Nonetheless, Germany both offers blanket support and – but for a brief hesitation once British intentions become clear – renews it throughout Austria's dilatory efforts at approving and realizing mobilization throughout July. Some observers attribute this unconditional support to a *desire* for war,[44] yet the German leadership is nothing if not calculating and frugal – that is, mindful of the costs and risks of war.[45] Why embark on a course of action whose results were understood to be so (potentially) disastrous?

The answer lies not in Germany's position of strength in July 1914 (which is considerable) but where it believes it *will be* in 1917, with Russia's rearmament complete and Germany's own fiscal limitations in meeting the threat of Entente arms finally reached. After years of waste competing with the British for mastery of the oceans, Germany has strained its finances to the brink, expanding its army with a historically large investment in 1913. Its credit rating has fallen correspondingly, yet Russia's rating has continued to rise, and the vise grip of the Franco-Russian Entente will only tighten in the coming years.[46] The German political class sees two possible ways out of this dilemma. One entails political liberalization that would compromise its dominance in the *Kaiserreich*, the other prevention of relative decline. Not preventive war, necessarily, but some means by which to arrest the Tsar's expansion into the region that could dramatically increase Russian power: the former Ottoman lands of southeastern Europe. A preventive war will be enormously costly, but the July Crisis offers Germany a unique opportunity: the chance to see Russia shut out of the Balkans (and cheaply, if Germany can stay out of the war), Austria's position bolstered if the conflict remains localized, and, if Russia intervenes, the guarantee that Austria-Hungary can hold the Eastern Front while Germany unleashes the Schlieffen Plan in the West. (If there were a textbook definition of a small margin for error, this would be it.) Supporting Austria-Hungary gives Germany a chance – however small, however risky – of realizing its first-best outcome of the July Crisis: shutting Russia out of the Balkans and offsetting a great deal of the military consequences of Russian rearmament. For Germany, "victory [is] possible either on the field of battle or at the conference table,"[47] but it prefers

---

[44] Fromkin (2004) is a recent example of this argument.
[45] Mulligan (2014).
[46] Levy (2014, p. 155).
[47] Herwig (2014, p. 23).

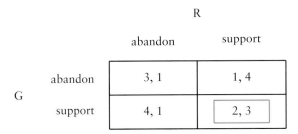

Figure 4.4 Germany and Russia in the July Crisis.

the cheaper option if possible. Russia, for its part, is well aware that an Austrian success in the Balkans could shut it out for decades, successful rearmament notwithstanding.[48]

Figure 4.4 shows that Germany's options are to support the Dual Monarchy, committing itself to a war against Russia if necessary, or to abandon it, leaving Austria to fight alone if Russia pledges itself to Serbia's survival. Russia, on the other hand, must support or abandon Serbia. It most prefers that Germany abandon Austria, leaving Russia free to defend its Balkan protégé, but it prefers war with Germany to leaving Serbia to face the combined might of Germany and Austria.[49] Germany's most-preferred outcome is for Austria to crush Serbia unmolested, shutting Russia out of the Balkans via a local "diplomatic revolution" and possibly splitting the Entente.[50] Germany does, though, prefer that this happen with a promise of support in order to keep the Austro-German alliance healthy. Germany receives 4 if Austria crushes Serbia alone with stated German support, and 3 if it happens without German support. If Russia attacks an abandoned Austria, Germany gets its worst outcome (1), while its third-best outcome (2) is available if it supports Austria in the face of a Russian attack. This is consistent with the image of Germany as a power in relative decline: refusing war with Russia allows an unfavorable shift in power to continue, both via the continued progress of the "Grand Programme" and a substantial reduction in Austrian power. On the other hand, Russia's most-preferred outcome is to support Serbia while Germany abandons Austria (4), followed by each side supporting its protégé in a Continental war (3), trailed by its worst outcome: any situation in which Serbia is abandoned to its fate (1).

---

[48] Levy and Mulligan (2017, p. 741).

[49] This reflects, with adjustments for the model in this chapter, Levy's (1990–1991) characterization of German and Russian preferences in 1914. Germany prefers localization, but a general war is preferable to allowing Austria to face Serbia and Russia alone (pp. 160–161), while Russia prefers that, if an Austro-Serbian war breaks out, it can defend Serbia without German interference, but it will tolerate a general war rather than see the Serbs – and its own influence in the region – go under (p. 157).

[50] See Levy (2015, p. 210).

PROPOSITION 4.3   *The strategy profile (support; support) is a Nash Equilibrium.*

Proof   For (support; support) to be a Nash Equilibrium, it must be the case that

$$u(support; \text{support}) \geq u(abandon; \text{support})$$

for each player. This inequality is satisfied for G because $2 \geq 1$, and it is satisfied for R because $3 \geq 1$. No player has a profitable deviation, so (support; support) is a Nash Equilibrium.   □

The unique equilibrium of (support; support) in the Russo-German game may not be surprising to us by now, but its necessary connection to the equilibria of the Austro-Serbian and Russo-Serbian games in Figures 4.2 and 4.3 makes it illuminating. Each side supports its protégé, with Germany and Russia refusing each other's last-minute entreaties to back down. If Germany withdraws support for Austria, Russia will fall upon Austria with superior numbers, saving Serbia and dealing a catastrophic blow to the Hapsburg Empire. Ironically, this ensures that Austria has skin in the game – that it will be a part of a German preventive war against Russia – when in previous twentieth-century crises such support wasn't in the offing.[51] Likewise, if Russia backs down, it avoids war with Germany, but Austria can crush Serbia and effectively shut Russia out of the Balkans, hobbling the European resurgence on which it has focused after the humiliation of 1905. We can verify that this is also the unique Nash Equilibrium, because each side will support its protégé if the other abandons its ally, and neither will stand aside while the other supports its protégé alone.

What does this teach us about how the Austro-Serb crisis became a general European conflagration? Germany and Russia went to war in 1914 because neither could credibly promise not to withdraw support for its smaller partner. As a result, *both* sides can be characterized as fighting a preventive war. But without appreciating the implications of an Austro-Serbian war for the Russo-German relationship, this fact looks paradoxical.[52] While it's easy to look to the alliance system as the key factor explaining the outbreak of general war,[53] the logic supporting

---

[51] See Stevenson (1997) and Clark (2012).

[52] See Snyder (2014) for the paradox claim, then Levy (2015) (with Snyder's [2015] response) and Levy and Mulligan (2017) for arguments that the Austro-Serbian war removes the paradox.

[53] See Christensen and Snyder (1990) as well as Vasquez (2014) for a more recent statement of the argument.

the equilibrium in Figure 4.4 and its grounding in the equilibria of the Austro-Serbian and Austro-Russian crisis games reveals a different line of reasoning. Germany and Russia went to war over the implications of the Austro-Serbian war for their *own* power transition, Germany to arrest Russia's rise and Russia to preserve its own chance to rise. Both Germany *and* Russia launched preventive wars, thanks to the strategic interconnectedness of the international system. Whether or not Germany was tied to Austria by a formal alliance, whether or not Russia felt responsible for the security of a fellow Slavic state, the problem of shifting power would still have pushed them to war, since the source of shifting power was an Austro-Serbian war.[54] The July Crisis offered Germany a chance to secure the gains of a preventive war against Russia on the cheap, without launching a direct assault on the Tsar's empire, but Russia's desire to complete the "Grand Programme" led it to embark on its own preventive war against Germany – even though it would have preferred its power to grow unmolested. Rising powers in general wish to delay war so as to complete their rise with few complications,[55] but when declining powers can deny them the chance to grow, rising powers can attack first in hopes of preserving a status quo in which they rise. The expansion of the July Crisis into the First World War is just such a case.

4.2.2 Why 1914?

A satisfactory explanation of why the July Crisis became a general war must also tell us why other crises – say, the Moroccan Crises of 1905 and 1911 or the Balkan Wars of 1912–1913 – didn't. If we focus only on 1914, we risk identifying apparent causes of the Great War in 1914 that were also present in previous years yet failed to precipitate it. This is the risk of what social scientists call selecting on the dependent variable (i.e., the thing to be explained). Instead, if we want to understand why war occurs, we can't just look at wars alone; we've got to compare disagreements resolved by war to disagreements resolved peacefully. For the First World War, we have to ask why war came in 1914 but not 1905, 1912, or 1916. Why were Russia and Germany able to restrain themselves before Franz Ferdinand's death, as Ottoman power crumbled in Southeast Europe, but not afterward, when it could hardly crumble any further? The German desire for preventive war can be traced back at least as far as the formation

---

[54] The Russo-French alliance might explain why Germany attacked France first in its war plan, but suppose that there were no such alliance; Germany might've been even more eager to wage a preventive war against Russia, provided that it could trust France not to take advantage of the opportunity to recover Alsace and Lorraine.

[55] See Powell (2006).

of the Franco-Russian alliance in 1894, and German officials discussed it explicitly at what Chancellor Bethmann-Hollweg called a "war council" in 1912, yet war didn't come.[56] And Russian leaders, we know, were eager to delay a general European war as long as possible. General war, which few doubted would be long, bloody, and apocalyptic, was on the minds and lips of generals, diplomats, ministers, and monarchs, even popular novelists, for years before 1914. But if growing Russian power was such a concern – and it certainly was – why did Germany not maneuver itself for going on the attack well before 1914? The games in this chapter suggest an answer, but we've got to compare the July Crisis to previous opportunities for preventive war to be confident in it.

For us, the most important feature of the July Crisis is that the outcome of an Austro-Serbian conflict would impact not just the local distribution of power but also that between Russia and Germany. An Austrian victory over Serbia would blunt the effects of Russia's rise, shutting it out of the approaches to Constantinople, making any such newfound military power more difficult to use. This prospect encouraged Russia to fight a war to preserve a chance to complete its rearmament in a favorable environment. Germany, for its part, couldn't stand aside as Russia eliminated Austria-Hungary, its only effective ally after the Kaiser failed to renew Bismarck's Reinsurance Treaty with Russia in 1890, which would accelerate Germany's own decline relative to Russia. Without the prospect of an Austro-Serbian war doing Germany's preventive work for it, war might not have come in 1914, the latter's preventive motives notwithstanding. After all, Russia's rise and Germany's long-term inability to compete in the arms race were widely known before 1914; they were present when Austria annexed Bosnia-Herzegovina in 1908, when the Balkan Wars of 1912–1913 put Serbian power on the rise at Ottoman expense, and when Russia objected to the appointment of the German general Otto Liman von Sanders to the Ottoman army later that year. In each case, neither Germany nor Russia proved willing to instigate a broader war. During the Balkan Wars, Russia announced a "partial" mobilization aimed only at Austria-Hungary, and the crisis was resolved. Yet partial mobilization in 1914 set Russia on a collision course with the *Kaiserreich*. What changed to make the same policy preserve peace in one year but virtually guarantee war the next?

Figure 4.2 provides the answer. Promises of German support hadn't encouraged Austria to attempt a final reckoning with Serbia in previous

---

[56] Some analysts make a lot of the fact that this "war council" talked about the possibility of preventive war against Russia (e.g., Fromkin, 2004), yet Leonhard (2018, p. 54) notes that Bethmann used the label sarcastically, because civilian politicians weren't invited.

crises,[57] but by 1914, with one of the few advocates for peace murdered in Sarajevo and Austria's waning chances to crush its southern neighbor too tempting to resist, the Dual Monarchy was finally willing to let slip the dogs of war.[58] With the Serbian threat approaching its peak after two consecutive victories in the Balkan Wars, Austria's own impending fiscal and financial difficulties offered such a bleak view of the future that even moderates in Vienna fell in line with the militarists' calls for preventive war. Finally, after years of halfhearted support for German goals, Austria had sufficient skin in the game to be willing to fight, even in the face of near-certain Russian intervention. Germany could finally count on the Dual Monarchy to help hold the Eastern Front against Russia, making the military's long-sought preventive war feasible. That alignment of interests posed a sufficient threat to Russia that, rising power notwithstanding, the Tsar would abandon his strategy of waiting for power to finally shift in his favor. That Russia could (even should) have waited in 1914 is a popular idea,[59] but an Austrian victory in a localized war on Serbia would've rendered moot much of the "Grand Programme," and it would've done so by German design. Had Russia waited for war while Austria dismembered Serbia and consolidated Hapsburg dominance in the Balkans, it would've occupied a far less favorable strategic position; its prospects would've been worse, not better, the completion of rearmament notwithstanding. Thus, in July 1914, "[t]he Austrian desire for military action is *the essential difference* from the earlier crises" (emphasis added).[60]

Prior to July 1914, Austria had proved at best a hesitant German ally, but in the wake of the assassination crisis Germany could finally count on Hapsburg willingness to send an army into the field. But to say that Germany used Austria for its own purposes of starting a war misses the point. *If* Germany could deter Russia from mobilizing, and *if* Austria could crush Serbia and ensure Teutonic dominance of the Balkans and – ultimately – the remains of the Ottoman Empire in Europe, then Germany could strike a preventive blow against Russian power without firing a shot. This, as we saw in Figure 4.4, was Germany's first-best outcome of the July Crisis. Its inability in the face of competing Russian incentives to achieve that goal should not obscure for us the lure of localizing an Austro-Serbian war as an explanation for Germany's decision to take the plunge in 1914. Without credible Austrian participation, financially strapped Germany would face substantial difficulties in mounting

[57] Stevenson (1997).
[58] See Clark (2012) for a discussion of what it took for this "Balkan inception" scenario for the Great War to finally crystallize.
[59] See Snyder (2014) and Renshon (2017, pp. 223–232).
[60] Williamson (2014, p. 45).

a preventive war, and this fact proved critical in both the issuance of the "blank check" *and* in Russia's belief, confirmed by the Austrian ultimatum, that war with Germany was unavoidable.

Much ink has been spilled in the ensuing century about why, given the tremendous costs of the First World War, Germany and Russia were unable to **deter** each other from unleashing their war machines.[61] But this is the wrong question. Deterrence works on the presumption that one state would back down if only it knew the other side's willingness to fight – hence the need to make a deterrent threat to clarify one's intentions. Deterrence presumes that, absent a threat to retaliate, the recipient of the threat would carry out the proscribed action, i.e., that actors are deterrable.

DEFINITION 4.3   *Deterrence uses threats of punishment (e.g., war) to discourage another actor from taking a specific action (e.g., invasion).*

Yet Russian and German preferences over the Austro-Serb crisis clearly do not satisfy this requirement. When fully aware of the other's intentions, both sides still chose war over allowing the other side to support its protégé. Deterrence was beside the point, "bound to fail ... because the Germans believed that in 1914 they had a better chance of defeating any Entente combination than they would ever enjoy again."[62] The question of full versus partial Russian mobilizations is also misleading, because "Russian partial mobilization would eventually lead to a German mobilization because of the Russian threat to Austria, not because of the direct threat to Germany."[63] When driven to preventive war by a commitment problem, states will look back and regret the costs and destruction of war, but *not* because they wish they had known the other side's intentions. Their equilibrium reasoning doesn't look like deterrence failure. Had deterrence been possible, the reasoning would go, "If only we'd known that the other side would fight, we would've acted differently," but following a preventive war, the reasoning is, "If only the rising side could've promised not to use its power, we could've avoided this war." This fits with German and Russian decision-making at the time better than the reasoning behind deterrence failure, which we'll explore in more detail in Chapter 13.

What, then, distinguishes 1914 from previous opportunities for war? The answer is the unique constellation of interests that came together in the July Crisis, which saw Austria willing to use force to solve Serbia's commitment problem, thereby activating commitment problems for both Russia *and* Germany. In previous crises over French power in Morocco, carving up Ottoman lands in Europe, and growing German influence in

---

[61] See Zagare (2011, chapters 5 and 6).
[62] See Hastings (2013, p. 78).
[63] Levy (1990–1991, p. 181).

Constantinople, Austria wasn't committed to the fight, which discouraged Germany from unleashing a preventive war and allowed Russia to continue its post-1905 rearmament in peace. But after the Sarajevo murders, Austria was willing to cash a German blank check, activating the twin preventive wars between great powers that would within weeks drive almost the entire Continent to war. The strategic interconnectedness of the international system is a key part of the background; the outcome of an Austro-Serbian war would have had profound implications for great power politics, threatening to upend the balance of power that had held, however tenuously, since 1815. Some explanations for the outbreak of war focus on the belligerents' belief in the success of rapid offensives as helping bring the war about,[64] but those beliefs were also present before the July Crisis in military doctrines across the Continent,[65] and even once war came they were wishes, hopes, neither convictions nor firm beliefs; even the German general staff, which built a war plan on the rapid defeat of France, did so because of its confidence that war against Russia would, as ever, be long and bloody and difficult. We'll address this so-called cult of the offensive in greater detail in Chapters 5 and 8. In the final accounting, both Russia and Germany jumped into the breach to try and shape the future of that balance. Failing to recognize the link between the Austro-Serb crisis and Russo-German relations, failing to recognize the system's strategic interconnectedness, can only obscure this explanation for the war.

4.3 WHOSE FAULT WAS IT?

When the Entente imposed peace terms at Versailles in 1919, a bedrock clause of the treaty required that Germany admit fault for initiating the war.[66] This "war guilt" clause would justify harsh reparations and limitations on German arms, among other punitive terms, in the treaty itself. It would also prove a point of popular anguish inside Germany, where the public began and ended the war believing the conflict to be defensive or, at any rate, hardly Germany's fault alone.[67] The Treaty of Versailles would become fuel in the interwar period for the rise of the Nazi Party, which picked up the military's postwar rhetoric about a mythical "stab in the back" to account for Germany's defeat and for the eventual outbreak of the Second World War. The war guilt clause was contentious then – American president Woodrow Wilson only conceded to the idea of harsh

---

[64] See, e.g., Tuchman (1962).

[65] See, especially, Buttar (2014) and Philpott (2014), two remarkable accounts of the interaction of belligerent war plans.

[66] See Neiberg (2017) for a brief and insightful history of the Treaty of Versailles.

[67] See Watson (2014).

reparations in order to win support for his League of Nations proposals, and John Maynard Keynes published a major critique of the Treaty after leaving the negotiations in disgust in 1919 – and it remains so, especially in light of the Treaty's role in Germany's poisonous interwar politics.

What can the games in this chapter tell us about guilt, fault, or blame for starting the Great War? "Guilt," or "responsibility" as characterized in the treaty, implies that Germany *wanted* the conflict and that its decisions alone were sufficient to have brought it about. Some scholars accept this implicit line of reasoning, even going so far as to work from a murder-mystery metaphor to analyze the causes of the war,[68] but guilt is a difficult case to make in light of this chapter's analysis; the outbreak of general war depended on decisions for preventive war made not only in Berlin but also in Vienna and Moscow. Germany could in principle have undermined Russian power in the Balkans on the cheap if the Austro-Serbian war had been successfully localized. And German actions in the July Crisis, particularly its express desire for Austria to strike quickly (which Austria manifestly failed to do), are consistent with the idea that Berlin would accept war if localization failed, but that localization was still its most desired outcome. Germany *did* voluntarily issue the blank check that emboldened Austria to launch a long-desired preventive war against Serbia, but *not* in the hopes of touching off a cataclysmic general war involving all the great powers.

If Germany didn't want or explicitly pursue war, then the question of guilt appears not only beside the point but also misleading. Germany's decision to mobilize against Russia and France depended on decisions made in Vienna and St. Petersburg, just as decisions in those capitals depended on actions taken in Berlin. No single decision was sufficient to have brought about a general war from the July Crisis, because the Austrian, German, and Russian decisions for war form part of an equilibrium in which each decision depends on the other. With multiple necessary conditions for war satisfied in different capitals, the question of blame or guilt loses much of its urgency.[69] More importantly, searching for a guilty party doesn't just fail to explain the war; it also blinds us to the very real strategic problems facing decision-makers in 1914, in years before and after, and in our own time. The war was tragic, bloody, and destructive, but it didn't require evil, unlimited ambitions to come about. Failing to recognize that, failing to put ourselves in the heads of the decision-makers in real time, can blind us to the very real possibility that modern great powers may find themselves once again faced with such a thorny strategic problem.

[68] See Fromkin (2004).
[69] See also Levy (2014, pp. 148–149).

4.4 ON "UNWINNABLE" WARS

When Germany launched its preventive war in 1914, it expected that its ability to defeat the Entente powers had peaked and would soon decline. From a preventive standpoint, this makes sense, but it overlooks something critical: the peak was still pretty low. France, Russia, and Britain could muster a larger total population, greater aggregate wealth, secure seaborne trade, and reliable credit in a way that the Central Powers could not, Germany's superior battlefield effectiveness notwithstanding.[70] Germany and Austria-Hungary's prospects weren't going to improve, but they were *already bad*. Some estimates at the time, in fact, put the chances of success at no higher than 50 percent. Germany's ability to survive a long war, an attritional fight to the finish, was clearly in doubt. And yet, in Bethmann's words, his country still took a "leap into the dark." With the odds against Germany, why not remain at peace?

PUZZLE 4.2 *Why did Germany accept a war with such a small chance of victory?*

On August 4, as German troops were crashing into Belgium on the way to France, Prussian War Minister Erich von Falkenhayn told his Kasier, "Even if we go under as a result of this, it was beautiful."[71] That's hardly the picture of optimism from one of the men that helped make war possible. Does our story in this chapter give German leaders too much credit for being frugal and calculating? Should we attribute their willingness to fight a world war to a miscalculation or, worse, a willful disregard for the realities of the balance of power? A pathological attachment to honoring alliance commitments or to preserving prestige? Or to simple national hatred? Tempting as it might be – and plenty of analysts have succumbed to that temptation – the answer is no. Explanations like this are at best unnecessary or self-serving but also, tainted as they are by a hundred years of hindsight, misleading.

To see why, let's dig a little deeper into the incentives that drive states to preventive war. When a state fights a war to arrest, end, or reverse its loss of power relative to a rising opponent (recall Definition 2.13), its chief concern is *preventing* its position from getting worse. Fighting to preserve a dominant position might make intuitive sense to us, but fighting to preserve even a weak position can be attractive when future decline is basically certain. To the minds of the German leadership, Russian resurgence and Austrian weakness would lead almost inevitably to a collapse of great power status. If remaining at peace makes ultimate ruin a near certainty,

---

[70] See Ferguson (1999, chapters 4, 5, and 9).
[71] Quoted in Hastings (2013, p. 118).

then an alternative that offers even slightly better odds of arresting decline – that is, a war that promises at least some chance of subduing one's enemies – looks like a worthwhile gamble. Certain decline from the status quo can encourage states to roll the iron dice of war, even when those dice are weighted against them. Germany may have been pessimistic about its chances of defeating the Entente in 1914, but a last best chance is still a last best chance, even when "best" looks pretty grim. The more the odds are shifting against a declining state, the more desperate it may become, accepting increasingly risky gambles in hopes of preserving its position. In Berlin, "war was viewed as both apocalyptic fear and apocalyptic hope."[72] We'll see that play out several times for Germany over the course of the war.

Indeed, Wilhelmine Germany isn't alone in the historical record for launching a preventive war when the odds weren't exactly favorable. Japan went to war twice in the twentieth century with what it calculated as 50–50 chances of victory, successfully against Russia in 1904 and disastrously against the United States in 1941.[73] In each case, Japan sought to preserve some chance of averting future decline, to stifle Russian encroachment into Manchuria in the Russo-Japanese War and to knock the United States out of the Pacific before it would reach peak naval capacity during the Second World War. Germany indeed acted out of a pessimistic acceptance of *future* weakness, which made long odds in the present more attractive by comparison. This would lead to both a daring war plan aimed at trying to win quickly, before the Entente could fully mobilize, and, as the war dragged on, a series of increasingly disastrous gambles on military aims and strategy aimed at preserving some chance of survival in the face of looming catastrophe.

4.5 CONCLUSION

A popular trope about the First World War sees it as inadvertent, an accident, a war that no state wanted yet all slid into unwittingly. Not surprisingly, the politicians that made early decisions for war – especially in Germany – were early proponents of this view. This image sits uncomfortably alongside another popular narrative, i.e., that Germany wanted and consciously brought about a world war, but we've shown in this chapter that neither of these characterizations is correct. As Jack Levy notes in his study of the July Crisis,

---

[72] Herwig (2014, p. 21).
[73] On the Russo-Japanese War, see Connaughton (2003) and Streich and Levy (2016), and on the Pacific War, see Hotta (2014) and Paine (2012).

the image of World War I as inadvertent and the image of World War I as the intended consequence of Germany's drive for world power are both exaggerated. Germany wanted a local war, but neither Germany nor any other great power wanted a general European war with British involvement.[74]

To be sure, Germany was willing to risk a general war in its management of the July Crisis, but its most desired outcome, the elusive item at the top of its wishlist, was a localized Austrian war on Serbia that would both shore up Hapsburg power and sharply diminish the Russian threat in the Balkans. Germany's leaders knew war to be costly, wasteful, and potentially ruinous – they even expected the war against Russia to be long and difficult – yet they acted out of a "rational pessimism"[75] over their ability to compete with their great power rivals in the face of a rapid Russian rise and their own deteriorating fiscal position.[76] Yet this preventive war became possible only when Austria was itself committed to war and when Russia could not stand aside and see itself shut out of the Balkans. By backing Serbia, Russia denied Germany its first-best outcome of a localized Austro-Serbian war, but Germany could prevent its worst outcome – Tsarist troops pouring into the Balkans and smashing Hapsburg power – by activating plans for war against the Entente.

Viewing the war in this way resolves several puzzles, including the apparently incompatible claims that both Russia and Germany had preventive motives in escalating the July Crisis and why an issue of fairly small stakes – an assassination in a region full of them – could ultimately draw in the major military powers on the Continent. It also explains why German leaders could quite rationally choose to unleash a war in which they knew their chances of victory to be small, though vanishing with each passing year. We'll see in subsequent chapters that this initial pessimism goes a long way to explain what seems like an extreme German taste for risky, ultimately disastrous, military gambles. Yet with only Serbia, Austria, Germany, and Russia in the fight, we're looking at a general European war. Not yet a world war. France's decision to join the war isn't all that puzzling; Germany declared war on France before declaring war on Russia, and France was bound by alliance to fight alongside Russia. It's the British decision to fight, to implement its long-planned blockade of German ports and to send the British Expeditionary Force into the line on the Western Front, that will make this incipient conflict a true *world war*.

---

[74] Levy (1990–1991, p.154).
[75] Harrison (2016).
[76] See McDonald (2009, p. 232).

4.6   EXERCISES: SYSTEM EFFECTS

More than almost any other, this chapter highlights the strategic interconnectedness of the international system. Events in one corner of the system can shape events in another, such that we can't explain what happens in the Russo-German game of Figure 4.4 without some understanding of what happens in the Austro-Serbian game of Figure 4.2 and the Russo-Austrian game of Figure 4.3. The international system isn't understandable as the mere sum of its parts,[77] and to see how these systems effects work in practice, we can take each game in this chapter and see just how robust its Nash Equilibrium is to changing preferences – preferences that, as we noted above, depend on the equilibria of other games. If the outbreak of general war depended on a network of incredible commitments, then it's useful to think counterfactually and make each commitment credible – Serbia's, Russia's, and Austria's – to see what happens to the other player's strategies. In this way, we can enrich our explanation of why war came when it did in 1914 and pin down what it would've taken to avert or delay it.

Let's start with the strategic problem at the root of the July Crisis, the Austro-Serbian game given by Figure 4.2. In the historical record, preventive war breaks out in this game for two reasons: (1) Serbia's inability to commit to honoring Austria's ultimatum and (2) Austria's willingness to use force to solve that commitment problem. Exercises 4.1 and 4.2 force us to think about the role of rising Serbian power and the German blank check, respectively, in shaping outcomes in the July Crisis.

EXERCISE 4.1   *Identify a preference ordering for Austria that supports (pass; refuse) as a Nash Equilibrium, then prove the existence of that equilibrium.*

EXERCISE 4.2   *Identify a preference ordering for Serbia that supports (pass; honor) as a Nash Equilibrium, then prove the existence of that equilibrium.*

What do these exercises tell us about how the outcome of the assassination crisis depended on the anticipated outcomes of other games in the chapter?

Next, let's turn to the Russo-Austrian game depicted in Figure 4.3, where neither side could, in 1914, resist the temptation to support or attack Serbia.

EXERCISE 4.3   *Identify a preference ordering that supports (pass; pass) as a Nash Equilibrium, then prove the existence of that equilibrium.*

---

[77] Braumoeller (2012); Jervis (1997).

EXERCISE 4.4   *Identify a preference ordering that supports (pass; attack S) as a Nash Equilibrium, then prove the existence of that equilibrium.*

With these games specified and solved, we can think about what it would've taken for (1) either Russia or Austria to leash the dogs of war or (2) Russia to stand aside while Austria invaded Serbia. Which of these new equilibria, if any, would alter the equilibrium of the Austro-Serbian game in Figure 4.2?

Finally, consider the Russo-German interaction captured in Figure 4.4, where in the chapter's narrative each side is driven to fight what it believes (rightly) to be a preventive war.

EXERCISE 4.5   *Identify a preference ordering that supports (abandon; abandon) as a Nash Equilibrium, then prove the existence of that equilibrium.*

EXERCISE 4.6   *Identify a preference ordering that supports (support; abandon) as a Nash Equilibrium, then prove the existence of that equilibrium.*

EXERCISE 4.7   *Identify a preference ordering that supports (abandon; support) as a Nash Equilibrium, then prove the existence of that equilibrium.*

Exercises 4.5–4.7 imply different counterfactual stories about how a war between Russia and Germany in 1914 might've been averted. How does each alternative equilibrium relate to changes in the historical record? Specifically, what would need to be different about the Austro-Serbian and Russo-Austrian games to bring about a different Nash Equilibrium in the Russo-German game, the one that would transform the July Crisis from a mere regional incident into the spark that would burn down the international order?

5 The Theory of War II: Information Problems

[I]ndividuals may be faced with uncertainty about the consequences of their choices, so their choices are not implied in any straightforward way by their preferences over outcomes.

R. Harrison Wagner,
"Who's Afraid of Rational Choice Theory?"

In this chapter we expand our analytical toolkit, introducing games in which players are uncertain over each other's preferences. To do this, we'll return to the puzzle we addressed in Chapter 2:

> Conflicts typically end in peace settlements, so why do states sometimes fail to reach those settlements before waging wasteful wars?

Our first solution to this puzzle relied on the legal anarchy of the international system to develop a model of preventive war. In this chapter, we'll develop a second solution around the idea that states' preferences are often hard for others to know, especially when they have incentives to lie about their preferences. We'll show that war can break out when one state can't make an accurate guess about what bargains its opponent will accept in lieu of war, leading it to demand concessions that the other side turns out to be unwilling to grant. If a state truly is willing to fight over some issue, it may be unable to convince its rival of that fact. It would certainly bluff about its willingness to fight if it weren't resolute, provided it would be believed, which ensures that its opponent *won't* believe even honest statements of a willingness to fight. In addition to shifting power and de jure anarchy, uncertainty and obstacles to communication can also explain the outbreak of wasteful, inefficient war.

Developing our second explanation for war requires that we introduce Bayesian games, in which players might be uncertain over each other's pay-offs – and, as a result, the consequences of their own choices. Incorporating uncertainty into strategic-form games requires that we introduce some new conceptual machinery, including private information and basic probability theory, the latter in the form of Bayes' Rule. This will help us develop the concept of *Bayesian Nash Equilibrium*, which tells us how players devise strategies in light of uncertainty about other players' preferences. Our goals in this chapter are to

- demonstrate how to identify a Bayesian Nash Equilibrium;
- use Bayes' Rule to refine beliefs on the basis of new information;
- show how uncertainty over a state's preferences can lead to war;
- introduce the principal-agent problem as a model of domestic politics.

We'll set up some key applications of game theory for use in later chapters, where the characters in our story are often poorly informed about each other's goals and intentions, and where they have incentives to use that ignorance to deceive one another. In addition to explaining the link between uncertainty and war, we'll explore an application of Bayesian games in which we use public uncertainty over government preferences to explain some puzzling bits of waffling in France and Germany when the guns of August should have otherwise been booming. As noted by the august Harrison Wagner in this chapter's epigraph, choices made under uncertainty can often lead players to outcomes, like wasteful wars, they surely would've avoided if they had more information. We'll see early on in our discussion of war as an information problem that it poses serious difficulties for making inferences ex post about people's goals and the effectiveness of their strategies – that is, with the notorious, distorting "benefit" of hindsight.

Key Terms for Chapter 5

- Belief
- Private Information
- Expected Utility
- Bayesian Nash Equilibrium
- Information Problem
- Cheap Talk
- Separating Equilibrium
- Principal-Agent Problem
- Pooling Equilibrium

5.1 UNCERTAINTY AND BAYESIAN GAMES

For each strategic problem we've encountered thus far, from the arms races of Chapter 3 to the preventive wars of Chapter 4, uncertainty hasn't been important. We've studied games of complete information (Definition 2.4) in which players know enough about each other's preferences to gauge their likely strategies, and while uncertainty may be *present* in these interactions, it's not been *necessary* to explain them. As such, we've not yet modeled uncertainty.[1] Nonetheless, politics is often an information-poor environment, and sometimes uncertainty *is* relevant for explaining the outcomes of strategic interactions. Candidates for elective office may have only a vague sense of their opponents' fund-raising capacity or get-out-the-vote operations; coup plotters may be in the dark about whether other officers, as well as key parts of the army, security services, or population will support them at the appointed hour; governments may be uncertain over whether tariffs on a particular product will be enough to spark a trade war with countries making that product; legislators may agonize over whether they will, when the tallies finally pop up on C-SPAN, have enough votes to win passage of key legislation; and states and their leaders can be uncertain over how much their rivals value disputed territory or how long they can sustain public support for a concerted war effort. If a Nash Equilibrium depends on players having some basic knowledge of each other's strategies, how can we say anything about equilibrium when players don't know each other's preferences?

In Chapter 2, we defined games in terms of players, actions, outcomes, and preferences. When players choose strategies that allow them to do as well as possible in light of all other players' strategies, then that strategy profile constitutes a Nash Equilibrium (Definition 2.7). But Nash Equilibrium takes as given that the players know each element of the game, including other players' strategies. This knowledge forms part of the common conjecture (Definition 2.8) over how actors will play the game, a necessary part of Nash Equilibrium and the very stuff of the social world – ideas, identities, roles, norms, and cultural practices.[2] Players can't devise best responses to each other's strategies if they don't know what those other strategies are. One potential source of uncertainty over strategies may be another player's preferences (Definition 2.3). Figure 5.1 presents a variation of our now-familiar crisis bargaining game (Definition 2.2) in which A chooses how much territory to demand (half or all) and B chooses how much it is willing to concede (half or all). If A demands more than B is willing to concede, i.e. (half; all), then there's a war for the territory, but if A demands *no more* than B is willing to concede, then A gets the amount of its demand (but no more) in a settlement. If A demands half and B is willing to concede half, the land is split in half; but if A demands half and B is willing to concede all, A still only gets half (and clearly may regret not having demanded all). We found a Nash Equilibrium of a similar game in Figure 2.3, where A knew how B would respond to a demand for all the

---

[1] Recall that a model should include only as many moving parts, as many details, as necessary to serve its goals.

[2] Again, Watson (2013) and Morrow (2014) provide excellent treatments of the content and importance of the common conjecture.

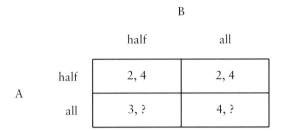

Figure 5.1 A game with unknown preferences.

territory. In Figure 5.1, though, A *doesn't* know how B ranks conceding half (which provokes a war) versus conceding all if A demands the whole pie. A, it seems, can't devise a strategy, because it knows neither B's likely response to nor its own payoff for demanding the whole pie.

How can we find a Nash Equilibrium under these circumstances? The short answer is that we can't. Without a minimum level of shared knowledge, Nash Equilibrium breaks down. We need a way to integrate country A's uncertainty over B's preferences into our model. To do this, we introduce the concept of *beliefs*, which represent a player's uncertainty about the true state of the world as a set of probabilities.

DEFINITION 5.1   *A **belief** is a player's subjective estimate of the probability that a certain state of the world is the true state of the world.*

Suppose that there are two possible states of the world. Either it'll rain in Austin this afternoon, or it won't rain in Austin this afternoon. I don't know which of these states of the world is the real one, though I'd like to know, and I can make a guess (helped along by a decades-long drought, to be sure). The subjective probability that I assign to either state, rain or no rain, will determine whether or not I grab my umbrella on the way out the door.[3] Turning back to the puzzle of war we posed in Chapter 2, suppose that country A believes that country B has one of two possible sets of preferences. Either the state of the world is such that B is resolute, in which case it prefers war to conceding the whole prize (3 > 1), or the state of the world is such that B is irresolute, in which case it prefers conceding the whole prize in lieu of war if A demands all (1 < 3). Then, suppose that country B knows its preferences, but country A doesn't know B's preferences. When one player knows its preferences yet others don't, we say that the the player in question has *private information*.

DEFINITION 5.2   *A player has **private information** over its preferences when it knows its own payoffs but other players do not.*

---

[3] If I'm honest, *determine* is a strong word here. I almost *never* remember my umbrella even when I think it's very, very likely to rain later in the day.

When B possesses private information, as it does in this example, we say that B is the "informed" player and A is the "uninformed" player.[4] As far as A is concerned, country B is one of two different players, or two player-*types*: resolute or irresolute. A may not know which type of country B it's facing, but it knows each type's preferences, so it *can* make an accurate judgment about the likely strategy of each possible type of state B. Think back to the rain example: I know the consequences of getting rained on and staying dry on the way to my office, so I know what each possible state of the world will be like – I just don't know, when I beat a path from the bus stop to the office, which state of the world I'll be in. Just like me and the weather, A knows that B will be either resolute or irresolute, just not which of those two ahead of time. This allows players to know each other's strategies despite their uncertainty over the true state of the world. They just need a guess over which player-type they're facing, and we can use the rules of probability to think about how A makes such a guess.

We model A's uncertainty about B's preferences as a subjective probability estimate, or A's best guess when it begins the game, over the chances that B is resolute or irresolute. Thinking about probabilities lets us retain the logical precision and the mathematical substance of game theory. It demands a little more of us mathematically, but only a little: a single variable representing the extent of A's uncertainty, as opposed to the fixed numbers (3, 4, whatever) we've seen to this point. Let's say that A's initial, or *prior*, belief that B is resolute is simply r, which ranges between 0 and 1 since it's a probability. We can also write $Pr(\text{resolute}) = r$, where $0 \leq r \leq 1$. Since there are only two possible types of B in the radically simplified world of our model, A's prior belief that B is irresolute is the complementary probability, $Pr(\text{irresolute}) = 1 - r$. Using probabilities as a metaphor for uncertainty is remarkably flexible. Figure 5.2 shows that, when $r = 1$, A is certain that B is resolute, and when $r = 0$, A is certain that B is irresolute. If either $r = 1$ or $r = 0$, Figure 5.1 reduces to a game of complete information like those we've seen in previous chapters, because A knows B's type, which helps it fill in the missing payoffs. But when r falls in between zero and one, A weighs the chances that B is resolute or irresolute when guessing B's strategy and devising a best response. When $r = 3/4$, A believes there's a 75 percent chance that B is resolute and only a 25 percent chance that B is irresolute. Finally, when $r = 1/2$, A is maximally uncertain over B's type, believing it equally likely that B is resolute or irresolute.

---

[4] In a technical sense, we assume that a nonstrategic player, Nature, has chosen B's preferences and informed B of that information, but it has opted not to give the same information to A.

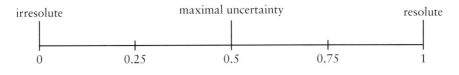

Figure 5.2 Uncertainty and subjective probabilities.

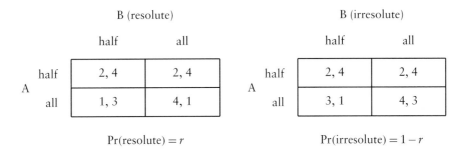

Figure 5.3 An example of a Bayesian game.

By thinking in terms of different player-*types*, or individual players with identifiable payoffs and strategies, and A's subjective *beliefs* about which player-type of B it's facing (resolute or irresolute), we can write down a much more useful version of the game in Figure 5.1. In our new formulation (shown in Figure 5.3), A is uncertain over whether it's playing the game at left, where B is resolute, or at right, where B is irresolute. For A, the question is simple: is its opponent willing to go to war rather than make big concessions? A's beliefs let it calculate the risk of behaving as if B is one type and not the other, and this – combined with A's ability to identify each type of B's strategy – allows it to formulate a best response consistent with our notion of Nash Equilibrium, despite A's uncertainty over B's specific type. A little learning-by-doing will help this make more sense.

Figure 5.3 is an example of a *Bayesian game*, in which one player is uninformed, entering the game with some subjective beliefs about the informed player's type.[5] This game has three players, even as it represents a world with only two, because it allows us to represent A's uncertainty as a guess over which of two possible types of B it faces. In contrast to the games of complete information in Chapter 2, Bayesian games entail *five* elements:

1 **player-types** who make choices in pursuit of some goals
2 **actions**, or courses of action, available to each player

---

[5] For some of the original work on Bayesian games, see Harsanyi (1967).

3 **outcomes** produced by the combination of each player's chosen action
4 **preferences** by which each player ranks possible outcomes of the game
5 **beliefs** that assign probabilities to each of a player's possible types

A Bayesian game defines who's involved in a strategic interaction (player-types), what options they have (actions), the consequences of their choices (outcomes), how they rank outcomes against the achievement of their goals (preferences), *and* what each player knows about the other's preferences (beliefs). It's a small generalization of the games we've used previously, but it opens up several more paths of analysis to us as the characters in our story confront the confusing, chaotic, low-information environment of the first major war of the twentieth century. Bayesian games are named for Thomas Bayes, an eighteenth-century English minister who published a single mathematical work (and posthumously at that) that proved one of the fundamental theorems of probability theory. But more on that later.

Uncertainty over player preferences introduces one more wrinkle, because it requires some adjustments in the way that we write down payoffs. In previous chapters, we've assumed that players know exactly how choices translate into outcomes. When they know other players' preferences, they can infer how their opponents will respond to a given strategy. Think back to the game in Chapter 3. If both sides choose to build in the Anglo-German naval race game, both sides expect a payoff of 2. The game in Figure 5.3 isn't so simple. What if A demands all of the territory? A doesn't know B's type, but it can immediately work out how each type of B will respond, conceding only half if resolute and conceding all if irresolute. But how does A calculate its own payoffs, which depend on B's type?

To answer this question, we need to reference mathematicians of more recent vintage than Reverend Bayes. In their pioneering early work on game theory (which really did begin with an analysis of the best ways to play parlor games), John von Neumann and Oscar Morgenstern developed a simple method for thinking about choice under uncertainty called **expected utility** (denoted EU as opposed to *u*), or what we'll also call "expected payoff."[6] Von Neumann and Morgenstern showed that, if we know A's beliefs and how it ranks possible outcomes, we can represent the *expected* value of any given choice with a simple weighted average, or what you might remember from a mathematics class as an expected value.

---

[6] "Utility," as we noted in Chapter 2, is a bit misleading as a way to characterize preferences, because it implies that there's something out there called "utility" that players seek to gain or make more of. But that's not right. Payoffs, which can be thought of as "amounts" of utility, if we wish, are metaphors for whatever it is that players actually value, and we don't need to take a position on that.

DEFINITION 5.3   *The **expected utility** of an action is the sum of the payoffs for each possible outcome multiplied by the probability of each outcome occurring.*

Let's see how this works in practice. If A knows that a resolute B will concede only half in response to a demand for all the land but that a resolute B will concede all, A's expected payoff for demanding all the land is

$$EU_A(\text{all}) = \text{Pr(resolute)} \times 1 + \text{Pr(irresolute)} \times 4.$$

Given what we know about 1's prior beliefs, we can also write it as

$$EU_A(\text{all}) = r \times 1 + (1 - r) \times 4.$$

Thus, a player's expected payoff for a given choice can be written as the sum of the payoff for every possible outcome weighted by the probability with which that outcome comes to pass: a simple weighted average, not unlike the one you'd use to calculate a grade. Thanks to its knowledge of each possible type of B and its beliefs over those types, A knows that demanding all the disputed territory will lead to a war (and a payoff of 1) with probability r, but it will lead to peace in which B yields the whole pie with probability $1 - r$. When r is high, A is relatively confident that B is resolute (and thus willing to go to war), which decreases the expected value of this bold bargaining position. On the other hand, when r is low, A is relatively more optimistic that B is irresolute (and thus willing to yield the territory), which increases the expected value of demanding all the disputed land. It's worth noting now that, in contrast to payoffs under complete information, expected utility implies cardinality; that is, an expected utility of 0.5 really does represent something twice as attractive as an expected utility of 0.25. To see why, suppose that A gets 5, rather than 4, from controlling all the land; its rank-ordering over outcomes is the same, but its expected utility increases to $r \times 1 + (1 - r) \times 5$ – which can alter the relative attractiveness of other actions. Therefore, when we're dealing with payoffs for uncertain outcomes, even when we compare them to payoffs for certain outcomes, the magnitudes of the payoffs we assign to our players matter, not just the ordering. Armed (no pun intended, I swear) with knowledge about A's beliefs and her expected payoffs for choices with uncertain outcomes, we can now develop a way of solving games with private information, called Bayesian Nash Equilibrium, that will lead us to our second solution to the puzzle of war.

5.1.1   Bayesian Nash Equilibrium

Before we solve the Bayesian game in Figure 5.3, it's worth adding some substantive heft to our discussion by returning to the puzzle that motivated both this chapter and Chapter 2, which will help us see how Bayesian Nash Equilibrium works as both a solution concept and a way to resolve puzzles about strategic interactions under uncertainty. To wit: why do countries go to war, expending sometimes catastrophic but always wasteful levels of blood and treasure, in the service of writing down new peace settlements that they could in principle have written down beforehand? Why do countries fail to reach mutually agreeable bargains that avert war, only to fight, reach mutually agreeable bargains, then look back with predictable regret on all the waste that led to the new settlement?

PUZZLE 5.1   *Why do states sometimes fail to reach peaceful settlements before fighting wars they know to be costly and wasteful?*

The commitment problem helped us understand the escalation of the July Crisis as a special, albeit unusually complex, case of interlocking preventive wars (Chapter 4). But promises rendered incredible by shifting power aren't the only paths by which calculating, frugal leaders can find themselves waging wars whose costs they'll surely come to regret ex post. That means we need to write down a model where commitments are credible – that is, where power isn't shifting such that an agreement today will only erode tomorrow in the face of another side's rising power. If we can produce war in a model with credible commitments, then we'll know that we have a different mechanism, a different explanation, a different path to war than the one we explored in Chapter 2. We'll start by exploring a possibility uniquely suited to Bayesian games: what if countries simply don't know, and can't communicate, what concessions they're willing to make to avoid war?

Preferences are unobservable. They're *subjective* rankings over potential outcomes, existing only in the minds of the actors in our story and in many cases knowable to others only if our actors choose to be honest about them (a dubious proposition, to be sure). What does this mean for the outbreak of war? Let's return to our Bayesian game of crisis bargaining, reproduced in Figure 5.4, where A is uncertain over which game it's playing: on the left, where B is resolute, or on the right, where B is irresolute. When B is resolute, the game looks just as it does in Figure 2.2. Peace obtains only if A doesn't demand more than B is willing to concede, but can win no more than it demands, even if B is willing in principle to concede more. As such, A's best outcome is to win the whole prize (4), and second-best is to win only half (2), while war against a resolute B willing to mount a defense of the disputed land is the least attractive outcome (1); likewise, a resolute B's best outcome is to yield only half (4), but he prefers a fight (3) to seeing A win the whole pie. If B is resolute, fighting is more attractive than yielding all the land, but if B is irresolute,

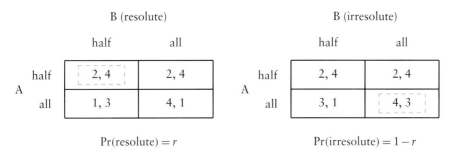

Figure 5.4 Information problems and war.

war is less attractive for itself but more attractive for A. Military power is relative: the less attractive fighting is for B, the more attractive it will be for A. This is the key difference between the resolute and irresolute types of B, because the latter would rather yield all the land (3) than fight in an attempt to retain it (1). And to make matters worse, war against an irresolute type of B is more attractive for A, who ranks war against an irresolute B as its second-best outcome (3). Thus, A wants to grab as much territory as possible without provoking a war, while B wants to keep as much land as possible. However, A doesn't know whether demanding all the land will result in its first-best outcome of full concessions (4) or its worst outcome of war against a resolute type of B (1).

How should we solve this game, and what does it teach us about war? Let's begin by looking at how the game *would* play out under complete information. If A knows it's playing the game on the left, then we would find a unique Nash Equilibrium (Definition 2.11) at (half; half). Knowing that demanding all will lead to a war against a resolute B unwilling to concede the whole pie, A demands only half. B, meanwhile, has no reason to deviate from a strategy in which it concedes as little as possible. If, on the other hand, A knows that it's playing the game on the right against an irresolute B, the unique Nash Equilibrium is (all; all). Aware that B can't credibly threaten a war that yields its own worst possible payoff, A demands all rather than half, which would avert war but leave A with less territory than it wants; B, for its part, prefers to yield rather than concede only half and end up fighting a war. In each case, A knows precisely how much it can demand of B without provoking a war, and it does just that, gaining only so much territory as it can while avoiding the waste and risk of armed conflict. Like the example Nash Equilibrium in Figure 2.3, war doesn't occur when countries know each other's preferences and when the distribution of power isn't shifting. Our problem in this Bayesian game is that A *doesn't* know whether it can demand the whole pie without provoking a war; if it demands all and B turns out to be resolute, then

A may get a painful war it could've avoided if only it had demanded a smaller share of the pie.

To solve this game in light of B's private information, we need a solution concept that integrates the uncertain player's beliefs about player-types. In a **Bayesian Nash Equilibrium** (or BNE), players choose strategies that ensure they're doing the best they can in light of what they *believe* other players are doing – given that they can only make a more or less informed guess about other players' strategies. Equilibrium reasoning is similar to that in Nash Equilibrium. An *informed* player reasons, "The other player is choosing action Z, so it's best that I choose action X, because option Y wouldn't be a better response to Z." An *uninformed* player, however, reasons slightly differently: "I'll choose action Z, because the average response of the other player's types is better for me than the average response of the other player's types if I choose action W." Just as they are in a Nash Equilibrium, strategies in a Bayesian Nash Equilibrium are *mutual best responses*. Strategies (outcomes aside) are in a kind of mutual balance, and the equilibrium is self-enforcing (Definition 1.6) because neither player can gain or profit from changing its strategy. The only difference is that one player chooses while uncertain over the other's strategy.

DEFINITION 5.4   *At a **Bayesian Nash Equilibrium** each player-type does as well as she can, given what she believes about what all other player-types are doing.*

Calculating a Bayesian Nash Equilibrium isn't much different in principle than calculating a Nash Equilibrium. We still identify candidate strategy profiles and check to see whether players have *profitable deviations* from them, though one player chooses its strategies in light of expected, not certain, payoffs. If no player-type has a profitable deviation, then the set of strategies in question exists in equilibrium. Our way in to finding a Bayesian Nash Equilibrium of the game in Figure 5.4 is the informed player, country B, whose best responses to A's demands are easy to identify. If A demands half, then B receives its best outcome of 4, however much it is willing to concede; it's indifferent over its choices if country 1 demands half. If A demands all the territory, however, B's best response depends on its type: the resolute type concedes only half, touching off a war that's more attractive than full concessions (3 > 1), but the irresolute type concedes all rather than half, which would touch off a war it must, under any circumstances, avoid (3 > 1). Knowing that A would demand only half if it believed B to be resolute, the resolute type would like to convey the truth about its willingness to wage that war. But the fact that B could just as easily proclaim its willingness to refuse extensive concessions if it *weren't* the resolute type means that A's uncertainty remains unresolved. We'll talk more later about this incentive to bluff about private information and how it creates a corresponding incentive for others to disbelieve.

What does this mean for A's strategy, which depends on its calculations of a best response? Uncertain over B's type, it can nonetheless guess each type's best response should B turn out to be that type. A faces what we call a risk-return trade-off: the more A demands, the better the deal it gets if country B meets those demands, but larger demands also mean that B is less likely to accede to them.[7] A demand of all can only be conceded by the irresolute type, but a demand of half will be conceded regardless of B's type. Demanding half is a risk-free way to ensure that A avoids the worst outcome of war against a resolute B, because this smaller demand, this less aggressive bargaining posture, is sufficient to ensure acceptance whether B is resolute or irresolute. Country A thus has to choose between demanding half, which avoids war but wins only small concessions, and demanding the whole pie, which entails some risk that B will turn out to be the resolute type that refuses to concede – thereby touching off a war whose costs both are sure to regret.

To see when A will make that risky proposal, we can make a simple expected payoff comparison. If it demands half, A receives 2, because B will concede exactly that much regardless of type, but if A demands all, it has to weigh the war that follows the resolute type's rejection against the irresolute type's acceptance. Therefore, A will demand all, running a risk of war, when the following inequality is satisfied:

$$\text{EU}_A(\text{all}) \geq u_A(\text{half}) \Leftrightarrow r \times 1 + (1 - r) \times 4 \geq 2.$$

The left side of the inequality is A's expected payoff for demanding all: if B turns out to be resolute (which happens with probability r), it concedes only half such that war breaks out, but if B turns out to be irresolute, it concedes all, preserving peace and yielding A's best outcome. The right hand side, of course, is A's payoff from demanding only half, which is sure to win a concession, albeit a small one, regardless of B's preferences. Doing the math, we can solve for r, which will tell us what A must believe about B's preferences in order to make running a risk of war attractive. Solving this inequality for r shows that A will risk war when

$$r \leq \frac{2}{3},$$

or when it is confident enough that B is irresolute (i.e., willing to concede the whole of the disputed territory). If A is sufficiently doubtful over B's

---

[7] On the risk-return trade-off, see Powell (1999, chapter 3).

willingness to fight, then A will choose to risk war, demanding all the territory in a calculated gamble that goes awry if B really does turn out to be resolute.

Proposition 5.2 characterizes this Bayesian Nash Equilibrium, which entails A's strategy, its beliefs r, and a strategy for each player-type of B. Note that row and column player strategies are still separated by a semicolon, while different *types* of the column player are separated by commas.

PROPOSITION 5.1   *The strategy profile (all; half, all), with beliefs $r \leq 2/3$, is a Bayesian Nash Equilibrium.*

Proof   For (all; half, all) to be a Bayesian Nash Equilibrium, it must be the case that

$$u_B(\text{all}; \textit{half}, \text{all}) \geq u_B(\text{all}; \textit{all}, \text{all}) \quad \text{and} \quad u_B(\text{all}; \text{half}, \textit{all}) \geq u_B(\text{all}; \text{half}, \textit{half})$$

for the resolute and irresolute B, respectively, and that

$$\text{EU}_A(\textit{all}; \text{half}, \text{all}) \geq u_A(\textit{half}; \text{half}, \text{all})$$

for A. The first inequality is satisfied because $3 \geq 1$, and the second is satisfied because $3 \geq 1$. The final inequality is satisfied only when $r \leq 2/3$. When $r \leq 2/3$, no player has a profitable deviation, so (all; half, all) is a Bayesian Nash Equilibrium.   □

When $r \leq 2/3$, we have a BNE with strategies (all; half, all), where A demands all, the resolute type of B concedes only half (leading to war) and the irresolute type concedes all. On the other hand, when $r > 1/2$, or when A isn't so optimistic that B is willing to concede the whole pie, we have a peaceful equilibrium – that is, one with no risk of war – of (half; half, half) with beliefs $r > 1/2$, because A is unwilling to risk touching off a war. Settling for its third-best outcome of 2 is more attractive than running too large of a risk that it ends up in a war against the resolute type of B, which is A's worst possible outcome.

PROPOSITION 5.2   *The strategy profile (half; half, half), with beliefs $r > 1/2$, is a Bayesian Nash Equilibrium.*

Proof   For (half; half, half) to be a Bayesian Nash Equilibrium, it must be the case that

$$u_B(\text{half}; \textit{half}, \text{half}) \geq u_B(\text{half}; \textit{all}, \text{half}) \quad \text{and}$$
$$u_B(\text{half}; \text{half}, \textit{half}) \geq u_B(\text{half}; \text{half}, \textit{all})$$

for the resolute and irresolute B, respectively, and that

$$\text{EU}_A(half; \text{half}, \text{half}) \geq u_A(all; \text{half}, \text{half})$$

for A. The first inequality is satisfied because $4 \geq 4$, and the second is satisfied because $4 \geq 4$. The final inequality is satisfied only when $r > 1/2$. When $r > 1/2$, no player has a profitable deviation, so (half; half, half) is a Bayesian Nash Equilibrium.   □

The procedure established in Chapter 2 of proposing candidate equilibria and checking for profitable deviations will show that these are the game's only BNE. (Doing that explicitly as a set of exercises would be useful at this point.) When A is optimistic about B's unwillingness to fight, we have a potentially violent equilibrium in which A risks war with its bargaining posture, and when A is more pessimistic, we have a peaceful equilibrium in which she demands (and receives) only so much as a truly resolute type of B would yield. By introducing a variable into the equation – in this case, A's beliefs abut B's type – we can refine our understanding of uniqueness (recall Definition 2.11). As you can see in Figure 5.5, there are some values of r for which each equilibrium is unique, where the BNE in question is the only plausible way to play the game. However, when A is neither too optimistic nor too pessimistic, or when $1/2 \leq r \leq 2/3$, both equilibria exist; therefore, they are not unique for this range of possible beliefs that A might hold. Bayesian Nash Equilibrium can tell us that both equilibria exist, and our proofs can tell us *why* they exist, but neither can tell us which of the two is more likely to be played. For insights into the problem of overlapping (or multiple) equilibria, we'll drop some hints in Chapter 6 and then deal with the problem more thoroughly in Chapter 10. For now, what's important is that A responds to the risk-return trade-off by staking out an aggressive bargaining posture only when it has reason to doubt B's resolve. And when A's calculated gamble doesn't pay off – that is, when B does happen to be resolute – the two sides end up in a war.

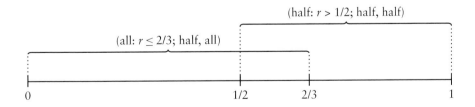

A's belief that B is resolute (r)

Figure 5.5 Unique and overlapping equilibria.

When war occurs in our Bayesian Nash Equilibrium, it's manifestly tragic, wasteful of blood and treasure in the way that preventive wars are in the games of Chapter 2. Both sides can look back with regret on a peaceful settlement not reached; A and a resolute B (the type that it ends up in a war with) would both have been better off striking a deal in which half was demanded and half was yielded. Yet as noted in this chapter's epigraph, a player's preference ordering (like A's preference to seize all the land it can while avoiding war) doesn't tell us much on its own about how A ends up waging a war. A, the uninformed player, receives its worst outcome of 1. And while the informed, resolute country B is better off in war than it would be acceding to A's aggressive demands, it can still look back at the game after the war and wish that it hadn't had to fight in order to prove that it deserves better terms than A had on offer. Had A demanded half and the resolute B conceded it, payoffs would've been (2,4); to verify, check the payoffs in Figure 5.4. In that event, both would have been better off than they are after the war that breaks out in equilibrium and leaves them with payoffs of (1,3). War destroys the very things that states value when they wage it. It shrinks the total pie to be divided as it does in Figure 2.4, and yet states can fail to reach peaceful bargains when they're unsure what terms their opponents will accept in lieu of war.[8]

5.1.2 Information Problems and War

We now have a second solution to the inefficiency puzzle of war: information problems. When one state is unsure of what bargains its opponent accepts in lieu of war, it faces a risk-return trade-off. Modest demands ensure a peaceful settlement, but the returns are, of course, modest. Aggressive demands pay off big when they're met, but they're more likely to result in war than modest demands. War occurs when one state demands more than the other is willing to concede, a war that could have been averted if only the informed side had been able to credibly communicate its resolve – i.e., its willingness to fight rather than make painful concessions. Only after fighting can A be properly subject to B's taunt of "I told you so," but the fact that it took a war to figure this out is tragic. But if it's a lack of information (information that the other side has, by the way) that prevents states from reaching deals that both would prefer to war, why not just share the relevant information?[9] In this chapter's game, peace is possible as long as states can reveal their preferences, yet they sometimes don't. Why can't a state willing to fight rather than make big concessions simply tell the

---

[8] For good measure, see Fearon (1995).
[9] If that occurred to you while reading the previous section, then good job. The problem of credible communication is a major research agenda in political science.

other side that fact, cut an efficient deal, and move on? We'll address that puzzle in this section, completing our discussion of information problems by showing that "[t]he cause of war cannot simply be lack of information, but *whatever it is that prevents its disclosure*."[10]

PUZZLE 5.2   *If states can avert war by communicating their true preferences over war and peace, why don't they communicate them?*

To make this puzzle a bit clearer, let's return to the Bayesian Nash Equilibrium of the game in Figure 5.4, where war breaks out when A's optimism leads it to demand the whole pie of B, before that optimism is shattered by the realization that B is in fact unwilling to part with the disputed land without a fight. Let's suppose that the players have a chance to communicate before the game by simply (and at no cost) stating their preferences up front. A's preferences are known, but B's aren't, which makes this opportunity to communicate potentially valuable. When B is resolute, it has every incentive to reveal its true, privately known preferences. If A knows that B is willing to fight and that it'll be much the worse for wear if the two come to blows, A will demand only half of the disputed land. Thus, if we give B a chance to say "I'd rather fight than yield the whole pie" when it's resolute, it would surely say that very thing. So far, so good. It's information that A would like to have and that a truly resolute B would love to reveal. Surely that would be enough to convince A that it needs to limit its demands. Sadly, it isn't. If simply claiming to be resolute is enough to convince A to moderate its demands, then B will say that even if it *isn't* truly willing to fight, even if it's the irresolute type. Why reveal a lack of resolve, a truth that would force B to yield the whole of the disputed territory, if it can simply and easily lie about its preferences, if it can bluff, holding on to more of the territory that it values without having to fire a shot in its defense?

This incentive to dissemble, to misrepresent or lie about one's private information, creates a corresponding incentive for the other side to disbelieve. If an informed leader would *claim* a willingness to fight even if she weren't willing to fight, why should her opponent believe her when she draws a line in the sand? When one side has an incentive to lie about its preferences (and therefore its likely strategy) in the service of trying to influence the other player's strategy, the players face an **information problem**.

DEFINITION 5.5   *An **information problem** exists when one player's incentives to lie about privately known preferences encourage others to disbelieve it.*

[10] Fearon (1995, pp. 390–391, emphasis added).

The information problem in this chapter emerges from incentives to claim a willingness to fight whether or not states actually *are* willing to fight. Irresolute states would bluff about their willingness to fight if it would work, and this encourages their opponents to discount their statements. An incentive to lie creates a corresponding incentive to disbelieve. A could receive a pregame message from B stating, "I'd rather fight than yield the whole pie," yet A would have every reason to discount it by reasoning to itself, "That's exactly what B would say if it were bluffing. I've got no reason to believe this." An irresolute B simply has too much at stake – the difference between keeping the whole of the disputed territory and holding on to only half – to be honest about its preferences. Yet if A knows that B will bluff about its willingness to fight, then it discounts B's statements to the point of ignoring them, relying only on its prior beliefs as it faces a risk-return trade-off in setting its demands.

To see how this works in practice, we can draw on Bayes' Rule, the equation that made the good reverend justifiably famous (albeit after his death and some heavy editing of his work by a fellow scholar). Bayes' Rule uses the laws of probability to show how beliefs – say, A's estimate of the chances that B is resolute – change as a result of new information.[11] Beginning with *prior* beliefs, we can introduce some new information, then use the laws of conditional probability to see whether and how that leads to different *posterior* beliefs. Bayes' Rule lets us calculate the probability that event R is true, given event S and knowledge of how likely it would be to observe S if R were (and weren't) true. If we want to know $\Pr(R|S)$, or the probability of R given that S occurred, Bayes' Rule gives us

$$\Pr(R|S) = \frac{\Pr(R) \times \Pr(S|R)}{\Pr(R) \times \Pr(S|R) + \Pr(\neg R) \times \Pr(S|\neg R)},$$

where $\neg R$ represents the probability that R isn't true. The probability that R is true given that S has occurred is simply the ratio of the probability that we'd see R and S together (the numerator) to the probability that we'd see S in any case – that is, whether or not R is true (the denominator). Bayes' Rule tells us that if S is likely to occur only if R is true, then seeing S should *increase* our confidence that R is true; if S is likely to occur only if R is untrue, then seeing S should *decrease* our confidence in the truth of R; and if S is equally likely to occur whether or not R is true, then it shouldn't

---

[11] Using the same mode of learning across multiple models ensures that, when we study Bayesian games, the equilibria we find aren't an artifact of any quirks in our model of beliefs but the result of the important features of the strategic settings that we define with our models.

change our beliefs at all. The key factor in this process of *belief updating* is whether S occurs at different rates when R is true and untrue.[12]

Now let's return to the problem of pregame communication in our model of crisis bargaining. If A knows that B would claim to be resolute even when it isn't, then we can apply Bayes' Rule to A's prior belief about B's resolve – and show that A won't alter its beliefs in response to B's statements. Let's call R the event that B is resolute, $\neg R$ the event that B is irresolute, and S a diplomatic message stating "I'd rather fight than yield the whole pie." What we want to know is $\Pr(R|S)$ – looks familiar, right? – the probability that B is resolute given that it has issued a diplomatic statement of resolve. With Bayes' Rule and some knowledge of B's incentives to lie, that's easy. A's prior belief that B is resolute is r, such that $\Pr(R) = r$ and $\Pr(\neg R) = 1 - r$, respectively. We also know that B will claim to be resolute whether or not it truly is, so $\Pr(S|R) = 1$ and $\Pr(S|\neg R) = 1$. If we substitute this information about A's beliefs and B's incentives to lie into Bayes' Rule, we get

$$\Pr(R|S) = \frac{r \times 1}{r \times 1 + (1 - r) \times 1} = r,$$

which shows that, after hearing B claim to be resolute, A's posterior belief in B's resolve is r. Its prior belief remains unchanged as it becomes A's posterior belief. A goes into potential pregame communication believing that B is resolute with probability r, but B's incentive to lie ensures that A leaves pregame communication with the same belief. And when A's belief is optimistic enough that B is irresolute ($r \geq 2/3$), it stakes out a bargaining position that entails a risk of war.

Why can't B communicate its resolve when it's truly willing to fight? B's pregame statement of resolve is uninformative, because it's **cheap talk**. Simple diplomatic communication, which ranges from speeches to diplomatic telegrams to ambassadorial meetings, is essentially costless; whether one utters a truth or a falsehood doesn't alter the ease or expense or difficulty or pain of sending the message.

DEFINITION 5.6   *Cheap talk is communication that is costless regardless of its content (e.g., its truth value).*

---

[12] It's also eerily telling when we think about how authoritarian politics can infect even democracies with a free press. Those who would undermine the opposition on which democracies and republics thrive try not to challenge the facts reported about their corruption, ignorance, or unfitness for office but to delegitimize the source – to make their followers believe that everyone lies, that everyone is biased, and thus to reject even the truth when it stares them in the face. Did Chancellor Palpatine deny that he was seeking ultimate power? No. He just delegitimized the Jedi.

As a result, there are no real disincentives to lying when states bargain in the shadow of possible war. The worst that can happen for B is to have its bluff called when A eventually demands the whole pie, but that's what happens if A knows B's true preferences anyway. Why not lie, then? When diplomatic communication is cheap talk, rival states have little reason to believe one another when they say they're willing to fight – even when they're telling the truth. We'll see this time and again throughout our discussion of the Great War, as states that truly are willing to fight, or to hold out one more month or one more year in a grinding war of attrition, have trouble convincing their opponents of that fact.

The problem, from our perspective of explaining why A can't believe B when it says it's willing to fight, is that a truly resolute B has no way of *separating*, or distinguishing itself, from an irresolute version of itself. A resolute type of B needs some action that it can take that it wouldn't take if it were irresolute, but diplomatic statements of belligerent intent – no matter how overheated – don't do the trick.[13] Our Bayesian Nash Equilibrium described in Proposition 5.1, though, provides a hint as to how players *can* reveal their types when they have incentives to lie. In this **separating equilibrium**, player-types take unique actions that allow uninformed players to distinguish types by their actions – though, sadly for those wanting to avert war in this example, only after those actions have been taken.

DEFINITION 5.7   *At a **separating equilibrium**, player-types take unique actions that distinguish them from other types.*

When A makes the risky proposal that B rejects only when it's resolute, then there's something to be learned. Demanding all means that B yields half and fights a war only when resolute, which forces types to separate. If we label B's choice to play "half" event F, then we have a different application of Bayes' Rule, because $\Pr(F|R) = 1$ and $\Pr(F|\neg R) = 0$. Therefore, A's posterior belief that B is resolute after seeing B fight a war is

$$\Pr(R|F) = \frac{r \times \Pr(F|R)}{r \times \Pr(F|R) + (1-r) \times \Pr(F|\neg R)} = 1.$$

That is, A can infer B's type perfectly from its response to a demand for the whole pie, because B is only willing to fight a war when resolute; A can likewise learn that B is irresolute if it yields the whole prize when A demands the whole prize. But that's true only in the equilibrium in which different types of B take different actions, i.e. (all, $r \leq 2/3$; half, all). In the (half, $r > 1/2$; half, half) equilibrium, B plays half regardless of its type, and A can learn nothing. The consequence of mimicking the

[13] Ever wonder why other countries rarely believe North Korean threats? Here you go.

resolute type is a costly war that an irresolute B would do anything in its power to avoid, so it's got no incentive to bluff – rather, the threat of ending up in a war keeps B honest. When actions aren't costless, they can convey information that states would otherwise have incentives to obfuscate.

In this example, the very tragic outcome that motivated our puzzle – an avoidable war – reveals the information that the states needed to begin with. That'll have a lot to do with how we explain the duration and termination of war in Chapter 12, so keep the informational value of war in mind; this isn't just another in the long litany of tragic outcomes we're learning to explain. In fact, the informational result of the violent equilibrium points to actions short of war that might help resolute states reveal themselves as such. These actions, called *costly signals* in deliberate contrast to cheap talk, can help states reveal a willingness to fight, to separate or distinguish themselves from irresolute types, because they surely wouldn't countenance taking such actions if they weren't truly willing to bear the costs and risks of war.[14] As long as the costs borne can be recouped by war, or as long as they make backing down from threats to fight painful, many actions can serve as costly signals of resolve. Arms buildups,[15] military mobilizations and deployments,[16] "tripwire" forces stationed in far-flung locales,[17] alliance commitments that invoke reputations for reliability,[18] and public threats that put leaders at risk of electoral punishment for failing to follow through[19] can all help distinguish resolute states from those unwilling to fight, all because irresolute states would be unwilling to bear the costs associated with following through on their threats. When, for example, American President Clinton threatened to invade Haiti in 1994 unless the military junta reinstalled elected president Jean-Bertrand Aristide, he did so publicly, staking his political reputation – and thus his electoral prospects – on following through with the threat if necessary. Backing down in the face of the junta's intransigence would've been so politically painful that the junta judged his threat credible, and the United States and Haiti averted war, precisely because a president unwilling to follow through on the invasion threat wouldn't have made it so publicly. When states or their leaders can find ways to convey their resolve in ways that irresolute states wouldn't countenance, they can avert

---

[14] For foundational works on this topic, see Jervis (1970), which is well written but tempered by a frustrating dose of disequilibrium reasoning; Spence (1973); and Fearon (1994, 1997).

[15] Fearon (1997).

[16] Slantchev (2005).

[17] Schelling (1966).

[18] Morrow (2000).

[19] Fearon (1994, 1997).

war by disabusing their opponents of their optimism and the attendant willingness to risk war.

5.2 WHY DID FRANCE AND GERMANY HESITATE?

Bayesian games can also shed some light on a puzzle linked directly to the tightly wound climax of the July Crisis, where two decisions stand out as puzzling in light of the widespread belief that generals and politicians alike were committed to a "cult of the offensive"[20] or "war by timetable."[21] Germany, as it geared up for a two-front war, delayed at Bethmann's insistence its own mobilization until it could confirm that Russia had, in fact, ordered a mobilization of its own. Not until mobilization placards were reported in the western reaches of the Tsarist Empire did Germany put its daring war plan fully, legally, and irreversibly into motion.[22] To the west, France, which expected to be an early German target in that same two-front war, ordered its army to deploy ten kilometers behind the German border – without railways, reservists, forts, or requisitioned horses – as ultimatums, rebuffs, and last-ditch proposals for mediation sizzled through the telegraph cables linking the European capitals.[23] Both countries believed hostilities inevitable, yet rather than let slip the dogs of war, they leashed them. Why delay? Why would forgoing an apparent first-strike advantage in a war deemed inevitable, to say nothing of effectively yielding parts of one's own territory to an imminent enemy advance, be desirable to a public that presumably also wants to avoid national dismemberment or foreign domination?

PUZZLE 5.3   *Why did Germany and France delay the implementation of war plans predicated on attacking as quickly as possible?*

To resolve this puzzle, we need to think about not just military strategy but also the domestic politics of the war effort, because Germany's delayed mobilization and France's withdrawal from the soon-to-be-violated border were both guided by a desire to ensure broad public support. As we saw in Chapter 4 (and will again in Chapter 8), many belligerents, France included, entered the Great War hoping to achieve a quick victory but remained mindful of the risks that it would become a long, bloody war of attrition. Some weren't as hopeful: Germany needed to win quickly in France, because it expected the war against Russia to be murderously

---

[20] Van Evera (1984).
[21] See Taylor (1969).
[22] For this and more on the German decision to activate its war plan, see Herwig (2014, chapter 2).
[23] See Stevenson (1996, pp. 389–392) and Hamilton and Herwig (2004, p. 124).

long and difficult.[24] If the war dragged on, national leaders knew they'd need support from the publics that would provide the soldiers, laborers, bond purchasers, and able bodies that would sustain the war effort. Part of the public would support the war regardless of its aims, but others might not be so quiescent. If conscripts refused to muster or if they deserted, if workers laid down their tools or resorted to sabotage, if socialist and social-democratic parties made trouble in the legislature or called supporters to the barricades, and if domestic peace were poisoned by an unpopular conflict, the war effort might be fatally compromised. Belligerent governments, no matter how autocratic their institutions (and Germany's Prussian institutions were pretty autocratic when it came to the military), knew that they needed the support, or at least the acquiescence, of the working class for a successful war effort. Some belligerent governments managed it better and for longer – if only just enough longer – than others, but to win that support governments had to convince key parts of the public that the war was a defensive one, not an aggressive bid for empire. Only by painting the war as defensive did the French and German leaderships believe that they could bring enough of the public along with them into the maelstrom.

Taking this to a more general model of domestic politics, the problem is that the government knows its true aims in the war, but the public doesn't. And to make matters worse, an information problem (Definition 5.5) stands in the public's way of making the right decision over supporting the war effort: if the government's aims are truly defensive, it would say so, but if its aims are aggressive, it would certainly deny it in hopes of bringing along the wary, typically anti-nationalist and nominally pacifist socialist and workers' parties. This is a special case of what's called the **principal-agent problem**. A principal (the public) would like to delegate a task (national defense) to an agent (the government), but the principal is unsure of just how far the agent's preferences diverge from its own.

DEFINITION 5.8   *A **principal-agent problem** exists when a principal wishes to delegate a task to an agent with private information over its preferences.*

This makes delegation – or, in this case, supporting the war – risky. The public prefers to support a defensive effort and to oppose an aggressive one; if it supports the war only to see the government pursue expansionist or imperial aims, the public regrets its support, but if it fails to support the government in a defensive struggle, it regrets weakening what turns out to have been a war effort worth supporting. The problem for the public is to

---

[24] Napoleonic France provided a century-old precedent for that, as it happened.

choose whether to support a government that may be honest yet has every incentive to lie about its war aims. The government thus has an informational advantage, which creates an information problem (Definition 5.5), putting the public at a corresponding informational *disadvantage*.

A common application of the principal-agent problem is the relationship between employer and employee, where the former has to find a way to incentivize the latter to work hard when the employee might prefer to work much less than the boss would like. If the boss knows her employee has the same preferences over how hard to work (which is probably pretty rare), or if she has time to watch employees around the clock, then there's little to worry about. But the boss can't be sure, so she has to work out some kind of compensation scheme – a contract, which works like a publicized contingency plan, or a strategy (Definition 2.5) – that may be a hassle to put in place but which may, if well designed, discourage the employee from slacking off when the boss isn't looking. She may pay by the hour or by output, and she may threaten to fire her employee if he fails to meet those standards. The hope is that a good contract can either change a slacker's incentives such that he behaves like a good employee or force him to reveal his type and get a well-deserved sacking. And the public's problem in our model isn't too different from the employer's contracting problem. It may not be able to replace the government in the *Kaiserreich* as easily as it can in France, but in both cases the public can threaten to deny the government something it wants, i.e., support for the war, in hopes of disciplining the government's policy choices.

Principal-agent problems entail private information, so we can model them with Bayesian games. Dispensing with proper names for now, Figure 5.6 depicts an uninformed public (P) and an informed government (G), where the government has defensive aims with probability d and expansionist aims with probability $1 - d$. With war inevitable, the government must decide whether to move "now" by trying to mobilize first, or to "wait," allowing the enemy to make the first move. Suppose that the public has two possible strategies: unconditionally supporting "either"

		G (defensive)			G (expansionist)	
		wait	now		wait	now
P	either	4, 3	5, 4	either	3, 3	2, 4
	neither	1, 1	1, 1	neither	3, 1	3, 1

Figure 5.6 The principal-agent problem in military strategy.

or "neither" strategy. This creates eight possible outcomes: waiting with support, moving now with support, and making either choice without support, where the lack of support undermines the distinction between moving now and waiting. For the government, waiting sacrifices the ostensibly vital initiative in a war of conquest, and it can slow both deployments and reaction times in the event that the army plans to go on the defensive. Whatever they wish to pursue – even if it's horrible for their subjects, like throwing up punishing tariffs and provoking a trade war – governments would prefer support or, at a minimum, the absence of public opposition. Thus, regardless of its type, the government most prefers to implement its plan now and with public support (4), followed by waiting and still securing public support (3), and the outcome it most wants to avoid is a fatal loss of public support (1). Finally, the public's preferences depend on the type of government it supports or opposes; the public is happy to constrain an offensive war by refusing support but fears undermining a defensive war. Its best outcome is to support a defensive government that doesn't wait (5), followed by supporting a defensive government that waits (4), then an expansionist government that either waits or must face opposition (3), and then by opposing a government that aims only at a defensive war (1).

Faced with these incentives and available strategies, how will government and public play the game? Proposition 5.3 characterizes two Bayesian Nash Equilibria, one of which exists when the public believes that the government is likely enough to have defensive aims, and another that exists when the public is less confident that it's not dealing with an expansionist government.[25] When $d \geq 1/5$, the public is confident enough that the government has defensive aims, and we see an equilibrium at (either; now, now) in which P offers blanket support; this saves the war effort, but it forces the public to tolerate a risk that, if the government turns out to be expansionist, it's just jumped into a war effort that it'll regret being part of. On the other hand, when $d \leq 1/5$, the public is more suspicious, and it refuses to support the war effort, restraining an expansionist government but tying the hands of a defensive one. As solutions to the principal-agent problem go, neither of these options is great, because both entail some chance of regret, either by allowing an expansionist war to get rolling or by compromising what would've been a genuinely defensive war effort.

---

[25] There's a third BNE as well, at (neither: $d \leq 1/4$; wait, now), but it's similar enough and exists under conditions similar to (neither; now, now) so that we can focus only on the latter without losing any insight. In Chapter 10, we'll see that multiple equilibria can be useful for answering some questions, but not so much in this case. Still, proving its existence is a worthwhile exercise if you want some practice.

PROPOSITION 5.3   *The strategy profile (either; now, now), with beliefs $d \geq 1/5$, is a Bayesian Nash Equilibrium, and (neither; now, now), with beliefs $d \leq 1/5$, is a Bayesian Nash Equilibrium.*

Proof   For (either; now, now) to be a Bayesian Nash Equilibrium, it must be the case that

$$u_G(\text{either}; now, \text{now}) \geq u_G(\text{either}; wait, \text{now})$$

for the defensive G,

$$u_G(\text{either}; \text{now}, now) \geq u_G(\text{either}; \text{now}, wait)$$

for the expansionist G, and

$$u_P(either; \text{now}, \text{now}) \geq u_P(neither; \text{now}, \text{now})$$

for P. The first and second inequalities are satisfied because $4 \geq 3$. The final inequality is satisfied only when $d \geq 1/5$. When $d \geq 1/5$, no player has a profitable deviation, so (either; now, now) is a Bayesian Nash Equilibrium.

For (neither; now, now) to be a Bayesian Nash Equilibrium, it must be the case that

$$u_G(\text{neither}; now, \text{now}) \geq u_G(\text{neither}; wait, \text{now})$$

for the defensive G,

$$u_G(\text{neither}; \text{now}, now) \geq u_G(\text{neither}; \text{now}, wait)$$

for the expansionist G, and

$$u_P(neither; \text{now}, now) \geq u_P(either; \text{now}, \text{now})$$

for P. The first and second inequalities are satisfied because $1 \geq 1$. The final inequality is satisfied only when $d \leq 1/5$. When $d \leq 1/5$, no player has a profitable deviation, so (neither; now, now) is a Bayesian Nash Equilibrium.   □

But this isn't quite right for solving our puzzle, because we need to find a different equilibrium, one at which the government waits, the public supports, and the government believes that it couldn't have secured support without waiting. The game in Figure 5.6 can't produce such an equilibrium, and the last missing piece is the reason why: the public's strategy in both France and Germany seems to be conditional, supporting if the government waits but refusing if the government moves now. In other words, the French and German publics seem to have had a better solution to the principal-agent problem than we gave them in Figure 5.6, and this induced a strategy

		G (defensive)				G (expansionist)	
		wait	now			wait	now
	either	4, 3	5, 4		either	3, 3	2, 4
P	wait	4, 3	1, 1	P	wait	3, 3	3, 1
	neither	1, 1	1, 1		neither	3, 1	3, 1

Figure 5.7 Solving the principal-agent problem in military strategy.

on the part of the agents in our story of waiting in order to secure that support, even if it would compromise offensive war plans. This tells us we should look for a **pooling equilibrium**, where the government takes the same action regardless of its type.

DEFINITION 5.9   *At a **pooling equilibrium**, player-types take the same action, which fails to distinguish them from other types.*

In contrast to the separating equilibrium we found in the previous section, the public won't be able to update its beliefs over the government's type. The analogy with employment contracts may be a bit strained here – who cares if an employee is secretly lazy but still does the work well enough? – but the intended effect of this conditional support strategy is the same as a threat to fire an underperforming employee: in order to win the principal's favor, the agent acts as the principal would like it to and gets the support it wants.[26]

Figure 5.7 fixes this problem by introducing a third strategy for the public, labeled "wait" to indicate that it'll support the war effort only if the government waits, if G forgoes the benefits of an easy first strike and lets the blame (such as it was) fall on the enemy for shooting first.[27] If both public and government play "wait," then the outcome is identical to (either; wait), and if the government moves now while the public plays "wait," we see payoffs identical to (neither; now). This is a departure from our previous games, where we give players only two options, but the rules of mutual best responses – the underlying logic of equilibrium – still apply. It's a simple substantive change, representing a more sophisticated strategy, and it captures precisely the rule of thumb that the French and German publics seem to be using (or, at a minimum, that their governments believe them to be using) in 1914. And as we can see in Proposition 5.4, this option changes the outcome pretty substantially.

---

[26] The game, and thus the story, ends there for now, but we'll see in Chapter 14 that some aggressive governments can't fool their publics forever.

[27] Speaking of which, Han shot first.

> PROPOSITION 5.4   *The strategy profile (wait; wait, wait) is a Bayesian Nash Equilibrium for any prior beliefs d.*

Proof For (wait; wait, wait) to be a Bayesian Nash Equilibrium, it must be the case that

$$u_G(\text{wait}; \textit{wait}, \text{wait}) \geq u_G(\text{wait}; \textit{now}, \text{wait})$$

for the defensive G,

$$u_G(\text{wait}; \text{wait}, \textit{wait}) \geq u_G(\text{wait}; \text{wait}, \textit{now})$$

for the expansionist G, and both

$$u_P(\textit{wait}; \text{wait}, \text{wait}) \geq u_P(\textit{either}; \text{wait}, \text{wait})$$

and

$$u_P(\textit{wait}; \text{wait}, \text{wait}) \geq u_P(\textit{neither}; \text{wait}, \text{wait})$$

for P. The first and second inequalities are satisfied because $3 \geq 1$. The penultimate inequality is satisfied because $d(4) + (1-d)(3) \geq d(4) + (1-d)(3)$, and the final inequality is satisfied because $0 < d < 1$. For all values of d, no player has a profitable deviation, so (wait; wait, wait) is a Bayesian Nash Equilibrium. □

In this BNE, the public manages to solve the principal-agent problem more effectively than it can in Figure 5.6, because it's tailored a conditional strategy that forces the government to wait, either delaying mobilization or standing back to let the other side cross the Rubicon first, if it wants public support. This allows the public to support a government that has defensive aims, albeit with the sacrifice of delaying implementation of the war plans, and to at least restrain the expansionist type, forcing it to wait and making an offensive war harder to launch. It's not a perfect solution; few solutions to anything in politics can be, because they typically involve trade-offs over scarce values. But this strategy does allow the public to avoid the regret of either (1) supporting an expansionist war without without so much as forcing a delay or (2) compromising a defensive war effort with a crudely applied strategy of opposition, and it does so by eliminating the government's informational advantage. Furthermore, (wait; wait, wait) is an equilibrium for any value of d, i.e., regardless of how much or how little the public knows about the government's true war aims. An expansionist government would *like* to convince the public that it merits support by claiming defensive intent. It's got a clear incentive to lie, but if the public can use its threat of opposition to force the government to wait, then it can at least blunt the impact of an offensive war plan it doesn't want to support and still support a defensively minded government, all while not really needing to know the government's type – at least in the short term.

Returning to our motivating puzzle, both France and Germany play wait in 1914, the former's generals deploying well behind the German frontier, the latter's civilian leaders antagonizing the generals by waiting for clear signs of a Russian mobilization before declaring war. Their aims, though, were quite different: France to, at a minimum, recover Alsace-Lorraine and Germany to reduce the Low Countries and upset the balance of power between itself, France, and Britain.[28] France's war aims are more revanchist than expansionist, so let's suppose that it's a defensive type (but note that the argument wouldn't be harmed if we put it in the aggressive bin). Germany's aims are more expansive, though, and the government knows that upsetting the European order won't be terribly popular with the working classes, so we'll say that it's an aggressive type. We have two different types playing the same strategy (that is, pooling) that prevents publics from learning their government's aim from early mobilization decisions. (Granted, even defensively minded governments would like to earn support *and* move now, but the information problem prevents them from having this cake and eating it, too.) Large swathes of both publics – nationalists, monarchists, socialists, and liberals alike – support the war effort if not with wild enthusiasm then with grim determination, especially in the early years, accepting the narratives from their respective governments that the war is defensive, designed to ward off threats to the nation's survival.[29] For key parts of the French public, the Germans clearly started it, and for equally critical parts of German society, the Russians were just as obviously at fault.

Principal-agent models have proven useful for thinking about how domestic politics influences international politics, because they draw our attention to (1) the extent to which leaders' preferences differ from the publics whose support they need to implement policy and (2) the extent to which the public can discipline its leaders by punishing failed policies. Leaders are, after all, politicians; they'd rather retain office than lose it.[30] Our puzzle in this section was an easy case for the principal having leverage over the agent, because both democracies and autocracies relied on mass armies in 1914. But sometimes a state's political institutions make it harder

---

[28] We'll talk more about what that balance of power entails in Chapter 6.

[29] On the nature of support for the war in belligerent nations, see Philpott (2014, chapters 1 and 4), and for the German reaction to early Russian incursions, see Watson (2014, chapters 2–4).

[30] Like any assumption, this one isn't everywhere and always true, but on average, it's *massively* safe to make.

to discipline the leadership. It's fairly easy in democracies for the public to punish bad behavior in that voting is easier, if less romantic, than starting your own rebel group, being the first person at the barricades, or mounting a coup. Autocrats, on the other hand, can rely on repression and the co-optation of other elites to insulate themselves from punishment at the hands of the public; often, the only principals able to discipline an autocrat are members of his own military or political elite.[31] This distinction, between democratic publics able to punish their leaders and autocratic publics unable to do so, has been put forward as an explanation for why democracies win so many of the interstate wars they fight: the threat of losing office encourages them to avoid wars they're likely to lose and, if war can't be avoided, to try especially hard to win. Autocratic leaders are harder to remove, by contrast, and they can survive military defeats in office that would otherwise topple elected leaders.[32] Nonetheless, the principal-agent problem can loom large over democratic politics when leaders can exaggerate threats or, at the extreme, start (or continue) international wars in order to convince the public to support them or grant greater political power.[33] We'll talk more about the link between domestic international politics in Chapter 14, but for now it's worth noting that throughout the First World War, governments leveraged informational advantages about foreign policy in order to sustain public support. The German public, for example, received a steady stream of misleadingly good news early in the war, and it took years (and everything between here and Chapter 14) before the spell was finally broken and the chances for victory against the Entente were revealed at home for what they were: grim.

5.3   CONCLUSION

We began this chapter by asking (again) how calculating, frugal leaders can find themselves engaged in wars that they know will be wasteful,

---

[31] On the ease with which elites can punish autocrats, see Weeks (2008). This line of reasoning isn't to say that elections *always* produce the best leaders or that voters always punish elected officials for bad policy, but free and fair elections are associated on average with better economic growth and respect for human rights compared to countries without them (Bueno de Mesquita et al. 2003; Davenport 2007; Ritter 2014).

[32] See, inter alia, Bueno de Mesquita et al. (2003) and Reiter and Stam (2002). It's not so clear, though, that the differences should be all that great, since autocrats trade a lower risk of losing office for a higher risk of exile, jail, or death – as opposed to the lecture circuit – upon losing power. On the prospective effects of those consequences on conflict behavior, see Chiozza and Goemans (2011).

[33] See Arena (2015); Downs and Rocke (1994); Saunders and Wolford (n.d.), and Smith (1996, 1998) for stories not unlike Palpatine's manipulation of the Clone Wars to accrue power and, eventually, destroy the Old Republic from within through an artful manipulation of poor old Jar Jar Binks.

only to end up committing to peace settlements not all that different from the ones they turned down before fighting. This chapter's answer to the puzzle relies on the inherently unobservable nature of preferences and the challenge of communicating them in the face of incentives to bluff in hopes of convincing one's opponents to offer better terms than they otherwise might. This incentive to lie makes diplomatic communication difficult, and it leads states to fight wars that could be avoided if only they had been able to communicate their private information. In 1991, for example, a broad coalition led by the United States was unable to convince Iraq of its ability to eject the latter's forces quickly and easily from Kuwait, and it could prove its ability to do so only through war. Tragically, Iraq entered the war believing that it could bog the coalition down in the rough terrain west of Kuwait in something very much like the trench warfare that came to dominate the Western Front in the First World War, and which Iraq had experienced in its recent war with Iran.[34] Eight years later, another US-led coalition went to war against a Serbian government doubtful of its stated willingness to bomb and then, if need be, invade it into submission over ethnic cleansing in the breakaway region of Kosovo; however much the coalition said about its willingness to wage a lengthy war, Serbia didn't believe those statements until they were backed up with costly actions (that is, preparations for an invasion through Albania) that a bluffer wouldn't countenance. In each case, war occurred because a truly resolute actor willing to pay the costs of imposing its will, could convince its opponent only by doing the very thing in question: launching a war.

We introduced a new modeling tool, Bayesian games, to solve this puzzle as well as one about curious decisions to delay the implementation of war plans once hostilities were inevitable. By taking seriously players' uncertainty about each other's preferences, we showed that limited information on its own isn't enough to explain war. States must also be unwilling or unable to share the information whose revelation would allow them to avert military conflict. We used the laws of probability embedded in Bayes' Rule to show that the key to credible communication is for states to find a way to make bluffing about their resolve too expensive. Simple diplomacy, or words divorced from action, is often cheap and too easily dismissed, but words matched with costly deeds – like military mobilizations or public efforts to stake one's political survival on the outcome of a crisis – can discourage bluffers from lying about their willingness to fight. In subsequent chapters, we'll encounter several different mechanisms by which states can send credible signals of both their willingness to fight and, at times, their willingness to *resist* the temptation to fight. In this

---

[34] On the Iran-Iraq War, see Razoux (2015).

chapter, the key problem was for resolute states to prevent uninformed states from pushing them too far, a challenge made all the more difficult by an irresolute state's incentive to bluff. But you can probably imagine pretty easily that our discussion of the commitment problem in Chapters 2 and 4 suggests that the *opposite* problem can also exist: states with truly limited aims may have trouble convincing their opponents that they don't have aggressive, expansionist aims. In the next chapter, we'll use our knowledge of Bayesian Nash Equilibrium to see that, as their forces marched through Belgium on their way to a clash with France, German leaders faced an incredibly high-stakes problem of conveying not resolve but restraint.

5.4   EXERCISES: THE UN AND PUBLIC OPINION

Bayes' Rule will be useful again in later chapters, so in this section we'll get some more practice, using it to understand when and how international institutions, like the United Nations Security Council in the postwar era, can shape public support for war.[35] The UN Security Council discusses and passes (nominally binding) resolutions on matters of international peace and security. It has fifteen members, but substantial power rests with the five permanent members – the United States, Great Britain, France, China, and Russia, or the P5 – who can veto any resolution brought before the council. You might think that this is a recipe for gridlock, as rival great powers can simply block each other's proposals whenever they wish. But the P5's very ability to publicly block or support one another when, for example, one seeks approval to go to war can actually shape the public's willingness to support a proposed war.[36]

Suppose that your government has gone to the Security Council to seek approval for using force against country X. You know which permanent members tend to support your country and which tend to oppose it, but you're uncertain over whether this war is a good idea. Will it restore or prop up the status quo, like the 1991 Gulf War, or upend it with potentially disastrous consequences, like the 2003 Iraq War? Let's say, for the sake of argument, you'd prefer to support the former, limited kind of war and to oppose the latter. If your government has truly limited aims, it would say so, but to win your support it would also claim to have limited aims if it didn't. Your government confronts a clear information problem (Definition 5.5), but as it happens the reaction of the other P5 members can sometimes help solve it, and Bayes' Rule can show us how. Let's say

---

[35] Forgive the temporal jump, but this will help set up our later discussions of the UN in Chapters 6 and 15.

[36] This discussion leans heavily on Chapman and Reiter (2004) and Chapman (2011).

that your prior belief that the war will be limited (event l) is $\Pr(l) = 0.5$. Next, suppose that your government has gone to the Security Council, where country Y vetoes the resolution (event yv), nominally on the ground that it's aims aren't limited (event $\neg l$) or what we'll call expansive. Will this change your belief about the desirability of supporting the policy? Writing out Bayes' Rule gives us

$$\Pr(l|yv) = \frac{\Pr(l) \times \Pr(yv|l)}{\Pr(l) \times \Pr(yv|l) + \Pr(\neg l) \times \Pr(yv|\neg l)},$$

which is the ratio of a probability that a Y opposes a truly limited war to the probability that Y would oppose your government regardless of the aims of the war. Next, let's define two variables, $g = \Pr(yv|l)$ and $b = \Pr(yv|\neg l)$, representing the probability that country Y would oppose a limited war and that it would oppose an expansive war. After some substitution, we have

$$\Pr(l|yv) = \frac{0.5 \times g}{0.5 \times g + 0.5 \times b},$$

which after multiplying both numerator and denominator by 2 gives us

$$\Pr(l|yv) = \frac{g}{g+b}.$$

Now, what have we learned? Your new estimate of whether the intervention has acceptably limited aims is another ratio, depending on whether country Y would behave differently with respect to limited and expansive wars. If $g = b = 1$, meaning that Y would oppose *anything* your government proposes, perhaps because it's a major geopolitical rival, then $\Pr(l|yv) = 0.5$; your beliefs won't change. You've got clear reason to discount Y's opposition, which is consistent with patterns of public support in the United States: opposition from expected sources, like Russia and China, doesn't have much of an impact on public support for war.

But suppose that country Z also opposes (event zv) your government's proposal, and suppose further that Z is typically a source of support – maybe it's a fellow member of the status quo coalition – and really dislikes coming out against your government and revealing any kind of crack in the coalition. If it *will* oppose, though, then it truly thinks a proposed war is a bad idea. So, let's say that for Z, $g = 0.1$ and $b = 0.75$, such that it rarely opposes your government over limited wars but will, however painfully, oppose your government over expansive wars. Our new equation is

$$\Pr(l|zv) = \frac{g}{g+b} = \frac{0.1}{0.1 + 0.75} \approx 0.12,$$

which means that your belief that the war is worth supporting falls precipitously, from 0.5 to roughly 0.12. Since country Z responds differently to limited and expansive wars – supporting your country in virtual lockstep for all but the most ill-conceived adventures – its opposition is highly informative. Therefore, when rivals oppose your country in the Security Council, it barely registers, because they'd vote against you regardless of the aims of the war, but when friends oppose your country in the Security Council, you take note, because they've got incentives to oppose only when the proposed war is a really, really bad idea. Indeed, the threat of a French veto, which might've undermined support at home and abroad, discouraged the United States from seeking out the much-discussed "second resolution" approving the Iraq War of 2003.

Now, let's do some exercises focused not on opposition but support. Your prior belief remains the same, $\Pr(l) = 0.5$, but now you've got to judge the policy based on statements of support from countries J (event js) and K (event ks).

EXERCISE 5.1 *Suppose that* $\Pr(js|l) = 1$ *and* $\Pr(js|\neg l) = 0.9$. *How does your belief about the war's aims change, if at all?*

EXERCISE 5.2 *Suppose that* $\Pr(ks|l) = 0.75$ *and* $\Pr(ks|\neg l) = 0.1$. *How does your estimate of the probability that the policy is good change, if at all?*

With these calculations complete, you can see an emergent pattern: support from friends and opposition from rivals isn't very informative, but support from rivals and opposition from friends often *is* very informative. The Security Council can thus inform both domestic and international opinion about the desirability of supporting any given use of force, not because its resolutions have teeth (they don't in any real sense), not because it's representative of global public opinion (it isn't), and not because it's an effective forum for deliberation (much of the action is behind the scenes), but because it allows the great powers to take visible public actions that can, when they come from unexpected sources, be highly informative. As we'll discuss later, the Security Council is an important part of the current global balance of power – and one without an analogue in the time of the First World War.

6 A Scrap of Paper: Belgium, France, and British Entry

> *[Bethmann] said that ... just for a word "neutrality," a word which in war time had so often been disregarded just for a scrap of paper, Great Britain was going to make war on a kindred nation.*
>
> Sir Edward Goschen,
> August 6, 1914

With the Continental powers on a collision course in 1914, the question of whether Great Britain could maintain its tradition of "splendid isolation" was very much up in the air. Even its eventual French and Russian partners agonized, as they traded declarations of war with Germany, over whether British help would be forthcoming.[1] The United Kingdom ultimately joined the war in support of France and Russia, yet the manner in which British intervention came about is still puzzling:

> Why was it Belgium's peril, not France's, that convinced Great Britain to intervene in a general European war?

Why, in other words, was a looming threat to France, long the main counterweight to German ambitions in Western Europe, insufficient to bring the British public and Cabinet into the war, while Germany's invasion of "gallant little Belgium" did the trick? Had France gone under, German ascendance on the Continent would have been assured, and Belgium's fall before the fearsome German war machine was preordained. Yet it was a German invasion of Belgium that convinced the British to fight, *not* the possibility that Germany would defeat another European great power. Our solution to this puzzle, which links British entry into the war to the 1839 Treaty of London that guaranteed Belgian neutrality, will teach us a few things:

- how states choose sides in ongoing wars;
- what the balance of power is, and how it relies on international law;

---

[1] See Hastings (2013, p. 85) and Levy and Mulligan (2017, p. 744).

- how "wishlists" of war aims have a real effect on international politics;
- how states try to reassure others about their intentions.

We'll see in this chapter that international law played a decisive role in bringing Great Britain into the First World War, even though international law is generally unenforceable, toothless in the face of de jure international anarchy. By virtue of being public, international law helped the great powers settle on a commonly held view that an invasion of Belgium would be tied to a desire to dominate Europe, and thus to unhinge the balance of power designed to keep the peace on the Continent. Germany's violation of Belgian neutrality, which would almost certainly be followed by British retaliation, convinced the British that Germany's aims were not as defensive as Germany insisted. Rather than trust that Germany wouldn't pursue the ultimate "enfeeblement" of its enemies invoked in Chancellor Bethmann Hollweg's notorious *Septemberprogramm* issued a few weeks into the war – often dismissed as a mere "wishlist" – the United Kingdom embarked on its own preventive war aimed at preserving the European balance of power and, in the minds of its leaders, Britain's survival as a great power. Along the way, we'll use our newly expanded toolkit to analyze Bayesian games in which players are uncertain over each other's preferences. We'll then use those insights to learn about the workings of the European balance of power, international law, and the thorny problem of reassurance.

Key Term for Chapter 6

- Balance of Power

6.1 THE DEFENSE OF BELGIUM

Great Britain's entry into the First World War looks inevitable in hindsight. 1904's Entente Cordiale resolved outstanding colonial issues and cemented an alignment with Britain's longtime French rival, and though the Entente fell short of a binding alliance commitment, it set the stage for subsequent military talks in the years before the Great War. Furthermore, any German drive to end its diplomatic encirclement with a war aimed to dominate Europe was fundamentally intolerable to the British, whose survival as a great power – on their tiny collection of islands floating just off the northwestern edge of Europe – depended on the perpetuation of a balance of power system in which no single power could rule the Continent.[2] If Germany defeated both republican France and Tsarist Russia, as seemed

---

[2] See Gulick (1967) on the classical European balance of power.

possible in the early weeks of the war, then Britain's future security would surely be jeopardized. After subduing France, a victorious Germany could dominate the Channel coast, deny British access to the Continent, encircle the British Isles, and then separate Britain from the colonies whose exploitation sustained it as a great power. Why *wouldn't* Britain join a war to stifle a German bid for European hegemony?

In 1914, the answer to that question wasn't so straightforward. With the exception of the Crimean War, British neutrality during European great power wars had been the rule since Napoleon's final defeat in 1815.[3] One Continental adventure in the previous century hardly signaled a desire to intervene when the other great powers went to war. Furthermore, France, the most democratic state in Europe, had since 1894 been allied with the Continent's least democratic state, Tsarist Russia; this did little to endear the British public to the French cause. And if Russia's weak democratic credentials weren't enough, it was also a major rival for Britain in the "Great Game" of imperial politics in Central Asia. The British commitment to France through the Entente was also intentionally weak.[4] In the final accounting, Britain wasn't bound legally to France's defense (as Foreign Minister Sir Edward Grey was wont to point out when pressed), recent military talks discussed only a division of naval effort by which the Royal Navy would defend France's northern coast, the British ruling house of Saxe-Coburg and Gotha was itself German,[5] and both public and Cabinet were initially hostile to the idea of joining the war at all. Recent naval exchanges had increased optimism, especially in Berlin, that an Anglo-German rapprochement was at least possible. In fact, Chancellor Bethmann-Hollweg would hold out faint, though vain, hope that an Anglo-German understanding might emerge even in the waning hours of peace. Finally, Germany had defeated France decisively in 1871, detaching the territories of Alsace and Lorraine, and Britain's great power status had been unaffected. Why, then, should the British Empire even care if Germany and France once again went to war?

Britain's First World War would also prove to be ruinously expensive, in terms of lives wasted on a mostly indecisive battlefield, Pounds diverted from the national treasury, and debts to the war's American financiers. Hopes of victory (and the promise of reparations) kept the Empire together, but the demands placed on subject peoples during the war would only intensify their calls for independence and self-government.[6] Sending the

---

[3] See Abbenhuis (2014).

[4] In French, *entente* means "understanding" or "intention" – a far cry from an alliance, which commits states to certain actions with written, ratified treaties widely understood to be legally binding (see Morrow, 2000).

[5] It would only rename itself the House of Windsor, distancing itself from Germany, in 1917.

[6] See Manela (2009) and Gerwarth and Manela (2015).

small British Expeditionary Force (hereafter, the BEF) to plug holes in Franco-Belgian lines retreating in the face of a massive German onslaught early in the war would prove to be only a drop in the bucket. Furthermore, about 700,000 British soldiers would die over the course of the war, even as the British homeland went largely untouched but for some sensational, shocking, and mostly ineffectual Zeppelin raids. After the war, domestic politics would descend into bitter recrimination, as citizens, soldiers, generals, and politicians competed to apportion blame for a war that killed many and maimed more – yet served only, in the end, to do little more than preserve the international and domestic balances of power. To the democratically minded, the war failed to unseat Britain's traditional elites. All this, because Germany invaded a minor power in August 1914 on the way to yet another war against France?

It's also possible to read the war spawned by the July Crisis as something less than a German drive for hegemony. Doing so has become a popular trope in the intervening century, and it's not without some *prima facie* merit. As we argued in Chapter 4, Germany's first-best outcome was to see its Hapsburg partner crush Serbia unmolested, but once Russia acknowledged on July 31 that its mobilization was too far advanced to call back, Germany was forced to activate its own contingency plans for general war: an updated version of the now-infamous Schlieffen Plan (about which more in Chapter 8). Anticipating a slow Russian mobilization, Germany aimed to first neutralize the quick-to-mobilize French army before wheeling East to meet the slow-to-mobilize Russian steamroller – all in hopes of avoiding the strategic nightmare of a two-front war. Before it came to general war, though, Germany issued ultimatums to Paris and St. Petersburg on July 31, demanding that they halt their own respective mobilizations. With no satisfaction forthcoming, Germany finalized its mobilization on August 1 and declared war on France on August 3. This failed attempt to coerce a halt to Russian mobilization, which was genuine even if Germany did aim for a long-term hobbling of Russian power, was prominent in the German narrative of defensive intent. The Kaiser's embassy in London also blamed Russian mobilization for the breakdown of last-ditch British mediation efforts, claiming that "We could not idly watch Russia mobilizing on our frontier."[7]

And yet, with the Continent's largest army coiled to strike at France and afforded some breathing room while the Russian armies continued an ostensibly sluggish mobilization in the east, Britain's Cabinet dithered. Only a few voices (including a young Winston Churchill) called for intervention on France's behalf. A great many more recoiled at the idea of

---

[7] Quoted in Mombauer (2013, p. 501, Document 307).

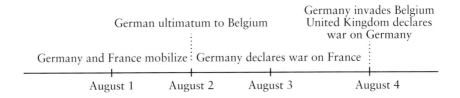

Figure 6.1 The violation and defense of Belgium, August 1914.

fighting for France alone. Foreign Minister Sir Edward Grey asked David Lloyd George, future Prime Minister, how he would feel if France were overrun. The latter asked in response how Grey would feel if Tsarist Russia overran Germany.[8] Split between interventionists worried over Britain's long-term position as a great power if Germany dominated the Continent and a "Little Englander" faction that held on, with the public, to the hope of continuing the tradition of splendid isolation, Britain's decision hung precariously in the balance.[9] As shown in Figure 6.1, only on August 4, a full day after Germany's declaration of war and several days after such a war was believed to be inevitable – an eternity in the overstuffed days of the July Crisis – did Britain declare war on Germany.

Why the delay? Why did Britain maintain a veneer of – at times waffling, at times callous – aloofness as France stared down the prospect of war with Germany until the 4th, when, with the guns of August already firing, it finally entered the fray? The answer, it seems, was Germany's choice on August 2 to make certain demands of its small, legally neutral Belgian neighbor whose territory sat along the ideal marching route for a massive envelopment of the French army. Critical parts of the ultimatum read thus:

1 Germany contemplates no act of hostility against Belgium. In the event of Belgium being prepared in the coming war to maintain an attitude of benevolent neutrality toward Germany, the German Government will bind itself to guarantee ... the possession and independence of the Kingdom in full ...

2 Germany undertakes, under the above-mentioned condition, to evacuate Belgian territory as soon as peace has been concluded.

3 If Belgian adopts a friendly attitude, Germany is prepared ... to purchase for cash all necessities required by her troops ... and to make good any damage that may possibly have been caused by German troops.

Should Belgium oppose German troops, ..., Germany will, to her regret, be compelled to consider Belgium an enemy.[10]

[8] McMeekin (2013, p. 360).
[9] And as the Brexit referendum of summer 2016 made clear, the modern incarnation of the Little Englanders is alive and, surprisingly, well.
[10] Quoted in Mombauer (2013, p. 533).

In other words, King Albert of Belgium was to order his army to stand aside while German troops marched through and occupied parts of his territory on the way to a bigger clash with France. Once peace was secured, German troops would nominally leave. But if Belgium chose to resist the inevitable, "the future regulation of the relations between the two States must be left to the decision of arms."[11] As Europe waited with bated breath, King Albert announced on August 3 his intention to reject the ultimatum, earning his country the epithet "gallant little Belgium" and swiftly turning opinion in the British Cabinet, Parliament, and public toward war.

Dramatic though it was for the public to rally to the defense of a weak state menaced by a strong one in affirmation of the principle of right over might, the shift in British opinion wasn't a complete volte-face. Belgium was, like the Netherlands, a buffer state caught between a triangle of great power rivals.[12] Britain, Germany, and France could each use Belgium's ports and plains to menace the other, and this mutual mistrust led them to guarantee Belgium's perpetual independence and neutrality in the Treaty of London in 1839.[13] Suspicion had also been building since at least July 31, when Bethmann had pointedly chosen not to guarantee Belgian neutrality in an exchange of notes with British ambassador Sir Edward Goschen, even as he made the same guarantee for the Netherlands. As sins of omission go, this one looks historically grave.[14] The Cabinet then approved a final warning on August 1 that Britain would not stand aside in the event of a violation of Belgian neutrality, prompting no small amount of panic among the (largely sidelined) civilian leadership in Berlin. But Germany's ultimatum was written, and nothing would stop its being sent. Once Belgium's decision to resist was announced and German troops attacked the fortress of Liège, it was too late: the British Empire would join the war against Germany with the full-throated backing of the pacifist Radical and "Little Englander" factions, as well as the public that would provide the votes, labor, and lives required to sustain the effort of a general war.[15]

The cynicism left in the wake of wartime anti-German propaganda notwithstanding, it was Belgium's peril that appears to have finally drawn the British Empire into the war. "The deciding issue," then, "was Belgian neutrality."[16] Without Germany's march into neutral Belgium, significant

---

[11] Mombauer (2013, p. 533).

[12] For a somewhat different take on buffer states, see Fazal (2007).

[13] See Partem (1983, p. 24).

[14] To make the point a little finer, imagine this simplified version of the exchange. Goschen: "Will you guarantee Belgian neutrality?" Bethmann: "We'll leave the Dutch alone." Goschen: "..." That's about the long and the short of it (see McMeekin, 2013, p. 278).

[15] See Hull (2014, p. 36) and McMeekin (2013, p. 374).

[16] McMeekin (2013, p. 333).

(and potentially decisive) elements of the British government and public would have found it difficult to commit the anathema of participation in a European war. Yet on the surface it would seem to strain credulity to argue that the fate of a single minor power among many, on a Continent where the weak had long suffered at the hands of the strong, should be *more* important to another great power (like the United Kingdom) than the fate of a major military power (like France). Furthermore, British claims to a principled commitment to international law – here invoked by Germany's disregard for Belgium's right to remain neutral – are (were, and remain) easily cast as self-serving. Bethmann's famous accusation, as reported by British ambassador Edward Goschen in this chapter's epigraph, that Britain was consigning Europe to a world war because of a mere "scrap of paper" guaranteeing Belgian neutrality certainly fits the bill.

But as we'll show in this chapter, international law and the balance of power *do* explain why Belgium is key to explaining British entry into the Great War. They'll do so, however, in an unexpected way. The resolution of the puzzle requires that we look in two places: (1) the dusty old Treaty of London that guaranteed Belgian neutrality and (2) a September 1914 statement of German war aims all too often dismissed as a "mere wishlist." The former established common expectations about the consequences of any one great power (Germany, France, or Britain) violating Belgian neutrality, and the latter represented not a flight of fancy, not a power-political daydream, but precisely the outcome that Britain believed Germany couldn't resist imposing if it *did* conquer Belgium. Each of these elements is critical to understanding British entry, though in what follows we'll work through them in reverse-chronological order, beginning with Britain's strategic problem in 1914, Germany's war plan, and an old treaty recognizing Belgian independence.

6.2 EXPLAINING BRITISH ENTRY

The century since the First World War has spawned what we can charitably call an excess of hindsight. That shouldn't be surprising, given the tremendous dislocation and destruction wrought by four years of apocalyptic, near-total war. But the understandable regret over the war's costs has obscured the reasons states joined it, the United Kingdom in particular. Some accuse the British of waffling and failing to deter Germany's bid to break the Franco-Russian alliance, and others assert that it joined the war – maybe after waffling, maybe after remaining cynically aloof – only to further its own imperial ambitions at German expense.[17] Neither of these

---

[17] For recent examples of the species, see Ferguson (1999) and McMeekin (2013).

attempts at iconoclasm, though, can explain why Britain joined the war when and how it did: not when it was evident that German troops would soon attempt to invest France, but only once it was clear that they would march across Belgian territory to do so. It's tempting to dismiss Belgium as a mere pretext for more cynical explanations of British belligerence, but if preventing German dominance in the Low Countries were less important, then intervention should've come sooner, once war with France and Russia was clearly in the offing. France, to be sure, wouldn't have complained about an earlier, bolder sign of British commitment, yet Britain delayed. Why?

PUZZLE 6.1   *Why was Great Britain unmoved by a German threat to* France, *but driven to intervene in the European war by a German threat to* Belgium?

Explaining Britain's decision to intervene, which takes the European war global, requires that we explain both (1) how it comes to believe that joining the war against Germany is worthwhile and (2) how it's Belgium's peril, not the prior threat to France, that leads Britain to that belief. We'll model a situation in which Great Britain begins the game unsure over the value of joining a war against Germany: if Germany hopes only to fend off a Franco-Russian attack, then standing aside makes sense for Britain, but if Germany's hope is to cripple its Continental enemies and dominate the Channel ports, whose independence guarantees Britain's security, joining the war is worthwhile. The question boils down to one of restraint: are German aims truly defensive? If mere claims of defensive intent will keep Britain out of the war, Germany has an incentive to lie about hegemonic intentions if it has them; it has an information problem (Definition 5.5). That incentive to lie, of course, creates a corresponding incentive to disbelieve. How can Britain judge Germany's intentions when the latter would *claim* benign intent no matter the truth?

We'll show that a key part of resolving this puzzle comes from the arcane world of international law and treaty-making. Decades of dismissing the importance of international law, especially in light of the failures of neutrality in World War II,[18] have made it easier to read British protestations over Germany's violation of Belgium's neutral status as disingenuous. But we'll argue that the entrenched, widespread expectations embedded in 1839's Treaty of London ensured that Britain, Belgium, and Germany could choose their own strategies based on accurate conjectures about what the others were likely to do. The common conjecture (see Definition 2.8), of course, is one of the bedrocks of Nash Equilibrium. Shared under-

---

[18] See Wylie (2002, chapter 1).

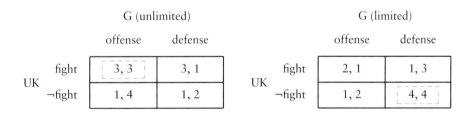

Figure 6.2 German goals and Britain's strategic problem.

standings of strategies and likely reactions have to come from *somewhere*, and in the complex, strategically interconnected world of the international system, treaty law can help define, change, and bolster the common conjecture. A treaty may well be "a scrap of paper," but its value in coordinating expectations and, in this case, convincing states of the value of joining wars is all the more remarkable for the law's apparent toothlessness. Thanks to its role in shaping the common conjecture, international law not only helps resolve our puzzle about British intervention but also sustains the very balance of power systems that we often think of as too hard-nosed, too calculating, too cynical, to bother with the niceties of international law.

6.2.1 Solving the Puzzle

We'll begin with the United Kingdom's dilemma, which entails choosing whether or not to fight alongside the two countries directly under the German hammer in the West: France and Belgium. When Germany unleashes its war plan on the Western Front, Britain must decide whether to fight, joining France and Belgium, or to stand aside (labeled ¬fight in Figure 6.2). Germany, meanwhile, must choose to play offense or defense. If it plays offense, it seeks in victory to reduce France as a great power and to absorb Belgium, to unhinge the balance of power in Western Europe, thereby posing a potentially existential threat to Britain. If, on the other hand, Germany plays defense, it seeks only to preserve the balance of power in Western Europe, fighting a holding action against French attacks aimed at retaking Alsace and Lorraine. The question for the United Kingdom is whether Germany can, free of any constraints, credibly promise *not* to pursue Continental hegemony through an offensive strategy if given the opportunity. In other words, can "Britannia really stand by and allow Germany to control the southern Channel coast and to acquire access to the Atlantic?"[19] Thus, we can think of Germany as one of two player-types (recall Chapter 5), one with *unlimited* goals and one with *limited* goals,

[19] Herwig (2014, p. 32).

and Britain is unsure which type of Germany it faces in 1914. If Germany's goals are limited, Britain prefers not to fight, saving the costs of war while Europe recovers its own balance of power, but if Germany's goals are unlimited, Britain prefers to enter the war, cutting down a future threat alongside France and Belgium rather than face a victorious, aggrandizing Germany that controls the Channel ports.[20]

Figure 6.2 presents Britain's dilemma in a strategic-form game. Either Germany has unlimited ambitions (as it does on the left) or limited ambitions (as it does on the right). If Germany's goals are unlimited, then its choice is simple: it prefers to play offense no matter what Britain chooses to do. A Germany with unlimited goals will seek to dominate the Continent if given the choice, whether or not Great Britain chooses to intervene. As such, in the game on the left, where its aims are unlimited, Germany's best outcome is to play offense unmolested (4), while playing offense in the face of British intervention (which yields 3) remains preferable to any outcome of playing defense, for which Germany receives 2 if Britain does not intervene and 1 if Britain does. Great Britain, for its part, prefers fighting a Germany with unlimited aims, regardless of German strategy, because *any* threat to dominate the Continent is intolerable. Therefore, Britain receives 3 for any outcome in which it fights and 1 for any outcome in which it stays on the sidelines against a Germany with unlimited aims. If the United Kingdom *knows* that Germany's ambitions are unlimited, then it's easy to see how this game will be played. Both sides have a dominant strategy: Germany plays offense regardless of Britain's choice, and Britain fights whatever Germany does. The dashed line highlights this strategy profile of (fight; offense), but recall that it's only a potential equilibrium because Britain isn't certain that it's playing the game on the left. Rather, it's possible that Britain and Germany are playing the game on the right, where Germany's aims truly *are* limited, more in line with the old, conservative, tried-and-true Bismarckian foreign policy that the impetuous Kaiser Wilhelm seems to have rejected.

In the game on the right, where Germany's ultimate aims are limited to preserving the balance of power, its best outcome is to play defense while the British remain aloof (4), and its worst outcome is to play offense and provoke the British to fight in the process (1). With limited aims, playing defense even in the face of British intervention is Germany's second-best outcome (3), while second-worst is playing offense as Britain remains aloof (2). Limited goals imply no designs on unhinging the balance of power in Western Europe, so Germany always prefers defense to offense, and it is always better off if the British do not intervene. Britain's prefer-

---

[20] For another game-theoretic treatment of this problem, albeit without the direct application to the First World War, see Powell (1999).

ences when faced with a limited-aims Germany are similar. It most prefers to stay out while Germany plays defense (4), will prefer to fight if Germany plays offense by, say, subjugating Belgium (2), but it most wants to avoid an unnecessary intervention or a failure to fight if Germany does play offense (1). The dashed line indicates that there would be a unique Nash Equilibrium to this game as well, if only Britain knew it were playing it: (¬fight; defense).[21] A Germany known to be committed to the current balance of power in the West can be trusted to play defense, and in that case the United Kingdom is happy to preserve its splendid isolation.

The problem for Britain in the July Crisis is that it's not sure whether Germany's aims are limited or unlimited. Germany knows the true extent of its aims, but Great Britain lacks that information. If Germany's aims are truly unlimited, then joining the war now, with French and Belgian (and Russian) help, is attractive for Britain. But if Germany has genuinely limited aims, joining the war is a waste – something that Britain will surely come to regret, given the costs and risks of waging great power war.[22] Given Britain's desire to prevent a Continental hegemony, a Germany with unlimited aims has strong incentives to lie about its preferences: if it has unlimited aims and can convince Britain that it doesn't, then it can count on Britain to play ¬fight, allowing it to dominate the Continent unmolested – or, at a minimum, quickly enough to render futile any resistance launched from across the Channel. That is, Anglo-German relations are characterized by an information problem (recall Definition 5.5), and the *Kaiserreich*'s incentives to lie about its goals creates an incentive for the British to disbelieve German claims of limited intent.

Such claims are many and loud as the knot of war tightens in the remaining days of peace, but they fall on largely deaf British ears. Germany accuses France of already violating Belgian neutrality – dubious, given France's long-standing assurances to Britain that it will do no such thing *and* the order (recall Chapter 5) to keep its troops well back of the border. And German requests to trade Belgian and French territorial integrity for British neutrality ring hollow, "crude and almost childlike," to Prime Minister Herbert Henry Asquith, who believes that a German bid for Continental hegemony can't be ruled out.[23] To be sure, many in the British Cabinet and public *wish* German statements of limited aims to be true, if only because it will excuse them from joining a costly European war. But they also know that this is precisely what Germany would say if it wished

---

[21] You can prove the existence and uniqueness of these complete-information equilibria by following the procedures established in Chapter 2.

[22] The debate, to this day, isn't entirely settled (see, e.g., Ferguson, 1999). But, as we'll see, what Britain *believed* at the time was more important than what a century's worth of hindsight might lead observers to infer. Hindsight isn't 20/20; it's distorting.

[23] Hastings (2013, p. 77).

to lull Britain into a false sense of reassurance, only to exploit British neutrality in aid of conquering Belgium and reducing France. This inability to reassure others of defensive intent is central to Germany's information problem; if its aims truly are limited, it will say so, but if its aims are unlimited, it will refuse to admit it, proclaiming limited aims in hopes of appearing unthreatening.

Following the definition of Bayesian games we established in Chapter 5, we'll say that Britain begins the game with prior beliefs that assign probabilities to each of Germany's possible types, such that

$$\Pr(\text{unlimited}) = q \quad \text{and} \quad \Pr(\text{limited}) = 1 - q.$$

Thus, Great Britain begins the game believing that Germany has unlimited aims with probability q, which we'll assume is not so high that Britain will intervene in equilibrium. We do this because, if we are to explain how Germany's invasion of Belgium leads Britain to intervene on the side of the Entente, Britain must be unwilling to intervene absent an attack on Belgium. (Otherwise, there's nothing to explain, and Britain would've gotten involved days before it actually did.) So, we look for a Bayesian Nash Equilibrium involving strategies of (¬fight; offense, defense).

PROPOSITION 6.1   *The strategy profile (¬fight; offense, defense) is a Bayesian Nash Equilibrium when $q \leq 3/5$.*

Proof   For (¬fight; offense, defense) to be a Bayesian Nash Equilibrium, it must be the case that

$$u_G(\neg\text{fight}; \textit{offense}, \text{defense}) \geq u_G(\neg\text{fight}; \textit{defense}, \text{defense})$$

for the unlimited G,

$$u_G(\neg\text{fight}; \text{offense}, \textit{defense}) \geq u_G(\neg\text{fight}; \text{offense}, \textit{offense})$$

for the limited G, and

$$u_{UK}(\neg\textit{fight}; \text{offense}, \text{defense}) \geq u_{UK}(\textit{fight}; \text{offense}, \text{defense}).$$

The first inequality is satisfied because $4 \geq 2$, and the second is satisfied because $4 \geq 2$. The final inequality is satisfied only when $q \leq 3/5$. When $q \leq 3/5$, no player has a profitable deviation, so (¬fight; offense, defense) is a Bayesian Nash Equilibrium.   □

To prove the existence of this equilibrium, we first need to verify that the strategy we assign to each of Germany's possible types is a best response to Britain's strategy. The unlimited type is more than happy to play offense if Britain doesn't fight, because playing defense would waste an opportunity for aggrandizement ($4 \geq 2$), and the limited type is also sure to play defense, because going on offense, even if Britain chooses not to fight, remains unattractive ($4 \geq 2$). Finally, we make an expected utility comparison to see when Britain will refuse to fight, or $\text{EU}_{\text{UK}}(\neg\text{fight}) \geq \text{EU}_{\text{UK}}(\text{fight})$, which we can also write as

$$q \times 1 + (1 - q) \times 4 \geq q \times 3 + (1 - q) \times 1.$$

Some quick algebra shows us that Britain refuses to fight when $q \leq 3/5$, or when it doesn't believe it too likely that Germany has unlimited aims. So, when

$$\Pr(\text{unlimited}) \leq \frac{3}{5},$$

Britain's prior belief that Germany will, if given a chance, unhinge the balance of power in Western Europe is low enough that standing aside while Germany fights yet another war against France poses a small but acceptable risk. This hesitance to intervene approximates the position of the British public and the Little Englander faction in the Cabinet before Germany's ultimatum to Belgium. Our task in solving this chapter's puzzle is to see how the invasion of Belgium can convince Britain that Wilhelmine Germany does, in fact, have unlimited aims – to change this calculation such that fighting becomes Britain's best response to the outbreak of the war.

We know that something must change Britain's beliefs about Germany's ambitions. It's not enough, though, to speculate. Solving this puzzle demands that we write down two Bayesian games, similar to the system of games we analyzed in Chapter 4, one involving Germany and Belgium, the other revisiting the Anglo-German game of Figure 6.2. In each case, we'll give Britain and Belgium prior beliefs that Germany has unlimited aims with probability q. The equilibrium of each component game once again depends on the equilibrium of the other, and we want to establish the equilibrium existence of several strategies. First, we want to show that Germany violates Belgian neutrality only when it has unlimited aims and that it honors Belgian neutrality when it has limited aims. Second, we want to show that Germany's strategy changes Britain's beliefs, raising its estimate of $\Pr(\text{unlimited})$ from somewhere below $3/5$ to something sufficiently higher to justify intervention once Germany violates Belgian neutrality. Finally, we want to show that Belgium resists the German invasion, bleak prospects of holding fast against Germany's right hook notwithstanding. If we can show that these strategies exist in equilibrium, we can explain why the threat to Belgium draws Britain into the war.

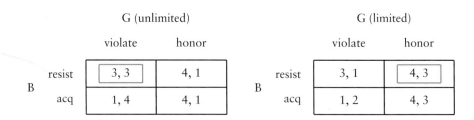

Figure 6.3 German strategy and Belgian neutrality.

We'll begin with the question of Belgium's neutrality and its decision to fight Germany, characterized in Figure 6.3. Germany debates whether to violate Belgian neutrality on the way to France, rather than simply fight on the Franco-German frontier, which honors Belgian neutrality. Belgium, for its part, must decide whether it will resist or acquiesce in a German invasion. If Belgium plays resist, then it will fight in the event of a German invasion (for which it expects French assistance), and if it plays "acq" (or acquiesce), it stands aside as German columns rush through its territory on the way to their clash with France.[24] Note that, should Germany honor Belgian neutrality, then this contingency isn't activated. Like Britain, Belgium is also unsure whether Germany's aims are limited or unlimited, but for the sake of argument we'll say that its main priority is avoiding armed attack; Germany's ultimate aims won't matter much for King Albert with Prussians and Bavarians patrolling Belgian streets. Regardless of Germany's aims, Belgium receives 4 if its neutrality is honored. If Germany attacks, Belgium's payoffs depend on its strategy: resistance and the chance of survival it preserves yields a 3, where acquiescing to a German invasion yields its worst payoff of 1. The difference between resistance and acquiescence hinges on what Britain will infer from the violation and then do in response; failing to resist forfeits neutrality in the future, just as surely as resisting and losing makes neutrality moot. In any case, German promises to preserve Belgium's territorial integrity in its ultimatum are believed wholly incredible.[25]

Germany's payoffs depend on its type and Belgium's strategy. They're also shaped by Britain's strategy in the linked Anglo-German intervention game, the equilibrium of which dictates that Britain fight if Germany attacks Belgium but remain aloof if Germany attacks only France. Let's begin with a Germany with limited aims, which has a dominant strategy of playing defense in the Anglo-German game and which recoils at the prospect of provoking British intervention. This type, on the right in

---

[24] France has been given short shrift in this narrative, but not because its army wasn't top-notch. The French acquitted themselves pretty well, all else equal.
[25] Hull (2014, pp. 32 and 33).

Figure 6.3, is happiest honoring Belgian neutrality and focusing its efforts on containing the inevitable French offensive on the shared Franco-German border. France isn't expected to violate Belgian neutrality unilateraly, thanks to a well-known policy of no first violation and a 1911 comment from British Foreign Minister Grey that his public would surely demand intervention against whichever side violated Belgian neutrality.[26] Therefore, if a Germany with limited aims honors Belgian neutrality, it receives 3, but if it violates (which it might do for military expediency), then it receives 2 if Belgium acquiesces (which nonetheless risks British intervention) and 1 if Belgium resists and potentially ties down the invasion force. With unlimited aims, on the other hand, Germany's best option is to violate Belgian neutrality and win its acquiescence (4), though a resisted violation (which also entails British intervention) is still the next best outcome (3). Worst for its unlimited aims is to honor Belgian neutrality (1), which holds out no hope of restructuring the European balance of power.

What does this mean for German strategy in the West? The difference between limited and unlimited aims, as seen in Figure 6.3, is that the threat of British intervention is sufficient to deter Germany from invading Belgium if its aims are truly limited. A Germany with limited aims has a dominant strategy – honoring Belgian neutrality, avoiding British intervention, and focusing its efforts on the Franco-German frontier. If it has unlimited aims, however, Germany's incentives change; it has a dominant strategy of violating Belgian neutrality, British intervention be damned. Belgium, for its part, has its own dominant strategy. Planning to resist in the event of German attack is never a worse bet than acquiescing, regardless of Germany's type. Therefore, we have a simple Bayesian Nash Equilibrium of (resist; violate, honor) that does not depend on Belgium's beliefs about Germany's aims.

PROPOSITION 6.2   *The strategy profile (resist; violate, honor) is a Bayesian Nash Equilibrium regardless of Belgium's prior beliefs.*

Proof   For (resist; violate, honor) to be a Bayesian Nash Equilibrium, it must be the case that

$$u_G(\text{resist}; violate, \text{honor}) \geq u_G(\text{resist}; honor, \text{honor})$$

[26] On the former, see Hastings (2013), and on the latter, see Hull (2014, p. 31). Avoiding Belgium to keep the British happy was even part of Joffre's Plan XVII (Leonhard, 2018, p. 44), but since Germany didn't know this particular detail, we can't use it to justify Germany's information in the game; France's public statements, though, suffice in this case.

for the unlimited Germany,

$$u_{\mathrm{G}}(\text{resist}; \text{violate}, \textit{honor}) \geq u_{\mathrm{G}}(\text{resist}; \text{violate}, \textit{violate})$$

for the limited Germany, and

$$\mathrm{EU_B}(\textit{resist}; \text{violate}, \text{honor}) \geq \mathrm{EU_B}(\textit{acq}; \text{violate}, \text{honor})$$

for B. The first inequality is satisfied because $3 \geq 1$, and the second is satisfied because $3 \geq 1$. The final inequality is satisfied because

$$q \times 3 + (1-q) \times 4 \geq q \times 1 + (1-q) \times 4$$

is true for any value of q. No player has a profitable deviation for any value of q, so (resist; violate, honor) is a Bayesian Nash Equilibrium.   □

Now that we've established that these strategies exist in a BNE, our next step is to compare them to the historical record: a German violation of Belgian neutrality that occurred with essentially complete knowledge that the British would be unable to remain aloof if Belgian territory were overrun with German troops. How plausible is this equilibrium? Civilian leaders' wishful thinking about British aloofness notwithstanding, General Helmuth von Moltke and his German general staff aren't "unduly troubled" at the prospect of violating Belgian neutrality, "because they had long believed that Britain would fight against them in any case."[27] In other words, Germany *knows* that Britain will defend Belgium; it just doesn't care.[28] Germany's actions indict it in Belgian and British minds, even as its words declaim its defensive motives in the war. It violates Belgian neutrality *in full knowledge that it will provoke the British to intervene*, which Germany will only do if its aims are truly unlimited – that is, if it aims to swallow Belgium and enfeeble France. Why provoke war with the British Empire – its wealth, its navy, and its potentially limitless access to manpower (thanks to its imperium) and credit (thanks to the United States) – if Germany *weren't* making a bid for Continental hegemony? War with Britain in service only of holding off French and Russian attacks would make little sense, and Belgium isn't alone in making this calculation: the British government and public do as well.

As we saw in Chapter 5, we can represent this learning process, this updating of Belgian and British beliefs, with Bayes' Rule. If Germany violates Belgian neutrality only when it has unlimited aims, then Britain can use Germany's treatment of Belgium in Figure 6.3 to judge the value of

---

[27] Hull (2014, p. 25).
[28] Ludendorff acknowledged as much in a 1912 planning document reflecting on Germany's tenuous strategic position (Leonhard, 2018, p. 43).

joining the war. In other words, Great Britain can learn which game in Figure 6.2 it's actually playing. Bayes' Rule characterizes Britain's belief that Germany's aims are unlimited after observing a violation of Belgian neutrality, as

Pr(unlimited|violate)

$$= \frac{q \times \text{Pr(violate|unlimited)}}{q \times \text{Pr(violate|unlimited)} + (1-q) \times \text{Pr(violate|limited)}},$$

which, after some algebra, we can see equals 1. If Germany violates Belgian neutrality in full knowledge that it'll provoke British intervention, then Britain can learn about Germany's aims: only a Germany with unlimited aims would take such an action. From a prior belief that Pr(unlimited) = 3/5, Great Britain's updated beliefs now indicate that Pr(unlimited) = 1. It's now confident that Germany has launched a bid to dominate the Continent, to replace its own long-running nightmare of encirclement with Britain's strategic nightmare of being cut off from the Continent.

As shown in Figure 6.4, the separating BNE of the German game against Belgium resolves the uncertainty at the heart of the Anglo-German game. When Britain chooses between fight and ¬fight, it now knows which game it's playing, because it's convinced that German aims are unlimited. Germany attacks Belgium only when its aims are unlimited, and it honors when it has limited aims. Player-types *separate* (Definition 5.7), taking actions unique to their type and revealing their private information (i.e., their preferences) to other players. When Germany issues its ultimatum to Belgium – and, beforehand, when Bethmann refuses to guarantee Belgian neutrality to the British ambassador – Britain comes to believe that it's facing a Germany bent on dominating the Continent, undeterred by the prospect of war with the British Empire. After observing Germany's strategy on what will become the Western Front, Britain knows which game it's playing. As such, it can tailor its strategy to German behavior. If Germany honors the Treaty of London, Britain believes that it's playing the limited game on the right, where Germany has a dominant strategy of playing defense and where Britain's best response is not to intervene (4 < 3). But a

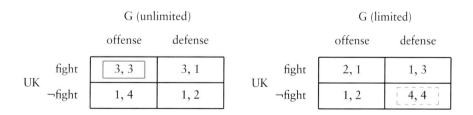

Figure 6.4 Germany's aims and British intervention.

violation of the Treaty of London reveals that the true game is on the left, where a Germany with unlimited aims has a dominant strategy of playing offense, leaving Britain with a best response of fighting ($3 \geq 1$) – throwing the British Expeditionary Force into the path of the German army as it crashes through Belgium and into France, turning what began as a regional war in the Balkans finally and fully into the First World War.

PROPOSITION 6.3   *The strategy profile (fight; offense, defense) is a Bayesian Nash Equilibrium regardless of Britain's prior beliefs.*

Proof   For (fight; offense, defense) to be a Bayesian Nash Equilibrium, it must be the case that

$$u_G(\text{fight}; \textit{offense}, \text{defense}) \geq u_G(\text{fight}; \textit{defense}, \text{defense})$$

for the unlimited G,

$$u_G(\text{fight}; \text{offense}, \textit{defense}) \geq u_G(\text{fight}; \text{offense}, \textit{offense})$$

for the limited G, and

$$u_{UK}(\textit{fight}; \text{offense}, \text{defense}) \geq u_G(\neg\textit{fight}; \text{offense}, \text{defense}).$$

The first inequality is satisfied because $3 \geq 1$, and the second is satisfied because $3 \geq 1$. The final inequality is sure to be satisfied when $\Pr(\text{unlimited}) = 1$, because $3 \geq 1$. No player has a profitable deviation, so (fight; offense, defense) is a Bayesian Nash Equilibrium.   □

Why do Germany's attempts at reassurance, its constant declarations of limited aims, fail? Our model shows that Germany takes an action that Britain believes Germany surely won't take – using neutral Belgian territory in an invasion of France – if its goals are as defensive as Berlin claims. Germany's actions give the lie to its words, and critical elements of the British public and Cabinet fall in line with the interventionists, switching from the wary aloofness that sustains a decision not to fight in the first Anglo-German game of Figure 6.2 to a wholehearted willingness to stifle a German attempt at Continental hegemony. The Treaty of London's guarantee of Belgian neutrality is the bellwether by which France, Britain, and Germany can interpret one another's actions: knowing that crossing into Belgium may provoke the other guarantors into opposition, any state that does so must be bent on overturning the tripartite balance of power sustained by the Treaty. The power that controls Belgium's plains or Channel ports can menace the other two, and this is what makes Belgium special:

the balance of power hinges on it.[29] When times are good, i.e., when no single power has hegemonic intentions, each side can commit credibly not to swallow Belgium. But when times are bad, when one power has hegemonic designs that it quite reasonably doesn't want to broadcast, it must control Belgium if it's to defeat the other two. And making *that* bid is enough to convince the others that the balance of power itself is under threat.

We now have a solution to the puzzle of why Britain enters the war *and* why an impending attack on Belgium is sufficient to precipitate it while an impending attack on France isn't. It is Germany's threat to the European balance of power – a balance that guarantees Britain's survival as a great power via Belgium's neutrality – that provokes British intervention. Germany's bid to control Belgium, made in the face of certain intervention, convinces Britain that the threat of strategic isolation is real. Franco-German wars may be nothing new in 1914, but the threat to Belgian neutrality is a different animal entirely, because Germany will be unable to resist the temptation to remain in Belgium and cement its domination of Western Europe. Thus, "it was not a disaster to France which petrified the 'interventionists [in the Cabinet],' but the consequent isolation and defeat of Britain."[30] Weeks after the war breaks out, Bethmann's private secretary Kurt Riezler will draft what comes to be known as the *Septemberprogramm*, a list of war aims that includes the annexation of Belgium and Luxembourg, permanent sovereignty over Poland, the partial dismemberment and disarmament of France, the creation of subservient buffer states out of Russian territory in the east, a pan-European customs union called *Mitteleuropa*, and an expansion of the German colonial empire. This amounts, in no uncertain terms, to the destruction of the prevailing balance of power. Later, Germany ends up with the chance to implement only part of this scheme by imposing a harsh victor's peace on Russia in early 1918, and some scholars dismiss the *Septemberprogramm* as a mere wishlist.[31] But that, for Britain in 1914, is precisely the point. What Germany *would* do if unconstrained in the de jure anarchy of the international system, the outcome it most prefers, is precisely what Germany can't promise not to pursue in victory over Belgium – and precisely what Britain will do all it can to prevent. The *Septemberprogramm* is the written manifestation of the commitment problem that drags Britain into the war against Germany.

---

[29] For an excellent recent discussion of the unique lives of buffer states, see Fazal (2007).
[30] Kennedy (1980, p. 427).
[31] See Stevenson (2012, p. 845) for a brief discussion of the debate over the memorandum's significance.

6.2.2   Was It Law or Self-Interest?

Britain couched its defense of Belgian neutrality in terms of upholding the sanctity of international law, of standing up for small states and the principle of right over might, in speeches before Parliament and in domestic and international propaganda. But we, like many an observer since, might still reasonably ask whether international law really mattered at all. International law is mostly toothless in the absence of a common authority with the remit to police and punish states for breaking the rules (recall Chapter 1). And if that's the case, why care about it? Why crow about violations when might – that is, military force – is the ultimate arbiter of who gets what in international politics? Was Germany's violation of the Treaty of London merely a pretext for a British attempt to prolong its reign as the dominant imperial power? Or was it, as Bethmann implied when he accused Britain of going to war over "a scrap of paper," the residue of a utopian dream, of idealists hoping to impose the niceties of domestic law on a gritty, dangerous, and anarchic international system?[32]

Answering this question is less straightforward than it might appear. Great Britain's decision to intervene was consistent with commitments to which the the Treaty of London bound it, but joining the war also fit with what Britain believed to be very much in its interests: not saving Belgium per se, but thwarting the achievement of a European hegemony that Germany would be unable to turn down if given the chance. Germany's ambitious, revolutionary *Septemberprogamm* may have been a wishlist, but for that reason it represented precisely what Britain wished to deny Germany the chance to impose on its enemies. It's important to note, though, that Britain may not have arrived at this conclusion – that Germany's claims of limited aims were hollow – if the law hadn't been violated. International law requires self-enforcement, but that doesn't mean that it must be complied with to affect state behavior. It can shape which strategies states choose and, as a result, which equilibria best characterize the historical record. Breaches of the law can be valuable because they're informative, revealing to other states how they should interpret the actions of those that cast compliance to the wind and break the commonly known rules of international law. International law can act as a collectively agreed red line that, when crossed, helps states make accurate conjectures about how others will react – a necessary element of any Nash Equilibrium.

International law needs neither teeth nor compliance to influence state strategies. As we've seen since Chapter 2, and implicit in our discussions about international politics from the beginning, a key feature of

---

[32] See Carr (1964) and, for a more polemical treatment of the matter, Mearsheimer (1994–1995).

equilibrium reasoning and behavior is the *common conjecture* (Definition 2.8), the agreed set of roles, norms, identities, and likely reactions that help states choose the strategies that they play in equilibrium. In every model we've discussed so far, from the Anglo-German naval race to the July Crisis, we assume that states can readily guess what strategies each is likely to play; states in arms races expect that each side would build unilaterally if allowed, declining states gauge that rising states will be unable to resist temptations to use newfound power in the future, and guarantors of small states' neutrality keep a watch for potential violations. It's reasonable, though, to ask *how* states come to know these things about one another. Sometimes, they can reason to a common conjecture simply by knowing the other's goals and knowing that the other knows their goals, and so and on. That's easy for simple, two-player interactions like arms races, but when states have to gauge the likely reactions of multiple states both today and long into the future – as the British, Germans, and French did when they guaranteed Belgian independence in 1839 – a common conjecture can be more difficult to establish.

As we'll see explicitly in Chapter 10, some games can be played in multiple, equally rational ways, and states can only guess what each other will do by engaging in some kind of pregame coordination of their expectations. The problem is magnified by situations, like the July Crisis or the crisis of Belgian neutrality, in which several states play each other in distinct games with linked equilibria. How, for example, can Germany know that Britain will draw inferences about the extent of its aims simply by watching for violations of Belgian neutrality? How can Belgium be certain of British assistance in the event that it resists what is, for all intents and purposes, an inevitable military catastrophe? The answer, in this case, is the Treaty of London, by which the great powers agreed to guarantee Belgian neutrality – that is, the inviolability of its territory in the event of war between the guarantors – by threatening force against the violator. By making public a commitment that might otherwise be private, each party to the treaty assesses a greater chance that the others will use force against it in the event of a violation. This, in turn, deters it from opportunistic violations for matters of simple military expedience. However, if a guarantor violates Belgian neutrality despite the knowledge that it has raised its chances of provoking intervention, then others can draw the inference that its aims are unlimited, just as Britain did in 1914. This process of drawing lines in the sand and daring states bent on unhinging the balance of power to cross them defines the common conjecture by which states can make judgments about each other's likely behavior when formulating strategy. Without international law, which makes those intentions public, Britain would be less confident in reading the German invasion of Belgium as a bid to dominate the Continent than as a simple matter of improving its odds in a defensive war against its old French rival.

International law creates stable expectations of state strategies, defining the common conjecture that sustains and explains the prevalence of particular equilibria. By helping states make accurate guesses about each other's strategies, it defines the common conjecture throughout the international system: when, for example, states will guarantee each others' neutrality only when others will stand beside them, a public record of commitments to do so can influence other states' beliefs just enough to sustain an equilibrium in which large numbers of them come to the aggrieved neutral's aid. International law, then, defines and coordinates the expectations that are key to the definition of any equilibrium that we might use to explain patterns of war, peace, and diplomacy. Without it, states have trouble guessing each other's strategies and formulating their own best responses. Without the Treaty of London – without a shared expectation that signatories would only violate Belgian neutrality if they truly had unlimited, hegemonic aims – we can imagine the games in Figures 6.3 and 6.4 playing out differently, up to and including a much longer and potentially more fraught process of bringing Britain into the war. Indeed,

> What mattered in the rhetoric of July 1914 was less political philosophy [i.e., "public ethics" and "just war"] and more an embryonic sense of international law, less the abolition of war and more its containment.[33]

What does this mean for the question with which we began this section? Perhaps surprisingly, it means that both prominent takes on the role of Belgian neutrality are partially correct; Britain manifestly entered the war for power-political reasons, hoping to preserve its great power status against a German bid for Continental hegemony, but it was only able to draw that inference because of widespread agreement, created by the Treaty of London, about the meaning of a German violation of the law. Britain's commitment to the specifics of international law, especially the rights of small states – popular victims of great power jealousies and ambitions – may not have been sincere, but its belief that violation of the law revealed critical information was firm. Absent the Treaty of London, Germany might have felt freer to invade Belgium, and the rapid change in British public and Cabinet opinion in favor of war would've been less likely. Therefore, Britain acted in the interests of a stereotypically cold, hard calculation of power, but this decision was made possible only because of a belief that other states knew and conditioned their own strategies on the specifics of international law.

---

[33] Strachan (2014, p. 433).

Another way to read these models, in fact, is that international law is far from toothless. It is, instead, a key part of the international system. Great powers may not view the law as consistently binding, but they take seriously its effects on the shared beliefs, the common conjectures that sustain their strategies in equilibrium. When the great powers play equilibria in which they try to prevent one's dominance over the others, they rely on information about each other's ultimate ambitions that can be provided by their willingness to break the rules. Breaches of the law, far from an indictment of its effectiveness, actually make it effective, by sustaining the balance of power system that continues to characterize great power politics. To ask whether Britain acted out of commitment to international law or callous self-interest is to ask the wrong question, because international law helped it make decisions about what strategies were in its interest. Indeed, the history of the Great War itself testifies to the importance of international law as a device that shapes expectations and state strategies. As noted above, France reassured Britain in 1911 that it would resist the temptation to be the first violator of Belgium, because it knew the likely British response. Even more telling, German military officers and international jurists viewed their war aims in an explicitly legal sense: "In short Germany was, or after its victory soon would be, the sovereign lawgiver to the world."[34] That's hardly the language of limited foreign policy aims, but neither is it the language of a state that believed international law to be mere "scrap[s] of paper."

6.3 WHAT IS THE BALANCE OF POWER?

One of the more enduring concepts in the study of international politics is the "balance of power," though (like war itself) its use in a dizzying array of contexts by both decision-makers and scholars over the centuries has done a lot to cloud its meaning. It's been called everything from an institution that defines the rules within which states choose their strategies[35] to a recurrent collective pattern that emerges from states' individual efforts to ensure their survival[36] to a dangerous folly based on the cynical belief that right makes might – an argument made by both academics and characters in this very text like Woodrow Wilson.[37] Some observers and decision-makers even use terms like *equilibrium* to describe it, though what they mean in applying that term is typically less precise than the sense in which we use it here; remember that, for us, whether strategies are in equilibrium

---

[34] Hull (2014, p. 271).
[35] Bull (1977).
[36] Waltz (1979).
[37] On the former, see Vasquez (1999), and on the latter, see Tooze (2014) and Knock (1995).

has no connection to whether the outcomes they produce look in any way like an "equilibrium."[38] Whatever the balance of power is, countries care enough about it to go to war to either preserve or unhinge it, often at tremendous cost.[39] It's a slippery concept, but we can use the logic of equilibrium to get a bit of a handle on a definition that's useful for our purposes. Ours is slightly different from other definitions, emerging as it does from our model of the international system outlined in Chapter 1, so it's worth elaborating. What do we mean when we say that Germany sought to upend the balance of power, or that Great Britain went to war to defend it? What *is* the balance of power?

We can use our understanding of games, strategies, and equilibrium, along with some clues from the story so far, to sketch out an answer to this question. Traditionally, a balance of power has been associated with a situation in which no single power, alone or in concert with others, can dominate or threaten the survival of the remaining great powers.[40] This implies that a balance of power arises from a set of equilibrium strategies chosen by calculating, frugal leaders in light of their own military power and beliefs about each other's strategies. States value their places in the hierarchy, and they temper their desires to improve their position against the costs of doing so, which at the extreme can entail military defeat and occupation – as Napoleonic France, Nazi Germany, and Imperial Japan all learned when their respective bids to shake up the hierarchy were thwarted. When power is balanced, positions in the global power hierarchy are stable, because those states that might wish to climb the ladder expect to be met with a balancing coalition, i.e., a collection of states that will line up to defend the status quo against challengers. Therefore, a balance of power is made up of shared beliefs, a common conjecture, about the likely alignments in and outcomes of hypothetical wars between the great powers. As such, the balance of power has elements of both power *and* ideas, which define the strategies states choose that produce it.[41] It supports an equilibrium in which the great powers stay at peace with one another, avoiding that hypothetical general war.

DEFINITION 6.1   *A **balance of power** is a shared belief that a general war to reorder the international hierarchy would be too costly to pursue.*

---

[38] For a useful statement of this problem, see Schroeder (1989).

[39] There's also a sense in which it's used as a synonym for the distribution of power – that is, who has how much power relative to whom – but since a distribution can be either balanced or imbalanced, it's not a definition we want to use here. Terms like *balanced balance* and *imbalanced balance* would just obfuscate more than they would clarify.

[40] See, e.g., Gulick (1967).

[41] As we'll make more concrete later, it's a function of beliefs about likely coalitions in a general war.

If a balance of power is sustained by a common conjecture about the nature of a general war, then changes in those shared beliefs can upset the balance. The outcomes of future wars depend on both material factors like financial and military power, which shape the size and quality of armed forces, as well as beliefs about future alignments and the scope of states' aims. Great powers went to war in the nineteenth century, for example, over German unification and Russian ambitions in the lands of the Ottoman Empire, but they avoided general wars in the belief that the balance itself wasn't under threat.[42] By 1914, though, Germany (with Austria's help) launched a two-front war against Russia and France *and* provoked a balancing response from Great Britain. What changed? Our story so far points us in the direction of changes in the power, preferences, and beliefs that supported the pre-1914 balance of power. Chapter 4 argues that Germany fought to preserve its place in the hierarchy against an expected fall. With Russian power recovering and its attention turning from East Asia back to Europe, bolstered by an 1894 alliance with France that emerged from Germany's own failure to renew a treaty with Russia in 1887, both power and alignments were shifting against Germany – presaging a preventive war in which Germany would try to preserve its place in the hierarchy by knocking its rivals down. Britain, the traditional holder of the ring in the European balance, foresaw a shift against its own position in a potential German victory over France and Belgium, in a particularly costly implication of the strategic interconnectedness that characterizes the international system. Therefore, changes in the expected alignments and outcomes of a possible general war, one that would see Germany's prospects steadily diminish if it didn't take advantage of the July Crisis *now*, led to a war that broke and ultimately reshaped the balance of power. By contrast, in the Sino-centric order that characterized East Asia before the late nineteenth century, the long-standing, overwhelming, and well-known dominance of Chinese power helped preserve peaceful relations between the center and other states – Korea, Japan, and Vietnam – with far fewer violent interruptions than the more fluid European balance.[43]

The balance of power comes down, ultimately, to beliefs about a hypothetical war between the great powers. As such, some key elements shaping those beliefs that define a balance of power will be (1) the number and alignments of great powers and (2) rules of thumb for judging intentions – say, whether one seeks to preserve or overturn the balance – defined by long-standing practice or, as we saw in this chapter, international law. When the number, military strengths, and alignments of great powers are basically stable, supporting a belief that launching a war to reorder the

---

[42] For an excellent recent survey of the century, see Evans (2016).
[43] For an excellent analysis of this period, see Kang (2010).

hierarchy will be ruinous or prohibitively costly, then a balance of power exists, and it supports peace among the great powers in the sense of avoiding a general war. But these commitments can unravel if expectations about the nature of a hypothetical general war begin to change. Great powers may fear falling from the ranks due to their own collapse, like the Soviet Union in 1991, or the rise of a competitor, like Germany vis-à-vis Russia in 1914. New great powers of uncertain alignment may rise, like Germany, Japan, and the United States in the late nineteenth century and China and India in the early twenty-first, radically changing expectations about the sides, scope, and potential costs of great power wars to come. In each case, uncertainty over alignments and intentions or shifts in the number of great powers – that is, the makeup of those coalitions committed to defending the status quo and those to overturning it – can begin the process by which ambitious rising powers or fearful declining powers try to unhinge the balance and establish a new order.

Not all changes in numbers and alignments are sufficient to touch off a general war. But if we think about maintaining the balance of power as a kind of multilateral bargaining problem, we can gain some purchase on when it's likely to be unstable. The Soviet Union collapsed in 1991, yielding its Eastern European empire to independence and a Russian successor state whose economic and military power was a shadow of its former self, but reassurances from the remaining great powers appear to have been sufficient to discourage its leaders from launching a last-ditch preventive war.[44] Germany achieved long-desired unification in the latter half of the nineteenth century by winning a series of wars against Austria, France, and smaller German principalities, but by honoring legal commitments like 1839's Treaty of London, it managed to convince Russia and Great Britain that it didn't (yet) pose a serious threat to the balance of power. Prussia may have supplanted Austria as the dominant power in Central Europe and detached Alsace and Lorraine from France, but it posed a limited threat to the great power hierarchy, and it was able to convince other states of this fact. Neither change represented such a substantial reordering of expectations that the other great powers considered a general war. But when such changes *do* shift power and expectations sufficiently, we see the cataclysmic wars that redefine and reorder the international system, like the Napoleonic Wars, the world wars of the twentieth century, and the Third World War that the great powers have thus far avoided (cross those fingers) since 1945. But how do states that truly are committed to preserving the balance of power, those that can grow in power but *not* pose a threat to others, reassure their opponents and avoid destabilizing wars?

---

[44] On the risk of a violent Soviet collapse, see Sarotte (2009) and Plokhy (2014).

6.4 REASSURANCE AND INTERNATIONAL POLITICS

Great Britain entered the First World War when it did because it came to believe that German aims were not limited and defensive but unlimited and hegemonic, Berlin's protestations notwithstanding. Britain's war was preventive, but had Germany managed to signal defensive intent, it might have come even closer than it eventually did to crushing France.[45] The chance to discourage balancing is a powerful incentive to lie about one's aims – about the willingness to exploit today's cooperation or quiescence tomorrow – and that creates for states with benign intentions a difficult problem of reassurance. When states with truly limited aims fail to reassure others fearful of their intent, they can fall victim at one extreme to unnecessary preventive wars. But they can also encourage mistrustful sates to balance against them in a variety of other ways, including the denial of trade and economic cooperation, the formation of coalitions aimed at containment, military support for one's enemies, and obstruction in international institutions.

The problem of reassurance is a species of information problem (Definition 5.5) similar in kind to the challenge of signaling resolve we encountered in Chapter 5. Like resolute states whose threats are discounted, those with limited aims can find themselves treated like they have unlimited aims. Iraq, for example, faced just such a problem during the crisis of 2002–2003 that led ultimately to an Anglo-American invasion launched from Kuwait in 2003. Though its nuclear, chemical, and biological weapons programs had been halted for good after an American-led air campaign against it in 1998, Iraq refused full cooperation with United Nations inspectors for years, failing to reveal its lack of weapons programs because it had to maintain an image of military prowess to its neighboring rival, Iran.[46] Suspicion of Iraqi weapons programs was widespread, and with the United States more willing after 2001 to pursue a preventive war it had been considering for over a decade, Iraq was unable to reassure its enemies over its ability to build weapons of mass destruction, prompting a preventive war that toppled its government and plunged the country into years of insurgency, civil war, and sectarian strife. Tragically, it was only after the invasion that it became clear that Iraq had ended its pursuit of weapons of mass destruction years beforehand.

How can states with truly limited aims reassure those that would otherwise balance against (or simply invade) them? Just like signaling resolve requires doing something that an irresolute state wouldn't do, reassurance requires taking steps that a state wouldn't take if it didn't have hostile,

---

[45] For more on that, you've got to wait until Chapter 8.
[46] See Ricks (2006).

unlimited, or expansionist intent. Germany's bid to misrepresent its ambitions failed in 1914, thanks in large part to the line in the sand drawn by the Treaty of London, but in prewar crises over Morocco in 1905 and 1911, when its goals genuinely were limited, it was able to convey that by releasing conscripts from the army – by publicly and consciously limiting its own military power, which it *wouldn't* do if it were bent on pushing the button on the Schlieffen plan.[47] Publicly limiting the ability to use military force can serve as a credible signal of restraint, of a willingness to abide by the status quo. The Soviet Union managed a similar feat of reassurance in the late 1980s and early 1990s, as it offered unilateral cuts in its nuclear forces and negotiated steep reductions in conventional arms, reducing the fears of its Western rivals that it might respond to its deepening economic decline by launching a preventive war[48] – a preventive war, it is to be noted, that would've been prompted by the terrible realization that it couldn't win an arms race – just like Germany in 1914.

Reassurance is also tied intimately to relations between great and minor powers, especially in the unipolar era that followed the fall of the Soviet Union and the rise of the United States to sole superpower status. Unchallenged militarily, economically, and ideologically, the United States exercised an unprecedented freedom of action after the end of the Cold War. Power, though, is inherently threatening, and the collapse of America's main rival created *more* opportunities for other states to distrust its intentions. When going to war to restore borders or stop ethnic cleansing, expanding its alliance network, or shifting the deployment of a historically powerful military machine, the United States had to find ways to reassure numerous states fearful that it might turn its gaze on them in the future. In other words, the United States had to discourage other states from balancing against it. Beginning in the post–World War II era, it frequently sought the approval of other great powers in the United Nations Security Council for the use of force. This signaled to potentially fearful states that American aims were limited; if its great power rivals were willing to go along – as they were with overturning the Iraqi invasion of Kuwait in 1991 – then surely the global status quo wasn't under threat.[49]

Great powers can also choose coalition partners wisely, building coalitions that can credibly put on the brakes (or even disband) after achieving their initial aims, which reduces the threat posed to potentially fearful outsiders.[50] The United States, for example, consciously excluded Chiang Kai-Shek's Taiwan from its Korean War coalition in 1950 as a way

[47] See Stevenson (1997).
[48] See Kydd (2005, chapter 8).
[49] See Voeten (2005).
[50] See Wolford (2015, chapter 5).

to signal to mainland China that its goals were limited to the Korean Peninsula – and not to giving Chiang a blank check to restart the Chinese Civil War.[51] Similarly, in 1991, as it built a coalition to eject Iraq from Kuwait, it relied on military, logistical, and basing support from regional powers that would refuse to participate in an extensive campaign of toppling the Iraqi government, like Saudi Arabia. It also pointedly excluded Israel, despite the latter's considerable military power and shared hostility to Iraq, and secured Soviet assent in the United Nations Security Council. These steps both limited the coalition's aims and its military power, but by doing so they reassured neighboring states. Iran could infer that balancing was unnecessary, while Turkey and Syria could judge that participating today wouldn't come back to bite them via expansive American aims in the future.

Great powers are defined by their considerable military power and freedom of action. Yet that very ability to pursue their ends unilaterally means that they must reassure potential adversaries in order to maintain their positions in the hierarchy and to preserve the global order that supports the hierarchy. Great power status is only manageable and affordable when potential balancers can be reassured that significant military and economic power will be wielded with restraint. Power itself is threatening, and to the extent that great powers can tie their hands against using that power or take other costly steps to convince those that fear them that their aims are truly limited, they can sustain that power peacefully. When they fail at reassurance, they can provoke widespread opposition, from the defection of allies or client states to rival great powers to the outbreak of costly, destructive wars.

6.5 CONCLUSION

Britain's decision to declare war on Germany, which entailed the deployment of the British Expeditionary Force and a blockade of German ports (about which more in Chapter 10), turned a European war into a truly global one. The United Kingdom would not only draw on its extensive network of colonies for money and manpower but also pursue further imperial interests around the world, including an expansion of its influence in the Middle East,[52] but its intervention was hardly foreordained after a century of near-exclusive neutrality in European wars. Yet Britain *did* go into the line with the Entente in August, not because Russia or France were about to grapple with the Central Powers, but because neutral Belgium

[51] Stueck (1995, 2004).
[52] See McMeekin (2015).

would soon be shaken by the footfalls of massed German boots. To solve this puzzle, we looked to the 1839 Treaty of London. Its guarantee of Belgian neutrality established the shared expectations that supported an equilibrium in which Britain was able to learn about German expansionism – and then decide that joining the Entente's war effort was in fact in its interest. It's tempting to dismiss international law as irrelevant in the face of a war that did so much to rend the social and legal fabric of the international system, but what the violation of Belgian neutrality represented – an end to the triangular balance between France, Germany, and Britain in Western Europe – is key. "Belgium defined the central issues" of Britain's war.[53]

Our analysis of British intervention focused on the fate of a small country sandwiched between three great military powers, but the insights also showed us something about the politics of great power coalitions, the relationship between the balance of power and international law, and the problem of reassurance. When the Entente and the Central Powers went to war in August, each side did so preventively, as we saw in Chapter 4 for the early entrants and in this chapter for Great Britain. There wasn't much doubt by early August that this war might prove disastrous even in victory, but that the fighting would last so long (and be so indecisive), that it would kill or maim so many, and that it would upend the international system itself would be a surprise. All sides *feared* that the war might turn into a long, bloody slog, and they took steps to mitigate that risk. Germany, for example, entered the war with plans for the offensive, for waging a war of maneuver backed up by recent advances in firepower and mobility hoping to strike a knockout blow against France in a matter of weeks before turning and facing Russia. But as we've seen thus far, one side's goals in a strategic interaction can often be denied by another, and in the following chapters we'll trace the war's evolution from one of maneuver to the taxing, indecisive stalemate that it would become for most of the next four years.

---

[53] Hull (2014, p. 41).

7 Troubled Partnerships: Coalitions at War

> *To count on the intercession of our ally!! What an illusion.*
>
> Count Alfred von Schlieffen.
>
> *There is only one thing worse than fighting with allies, and that is fighting without them.*
>
> Sir Winston Churchill

Its carnage, scope, and duration may have been surprising, but the Great War that broke out in 1914 was no bolt out of the blue.[1] The power-political fault lines were more or less known, sides were drawn up, and war plans worked out often many years in advance. The Central Powers of Germany and Austria-Hungary had a decades-old alliance, though the Triple Entente was of more recent vintage, and the still-newer British commitment was questionable right down to the wire. This poses a puzzle for how each coalition behaved in the first weeks of the war:

> Why did Britain and France find military cooperation easier than Germany and Austria in the opening weeks of the war?

In other words, why did the newer coalition, centered on an uncertain commitment from an ally whose territory wasn't under direct threat and riven with precariously dormant imperial rivalries, keep all its armies in the line on the main front, while the venerable alliance of Germanic powers failed to cooperate in meeting their primary threat of a major Russian offensive? Despite an early hiccup, both Britain and France honored their commitments at the Battle of the Marne, while Austria refused German requests to put the Serbian campaign on hold to face Russia together, and Germany itself surprised Austria by limiting its initial commitments to the war against Russia. The games we write down in this chapter to solve this puzzle will teach us a few things:

---

[1] I'm shamelessly borrowing a metaphor from Fromkin's (2004) prologue here; it's as good a metaphorical use of St. Elmo's Fire as you're likely to find in a popular history of the July Crisis.

- how cooperation can fail when all parties want the same outcome;
- the costs and benefits of coalition-building in international relations;
- how private goals can sustain cooperation when shared goals can't;
- how coalitions form, when they succeed, and when they fail.

We'll see in this chapter that both the Entente and the Central Powers – indeed, all military coalitions – face a basic *collective action problem*, in which the shared goal of military victory isn't sufficient to discourage partners from trying to shift the costs of fighting onto each other. International cooperation is costly, from contributing troops to a war effort to lowering trade barriers to limiting greenhouse gas emissions, and when the benefits of military victory, access to markets, or clean air accrue even to those that don't contribute to them, countries have individual incentives to shirk even when they'd all be better off solving the problem together. Cooperative obstacles to coalition war efforts are a specific case of something more general, and we'll introduce a series of models in this chapter that both define the collective action problem and identify potential solutions. We'll show that the weaker alignment of interests between Britain and France, far from hampering cooperation, actually helped *solve* their collective action problem; each had a private interest in securing a position of power at the postwar peace conference, which drove them to sustain a major war effort. Meanwhile, the solitary dominance of German preferences in its coalition ensured that Austria had no individual incentive to cooperate, dooming the Central Powers to a major cooperative failure that saw Germany weaken its Western flank to shoulder a disproportionate and potentially ruinous share of the burden in the East.

Key Terms for Chapter 7
- Collective Action Problem
- Selective Incentive
- Military Coalition
- Alliance

7.1   COOPERATION IN RIVAL COALITIONS

After the flurry of mobilizations, counter-mobilizations, and declarations that saw all of Europe's major powers enter the war, it's tempting to think all that was left was to execute the war plans – in other words, that the politics of the war might stop. That would be a mistake: each major power's plans depended on a mix of things it could control directly, like the movement of its own troops, and things it couldn't, like the cooperation of its coalition partners. Germany's plan, as we've noted, was to hurl most of its forces West, through neutral Belgium, in an attempt to repeat its success in the Franco-Prussian War of enveloping and shattering the French army; but this depended on the success if its own small force holding onto East Prussia *and* the willingness of the Dual Monarchy's Commander-in-Chief, Franz Conrad von Hötzendorf, to take his eyes off the prize in Serbia and tie down Russian forces on his northern frontier in modern-day Ukraine and Poland. Meanwhile, France's Plan XVII, hatched by the imperturbable French C-in-C Joseph Joffre, aimed to smash through the German center on the countries' common frontier; in the early going, France would depend on Russian troops falling upon Germany in the East, but once the German plan carried the day in the West, it would also depend heavily on British troops staying in the line, protecting Paris, and participating in the first great counterattack of the war. But while the Central Powers appeared more tightly aligned than the Entente in peacetime, their coalition would turn out to be a cooperative disaster, while their otherwise waffling rivals would prove far more adept at sharing the burdens of waging war.

It's fair to say that the Central Powers had seen general war coming for years, as the Franco-British-Russian Entente tightened and as France financed military buildups in both Russia and Serbia. By 1905, the German general staff had settled on a plan, bearing the name of its retiring Chief of the General Staff Count Alfred von Schlieffen, that prioritized knocking France out of the war in a matter of weeks – forty days after mobilization, to be precise – before turning east to meet the slow-moving Russian mobilization.[2] By 1914, Russian rearmament had progressed sufficiently to speed up its mobilization times, which placed even greater importance on one piece of Germany's plan for the Eastern Front: a reliance on Austrian arms to tie down the Russians. Austrian decision-makers fully expected to bear the brunt of Russian attacks early in a war, and Conrad assured Moltke in the months leading up to the war of his intent to devote the majority of his forces to that front (and not against Serbia) while he waited for Germany to sweep France aside in the West.[3] Russia was the acknowledged common enemy in the East, it posed a far greater threat to the Dual Monarchy's survival than tiny Serbia, and the Central Powers' planning, spotty though it was on specifics, acknowledged this. If Austria could weather Russian attacks early, it would eventually receive German support, enabling it to secure its position in the Balkans and its own survival.

Yet as soon as war became imminent in July 1914, fissures started to show in the Teutonic alliance. Austria's mobilization, slowed by the large number of troops on harvest leave (bringing in food they'd need on campaign), failed to achieve anything resembling the rapid July victory over

---

[2] More on the Schlieffen Plan, and just how much Moltke changed it, in Chapter 8.
[3] Herwig (2014, pp. 47–53).

Serbia on which Germany's blank check was predicated. With war declared on July 27 and the Tsarist armies on the move days later, there was no turning back. Germany relied on Austria to turn its attention East, to honor its pledge to wheel around from Serbia and face the Russians. Conrad, however, chose a different course of action with his three army groups. *Minimalgruppe Balkan*, the army tasked with crushing Serbia under General Oskar Potiorek, stayed in the south and received the bulk of Austria's reserves in the form of *B-staffel* – which Germany expected to head north to assist *A-staffel* forces facing down the Russians. Not two formations but one would face the oncoming Russians in Galicia.[4] Three attempts to invade Serbia would fail through the fall, while at the same time undermanned, outclassed, and outgunned Austrian forces staggered from disaster to disaster in their attempt to contain Russian offensives that would eventually capture the fortress city of Lemberg. Austria's war turned into a catastrophe on two fronts, prompting Germany to begin diverting troops to the East as early as August 25. And by late September, newly installed Chief of the General Staff Erich von Falkenhayn would raise a new 9th Army tasked with reversing Austrian losses and leading a push into Russian Poland.[5] Military cooperation on the Eastern Front had proven a dismal failure, and over time Germany would not only send troops but also command authority to the erstwhile Hapsburg front.

Meanwhile, on the Western Front, Entente generals were only slowly beginning to realize the scale of the German right hook swinging through Belgium and preparing to turn and plunge itself into France's left flank. (In Map 7.1, H. G. Wells – yes, *that* H. G. Wells – refers to the German movements as the "original" plan, but as we'll see in Chapter 8, this turned out to be an improvised change; the Schlieffen concept had the right wing waiting before turning south.) Casualty rates had been astronomical, historically so, though largely kept from public view. The French Commander-in-Chief, Joseph "Papa" Joffre, had first gambled on striking at what he believed would be the German center in the Ardennes, then upped the stakes by ordering a dramatic retreat and reorientation east of Paris to meet the tip of the German spear head on. We'll talk more about Joffre's great retreat in Chapter 8, but for now it's worth focusing on a key part of Joffre's plan to save France: General Direction No 2. Joffre envisioned a counteroffensive that would take advantage of an unexpected German turn south with a newly formed French Sixth Army east of Paris and the four divisions of the British Expeditionary Force (BEF), recently arrived, even more recently bloodied, and under the command of Field Marshal Sir John French. German commanders appeared unaware of their vulnerability to

---

[4] Philpott (2014, p. 46) and Herwig (2014, pp. 53 and 55).
[5] Philpott (2014, p. 65).

Map 7.1 The German sweep through Belgium, August 1914. From Wells (1922).

French Sixth Army, and if the BEF could march north from its position southeast of Paris, with French Fifth Army to its right, German combat power in France and Belgium could be dealt a serious, if not fatal, blow. General Direction No. 2 might cap off the grand retreat by saving Paris, if only the Entente troops could regain their footing and the BEF stay in the line.

The promise of going on the offensive notwithstanding, Sir John dropped a bombshell on Joffre in a memo that read:

> I feel it very necessary to impress on you that the British Army cannot under any circumstances take its place in the front line for at least ten days. I require men and guns to make good casualties ... You will understand that I cannot meet your wishes to fill the gap between the [French] Fifth and Sixth Armies.[6]

After taking serious casualties in the early going, worried about salvaging a presence near the Channel ports in Belgium, and feeling abandoned by his allies, Sir John wanted no more than to retreat, lick his wounds, and

---

[6] Quoted in Hastings (2013, p. 251).

try to hold on to the Channel ports.[7] Needless to say, Joffre was not impressed with Sir John's refusal, which threw the possibility of an effective counteroffensive up in the air.[8] Joffre would likely have to cancel the offensive and simply hope that the German attack would break against French defensive positions – as opposed to turning back in retreat.[9] "By the end of August Anglo-French cooperation in the field had all but ceased."[10] Relying on an order from Secretary of State for War Horatio Herbert Kitchener, the retired general who'd earned fame by crushing revolts in colonial Sudan, to preserve his forces, Sir John seemed bent on pulling his small force out of the line. And yet with French armies crashing into the German right, the BEF ultimately *did* march forward, meeting its obligations and threatening to slide right into a suddenly yawning gap between German First and Second armies, prompting a retreat that would stabilize the lines in France for years to come.

The British met their obligations, but why? And if the Entente could sustain effective military cooperation, why couldn't Germany and Austria? If any coalition should've had problems getting its act together, it's not unreasonable to guess that it should've been Britain and France on the Western Front – not the Central Powers that faced down Russia. First, the French and the British were ancient rivals. They'd fought one another countless times over the centuries (and once *for* a nearly a century), and one of those wars put a French king on the English throne in 1066. Having abandoned the idea of conquering one another, they'd only recently begun to patch up their outstanding issues by negotiating the Entente Cordiale in 1904. Nonetheless, few Britons spoke French, and fewer French cared to know English. Second, Britain came late to the French cause, after some weeks of very public waffling, and at least in the early going its commitment to the war on land would be limited to the relatively small British Expeditionary Force (Britain being a naval power, it typically had no need for the massive standing armies of the Continental powers). Pulling out when the going got tough would be tempting and easily rationalized. Relatedly, prewar coordination on where the British would land and who would command the coalition forces was, for all intents and purposes, nonexistent.[11] Finally, while France and Belgium fought for their own land, the British Isles were hardly under threat unless Britain *did* make an enemy of Germany and Admiral Tirpitz's risk fleet. How long would the public remain willing to bleed for someone else's home territory, not its

---

[7] Philpott (1996, p. 22).

[8] You read that correctly: the British general most willing to abandon his French allies – and who spoke no French himself – was named "French." You can't make this stuff up.

[9] See Hastings (2013, chapter 9).

[10] Philpott (1996, p. 24).

[11] See Weitsman (2003, p. 102).

own scepter'd isle? And why should the Empire's defense be sacrificed by diverting men and materiel to an army when Britain had relied for so long on a peerless navy and prudent neutrality?

Imperial Germany and the Dual Monarchy, on the other hand, would seem to have everything going for them. The two leading Germanic powers spoke the same language and shared a common culture, and both retained the trappings and much of the substance of *ancien regime* autocracies committed to the so-called monarchical principle. Cultural affinities notwithstanding, their strategic ties were also strong. Despite coming to blows as Prussia achieved the longtime dream of unifying Germany at Austria's expense in a series of mid-nineteenth-century wars, their current alliance (inked in 1879) was one of the longest-lived in Europe.[12] If general war came to Central or Eastern Europe pitting Slav against Teuton, no one doubted that Germany and Austria-Hungary would line up on the same side. In fact, the Central Powers needed each other, because in 1914 they had almost no one else. Italy was unlikely to invoke the Triple Alliance to enter the war on their side (more on that in Chapter 9), and Germany needed Austria to shore up its southern flank just as much as Austria needed German support to withstand a long war against Russia. Unlike the British and the French (and, by extension, the British and the Russians), the Germanic powers had no major imperial rivalries to speak of between them, and Austria more or less happily followed the German line in the alliance with respect to matters in the Balkans.[13] Finally, they faced a significant, shared, almost existential threat: rising Russian power in the East. If anything could guarantee close cooperation in the coming war, surely the Central Powers' combination of cultural, political, and strategic affinity would do the trick. Right?

Wrong. While the British lined up beside their French and Belgian partners and began the process of building a viable land army almost from scratch, Austria tried to implement two plans at once – sending some formations to face the Russians, while others remained focused on a Serbian campaign that had become a sideshow. Each was tempted by the prospect of skimping on the military efforts required by its coalition partner, but only Britain resisted the temptation. The deck apparently stacked against it, the Entente pulled off the necessary military cooperation to achieve a stunning success on the Western Front that could scarcely have happened without the British staying in the line. Meanwhile, with everything

---

[12] The longest-lived alliance, then and now, is that between England and Portugal, in force since 1373 but for a sixty-year interruption straddling the turn of the sixteenth and seventeenth centuries, when Portugal was in political union with Spain.

[13] It had, of course, been less than eager to offer Germany support in the prewar Moroccan crises (Stevenson, 1997).

seemingly in place to ensure that Austria would line up alongside Germany against the shared (and more serious) threat of Russian invasion, the Dual Monarchy dithered, embarrassing itself in a failed bid to crush Serbia and leaving Germany, its only ally, holding the bag on *two* fronts against *three* other great powers. But why? What was so different about politics in the Entente that the weakest link in its chain held, while an apparently stronger link in the Central Powers' chain broke? We'll show in the next section that many of the apparent disadvantages we identified for the Entente, as well as the advantages held by the Central Powers, had quite the opposite effect.

7.2 EXPLAINING WARTIME COOPERATION

In the early weeks and months of the war, described in Figure 7.1, both the Entente and the Central Powers showed some troubling signs of cooperative breakdowns that could have proven fatal for their war efforts. In this section, we'll show how the Entente ultimately overcame its major cooperative obstacle while the Central Powers, whose stakes were no less serious, did not. To do that we have to develop an understanding of why cooperation over such high stakes, even national survival, could be so fragile in the first place.

PUZZLE 7.1 *Why were the Entente powers able to cooperate on the Western Front, while cooperation broke down between the Central Powers in the East?*

Each rival coalition was made up of great powers, each could draw on reserves of wealth greater than the average country, and each of them made conscious decisions to enter the war. Yet once the chips were down, only the Entente managed to draw substantial military efforts from both members after some initial cooperative hiccups. Britain and France had none of the apparent cultural, political, or strategic advantages of Germany and Austria, who *couldn't* cooperate well, so what are we left with as an explanation? One strand of the popular narrative has attributed the Entente's recovery to the surrender of Sir John's weak nerves to Papa

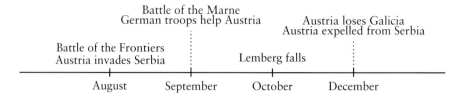

Figure 7.1 Coalition warfare, 1915.

Joffre's "Olympian calm," "iron will," and impassioned plea for cooperation and the preservation of British honor.[14] But not every coalition
has had a Joffre to browbeat its laggards into fighting, and cooperative
problems are most often solved without the timely intervention of a musta-
chioed walrus of a Frenchman wielding the right turn of phrase. This same
popular narrative also has the Central Powers lacking anything resembling
the charismatic leadership of the Western powers as they fell prey to a
combination of Austrian incompetence and venality. There's a facile sheen
of credibility to this explanation, but it doesn't really mesh with our understanding of the characters in our story as frugal and calculating. Plenty of
coalitions have cooperated, while plenty others have failed to, both with
and without their own versions of Joffre, French, Falkenhayn, and Conrad.
So it's important to begin with what we know in general about wartime
cooperation, whoever happens to be in charge.

Let's start by thinking about coalition warfare in the abstract, with
no proper nouns yet. Suppose that two coalition partners, A and B, must
choose how much effort to devote to fighting a common enemy. Effort decisions involve the number of troops in the line, investments in their supply
chains, and how many reserves of soldiers, ammunition, and money are
to be fed into the battle after the inevitable initial losses. The more effort,
the harder a partner fights. The greater each partner's effort, the better the
coalition's chances of success, whether that entails beating back an invasion
or puncturing and then breaking through an opponent's lines. The chances
of success are highest when both partners choose high effort, lower when
only one does, and dire when both choose low effort. Yet military effort is
costly. Armies must be fed, supplied, and coordinated, and their casualties
replaced with fresh recruits – and every soldier, shell, dollar, and machine
gun thrown into this battle can't be used in others. Each partner weighs
the costs of military effort in any given battle against the increased odds of
success, but the collective nature of the war effort introduces a major complication. If the coalition wins the battle, both partners enjoy the benefits
of the outcome whether or not they contributed significantly to the victory. A battlefield victory is thus a *collective good*, because its benefits are
diffuse: one partner can't be excluded from enjoying a successful defense,
encirclement, or breakthrough even if it contributed little to the fight.[15]

When the costs and benefits of the coalition's war effort are structured
this way, preferences in Figure 7.2 resemble the Prisoner's Dilemma that
we encountered in Chapter 3. Each partner prefers that the other shoulder
most of the burden, and its best outcome is to put in low effort while its

---

[14] See, in particular, Hastings's (2013) account of the first four months of Britain's war.
[15] See Olson (1965) for the classic statement of this problem, as well as Olson and
Zeckhauser (1966) for an application to peacetime military spending in alliances.

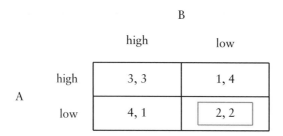

Figure 7.2 Coalition war efforts as a collective goods problem.

partner puts in a high effort, trading off a reduced chance of success today in order to husband resources for the future (4). Worst is to shoulder the burden of high effort alone while one's partner gives low effort (1). In the middle, mutually high efforts are better than mutually low efforts (3 > 2); for mutually high efforts, both sides pay the costs of producing a higher chance of success, but if both sides shirk and choose mutually low efforts, the overall chances of success plummet and the coalition courts disaster. Think of it this way: if both partners put in high effort, they can secure a 75 percent chance of success wth the burdens of blood, treasure, and forgone opportunities on other fronts shared fairly evenly; if only one exerts high effort, the chances of success fall to 50 percent while the hardworking partner shoulders a ruinous share of the burden; and if neither side puts in high effort, they minimize their exertions but secure only a 25 percent chance of success. When cooperation is individually costly and produces a good from which neither can be excluded – that is, when the benefits are diffuse but the burdens concentrated – we say that our partners face a **collective action problem**.

DEFINITION 7.1   *When a collective good requires individually costly cooperation to produce, there exists a **collective action problem**.*

Absent a solution to the collective action problem, the unique Nash Equilibrium of (low; low) is predictable: both sides exert low effort, saving themselves the burden of providing an effective defense on their own, but reducing the coalition's overall chance of success. (We won't reproduce the solution here, because it's isomorphic to the proof of Proposition 3.2.) Sir John certainly wants to limit his efforts in the upcoming clash if he gets the chance; he'd much rather save the BEF while France defends its own capital from the German onslaught, forcing on General Joffre the terrible decision of throwing everything into the defense of Paris, which risks losing the war, or limiting the French effort – and chances of success in the short term – in hopes of being able to put up a better fight another day. In the East, the Dual Monarchy's preferences aren't all that different;

Conrad would much rather focus on crushing Serbia than wheel the whole of the Hapsburg army east to face Russia when Germany can carry a large chunk of the burden on its own. Conscious of its own costs for fighting a two-front war, Germany also desires to shift the early burden of fighting Russia onto Austria while it deals with the French and British in the West. Therefore, for both the Entente and the Central Powers, each coalition will be better off if each partner can commit to higher efforts, but the temptation to shirk and make a weaker effort has the potential to drive collective efforts down in a tragic underprovision of coalition war efforts.

But while these underlying temptations exist on both sides, only the British and the French appear to find a solution that keeps both armies in the line and sharing the costs of a substantial military effort. Sir John's waffling notwithstanding, the BEF *does* rejoin the French fight at the Battle of the Marne, marching into a gap formed between German First and Second Armies that will prove decisive in throwing back the rapidly advancing invaders (for more on this, see Chapter 8). On the Eastern Front, Austria divides its efforts between Russian and Serbian fronts, to predictably disastrous effect. However, this initial cooperative failure is partially corrected, not because the Central Powers manage to work together, but because Germany pulls some units from the Western Front and assumes a large chunk of Austria's military responsibilities.[16] The collective good of a stout, if porous, resistance to the Russian onslaught is provided, not by collective but by unilateral action. Our challenge is to explain this difference: why did the Entente manage to cooperate, while the Central Powers saw one partner effectively take over the other's war effort?

7.2.1 Solving the Puzzle: The Entente

Let's start with the Entente. Why do the British ultimately come around to do their bit at the Battle of the Marne? Does Sir John have a change of heart – one in which he stops caring about preserving his troops and supplies in the face of the war's shocking early casualty rates? Does the sheer force of Joffre's personality (and it *was* a forceful one) do the trick? Probably not. The focus on Sir John, his nerves or lack thereof notwithstanding, is a bit of a red herring. Interpersonal rivalries between generals can make for compelling storytelling, but French's desire to preserve his fighting force and to prioritize the defense of the Channel ports – Britain's lifeline as a great power – is more than understandable.[17] The key, for us, is that when the chips are down, it isn't the BEF commander's priorities

---

[16] Keep an eye on the theme of creeping German control over Austrian war efforts. It'll spark some understandable tensions that emerge again later in the war.

[17] On British defensive priorities, see Philpott (1995).

that win out, but those of his political masters in London. Whether to keep the BEF in the line on the Western Front isn't entirely General French's decision to make. To be sure, the Cabinet, especially Kitchener, is sensitive to immediate battlefield outcomes and the risk of losing the BEF before the New Army can be stood up and trained. But the government's goals are broader than Sir John's, and it has the authority to dictate foreign and military policy (a standard feature of healthy democratic political systems).[18] Just like soldiers don't have too many interests in common with the commanders that tell them where to go and whom to shoot, generals are often out of sync with the civilian leaders that tell them whom to fight, what for, and when to stop. Generals are understandably concerned with *battlefield* outcomes, but civilians are often concerned with how those military outcomes translate into *political* outcomes.[19]

If Sir John's preferences approximate the collective action problem of Figure 7.2, what can we say about his government's preferences? How do the civilian leaders directing their generals in the field value the outcomes of the early battles on the Western Front? Where both Sir John and Papa Joffre are concerned with the immediate problems of allocating effort to maximize their chances of success while minimizing costs, their respective governments are concerned with both the war *and* its aftermath. The influential nineteenth-century Prussian thinker Carl von Clausewitz was already famous by 1914 for theorizing about war as a political instrument, a means (albeit a wasteful one) to an end – and to their credit the civilians in the Entente capitals often keep their eyes on the distant prize of reaching a favorable settlement even when tempted by the short-term exigencies of the battlefield.[20] Cooperating in the war effort may be expensive and risky, but the outcome of a successful coalition effort on the Marne is about more than just a chance to halt the German advance. For Britain in particular, cooperating in Joffre's offensive is about sustaining the Entente beyond a single battle and securing a place at the negotiating table when the time comes to make peace – a seat from which it will command far less influence if it doesn't pay in blood like its partners France, Russia, and Serbia. Postwar negotiations among the victors are often difficult, and in many cases what a state walks home with after victory has a lot to do with

---

[18] Civilian control of the military is one of the bedrocks of stable democracy, and you can see the desire to limit the power of the state, with its monopoly on the use of physical violence, through just such a mechanism in the earliest documents of American democracy.

[19] This can create no small amount of tension between them during wartime. Hastings (2013, p. 224) notes that BEF commander "Henry Wilson ... once told [General] French that [War Minister] Kitchener was as much the enemy of the BEF as Moltke or Falkenhayn."

[20] See Clausewitz (1976), and for a compelling recent interpretation of Clausewitz, see Wagner (2007).

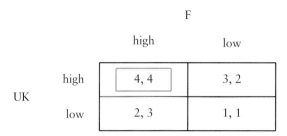

Figure 7.3 Private benefits for cooperation on the Western Front.

what it brought to the table in the first place.[21] There are some ancillary benefits, including developing an experienced army and officer corps on the fly, but the key to Britain's preferences is that fighting can produce *private* benefits that it can't enjoy if it abandons its partner in the field. We call these individual rewards and punishments that accrue, respectively, to those that do and don't contribute **selective incentives**, and they are often critical to seeing collective goods provided.[22]

DEFINITION 7.2   *A **selective incentive** is a private benefit or punishment received by an actor that, respectively, does or doesn't contribute to a collective good.*

To see how selective incentives work, let's look at the game in Figure 7.3, where actions are the same as in Figure 7.2 but where the British and French governments, not their generals, make decisions. The battlefield consequences of high and low efforts remain unchanged, but in this game our players consider the political consequences of their decisions as well. High efforts may be costly, but they carry a specific benefit that can't be attained in any other fashion: a privileged spot at the table to negotiate the peace settlement. Britain and France are colonial empires with global reach, and their interests in the war, both in terms of what can be gained and what can be lost, extend far beyond Flanders and northern France.[23] His own colorful battlefield history notwithstanding, Kitchener saw things differently from London, believing that refusing battle in the short term was contrary to Britain's interests. "Leaving the continental powers to decide the land war for themselves" was out of the question; "Britain already had the lion's share of the world, [and] she intended to keep it and take more if it was offered."[24] Each partner has a stake in

---

[21] See Plokhy (2010) and Tooze (2014).
[22] See Olson (1965, p. 51). And see Ostrom (2015) for a lengthy treatment of institutional solutions to the collective action problem, many of which involve special instances of selective incentives.
[23] See Weitsman (2003, p. 105).
[24] Philpott (2014, p. 67).

overseeing the distribution of the spoils of victory, but skimping on the war effort lowers the chances of victory and means being at best ignored and at worst punished in the peacemaking process. Therefore, both Britain and France place additional political value on sustaining high military effort and avoiding the "politically untenable" course of abandoning the coalition.[25] This reorders their preferences over possible outcomes of the impending Battle of the Marne. Best for each side are mutually high efforts (4), which offers the best chance at battlefield success in addition to guaranteeing political influence after the war, and worst for each side are mutually low efforts, which reduces the chances of both victory and postwar political clout (1). In between these outcomes, though, we can see hints of the old Anlgo-French imperial rivalry, which may reignite if they must carve up the globe as victors.[26] If collective action is to fail at the Battle of the Marne, then each partner prefers that it be the one seen to make the high effort, so each gets 3 for being the only to give high effort and 2 for giving low effort while the other gives high effort.

Figure 7.3 shows we're no longer in the Prisoner's Dilemma world in which each partner would like to husband its own resources while the other bears the burden. Rather, both Britain and France have a dominant strategy of high military effort; no matter what the other does, each is better off giving high effort. If one contributes, then the other must in order to guarantee that it won't be locked out of the settlement, and if the other doesn't contribute, then being the only one making a high effort can still pay political dividends down the line should the tide turn and the Entente negotiate peace as victors. This underlying competition for influence ensures that the coalition's motives are mixed, but since each side wants to reap the rewards of high effort and certainly doesn't want to let its partner be the only one to do so, the equilibrium turns out to be a cooperative one in which the collective good of mutually high efforts is provided. Indeed, the Cabinet's response to Sir John's desire to withdraw the BEF was an explicit order to stay in the line and preserve "Anglo-French solidarity," even at tremendous cost.[27] Joffre may have credited his own impassioned pleas for bringing Sir John along, but of course the decision was the Cabinet's – and it was determined to turn the horrific costs of the early weeks of the war into an eventual strategic and power-political victory.

PROPOSITION 7.1   *The strategy profile (high; high) is a Nash Equilibrium.*

---

[25] Philpott (1996, p. 25).

[26] On the "tacit neutrality" that governs coalition partners, see Gamson (1961), and on the bargaining problems associated with victory, see Wolford (2017).

[27] Hastings (2013, p. 298).

Proof   For (high; high) to be a Nash Equilibrium, it must be the case that

$$u_{\text{UK}}(high;\text{high}) \geq u_{\text{UK}}(low;\text{high}) \quad \text{and} \quad u_{\text{F}}(\text{high};high) \geq u_{\text{F}}(\text{high};low).$$

Both inequalities are satisfied, because $4 \geq 2$. No player has a profitable deviation, so (high; high) is a Nash Equilibrium.   □

The unique Nash Equilibrium of the Entente's game is (high; high), because neither side wishes to reduce its effort and be left out of the political benefits of negotiating the postwar settlement; for each player, $4 > 2$ ensures that these actions are best responses. The contrast with the game in Figure 7.2, where purely military incentives created a collective action problem, is instructive: without the added incentive to gain a leg up in postwar negotiations (a goal that's as farsighted as it is selfish), the British might reduce their effort on the Western Front and force the French to either do the same or bear the whole burden. Strange as it sounds, the interests that Britain and France have in common make cooperation difficult, because each would like to shift the immediate burden of fighting Germany onto its partner. Rather than doom them, their private interests in the outcome of the battle save Britain and France from a major cooperative failure. The divergence in their interests, the pursuit of which demands seats at the peace conference, enables them to cooperate in a dramatic victory that stops the German advance cold at the River Marne – then freezes it in place along the River Aisne for much of the next four years.

7.2.2   Solving the Puzzle: The Central Powers

The Entente averts a major cooperative failure on the Western Front because both the British and the French have private incentives to maintain a high level of effort. On the Eastern Front, the Central Powers aren't so lucky. With Austrian forces divided between Serbian and Russian campaigns – and faring poorly in both – Germany makes the fateful decision to divide its own military efforts, sending armies and attention east in the process of shouldering nearly the entire military, financial, and political burden on the Eastern front – subsidizing, manning, and commanding on its own what should be a collective war effort against Russia. By late September, in fact, a new German army will head East, tasked with plugging gaps in Austria's lines in Galicia and leading a push into Russian Poland.[28] The Central Powers avert mutually low efforts against Russia, but *not* because they overcome their collective action problem together. The Germans simply shoulder most of the burden while Austria staggers from disaster to disaster in its attempts

---

[28] Philpott (2014, p. 47).

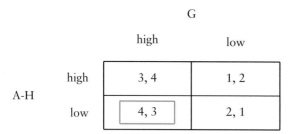

Figure 7.4 Germany shoulders the burden on the Eastern Front.

to both subjugate Serbia and stem the rising Russian tide. This is a stark contrast to the Entente, where both major powers would have chosen high effort regardless of the other's strategy. Our task now is to explain why cooperation fails, leaving Germany holding the bag while its Austrian partner, whose own subpar military might gives it a much smaller margin for error, shuffles along much as it did before.

The game in Figure 7.4 represents the strategic situation facing Germany and Austria in the early weeks of the war, where each hopes to fend off an imposing, westward-marching opponent. The purely military consequences on the front in question, where Germany and Austria each face Russia, are the same as in Figure 7.2; both countries need to resist a Russian invasion, but where Germany is concerned with France and Britain in the West, Austria still has eyes for Serbia to its south. Their chances of successfully repelling the Russian invasion in preparation for their own offensive are greatest when both devote high efforts to the Russian front. The coalition's prospects fall if only one side makes a full effort, and they plummet if neither side chooses high effort. For Austria-Hungary, high effort means wheeling around to face Russia with the full force of its armies, and low effort diverts resources and attention to its adventure in Serbia. The distinction between high and low effort for Germany looks different – it is, after all, also trying to knock France out of the war at the same time. High effort throws as many troops as possible against the Russians, given the constraints imposed by the prioritization of the Western Front, and low effort means stripping the Eastern Front still further of its own forces. Each side would like in principle to shift some of the burden to the other, given its multiple priorities, raising the specter of a collective failure on the Eastern Front.

So far, the Central Powers' collective action problem is little different from the one facing the British and the French. But the political incentives that drive high levels of effort on the Western Front are simply absent in the East. Let's start with Austria, whose leaders don't have quite the same expectations heading into the peace conference that Germany does.

The Dual Monarchy has been the junior partner in the alliance with Germany since its inception. Even in victory, that's likely to remain the case after 1914. It will be Germany that dominates Western Europe, Germany that garrisons new lands in the East, Germany that dominates the Continent economically through its *Mitteleuropa* scheme – and Germany that remains ascendant among the Central Powers.[29] In fact, throughout the war Germany proves to have no compunction about offering Austrian territory to induce neutrals to join the Central Powers (but more on that in Chapter 9).[30] Therefore, Austria has little political incentive to turn its attention away from Serbia, and its preferences resemble those of the collective action problem in Figure 7.2. Its first-best outcome is for Germany to shoulder the burden of high effort alone (4); second best is mutually high efforts, since any outcome with a high German effort is better than the potentially disastrous outcomes without full German participation (3); and mutually low efforts, which allows it to at least deal with Serbia (2), are preferable to being the only power making a high effort against the Russians (1). Regardless of Germany's strategy, then, the Dual Monarchy is better off choosing low effort, focusing its energies on the ostensibly more manageable task of crushing Serbia; it expects no private benefits from contributing to the collective good of holding back the early Russian offensives.

Next, the same disparity of political power in the coalition that limits Austria's political stake in the military effort increases Germany's. If high effort can't be sustained against Russia, then the bid to knock France out of the war early is moot. What's the point of menacing Paris if Tsarist armies are encamped on the outskirts of Berlin? An Austrian collapse at Russian hands would be equally catastrophic, sowing doubts about the Central Powers among neutral states in the Balkans and encouraging them to line up with the Entente.[31] It's therefore best, in German eyes, for both partners to commit as much as they can to the Russian front, though of course it disagrees with Austria over how much effort "can" be spared on the Serbian front. Germany's most preferred outcome is thus a mutually high effort against Russia (4). But given the need to hold back Russia while the plans on the Western Front have a chance to come to fruition, Germany's second-best outcome is to provide a high effort on its own (3), effectively taking over management of the Eastern Front if Austria's effort falters. Germany prefers, however, that it be the one to provide high effort if it's going to be unilateral, rightly not trusting the effectiveness of unaided

---

[29] Herwig (2014, p. 53).
[30] See Weitsman (2003, pp. 93–95) for a discussion of how German dominance of the coalition affected Austria's willingness to cooperate throughout the war.
[31] For more on choosing sides in wars, see Chapter 9.

Austrian arms (2), and of course the outcome it must avoid at all costs is mutually low war efforts (1). Unfettered by competition with its junior partner, Germany cares most about ensuring high military efforts on the Eastern Front, and Figure 7.4 shows that it has a dominant strategy of putting forth high effort.

How do these incentives add up? First, it's worth verifying that (high; high) can't be a Nash Equilibrium, because it sheds light on why the Central Powers fail to cooperate as effectively as the Entente.

PROPOSITION 7.2   *The strategy profile (high; high) is not a Nash Equilibrium.*

Proof   For (high; high) to be a Nash Equilibrium, it must be the case that

$$u_{AH}(high; \text{high}) \geq u_{AH}(low; \text{high}) \quad \text{and} \quad u_G(\text{high}; high) \geq u_G(\text{high}; low).$$

But $u_{AH}(high; \text{high}) \geq u_{AH}(low; \text{high})$ requires $3 \geq 4$, which is untrue. At least one player has a profitable deviation, so (high; high) cannot be a Nash Equilibrium.   □

Unsurprisingly, given its dominant strategy of low effort against Russia, Austria-Hungary has no incentive to devote serious effort in the game in Figure 7.4. Germany would be happy to see this equilibrium played – note that it receives its highest possible payoff if Austria's high effort matches its own – and has no profitable deviation. But Austria manifestly does, and as such it can't credibly promise to throw its share of the weight into the path of the advancing Russian army.

Next, the highlighted strategy profile in Figure 7.4 shows that the unique Nash Equilibrium of this game is (low; high), consistent with our understanding of the failure of collective action on the Eastern Front. Austria-Hungary chooses low effort, securing its first-best outcome of shirking on the Russian front because it knows that Germany will choose high effort on its own (4 > 3); and Germany, aware of Austria's low effort, chooses high effort unilaterally rather than risk a complete collapse on its Eastern Front (3 > 1).

PROPOSITION 7.3   *The strategy profile (low; high) is a Nash Equilibrium.*

Proof   For (low; high) to be a Nash Equilibrium, it must be the case that

$$u_{AH}(low; \text{high}) \geq u_{AH}(high; \text{high}) \quad \text{and} \quad u_G(\text{low}; high) \geq u_G(\text{low}; low).$$

The first inequality is satisfied because $4 \geq 3$, and the second is satisfied because $3 \geq 1$. No player has a profitable deviation, so (low; high) is a Nash Equilibrium.   □

At this equilibrium, Austria can't credibly promise not to split its efforts between Serbia and Russia, while Germany can't promise not to come to Austria's aid when the latter finds itself bogged down in its own two-front war. Germany's stake in the outcome of the Russian war is simply too high, and rather than save itself from the costs of producing the collective good of a stout Eastern Front defense, it provides the good alone and imperfectly, because the alternative is to fatally compromise the overall war effort against the Triple Entente. The Kaiser's troops are fully engaged in Austrian Galicia by September 25, trying to stem the tide against Hapsburg defeats that came early and often, and even as more German units stream in through the fall, Austria tries to invade Serbia a *third* time – still happy to push the heaviest burdens for its own safety onto its more powerful partner.[32]

Even as its front nearly collapses in Galicia, even as it continues to flail against a stout Serbian defense, Vienna refuses the kind of cooperation desired in Berlin. Why? Germany simply has no leverage over the Dual Monarchy, because the leadership in Vienna knows its powerful patron will bear the risks so it doesn't have to. Absent the knowledge that Germany could and would pick up the slack, Austria can take riskier actions than it otherwise would – like skimping on a defensive effort against the massed Russian army – without those guarantees. This isn't the first time that Austria's been emboldened by its dependence on Germany (remember Chapter 4), nor will it be the last, but it offers an interesting contrast to the Entente, where a coalition of political equals could each find a selective incentive to contribute to the collective good. But with Germany poised to dominate Austrian foreign policy even in victory, Austria has no added incentive, like the promise of a commanding presence at the eventual peace conference, to hurl the full force of its military might against the Russians.[33]

7.3 ON SOLVING COLLECTIVE ACTION PROBLEMS

Collective action problems are a persistent feature of politics, from the personal to the national to the global. Yes, coalition partners must solve them if they're to give themselves their best chance at military victory, but

---

[32] See Herwig (2014, pp. 87 and 109).

[33] In matters that'll be important for Chapter 14, the fear of being subordinate to Germany even in victory will lead Vienna to send out (mostly) secret feelers for a separate peace both before and after the Central Powers' victory over Russia in 1918 (Stevenson, 1988).

collective goods exist in a variety of other contexts. At the global level, collective goods include a reliable global trading system, an environment free(ish) from pollution, well-functioning institutions for dispute settlement, and a general absence of disruptive civil and interstate wars – which themselves can have negative consequences for trade, the environment, and physical security well beyond the neighborhoods in which they occur. The problem with each of these goods, as you might suspect, is that their benefits are diffuse and the costs of producing them are concentrated. Any potential beneficiary would like, in principle, to push the burden of providing these goods onto others so that she can enjoy the good for free. That is in principle a sizable obstacle to cooperation, yet international or global collective goods often *are* provided, if sometimes haltingly and incompletely. Our example of coalitions at war can tell us a lot about how collective goods can be provided more generally.

The Entente's collective action problem was solved on the Western Front by selective incentives that outweighed the individual costs of contributing to the war effort. For Britain, and to a lesser extent France, the promise of a seat at the conference table and preserving a reputation as a reliable partner was enough to overcome the short-term costs of fighting. But selective incentives don't have to be rewards; threats of punishment can also encourage contributions to public goods. For example, most of us pay taxes – the sine qua non of government-provided collective goods such as an effective legal system, competitive markets, national security, and usable infrastructure – not because we like paying them, but because there are steep penalties associated with refusing to contribute. Absent a central authority to punish noncontributors, however, punishment as a solution is harder to find in the international system. The League of Nations, which we'll say more about in later chapters, famously failed to check German, Italian, and Japanese expansionism in the 1930s because no single state wanted to pay the costs of confronting them when the effort might've been sloughed off onto others. The World Trade Organization (WTO), however, does have a record of using punishments to encourage states to contribute to the collective good of mutually low trade barriers. When one state imposes a tariff designed to protect domestic producers – sheltering an inefficient business at the expense of its own consumers and the efficiency of global trade – the WTO can authorize retaliation, helping other states target the rule-breaker with tariffs of their own. By coordinating beliefs among other states, it helps ensure that the punisher isn't punished itself by others for starting a trade war, and the risk of authorized retaliation discourages states from imposing some tariffs in the first place.[34] Just as

---

[34] See Reinhardt (2001).

we saw in Chapter 6, commonly agreed rules can help states settle on equilibria in which it's safe to punish, and therefore easy to deter, failures to cooperate. Thus, the collective good of an efficient trading system in which goods can move freely and affordably, but which governments have incentives to flout when it benefits them politically, can be sustained by threats of punishment for those that try to unilaterally cheat. This mechanism is similar to the workings of multilateral arms control (Chapter 3) and neutrality laws (Chapter 6), where threats of punishment may deter unilateral incentives to engage in arms buildups or to expand the scope of ongoing wars.

Next, the ease with which collective action problems may be solved also depends on what we might call the mode of their production.[35] Some goods, like globally low barriers to trade, require the cooperation of large numbers of countries, but others can be provided by fewer states, or *k*-groups, that are uniquely positioned or willing to produce a collective good.[36] Germany on the Eastern Front was a *k*-group of one, in that it could shoulder nearly the entire burden, but larger *k*-groups exist in other contexts. For example, the great powers have in recent years cooperated in curbing piracy off the East African coast, largely because only they possess the requisite naval forces, despite the fact that numerous other countries benefit from such policing. Likewise, a small group of wealthy countries contributes to the International Monetary Fund in return for influence over the disbursement of funds, in hopes of providing the global collective good of a stable international monetary system.[37] Finally, hegemonic states that sit at the top of the global power hierarchy, like the United States after the Second World War and Great Britain before the First, often shoulder a disproportionate burden in securing freedom of the seas, setting global economic standards, and providing order far from home to keep the global economy humming.[38] They're uniquely positioned, thanks to their wealth and power, *and* uniquely compensated, granted prestige and authority over others' policies, for providing these collective goods – but as we've already seen, especially in Chapter 4, the rights and privileges accruing to the states at the top of the global power hierarchy are so lucrative as to create some dangerous competition for spots at the top.

Finally, some goods require multiple different inputs to be produced, and when states differ in their ability to provide each component of the

[35] With all due apologies to Mr. Marx, of course.
[36] The terminology of a *k*-group is due to Schelling (1978, pp. 213–243) and is also related directly to collective action by Hardin (1982). Olson's original term appears to have been "intermediate" group.
[37] Debates over the effectiveness of the IMF notwithstanding – and there are many, some useful and some less so – all countries are generally better off when the number of them experiencing financial crises is minimized.
[38] See Gilpin (1981), Keohane (1984), and Kydd (2005).

good, they can find cooperation relatively easy. Stepping back from the narrow question of individual Entente contributions to the war on land, Britain, France, and Russia also had to wage a naval war if the Austrian and German fleets were to be neutralized and the flow of supplies both to and between the Entente powers sustained.[39] The Russian navy had received less attention than the army in the post-1905 recovery, and the French fleet, though no slouch, would be unable to bottle up the Austrians in the Adriatic, guard ships ferrying troops from Algeria to the homeland, and defend the Channel coast. But Britain, a minor land power yet dominant naval power, was uniquely positioned to shoulder more of the naval burden in the North Sea while France and Russia made proportionately larger contributions to the land war. In this case, no partner could safely shift the burden of its unique contribution onto another – like Germany and Austria tried to do with their nominally interchangeable land forces – and specialization cemented a basically sustainable collective Entente war effort even beyond Russia's spasmodic, catastrophic defeat in 1917–1918. Specialization has also played a prominent role in subsequent collective military efforts, from the American specialization in naval warfare and strategic bombing in NATO war plans during the Cold War, to Kuwait's provision of basing and staging support for the 2003 Iraq War while the United States and Britain provided the combat power, and to the NATO intervention in the Libyan civil war, where the United States provided refueling and targeting support to European warplanes flying most of the combat sorties. By contrast, where contributions require less specialization, like the NATO effort in Afghanistan in the wake of the toppling of the Taliban government, cooperation is more difficult.[40] Therefore, when countries can specialize in the production of parts of a collective good, they can sustain collective action even when the private costs of contributing are large, because there may be no one else onto which they can shift the burden.

Whether through selective incentives, the emergence of k-groups, or specialization in tasks, collective action problems are generally solved by altering individual, private incentives to cooperate. Sometimes, those individual incentives can come in the form of genuine civic-mindedness, which makes some individuals very willing to bear the burdens of contributing to the public good; it's possible, even perfectly rational, to enjoy bearing the burdens of contributing a collective good. But in many cases, especially the high-stakes military-diplomatic ones on which our story is focused, the costs of contributing to a public good can be more daunting – even

---

[39] Much of the discussion of naval strategy in this book draws on Sondhaus's (2014) recent, and lucid, study.

[40] For a thorough and insightful treatment, see Saideman and Auerswald (2014).

when survival is nominally at stake, like it was for the Dual Monarchy in 1914. When the costs of contributing to a collective good are sufficiently daunting, countries require some kind of individual compensation, a private benefit to activate (or less charitably, provide a rationalizeable story for) public-mindedness. Political authority over the spoils of victory; the prestige, rights, and privileges that come with the role of global hegemon; and the knowledge that, without one's own specialized contribution, the whole effort might fail have all proven effective (at times) in getting otherwise hesitant states to pull their weight in the production of international collective goods.

7.4 COALITIONS AND INTERNATIONAL POLITICS I

We encountered the great power coalitions at the center of this chapter when they were already at war, but military coalitions shape international politics even during peacetime, because they establish expectations about the sides, costs, and outcomes of possible wars. Coalitions support the balance of power (recall Definition 6.1), which provides a rough guide to who gets what in international relations. The Entente and the Central Powers are specific examples of the more general class of military coalitions, which we'll define as groups of states that will wage war together (if necessary) to achieve a common goal. That goal may be defending, unhinging, or restoring the balance of power, securing or reversing territorial conquests, bolstering or toppling foreign governments, or keeping the peace between other warring factions. The waste of war ensures that coalitions hope to achieve these goals without having to fight for them, but if it comes to a contest of arms, fighting with partners allows countries to bring more power to bear than they could alone. Like arms races (Definition 3.1), coalition-building is an attempt to shape the outcomes of possible (and sometimes ongoing) wars. As we've seen, however, sustaining military cooperation when threats are called in and armies must enter the field can be a major obstacle even when coalition partners share common, high-stakes goals like the defeat of a powerful enemy. The difference between stability and upheaval, between peaceful change and war, often comes down to just how well coalition partners can secure, sustain, and reward cooperation.[41]

DEFINITION 7.3   *A **military coalition** is a group of states that threatens (and may use) collective military force for common ends.*

---

[41] For an expanded analysis of what military coalitions are and how they behave, see Wolford (2015). For earlier treatments, see Starr (1972) and Ward (1982).

Coalitions have participated in 40 percent of all interstate wars since the final defeat of Napoleon in 1815[42] and in about one quarter of all crises that could've escalated to war since the end of the Second World War.[43] The average military coalition has two members, but a few are massive. Roughly a dozen states participated on the side of the Entente in the First World War, as well as in American-led campaigns against Iraq (1991) and Kosovo (1999) in the first decade after the Cold War, and nearly two dozen contributed to Allied victory in the Second World War.[44] Coalition members can contribute combat forces, like the British and Americans during the invasion of Iraq in 2003, as well as basing, staging, and logistical support, like Kuwait in the same war. Coalition partners increase available military power, reduce the costs of war, and even help legitimize a side's aims. But when coalitions bargain with other states over withdrawing from or ceding territory, submitting to weapons inspections, ending ethnic cleansing, replacing their governments, or ending support for foreign rebels, members also negotiate internally – over the demands of the target, the sizes of their contributions, and the distribution of the spoils. When they work together, coalitions have a staggering record of military success.[45] Nonetheless, partners often compete to limit the costs of cooperation, from blood and treasure to destruction and displacement, and the consequences of that competition can be dire.

Some of the oldest work on the topic focuses on balancing coalitions, or those groups of states that band together to deter (and, if that fails, defeat) challenges to the balance of power.[46] When the prevailing international hierarchy is defended by a strong, well-established coalition – say, the American alliance network in the post–World War II era – then challenges can be discouraged, a balance of power sustained, and great power peace preserved.[47] But when the status quo coalition's ability to cooperate is uncertain, potential challengers may become optimistic that they can safely demand more territory or prestige (see Chapter 5). Dissatisfied powers like Nazi Germany, Imperial Japan, the Soviet Union, Communist China, and post-Yeltsin Russia, for example, have all tested the limits of the status quo coalition's cooperation when its ability to act collectively has fallen into question. Even when the status quo coalition's membership is changing or growing more powerful, potential challengers may be tempted into preventive wars (recall Chapter 2) to take advantage of temporary weakness or to arrest a slide down the rungs of the

---

[42] See Sarkees and Wayman (2010).
[43] See Wolford (2015, chapter 2), Wilkenfeld and Brecher (2010), and Palmer et al. (2015).
[44] Again, see Sarkees and Wayman (2010).
[45] See Morey (2016).
[46] See, e.g., Morgenthau (1967) and Waltz (1979), in particular.
[47] For a similar argument, see Rosecrance (2002).

global hierarchy. It was, after all, Russia's growing power and Britain's embrace of the Entente that helped drive Imperial Germany to challenge the international hierarchy in 1914. Great power politics are multilateral and more complex than the simpler models of crisis bargaining we analyzed in Chapters 2 and 5, but the frictions that drive states to war are the same: the risk that a balance of power collapses into violence rises and falls with changes in the expected outcomes of hypothetical great power wars.[48] The specific sources of uncertainty or shifting power may differ in a multilateral context, but the reasons they undermine efficient bargains and drive states to war are the same.

Coalitions are most effective at deterring challenges to the status quo when they can solve an acute collective action problem. Containing a rising or revisionist challenger may mean the difference between peace and war, a matter of life and death for some states, but it's also expensive and dangerous. Even states fully invested in preserving the status quo prefer to pass the buck if they can, letting others take up the slack of nipping nascent challenges in the bud.[49] When revisionists find the status quo coalition's ability to cooperate wanting, they test, probe, and try to peel off its members in attempts to undo the balance of power. Nazi Germany famously did this by first remilitarizing its western frontier in violation of the Treaty of Versailles, then winning French and British consent to its annexation of Czechoslovakia, and capping it off by colluding with Soviet Russia, an ostensibly implacable ideological foe, to invade and partition Poland in 1939 – shattering the interwar balance of power and giving Germany a free hand to invade and conquer France the following year.[50] In the early twenty-first century, Russia, an autocratic power stripped of its empire by the collapse of the Soviet Union, attempted something similar, searching for fractures in the Atlantic alliance (that is, NATO) after invading Crimea and participating in a civil war in Ukraine. Russia threatened the Baltic States and supported right-wing nationalist and racist movements throughout Europe and North America, including France and the United States, all in hopes of undermining the coherence of the Western, democratic bloc arrayed against it. As of this writing, its success in doing so remains an open

---

[48] And if the Marxists in the room will allow us to do some minor violence to the basics of materialism, the international balance of coalitions, or the sides in a hypothetical war, are the substructure of international politics, and the bargains struck because of those expectations – and the consequences of trying to strike bargains inconsistent with those expectations (war) – are the superstructure of international politics.

[49] See Christensen and Snyder (1990) and Mearsheimer (2001).

[50] For a riveting account of Germany's "strange victory" over France, see May (2000). For a long and accessible history of the global Second World War, see Hastings (2012), and for a treatment of its place in a half-century of conflict in Asia, see Paine (2012).

question. But what separates those coalitions that can credibly promise to cooperate from those that can't?

We can answer this question by breaking it into two components: coalitions must first (1) solve their collective action problem and then (2) convince potential opponents that they've solved it. We can immediately recognize an information problem here (Definition 5.5), because a coalition would obviously *claim* to an enemy that it's solved its collective action problem even if it hasn't. As we saw in Chapter 5, convincing an opponent of a willingness to wage a wasteful war – and in the case of a coalition, wage a wasteful war *together* – requires taking costly actions that one wouldn't otherwise take. One way in which states try to solve both problems at once are alliances, written agreements by which they codify wartime obligations.[51]

DEFINITION 7.4   *An **alliance** is a written agreement that stipulates how states are to behave during wartime.*

Alliances are contracts; they're viewed by their signatories as legally binding, they're (typically) part of the public record, and they stipulate what actions states are obliged to take in the event of certain contingencies. In a defensive alliance, for example, states may agree to come to one another's aid in the event of armed attack by another state. The Triple Alliance out of which the Central Powers emerged in 1914 was a nominally defensive alliance, as was the Franco-Russian alliance that threatened to encircle it. Contemporary examples include alliances between the United States and Japan, the United States and South Korea, and NATO, each a key element in the balance of power after the Second World War. Alliances solve the collective action problem in part by their very publicity, as partners stake their individual credibility in making future commitments on their willingness to honor their obligations.[52] This addresses each part of the information problem. First, by giving each member a private stake in coming to its partners' defense, alliances create selective incentives that facilitate cooperation. Second, by making these incentives public, they also signal to potential enemies that the coalition is likely to fight together when their commitments are activated.

Alliances aren't perfect solutions, though. Even allied coalitions, a minority of all coalitions formed since 1946, face the problem of distributing the costs and benefits of war when conflict is imminent. Britain and France debated how best to face Nazi Germany after declaring war in 1939 despite a preexisting alliance designed with precisely that

---

[51] See Leeds, Long, and Mitchell (2000) and Morrow (2000), and keep this definition in mind the next time you hear *alliance* or *ally* tossed around casually on the news.
[52] See Leeds (1999), Gibler (2008), and Benson (2012).

contingency in mind,[53] the United States limited its war aims against Iraq in 1991 in order to secure Saudi support,[54] and in 1999 Britain and the United States agreed to threaten not a ground campaign but an air war to coerce Serbian forces to leave the breakaway province of Kosovo.[55] Indeed, since the costs of war fall unevenly across their members, coalitions must sometimes water down their threats, commit to cheaper military options, or limit their war aims in order to keep the costs of cooperation down. As a result, they may secure the cooperation of their more hesitant partners, yet only create doubts in their opponents' minds about their willingness to see a war through to its conclusion. Like Iraq in 1991 and Serbia in 1999, a coalition's opponent may not doubt the threat of war but may suspect that the coalition won't have the stomach to wage a long war, leading opponents to choose intransigent bargaining positions that increase the risk of a war in which they suspect they can simply wait out a fractious coalition.[56] Coalitions thus face a trade-off between solving their own collective action problems and convincing their opponents of just how willing they are to wage a long, bloody war.

Coalitions are sometimes more, but occasionally less, than the sum of their parts. When they can publicly solve the collective action problems that will tempt their members to skimp on war efforts when their promises are called in, they can successfully deter their opponents from seeking to overturn the status quo or convince their opponents to revise the status quo peacefully in their favor. Alliances can help by creating private costs for refusing to cooperate, but sometimes coalitions must solve the collective action problem by limiting the costs of cooperation, which can sow the very doubts about their resolve, of which they wish to disabuse their opponents. As we'll see in later chapters, the specific challenges of coalition warfare, from sustaining cooperation to compensating partners for their wartime burdens, will be a persistent part of the narrative of the First World War, the negotiations of the peace settlement, and the challenges of preserving that settlement in the interwar years.

7.5 **CONCLUSION**

From the first shells lobbed by Austrian guns into Belgrade to the last exchange of fire on the Western Front on November 11, 1918, the First World War was a contest of coalitions. Even (and especially) when the stakes are high, coalition warfare produces collective action problems that

---

[53] See Hastings (2012, chapters 2 and 3).
[54] See Atkinson (1993) and, for an explicit theoretical treatment, Wolford (2015, chapter 3).
[55] See Clark (2001, chapters 6 and 7).
[56] See Wolford (2015, chapter 4).

talented generals and politicians can find it difficult to solve. As evidenced by the epigraphs that opened this chapter, even those leaders that manage successful coalition war efforts (and were part of two) can find them frustrating and maddening. When Count von Schlieffen chose not to share too many of the details of his plan with Austrian officers, he noted presciently,

> alliances produce relatively little owing to the desire of each member to pass the lion's share of the work on to the others [and] to reserve for oneself spoils.[57]

Schlieffen's pessimism would prove warranted on the Eastern Front, but in this chapter we showed that coalition warfare wasn't all doom and gloom for the Entente on the Western Front. Yet it wasn't public but private gains, not collective but individual goals, not charitable but selfish motives, that solved the Entente's collective action problem on the Western Front in 1914. Britain and France had strong individual motives to contribute to the joint war effort, but Austria's subordinate role in its alliance with Germany effectively doomed the latter to shouldering most of the burden against Russia – precisely because Austria gained little extra from putting in effort that Germany would eventually devote itself.

The picture we've painted thus far of Entente cooperation is a rosy one, but it's worth keeping in mind that the war in the West began with a series of crushing German victories and humbling French defeats. Likewise, while the Austrians struggled mightily against the Russians in Galicia, Germany would respond to the Russian invasion of East Prussia with a quickly lionized (if somewhat exaggerated) victory at the Battle of Tannenberg that would begin to build the legend of the two men that would soon come to dominate the German war effort: Paul von Hindenburg and Erich Ludendorff. If the Central Powers needed a quick victory before the full weight of Entente wealth and manpower could be brought to bear, it looked in the early weeks of the war like they just might pull it off. By late August, though, their prospects had changed, with Germany seeming to snatch stalemate (in a two-front war, no less) from the jaws of what should've been an intoxicating victory. In the next chapter, we'll develop the game-theoretic tools that'll help us figure out just how the fast-moving, if historically bloody, war of maneuver that seemed to favor Germany in August turned into the static, attritional struggle that would over the long run favor its enemies.

---

[57] Quoted in Herwig (1990, p. 273).

8 The Best-Laid Plans: Attrition's Static Horror

> *No plan of operations extends with certainty beyond the first encounter with the enemy's main strength.*
>
> Helmuth von Moltke (the Elder),
> *Moltke on the Art of War*

> *But perhaps I was destined for a more glorious end, one worthy of envy, as Victor Hugo said – like, for example, being pounded, shredded, asphyxiated, blown to bits in a cloud of smoke.*
>
> Corporal Louis Barthas,
> *Poilu*

This chapter addresses one of the First World War's most defining tragedies and enduring controversies: the singular, apparently inescapable horror of attritional warfare on an industrialized battlefield.

> Why did the First World War become a grinding contest of attrition from which the belligerent parties couldn't seem to escape?

Trench warfare on the Western Front, with its long stretches of boredom punctuated by deafening artillery barrages, panicked searches for gas masks, and futile dashes "over the top" across No Man's Land, was static and bloody and indecisive. A nearly uninterrupted front of opposing trenches snaked from the Franco-Swiss border to the Belgian coast, the neat circular line of siege warfare cut, mangled, and draped across the continent. A drawn-out wearing down process supported by sustained industrial mobilization, what the French called *grignotage* and the Germans *Materialschlacht*, dominated both Western and Eastern Fronts for nearly four years, despite the availability of heretofore unimaginable firepower, rapid communications, and – thanks to railways – mobility. Our task in this chapter is to explain why a war that most hoped to win quickly could begin with so much movement, embodied by the German army advancing within twenty-five miles of Paris scarcely a month after declaring war, before settling into the slow-burning, nightmarish, attritional stalemate that would be broken only years later. Solving this puzzle will teach us a few things:

- why countries deliberately create uncertainty about their strategies;
- how attrition, for all its horror, became a stable (if costly) equilibrium;
- why both Western and Eastern Fronts proved equally indecisive;
- how military secrecy can create the uncertainty that causes war.

By tracing the evolution of the lightning advances of the early weeks of the war into an enduring, painful stalemate, we'll show how France was so grievously outflanked by the German sweep through Belgium, how it was able to recover so quickly and pull off a remarkable victory on the River Marne, and how Germany made the subsequent decision to retreat to the River Aisne and dig in – to bite and hold in the Belgian and French lands it still controlled. We'll show that attrition was a decision made on both sides to *save* lives, to reduce the rate of loss that defined the early battles of the war in which frontal assaults ran into the teeth of modern firepower and, even if successful, were impossible to follow up in the face of swift and savage counterattacks. Strategies of attrition were in equilibrium for the first three years of the war because the best available alternatives would court disaster. Attrition was a trap from which the belligerents would find it remarkably difficult to escape, even as its promises of victory could be realized only well past the horizon when it first settled in during the winter of 1914–1915. We'll also address the age-old question of just how "futile" attritional strategies were, how the Eastern Front could look so much different than the West and yet prove no more decisive, and how military strategy affects broader patterns of international politics.

> **Key Terms for Chapter 8**
> - Strategy of Attrition
> - Pure Strategy
> - Mixed Strategy
> - Mixed Strategy Nash Equilibrium

8.1   FROM MANEUVER TO ATTRITION

Chapter 6 introduced us to one small part of the great Allied retreat, where French and British troops lay in wait east of Paris for the unsuspecting tip of the German spear. The Battle of the Marne followed the first few bloody, confused weeks of fighting generally called the Battle of the Frontiers, when the French and German war plans first collided. These intricate plans, difficult to change once set in motion and predicated on the possibility of rapid victories that manifestly didn't come to pass, have received a century's worth of scrutiny, scorn, and regret over their costs and apparent shortcomings. France and Russia planned to go immediately on the offensive once war had been declared, the former getting out of the gate first while the latter's mobilization spun slowly up. Germany, anticipating a two-front war, went with Moltke's updates of the Schlieffen Plan, named for the former Chief of the General Staff that proposed a radical solution to encirclement by the Franco-Russian alliance. This plan, as we've noted, envisioned a swift march through neutral Belgium (Schlieffen's original also envisaged going through the Netherlands) that would allow a colossal envelopment and rapid destruction of the French Army, mirroring Carthage's famous victory over Rome at Cannae in 216 BCE.[1] With France crushed by the fortieth day after mobilization, the extensive German rail network would then swing the bulk of the invading forces back east in time to join the Hapsburg armies already working to stifle what was expected to be a slower-moving Russian mobilization. Keeping our focus momentarily on the Western Front, Germany hoped to swing north of the main concentration of French forces, while France hoped to drive into and smash the German center, opening up a route to retaking Alsace-Lorraine while Russian columns took advantage of the division of German forces to march through East Prussia and toward Berlin. Those were the plans, at least.

The early weeks of the war, especially in the West, seemed to vindicate Moltke's modifications to Schlieffen's concept (recall Map 7.1).[2] After the daring capture of the Belgian fortress of Liège, German armies poured across the Belgian and Luxembourgish frontiers, throwing back Belgian defenders and, fearing *francs-tireurs*, burning villages and executing civilians in atrocities that would prove a gold mine for Entente recruitment propaganda throughout the war. (Interestingly, crimes against civilians ceased almost entirely once German forces crossed into France.)

[1] This battle might be among the most fetishized in the European military tradition, and not without reason. But its hold on the German general staff in the First World War might've been a bit too strong (Keegan, 2000).

[2] The Schlieffen Plan has been controversial from the beginning. After making the postwar rhetorical rounds as the plan that, if followed properly, would've won the war, its true shape took form only after its discovery in the American archive of documents captured during the Second World War (Zuber, 1999). Its implementation in 1914 had been modified substantially from its origins – reasonably so, since Russia had recovered from the 1905 weakness on which Schlieffen's memorandum was predicated. But that hasn't stopped political scientists from arguing whether its focus on the offensive, whether or not it would end the war or merely set up the long struggle against Russia, caused the war (Lieber 2007; Snyder and Lieber 2008). As we'll see later in this chapter, it's not clear that beliefs in the importance of going on the offensive were enough to cause war absent shifting power between Austria and Serbia.

While Germany exulted in initial successes in Belgium, French troops crossed into Alsace-Lorraine, only to withdraw after the Battle of Mulhouse. In a symptom of widespread early optimism, the Kaiser declared Germany's successful defense of Lorraine as "the greatest victory in the history of warfare."[3] Joffre's Plan XVII, which envisioned a drive into the German center, the hinge around which the expected Belgian crossing would swing, proved disastrous. French troops, badly mauled in their first encounter with the German army, nonetheless stayed on the attack only to suffer shocking casualties at the hands of accurate rifle fire and, especially, the machine gun. In fact, the first weeks on the Western Front, in which massed frontal attacks confronted well-positioned machine gun and artillery fire, would see the highest casualty rates of the war until the last desperate months of 1918. Not until numerous reports came in confirming that German forces were marching much farther into Belgium than Plan XVII accounted for, that Moltke was attempting a more ambitions envelopment than Joffre expected, did the Entente realize its own peril. The French government abandoned Paris hastily for Bordeaux, Sir John French started brooding about withdrawal, and the onus of saving France fell upon the broad shoulders of General Joseph Joffre.

Once Joffre realized that the main German effort was swinging much farther north than Plan XVII anticipated, he ordered a large-scale retreat that would set up the fateful Battle of the Marne in early September. The French rail network would allow an astonishingly rapid redeployment of forces to the west, complemented by the BEF halting its own retreat (recall Chapter 7) and the creation of a new French Sixth Army northeast of Paris, of which German forces were as yet unaware. After turning south well short of Paris, deviating from the plan to pursue what they thought was a beaten French Army, German forces would find themselves losing coordination as Germany's First Army wheeled to face French Sixth, creating a gap between itself and the trailing German Second into which the recommitted BEF could march almost unopposed.[4] In response, German forces would beat their own (soon to be controversial) retreat, initially establishing themselves on the heights overlooking the River Aisne. But unlike the Entente after the Battle of the Frontiers, they didn't prepare an immediate counterattack. Rather, German troops got the order to dig in, to bite and hold in place. Early trenches were hasty, shallower than the near-permanent underground residences they would soon become. Nonetheless, the grim logic by which both sides would confront one another for

---

[3] The parvenu trumpets *all* events, even failures, as triumphs and cares not when opponents point out the truth; the enthusiasm of his supporters is all that matters. Wilhelm would make similar mistakes in 1918, with the irony even thicker.

[4] See Hastings (2013, chapters 9 and 10).

the next several years was evident as soon as the First Battle of Ypres in November, when the British and Germans traded artillery bombardments designed to soften up the other's defenses, only to find that infantry still fell in large numbers before dug-in machine guns and high-volume rifle fire. The first few weeks of the war made one thing abundantly clear: defense, for the foreseeable future, would dominate offense on the modern battlefield.

Trench warfare commands most of the attention in the popular Western narrative of the Great War, and not without reason. To the soldiers that sheltered in, scampered between, leapt out of, and died trying to reach the trenches, the Great War was a horrific, dehumanizing, pitiless folly.[5] No single dash through the mud and craters and rotting corpses of No Man's Land between opposing trenches (sometimes as few as thirty yards apart), no breakthrough, however dearly purchased, proved more than a prelude to the next plunge, the next feverish dash, the next collapse in the face of a withering counterattack. Trenches were protected in front by tangles of barbed (and sometimes piano) wire, sloping parapets, and machine gun emplacements; behind by secondary and tertiary trenches, staggered machine gun emplacements with fields of fire designed to punish enemy breakthroughs, and farther back by artillery that would either target attackers, other artillery batteries, or the opponent's wire. Trench warfare, whether in the chalky soil of the Belgian plain or the scorched beaches of the Gallipoli peninsula, promised little more than misery for the troops in the line. The mud, the stench, the fear, and the boredom – to say nothing of the shell-shock caused by hours of artillery bombardment – became a metaphor for the war itself: interminable, uncivilized, and apparently pointless. And that only makes the widespread commitment to attrition all the more puzzling.

The First Battle of Ypres in October and November 1914 helped open the war's attritional phase, but the 300-day Battle of Verdun – the longest battle of the war – would see Germany go on the offensive with the explicit aim not to conquer more French territory but, in the words of General Erich von Falkenhayn, to "bleed the French army white." If Joffre's army couldn't be smashed in the field, surrounded, or forced to surrender, it would have to be destroyed, man-by-man. With the Eastern Front relatively quiet after a major Austro-German offensive near Gorlice-Tarnów in Poland failed to shatter the Russian army, and with a sizable Entente offensive likely in the works for mid-1916, Falkenhayn embraced attrition wholeheartedly, hoping to break the French army in the field or, at a

---

[5] Unless you happened to be Ernst Jünger. The author of *In Storms of Steel* seems to have been one of the only frontline soldiers to have loved combat in the First World War.

minimum, the public's will to continue the fight on the home front. His orders famously described an attack only "in the *direction* of Verdun" [emphasis mine]. This lack of a clear aim to capture fresh territory has brought him in for no small amount of postwar criticism, not unlike British General Sir Douglas Haig's characterization of his own strategy as simply "killing Germans." Capturing Verdun was beside the point, which was simply to draw in and kill as many Frenchmen as possible. Both France and Germany suffered hundreds of thousands of casualties over the nine-month battle in which fortresses like Douaumont and Vaux changed hands indecisively and nearby villages were reduced to fields of craters that bore more resemblance to the pitted surface of the moon than lush, green north-eastern France.[6] The battle would lead France to ask Russia and Britain to rush the launches of their own planned offensives to relieve pressure around Verdun, resulting in the First Battle of the Somme in the West and an initially successful but (again) ultimately indecisive Russian offensive named after its commander, General Aleksei Brusilov, in the East. Verdun would not break the French army as Falkenhayn had hoped, and when German forces broke off the battle in December, little had changed on the ground. France held on to both Verdun and its will to fight, and the war continued with no end in sight. No one seemed to have a solution to the problem of breaking the attritional deadlock.

Before we analyze it in detail, it's worth pinning down exactly what we mean when we talk about "attrition" and military strategies built around it. Its Latin root is *atterere*, which means "to rub against" in order to create friction, or simply "waste," depending on the context.[7] The French called it *grignotage*, which translates as "gnawing away," the Germans *Materialschlacht*, which ties the importance of industrial output to *Shlacht*: "battle" or, as part of this compound word, "slaughter." Each term gets at the ends of a **strategy of attrition** – that is, to wear down or sap the enemy's ability to resist – but the second pillar of attritional strategy is that the pressure must be sustained, pinning the enemy in place with constant pressure, forcing her to give battle and use up her reserves in the process.

DEFINITION 8.1   *A **strategy of attrition** prioritizes wearing down an enemy's ability to continue the fight through sustained pressure.*

This sustained, if at times low-intensity, pressure, aimed not at an immediate military decision but at laying the groundwork for one in the distant

---

[6] It's still striking today, where fields of craters now have a light covering of grass and the occasional marker showing which buildings used to stand where in now nonexistent villages.

[7] Or, if I'm being honest, one uses Merriam-Webster for the origin of *attrition* and Google Translate for the translation of *atterere* into English.

(sometimes years-distant) future by chewing up an opponent's ability to continue the fight, is the essence of attrition. It aims to win only one battle: the last one. To the men in the trenches and impatient civilians suffering the privations of war at home, its application in any one battle or for any short period of time smacks of giving up – of abandoning any pursuit of what we'd conventionally call military "victory" (for more on that, see Chapter 11). We'll see in this section that attrition can, indeed, produce long and bloody wars that stay locked in stalemates but that it has its own grim strategic logic.

But why *this* set of strategies? Why did the war settle into an apparently mindless attritional contest? Surely *someone* could've come up with a better way. One possibility is the quality of 1914's military leaders. From the trenches to the streets to the halls of government, the men that managed the war – generals and civilians alike – were called butchers, murderers, devils, and fools. Even before peace negotiations could get under way, civilians chided generals for their lack of imagination, their blindness, and their detachment, and doing so was good politics; even the victors looked with regret on the appalling costs of the war. But good politics is rarely good political science. This criticism assumes that the generals *wanted* attrition rather than entertain the possibility that they might've merely tolerated it, accepted it as the least bad of their options – that it was a tragic equilibrium, not a tragic failure of imagination. Another possibility is that the force-to-space ratio on the Western Front, a short front that ran from the Swiss border to the Belgian coast, packed densely with men and steel, made a war of "maneuver" as opposed to attrition impossible. But this distinction between maneuver and attrition doesn't get us very far once we look beyond the Western Front. Maneuver was easier in the wide open, less populated spaces of the East, but even the dramatic 300-mile advance enabled by the Central Powers' Gorlice-Tarnów Offensive of early 1915 failed to break the Russian army, which escaped "beaten but not destroyed" despite suffering around 2 *million* casualties.[8] Their operational differences to the contrary, both fronts were indecisive, and in the case of Germany, their battles were planned and directed by many of the same individuals. It strains credulity to say that Ludendorff and Falkenhayn were different men in Belgium and France, East Prussia and Romania. In East and West, breakthroughs would either quickly outrun supply lines or face savage counterattacks enabled by the rapid movement of men and materiel behind the front, leading both rival coalitions to focus not on conquering territory, not on defeating their opponents in dramatic battles of encirclement, but of wearing them down, killing more men than

---

[8] Herwig (2014, pp. 144–149).

could eventually be replaced in a long, slow war of attrition. Our challenge is to explain why attrition emerged and why its grip on strategy was so tight.

8.2 EXPLAINING ATTRITION

Our goal is to explain the onset and survival of attrition as an equilibrium, as the product of strategies accepted by calculating and frugal leaders as a best response to an opponent's strategy and over alternatives that would have been even worse – not as the product of an implausibly collective folly or failure of leadership.[9] To do that, we'll leverage some crucial facts about the early weeks of the war, in which attrition hadn't yet been embraced, for comparison to the fateful decisions over the fall and winter of 1914–1915, whose major battles are given in Figure 8.1, that would define the remainder of the war. This requires that we frame our initial puzzle a little differently.

PUZZLE 8.1   *What led all the belligerents to adopt strategies of attrition?*

Our question emphasizes two key ideas: (1) every belligerent embraced attrition, not because its leaders had an inherent preference for it (their individual hopes for quick victories to *avoid* attrition certainly belie that), but (2) because it seemed a better option than trying to win the war quickly, which would have entailed battles that were far costlier and less predictable. As we'll see, the war would've been attritional whether or not the belligerents accepted static warfare; they simply would've sustained intolerable casualty rates if they'd tried to remain on permanent offensives. If we can explain the choice to simply "kill Germans" or "bleed France" as part of an equilibrium, we can not only explain attrition's onset and duration but also its implications for how the war would eventually end – that is, what it would take for at least one side to abandon its commitment to attrition for a different strategy aimed not at bleeding but actually, finally smashing the other side. We'll analyze a pair of games that allows us to get into the heads of generals and politicians, to think through their dilemmas in "real time," and to gain some fresh insight into an old question.

We'll begin with the primary alternative to attrition that the Russians, Germans, Austrians, French, Italians, Ottomans, and British all attempted in the early months of the war: an all-out commitment to the offensive, to massed assaults sometimes sought head-on and sometimes pursued

---

[9] Really. "Failure of leadership" is typically a vacuous criticism, just like a "lack of political will." Both are less precise ways of saying "she didn't have any interest in doing what I wanted her to do, and I, one of her opponents, disapprove of the choice she made."

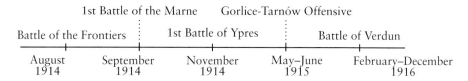

Figure 8.1 The path to attrition, 1914–1916.

through encirclement, in the impatient pursuit of a decisive engagement. We'll write down a variant of what's known as the Colonel Blotto game, which reveals some of the challenges of choosing military strategies but also explains how Germany would seemingly achieve so much through mobile warfare in the first weeks of implementing Moltke's updated Schlieffen Plan. We'll show that initial German successes and French setbacks were both the result of a fog of war created by the actions of both sides, of similar gambles, neither of which ultimately paid off once the realities of industrial warfare made themselves manifest. In the process, we'll see that much of the postwar effort to judge the acumen of First World War generals based on the outcomes of their early campaigns isn't all that illuminating. After a rapid Entente retreat and French-directed redeployment, which demonstrated in dramatic fashion the difficulties of following up offensive successes, both sides abandoned the consistent use of massed frontal assaults in favor of strategies of attrition. We'll show that attrition as an equilibrium can be understood as a conscious move away from the costlier strategies that preceded it. Thanks to the dominance of defensive technology in the early years of the war, all belligerents accepted (with varying degrees of reluctance) the necessity of attritional strategies designed to limit their own casualties while eating slowly away at the enemy's reserves, forgoing all-out bids for victory in return for trying to hasten the other side's collapse. We'll see that this decision not to seek ultimate victory in every battle explains postwar recriminations over the war's staggering costs and how the distinction between strategies of maneuver and attrition can be false. We'll also presage the manner in which the war eventually ends for both Russia, whose armies retire (but aren't wiped out) in 1917, and Germany, whose will to fight is exhausted (even as its armies remain nominally intact) in 1918.[10]

8.2.1 Solving the Puzzle: The Frontiers

The conventional story of the Great War's beginnings is familiar, rooted in plans for maneuver warfare characterized by rapid, rail-mobile advances

---

[10] On the latter, see Chapter 14.

G

	left	right
left	1, 0	0, 1
right	0, 1	1, 0

F

Figure 8.2 Military strategies on the Western Front.

that can encircle and destroy enemy formations (if they don't surrender). What some analysts call the "cult of the offensive" seems to grip every belligerent general staff.[11] But the opening weeks are a study in dashed hopes. (I say "hopes" here because conventional claims of a short war illusion among the relevant decision-makers are probably overstated.[12]) Each belligerent hopes, aims, and very much tries desperately to win quickly, but there are few illusions about the consequences of a bid that fails before Christmas: a long, bloody contest that will, in Bethmann's words, destroy European civilization. That no belligerent succeeds in its attempts to win the war quickly seems at first surprising, especially given Germany's early successes in slicing through Belgian and French resistance at Joffre's left. But we can begin to make sense of the patterns of early successes and setbacks – and how they turned eventually into a lengthy attritional death-grapple – if we take seriously the basic strategic problem of allocating forces for attack or defense. Working out the strategic logic of the Battle of the Frontiers, the first and last gasp of maneuver warfare on the Western Front until 1918, will shed light on the limits of military strategy in the face of what turns out to be substantial structural obstacles to decisive breakthroughs or encirclements in the brave new world of industrial war.

Figure 8.2 represents the interaction of German and French war plans on the Western Front. Both belligerents build their plans around going on the offensive, but each has a different idea of how best to *use* the offensive. Neither belligerent can cover the entire front effectively – even with millions of men under arms at the staggering levels that emerge later in the war, troops are a scarce commodity not to be wasted – so it must choose where to concentrate its effort. France, under Plan XVII, aims to strike German formations at center mass, to land a decisive blow at the enemy's strongest point, unraveling whatever attempt at encirclement Moltke might have cooked up. On the other side, Moltke's commitment

---

[11] See Van Evera (1984).
[12] See Farrar (1973).

to the Schlieffen principle means that he aims to bypass the main French force, swinging through Belgium before pivoting and descending on Paris in a massive envelopment that will surround and then destroy the French army (and whatever "contemptible little" British force might be in the area).[13] Translated into a simple game in the strategic form, if each player has the choice of playing left or right (or any pair of options in which enemies can either block or outflank the other), France's best outcome is to match the German move, meeting left with left and right with right in order to ensure that it confronts the main German force, while Germany's best outcome is to play France's opposite, swinging right if France goes left and left if France goes right. This implies a simple set of payoffs. For any outcome in which France parries the German thrust, it receives 1, and for any outcome in which it gets flanked by the German attack, it receives 0. Germany, for its part, receives 1 for any outcome in which it attacks the area France leaves vulnerable and 0 for any outcome in which its axis of advance collides with the main concentration of French troops.

Each side's incentives are clear – France wants to match Germany's move, Germany wants to do the opposite – but how they add up to produce an outcome is far from obvious, given the intuition about equilibrium that we've developed thus far. Information is complete and symmetric, so Bayesian Nash Equilibrium (Definition 5.4) doesn't apply, but if we look for Nash Equilibria (Definition 2.7) as we've done thus far, we'll come up empty. Suppose that both play left. Can a strategy profile of (left; left) be a Nash Equilibrium? France is happy, because it receives 1, while deviating to right would yield 0, but Germany clearly has a profitable deviation; if France plays left, then Germany can do better by playing right, which yields its best outcome. You can probably see where this is going: no matter which pair of actions we choose, either France or Germany has an incentive to deviate from the proposed strategy. France will match Germany if it knows where the latter will attack, and Germany will evade France's main thrust if it knows where that attack is coming from. Common knowledge of other players' strategies, a fundamental element of Nash Equilibrium, seems to undermine the possibility of pinning down a pair of strategies that actually are in equilibrium. The problem, as we'll show next, is that we're limiting our players thus far to **pure strategies**.

DEFINITION 8.2   *In **pure strategies**, players take one and only one action with probability one and all other actions with probability zero.*

---

[13] Hastings (2013, chapter 6).

But as stated in Proposition 8.1, this game can have no Nash Equilibria in which players are certain of each other's choice over playing left or right.

> PROPOSITION 8.1 *There exists no Nash Equilibrium in pure strategies.*

Proof For some arbitrary profile of pure strategies to be a Nash Equilibrium, it must be the case that no player has a profitable deviation. Each strategy profile requires $0 \geq 1$ for the player that receives 0, which is untrue. One player is sure to have a profitable deviation from any such strategy profile, so there can be no Nash Equilibrium in pure strategies.   □

How do we calculate a Nash Equilibrium under these circumstances? The answer is simple and intuitively satisfying. Suppose, for example, that you're tasked with destroying another country's combat forces as quickly and as easily as possible. The enemy army is roughly a match for yours, so it'll pose a serious challenge. You and your general staff will work out a plan, one that involves either targeting or encircling the enemy's center of gravity. Then, under most circumstances you'll be sure *not* to broadcast your plan to the opposing army, because one surefire way to make sure that the enemy can blunt the effectiveness of your strategy is to prepare for it. If your enemy knows you'll try to outflank her, she'll move to block your advance, and if she knows you'll go for a frontal attack, she won't bother reinforcing her flanks and can meet you at full strength. Your best bet as a military planner, then, is to avoid tipping your opponent off – to keep your plans a secret. In 1991, for example, the American-led coalition that ejected the Iraqi army from Kuwait staged a feint, placing ships near the Kuwaiti coast to make Iraq fear an amphibious assault, while the main force swung west of Kuwait in order to encircle, then destroy the Iraqi army.[14] Likewise, in 1914, there isn't much doubt in France that Germany will swing through Belgium, but just how far west the right hook will go before turning south isn't information to which Joffre is privy.

What does keeping one's plans secret look like in the model of Figure 8.2? First, remember that we're using the model as a metaphor, so don't worry too much about fidelity to details. Second, we can think about each player's goal as generating uncertainty in the other's mind about where it plans to move, left or right. We know from Chapters 5 and 6 that uncertainty can be usefully represented as a set of probabilities. But in this case, players generate the uncertainty themselves, engaging in **mixed strategies**, randomizing over their possible actions to keep their opponent guessing about their own best response.

---

[14] For some contemporary accounts, see Freedman and Karsh (1991) and Atkinson (1993).

DEFINITION 8.3 *In **mixed strategies**, players play each of several actions probabilistically (i.e., with a probability less than one).*

If, for example, France can't guess which way Germany is likely to attack, then it can't perfectly match its attack to the German center of gravity. Likewise, in poker, you try not to tip your hand lest an opponent realize either that it makes sense to fold or to keep upping the ante. In American football, play calls are kept secret – and passing plays switched up with running plays – to make sure that defenses can't perfectly guess the proper formation and stifle the offense; likewise, defenses don't use the same scheme every time, lest they be picked apart by an appropriately chosen offense. And the surest way to lose at Rock-Paper-Scissors is, of course, to tip your opponent off about which option you'll choose. If a player wants to generate uncertainty in the mind of another player, to keep him guessing as to where she'll attack, or where she'll establish the strongest defense, then in terms of our model she needs to do exactly what a poker player, a football coach, or a Rock-Paper-Scissors maven would do: randomize. The same holds true for the other player, who also randomizes over his available actions, such that each player effectively rolls the dice over which direction to attack and then keeps that information secret from the other. Keep in mind that this is, of course, a metaphor; Moltke doesn't flip a coin to determine how much of Belgium to violate, but his decision-making process *is* kept secret from the French, who can only guess where the German blow will fall.[15] Secrecy ensures that, for all one's opponent knows, her choice is pulled out of a hat.

When both players randomize, they blunt any advantage that the other might gain from knowledge of their specific actions. They do, however, have some guess over the probability with which the other player chooses among her actions. This ensures that they still know each other's strategies, as they must for us to preserve the logic of Nash Equilibrium. It's just that, in this case, those strategies entail randomizing over available actions to render the other player's strategy as ineffective as possible. This is the essence of a **mixed strategy Nash Equilibrium**, in which players' best responses are to randomize over their available choices.

DEFINITION 8.4 *At a **mixed strategy Nash Equilibrium**, players do as well as they can (randomizing their actions), given what all other players are doing (randomizing their actions).*

How can randomized strategies constitute mutual best replies? The key is to think about what could make a player willing to randomize between two

---

[15] Even once the plan was executed, what actors saw, like in Map 7.1, wasn't the initial German strategy.

actions: she must believe that it makes no difference which one she chooses. If that's the case, then in Figure 8.2 she's free to play left with any probability and right with any complementary probability, because the other player is randomizing just at the rate that makes her indifferent; left or right yields the same payoff in expectation. Therefore, her best response is to make the other player indifferent, so that he's forced to mix over his available choices and can't tailor them to what he believes about her likely strategy. If that's a bit technical, just focus on the intuition: each player needs to keep the other guessing and prevent its opponent from attaining its best outcome (which entails the worst possible outcome for the player in question).

What does this mean for Germany and France in Figure 8.2? In a technical sense, each player must choose probabilities of playing left and right that will render the *other* player indifferent over its own choice of right and left; neither can take advantage of knowledge of the other's choice, nor can it do better by choosing a different rate of right or left, since both are indifferent. Mixed strategies are a little more demanding mathematically than pure strategies, so it's worth working through the formalities in detail. But the logic behind them – the absence of any better response to the other player's strategy – remains the same. To find France's strategy, let's suppose that it plays left with probability ℓ and right with probability $1 - \ell$. To choose the correct probability, it needs to render Germany indifferent over its choice of where to attack. Germany's expected payoff for choosing left is $\Pr(\text{France plays left}) \times 0 + \Pr(\text{France plays right}) \times 1$, or, after substitution,

$$\ell \times 0 + (1 - \ell) \times 1.$$

This must be set equal to Germany's expected payoff for choosing right, which is $\ell \times 1 + (1 - \ell) \times 0$. Therefore, to find France's mixed strategy, we solve

$$\ell \times 0 + (1 - \ell) \times 1 = \ell \times 1 + (1 - \ell) \times 0,$$

which yields $\ell = 1/2$. If France can lead Germany to believe that it's equally likely to play left or right, then it prevents Germany from knowing whether its own choice of playing left or right can achieve a proper flanking maneuver when it unleashes its armies on the Western Front.

But, of course, this is only half of what we need to find a Nash Equilibrium in mixed strategies: we must also show that Germany randomizes, rendering France uncertain over where the attack will come (and justifying its own choice to randomize where it allocates the bulk of its own forces). If Germany plays left with probability γ and right with probability $1 - \gamma$, then France is indifferent over playing left and right when

$$\gamma \times 1 + (1 - \gamma) \times 0 = \gamma \times 0 + (1 - \gamma) \times 1.$$

Solving for γ, we find that Germany's best response is to play left with probability $\gamma = 1/2$ – that is, Germany must keep France guessing as to where it's aimed the tip of its spear. When both players randomize in this fashion, rendering the other indifferent over their own choices, they prevent their opponent from perfectly guessing, and thus perfectly undermining, their strategy. Neither player can do better than randomizing, because as soon as one player's action is predictable, the other can take advantage of it. Therefore, the game in Figure 8.2 has a mixed strategy Nash Equilibrium that we can write as (1/2 left; 1/2 left), such that the row player (France) plays left with probability one-half and the column player (Germany) plays left with probability one-half. The key for each player is to minimize the chances that its opponent walks away with its first-best outcome (which is also the player in question's worst outcome). It's possible that games with mixed strategies also have Nash Equilibria in which players don't mix, but as we showed in Proposition 8.1, that's not the case in Figure 8.2; (1/2 left; 1/2 left) is unique.

PROPOSITION 8.2   *The strategy profile $(\frac{1}{2}left; \frac{1}{2}right)$ is a mixed strategy Nash Equilibrium.*

Proof   For $(\frac{1}{2}left; \frac{1}{2}right)$ to be a Nash Equilibrium, it must be the case that

$$EU_F(left) = EU_F(right) \quad and \quad EU_G(left) = EU_G(right),$$

which ensures that no player has a profitable deviation. Let F play left with probability ℓ and G play left with probability γ. The first equation is satisfied when

$$\ell \times 0 + (1 - \ell) \times 1 = \ell \times 1 + (1 - \ell) \times 0 \Leftrightarrow \ell = \frac{1}{2},$$

and the second is satisfied when

$$\gamma \times 1 + (1 - \gamma) \times 0 = \gamma \times 0 + (1 - \gamma) \times 1 \Leftrightarrow \gamma = \frac{1}{2}.$$

No player has a profitable deviation, so $(\frac{1}{2}left; \frac{1}{2}right)$ is a mixed strategy Nash Equilibrium.   □

Now, what does this equilibrium tell us about the initial moves on the Western Front? How, in what will become known as the Battle of the Frontiers, is France so badly outflanked by a German army that it knows will try to advance through Belgium? First, the model tells us why Germany doesn't telegraph its intentions to France about a wide sweep through Belgium and why Joffre, for his part, can reasonably gamble on attacking what he thinks likely to be the German center near the Franco-German border. Joffre makes a guess as to the best place to make the French thrust, hoping he'll smash into the German center mass and retake Alsace-Lorraine while the Russians march relentlessly toward Berlin. But he can't afford to be perfectly predictable, lest Moltke know exactly how to outflank the French like his uncle did during the Franco-Prussian War. Likewise, Moltke has to choose just how may troops to try and cram through the tiny corridor provided by the Belgian-German border (narrowed by his decision not to violate Dutch neutrality, as Schlieffen had planned), how many to leave near the common border with France, and how to ensure that France doesn't know precisely how he balances these priorities. Secrecy with respect to the allocation of force, where to strike and where to hedge, where to concentrate and where to feint, is the essence of mixed strategies in the Battle of the Frontiers.

France is outflanked because it attacks what turns out not to be the key part of the German line, but the German left – here snatching some German territory and losing it again, bloodying itself in the process but doing nothing to stop the rapidly swinging right hook that throttles the Belgians and the weak French left on the way to a deep dive toward Paris. Put simply, France is outflanked because it has to gamble on where to concentrate its attack; Moltke certainly isn't going to clarify precisely what Joffre can do to interpose himself between German First and Second Armies, the tip of the spear flying through Belgium. Likewise, Moltke's moves represent a high-stakes gamble of their own; he must hope that Joffre doesn't deploy in such a way as to blunt the march through Belgium, but he also has to keep enough weight on his left to ensure that even a mis-directed French attack doesn't succeed in snatching large parts of southwestern Germany. (It surely won't do to sit atop part of northern France while French boots march triumphantly across the Rhineland and Bavaria.) Moltke does, controversially (but only after the fact) weaken the right hook on the eve of war, diverting some troops to his left, but this is in keeping with the logic of the mixed strategies that dominated prewar planning: necessary gambling on where to concentrate forces, keeping one's own plans a secret and hoping that they offer an advantage over the other side's equally secretive strategizing. In a very real sense, countries *create* much of the famous "fog of war" on their own.[16]

The game in Figure 8.2 should also induce some caution in judgments over the military effectiveness of particular strategies and the competence of particular strategists. If we think about how mixed strategies should

---

[16] For one of the earliest discussions of the fog of war, see, as always, Clausewitz (1976).

produce outcomes, then the chances that Germany would play right while France plays left, which means that Germany successfully gets around the French flank, are the product of the probability that Germany plays right (1/2) and the probability that France plays left (1/2). Multiply them together, and we get 1/4, and this is true for *each possible outcome of the game*. Having unleashed his version of the Schlieffen Plan, Moltke knows his chances depend on where Joffre will interpose his forces – and, given that Germany can only achieve local superiority in the number of divisions thrown into the battle, this is a significant gamble; in our model, it has a 50 percent chance of success. Likewise, Joffre's odds, having chosen to implement Plan XVII in hopes of knocking the German army on its heels, are also just about even. Neither general deliberately chooses a strategy with long odds of success – and, when national survival is at stake, a 50–50 shot is definitely a gamble – but given his opponent's own mixing strategy, it's about the best for which he can hope. As ever, strategies and the outcomes they produce, from the ballot box to the battlefield, are interdependent.

This game makes manifest the value of studying events as if they occur in real time, free of the constraints of hindsight. It makes little sense to attribute either brilliance to Moltke or buffoonery to Joffre, because their strategies dictated that the outcome could've gone either way. It would, in a very real sense, be like labeling someone brilliant for calling "heads" before a coin flip comes up "heads," or to discount their intelligence had they called "tails."[17] Mixed strategies – the secrecy, obfuscation, and prioritization that characterize the making and execution of military plans – are designed to present one's opponent with something like a coin flip and to ensure a coin flip's odds for oneself, because tipping your hand would be even worse. Seen in this light, the interaction of the Schlieffen Plan and Plan XVII doesn't tell us too much about which strategy was "better," only that one general's roll of the dice worked out. Thinking in real time, confronting the same choices and constraints as the characters in our narrative, shows that the outcome of the Battle of the Frontiers – a looming French defeat – is a misleading, distorting vantage point from which to evaluate the military strategies of 1914, much less to explain them. The same Joffre that we might castigate for Plan XVII also manages a large-scale retreat and repositioning of his forces that ends up saving France on the River Marne from a disastrous German envelopment. But as we'll see next, this last gasp of Moltke's offensive would lead to a dramatic change in belligerent strategies.

[17] That doesn't stop people from doing it, of course, but it still doesn't make any sense.

8.2.2 Solving the Puzzle: After the Marne

Germany's bid to win the war in forty days with the Schlieffen Plan comes up empty once the Entente manages a rapid retreat and redeployment along the River Marne, where the German advance finally grinds to a halt. Notably, one of the keys to this redeployment – rail transport – will prove critical in the onset of a new, more static, attritional phase of the war. After Germany's retreat to the River Aisne, the war in the West sees a series of desperate attempts by each side to turn the other's flank in a cascading series of failed offensives that creeps northwest until terminating near the impassable marshes of the Belgian coast. This "Race to the Sea" fixes the Western Front in place along a line roughly matching that of Map 8.1, closing off the possibility of encirclement without first achieving a breakthrough on a now continuous, unbroken front. November's First Battle of Ypres establishes the template for trench warfare, which reduces heretofore ruinous casualty rates but seems to foreclose the chance for any offensive to succeed, however large and intricately planned. Long odds of a sustainable breakthrough notwithstanding, the slow wearing-down process of attrition becomes the rule on the battlefield for the next four years. In this section we'll answer two questions. First, to what extent did strategies of attrition make military-strategic sense, and, second, why was it so durable despite its grave social, psychological, and political costs?

Thus far, we've talked about attritional strategies, like Falkenhayn's desire to bleed the French army white, in isolation, in terms of a country's individual incentives to pin its opponent in place and bleed its reserves rather than drive to its capital or shatter its army in the field with a single, name-in-the-history-books coup de grace. But strategies don't exist in isolation. They're part of strategy *profiles*, chosen and sustained in equilibrium – and attrition was certainly sustained in the Great War – only insofar as they're a best response to what other players are doing (Definition 2.7). To understand the logic and durability of attrition, we should ask what was France doing that shaped Falkenhayn's response at Verdun, and vice versa. And why was Haig willing to casually describe his strategy as "killing Germans," with said Germans giving battle under those conditions? Both sides, Entente and Central Powers, settled on strategies of attrition, and it bears asking why that was the case. Otherwise, we can only explain incentives to use attrition, but not its occurrence, not least because neither side would choose attrition unless it has to. If one side adopts attrition, why should the other, and why adopt it given knowledge that the other will? What are the forgone alternatives that each rival coalition decided would have been *worse* than the war we saw? What problem was attrition meant to solve? Only by answering these questions can we understand not

THE WESTERN BATTLE LINE, JANUARY 1, 1915

Map 8.1 The Western Front after the Race to the Sea, 1915. From Reynolds, Churchill, and Miller (1916).

only the adoption of but also the dogged commitment to ostensibly futile strategies of attrition.

To that end, Figure 8.3 characterizes the strategic problem facing the Entente and the Central Powers once attrition sets in. Each side must

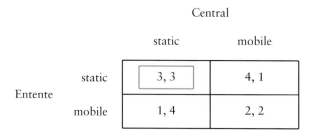

Figure 8.3 The grim logic of attrition on the Western Front.

choose between a static strategy of attrition, which entails maintaining a dogged defense-in-depth based around thinly held front lines and a network of layered trenches, launching the occasional offensive to pin the opponent in place and drain its reserves, or a mobile strategy, which entails abandoning constant pressure along the entire front in favor of concentrated frontal attacks in the vein of the Battle of the Frontiers. If both sides play static, we see the Great War with which we're familiar: a grinding stalemate of individually indecisive battles and soldiers killed and maimed in vain, but one that fixes the opponent in place with constant pressure rather than allow a concentrated assault that might break through a weakened trench system. Should one side go mobile, even if denuding the front at one point entails massing for a major attack elsewhere, and the other remain static, the weakening of the defensive system can presage a breakthrough that can't be contained as easily as it could with a properly manned trench system; alternatively, if it manages to launch a major offensive, it will run into a virtually impenetrable static defensive system maintained by an enemy playing static. If both sides go mobile, if they let up on the constant pressure of attrition, then we see a return to the equally indecisive battles with the vastly higher, unsustainable casualty rates that we saw in the Battle of the Frontiers. The apparently elusive war of maneuver might be restored, but at the cost of allowing enemy forces to spill through temporary gaps and achieve the type of routs or encirclements that France narrowly escaped in August.

Each side's preferences are easy to guess when we lay the options out this way. A belligerent most prefers static attritional pressure while the other goes mobile, because it can apply the full weight of its firepower on a massed, vulnerable body of onrushing bodies and eat substantially into the enemy's reserves (4). Its worst outcome is to be the only side that goes mobile, allowing the other side space and time to concentrate and execute an offensive free of the threat of effective counterattack *or* to chew up an attempted frontal assault with its sustained attritional system. Only slightly better is both sides going mobile, which returns the belligerents to the preattrition battlefield (2), and the second-best for each is a mutual maintenance of static attritional pressure (3), where each side is pinned down by the need to defend against occasional offensives and engages in occasional offensives of its own to eat into the enemy's reserves. Like Germany's effort at Verdun, the Franco-British push at the Somme, and the Russian Brusilov Offensive, these occasional offensives can be large, but their goal is not to capture territory per se, and they aren't as large as they could be if the front were denuded for the largest possible concentrations of force (as would be required for a mobile strategy in Figure 8.3). None of these outcomes, of course, are inherently desirable (and if we're being honest, "desirable" is in any case out the window once you're in a war for survival), but the game does allow us to see that the Entente and Central Powers aren't left with many good options for military strategies after the Battles of the Marne and the Frontiers. But Figure 8.3 can help explain just how our belligerents can find themselves trapped in an attritional equilibrium with no good way out. The unique Nash Equilibrium is (static; static), and it's easy to see why; should either side try to go mobile, the other's steady pressure on the front is no longer balanced, allowing the elusive breakthrough that neither side could achieve (and for which soldiers, politicians, and civilians longed) or suffering unsustainable losses in a foolhardy massed offensive. Mutual attrition isn't either side's most-preferred outcome, but the alternative of relenting unilaterally in hopes of going mobile is much worse (3 > 1).

PROPOSITION 8.3 *The strategy profile (static; static) is a Nash Equilibrium.*

Proof For (static; static) to be a Nash Equilibrium, it must be the case that

$$u_E(\textit{static}; \text{static}) \geq u_E(\textit{mobile}; \text{static})$$

and

$$u_{CP}(\text{static}; \textit{static}) \geq u_{CP}(\text{static}; \textit{mobile}).$$

The first inequality is satisfied because $3 \geq 1$, and the second is satisfied because $3 \geq 1$. No player has a profitable deviation, so (static; static) is a Nash Equilibrium. $\qquad\square$

The uniqueness of (static; static), which you can check yourself, explains why it's so difficult to exit attrition. But Figure 8.3 also shows that it's not even clear that both sides would be better off if they *could* each commit to abandoning static warfare. Each gets 2 if both go mobile, if only because both are burning through men and materiel faster and risk losing control of the battlefield much more quickly than they would under the brutal logic of static attritional warfare. But if one's opponent is willing to go mobile, then the other belligerent has a clear profitable deviation from (mobile; mobile) by unleashing attrition on an adversary that has chosen to walk directly into the teeth of modern firepower. Seen in this light, attrition isn't even tragic in the sense of there existing an alternative set of strategies that would leave both sides better off. There's a commitment problem at the heart of attrition, to be sure, in that neither side can promise to go mobile if the other will (since 4 > 2). But unlike the Anglo-German naval race we analyzed in Chapter 3, where committing not to build more dreadnoughts could save waste and maintain the distribution of naval power, there's no ostensibly better alternative to attrition that the players wish they could've played. A strategy profile of (mobile; mobile) would either continue the pain of war indefinitely *or* bring back the staggering costs of massed frontal attacks.

Strange as it might seem, and frustrating as it is for the men in the trenches and the civilians on the home front, attrition is evidence that both the Entente and the Central Powers are playing a calculated long game. It enables breakthroughs, perhaps even successful ones, *if* the other side relents, but in equilibrium, with both sides committed to static warfare, the best that either side anticipates is forcing the enemy to burn up its reserves faster than they can be replaced while trying to conserve its own. Then, if the other side breaks, if its ability to manage a defense-in-depth is compromised, one of the occasional offensives can achieve a lasting breakthrough – but that's only possible if pressure is constant but conservative, pinning the opponent in place and making her expend more blood and treasure than she can ultimately sustain. And, as Falkenhayn notes before Verdun, with the horrific casualty rates of the Battle of the Frontiers still fresh in his mind,

> Our precise problem is how to inflict heavy damage on the enemy at critical points at relatively small cost to ourselves. But we must not overlook the fact that *previous experience of mass attacks in this war offers little inducement to imitate them.* [emphasis added][18]

Attrition wasn't about individual battles but a larger campaign, conserving one's own manpower and materiel while wearing down the enemy's. It wasn't a contest for territory but a contest of mobilizations. Only once one side's reserves were finally burned up or its soldiers unwilling to fight – and the two would prove later in the war to be related – could a breakthrough be sustained and battlefield victory made meaningful. The ability to manage quick, effective counterattacks like never before (and strategies that made use of that possibility) rendered an early twentieth-century Cannae a practical impossibility. The Kaiser himself seems to have seen this clearly, noting "One must never utter it nor shall I admit it to Falkenhayn, but

---

[18] Quoted in Horne (1923).

this war will not end with a great victory."[19] No one much *liked* attrition, and even if it made strategic sense, its architects weren't safe from political attacks by other ambitious commanders; General Wilhelm Groener, for example, lamented Falkenhayn's "homeopathic tactics" at Verdun, but it's not clear that he, or anyone else, could've done much better.[20] Until such time as one side couldn't mount effective counterattacks, or until such time as new technology or tactics ensured that breakthroughs could be followed up in the face of modern firepower, attrition would rule the battlefield. And rule it did, in the West *and* the East, whether the face of battle was static trench warfare or dramatic but ultimately indecisive campaigns of maneuver.

8.3 ATTRITION *AND* MANEUVER IN THE EAST

Attrition is associated in the popular mind with the trenches in France and Belgium, but we misunderstand it when we associate it *only* with static warfare. Recall that our definition of attrition (Definition 8.1) says nothing about whether it's a war of maneuver or one of static engagements. Both can be and *were* attritional in the First World War. Attritional strategies aren't designed to win every battle – only the last one. Contrary to the popular image gleaned from the Western Front, attrition can take many forms, including strategies of maneuver that were practically excluded in the West after the completion of the Race to the Sea. In the vast spaces of the East where the Central Powers faced Russia, the front was far more fluid, lurching back and forth hundreds of miles at a time, yet operational successes still failed to bring about strategic decision. The hallmark of attrition is that victory can only come on the heels of destroying nearly all of enemy's combat power. After effectively taking over the Austrian war effort, Germany in spring 1915 launched a major offensive around Gorlice-Tarnów in modern Poland (near the dashed line east-southeast of Krakow in Map 8.2), hurling Russian armies back three hundred miles and knocking two million enemy soldiers out of the war. The offensive saved the Dual Monarchy from collapse after a series of disastrous defeats, facilitated the conquest of Serbia, and secured the rail link with Constantinople (which had come in on the side of the Central Powers in 1914), but it failed in its goal of encircling and destroying Russian armies, which escaped before the onset of the fall rainy season.[21] The Gorlice-Tarnów Offensive's

[19] Herwig (2014, p. 191)
[20] Herwig (2014, p. 191).
[21] Herwig (2014, p. 148). It seems that it's not just Russian snows that bog down would-be conquerors.

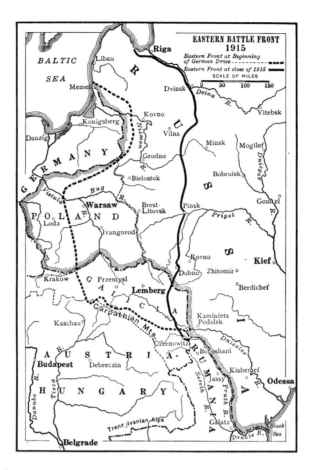

Map 8.2 The Eastern Front before and after the Gorlice-Tarnów Offensive, 1915. From McMurry (1919).

combination of maneuver and attrition is hardly unique in the East, but it helps shed light on why attrition set in and how it was eventually broken.

The contrast between East and West, between the respective stasis and fluidity of their fronts, is notable precisely because of their major underlying similarity: the basic indecisiveness of the fighting, the elusiveness of any single decisive blow, a Cannae or a Sedan that would knock an opponent out of the war. On both fronts, breakthroughs were difficult to follow up due to the application of modern firepower and the rapid movement of men and materiel behind the front, rendering breakthroughs (even the dramatic ones on the Eastern Front) nearly impossible to exploit. Part of it, to be fair, had to do with the Russian army's freedom of retreat, but the fighting was no less indecisive when Russian offensives pushed into the more constricted areas of East Prussia and Austrian Galicia. On the Western Front, Fort Douaumont changed hands several times over the course of the Battle of Verdun, just like the Galician cities of Lemberg and Przemysl on the Eastern Front, captured and besieged and liberated and back again several times throughout the war. While generals on the Western front bemoaned their inability to restore maneuver, their counterparts in the East had plenty of it – and none of the decisiveness that both sides sought. If attrition dominated the battlefield even in the presence of maneuver, not just when the fighting was essentially static as it was on the Western Front, we're left with other factors in common between East and West to explain why attrition set in and stayed in. The prime candidates are the technology of industrial war, from machine guns to massed artillery to rail mobility, and prevailing tactics and operational concepts that dictated how those technologies would be used.

The First World War saw the first widespread and sustained use of several technologies that had debuted in earlier wars but had never been used in combination by so many belligerents with the financial and demographic resources of the great powers. A hand-cranked forerunner of the machine gun, named for its inventor Richard Gatling, helped the United States win the American Civil War, and more modern variants supported Japan's shattering victories over Russian forces in Manchuria in 1904 and 1905. Artillery had seen major improvements in both range, targeting, and destructive capacity in recent years, from long-range guns mounted on rail cars to massive siege mortars that could reduce enemy strongpoints (like the forts at Liége) with high-trajectory shells. Finally, both men and materiel could be moved by a dense, efficient rail network that had not yet been used for the destructive ends of a general European war.[22] The great powers in 1914 wielded unheard-of levels of firepower and armies of unprecedented size, and they could deploy both of them quickly and for an extended period of time. Breakthroughs were, as a result, both enormously costly and difficult to convert into lasting success. Artillery might blast gaps in the the opposing side's wire or disorient the soldiers manning its trenches (such was the goal of "hurricane" bombardments, which benefit from a cool name, if we're being honest), but after wading through No Man's Land, scampering up the opposing parapet, and leaping into the enemy's trench, attacking troops, thus isolated from their own supply and communications lines, would face withering fire from machine gun emplacements in the second trench line and savage counterattacks from the enemy's rail-mobile reserves. In the early weeks and months of the war, massed frontal attacks proved useless against the mechanized typhoon of

---

[22] Not that states weren't concerned about the military potential of railroads. The impending completion of the Trans-Siberian Railway through Manchuria helped push Japan toward preventive war in 1904, and Russia had at one point intentionally left its rail network in Poland weak to make advances difficult for future invaders.

modern firepower, and armies would develop what we now call combined-arms tactics in subsequent years that would produce more effective combinations of aerial reconnaissance, artillery fire, and infantry assaults supported by the first tanks. But it wouldn't be until belligerents ran out of reserves or the army in the field's willingness to fight – as would happen to Russia in 1917 and Germany in 1918 – that attrition would finally be broken and the exhausted sides subject to unstoppable offensives. Then, and only then, would belligerents have a profitable deviation from their strategies of attrition. But our story is several years away from that yet.

8.4 MILITARY STRATEGY AND INTERNATIONAL POLITICS

The military plans with which belligerents entered the First World War have received perhaps an undue amount of scrutiny, especially by politicians trying after the fact to frame decisions as out of their control, driven by unchangeable timetables forced upon them by militaries that snaked free of civilian control.[23] "War by timetable," by which states were dragged into the war by the now-or-never imperatives of the desire to win quickly, has come in for just as much criticism as attrition in the century since the war. As we've seen, the First World War probably wasn't *caused* by military strategies – shifting power in Eastern Europe was sufficient, as we showed in Chapter 4 – but the embrace of attrition in the face of defensive advantages certainly shaped its duration, its course, and its cost. Thanks in part to a lengthy debate over the causes of the First World War, political science has in recent years linked military strategies to a number of important patterns in international relations, from war duration and outcome to the effectiveness of deterrence (conventional and nuclear) to the creation of private information that can lead to the outbreak of war due to information problems.

One popular argument has it is that, by 1914, the technology of defense was dominant over the technology of offense, were we can take "technology" to mean both tools (machine guns, artillery, railroads) and ideas (tactics and doctrine). The war began, so this argument goes, because faith in the offensive was misplaced – and widely so.[24] But as the belligerent nations soon discovered, offensives were difficult to convert into larger successes, and it was easier to defend ground than to capture

---

[23] Political speech, whether in stump speeches, exculpatory memoirs (though I suppose the adjective there is redundant), or exclusive interviews, is inherently strategic, plagued with incentives to misrepresent (remember the relevant parts of Chapter 5). Blame-shifting is rarely innocent, and we should be careful in trusting claimed or ascribed motives contained in political speech.

[24] See Van Evera (1984).

it with a fresh attack. This favored strategies of attrition, which diluted the importance of any battle that wasn't the last one. Scholars have since attempted to tie changes in the relative attractiveness of attack, or the "offense-defense balance," and the ability to distinguish offensive from defensive advantages, to broader patterns of war and peace.[25] That effort has proven challenging, though. Many technologies can be used for offense or defense, depending on the strategies with which they're employed – railroads, for instance – and nor is it clear why the ease of attack or defense should lead states to choose a costly war when negotiations are possible. Still, the theories of war developed in Chapters 2 and 5 offer some hints. First, offensive advantages may lead to war if they're large enough to create a commitment problem. Suppose, for example, that some shock to military technology creates a situation such that the side attacking first is almost certain to win, but that advantage evaporates if the opportunity to attack is forgone and transferred to one's rival. In that case, power might be shifting enough to justify launching a war from a temporary position of strength, but this logic also describes how first-strike advantages (not any particular distinction between offense and defense) might lead to war – so it's not clear that this would be a story about the offense-defense balance per se.[26] Second, we can imagine that crisis bargaining might break down because of *disagreements* about the relative balance of offense and defense, say if an attacker believes she can take more of a target's land than he can defend, but in this case it's not the offense-defense balance causing war but something more general: private information about the attractiveness of war, with which we're already familiar.

Recent work on military strategy has also begun to link it to some of the very processes that make peaceful bargains difficult to reach by *creating* information problems.[27] As we saw in our analysis of the game in Figure 8.2, states have incentives to hide the specifics of their military strategies from one another, because their planned lines of advance, the locations of defensive works and reconnaissance assets, or even the existence of a plan for surprise attack all have a bearing on the outcome of a war – but this information is useful only if it's not shared. Imagine, for example, that Japan had announced to Russia days beforehand that it planned an attack on Port Arthur in 1904; rather than the stunning strategic success that began the Russo-Japanese War, Japan might have found a port either fortified or emptied of enemy vessels already on the move

---

[25] See, inter alia, Jervis (1978) and Van Evera (1998), and for a skeptical take, see Lieber (2000).

[26] See Fearon (1995, pp. 402–404).

[27] See Meirowitz and Sartori (2008) for an explicit analysis of a conjecture that appeared in Fearon's (1995) treatment of uncertainty and war.

to counter Japan's opening gambit. The advantage of surprise blunted, it's possible that Japan would have been unable to make significant gains at its opponent's expense. Tragically, the very information that might avert some wars, from plans for daring surprise attacks to the specific allocations of tanks, artillery pieces, strategic bombers, and naval tonnage that states will take to war, is often kept secret lest its military advantage melt away. Therefore, military technology – regardless of the offense-defense balance – can lead to war not directly but by encouraging states to create the very information problems that can undermine their ability to find peaceful settlements in crisis bargaining.

In addition to the outbreak of war, the strategies that states choose in light of technological, geographical, demographic, and domestic-political factors can shape the duration, outcome, and scope of war. In the First World War, belligerents adopted strategies of attrition that undoubtedly made for a longer war than would have been the case if they'd never abandoned massed frontal assaults, but those strategies made sense given prevailing technology. Iran and Iraq, in their bloody war in the 1980s, also adopted strategies of attrition, aiming to undermine the other's ability to continue the war rather than seek a sweeping knockout blow for which neither was equipped; the result was an eight-year war of mostly indecisive efforts to break the other's will to resist that drew no small number of contemporary comparisons to the First World War.[28] Insurgent movements also frequently adopt guerrilla warfare, refusing battles that risk defeat against conventionally equipped forces and choosing instead to bleed away their enemy's will to fight. In each case, structural features of the conflict, from terrain to technological advantages to resource constraints, encourage states to choose strategies that shape the duration and the potential outcome of the war. If a short war will be ruinous, then one belligerent may do its best to lengthen it, and vice versa. In the Gulf War of 1991, for example, the American-led coalition chose a strategy of maneuver built around an armed sweep through southern Iraq in order to cut off the latter's armies occupying Kuwait, while Iraq – vainly, as it turned out – attempted to entrench and turn the war into a long stalemate of which enemy publics would hopefully grow tired. Attrition, in the sense of trying to outlast one's opponent, is a general feature of warfare, but the extent to which states embrace attrition as their primary strategy varies according to their strategic environment.[29] When states choose maneuver strategies

---

[28] In fact, the Iran-Iraq War featured not only attritional trench warfare but also other Great War hallmarks, such as chemical weapons and crushing indebtedness to foreign creditors.

[29] On the first claim, see Langlois and Langlois (2009), who show that a positive relationship between one side's per-period costs of war and the other's probability of giving is present, on average, in wars since 1815.

and match them to the right terrain, wars tend to be short and victorious, but when states engage in strategies aimed at merely inflicting casualties – sometimes to blunt others' advantages in maneuver, sometimes because maneuver is too costly for both sides – wars tend to be longer and end in costly stalemates.[30] The contrast to the First World War is instructive; had the major belligerents *not* opted for attrition after seeing their bids for quick victories fail in 1914–1915, they might have burned through their fighting capacities much sooner and with much less of a chance to control the outcome.

If military strategies can shape the cost and duration of war, then what an opponent believes about how a state will prosecute a war can affect calculations over whether to initiate a crisis or mount an attack in the first place; that is, military strategy may be linked to a state's ability to deter attacks against either itself or its partners. The link between military strategy and deterrence took on major importance in the Cold War. Recall from Chapters 4 and 5 that deterrence entails clarifying for a potential attacker that the costs of challenging the status quo will be too great. One way to achieve this is to make sure that an invader pays significant costs for trying to gain territory, as NATO aimed to do by improving its conventional military capabilities in the 1980s with respect to the Soviet Union. The Red Army and its allies could muster a much larger force than NATO, but the latter tried to substitute quality for quantity – better tanks, stealthier aircraft, faster communications, superior training – and the promise of inflicting unsustainable casualties on Warsaw Pact forces if they started pouring through the Fulda Gap onto the West German plain. Thus, NATO's deterrent strategy in Europe was one of attrition, those same countries' experience with it during the Great War notwithstanding, because it promised to make any Soviet attack on the West murderously, prohibitively costly.[31]

The Cold War also saw states grapple for the first time with the thornier problem of nuclear deterrence, which required military strategies that would make the incredible (a war that might damage human civilization beyond repair) credible (or at least likely enough in the event of a challenge to the status quo division of Europe that neither side would attempt it).[32] How, for example, could the United States credibly threaten nuclear war to prevent a Soviet invasion of West Germany when

---

[30] See Bennett and Stam (1996), and for a report on the same model's eerily accurate predictions over the length of the conventional phase of the 2003 Iraq War, see Bennett and Stam (2006).

[31] See Mearsheimer (1983, pp. 206–208).

[32] Thomas Schelling analyzed ideas of brinkmanship in the 1950s and 1960s that shape the study of international conflict and the practice of international security to this day. See, in particular, Schelling (1966).

the stakes were clearly so much lower than the consequences of such a war? The United States devised strategies such as President Dwight Eisenhower's Massive Retaliation, which in the 1950s promised an all-out nuclear assault in the event of attacks on NATO allies, to Kennedy's Flexible Response, which viewed Massive Retaliation as incredible and sought to find other ways to use nuclear and conventional weapons to bolster the defense of the American alliance network. Nuclear weapons, thanks to their awesome destructive power, have proved almost useless as tools of coercion, convincing other states to change their behavior or to make concessions under pain of attack, but they *are* the ultimate tool of deterrence, of convincing one's enemies not to push one's back up against the wall.[33] Recent debates over national missile defense systems, which may undo the mutually assured destruction (MAD) on which great power deterrence has rested since the early Cold War, also boil down to questions of military strategy.[34] As we'll see in Chapter 14's discussion of peacemaking and reestablishing the balance of power after major wars, the shadow of nuclear weapons alters the paths of international politics even when their use isn't on the horizon.

8.5 CONCLUSION

We tend to think of the First World War as one of static, indecisive trench warfare that lasted far longer, cost more lives, and poisoned more societies than it should have. In the Atlantic democracies, this image owes much to the dominance of the Western Front in media, history, and shared memory. But just like judging military strategists for failing to act on information they didn't have and couldn't get, we draw faulty conclusions about the war when we look only at the relatively short and densely packed Western Front; combat in the First World War was strategically indecisive almost everywhere, from the fields of Flanders to the plains of Eastern Europe to the craggy heights of the Caucasus. Breakthroughs and encirclements, however dramatic and however sweeping, either faltered in the face of counterattacks enabled by swift rail transport or outran their supply lines, only to see their quarry withdraw and live to fight another day. With battle itself indecisive, strategists in all the major belligerent nations quickly realized that only winning the *last* battle could bring victory. Short of major technological or doctrinal breakthroughs that could neither be waited on nor plucked out of thin air, only breaking the enemy's army in the field,

---

[33] See, inter alia, Fuhrmann and Sechser (2014) and Sechser and Fuhrmann (2013, 2017).
[34] See Powell (2003).

killing more of her troops than she could replace, could win the war.[35] Both maneuver and static warfare were indecisive, but in the concentrated conditions of the Western Front, the former was far costlier – prompting both sides to entrench and try to wear each other down with artillery and occasional attacks rather than the frontal assaults that wrecked entire peacetime armies in 1914. Attrition became the rule for most of the war, not because generals and politicians were uniquely incompetent, not because the Western Front was too short or the Eastern Front too long, but because the limitations of the offensive made attrition, *grignotage*, or "killing Germans" part of a slow-burning, brutal equilibrium in which millions of soldiers were counted not too differently than the millions of tons of steel that went into producing the instruments of their death on the battlefield.

Attrition was an equilibrium, a self-enforcing product of strategies in balance that was not easily escaped, and a horrifically costly and traumatizing one at that. That it was costly and dehumanizing, that every battle that bled both sides in service of the bleeding alone, and that none of its proponents believed it could lead to a quick victory, explains the regret, the recrimination, and the befuddlement that follows almost any tragic equilibrium ex post. But explaining strategies, much less judging them, in terms of the outcomes they produced is also folly, and it blinds us to the explicable politics, the strategic dilemmas that characterize not just the Great War but any war about which we wish to learn (past or present). Take Papa Joffre. It's possible that "[h]ad Joffre fallen dead on September 1, history would remember him only as a bungler and butcher."[36] But this chapter has shown that the mere fact of France getting outflanked during the Battle of the Frontiers – even ignoring Joffre's redemption on the Marne – isn't sufficient basis for making such a claim. Likewise, the war of attrition that set in after his management of the Miracle on the Marne is better understood as the equilibrium product of strategic incentives that favored the defensive and, hard as it is to believe, a desire to *minimize* casualties after a few opening months that nearly destroyed every belligerent's peacetime army. The remaining years would see each rival coalition press for ever more extensive levels of social and military mobilization, all in the service of lasting one more year, month, or week than its opponents. Attrition is most of the time a game of waiting, only occasionally one of winning. Not until 1918, when technological and doctrinal changes would make offensives sustainable – and when American troops would be on the ground in sufficient numbers to allow British and French forces to sustain major war efforts despite their own flagging resources and resolve – would the

---

[35] See Philpott (2009, 2014) for a sobering analysis of the making and implementation of strategies of attrition in the First World War.

[36] Hastings (2013, p. 290).

attritional stalemate finally be broken. Before telling that story, however, we must explain why other countries, including Italy, the Ottoman Empire, Japan, and China, all found themselves not dragged into the maelstrom but willing to leap directly in.

8.6   EXERCISES: ARMAMENTS AND MILITARY SECRECY

Our example of mixed strategies in the Colonel Blotto game of Figure 8.2 was almost too straightforward, because when players randomized their choices, they did so by taking each available choice (left and right) with equal probability. But we noted that randomization doesn't imply equal probabilities for every action – only that we can describe actions as chosen according to some probability distribution, whether it's a fair coin, a twelve-sided die, or a rule that assigns different numbers to the first letter of each paragraph in a book. In a different strategic-form game, rendering one's opponent indifferent might, for example, entail playing left with probability 1/8 and right with probability 7/8, or 4/10, and 6/10, and so on. The mixed strategy NE of Figure 8.2 entailed players metaphorically flipping a fair coin, but every unfair coin can also be flipped to produce a randomized outcome.[37] Any mix of probabilities can work as the product of randomization, which we can demonstrate by returning to an idea we first encountered in Chapter 5: that countries, despite the possibly dangerous consequences (like a catastrophic war) of uncertainty over military capabilities, might have strong incentives to keep their armament decisions secret from one another. The United States, for example, kept the existence of radar-evading stealth aircraft like the angular, faceted F-117 and otherworldly, flying-wing B-2 secret for years; but why not let one's opponents *know* that you can evade their radars? Wouldn't a publicly known advantage redound to the benefit of the United States.[38]

PUZZLE 8.2   *Why do states keep important military advantages secret?*

To solve this puzzle, let's bring back our long-suffering territorial disputants, countries A and B, who know they'll confront one another in a future crisis and so must make armament decisions – say, whether or not to increase the size of the army. Let's suppose commitment problems due

---

[37] Strictly speaking, a coin that came up "heads" or "tails" every time would be the result of a random process, but it would be a degenerate one; players' actions would become entirely predictable, and so we wouldn't see mixing strategies in equilibrium.

[38] By designation, the F-117 was a fighter, but it was in reality an attack aircraft, capable of dropping a limited, if precision-guided, payload; the B-2, by contrast, was properly designated as the bomber that it is, designed to penetrate Soviet airspace and track down mobile ballistic missile launchers.

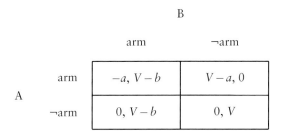

Figure 8.4 Arming to change and defend the status quo.

to shifting power aren't part of the story, in the sense that no state can interrupt the other's arming decision; states choose levels of armaments with an eye to one simple fact: the state with a military advantage will do better in the upcoming crisis, whether or not it escalates to war.[39] We'll suppose that, at the status quo distribution of power, B has the advantage; unless A boosts the size of its army, B retains the advantage, and it can retain it in the face of A's boost if it boosts its own land forces. Suppose that B controls a prize worth $V > 0$. Furthermore, boosting the size of the army is costly, such that A pays $a \in (0, V)$ and B pays $b \in (0, V)$ to raise, equip, and train new formations. When $a < b$, A can arm more efficiently than B; when $b < a$, B can arm more efficiently; and when $a = b$, they can arm with equal efficiency.

Figure 8.4 models this problem in the strategic form. Each side chooses whether or not to arm, which entails four outcomes. If both arm, each spends on new land forces, but B retains its advantage because it takes appropriate countermeasures; in this case, that's raising more divisions, but in the previous example that might mean aggressively developing counter-measures for enemy stealth technology. This outcome means that B retains control of the disputed land, so payoffs are $(-a, V - b)$. If A arms and B doesn't, A can seize the prize from B at the cost of arming, resulting in $(V - a, 0)$. If A doesn't arm but B does, A lives with a status quo that B preserves with arming it didn't need to engage in, such that payoffs are $(0, V - b)$. Finally, if neither arms, the status quo of $(0, V)$ stays in place. A's problem is pretty stark: if it can arm without provoking B to take countermeasures, then it can go on to exploit its military advantage,

---

[39] We know from Chapter 5 that, if each side knows the other's resolve – which in this case we'll say depends entirely on military capabilities, or armaments – then they can strike a peaceful bargain in which the stronger side gets a better deal. But if states are uncertain over each other's capabilities, then it's possible that one player demands more than the other will concede, leading to war. In either case, states are better off if they've achieved a unilateral advantage in military capabilities over the other. Remember what Mao said about the sources of political power.

but if B arms as well, then it's wasted time and energy and resources on the fool's errand of adding capabilities that are essentially useless on arrival.

EXERCISE 8.1   *Prove the existence or nonexistence of Nash Equilibria in pure strategies of the game in Figure 8.4.*

EXERCISE 8.2   *Prove the existence or nonexistence of Nash Equilibria in mixed strategies of the game in Figure 8.4.*

Completing both exercises gives us a compelling, if potentially tragic, solution to our puzzle. If states build predictably – say, if A plays a pure strategy of arming – then their opponents can take countermeasures and eliminate the advantages of unilateral arming. That, for example, is why the United States went to great lengths through the 1980s to keep the design details of its rumored but unacknowledged stealth aircraft under wraps: revealing the advantage would've encouraged countermeasures. Therefore, A arms in secret, randomizing between arming (with probability b/V) and not (with probability $1-b/V$) to blunt any advantage its opponent might gain from learning the truth, because B would rather not waste money on raising the necessary divisions if it doesn't have to. The costs of countermeasures help keep B indifferent, and B keeps A indifferent with its own mixing strategy (arming with probability $1 - a/V$, not arming with probability a/V). In this application, countries arm because greater military power makes them better off for future crisis bargaining, even (and especially) if those crises escalate to war. And as long as the logic of measures and countermeasures characterizes armament decisions, then states may very consciously create the very uncertainty over military strength that can cause crisis bargaining to break down in war.[40]

The mixed strategy equilibrium of the armaments game in Figure 8.4 also makes another useful point: when players adopt mixed strategies, the probability with which they take any given action depends not on their own preferences but on their opponent's, on the preferences of the player they're trying to render indifferent. The probability with which B arms $(1 - a/V)$ depends not on its own costs of arming – costs that A renders irrelevant with its own mixing strategy – but on A's, and vice versa. B is more likely to arm when A's costs for arming are low, regardless of its own costs of arming, and the same is true for A, which arms with probability b/V. But the value of the prize (V), which intuition might tell us should encourage both parties to arm, A to capture it and B to

---

[40] See Meirowitz and Sartori (2008) for the model on which this much cruder one is based. They show that, even when arming under mixed strategies is sure to generate a risk of war, states will still do it.

keep it, has a differential effect on players' choices.[41] A is *less* likely to arm as the value of the prize increases, not because A doesn't care about gaining at B's expense but because A has to tempt B into, with some probability, *not* arming. Likewise, B is more likely to arm as the value of the prize *decreases*, not because it likes arming to defend invaluable territory but because doing so ensures that A can't gain more from arming to win valuable territory than from arming to gain less valuable territory. Consistent with Harrison Wagner's epigraph in Chapter 5, in this and many other strategic settings, we can't look at outcomes and infer from them that players choose strategies based simply on their own preferences.

---

[41] If you remember nothing else from this book, remember this: intuition, free of some logical checks, tends to be garbage.

9 Choosing Sides: Building Military Coalitions

Herr von Bethmann-Hollweg said that the aim of these concessions was to purchase our neutrality, and, therefore, gentlemen, you may applaud us for not having accepted them.

Antonio Salandra,
Italian Prime minister
May 23, 1915

Not even the victors walked away happy from the First World War. But postwar regret was especially intense for several countries that joined later, saw their hopes for aggrandizement frustrated, and yet might plausibly have saved themselves the trouble by staying out. Neutrality was a popular proposition in both Italy and the Ottoman Empire, and leaders in both states went to some lengths to preserve it in the war's early going. That both would ultimately choose to join the war, despite the popularity of neutrality and the lack of any immediate threat, is puzzling.

> Why did Italy abandon neutrality for the Entente, while the Ottoman Empire abandoned it for the Central Powers?

By the summer of 1915, an Italian drive for Austrian Trieste bogged down on the Isonzo River, while the Ottomans faced the Russians in the Caucasus and an Anglo-French force at Gallipoli. Yet neither Italy, its imperial designs frustrated and its postwar politics infected by Fascism, nor the Ottoman Empire, stripped of its imperium and replaced by a rump Turkish state, seemed to improve its lot by abandoning neutrality. So why did they join the war?

The solution to the puzzle draws our attention not to neutrality as the alternative to joining the war but to (1) the terms on offer from rival coalitions trying to lure them into the conflict and (2) the credibility of promises to follow through on these deals after the war. Solving the puzzle in this way will teach us a few things:

- how states compensate partners to build military coalitions;
- the importance of postwar considerations in wartime behavior;
- how states decide to honor or renege on alliance commitments;
- how even sworn enemies can find themselves on the same side in war.

We'll see in this chapter how each state's decision was the product of negotiations with potential coalition partners wielding promises and threats of varying degrees of credibility. States join coalitions when they're offered sufficient compensation for the prospective costs of war by coalition-builders that would rather not make such promises; just like states find themselves bargaining with potential enemies, they must also bargain with (frequently hesitant) potential partners to secure support against those enemies. Italy and the Ottoman Empire weighed the political inducements offered by the Entente and the Central Powers, abandoning neutrality for the side that seemed likelier to follow through on its promises at war's end, whether those promises entailed shares in the spoils of war or simply assurances not to pose a menace in the future. We'll show that this logic of coalition-building in the shadow of postwar commitments can also explain a curious feature of the war in East Asia: China's decision to join the same side in the war as Japan, the mortal enemy that had usurped China's regional position in 1895 and even in 1914 sat atop traditionally Chinese territory. After working through the logic of coalition building and war expansion in the First World War, we'll explore when and how states choose to abandon their alliance partners and how military coalitions in general shape international politics, conflict, and the balance of power.

9.1 ITALY AND THE OTTOMAN EMPIRE JOIN THE WAR

It's not hard to look at the Ottoman and Italian decisions to join the war, in October 1914 and May 1915 respectively (see Figure 9.1), and think that both countries might've been substantially better off in 1918 had they remained neutral. Italian battle deaths totaled around half a million, concentrated chiefly on its mountainous frontier with Austria-Hungary, yet dreams of imperial expansion into Africa on a par with other powers like

Figure 9.1 Other powers fall in line, 1914–1917.

Great Britain and France would be dashed even in victory, and its body politic would fall victim to the aggressive cancer of Fascism in the early 1920s.[1] To the east, about 300,000 Ottoman troops would die in battle – and over a million Armenians would die in forced marches and brutal military reprisals for suspected pro-Russian sympathies – in a war that would rage from the Caucasus to Egypt and the Levant to Mesopotamia and the Arabian Peninsula. The war would end with the Empire's domains divvied up among the victors and its Caliphate abandoned, replaced by a rump Turkish national state. By this reckoning, neutrality looks ex post like a much better deal for both states. Italy might've preserved its army, its treasury, and a (relatively) stable political life, and the Ottomans could've preserved the very existence of their ancient imperium. Yet each eventually rejected offers to guarantee its neutrality.

Still more puzzling, both countries began the war with rapid declarations of neutrality, Italy on August 3, 1914, and the Ottomans on August 4.[2] Even without the benefit (sorry, *distortion*) of hindsight, it's not hard to see why. As we saw in Chapter 6, neutrality comes with certain rights and privileges that a violator's enemies may be eager to defend when the stakes involve the balance of power, as they manifestly did in the Great War. On the military side, two facts became clear in the early weeks and months of fighting. First, none of the belligerents showed an inclination to threaten either the Ottoman Empire or Italy directly, focusing their attention chiefly on other belligerents in hopes of winning the short version of the war.[3] Second, even if that should change, waging a war of self-defense was proving easier than a war of conquest (see Chapter 8), and both countries could count on mountainous terrain to help protect parts of their vulnerable frontiers. Moreover, neutrality was popular with both publics and significant factions of both political classes, including the Sultan and the Grand Vizier in Constantinople and a majority of the Chamber of Deputies in Rome.[4] Remaining aloof, husbanding blood and treasure for the postwar period – staying neutral, that is – as the other great powers worked feverishly at tearing each other to shreds, had a lot going for it in late 1914. But neither government proved willing to defend that position.

The Ottoman declaration of neutrality followed Italy's by a day, but it joined the war seven months sooner, casting its lot with the Central Powers in late October 1914 by consenting to the use of German-crewed ships recently "purchased" for the Ottoman Navy to attack Russian naval forces

---

[1] On Italy's disappointments and its fractious postwar politics, see Kershaw (2015, esp. chapter 6).

[2] Stevenson (1988, pp. 47 and 45, respectively).

[3] See Chapter 10 for how the acceptance of a long war changed belligerent strategies pretty radically by creating new content in the common conjecture.

[4] Stevenson (1988, pp. 45–51).

in the Black Sea. The delay wasn't a consequence of mere bureaucratic slug-gishness. Ottoman officials from the nationalist Young Turk faction (for-mally the Committee for Union and Progress, or CUP) had, after months of trying to secure a treaty with *any* great power to shore up its declining strategic position, inked a pact with Germany on August 2 promising to enter the war as soon as Russia did.[5] The problem, of course, was that the Sultan and his Grand Vizier retained their inclinations toward neutrality. To make matters worse, Britain, the world's dominant naval power, had also entered the war on August 4, dramatically raising both the stakes and the threat posed to the Empire's vulnerable Aegean, Mediterranean, and Middle Eastern flanks. It was in light of British naval dominance that an Entente offer to guarantee Turkish territory in return for strict neutrality seemed attractive, even against German promises of military aid and gains at Russian expense in the Caucasus.[6] While the Young Turks worked to ensure eventual belligerence, the Ottoman government took possession on August 6 of the German cruisers *Goeben* and *Breslau* (renaming them *Yaviz Sultan Selim* and *Medili*) that would eventually lead the Empire into war, preserving the legal trappings of neutrality as the ships entered the Straits and set off alarm bells in Entente capitals.[7] Months later, with its naval position improved and the Grand Vizier outmaneuvered at the Sublime Porte by the Young Turks, the Ottoman Empire would approve naval attacks on the Russian fleet, prompting St. Petersburg to declare war on November 2 and setting in motion the ultimate destruction of the almost 500-year-old Empire.

In contrast to the long-frustrated Ottoman search for allies, Italy began the war legally bound to Germany and Austria-Hungary in the Triple Alliance, a product of Bismarck's desire to reduce the probability of fighting a two-front war. But thanks in large part to its partners' low expectations, Italy managed a basically painless announcement that, owing to the defensive nature of the Triple Alliance, it wasn't bound to support Austria in a war against Russia that would spring from an Austrian attack on Serbia. As early as July 27, Italy indicated to Germany and Austria that, unless compensation was forthcoming in the form of concessions in the *Italia irredenta* – Hapsburg lands in the Tyrol and Adriatic coast populated by Italian speakers – neutrality was the rule.

---

[5] Stevenson (1988, p. 45). This also illustrates a more peaceful response to declining relative power than preventive war: a preventive alliance.

[6] See Stevenson (1988, pp. 45–46).

[7] Acquiring battlecruisers like the *Goeben* and *Breslau* wasn't exactly compensation for the two dreadnoughts, *Reşadiye* and *Sultan Osman-ı Evvel*, the Ottomans had ordered from the British but which, on the outbreak of war, had been seized before shipment and integrated into the Royal Navy, renamed HMS *Erin* and *Agincourt* – but it did help spark the diplomatic bidding war that would ultimately bring the Empire into the war.

Throughout the winter and spring, as the war settled into a stalemate on Western, Eastern, and now Turkish and Caucasian Fronts, yet before the dramatic (temporary) success of the Gorlice-Tarnów Offensive, debate continued in Italy over the attractiveness of joining the war, helped along by a competing bid for Italian support from the Entente. The diplomatic bidding war continued throughout the spring, until in late April 1915, Italy signed the secret Treaty of London, promising to enter the war against its former Triple Alliance partners in return for many of the same territorial gains that were on offer from Germany and Austria at the time – and which Italy might have been promised only for remaining neutral or, at worst, merely pinning down the French Army and Navy on their common land and sea frontiers.[8] By May 20, with the not-so-secret London terms pitted against a proposal to remain faithful to the Triple Alliance, Italy's Chamber of Deputies voted overwhelmingly to join the Entente.[9] Yet mere months after securing the Central Powers' capitulation, Italian nationalists would see their frustrated desires for Trieste, other lands on the Dalmatian coast, a foothold in Anatolia, and colonial opportunities in Africa as the deepest wound of a "mutilated victory" resulting from the Entente's postwar betrayal.[10]

It's notable, and not just in light of their disastrous experiences of the war, that both Italy and the Ottoman Empire turned down offers from their eventual enemies to guarantee their neutrality – and failing that in Italy's case, to bring it into the war on the side of the Central Powers. In the early weeks of the war, "[t]he Entente offered to guarantee Turkey in return for strict neutrality,"[11] which looks after the fact like a missed opportunity of historic proportions. Likewise, Germany dangled several inducements in front of Italy, including gains in the *Italia irredenta*, throughout the spring, in hopes of achieving at least benevolent Italian neutrality and at most active belligerence against the Entente (which would have raised the costs of Entente naval predominance). Both the Ottoman Empire and Italy, it seems, turned down golden opportunities to simply hold on to what they had, perhaps to gain (if even in a relative sense, climbing up the hierarchies of power and prestige) as the other powers exhausted themselves in the fighting. What better way to climb up the rankings by default, when the alternative is a costly and potentially ruinous war? Those apparently

---

[8] Yes, that's yet *another* Treaty of London, not to be confused with the one that took its star turn pushing Britain into war against Germany in Chapter 6 or with the numerous other declarations of London that would commit Entente members against separate peaces or that would seek to impose restrictions on naval warfare.

[9] Stevenson (1988, pp. 57–58).

[10] See Kershaw (2015, chapter 3).

[11] Stevenson (1988, p. 46).

tantalizing choices notwithstanding, both threw themselves into the swirling, chaotic, all-consuming maw of the Great War. Why?

9.2 EXPLAINING COALITION BUILDING

The apparent value of neutrality aside, this chapter's decisions look easy to explain in retrospect. Italy coveted lands controlled by the Dual Monarchy, dominated by a Hapsburg Austria against which Italy had fought five times before 1915.[12] As such, it abandoned the Triple Alliance for the Entente, who pursued the compatible goal of breaking Germanic dominance of central and southeastern Europe. The Ottoman Empire, long fêted by Kaiser Wilhelm (often to the bafflement of the rest of the German political class) for its access to the Middle East, with an army (since 1913) and now navy both staffed with German officers, chose the side to which it had been more closely tied in the prewar years. How could things have been otherwise? These *post hoc* explanations are tempting, but that doesn't mean they're right. Both countries flirted with neutrality, which might've saved the costs of war; as such, the ex post argument for neutrality is just as compelling (if not more so) than the *post hoc* argument for choosing as they did. Neither the Ottomans nor the Italians fared well in the war or in the postwar carve-up that they watched largely from the sidelines, where "the sidelines" means "briefly fighting each other in Turkish Antalya during 1919–1921 while the British and French cemented their geopolitical dominance."[13] Just as they did in Chapters 2 and 5, the costs of war pose a serious puzzle to explaining the decision to participate in it, especially when ostensibly better options – e.g., guarantees of neutrality – seem to have been left on the table.

PUZZLE 9.1   *Why did Italy abandon neutrality for the Entente, while the Ottoman Empire abandoned neutrality for the Central Powers?*

Explaining the Ottoman and Italian decisions to abandon neutrality requires that we think of war expansion in a different way than we did in Chapter 6. British intervention looks like an immediate case of balancing against a power believed to have unlimited aims, but the Ottomans and Italians had more freedom of action. By late 1914, it was no longer about "gallant" small countries resisting Prussian militarism or great powers

---

[12] Sondhaus (2014, p. 22).

[13] Of course, that doesn't mean the British and French fought the war just to cement geopolitical dominance; had they wanted to do that, they wouldn't have waited for Germany and Russia to be as powerful as they were in 1914. "*Cui bono?*" no matter how satisfying the answers might be is a *terrible* guide for explaining international relations. Think of it as a fast lane to doing little more than affirming the consequent.

trying to preserve a long-standing balance of power. Staying out *was* an option down to the last minute, giving both Italy and the Ottomans some leverage over would-be partners. Indeed, the belligerents had numerous means at their disposal to alter the relative attractiveness of joining the war and staying out; neutrality isn't a decision that can be taken in isolation, as Belgium and Luxembourg learned (the hard way) in August. The Ottoman and Italian choices are best thought of as part of a strategic process of coalition building, of negotiations between potential military partners over how they will be compensated for bearing the costs of war in service of another's war aims. Countries join military coalitions when they can be compensated for the costs of war by a coalition-builder willing to pay the price, and in many cases that affords significant bargaining power to the potential partner.[14] Each decision to abandon neutrality – and then which side to join – depends on what Italian and Ottoman decision-makers will accept as compensation, what terms the Entente and Central Powers offer in return, and – as we'll show in this section – the credibility of the latter's promises to come through in the all-important postwar negotiations ... whenever those might come about.

In this section, we'll write down an inherently transactional model of constructing military coalitions, where a potential partner chooses between competing offers from two belligerent coalitions. The basic insight is simple: war is wasteful, and those with the choice don't join a costly conflict for free. Supporting a coalition's war effort is costly in terms of lives and treasure and forgone opportunities, and prospective partners generally require some form of compensation – shares in the spoils of victory, policy concessions, loans or cash to offset the costs and risks of fighting, etc. – in return for their cooperation.[15] We'll call these concessions "side payments" as a kind of easy shorthand.[16] Working out the process of coalition formation in a game-theoretic model will show us that the key to both Ottoman and Italian decisions over choosing sides in the Great War was not just the *attractiveness* of the specific compensation packages on offer by the Entente or the Central Powers, which were roughly similar in value, but the *credibility* of those promises after victory, once negotiations resumed from a new postwar position. States make decisions over both starting wars and joining them with an eye to the network of bargains that will characterize

---

[14] See, e.g., Wolford (2015) and Wolford and Ritter (2016).

[15] The models and examples in this chapter draw from Wolford's (2015) treatment of the politics of military coalitions, but they generalize them by modeling competing offers of cooperation from multiple coalitions and the credibility of those commitments (see, in particular, pp. 219–220).

[16] On side payments, as well as many other ideas about coalitions that the author has used – nay, pillaged – throughout his career, see Riker (1962). It's a brilliant piece of social science.

the new postwar international order, as well as the risks of betting that the status quo associated with neutrality will stay in place. The short-term allure of neutrality or the terms on the table notwithstanding, negotiations with potential coalition partners, about the terms of both belligerence and neutrality, are very much about shaping the postwar world and securing one's place in it. But the gains of any course of action are judged against others' inability, thanks to the de jure anarchy of the international system, to commit not to take advantage of their victories.

9.2.1 Solving the Puzzle

Building military coalitions is, at root, a transactional process. Bargaining over the terms of military cooperation resembles haggling between a buyer and a seller in a market. A buyer wants a product on offer from a seller, but the seller will only make an exchange if what the buyer's willing to pay is a price that the seller will accept. Negotiating military cooperation, though, adds a different layer of complication. It's true that the buyer (the country seeking military assistance) can set an attractive price (political concessions to cover the costs of war), but the seller (the potential partner) knows that even with its help the war may not be successful and, furthermore, the war may produce a favorable outcome even if it chooses not to help.[17] Generally, coalition-builders offer larger side payments to entice partners that have a larger effect on the chances of victory and to those that, perhaps because they'd be decisive in the war effort, can demand a higher premium than others.[18] The terms get all the more generous, as we'll see in this section, when a rival coalition competes for the assistance of the same partner, as both the Entente and the Central Powers found themselves doing over Italian and Ottoman participation in the war – both of which were thought critical in securing ultimate victory for each side.

Let's start with the dueling compensation packages that the rival belligerent coalitions have put before the Italians. The Central Powers, hoping that Italy can be induced to honor at least the minimal level of "benevolent neutrality" that could be read into the Triple Alliance in the context of an Austro-Serbian war, have offered Italy territorial gains at Austrian expense and vague promises of a presence on the Dalmatian coast.[19] Austria is of course reluctant in offering its own territory to its Italian rival, but it has little choice in the face of its dependence on Germany, who will also offer

---

[17] That is, wars inevitably have a collective-goods component, since the outcomes affect both participants and those that stay on the sidelines (recall Chapter 7).

[18] See Wolford (2015, chapter 3). For similar analyses of war-joining in which states are assumed not to bargain over the terms of their cooperation, see Altfeld and Bueno de Mesquita (1979), Gartner and Siverson (1996), and Morrow (2000).

[19] See Herwig (2014, pp. 152–155).

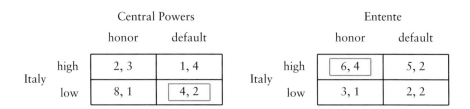

Figure 9.2 Italy chooses between rival coalitions.

Hapsburg lands to Romania later in the war in vain hopes of stabilizing the East.[20] The Entente, meanwhile, has offered up a very similar package of potential annexations; all Italy must do is abandon its neutrality for belligerency on the side of the Entente. If Italy says yes to one offer, it effectively says no to the other. It can't simultaneously maintain neutrality as hoped by the Central Powers and belligerency as hoped by the Entente, nor can it sustain neutrality and stave off Entente belligerency without some risk to its long, vulnerable coastline.[21]

We'll represent this dilemma by assuming that Italy must choose which game to play in Figure 9.2. It can align with the Central Powers, on the left, where it faces a choice between belligerence against the Entente (high involvement) and benevolent neutrality (low involvement), where it stays out of the war but likely faces constant pressure – not all of it of the polite variety – from both sets of rival belligerents to change its mind. On the other hand, it can align with the Entente by choosing to play the game on the right, where it enters the war against the Central Powers (and Austria-Hungary in particular) but chooses between high and low military efforts; the former is an aggressive, offensive war plan that tries to seize and hold Austrian territory, while the latter is a defensive effort that satisfies the Entente by draining Austrian resources and attention but produces lower odds of capturing the *Italia irredenta*. To keep things simple, let's assume that the side Italy chooses wins the war. This still gives Italy eight possible outcomes to consider, because after choosing a side, its new partners must decide whether to honor or default on the promised compensation package that tempts Italy to pay the costs of war.

Provided Italy accepts their offer, the Central Powers' best outcome (4) is to see Italy not just stay neutral but go to war against the Entente, but then renege on that bargain themselves in victory. Germany's enemies enfeebled, the Hapsburgs dominant in the Balkans, and the Adriatic an

---

[20] See Weitsman (2003, p. 94).
[21] Being shaped like a boot has some benefits, I suppose, but few of them have anything to do with safety from a seaborne attack.

Austrian lake, reneging on postwar commitments to an expansionist but generally weak Italy will be outrageously tempting. Honoring the pledges to Italy, which would entail transferring Austrian territory and giving up an extensive presence on the eastern shore of the Adriatic, is second best (3), since at a minimum Italy has helped defeat the Entente. If, on the other hand, Italy simply maintains neutrality, the Central Powers also prefer to default on their promises; they receive 2 and 1 for defaulting and honoring, respectively.

The problem for the Entente is rather different. If Italy puts forth a big military effort and ends up with Austrian territory, honoring the deal is fairly easy; Italy can keep what it captures. None of the Entente powers care too much about the disposition of the land in question, and defaulting on the bargain – depriving the Italians of their gains – would hardly be worth the additional effort of wresting it from them. Therefore, the Entente's highest payoff comes from honoring the deal with an Italy that did its part by making a substantial effort against the Dual Monarchy (4), and defaulting is less attractive (2). Any outcome with high Italian war effort is better than one with a low effort, in which defeating the Central Powers is costly and in which Italy likely won't have the requisite land in its possession. Dismembering Austrian territory is still attractive to the Entente, so we might assume that it would still be inclined to honor Italy's requests, though perhaps with much less enthusiasm and maybe to a much lesser degree. Therefore, let's assume that the Entente would lean toward default after an unsatisfactory Italian war effort, which nets 2 (less attractive than defaulting on an Italy that already controls the *Italia irredenta*). The Entente's worst outcome, then, is honoring the deal after Italy has put in a disappointing or half-hearted effort (1) – victory followed by additional wrangling at the peace conference that might produce another war.

Finally, how does Italy evaluate the possible outcomes of its alignment choices? Let's suppose that its most desirable outcome is to maintain neutrality as requested by the Central Powers and then see the latter's commitments honored at the end of a victorious war. In this case, Italy receives 8.[22] Joining the Central Powers also opens Italy up to its worst outcome, though, of high military involvement – i.e., active hostilities against the Entente – after which the Central Powers simply default on their promises, refusing to give up the promised territories (1). High involvement followed by Austria honoring its pledge is only slightly better, yielding a (2), because both of these outcomes entail the inevitably high costs of actively waging war against the Entente from the atypically

---

[22] Remember that payoffs here are strictly ordinal, so we're seeing a number like 8 simply because there are more options to consider; as long as it's still the highest payoff, we could substitute 80 in here, and nothing would change.

vulnerable geographical position of a peninsula facing down the world's most powerful navies.[23] Finally, maintaining neutrality while the Central Powers default is a middling outcome – saving the costs of active war against the Entente, at a minimum (4). Should it join the Entente, however, its second-best outcome is in play: high military effort that, while costly, leads to Italy possessing part of what it hopes to gain and an Entente decision to ratify those gains (6). Even if the Entente defaults, Italy might find itself in a war in which it's likely advantaged by holding the defensive in mountainous terrain, so high effort followed by an Entente default is not much worse (5). Low effort, though, ensures that Italy gains nothing and has to count on further wrangling (and possibly fighting) to get what it wants with the Entente's aid (3) or an Entente default (2), which is only one step above putting in high effort for a defaulting coalition of Central Powers. I never said that decisions over choosing sides in wars are simple – and it certainly wasn't easy for Italy, however obvious the decision looks through the cataract born of a century of hindsight.

How, then, will Italy choose? What game will it play? It's possible in principle to secure its best outcome (8) if it aligns with the Central Powers, but that depends on how Germany and Austria will behave in victory. There are relatively attractive possibilities that follow from joining the Entente, but again that hinges on the Entente's incentives to honor its commitments in victory. Let's start with the Central Powers, Italy's nominal allies offering to compensate it merely for maintaining a benevolent neutrality – allies that also happen to be better off reneging ex post on whatever promises they've made. Figure 9.2 shows that the Central Powers have a dominant strategy of defaulting, which should be quite easy, given that the promised concessions entail mostly Hapsburg territory that Italy would have one Hell of a time holding onto. Indeed, this line of thinking was pervasive in Vienna even as negotiations with Italy dragged on through the spring of 1915: "[Chief of Staff] Conrad, [Austrian Minister-President] Stürgkh, and [Hungarian Prime Minister] Tisza, as well probably as the Germans, also envisaged that promises extracted now under duress might be reneged on after the war."[24] And Italy can't help but be aware of the fact that whatever's been promised for the war's end can only be won by relying on the good faith of Austria and Germany; Italy repeatedly requests that the deal be executed immediately, but it's repeatedly rebuffed.[25] If Italy plays the game with the Central Powers, it expects Germany and Austria to default, and its own best response is to choose low involvement rather than

[23] The French were no slouches in the Med. Germany gets the lion's share of attention, thanks to its prewar competition with the British, but the French Navy would have helped the Royal Navy wreak havoc along Italy's almost indefensible coastline.
[24] Stevenson (1988, p. 55).
[25] Stevenson (1988, pp. 54–55).

waste active belligerence against the Entente when it won't be able to use victory to vault itself into an improved position among the great powers. Therefore, as indicated in Figure 9.2, the Nash Equilibrium of Central Powers alignment would be (low; default), where the Central Powers ride the denial of Italy's weight to the Entente to victory only to default on their prewar promises.

> PROPOSITION 9.1   *The strategy profile (low; default) is a Nash Equilibrium.*

Proof   For (low; default) to be a Nash Equilibrium, it must be the case that

$$u_I(low; \text{default}) \geq u_I(high; \text{default})$$

and

$$u_C(\text{low}; default) \geq u_C(\text{low}; honor).$$

The first inequality is satisfied because $4 \geq 1$, and the second is satisfied because $2 \geq 1$. No player has a profitable deviation, so (low; default) is a Nash Equilibrium. □

The Central Powers have no incentive to honor an agreement with a cooperative Italy, but we can see in the game on the right that the Entente *is* inclined to do so, as long as Italy puts in the requisite effort. This difference, of course, turns on the existence of a long-simmering Italo-Austrian rivalry that has no equivalent in relations with the Entente. If Italy puts in a high military effort after aligning with the Entente, it diverts Austrian forces from the Eastern Front and accelerates the attrition of the Central Powers' reserves; it also puts itself in a position to hold at least parts of the territory it hopes to control at the end of the war, so Italy has a dominant strategy of high military effort in the game at right. That's just as well for the Entente, which is happy to honor a commitment to allowing the annexation of the *Italia irredenta* under such circumstances; refusing Italy its spoils at this point by playing default would be counterproductive. Therefore, the unique Nash Equilibrium of the Entente alignment game is (high; honor).

> PROPOSITION 9.2   *The strategy profile (high; honor) is a Nash Equilibrium.*

Proof   For (high; honor) to be a Nash Equilibrium, it must be the case that

$$u_I(high; \text{honor}) \geq u_I(low; \text{honor}) \quad \text{and} \quad u_C(high; \text{honor}) \geq u_C(high; default).$$

The first inequality is satisfied because $6 \geq 3$, and the second is satisfied because $4 \geq 2$. No player has a profitable deviation, so (high; honor) is a Nash Equilibrium. □

This equilibrium nets Italy a payoff of 6. That's manifestly lower than the best it *could* do by aligning with the Central Powers, but it's the best option available; if Italy wishes to annex Hapsburg territory, the most credible route is turning down an offer from the Central Powers and pursuing a strategy that's costlier upfront – attacking Austria and, by extension, Germany – but which holds out the effective promise of Italy simply keeping what it captures, its partners' inclinations to honor or default on the bargain notwithstanding.

Faced with two options in which a fully realized, peaceful neutrality (however attractive in principle) is little more than a vain wish, one entailing a promise unlikely to be fulfilled and the other active belligerence against the very state at whose expense it wishes to gain, Italy's choice of abandoning neutrality for the Entente makes strategic sense. Looking at one game in which it's sure to receive a payoff of 4 and another in which it can secure 6, Italy chooses the Entente over the Central Powers. As Prime Minister Antonio Salandra puts it in his address of May 23 announcing Italy's entry on the side of the Entente,

> On the day when one of the clauses of the treaty was not fulfilled, ... to whom should we have addressed ourselves? To our common superior – to Germany?[26]

Even its signatories know that the Triple Alliance is "a fair-weather system," one that can really work only when the nascent Austrian-Italian rivalry isn't activated by, say, an Austrian war on Serbia.[27] It's rare in history that the stakes of a single major power–minor power war, like the one between Austria and Serbia, where the major power isn't as major as it used to be, can implicate the interests of so many other powers. If Italy is to bear the costs of belligerence (or vulnerable neutrality) in a general war, it's more inclined toward the deal most likely to be honored. Neutrality, in its leaders' estimation, will merely end with a German-dominated Europe in which Italian aims will be frustrated and in which it might lose even more to an emboldened Teutonic coalition.[28] This fear of German postwar dominance, as we saw in Chapter 7, explains more than the Dual Monarchy's lack of cooperative zeal on the Eastern Front; it also plays a role in rending the Triple Alliance before it can fight its first war together.

As it happens, the same logic that dictates Italy's alignment with the Entente can also shed light on the Ottoman Empire's decision to

---

[26] www.firstworldwar.com/source/italiandeclaration.htm.
[27] Stevenson (1988, p. 49).
[28] It might also risk eventual war with the Entente, since "the German army could not do the immediate damage to a neutral Italy that the Royal Navy could do to a belligerent one." See Stevenson (1988, p. 49).

abandon neutrality to honor what has thus far been an inconvenient – and unpopular if it becomes public – wartime pact with Germany. We don't require a separate game to describe the Ottoman decision process, though you're encouraged to write one down if you wish to check the logic, because we can see a remarkably similar process play out. Both Entente and Central Powers think that the Ottoman decision might one day decide the war, which drives them to offer as much as they can without breaking the bank, whether financially or politically. The Empire knows its decision is important to both sides, and it's determined like Italy to get as much as it can out of the bargain. But again the key distinction between the rival side payments isn't their content but the credibility of commitments to honor them after the war.

In stark contrast to Italy's decision, the Entente's compliance with its offer to the Ottomans is doubtful, because Ottoman neutrality might strengthen Russia – and give it an opportunity to gain and secure access to the all-important Turkish Straits that it will be fain to give up after the war.[29] From Germany, the Ottomans win promises of increased military aid and gains at Russian expense in the Caucasus. Looked at in this light, the decision is straightforward. Neutrality under Entente terms can only undermine the Ottoman position in what are bound to be future confrontations with a victorious Russian Empire, making any such guarantees of Turkish independence ring hollow.[30] The Empire has, by 1914, certainly fought its share of wars against Russian armies with an eye to renaming Constantinople "Tsargrad," so skepticism of the Entente's guarantees doesn't require clairvoyance.[31] On the other hand, siding with the Central Powers, which looks like a relatively safe bet on the war's outcome in the early going, will be based on terms far easier to be honored in victory.

States don't typically join costly wars merely for the sake of fighting, nor do they blindly take the largest offer on the table; they must balance the size of any offer against its credibility. The Ottoman foreign minister Talaat Bey – more famous for the orders that would lead to the deaths of nearly one million Armenian civilians during the war – put the Empire's dilemma thusly in his memoirs:

> My own position was that while much annoyed at the Black Sea affair
> [which began Ottoman belligerence], I nevertheless continued to believe

---

[29] Stevenson (1988, pp. 45–46).

[30] There's also the issue of the Entente's unwillingness to revisit the notorious "capitulations" that gave foreign powers rights in Ottoman territories, but that's not something the Central Powers are jumping to budge on, either, at least early in the war.

[31] On Russian ambitions to dominate the Straits and gain access to the Mediterranean, see Stevenson (1988) and McMeekin (2013, 2015). Pro tip: if ever you're inclined to convince someone that you *don't* want to conquer her capital, don't give it an aspirational name based on what you call your own despot.

that we should join with Germany. The Entente could give us nothing but the renewal of promises, so often broken, to preserve to us our present territory. Hence there was nothing to be gained by joining them.

Moreover, if we refused aid to our German allies now in the time of their need, they would naturally refuse to help us if they were victorious. If we stayed neutral, whichever side won would surely punish Turkey for not having joined them, and would satisfy their territorial ambitions at our expense.[32]

We've now shown that concerns about the eventual terms of peace and one's role in shaping them drive decisions to launch preventive wars before today's settlement erodes (Chapters 4 and 6), to cooperate in the face of otherwise strong incentives to leave one's partner in the lurch (Chapter 7), and, as we see here in Chapter 9, to join military coalitions even in the face of strong incentives to remain neutral or to join the other side. The Ottoman and Italian decisions over which side to join in the Great War illustrate this nicely. War was, for each belligerent, a means of shaping the terms on which it would live with its neighbors and the other great powers after the war – terms it might have been unable to secure by accepting its eventual enemy's requests for neutrality. The strategic interconnectedness of the international system drove both of these initially disinterested states into the war, because their fates were bound up with the other great powers whether or not they wished them to be.

9.2.2 Did Italy Break Faith?

When Italy sided with the Entente, signing the Treaty of London after spurning Austro-German advances, it (unsurprisingly) did itself no favors with its erstwhile partners in the Triple Alliance.[33] In his official response before the Reichstag, Bethmann spared no vitriol for Italy's decision to join the rival coalition, saying

> Italy has now inscribed in the book of the world's history, in letters of blood which will never fade, her violation of faith.

He added for good measure a nice summation of the putative consequences of violating treaties of alliance we discussed in Chapter 7:

> Italian statesmen have no right to measure the trustworthiness of other nations in the same proportion as they measured their own loyalty to a

---

[32] Horne, Source Records, and www.firstworldwar.com/source/talaat_entryintowar.htm.

[33] In typically monarchical fashion, Hapsburg Emperor Franz Josef declared, "The King of Italy has declared war on me" in an act of "perfidy whose like history does not know." The old man might have been angrier about Italy abandoning an alliance everyone knew it detested than he was about the murder of his own nephew. See www.firstworldwar.com/source/italywardec_franzjosef.htm.

treaty. Germany, by her word, guaranteed that the concessions would be carried through. There was no occasion for distrust.[34]

As we saw above, German offers of Austrian territory *did* occasion some distrust, but Bethmann's anger about what he labeled a significant breach of faith raises an important question: why did Italy abandon its partners in the decades-old Triple Alliance in the hour of their greatest peril, especially if doing so would sully Italy's ability to secure alliances and make commitments in the future? And what does this teach us about alliance commitments in general?

Alliances are contracts designed to shape the makeup of coalitions in future (and sometimes ongoing) wars (recall Definition 7.4). They're effective in this endeavor when they provide the right mix of carrots and sticks to make states work together when they have powerful incentives to renege on their commitments – i.e., when the bill comes due and they're asked to join a costly war on behalf of their partners. Alliance contracts are typically public (and secret treaties really took a beating in public opinion after the First World War). Establishing beliefs about who will side with whom when the fighting starts can sustain a balance of power by either minimizing the consequences of shifting power (by countering a rising side's newfound strength) or reducing uncertainty about the attractiveness of fighting (by disabusing potential opponents of their optimism).[35] Thus, an alliance system in which states tend to honor their commitments can be thought of as a collective good, and contributions to it (that is, the honoring of individual commitments) are encouraged by threats of refusing to believe a violator's future commitments.[36] That's a potentially strong selective incentive, and states do their part by investing time and effort only into alliances with partners they expect will be reliable, or that won't abandon them to their fate when enemy armies start massing on the border.[37]

States also try to reduce the risk of entrapment, of finding themselves obligated to join an emboldened ally's war they would rather not fight,[38] and just as with the risk of abandonment, they do so by being selective in their choice of allies and careful in the specifics of their obligations. They may limit their commitments to maintaining neutrality, to defending against attack (and even then only in response to attacks by certain states),

---

[34] See www.firstworldwar.com/source/italywardec_bethmann.htm.

[35] See Morrow (2000) on the rationale for making alliances public, Leeds (2003b) on alliances and deterrence, and Tammen et al. (2000) on the value of alliance-building in the face of rising powers.

[36] See Gibler (2008) for evidence that this occurs at the level of individual leaders being held accountable for their states' failures to honor alliance commitments.

[37] See Smith (1995).

[38] See Snyder (1984) and Snyder (1997).

even to attacking and carving up only specific enemies, but it's rare that they sign blanket commitments to military assistance under all circumstances. And this reticence is in the service of making it harder for their allies to abandon them and limiting the chances they'll be entrapped in undesirable wars.[39] For example, the United States carefully designed commitments to South Korea and Taiwan after the Korean War, refusing to support attempts to renew either the Korean War or the Chinese Civil War. It even went so far in Taiwan's case as to create deliberate ambiguity over whether aid would be forthcoming in the event of an attack, effectively leaving future decisions to defend Taiwan up to Congress, in hopes of restraining Chiang Kai-Shek's foreign policy.[40] Explicit attempts to prevent entrapment show that alliances can also be instruments of control, where states sign treaties with the explicit aim of tethering possible enemies to more desirable, and predictable, foreign policies.[41] The Austro-German alliance, for example, was born in the former's defeat at Prussia's hands in 1866, where the victor's terms included the signing of an alliance – an alliance that, as we've seen, could never perfectly subdue Austro-German rivalry.

As hard as they work to write down credible commitments with reliable allies, we shouldn't be surprised that states honor their alliance commitments at a pretty high rate – about 75 percent of the time.[42] Whether asked to join a war or to remain neutral, states generally honor their commitments, and given the costs of failing to, it would indeed be strange if they routinely ratified treaties they had no intention of honoring. In fact, even Italy's ostensible abandonment of the Triple Alliance is tough to read as a broken promise. The alliance was a defensive one, obliging Italy to fight alongside Germany and the Dual Monarchy only if the others were attacked unprovoked by other great powers; an Austrian invasion of Serbia, to the Italian mind, hardly fit the bill – as it would find itself joining an offensive war to strengthen its Hapsburg rival. Rare though they are, some broken promises have dire consequences. France and the Soviet Union, to take but one example, abandoned their commitments to defend Czechoslovakia against Germany in 1938, standing aside as Germany annexed first the Sudetenland (a Czech region with a majority of German speakers) and then the rest of the country, before turning against Poland in 1939.[43] What separates instances of broken promises, of violated commitments, from the more common cases in which states live up to their

---

[39] See Leeds (2003a).
[40] See Benson (2012, chapter 7).
[41] See Weitsman (2004) and Pressman (2008).
[42] Leeds, Long, and Mitchell (2000).
[43] For a general account of great power responses to German resurgence in the late 1930s, see Kershaw (2015, chapter 6).

obligations when pressed? In other words, when do states violate treaties that they at one time thought it wise to sign and ratify?

When states consider whether to honor an alliance commitment – say, when a partner is attacked – they weigh the immediate benefits of shaping the outcome of the war against the costs of fighting and the downstream benefits of being seen to uphold their commitments. Reneging becomes more attractive if a state's military and economic power has changed dramatically since signing the alliance; having grown strong enough to defend itself, it may not feel all that beholden to its partner, but having grown weaker it may be unable to recoup the immediate costs of war.[44] Likewise, when political institutions or the domestic coalitions that support them change, from democracy to autocracy or vice versa, states may seek new alignments, abandoning their former partners for new ones, like many states in Central and Eastern Europe did after the fall of the Soviet Union and the end of the Warsaw Pact. In some cases, these realignments may occur before treaties are invoked, with states merely abrogating or repudiating treaties before they can be caught in the act of honoring commitments.[45] Finally, the stakes of the war itself, as well as the compensation offered by its participants, can tempt states into violating previous commitments if they believe that they can be rewarded for backing a winner or if threats to punish them down the line are incredible. The Soviet Union, for instance, inked a nonaggression pact with Nazi Germany in 1939, allowing Stalin to share in the carve-up of Poland and mount his own invasion of Finland and the Baltics, as well as obligating him to stand aside in contravention of prior commitments when Hitler invaded France in 1940. Unprepared for war after years of domestic chaos, sweeping purges, and forced industrialization, Stalin abandoned his commitment to France, safe in the knowledge that he'd be unlikely to save it and that, should Germany turn against the Soviet Union, the Western democracies would be unable to continue the fight without his help. The calculation was brutally cynical, to be sure, but it's explicable in light of what Stalin believed would be minimal costs for violating commitments.[46]

Italy may not have violated its treaty obligations in a formal, legal sense in 1915. Considering Austria-Hungary to be the aggressor, it declared early neutrality once war with Russia and France became inevitable, but the incentives pushing it toward the Entente might have been strong

---

[44] See Leeds (1999) and Leeds (2003a).

[45] See, e.g., Leeds and Savun (2007) and Leeds, Mattes, and Vogel (2009).

[46] Abandoning France also had no small amount of extra attraction for the possibility of allowing the capitalist states to bleed by flinging themselves unaided against German fascism while the Soviet Union remained aloof. Stalin also killed his pet parrot with a pipe for mimicking his spitting style, so we shouldn't be surprised he'd make such a hard-nosed calculation (Kershaw, 2015, p. 272). The guy was a right *bastard*.

enough to lure it away from even a stronger commitment to the Central Powers. The Entente's demographic and economic power certainly favored it in a long war against Germany and the Dual Monarchy, its navies could menace the Italian coastline with ease, its offer of compensation to abandon neutrality was more credible, and the stakes of the war – survival as a great power – could reasonably shorten time horizons. Who cared about a reputation for upholding commitments if one wouldn't be around after betting on the losing side in a catastrophic global war? While Italy's decision to join the Entente isn't a clear case of a violated alliance commitment, the Teutonic powers' apoplexy notwithstanding, it does shed light on those relatively rare instances in which states have chosen not to uphold their obligations: when power or institutions have changed since the signing of the treaty and when the nature of the war itself minimizes the costs of violating commitments.

9.3 THE WAR IN EAST ASIA

Postwar peace negotiations represent both promise and peril, and the credibility of commitments that partners make ahead of time can explain why some states abandon neutrality and which side they choose. But the more general idea on which the game in Figure 9.2 rests – that choices made during wartime impact what and how much countries get in the eventual settlement – can also explain one of the war's most curious events. After two decades of steadily losing ground to a rising Japan, which toppled it from its place atop the regional hierarchy in 1895 in the First Sino-Japanese War (in which Japan gained control of Korea and Taiwan), and barely two unsteady years after toppling the Qing Dynasty that had ruled for two and a half centuries, the Republic of China joined the Great War on the same side as its Japanese enemy.[47] Pushed ahead by Foreign Minister Katō Takaaki, Japan had by November 1914 seized control of the German treaty port of Tsingtao on the Shandong Peninsula after a two-month siege, giving it effective command on the Yellow Sea.[48] And, thanks to political dominance in Manchuria since 1905, it could now approach Beijing from north and south on land. With the specter of further Japanese encroachments looming, China nonetheless sided *with* Japan by declaring war on Germany and Austria-Hungary in August 1917. Figure 9.1 places these events in the timeline of the Italian and Ottoman declarations of war.

---

[47] On the First Sino-Japanese War, see Paine (2003).

[48] Yes, it's *that* Tsingtao, home of the famous German-founded brewery. Its product is fine, as far as light lagers go, but this author prefers something a bit hoppier.

PUZZLE 9.2   *Why did China side with Japan in declaring war on Germany?*

Politics makes for strange bedfellows, sure, but at first blush it's hard to make sense of China's decision. It was in no position to fight in Europe as parts of its countryside descended into postrevolution warlordism, though it did actively send diplomats and laborers to help in factories and at the front (some of whom, after their often fraught experiences, would form the core of a revived postwar nationalist political class). China's limited military capabilities aside, rubber-stamping the Japanese presence on the Shandong Peninsula by refusing to give battle would only allow Japan to consolidate its hold on the area, which was crucial to Japan's position as a great power.[49] Italy and the Ottomans, after all, had gone to war against rivals that couldn't promise not to exploit them further in victory. If coalition partnership would only allow Japan to strengthen its position in Chinese territory – to say nothing of scooping up other German possessions in the Pacific at low cost – why should China join the war at all? Why not stay neutral, consolidate the new Republic of China government, and prepare to retake Shandong when the opportunity arose if, as the Chinese political class at the time could agree, "resisting Japan was its real goal"?[50]

China's path to belligerence was a long one, but it was tied not only to the question of Japanese presence but also to the credibility of Japan's 1914 promise to restore Shandong to China after the war.[51] Recovering Shandong bloodlessly, after Japan did the lion's share of the fighting, was certainly appealing on its face. But when Foreign Minister Katō issued Japan's notorious "Twenty-One Demands" in 1915 that discouraged China from joining the war, asserted enough economic and political rights to turn China into a vassal state, *and* ordered China to keep the negotiations secret; the game was up. Japan, China reasoned, would only want the extent of its demands kept quiet if it knew that the rest of the Entente would disapprove. China's leaders quickly inferred that Japan wouldn't give up its presence in China if it didn't have to, that its great power partners might be able to restrain Japan in those matters, and that the place at the postwar negotiating table Japan sought to deny it might be China's best hope of climbing a few rungs back up in the regional hierarchy. China publicized the Twenty-One Demands and won some softening of the

[49] For a discussion of the domestic politics of Japanese involvement, see Hamilton and Herwig (2004, chapter 8). Japan siding with the Entente wasn't a foregone conclusion, since, after all, siding with Germany might help balance against Russia, but the lure of easily conquering German colonies and preserving relations with Britain proved the decisive factors.
[50] Xu (2017, p. 247).
[51] Stevenson (1988, p. 43).

most extreme provisions, but by 1917 neutrality became untenable due to a sizable domestic outcry against creeping Japanese influence in northern China. By August 1917, several months after severing diplomatic relations, China declared war on Germany and Austria-Hungary.

Why take the fateful step of joining the war when the most it could offer was laborers, and when China would tie its own hands against military action to liberate Shandong? The promise of an eventual peace settlement, which would be the first truly global resetting of the balance of power in history, provides the answer. Japan and China wanted to get the same thing out of the First World War: China. The former initially joined because it could take German possessions (and because the Entente couldn't stop it from an overly charitable reading of 1902's Anglo-Japanese alliance), but it became committed over time to keeping China out in order to deny it standing in the postwar settlement – standing that China could only get, power it could only wield, if it had made some kind of contribution to the war effort. China's goal was to gain that leverage, the same kind of power that Britain sought to preserve by keeping its troops in the line on the Western Front (Chapter 7), to invoke the standards of self-determination already on the lips of the Western powers to tie Japan's hands against exploiting the war to further cement its hold on the Asian mainland. China couldn't credibly threaten a war to break Japan's hold on Shandong, but if it could earn standing in the peace negotiations, its leaders might achieve the same thing bloodlessly, by throwing not their own military weight but the combined authority of the other victorious powers behind an effort to halt Japan's imperial project in China.

As it happened, the victors at Versailles honored secret promises to allow a postwar Japanese presence in Shandong – a betrayal of China that actually helped sink ratification of the Versailles treaty in the American Senate – but Japan would eventually yield Shandong in 1922 as a result of pressure from the other great powers. However delayed, and however much it came with a series of other cascading disappointments in the interwar years, that was China's hope in siding with the Entente in the First World War: to gain a seat at the table from which it could bring the interests of other powers to bear in limiting Japanese aggrandizement at the expense of a more equitable regional balance of power. Even more so than in the Italian and Ottoman decisions, the overwhelming factor in China's alignment decision, as well as Japan's frustrated attempts to keep that alignment from happening, was the credibility, or lack thereof, of promises made during wartime and the chances that earning a standing in postwar negotiations could render such promises credible. Neutrality for China's young republic would have rested only on a patently incredible commitment by Japan to give up key parts of the very imperium it had been trying to build in Asia for decades. Therefore, belligerence *alongside* Japan became China's best hope for a power-political victory *over* Japan.

9.4 COALITIONS AND INTERNATIONAL POLITICS II

Chapter 7 told us why states might want to build military coalitions, from aggregating military capabilities to securing basing and staging rights to reducing the costs of war and building international legitimacy, but it also highlighted the challenges of sustaining cooperation once armies are in the field, casualties start to mount, and spending on the war begins crowding out other priorities. We saw how alliances can help solve some collective action problems by raising the costs of abandoning one's partners, but states can use positive inducements as well, offering side payments and concessions, to try and sustain cooperation. Germany struggled to offer inducements to its own allies, thanks in part to a political dominance among the Central Powers that would only grow after victory; it proved an obstacle both to Austria-Hungary's eager cooperation *and* to Italy's willingness to assist its Triple Alliance partners. The Entente, on the other hand, sustained cooperation more effectively because their wartime goals were to a large degree compatible; that is, each could satisfy some individual goals in the war without encroaching too far on its partners, lessening the severity of the collective action problem.[52] Yet the story so far begs the question of how states manage to strike such successful bargains with their coalition partners in the first place. Recent work in political science tells us a lot about who builds military coalitions, how they do it, and who joins them.

The story of war expansion we told in this chapter lays bare some of the key mechanisms at play in coalition building. First, a potential coalition-builder – or a coalition looking to add members – must ask itself three questions: "How much military assistance do I need, how much am I willing to pay for it, and who's willing to help at that price?"[53] States rely on partners for raw military capabilities, financial support, basing and staging rights, and the legitimation and diplomatic cover that comes from other countries' approval, each of which shapes in different ways their military prospects during war. But different contributions come from different partners at different prices, and potential partners can drive a hard bargain when a coalition-builder is desperate for help; when a potential partner is financially or militarily powerful, uniquely positioned geographically, or

---

[52] As we'll see, it takes the Bolshevik Revolution to finally make an already-defeated Russia ready to make a separate peace with Germany in early 1918.

[53] Wolford (2015, chapter 3).

when its support can win the assistance (or, at a minimum, the neutrality) of others, then it can demand better terms from a coalition-builder. The problem, of course, is that potential partners demand things that coalition-builders would rather not concede, like shares of the spoils of victory, concessions on other dimensions of foreign policy (like help against their own enemies), financial or military aid, a say in who else joins the coalition, and even adjustments to war aims, bargaining postures, and war-fighting strategies.[54] A military coalition forms when a builder (that is, a buyer) finds a partner's required terms (i.e., a seller's price) acceptable, and that process isn't always easy – especially in the looming shadow of a bloody, destructive, unpredictable war.

What do these coalition bargains look like in practice? One common way of securing cooperation is to negotiate over the spoils of victory or more immediate foreign policy concessions. Like the belligerents in the First World War, the Balkan League of Serbia, Greece, Bulgaria, and Montenegro agreed in 1912, albeit in terms that wouldn't prove stable, how to divide the lands they expected to capture from the Ottoman Empire in what would become the First Balkan War.[55] The Soviet Union requested a new infusion of military equipment, as well as promises of territorial adjustments in the region (chief among them Sakhalin Island, disputed with Japan), in return for promising to join the war against Japan after the prospective fall of Germany in 1945.[56] Turkey requested and received a package of financial and military inducements for participating in the 1991 Gulf War coalition, allowing the use of its airbases and the mere threat of opening a northern front to tie down a considerable number of Iraqi troops while their comrades-in-arms faced the rapid armored onslaught to the south. Sometimes, bargains aren't so easily struck. In 2003, when a smaller American-led coalition aimed to topple the Iraqi government, the terms on offer to Turkey – financial and military aid, as well as support for its bid to enter the European Union – proved insufficient, and the Turkish parliament refused to join the American coalition in a dramatic eleventh-hour vote.[57] Finally, just as some buyers can offer too little, some sellers can charge too much: the United States turned down offers of assistance from both Pakistan and Taiwan during the Korean War, because the former was tied to a request for a defense pact and assistance against

---

[54] Concessions like this are also present in alliance negotiations (see, e.g., Johnson 2015; Long and Leeds 2006; Poast 2012), which are a special case of coalition negotiations more generally.

[55] See Glenny (2012) and Hall (2000).

[56] Frank (2001).

[57] For a comparison of coalition negotiations with Turkey in 1991 and 2003, see Wolford (2015, chapter 3), and for discussions of both wars, see Freedman and Karsh (1991), Atkinson (1993), and Keegan (2005).

India in Kashmir and the latter risked allowing Chiang Kai-Shek to restart the Chinese Civil War – raising the specter for the United Nations-backed coalition of a Third World War against the combined might of the Communist bloc.[58]

Failing to secure a partner's cooperation can have an impact on the war indirectly in terms of forgone assistance or, even worse, a potential partner siding with one's enemy. But as we saw in Chapter 7, some partners require adjustments to war aims and bargaining strategies before offering their services, which can impact the course of crisis bargaining and the war itself in directly observable ways. In 1991, for example, the American-led coalition seeking to overturn the Iraqi annexation of Kuwait needed Saudi Arabian territory for a staging ground, but the Saudi royal family made clear that it would only allow the invasion to proceed from its territory if it wouldn't lead to a costly, chaotic breakup of Iraq (which remained a bulwark against Iranian ambitions in the region). As such, the United States committed not to drive all the way to Baghdad, securing critical Saudi support by promising not to include overturning the regional balance of power in its war aims.[59] Likewise, during three interventions in the Yugoslav Civil Wars of the 1990s, the United States assented to limited airstrikes as opposed to more extensive war efforts – like a ground invasion – in order to retain the support of key allies like Italy and Germany, whose proximity offered airbases from which to stage operations but which also put them at greater risk of retaliation or spillover effects.[60] Sometimes, these compromises lead to signaling failures, as we saw in Chapter 7, but commitments to limited war aims or war-fighting strategies can also discourage balancing and the further expansion of wars. Where Austria's association with Germany rendered incredible its own claims to limited aims in the July Crisis, keeping Taiwan out of the Korean War and the twin decisions to neither topple Iraq's government nor allow Israel into the Gulf War coalition in 1991 helped prevent the further expansion of those conflicts.[61]

So, what conditions are conducive to the formation of military coalitions? Great powers often find themselves building coalitions, because they frequently project power well beyond their borders, for which local basing and staging rights are critical, and to reassure potential balancers by winning widespread diplomatic support; Soviet assent to the 1991 Gulf War helped convince a wide number of states, for example, that the American-led coalition wasn't a threat worth balancing.[62] Indeed, the United States

---

[58] See Stueck (1995, 2004).
[59] See Atkinson (1993), Bush and Scowcroft (1998), and Kreps (2011).
[60] For a discussion of the Kosovo Crisis and War in particular, see Wolford (2015, chapter 4); for a discussion of this process in the Bosnian Wars, see Papayoanou (1997).
[61] See Wolford (2015, chapter 5).
[62] See Voeten (2005) and Chapman (2011).

has built coalitions almost by "default" after the end of the Cold War.[63] Preexisting alliance treaties,[64] as well as the perceived legitimacy of the operation and ethnic similarities, can lower the costs of winning a partner's support,[65] making coalitions easier to build. However, as coalition-builders need partners more desperately – say, when their military needs are large or when their leaders need to shore up their domestic position with a foreign policy success – they become less selective, paying higher prices to win the support of countries they'd otherwise not countenance as partners.[66] Britain and France, for example, cooperated with the Soviet Union after the latter's invasion by Germany in 1941, despite previous Nazi–Soviet collusion and the certainty of fraught future postwar negotiations, simply because there appeared no better path to victory.[67] And as we'll see later in our story, they accepted assistance from a United States openly ambivalent about (and sometimes hostile to) their aims in the First World War because, without a steady flow of dollars and (eventually) doughboys, the Entente might've lost the Great War.

9.5 CONCLUSION

When we talk about the expansion of war – that is, the addition of new belligerents to ongoing conflicts – we often use epidemiological terms like "spread," "diffusion," or even "contagion."[68] These terms can be powerful metaphors, but as we've seen in this chapter they elide something important about the way in which wars expand. War isn't contracted like the flu, nor does it burst forth out of the blue and despite all precautions like some kind of congenital time bomb. States often join conflicts consciously, as the result of a bargaining process by which they offer their military cooperation in return for side payments that can cover the costs of war, where those costs may be blood, treasure, or the perils of abandoning previous alliance commitments. Those countries engaged in war try to recruit assistance by shaping the terms by which potential partners enter the war. Absent a credible side payment, it's difficult to imagine any of the countries we focused on in this chapter joining in the manner or at the time that they did. Despite powerful incentives to remain neutral, the Ottoman Empire, Italy, Japan, and China all joined the Great War with an eye toward what they might gain as a result of belligerence and whether the

[63] Kreps (2011).
[64] See Wolford (2015, chapter 3).
[65] See Tago (2007) and Vucetic (2011b), respectively.
[66] See Starr (1972), Wolford (2015, chapter 3), and Wolford and Ritter (2016).
[67] Kennan (1984).
[68] See, e.g., Gleditsch (2002).

promises to make good on those concessions were credible. The first two joined by opting for the more credible of two packages of side payments made by rival coalitions, while the latter two joined in hopes of gaining advantages over each other at the ultimate peace conference, where each hoped to leverage the combined power of the Entente in determining the future of German holdings in China and, by extension, the future of China itself.

The difficulties of sustaining military cooperation notwithstanding (recall Chapter 7), the Entente and the Central Powers both engaged in a years-long competition for the allegiance of neutral powers whose contributions, however small in an absolute sense, might yet prove decisive in a long, close-run war of attrition.[69] Other neutral countries – including Bulgaria, Romania, and Greece – sought favorable terms on which to join the war, as did the leaders of would-be uprisings, including the Hashemites and al-Sauds, supported by foreign powers in the Ottoman Middle East.[70] That military cooperation comes with a price tag isn't surprising, but an appreciation of how states negotiate those prices and ultimately form coalitions (or don't) can shape whether states can get what they want in crisis bargaining without fighting, whether war drags on still longer, and ultimately whether coalitions end the war as victors or vanquished. Coalition-building, like arms-racing, is an attempt to shape the outcome of either ongoing or future wars, to manage and control the means of change in international relations. Securing that cooperation often requires concessions over what, precisely, a new peaceful order will look like. And as we'll see in later chapters, all the primary belligerents kept their eyes on the ultimate peace conference as costs and casualties mounted to no apparent end, domestic politics began to strain against the bonds of wartime unity, the Central Powers became more desperate to stave off defeat, and the European-dominated international order of the past became an ever more distant memory.

---

[69] This suggests another analogy between elections and war: in a close race, virtually everyone's vote is decisive, as is every event that sways votes right down to the end. Isolating one as decisive is logically equivalent to isolating any other.

[70] See, inter alia, Stevenson (1988) and McMeekin (2015).

10 Coordinating Caution: Naval War in the North Sea

Even the most successful result from a high sea battle will not compel England to make peace.

Admiral Reinhard Scheer

When you are winning, risk nothing.

Admiral David Beatty

This chapter returns us to the North Sea, where in 1912 the end of the Anglo-German naval race (Chapter 3) stabilized the distribution of power in Britain's favor. Yet for all the new capital ships laid down, christened, and commissioned, and despite each side's vulnerability to disruptions of seaborne commerce, the war in the North Sea was curiously limited to a few battles, from Dogger Bank to Heligoland Bight to Jutland-Skagerrak, that are more famous for being rare than for being decisive.

> Why did Great Britain and Germany wage a limited naval war, even as they devoted unprecedented levels of effort to a total war on land?

Great Britain and Germany were, by the outbreak of the war, the dominant naval powers in their respective coalitions, outclassing and outgunning all other belligerent fleets for most of the conflict.[1] Yet in an otherwise total war, where governments extracted heretofore unseen efforts from their populations and made concessions to win the military cooperation of states whose assistance they'd otherwise scoff at, the two navies that would seem to have the best chance of deciding the war by trying to eliminate the other's fleet made no serious attempt. Generals discouraged a live-and-let-live strategy in the oft-fragile discipline of the trenches, but admirals consistently forced just such a strategy on commanders and sailors otherwise spoiling for a fight.[2] But why?

---

[1] By the time the United States entered the war in 1917, its own shipbuilding program was on pace to give it the largest navy in the world by the early 1920s (Sondhaus, 2014, p. 252).

[2] Commanders and sailors on surface vessels, that is. For a few brief – but consequential – periods, German submarines were turned against Entente and neutral merchant shipping

Our model of naval strategy will both resolve this puzzle and teach us a few things along the way:

- how coordinating beliefs helps players choose among multiple equilibria;
- the role of "focal solutions" in solving coordination problems;
- how enemies set self-enforcing limits on the scope and scale of fighting;
- the importance of coordination problems in shaping the balance of power.

We'll show that the apparent anomaly of a limited naval war is a solution to something called a coordination problem in which players choose among multiple Nash Equilibria. The naval war we saw resulted not from any particular configuration of power or preferences but from tacitly created common knowledge about each side's strategies. In working through the logic of coordination, we'll see that there were, if not common, then coincident interests in limiting the naval war to support the relatively unconstrained land war. The problem for each side was to make a guess about the other side's strategy in what was an exceedingly low-information environment, where the credibility of communication was dubious at best. Both Germany and Great Britain were willing to wage a major naval war *if the other side would*, but they were also happy to keep the war limited *if the other side would*, because warships and trained crew were both critical to sustaining a long, grueling war effort and far more scarce than soldiers, machine guns, bullets, barbed wire, and shells. In the North Sea, the difference between a catastrophic total war between surface fleets and a cheaper, limited conflict depended on each side's expectations about the other's strategy and whether they could work out a tacit agreement in the absence of direct communication. That is, they had to create the common conjecture (Definition 2.8) on the fly, out of ready-to-hand features of the strategic situation. We'll show once again that ostensibly sensible individual incentives can add up to puzzling collective outcomes like, for example, two major powers locked in a battle to the death on the Continent refusing to use their formidable naval forces against each other. After discussing the naval dimension of the Great War, we'll show how a similar process explains equally curious limits on the scope of the Korean War, how it might do so again in a future great power conflict in the shadow of nuclear weapons, as well as how coordination problems and their solutions pervade international politics, from the drawing of borders to the preservation of peace between rival great powers.

(for details, you'll have to wait until Chapter 13), but the U-boats were never a serious threat to the Royal Navy, nor were British subs much more than a nuisance to the High Seas Fleet.

> **Key Terms for Chapter 10**
> - Coordination Problem
> - Focal Point/Solution

10.1 LIMITED WAR IN THE NORTH SEA

When general war finally came to Europe in 1914, the British and German navies were flush with newly built, musclebound dreadnoughts and their lightly armored, swifter (but equally well armed) battlecruiser cousins, crewed by sailors and officers eager to defend the national honor on the high seas. The British Empire controlled a global network of coaling stations and that connected it to the resources, money, and manpower of its far-flung colonies, giving it a unique capacity to blockade enemy coasts and project power to distant shores. Across the North Sea, the German "risk fleet" that Tirpitz had worked so tirelessly to build was a force in its own right. Smaller than the Royal Navy (though with better targeting systems for its shipboard guns), it could nonetheless pose a significant threat to the Royal Navy in port, to the English Channel, and to critical Entente shipping lanes. And yet the guns that echoed over the land for four years, hurling millions of tons of steel and high explosive and poison gas at enemy trenches, were mostly silent on the seas. Notwithstanding the years of shipbuilding and the dreams of admirals on both sides yearning to stamp their names on a modern-day Trafalgar, the clash between Europe's two most formidable navies, to say nothing of the exploits of the smaller fleets maintained by the other belligerents in the Mediterranean, Adriatic, Baltic, and Black Seas, proved to be underwhelming. As August 1914 dragged on with no major naval engagement in the North Sea, British sailors lamented that they'd ditched their furniture and flammable fittings overboard in late July, only to start replacing them a few weeks later once the frustrated reality of the war at sea set in.[3]

The war in the North Sea, the focus of this chapter,[4] saw only three sizable battles (see Figure 10.1) in which capital ships engaged one another as intended – at Heligoland Bight (1914), Dogger Bank (1915), and Jutland-Skagerrak (1916) – and none of them altered the course of the greater war. The British got the better of the Germans in the first two engagements, though as on land initial victories proved difficult to convert into broader strategic successes, as the Germans learned after a Pyrrhic victory in the

---

[3] Hastings (2013, pp. 356–357).

[4] Like Chekov's Gun hanging on the wall, if dreadnoughts are built early in the story (recall Chapter 3), they have to see action later, however limited it might be.

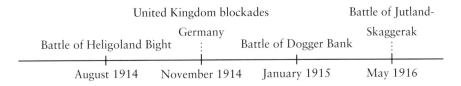

Figure 10.1 The war in the North Sea, 1914–1916.

third and largest battle. The British lost more ships at the Battle of Jutland-Skagerrak just west of Denmark, but even after failing to pursue a withdrawing German fleet, the Grand Fleet remained in control of the sea, and the High Seas Fleet was confined to the German littoral for most of the rest of the war, hiding behind a dense network of minefields and making only the occasional sortie toward the British Isles to shell coastal towns and assess whether the Royal Navy could be drawn into battle. German caution was evident well before 1916, though, in its refusal to attempt to interdict the British Expeditionary Force on its way across the Channel in the earliest days of the war. This seemed like precisely the kind of mission that Tirpitz might have envisioned for his vaunted risk fleet, yet it was studiously avoided.[5] Submarines, which would become infamous for sinking merchant ships (and help prompt American entry in Chapter 13), played only a marginal military role in these early battles, thanks largely to limited numbers and a prewar doctrine that saw them useful primarily as defensive weapons.[6]

The storied Royal Navy was also tied to a curiously cautious strategy. Faced with two options for strangling the import-dependent German economy by blockade, Great Britain chose the "distant" over the "near" option, laying a minefield between Scotland and Norway that lay along the horizon in Map 10.1. Its formidable reputation notwithstanding, Britain's navy was happy to stay away from the German-Danish littoral, cut off German access to vital seaborne imports, and contain German ships in the North Sea rather than patrol too close to the Continent,[7] questions over the legal status of such a distant blockade notwithstanding.[8] Enforcing

[5] See Sondhaus (2014, p. 116).

[6] That said, a German mine placed during Jutland-Skagerrak by a submarine outside the Grand Fleet's base at Scapa Flow in Scotland would eventually sink a ship carrying Secretary of State for War Lord Kitchener to Russia (Sondhaus, 2014, p. 225), killing him among 600 others and depriving the British of one of the few leaders to embrace the necessity of attrition to win the war (see Philpott, 2014). In death, he'd be blamed for a shell shortage that he'd been adamant about trying to avert. Wartime politics, like any other politics, is a dirty business.

[7] Philpott (2014, p. 197).

[8] According to the Declaration of London of 1909, which developed out of the London Naval Conference, blockades as a means of restricting enemy commerce had to be "effective" to be legal – that is, the blockading power had to be in complete control

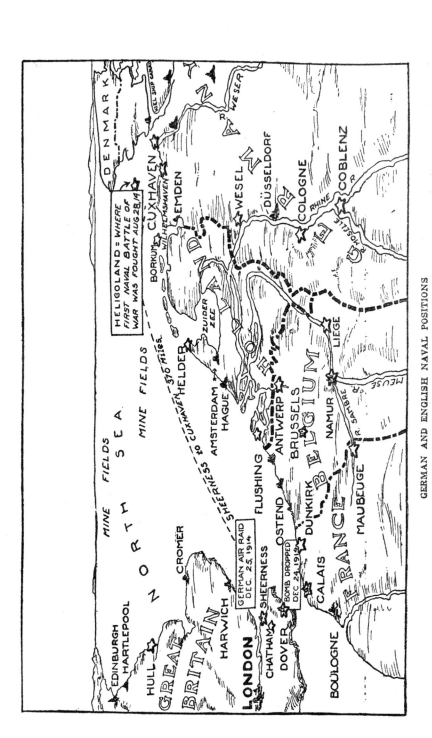

Map 10.1 Britain's blockade of Germany. From Reynolds, Churchill, and Miller (1916).

the blockade safe from concentrated German naval forces, clogging up the Channel and the seas between Scotland and Norway, the Royal Navy focused mostly on defense, mounting the occasional sortie in response to the occasional German raid on coastal cities.[9] Despite the moral outrage generated by coastal shelling and Zeppelin raids targeting civilians, the British never took the naval war to the Germans. The Grand Fleet never ventured closer to the German coast than it had to, as evidenced by Admiral David Beatty's controversial refusal to turn a tactical defeat into a potentially victorious strategic rout by pursuing withdrawing German ships after Jutland-Skagerrak.[10] An attack on the Continent, replicating 1807's Battle of Copenhagen in which a British fleet destroyed a Danish one and opened German lands to invasion, was possible, and Germany's dread of a repetition bordered on the pathological,[11] but such a threat never materialized. Indeed, "[i]n the first days of the war each navy expected, or feared, a bold strike from the other that never came."[12]

What makes the cautious British and German strategies so puzzling is that they seem to forgo a litany of opportunities to influence the course of the increasingly total war raging on land. Dependent as it was on imports that could be (and later were) slowed to a trickle by British blockade, Germany seems to have had every reason to try to break the British stranglehold before it became too tight.[13] Yet German sorties toward the British coast were few and far between. Even a feint toward interdicting the BEF in transit to the Continent might have diverted British attention to defending its coast rather than imposing a blockade, just as a more robust campaign of shelling the British coast might've done. Forcing the British to divert resources to containing the High Seas Fleet could have weakened its hold over Imperial shipping lanes, increasing the costs of extracting resources, wealth, and manpower from the colonies. After all, British control of the seas allowed it to bring 1 million troops from the colonies to the Continent with impunity, to say nothing of many more millions of tons of military stores, animals, and other personnel.[14] Still, Germany's commerce raiding efforts remained limited. The broad sweep of German naval strategy wasn't

---

over access to the closed ports in order to respect the rights of neutrals. While all the great powers signed the declaration, none ratified it, making its legal force questionable, and both Britain and Germany largely ignored it throughout the war (Sondhaus, 2014, p. 51).

[9] See Hastings (2013, chapter 11).

[10] Sondhaus (2014, p. 232).

[11] See Steinberg (1966).

[12] Sondhaus (2014, p. 114).

[13] Tempting as it might be to draw the comparison, the distant blockade and Germany's seeming quiescence isn't like Vader force-choking a helpless Captain Needa on the bridge of the *Executor*. Germany could, in principle, have put up more of a fight.

[14] Stevenson (2004, p. 200).

the search for a grand, decisive fleet-sized battle but a focus on guerrilla tactics based on mines and submarines, designed to avoid a direct attack on the Royal Navy.[15] German ships stayed mainly in port, officers and sailors atrophying (and toying with ideas of revolution) in the salt air hanging over the northern European coast while their compatriots in the army did the dirty if more exciting work of trying to bleed the Entente white or of dashing back and forth across the wide open spaces of Russian Poland. In fact, the surface fleet's most consequential action might have come not from battle but the refusal to seek it. The Kiel Mutiny of 1918 saw sailors refuse an order for a last-ditch engagement with the Royal Navy as the war lurched to its conclusion (for that, see Chapter 14), helping spark revolution and the fall of the Hohenzollern dynasty that had led Germany to defeat and its replacement by a more democratic government that would make peace with the Entente, only to be assailed by the autocratic forces that waged the war almost immediately after the armistice. It was hardly the denouement that Tirpitz and the Kaiser had in mind as they laid down dreadnought after dreadnought in the years before the war.

By refusing to give battle, by refusing to roll the dice at sea like it appeared so willing to do on land, Germany appears to have been complicit in the long, slow economic strangulation that eventually turned the public against the war.[16] Yielding the North Sea to British naval superiority for four years certainly looks like folly in light of the war's eventual outcome: German defeat in 1918 and the subsequent internment of the High Seas Fleet in the British Isles. Why did Germany wait until late October 1918, when defeat was all but a foregone conclusion and the navy primed for mutiny, to seek an ultimate decision with the Royal Navy? And why, for its part, didn't Great Britain flex its historically dominant naval muscle and impose a stricter blockade closer to German ports, strangling its civilian economy (and thus its labor pool) sooner and laying waste to a High Seas Fleet that could no longer hide? First Lord of the Admiralty Winston Churchill gave full-throated advocacy to an amphibious assault on the German coast, yet he was consistently denied the chance to open a new front on the Continent.[17] Why, in other words, did the limited war at sea look so little like the ostensibly unlimited war on land? Access to seaborne commerce sustained the Entente while its denial strained the Central Powers, yet Germany never seriously tried to isolate the British Isles until its final campaign of unrestricted submarine warfare in 1917, and the British Empire seems never to have seriously pressed the naval advantage it labored at great expense to maintain in the prewar naval race.

---

[15] Sondhaus (2014, p. 114).

[16] On the blockade and its effects on the German home front, see Herwig (2014), Philpott (2014), and Watson (2014).

[17] Hastings (2013, pp. 360–361). He'd get his way at the Dardanelles, eventually, but it would nearly sink his political career.

Why go to all the trouble of building expensive battle fleets with the express purpose of confronting each another, only to use them sparingly (if at all) when the war both sides prepared for finally came?

10.2 EXPLAINING LIMITS ON WAR

Frustrating as it was for the men crewing the ships, the German and British publics had to watch their prized fleets stay idle as armies flailed at one another in the ghastly, helpless stalemate on the Continent. It was especially strange for the average Briton, raised in a world of unquestioned naval dominance to expect as part of a "Trafalgar Complex" yet another Continental war to be resolved by yet another smashing victory for the Royal Navy.[18] But the reasons the public valued the Royal Navy – its role in maintaining the Empire, its legendary prowess, and its awesome firepower – also look like reasons to keep it far from European shores in a distant blockade: the cost of losing a single dreadnought, let alone a sizable chunk of the fleet, would be staggering. Doing so would require a diversion of resources, attention, and effort from maintaining links with the rest of the Empire during a war for survival that depended on those very Imperial possessions, from India, Malaya, and Singapore to Australia, New Zealand, and Canada. Indeed, the high costs of a naval war look like an elegant solution to this chapter's puzzle. German decision-makers also viewed the potential of a major confrontation as extremely costly, especially after defeat at Dogger Bank locked in a 3:2 ratio of British superiority in capital ships and drew back the curtain on the possibility of the Copenhagen scenario should the High Seas Fleet's ability to defend the coast be compromised.[19] Max Hastings captures the conventional story well, noting that

> for both sides, deterrence and defence, preservation of assets in being, became the dominant theme of the next four years, at the expense of offensive action.[20]

That rationale makes some *prima facie* sense: capital ships were valuable and difficult to replace, and "[t]he weaker side had little motive to risk annihilation, nor the stronger to risk nullifying its lead,"[21] so both Britain and Germany were inclined toward caution in using their priceless capital ships against one another. But this account is missing something. If each side knew that the other was so vulnerable – and there's little reason to believe that wasn't the case as cautious strategies were implemented year after year – then why not try to take advantage of the other's reticence? Why respond to an enemy's caution with caution of one's own, when a more aggressive option might force the enemy to play a difficult hand?

---

[18] Hastings (2013, p. 356).
[19] Sondhaus (2014, p. 139).
[20] Hastings (2013, p. 363).
[21] Stevenson (2004, p. 199).

PUZZLE 10.1   *Why did Great Britain and Germany wage a limited naval war while waging a total war on land?*

That a large-scale naval campaign might have proven prohibitively costly for both Britain and Germany is surely part of the answer to our puzzle, but we'll show in this section that it's not quite enough: the conventional story misses the crucial element of strategic interaction. Focusing simply on each side's high costs of fighting can't tell us what stood in the way of one side taking advantage of the other's unwillingness to risk large numbers of capital ships. True, a major collision might have been as wasteful and as unpredictable as the Battle of the Frontiers. British Admiral John Jellicoe, who could command the Grand Fleet at Jutland-Skagerrak, was "[t]horoughly aware of the unpredictability of a great naval battle fought with modern technology,"[22] but that doesn't mean neither side should stand idly by if the other decided to give battle. If British ships steamed for the German coast, or if attacks on the British seaboard were more than mere raids, then it strains credulity to claim that fleets would have refused to muster in defense. The unilateral incentive to save the costs of a large-scale naval war can only be realized if the other side chooses not to take advantage of the other's caution, and we'll show in this section that the easy story about the costs of losing capital ships gets something wrong about each side's preferences. We'll flesh out the story of the naval war by writing down and analyzing a pair of models – one focused on British and German preferences, the other on avoiding collisions on narrow sidewalks – and show that the amount of space between the limited, cautious naval war we saw and the grand, widescreen naval war everyone expected was very narrow indeed.

Despite their antagonism and willingness to seek out major engagements on land, Britain and Germany had strong incentives to *match*, as opposed to take advantage of, each other's strategy. We'll show that their goal was to keep the naval war limited if the other would, but to unleash the fury of their dreadnoughts' guns if the other indicated that battle would be given. Rather than avoid a naval version of the Battle of the Frontiers by changing the way battles were conducted (which resulted in attrition on land), the belligerents chose to avoid major battles almost entirely (or, if you prefer, digging trenches but doing so ridiculously far away from each other's artillery). The limited naval war arose from the solution to a coordination problem, in which there are multiple, equally rational ways to play the game (that is, the game has multiple Nash Equilibria) and where each side's beliefs about the other's strategy is the deciding factor in which equilibrium is played. Where the common conjecture supported

---

[22] Stevenson (2004, p. 205).

our equilibria thus far as part of the already-given background of the social world (recall Definition 2.8 and Chapter 6), in this chapter players actively try to shape the content of the common conjecture. The limited war in the North Sea, designed to avoid major engagements, could easily have been a total one built around large-scale fighting, even with the same sailors in the same gun turrets, the same leaders making strategy in London and Berlin for the same battle fleets, and the same publics waiting for news of the same war at home. Despite the fairly obvious fact that "commanders on both sides hesitated to risk their most powerful formations in what might turn out to be one final, decisive engagement" in order to support the broader effort of a long war,[23] the simple structure of outcomes, strategies, and preferences isn't always sufficient to tell us how a game will be played. Fragile as the equilibria of coordination games might be, they show how even mortal enemies can reach tacit agreement on how to limit war, despite the de jure anarchy of the international system that renders many promises of restraint incredible (recall Chapters 2, 6, and 9).

10.2.1 Solving the Puzzle

Writing down a useful model of naval warfare in the North Sea requires that we think a little differently about military strategy than we did in Chapter 8, where forces on land find themselves hoping, albeit in vain, for major breakthroughs. The enormous resources used by their armies mean that belligerents must devote less to their navies, placing an ever higher premium on protecting the expensive capital ships that guard coasts, shipping lanes, and troop transports. War (as I'm sure you're tired of hearing at this point) is instrumental and wasteful (Definition 1.1); belligerents hope to win each other's acquiescence at minimal cost, not to flog each other for the sake of flogging one another. Germany, outgunned by the British (a fact made painfully clear after the defeat at Dogger Bank) and fearful for its coastline, can ill afford to lose the High Seas Fleet. Even Tsar Nicholas II in Russia urges caution on his own Baltic Fleet in order to avert "a second Tsushima," referencing the Russian Navy's catastrophic defeat in the Russo-Japanese War.[24] Seaborne commerce, which requires constant protection, is also crucial to the Entente effort as their dependence on goods and manpower from their colonies – and, later, American troops – increases throughout the war. Neither side is eager to expend naval resources that are both critical to the war on land and, thanks to the cost and anticipated length of the war, difficult to replace. There are, however,

---

[23] Jeffery (2016, p. 124).
[24] Sondhaus (2014, p. 189).

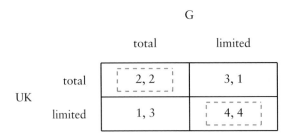

Figure 10.2 Naval strategy in the North Sea.

limits to each side's willingness to keep its navy on a purely conservative footing.

Figure 10.2 shows how these preferences structure British and German incentives for their respective war efforts in the North Sea. Both sides have the same options of total naval war, which for both means a concerted but costly effort to seek major engagements aimed at destroying the other's battle fleet, and limited war, which for the British means a distant blockade and for the Germans a retreat behind a protective cordon of littoral minefields, punctuated by the occasional guerilla-style raid on the British coast.[25] If both sides go total, they wage a war not unlike the Battle of the Frontiers in its staggering cost and unpredictability, risking precious dreadnoughts and battlecruisers that, once destroyed, leave merchant shipping and/or coastlines vulnerable. Each side receives 2 at a (total; total) strategy profile, which despite its costs is better than staying limited while the other goes total, which gives the side that goes total a chance – if even a slim one – of achieving naval dominance; the side that stays limited receives 1 at this outcome, while the side that goes total receives 3. Even waging a total war closer to the enemy's coast will be staggeringly costly given the defensive advantages of minefields and submarines, compromising the British ability to defend its network of coaling stations and the German ability to deter attacks on its coastline. Therefore, both Britain and Germany achieve their best outcomes of 4 at (limited; limited).[26] Each side most prefers a mutually limited naval war (4), which is more attractive than bearing the costs of going unilaterally total (3). Finally, each prefers participating in a total war (2) rather than leaving itself vulnerable if the other side decides to go on the offensive (1); it is this last element of belligerent preferences that the cost-tolerance story misses, and the omission isn't without consequences for explaining the limited war that we see.

---

[25] Sondhaus (2014, p. 114).
[26] For extended discussions of the naval war, see Stevenson (2004) and Sondhaus (2014). The latter, dedicated solely to the naval war, is eye-opening.

It might seem like we've taken some of the suspense out of the puzzle by setting up the game this way. Both players can achieve their best outcome by making the same choice, *and* that choice also happens to be the outcome we're trying to explain! You might've already guessed that this is too good to be true. If we follow the procedure for calculating Nash Equilibria, checking each possible strategy profile for profitable deviations, we uncover *two* strategy profiles, (total; total) and (limited; limited) as indicated by the dashed lines, from which neither Britain nor Germany has a profitable deviation. If Britain and Germany both embark on a total naval war, then neither can gain from unilaterally choosing a limited naval war, which would leave its fleet or its coast vulnerable to the total commitment of the other's naval efforts. Refusing to fight back against a committed assault from another great power is rarely a good idea. Therefore, we have a Nash Equilibrium at (total; total) because $2 \geq 1$ for each player, as stated in Proposition 10.1. But we're not done. Suppose that both players choose a limited war, the British maintaining a distant blockade (effectively ruling out the much-feared Copenhagen scenario), while the German fleet remains mostly in port, refusing to seek, much less give, battle. We can see immediately that (limited; limited) is *also* a Nash Equilibrium, because $4 \geq 3$. Neither player has an incentive to embark on a total war even to take advantage of the other's vulnerability, because preserving its fleet for the long haul of the war is paramount. Thus, we have two equally rational ways of playing the game and no way (yet) to say anything about which one will be played and why. Remember that the Nash Equilibrium solution concept (Definition 2.7) can tell us only whether a particular strategy profile is an equilibrium. It can't (and isn't designed to) tell us which one of several strategy profiles that satisfy the definition of a Nash Equilibrium will actually be played. For that, we require some extra machinery.

PROPOSITION 10.1   *The strategy profiles (total; total) and (limited; limited) are each a Nash Equilibrium.*

Proof   First, for (total; total) to be a Nash Equilibrium, it must be the case that

$$u_{\text{UK}}(total;\text{total}) \geq u_{\text{UK}}(limited;\text{total})$$

and

$$u_{\text{G}}(\text{total};total) \geq u_{\text{G}}(\text{total};limited).$$

Both inequalities are satisfied because $2 \geq 1$. No player has a profitable deviation, so (total; total) is a Nash Equilibrium. Second, for (limited; limited) to be a Nash Equilibrium, it must be the case that

$$u_{\text{UK}}(limited; \text{limited}) \geq u_{\text{UK}}(total; \text{limited})$$

and

$$u_{\text{G}}(\text{limited}; limited) \geq u_{\text{G}}(\text{limited}; total).$$

Both inequalities are satisfied because $4 \geq 3$. No player has a profitable deviation, so (limited; limited) is also a Nash Equilibrium.   □

Thus far, we've dealt almost exclusively with unique Nash Equilibria, with the exception of some overlapping equilibria in Chapter 5's model of crisis bargaining under asymmetric information. But the game in Figure 10.2 reintroduces this phenomenon of *multiple equilibria*, where one game admits of more than one logically equivalent solution. The unique equilibria we're used to by now are convenient in that they link a single strategy profile (which presumably contains the outcome we'd like to explain, like a limited naval war in the North Sea) deductively to a single set of actions, outcomes, and preferences. But sometimes a single set of actions, outcomes, and preferences isn't enough to yield a single prediction over how the game is to be played. The Anglo-German wartime naval confrontation appears to be just such a case, and even if one equilibrium is ostensibly "better" by some metric (efficiency, social welfare, appropriateness, ideological purity, or consistency with the whims of an angry deity that lives in a tree), the definition of Nash Equilibrium can't rule out the less attractive alternatives as long as players have no profitable deviations. This is another case in which the logical rigor of game theory is valuable, forcing us to think harder about why we can or can't rule out certain equilibria after "doing the math" and about where we can look to complete our explanations; without the model, we might reason to either of these outcomes informally, but we'd risk missing out on the other one ... and whatever else is required to explain why one occurs and not the other. *Nothing* in the logic of mutual best responses can tell us to expect (total; total) or (limited; limited), so we've got more work to do in generating an explanation – work that the casual explanation we discussed above missed – to resolve the puzzle. But lest multiple equilibria sound like a problem for solving this chapter's puzzle, try to think of them as a feature, not a bug. To see how, we'll need to dust off an idea we first discussed in Chapter 2, the common conjecture (Definition 2.8), which contains shared information about the social world in which games take place.

Why is the social background important for explaining the war in the North Sea? Remember that the common conjecture contains players' beliefs about each other's strategies, which help them to settle on the best responses that are central to Nash Equilibrium. But where the common conjecture in previous chapters told players that there was a single set of mutual best responses in a game, it tells players in Figure 10.2 that there are two sets of equally reasonable ways to play the game. One of them happens to be the outcome we want to explain (a mutually cautious naval war with fleets in port and sailors anxious to see battle), the other an outcome we might (and historical actors did) expect but don't see (a full-throttle naval war in which whole battle fleets are hurled at one another in a life-or-death-struggle for dominance of the North Sea). Yet both outcomes emerge from the same set of strategic conditions, with identical players, actions, outcomes, and preferences. How can we explain a limited naval war when the same conditions predict a total naval war with equal logical plausibility – that is, when two very different strategy profiles can both be a Nash Equilibrium? It's true that, going only on the existence of two Nash Equilibria, we can't explain either outcome.[27] Tempting as it might be at this juncture to throw our hands up and return to the drawing board, there's something to be learned from this strategic dilemma, commonly called a **coordination problem**. In situations like the game in Figure 10.2, multiple equilibria can be played that satisfy players' desires for either matching or corresponding strategies, and states need to coordinate their expectations on a set of shared beliefs about each other's likely actions if they are to identify mutual best responses.

DEFINITION 10.1 *A **coordination problem** exists when players want to choose corresponding strategies but there are multiple such equilibria to choose from.*

Coordination problems admit of multiple solutions, manifested in multiple equilibria, for the same set of actions, outcomes, and preferences. Which solution our players choose depends on what they believe about each other's strategy – that is, how they rely on and in many cases actively help construct the common conjecture.[28] The common conjecture is the basic set of ideas by which states understand international relations – definitions, meanings, practices, authority relationships, rules of thumb, strategies, etc. – anything that we could say makes up the shared culture, however limited or however extensive it might be, or the social world of international relations.[29] Chapter 6 showed us that international law and treaty-making is one source of common knowledge on which states

---

[27] Think about it this way. If a proposed explanation is consistent with two opposing sets of facts, then the explanation is clearly missing at least one piece that tells us when to expect one set of facts and not the other.

[28] You can imagine, in fact, that in many ways, shaping the common conjecture is the purpose of a great deal of what we commonly call political rhetoric. It is also a nice, clean logical basis for thinking about the social construction of reality.

[29] For one of the classics on the international system as a society, see Bull (1977).

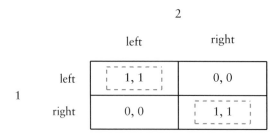

Figure 10.3 The sidewalk problem.

can rely in order to guess others' strategies and intentions. But in a low-information environment like an early twentieth-century naval war, with unreliable radios and battle fleets bristling with large and largely untried weapon systems, where there are no obvious rules or precedents to draw on, players have to flesh out, and may compete in fleshing out, the common conjecture on their own. When communication is limited but coordination is a must, players use knowledge ready to hand, from analogies to shared experiences to "obvious" strategies based on focal points to solve the coordination problem and settle on an equilibrium, all without direct communication. We'll see in this section that through a process of tacit (i.e., wordless) communication, even mortal enemies like Great Britain and Imperial Germany can settle on an equilibrium that limits the scope and scale of the war at sea.[30]

Before we return to the North Sea, we'll develop some intuition over how coordination problems are solved without direct communication by showing how focal solutions work in a radically different setting: the sidewalk. Suppose that two pedestrians, 1 and 2, who happen to be total strangers, approach each other on a particularly narrow sidewalk. There's only enough room for them to pass without colliding if they hew to opposite sides of the pavement – that is, if each keeps to her right or if each keeps to her left – and unless they play by the same rule, they collide. Figure 10.3 presents this strategic problem as a game, where each player has to choose as she approaches the other whether to walk on the left side or to walk on the right side of the sidewalk. We'll assume that these pedestrians care most about avoiding a collision, which is both a hindrance to getting to their respective pubs before happy hour ends and a source of public embarrassment, such that a pedestrian gets 1 if she passes the other without a collision but 0 if she collides with the other pedestrian. Just as it is for the game in Figure 10.2, there are two pure strategy Nash Equilibria to the sidewalk game, (left; left) and (right; right), highlighted in Figure 10.3

---

[30] For the pioneering work on coordination, tacit bargaining, and focal points, see Schelling (1960, chapter 3).

with the same dashed lines. (There's also a mixed strategy equilibrium that you can derive yourself if you're interested, but since this is a story about equilibrium selection, all the same arguments apply if we focus only on pure strategies.) Once again, nothing about Nash Equilibrium (Definition 2.7) can help us arbitrate between the two.

PROPOSITION 10.2   *The strategy profiles (left; left) and (right; right) are each a Nash Equilibrium.*

Proof   First, for (left; left) to be a Nash Equilibrium, it must be the case that

$$u_1(left; \text{left}) \geq u_1(right; \text{left}) \quad \text{and} \quad u_2(\text{left}; left) \geq u_2(\text{left}; right).$$

Both inequalities are satisfied because $1 \geq 0$. No player has a profitable deviation, so (left; left) is a Nash Equilibrium. Second, for (right; right) to be a Nash Equilibrium, it must be the case that

$$u_1(right; \text{right}) \geq u_{\text{UK}}(left; \text{right})$$

and

$$u_2(\text{right}; right) \geq u_2(\text{right}; left).$$

Both inequalities are satisfied because $1 \geq 0$. No player has a profitable deviation, so (right; right) is also a Nash Equilibrium.   □

How are our pedestrians to choose an equilibrium? Put simply, and in terms of a problem we face all the time, from narrow sidewalks to hiking trails to bike lanes to crowded hallways, which side of the road should they walk on if they want to get to the pub without colliding with a stranger along the way? The apparent predictive impasse in Proposition 10.2 shows us that they need some information, some kind of shared idea about whether each and the other should keep right or keep left, and whether each knows that the other knows that, which allows each to choose a best response to the other. Remember that best responses hinge on each player knowing that the other player will do, the other player knowing she knows it, as well as how she'll respond to it, and so on. That knowledge prevents them from colliding, but there's no law governing sidewalk pedestrianism (so far as I know) that can turn a strategy into an easily predictable and sustainable habit. So, assuming that our pedestrians can't shout out to one another, nor can they make gestures because their hands are full, what can they do? The idea of a **focal point** or focal solution, something easy and obvious to both players, suggests that players will settle on a strategy profile that relies on shared experience, shared culture, or something obvious and easily identifiable in the environment (like, say, "keep right" signs).[31]

DEFINITION 10.2   *A **focal point** or **focal solution** is a strategy profile based on some obvious, natural, or well-known feature of the situation that players can coordinate on without direct communication.*

In the sidewalk game, it's likely that our pedestrians rely on shared knowledge about their social environment, reasoning by analogy to similar situations that the other pedestrian is likely to have also encountered.[32] There may be no legal rule of the sidewalk, but there *is* in most locales an analogous legal rule of the road (right or left, depending on where you live). In the United States, our pub-bound pedestrians are likely to know this and to try "keep right" on the assumption that the other player will do the same and expect her to expect and act on that. That's all there is to it. There's some feature of the environment, in this case an analogous rule, that has the power, by virtue of being known and easily guessed in the absence of an alternative rule, of dictating which side of the road these two strangers will walk on.[33] A focal solution need not be terribly convenient, nor does it need to be fair; it just needs to be conspicuous. As Thomas Schelling has it, "[t]he rationale may not be strong at the arbitrary 'focal point,' but at least it can defend itself with the argument 'If not here, where?' "[34] The rule of the road is certainly conspicuous, and it may require one pedestrian to adjust more than the other – if, say, she starts out keeping left – but that inconvenience turns out to be less important than avoiding a collision, and if she expects that the other pedestrian is going to go with the rule of the road, she's got little choice but to abide by the same rule.

The sidewalk game illustrates that focal solutions aren't complicated. In fact, they *can't* be complicated if they're going to work. "Keep right" is a well-known, obvious benchmark that players are likely to expect others to know, and moreover it's easy to distinguish from "keep left" when other pedestrians abide by it. Dividing restaurant tabs down the middle, meeting back at the entrance to a market or bar, setting a meeting time at a nice round number, or waiting for someone at the tallest building in the area are all common, simple, conspicuous focal solutions for coordinating behavior. Each focal point is a piece of the social world that constitutes part of a shared culture, and in our example the rule of the road helps our players

---

[31] See Fudenberg and Tirole (1991, pp. 19–20).

[32] That friend of yours who insists on walking on one and only one side isn't someone that one a stranger would want to play this game with.

[33] Equilibria are essentially self-fulfilling prophecies, and this is perhaps nowhere more clear than in the case of coordination problems (Myerson, 1991).

[34] Schelling (1960, p. 70).

coordinate on the qualitatively distinct equilibrium of (right; right) instead of (left; left). That qualitative difference is critical; to be focal, a strategy profile needs to be easily distinguishable from alternatives. It has to stand out in some way, not only because other players are likely to think of it, but also so that players can tell what other players are doing.[35] In other words, "keep 50 percent to the right" won't really do in the sidewalk game. Differences in degree only make strategies harder to distinguish, and this is why we'd expect our pedestrians to hug the right side of the sidewalk pretty obviously, all in service of creating enough shared knowledge to manage their passage without a collision.[36] From very little prior information, the pedestrians coordinate their passage, hewing to the right in clear view of the other, wordlessly settling into an equilibrium selected not by any kind of hard-nosed calculation of costs and benefits but simply by coordination on shared cultural norms.[37]

Returning to the naval war in the North Sea, we can see the outlines of a solution to our puzzle. For most of the war, the vaunted battle fleets of the British and German navies avoid large-scale contact. The Royal Navy maintains its distant blockade while the German High Seas Fleet stays mostly behind a large minefield jutting out from Denmark into the North Sea, venturing out occasionally to shell the British coast or to see if the Grand Fleet can be drawn into a confrontation where German forces might have a local advantage. The one major fleet action of the war, the Battle of Jutland-Skagerrak, is the result of one of these raids, and while it ends in a tactical victory for Germany in that Tirpitz's force metes out more punishment than it takes, it's nearly a strategic defeat. After the battle, the German surface fleet never ventures back out in strength, as the focus of the naval effort shifts to interdicting allied shipping with unrestricted submarine warfare (for more on that, wait until Chapter 13). This is a tacit admission consistent with Admiral Reinhard Scheer's acknowledgment that "even the most successful result from a high sea battle will not compel England to make peace" and would likely fatally compromise the defense of the German coast even in victory.[38] Germany's decision to save its fleet is made easier, however, by the Royal Navy's decision not to pursue the campaign further once German ships chose to break off contact. Costly as Jutland-Skagerrak is, it clarifies for both sides

---

[35] Schelling (1960, p. 75).

[36] We've all been there. You're heading toward someone else on a path, you both end up trying to signal your intent about direction, yet you just awkwardly mirror the other's side-to-side lurches. Oof. Just try to make your side clear earlier and hope that the other person isn't too distracted.

[37] On culture as the very stuff that helps societies select among multiple equilibria, see Myerson (1991, p. 113).

[38] Sondhaus (2014, p. 228).

that neither intends to wage a total war in the North Sea that will risk fatally compromising the High Seas Fleet or forcing the British to weaken the naval defense of its Imperium to make good losses close to home. As British Admiral David Beatty had it after the battle, justifying British caution in a nod to the Entente's advantages in a long war, "[w]hen you are winning, risk nothing."[39]

For both sides, the logic in the North Sea is one of caution, because the war is expected to be long and the mutually costly outcome of a serious naval confrontation isn't really in question. But one side's caution might have tempted the other into boldness. Our model shows that *if* the British are willing to press the attack and try to annihilate the High Seas Fleet, Germany will have little choice but to give battle. Likewise, the Royal Navy will shoulder the burden of engaging in major fleet actions *if* the Germans wage war from a more aggressive posture. So the desire to husband naval capabilities by avoiding major engagements where possible, to preserve the massive fleets built at such tremendous expense since the years before the war (recall Chapter 3), isn't sufficient to explain why we don't see more than one major fleet action in the North Sea, because it can't account for the mutual and very real concerns that the other *might* try to take the war total.[40] An explanation for a limited war that neither side viewed as inevitable and that both were prepared to abandon for a more aggressive posture if need be must explain not only why the war remains limited but also why that second eventuality didn't come about. The models in this section allow us to do just that.

The strategic setting may admit the possibility of both limited and total naval war, but the reason that it remains limited, and the reason that Jutland-Skagerrak leads not to escalation but to a reaffirmation of the (limited; limited) equilibrium of the game in Figure 10.2 is that both sides engage in tacit communication that sustains the limited war equilibrium. First, by imposing a distant blockade, the British mark out a clear inability to easily implement the Copenhagen option, because its strategy is qualitatively distinguishable from a "near"-blockade that would've pressed on Germany's windpipe still further as it made British intentions to avoid major engagements less obvious. Second, by generally staying in port behind a protective cordon of undersea mines and testing British intentions with just a few limited sorties, Germany clarifies for the British its own strategy of limited naval war. The outcome may be slightly different, but the same logic supports our hypothetical pedestrians in Figure 10.3 sticking closely to the right edges of the sidewalk. The (limited; limited) equilibrium may not be a great one for Germany, because it enables the Entente to use its naval advantage to support the war on land, but coordinating on this equilibrium is still better than the alternatives. The logic of coordination demands that players

> must be ready to allow the situation itself to exercise substantial constraint over the outcome; specifically, a solution that discriminates against one party or the other or even involves "unnecessary" nuisance to both of them may be the only one on which their expectations can be coordinated.[41]

Thus, the mutual desire to avoid losses isn't enough to explain the war in the North Sea. Sensitivity to the costs of naval war is only part of an explanation that also requires a tacitly established common conjecture that guides the enemy fleets to a limited naval conflict.

The demands of sustaining the effort on land will lead the British and German fleets to wage a limited war, but only – and precariously – because each is able to figure out what the other side intends to do. Our analysis shows that the same strategic conditions, of high-class battle fleets bristling with modern weaponry and manned by sailors and officers eager to do their part to support the war effort, can just as easily lead to a chaotic and costly total war at sea with a simple, self-fulfilling shift in expectations. If either Britain or Germany comes to believe the other is bent on a major confrontation, it will adjust its own strategy, reinforcing expectations in the other of the need to take the war total, and so on, until they find themselves in a (total; total) equilibrium, even as the structure of the game itself remains the same. Fighting to survive as great powers by cutting the other (or the other's allies) down to size, Britain and Germany face a daunting problem, where a focal solution is all that stands between limited and total war from the English Channel through the North Sea and into the Baltic. When both sides have opportunities to alter the enemy's expectations about their willingness to throw a surface fleet fully into the war – from the distant blockade to the leashing of the High Seas Fleet to the refusal to follow up Jutland-Skagerrak – they revert instead back to the obvious, hard-to-mistake coordinating devices of distant blockade and defense of the German-Danish littoral. Had the long-war reality not shattered the short-war hope in the early going on land, it's possible that the strategic imperatives driving the naval war might look different, prompting us to write down a different game in Figure 10.2. As it happens, the need to maintain a lengthy war on land by preserving naval assets, combined with tacit coordination in the North Sea, can account for an otherwise surprising level of mutual restraint between what are in 1914 the two most powerful navies in Europe.

---

[41] Schelling (1960, p. 75).

272   10 Coordinating Caution: Naval War in the North Sea

10.2.2 Did the Dreadnoughts Matter?

Despite pouring staggering amounts of wealth into building dreadnoughts before the war, Britain and Germany hardly used them once declarations of war were exchanged and the turning of the attritional gears began grinding up the face of Europe. And if most of the familiar action of the Great War took place in the trenches while the world's largest battlefleets waged an anemic war on the North Sea hardly befitting their prewar prestige, it's worth asking about the extent to which the events of this chapter influenced the course of the Great War. Did the Germans waste the High Seas fleet by hiding it behind a cordon of undersea mines? And did the British forgo a chance to knock (i.e., starve) Germany out of the war sooner and more effectively by choosing the "distant" over the "near" blockade? On the first question, it's probably fair to say that the High Seas Fleet preserved its ability to deter at least a close-in blockade and at most a Copenhagen scenario by choosing not to fight in the face of restrained British preponderance; if there were any doubt that the German navy's best work would be deterrence along the littoral, the first Battle of Dogger Bank took care of that. But the second question, that the British blockade's effectiveness, setting aside questions of its legality under the law of the sea, is more contentious.[42]

London had worked out the idea of a distant blockade in the waning years of the Anglo-German naval race, acknowledging that Germany could do enough damage with its growing fleet that the costs of a tight, suffocating blockade along the coast would be prohibitive. Abandoning the legal strictures of the 1856 Declaration of Paris, which demanded that blockades be "effective" – in effect, smothering every German port – the distant blockade cordoned off the North Sea at the English Channel and the Norway-Scotland straits, leaving Germany's Baltic ports free.[43] Searching ships headed to and from Germany at a safe distance, the British began by paying lip service to the signed but unratified 1909 Declaration of London's distinctions between "absolute" contraband (military supplies and weapons), "conditional" contraband (dual-use goods like food and clothing), and noncontraband items with only civilian uses. But these definitions were rapidly abandoned, and by October 1914 even food was listed as absolute contraband in a clear nod to the fact that entire populations were to be mobilized for war.[44] As the contraband list grew, German merchant ships abroad at the outbreak of war remained interned in neutral ports,[45] limiting access to even noncontraband items, and the

---

[42] At least in the English-language literature.
[43] Herwig (2014, p. 283).
[44] Herwig (2014) and Sondhaus (2014, p. 51).
[45] Jeffery (2016, p. 132).

British continually tightened their grip, claiming the right to search ships bound for neutrals like the Netherlands (the Kaiser's "windpipe") and eventually barring them from calling at German ports, both violations of the laws of blockade and of neutrality rights.[46] Nonetheless, the blockade took time to take hold, to truly force food and materials scarcity on the *Kaiserreich*, and it remained subject to what the Royal Navy viewed as inconvenient political limits, particularly when American ships were allowed access to German ports for fear of getting on the wrong side of the Entente's biggest financier and potential ally.[47] Nonetheless, German imports were by 1917 so restricted that privation combined with "inflation, harvest failure, and over-expenditure on armaments were pushing the German economy into crisis."[48] But 1917 was a long, bloody, and frustrating time away from 1914.

The war on land may attract most of the ex post criticism when it comes to the conduct of the war (recall Chapter 8), but the British blockade has also come in for scrutiny by observers seeking a reason for the war's tragic cost and upheaval, both of which increased with, and in part because of, the length of the war. Some arguments dismiss the idea of a distant blockade doing much to harm a German economy that, for most of the war, could get things it needed from neutrals; to the extent that the German population faced privation, like the "Turnip Winter" of 1917–1918, it's often laid at the feet of a failure to organize the domestic economy, beset by an arcane federal structure, effectively to handle scarcity.[49] The German public, of course, was happy to blame rising food prices and the onset of rationing on the British, who came to be viewed as the primary enemy despite joining the war after France and Russia, and the German government had no problems with that attribution.[50] Another view has it that the blockade *could* have had a more profound impact on the war if it hadn't been distant, implemented piecemeal, and tightened only slowly over time – that is, if Britain hadn't failed to "grip the imperatives of total war."[51] The apparent logic of the argument here is seductive, going something like this: "The blockade worked, but it worked too late thanks to slow implementation and hesitance in London to truly turn the screws. Had the blockade been more aggressive, the war might've ended sooner." That line of reasoning is plausible in principle, but it elides something important about the analogy to the Battle of the Frontiers that we (as well as decision-makers in London and Berlin) made above.

---

[46] Herwig (2014, p. 283).
[47] Sondhaus (2014, p. 160).
[48] Stevenson (2004, p. 204).
[49] See Jeffery (2016, p. 132).
[50] See, in particular, Watson (2014).
[51] Hastings (2013, p. 359).

The model in Figure 10.2 tells us why the British would embrace the idea of a distant blockade, but it can also tell us something about the counterfactual: what would've happened in Great Britain *did* "grip the imperatives of total war" and adopt a more aggressive posture in the North Sea. The alternative to distant blockade wasn't a near blockade manageable if only London had the wherewithal (the unstated assumption of the "should've been more aggressive" criticism), but a potentially ruinous total war on the seas that risked compromising Britain's ability to support the war on land, where the war would ultimately be won, and continue a distant blockade if the attempt to impose a near one failed. Under these circumstances, in the face of the need to maintain shipping lanes and the threat to surface ships posed by German submarines and minefields, the distant blockade and its attendant slow effects were a lamentable choice (depending on your point of view) but a necessary one. "The action of naval power ... was slow, steady, always working, rarely dynamic and only after some time really effective,"[52] but when the Royal Navy's main contribution was to avoid a catastrophic outcome that remains off the equilibrium path – that is, an outcome that never occurs in a game – then judging its effectiveness and its role in shaping the war's outcome poses a serious inferential challenge.[53] The British knew that blockade would work, eventually, but it would certainly lack the panache of Trafalgar. But they had time, because the war on land had stalemated and should eventually turn on the Entente's access to more soldiers, more laborers, more money, and more industry. The cost of imposing their will directly on Germany through a total naval war would simply be too great in light of where their real strengths lay – not on the battlefield per se but in the mobilization of society and industry for total war effort.[54] The blockade was consequential – just ask the Germans – but the British didn't talk much about it, since legally they came off only slightly better than the Germans in their regard for neutral rights.[55]

It's easy to look at the British blockade, its politically necessitated leakiness and slow progress, and argue that the war might've been shortened if only the Royal Navy had been more aggressive. But that reasoning overlooks a torturous trade-off underlying the decision to pursue a distant

---

[52] Philpott (2014, p. 196).
[53] It's also catnip for those looking to make sloppy, flashy critiques.
[54] Philpott (2014, p. 198).
[55] See Sondhaus (2014, p. 368). In this case, the victors managed to win the propaganda war. But sometimes history is written by the losers: see the aftermath of the American Civil War, where the defeated slave states managed to control the narrative of the reasons for their rebellion (denying the sine qua non of slavery) and the circumstances of their defeat (painting inept strategic minds as something greater than what they were).

blockade: had the Royal Navy compromised its capacity to perform other roles by trying to either knock out the High Seas Fleet or strangle German commerce immediately, it would have squandered the Entente's advantages in the long war on land – which is where Germany would eventually capitulate. Being too aggressive with the Royal Navy might've forced a decision sooner, but it's not clear what the decision might have been if the (total; total) equilibrium emerged and superior British numbers collided in the North Sea with superior German gunnery, increasing the risks that the Entente would lose the war. The rationale for saving the Royal Navy, looked at this way, isn't too far removed from the rationale for adopting trench warfare to save lives after the catastrophe (and the unpredictability) of the Battle of the Frontiers. The longer the war dragged on, the better the Entente's chances, as time would reveal its natural advantages in wealth, demographics, finance, and, underlying all of the former, control of the seas. A short war was for the Entente far riskier. However counterintuitive it seems, we can see the distant blockade, the seemingly perverse leashing of the very Royal Navy that sustained Britain as a great power, as sustaining the Entente's advantages over the Central Powers. After the war, former Prime Minister Herbert Asquith, who led his country to war and lost a son at the Somme in 1916, would say, "with all deference to our soldiers, this war was won with sea power."[56] Far from being ineffective, or from shaping the course and outcome of the war only at the margins, the dreadnoughts proved worth the British investment, allowing the Entente to win on land while firing far fewer shells and losing far fewer lives than the armies in the ferocious, filthy, fetid hell of France and Flanders.

10.3 ON LIMITED WAR

The extravagant fleets more useful for blockade and deterrence, to say nothing of the wide expanse of the North Sea, may seem unique in facilitating a limited naval war in 1914. But limited wars – i.e., those in which belligerents manage by some agreement, tacit or otherwise, to restrict the scope, scale, severity, and savagery of the conflict – are not the exception but the rule. As puzzling as it seems on its face for great powers in a fight for survival to choose not to use all the means at their disposal, countries frequently wage war under clear limits to which they and their enemies both submit. War, thanks to its waste, creates a shared incentive not only to avoid it but also to limit its costs if fighting can't be avoided. If both sides wish to minimize their own costs for fighting or the risk that

---

[56] Sondhaus (2014, p. 348).

the war will expand to include other states, then they have a common (if that term seems too strange, think "coincident" instead) interest in placing limits on the actions they're willing to take in pursuit of victory. War, however, is a difficult environment for enemies to reach agreement on much more than the desirability of fighting one another, and this places a premium on tacit bargaining to work out the rules by which belligerents will wage war.

China and the United States, for example, managed to confine their two years of savage fighting to the eponymous peninsula during the Korean War, despite temptations for both sides to escalate or expand the war. China could have tried to divide the United Nations forces arrayed against its North Korean protégé by following through with plans to attack Taiwan, and the United States was tempted to bring the war to Chinese territory in hopes of stanching the flow of PLA troops into Korea. General Douglas MacArthur, in fact, proposed nuclear attacks on Chinese cities before President Harry Truman relieved him of command.[57] These temptations aside, the fighting remained confined to the Korean peninsula south of the Yalu River; chemical weapons weren't used, though that didn't stop Communist attempts to tar the UN with false accusations of the same;[58] and nor did the United States succumb to the temptation to use its nuclear advantage to compel Chinese troops to end their intervention when fortunes turned against it at the war's midpoint. Both Chinese and American preferences supported confining the stakes of the war to Korea, but of course neither would accept the other's unilateral attempt to gain an advantage, in a set of incentives that mirror German and British goals at sea in 1914–1918. Respecting these limits may have staved off a Third World War that would've quickly spread to Europe – North Korea only moved south, after all, with Stalin's blessing – and yet two bitter, ideologically opposed enemies with a historically large trust deficit did so with very little in the way of communication. How? With primacy on the Asian mainland at stake (a persistent source of great power conflict), the Soviets watching (and helping) with great interest, and Cold War paranoia at fever pitch, why *didn't* the Korean War become World War III?

China and the United States could've found themselves in a (total; total) equilibrium in a game much like the one in Figure 10.2, but instead they waged a relatively limited conflict that ended, roughly, where it all began near the Thirty-Eighth Parallel that had divided the Korean Penin-

---

[57] Issues of playing with (atomic) fire aside, that's one hell of a way to go out if you're getting sacked. It's probably fair to say that it surpasses in its political lunacy General George Patton's pronouncement of the need for a preventive war against the Soviet Union mere weeks after the Allied defeat of Nazi Germany in 1945.

[58] See Stueck (1995) and Wada (2013).

sula between Soviet and American zones of occupation at the end of the
Second World War. Schelling, in his classic analysis of the Korean puzzle,
attributes Sino-American tacit coordination to two factors: geography and
prevailing views about the nature of nuclear weapons.[59] First, the Yalu
River marked a clear division between Chinese and Korean territories that
United Nations forces respected by refusing to authorize "hot pursuit"
of Communist aircraft escaping across the frontier and by conspicuously
not interdicting Chinese reinforcements headed to Korea through Chinese
territory. The river was conspicuous, and while staying below it didn't
exactly make the United Nations war effort any easier, "[b]eggars cannot
be choosers about the source of their signal, or about its attractiveness
compared with others that they can only wish were as conspicuous."[60]
If the United States would not cross the Yalu, and likewise if China and
the Soviet Union didn't try to push the effective boundary south, then
the war could remain limited to the Korean Peninsula. Second, like the
curious absence of poison gas from Second World War battlefields despite
its ubiquity in the First, the qualitative distinction that existed (and still
does) in the popular mind between nuclear and conventional weapons
may have discouraged their limited use when, after some initial successes,
United Nations forces were hurled back from the Yalu and across the
Thirty-Eighth Parallel after Chinese intervention.[61] Any use of nuclear
weapons – no matter how limited – would've been viewed as indistinguishable from a full-scale embrace of general war. Far more than just "big
bombs," nuclear weapons could be focal only in their use or nonuse, not
in the degree of their use. "No nukes" was focal, conspicuous, and easily
distinguishable as part of a limited war, but "just enough nukes to fend off
China's advance in 1951, then no more" clearly wouldn't have been. The
analogy to Britain's distant blockade of German ports, which practically
ruled out a Copenhagen scenario, and the near blockade, which would've
made it easy, is striking. Therefore, one reason (among many), that the
otherwise savage, bloody, and high-stakes Korean War stayed localized
and limited to conventional arms was simply that geography and prevailing
beliefs about the nature of nuclear weapons facilitated coordination. In a
different place, and with more cavalier attitudes about nuclear weapons
(say, if the United States hadn't used two on Japan in 1945), the war, and
the world war it might've birthed, might've been radically different.

The Korean War may be one of the most dramatic examples of limited
conflict, but it has echoes in restrictions on American military strategy in

---

[59] See Schelling (1960, p. 76) for the specific claims and Chapter 3 as a whole for a discussion
of coordination and tacit bargaining that's yet to be surpassed. It's staggeringly good.
[60] Schelling (1960, p. 66).
[61] On this "nuclear taboo," see Tannenwald (1999, 2005).

the Vietnam War, in Soviet hesitance to cross into Pakistan to eliminate mujahideen safe havens during the Afghan War, the stability of the Line of Control that divides Indian and Pakistani Kashmir while offering an invisible shield to cross-border infiltrators, and even in the long-standing rituals of chase, pursuit, and shadowing between American and Russian pilots and submariners that prevented potentially risky local escalations during the Cold War. If the price of giving oneself a chance to win profitably is ensuring that the other's exposure to cost and risk is also limited, then both sides in a war may be willing to find some kind of tacit bargain restricting the scope, intensity, or scale of an otherwise brutal, destructive, and unpredictable contest of arms. We can't make much sense of either the ostensibly half-hearted war in the North Sea or the myriad self-imposed limits and boundaries containing great power conflict on the Korean Peninsula without recognizing that war is a wasteful way of doing things, and that belligerents often cross some serious national, ideological, sectarian, and political divides in placing limits on even fights to the death. Nearly all wars see belligerents submitting to some kind of shared limits on their conduct, and given our operating view of war as instrumental, wasteful, and *political*, it makes sense that we'd see calculating, frugal leaders engage in this kind of behavior. The problem is that we don't colloquially think about war like this – instrumental and therefore subject to political constraints – and as we'll see in Chapters 11 and 14, that failure to come to grips with war's political nature can lead to some misleading conclusions about how wars are conducted and how they ultimately end.

10.4   COORDINATION AND INTERNATIONAL POLITICS

Caution in the North Sea during the First World War and the precarious localization of the Korean War offer dramatic examples, but coordination problems in international relations are far from rare. Any time that states face a problem that admits of multiple solutions, each of which is better than failure to coordinate and all of which exist as Nash Equilibria, they face a coordination problem. Focal solutions can emerge because of precedent, analogy, or simply one party managing to frame the problem first.[62] There's no guarantee that coordination will help both sides come off equally well, but the key is avoiding a mutually worse failure to make corresponding choices. Coordination problems emerge when states must choose from a (sometimes bewildering) number of acceptable bargains, like standard weights, measures, and communications protocols, where

---

[62] Games have rules, and the actor that gets to define them may be at an advantage; it's no surprise that politicians fight so often over them.

each may have preferences for one particular deal over another but where the problem of finding an acceptable range of proposals has already been solved.[63] That doesn't mean, however, that coordination isn't contentious or that the problems it solves aren't high-stakes. In this section, we'll show how the logic of coordination can help us understand how states draw borders and how the United States and the Soviet Union worked out a set of rules that helped them avoid a superpower clash during the Cold War. But first, it's worth making an important distinction.

You might've noticed already that coordination problems are superficially similar to collective action problems (Definition 7.1) in that some coordination games produce tragic, inefficient equilibria. In the naval war game of Figure 10.2, for example, the (total; total) equilibrium leaves both players worse off than they would be in the (limited; limited) equilibrium (because 2 < 4). It can be tempting to make an analogy between the total war equilibrium and the (build; build) equilibrium of the naval race game in Figure 3.2, where the British and German empires regretted that they couldn't receive the higher payoffs (3 > 2) at (¬build; ¬build). In each case, players find themselves in a tragic equilibrium that they might've avoided if only they'd both adopted a more "cooperative" strategy, whether limiting the naval war or not building dreadnoughts.   But the similarities end here.[64] First, some coordination problems, like the sidewalk game in Figure 10.3, simply don't produce inefficient outcomes. Second, where collective action problems derive from incentives to take unilateral advantage of another player, coordination problems exist when conflicts of interest aren't so great. Finally, they're solved in very different ways. Solving a collective action problem requires altering players' payoffs such that they have private incentives to contribute to a collective good; a different configuration of beliefs can't change the fact that (build; build) is the unique Nash Equilibrium of the naval race game in Figure 3.2. But in the naval war game of Figure 10.2, two equilibria exist, and all that separates the inefficient (total; total) equilibrium from the more attractive (limited; limited) one is the content of the common conjecture; a different configuration of beliefs *can* move players from one equilibrium to another. But there's no "better" equilibrium in a Prisoner's Dilemma like the one that spawned the Anglo-German naval race, because no player can credibly promise to change

---

[63] This is in notable contrast to our model of crisis bargaining with private information in Chapter 5, where states don't initially agree on what the range of acceptable proposals happens to be.

[64] This doesn't stop political scientists from conflating the two with maddening frequency, but it's still important to fight the good fight. Coordination problems are distinct from cooperation problems, and they deserve a defender. What Liz Lemon is to good grammar on subway signage I am to the proper identification of coordination and cooperation problems.

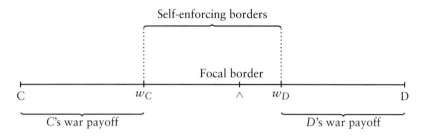

Figure 10.4 The coordination problem in bargaining.

strategies. When multiple equilibria exist, however, players can credibly change strategies, and finding a focal solution becomes key to solving the problem.

Now that we know what coordination problems *aren't*, we can see a bit more clearly what they *are* and how they shape international relations. First, coordination is fundamental to bargaining, including the process by which states negotiate over and establish borders – the very institutions that define the units of the international system (recall Chapter 1).[65] Suppose that two states (C and D) would like to define their mutual border, to divide a piece of land like they did in Figure 2.4 where each prefers more of the land to less. This time, though, we'll turn the (suspiciously) circular piece of land between them on its side, which allows us to think about bargaining along a one-dimensional line, represented in Figure 10.4. Let's suppose that C's capital is on the left end of the line, with D's on the right, and that a border is just a line dividing C's land on the left from D's land on the right. War would be costly, so if C and D fight, the total pie to be divided shrinks as it does in Figure 2.4, but in this case we'll say that war simply hollows out the middle of the line.[66] If war occurs, C gets everything to the left of w_C and D gets everything to the right of w_D, but fighting destroys everything in the middle (which is equivalent to the shrinking circle in Figure 2.4). If C and D avoid war, then they can draw a border anywhere along the line, saving the land destroyed by fighting, and any border drawn in between their two war payoffs leaves them – you guessed it – better off than if they'd fought a war. Since any border in this area leaves each side better off than it would be at war, we label them "self-enforcing borders" (Definition 1.6).

[65] Think of it this way: if constitutions use citizenship and residency rules tell us who is and isn't a member of a particular polity, then the mutual recognition of borders defines membership in the international system.

[66] This representation of bargaining in the shadow of war, popularized by Fearon (1995), has become one of the standard ways of representing the bargaining problem in political science. Throw a rock in a room full of people that study conflict, and you're more than likely to hit someone who's drawn a version of this figure in her own work.

This is a simple restatement of the war puzzle we addressed in Chapters 2 and 5, but even in the absence of bargaining frictions that cause war, it's still not obvious which border our two countries will draw. Any self-enforcing border is better than war, and both countries agree on this, but some leave C better and D worse off than others, and vice versa. Where will they draw the border? The likely outcome of a war decides where the range of self-enforcing borders happens to lie – in this case, in the middle, so we'd say that C and D are of about equal military strength – but the location of the border within this range comes down to something unrelated to the bargaining process itself: something conspicuous, something *focal*. A river, a mountain range, or a previous administrative division from a departed empire or a predecessor state can all serve as a focal point that helps countries C and D settle on a border; "features of the landscape [may] seem less important for their practical convenience than for their power to crystallize agreement."[67] Previous frontiers are so focal, in fact, that they can push states toward agreements without any meaningful connection to the military defensibility of the frontier or the nationalist preferences of those on either side of it; in fact, new borders that trace old ones are significantly less likely to be fought over later than those without such a strong coordinating effect – even those that should be more defensible militarily.[68] The point marked "focal border" in Figure 10.4 indicates just such a spot, something that commands attention and serves as a kind of self-fulfilling prophecy: both states expect the other to focus on the point, making it an attractive proposal that both are likely to accept, despite the fact that it clearly leaves D with more land than C. It's not all sunshine and light, however, as historical border precedents are also uniquely likely to produce territorial disputes down the line, and potentially violent ones at that, likely because of their ability to coordinate expectations about where borders "should" be.[69]

Finally, tacit communication and coordination is also prevalent in great power politics, where countries with little reason to trust one another nonetheless try to manage the balance of power peacefully in hopes of preventing general war. One of the most recent (and certainly high-stakes) examples occurred during the Cold War between the United States and the Soviet Union. The two superpowers outclassed the other great powers in their respective orbits in terms of military might and prestige, though the United States was far more powerful economically, and each possessed many thousands of nuclear weapons that could if used bring human

---

[67] Schelling (1960, p. 68).
[68] See Carter and Goemans (2011).
[69] See Abramson and Carter (2016).

civilization to a standstill.[70] After defeating Nazi Germany and Imperial Japan, the grand coalition that won the Second World War cracked in short order, and factions among the victors hardened into a rivalry between an American-led status quo coalition and an antagonistic Soviet-led coalition. Their spheres of influence abutted each other directly in divided Germany and indirectly in divided Korea, and the superpowers competed for the allegiance of unaligned states in the Third World, including eventual flashpoints like Cuba, where the placement of Soviet nuclear missiles would set off one of the most dangerous crises of the era. It had been centuries since the number of great powers sat only at two, and the most ready analogies were Athens-Sparta and Rome-Carthage – hardly cause for optimism, especially since the great powers had already fought two major wars in the twentieth century. And yet, ideological and power-political rivalries, deep mistrust and long memories of grievances, proxy wars and an ongoing arms race notwithstanding, the superpowers realized early on that a direct confrontation between them would be catastrophic. They had strong reasons to avert a new war, but their means of credible direct communication were often limited (that often happens to rivals, as we saw in Chapters 5 and 6).

These obstacles notwithstanding, the world survived the Cold War without a major great power conflict,[71] in part because the superpowers worked out their own rules of the road, just like our pedestrians in Figure 10.3 and like the British and German empires in Figure 10.2. Avoiding conflict was of paramount importance, and the superpowers found, haltingly and slowly and imperfectly over time, several tacit rules that allowed them to match one another's strategy, reducing the chances of an all-out war. Historian John Lewis Gaddis identified five rules that, by 1986, seemed to be operating as part of the "rules of the game" for the Cold War:

1   Respect spheres of influence.
2   Avoid direct [American-Soviet] military confrontation.
3   Use nuclear weapons only as an ultimate resort.
4   Prefer predictable anomaly over unpredictable rationality.
5   Do not seek to undermine the other side's leadership.[72]

The similarities with Anglo-German restraint in the North Sea are striking. The United States gave the Soviets a free hand in occupied Eastern Europe, much to the consternation of dissidents in Hungary (1956) and

---

[70] Those arsenals, by the way, are still around and still *huge*. I don't fear dying in a nuclear fireball as much as I did growing up in the 1980s, but I'm also not optimistic that those fears won't come back as the world slides back toward multipolarity.

[71] Though *with* a ton of movies about it, most of them only so much hot garbage.

[72] Gaddis (1986, pp. 132–139).

Czechoslovakia (1968), both of whom received Soviet invasions for their trouble, while the Soviet Union didn't attempt overt subversion of capitalist governments aligned with the United States in Western Europe.[73] After some close calls over Korea, neither side interfered directly with their own troops in the other's proxy wars, Vietnam for the Americans and Afghanistan for the Soviets, and over time both sides scaled back plans to use nuclear weapons as anything other than a last resort, making surprise attacks difficult. Furthermore, neither side took advantage of the other's domestic troubles, from precarious or ambiguous leadership transitions (frequent as the Soviet Union morphed into a gerontocracy) to scandals (Watergate, Iran-Contra) to assassinations (John F. Kennedy), resisting a temptation that might've put the other's back to the wall – all in the service, rhetorical language about global revolution and evil empires aside, of maintaining a restrained posture as long as the other side would do so as well.[74]

Finally, Rule 4 deserves some clarification, because it's laden with some very specific historical context. At the end of the Second World War, Germany and Korea were divided, unnaturally so, in arrangements that few, whether great powers or locals, thought optimal. Even Germany's capital, Berlin, isolated in Communist East Germany, was divided between East and West in a microcosm of the entire country. Closer to the United States, Communist Cuba hosted an American military base at Guantánamo Bay as part of a long-term lease that predated Fidel Castro's revolutionary regime.[75] These arrangements may have been complicated, tense, and crisis-prone, but they were also well known, conspicuous, and much preferable to any attempt to change them, which would've entailed a risky combination of strategies and all the nightmare scenarios that a war between the two most heavily armed and technologically advanced war machines the world had yet seen would entail.

Coordination problems are ubiquitous in international politics, but thankfully not all entail the risky tacit bargaining of wartime or superpower rivalry, because states often try to codify focal solutions in international law. Law helps define the common conjecture, as we saw in Chapter 6, by publicly proscribing certain practices like civilian targeting and prisoner maltreatment, as well as the violation of neutrals' rights. Making standards clear and public makes them focal, and those states interested in, say, preventing the maltreatment of their own prisoners can safely choose equilibria in which both sides honor the Geneva

---

[73] It did, though, take advantage of the naïeveté of a great many Western academics.
[74] Rule 5, by the way, manifestly didn't survive the American presidential election of 2016.
[75] Guantánamo's fame has turned to infamy, however, in the years since the September 11 attacks on the United States and the 2003 Iraq War.

Conventions, all thanks to the coordinating value of the law. If states can use the law to make better judgments about the value of joining wars, as Britain did in 1914, and when the information provided lets them select a different equilibrium than they would've in the law's absence, then we can talk once again about how international law – toothless and flimsy though it seems – can be a critical buttress of the balance of power. If law helps select equilibria, or if states can avoid confrontations simply by finding focal solutions in restrained strategies, then we can make a pretty strong argument that the balance of power rests not just on military capabilities but also ideas, on beliefs about who can do what to whom and why, on the very stuff of the social world of international politics. War may be the final arbiter of who gets what, but whether war influences international politics from beneath or on the surface depends in large part on both power *and* ideas, on the common conjecture that states use to make guesses about each other's strategies. A famous observation has it that "anarchy is what states make of it,"[76] and perhaps nowhere is this more true than when states can avert costly, wasteful conflicts – or fight only when doing so is truly worth it – with little more than a set of coordinated beliefs.

10.5 CONCLUSION

It's too tempting to criticize Britain's distant blockade and Germany's mine-field cordon as twin failures to appreciate the logic of total war. To do so is to overlook the importance of naval power in sustaining the war on land; Britain without its imperial network couldn't wage a long war, and a Germany unable to deter an attack on its North Sea coast would almost surely lose a long war. The challenge is figuring out why the British didn't take advantage of German caution and why, given Britain's long-run advantage, Germany didn't gamble on drawing the Royal Navy into a bigger battle or try to interdict the BEF on its way across the Channel. Belligerents hoping to avoid battle should be taken advantage of, or so one line of reasoning goes. But framing the war in the North Sea as a coordination problem shows that neither side had such an opportunity: each would fight a more aggressive naval war if the other would, but it would happily wage a limited war if the other would. And the primary factor favoring the latter over the former was the *focal solution* of a distant British blockade and the Germans staying in port at Wilhelmshaven, a pair of strategies that conveyed unambiguously that each had no intention of waging a total naval war as long as the other would also keep its distance, a restrained equilibrium made all the more striking by the fact that Britain

---

[76] Wendt (1992).

and Germany viewed each other as their *primary* enemy. All that stood in the way of a costly naval war that might've radically altered the course of the land war – and unpredictably so – was a shared idea that emerged from a tentative, fumbling, occasionally violent but mostly unambiguous exercise in tacit communication. Shared beliefs about a limited naval war, constructed on the fly by belligerents with little love for one another and less trust, helped create the war that we saw on land. Far from a disappointing failure to apply the logic of total war, the limited naval war was an integral part of sustaining the brutal attritional equilibrium that we examined in Chapter 8.

The attention lavished on Jutland-Skagerrak in the English-language literature notwithstanding, the First World War had no Trafalgar, no Salamis, no Tsushima, no Pearl Harbor, and no Midway. It lacked a major naval action on the surface, but it didn't need one. The slow, creeping, seemingly inevitable working out of the Entente's advantages in a long land war enabled by the sidelining of the surface fleets would eventually shift the focus of German naval planners to a weapon initially viewed as a defensive tool: the submarine. Its surface combatants boxed in by the Royal Navy, its leaders tired of bowing to American ideas about which ships headed to Britain could and couldn't be sunk, and the army sniffing a crushing victory over Russia on the Eastern Front, Germany would by early 1917 declare a war zone around Western Europe and begin sinking merchant ships with reckless abandon. This program of unrestricted submarine warfare was designed to bring Britain to its knees by cutting it off from its Empire and, ultimately, its major benefactor: the United States. Using one weapon where another fails isn't a bad strategy in principle, but as we'll see in Chapter 13, unleashing the submarines on Entente and neutral merchant shipping would precipitate the one major event that German leaders had been working hard to avoid for years: an American declaration of war.

11 The Theory of War III: Commitment and War Termination

A valid diagnosis of war will be reflected in a valid diagnosis of peace.

Geoffrey Blainey,
The Causes of War

Chapter 2 showed how commitment problems can stand in the way of settlements that save the costs of war, but it left hanging a thread that we've got to pick up as our narrative approaches the end of the Great War. We can't yet explain how war solves the bargaining problems that cause it in the first place – that is, how the act of fighting can create conditions for a settlement where none existed before. We'll tackle this problem by introducing dynamic games, which (1) allow us to model sequential moves more flexibly and (2) require that we learn the solution concept of Sub-game Perfect Equilibrium. The need for dynamic games will arise from our discussion of a puzzle inspired by a mismatch between how we often talk about war and how most wars actually end:

Why do most wars end in a compromise peace rather than total victory?

Most wars last several weeks or months, though a small few last several years. However long they drag on, a significant majority ends without a clear winner and an obvious loser. Nearly 70 percent of the time, flags aren't raised triumphantly over enemy capitals, victors don't swagger down conquered boulevards, and terms like "unconditional surrender" don't grace the text of peace treaties.[1] In other words, most wars don't look much at all like World War II.[2] Rather, both sides are left standing, governments and armies intact (if damaged), able but mutually unwilling to continue the fight. Sometimes, both sides can walk away claiming a moral or political victory. But why stop to reach a limited settle-

---

[1] See Slantchev (2004) and Wagner (2000, 2007).

[2] Given the staggering levels of destruction and brutality involved in that one (Kershaw 2012, 2015; Snyder 2010), we should probably be happy about that. To the extent it's viewed as a "good war," it's only because the baddies were really, *really* bad.

ment, a compromise peace, with a distrusted adversary? Why cut a deal when continued resistance, which may lead to a different outcome, remains possible?

Answering this question requires that we keep in mind why states go to war in the first place: not to kill and destroy for the sake of killing and destroying but to produce a fresh settlement, a bargain intended to either replace or restore the previous one, whether over who controls a piece of territory or who controls those who control that territory.[3] If war begins when today's bargain is no longer self-enforcing (Definition 1.6), then it ends when fighting leads belligerents to a deal that *is* self-enforcing – and this typically doesn't require one side to completely defeat and disarm the other. In this chapter, we'll extend the model of crisis bargaining and shifting power introduced in Chapter 2 to a dynamic setting that treats the beginning and end of war as distinct choices, saving a similar extension of our informational model of war (Chapter 5) for Chapter 12. We'll learn several things in the process:

- how to identify Subgame Perfect Equilibria in dynamic games;
- how fighting can make commitments credible that weren't beforehand;
- why some wars last so much longer than others;
- why civil wars endure longer than interstate wars.

This chapter is largely theoretical, but it sets up our analyses of the Great War's waning years in Chapters 13 and 14, where the expected outcome of the war, as well as the time it would take to get there, loomed larger than it had since those early days when short-war hopes were dashed in Flanders fields. The models will show us what's required for fighting to render incredible commitments credible, eliminating either the incentive or the ability of a rising state to renege on today's bargain, using the rigor of equilibrium analysis to make sure that our explanations for war are both consistent and complete – i.e., that they explain war's outbreak despite its cost and that they explain how fighting can solve the bargaining problem that sent armies into the field in the first place.[4] As we work out the logic of how states end wars driven by commitment problems, we'll address a related puzzle about why civil wars last longer on average than interstate wars, and we'll lay out some expectations over what to look for in later chapters as we try to explain the duration of the Great War, the manner in which it ended, and the (in)stability of the peace settlement that followed it.

---

[3] See Wagner (2007, chapter 4).
[4] On the requirements for consistent and complete explanations for war, see Leventoglu and Slantchev (2007).

> **Key Terms for Chapter 11**
> - Absolute War
> - Real War
> - Subgame Perfect Equilibrium
> - Subgame
> - Equilibrium Path

11.1 "REAL" AND "ABSOLUTE" WAR

When we talk casually about war, we're often drawn to ideas of winning and losing, of victory and defeat. And to be fair, examples *seem* to be everywhere. Germany surrendered unconditionally in 1945, and Japan a little less unconditionally later that year, after the largest and deadliest war in human history.[5] Argentina lost its bid to annex – or retake, depending on your sympathies – the Falklands/Malvinas Islands in 1982, and in 1991 the Iraqi army was forced out of Kuwait, its bid for annexation reversed in a matter of weeks. Most of us would call these wars defeats for one side and victories for the other, and from there it's a short leap to say that how wars end shouldn't be all that puzzling: they end when one side defeats the other on the field of battle. A short leap, but not one we should take, as it confuses war's military and political dimensions – to say nothing of the fact that the vast majority of wars don't end in unconditional surrender or the destruction of an enemy's capacity to resist.[6] Tempting as the analogy often is, war isn't like your favorite sport, where most games have a stipulated end and a winner is declared by rule. Wars generally end by mutual agreement long before a "winner" can be declared. This is what Carl von Clausewitz called "real" as opposed to "absolute" war, the former limited in the changes it produces and ambiguous in its outcome, the latter a rare ideal-typical case in which one side completely disarms the other.[7] But the two are related, because belligerents *choose* "real" wars in the shadow of what "absolute" wars would look like. Just as beliefs about how war will play out can influence the terms (and stability of) peace, we'll see in this chapter that beliefs about how an absolute war would finish can influence decisions to end wars before they become total.

---

[5] Good histories of the Second World War abound, but Hastings (2012) is a particularly good read, as is Paine's (2012) account of war in East Asia from 1911 to 1949. And if you want the Second World War through Churchill's eyes, see Hastings (2010).

[6] As we'll see in Chapter 14, there are even good reasons to make sure that one's opponent isn't fully disarmed at the end of the war.

[7] See Clausewitz (1976) for the unabridged version. For a recent interpretation, see Wagner (2007).

DEFINITION 11.1 *An **absolute war** sees one side defeat and disarm the other.*

DEFINITION 11.2 *A **real war** ends short of one side's defeat and disarmament.*

The historical record since Clausewitz's time – he watched Napoleon defeat Prussia at Jena on October 14, 1806 – only bolsters the case that war isn't what our colloquialisms imply that it is. Few wars are (or really ever have been) "declared" in a formal, legal sense,[8] and it's increasingly rare for them to end in formal peace treaties,[9] even as they continue to rearrange borders, replace governments, unhinge the balance of power, or upend rankings in the global hierarchy. The most striking patterns, for our purposes, involve how wars end. By one calculation, fully 64 percent of interstate wars between 1916 and 1991 ended with both sides still physically able to continue fighting.[10] This doesn't mean that some states don't come out better than others in attaining their ends. The 1991 Gulf War, in which an American-led coalition ejected Iraqi forces from Kuwait after the latter's attempt to annex the small petro-kingdom, was manifestly a success for the coalition. Nonetheless, it ended with the nominally vanquished Iraqi forces withdrawing across the old border beaten, bloodied, and reduced, yet still intact. It wasn't exactly the hammer and sickle hoisted over the Reichstag in 1945. Furthermore, the average war lasts just over a year, clocking in at about thirteen months, though the mean is pulled up by a few very long wars – like the one we're concerned with in this book – because the median war duration falls between 5 and 6 months.[11] We also know that wars between relative equals in terms of military capabilities and wealth tend to be long, democracies tend to do better than dictatorships as long as wars stay short, and wars of attrition tend to be longer than those in which maneuver is the order of the day.[12] But whether wars are short or long, limited or total, "real" or "absolute," almost all of them end in peace settlements of some sort, even if it's a total surrender. That alone makes a focus on the strictly military dimension of war outcomes misleading.

To see how, let's start by taking a closer look at our examples of ostensible victories. Nazi Germany resisted to the last, though Admiral Karl Dönitz, taking power after Hitler's suicide, still signed an instrument

---

[8] Fazal (2012).

[9] Fazal (2013). So all the dramatic talk of the Korean War not "technically" being over is mostly just that: talk.

[10] See Leventoglu and Slantchev (2007, p. 757), who use Slantchev's (2004) data to make this calculation.

[11] Slantchev (2004, p. 818).

[12] See Bennett and Stam (1996), Reiter and Stam (2002), and Slantchev (2004).

of surrender.[13] Imperial Japan surrendered with a sizable chunk of its army intact, garrisoning far-flung and isolated possessions, getting hurled back across Manchuria by the Red Army, and redeploying to face an American invasion force bearing down on the Home Islands in the wake of the nuclear attacks on Hiroshima and Nagasaki.[14] Argentina lost its bid for the Falklands, but British forces never landed on its shores,[15] and Iraq gave up Kuwait after four months of occupation – losing a sizable share of its combat power before securing a ceasefire with the coalition – yet mere days after the ceasefire Saddam Hussein declared his own victory in standing up to the assembled great powers and surviving in office.[16] In principle, Japan, Argentina, and Iraq could all have continued to fight in pursuit of an "absolute" war outcome, and their opponents – the Western allies and the Soviets, the United Kingdom, and a broad international coalition, respectively – could have pressed their advantages, yet they chose not to. Even in what we might think of as crushing defeats, these wars ended not because of a shattering military victory or dramatic collapse but because of a mutual agreement to call off the fighting.[17] But why? Fighting on could've produced a different outcome, yet these belligerents, like most others in a wide variety of contexts, stopped well short of one side disarming the other.

PUZZLE 11.1   *Why do most wars end in compromise peace rather than total victory?*

States rarely disarm one another, but it's important to think about why they might want to if we're to figure out how and why wars end short of such a total, "absolute" outcome.[18] Disarming an opponent renders it defenseless, allowing the one left standing, the nominal victor, to dictate terms – taking or doling out captured territory, replacing a vanquished state's government, seizing wealth or imposing indemnities, or simply removing a competitor for position in the global hierarchy.[19] That's

---

[13] For a harrowing account of the last act of the Second World War in Germany, see Kershaw (2012), and for a less than solemn look at Dönitz's accession to power, see the relevant sketch in *That Mitchell and Webb Look* (Mitchell et al. 2006).

[14] See Frank (2001) and Paine (2012).

[15] See Freedman (2005).

[16] See Freedman and Karsh (1991).

[17] And had the United States unleashed Operation Downfall, the planned amphibious invasion of Japan, casualties would've been horrific even by the standards of a war already known for breaking records in death, destruction, and human suffering (Frank, 2001).

[18] This discussion leans heavily on Wagner's (2007) discussion in his chapter 4.

[19] This is another place the sports analogy fails. As much as I'd like it to be the case that Kentucky could win a basketball game and fire the other team's coach, or bench the opposing team's best player for tournament season, that can't really happen under NCAA rules, as far as I know.

consistent with our view of war as instrumental, as a means of resolving disputes over the allocation of scarce goods in the international system, but it's not what tends to happen when states go to war. In the majority of wars, neither side has any serious intention of disarming the other: the United States and North Vietnam,[20] Iran and Iraq in their eight-year war,[21] Ethiopia and Somalia during the Ogaden War of 1977–1978,[22] the Anglo-French-Israeli attempt to seize the Suez Canal from Egypt in 1956,[23] and Russia and Georgia in the 2008 South Ossetia War,[24] to name just a few. But why fight a war, the ultimate promise of which is dictating terms to a prostrate opponent over a disagreement worth waging war to resolve, if disarming the other side, if eliminating its ability to resist, isn't even in the cards?

Answering this question requires that we recall two ideas established in Chapter 2: (1) war entails waste, and (2) it's not the only means by which scarce goods can be allocated.[25] States disagree over territory, resources, rights and privileges, and rankings in the global hierarchy, and occasionally they come to blows over them. But more often than not, they negotiate and strike bargains, finding peaceful settlements that either avert or, relevant for this chapter, end war. If war is instrumental, it's more useful to think about the desired end state of fighting not as military victory but as the thing that military action is intended to produce: a new settlement, a new allocation of goods or set of rules by which the belligerents will live in the future.[26] Wars are fought not for their own sake, but to influence the outcome of negotiations. Legal anarchy means that states can resort to war at any time, but they can *also* strike new deals at any time, and doing so can help them save the costs of continued war once they've already sent armies into the field. Wartime negotiations are fairly common, with diplomats meeting in conference rooms or leaders exchanging messages through intermediaries while soldiers slug it out on the battlefield – just like the United States and China did throughout the Korean War.[27] Even when formal negotiations are stalled, tacit bargaining continues; military force is applied with an eye toward making refusals to make concessions more painful for one's opponent, not always toward securing military victory per se. Several American bombing campaigns during the Vietnam War, for example, aimed to bring North Vietnam to the negotiating table, not

---

[20] Lawrence (2010).
[21] Razoux (2015).
[22] Tareke (2000).
[23] Kunz (1991).
[24] Antonenko (2008).
[25] We're *still* getting analytical mileage out of just those two assumptions. Not bad, right?
[26] Wagner (2000, p. 469).
[27] See Stueck (1995) and Wada (2013).

to destroy its forces in the field or clear South Vietnam of Communist insurgents.[28] Just like Britain and Germany worked to contain the costs of the naval war in the North Sea (Chapter 10), states also seek to strike war-ending deals when fighting is no longer necessary. Even knowing that they can influence their position for the final settlement can make them fight harder.[29] If war isn't instrumental, if war isn't *politics*, then we can't make much sense of the prominent role of intrawar negotiations, their failure and their success, in patterns of war outbreak, duration, and termination.

A few wars end in crushing military victories and total capitulation, but a great many more end in ceasefires or armistices or localized victories; some end rapidly and some impose years of punishment on the societies that wage them, but *all* wars produce a new bargain of some sort – and usually with signatures (sometimes compelled) from representatives of both sides. The Korean War lasted three years and ended with the border between North and South very close to where it began; the Iran-Iraq War did the same after nearly eight years; the Cambodia-Vietnam War ended with the former's Khmer Rouge government toppled; and the First Balkan War ended with the Ottoman Empire shedding most of its European holdings even as its survival as a polity was never in question. The rarity with which total disarmament is pursued is evidence of war's instrumentality. Likewise, the fact that wars end with the same phenomenon that usually averts them – negotiated settlements – tells us that war and diplomacy are tightly, intimately linked. Thus, the puzzle of how wars end, and why they tend to be "real" and not "absolute," is best solved by asking how and why states agree to end them and the terms on which they do so. It's useful to think of the beginning and the end of war as part of the same strategic process, one that begins with an act of agreement (that fighting is preferable to whatever proposals were on the table) and ends in another act of agreement (that the terms on offer now are better for both sides than continued fighting).[30] The fact that most wars aren't "absolute" indicates that fighting can render agreements possible that weren't beforehand, and once those agreements *are* possible, calculating and frugal decision-makers have every incentive to stop fighting, cut the relevant deal, and save the further costs of war. The cost, duration, and termination of war are linked, and if we're to work out a useful theory of how wars end, we'll have to confront these linkages directly.

The problem is that our explanations in Chapters 2 and 5 for war's outbreak beg the question of what fighting actually *does* to make

[28] Lawrence (2010).
[29] See Leventoglu and Slantchev (2007) and Wagner (2007).
[30] For excellent informal statements of this rationale, see Goemans (2000), Wagner (2007), and Reiter (2009).

settlements possible where they weren't beforehand, of what's so special about war that diplomacy sometimes needs its help to produce settlements. Our crisis bargaining models are perfectly adequate for explaining why war begins, because they collapse the entire conflict process into a single payoff. As long as it's ordered in a reasonable way relative to other outcomes in our players' payoff functions, we don't need to ask more of that setup if we're curious about how wars start.[31] But if we're curious about how wars end, then a theory of instrumental war must explain war's termination as well as its beginning. To learn about how and when wars end, we need to ask different things of our models. With a different destination in mind, we need a different map, and one that requires a more sophisticated mode of transportation at that. In the next section, we'll introduce dynamic games, which allow us to think more productively about how fighting might move belligerents from violent equilibria to peaceful ones, solving commitment problems where diplomacy unadorned with a concurrent contest of arms fails.

11.2 SOLVING COMMITMENT PROBLEMS

If war begins when a bargaining friction prevents a settlement from being struck without some preliminary fighting, then it stands to reason that war should end when fighting has cleared the initial obstacle to settlement. If negotiation and bargaining are the essence of politics, then they're also the essence and end goal of war. In this section, we introduce two new tools to help us think about how war solves commitment problems: dynamic games, in which we care about both the sequence of moves and how players adjust course in response to others' moves, and Subgame Perfect Equilibrium, the solution concept most commonly used to solve dynamic games of complete information. First, we'll walk through a game that's decidedly not about war, though far from apolitical, to get some practice with the need for and use of Subgame Perfect Equilibrium. Then, we'll tackle the bigger question of how war makes settlements that were impossible in the face of shifting power not only possible but also likely, obviating the need to fight to the finish just to secure a credible promise.

11.2.1 Subgame Perfect Equilibrium

Modeling the onset and termination of war as part of the same process, with distinct choices for each, isn't just a matter of introducing some

---

[31] See Powell (2004a).

you

	yes	no
never	1, 0	$\boxed{0, 1}$
if yes	-3, -3	0, 1
if no	$\boxed{1, 0}$	-3, -3
always	-3, -3	-3, -3

me

Figure 11.1 Extorting a dollar with a hand grenade.

realism to our theories of war.[32] Adding additional moving pieces to our models is only a good idea if we can learn something new from them, but the process of war termination turns out to be just one of those cases. We'll establish that in greater detail in the next section, but for now it's worth emphasizing that we want to ensure that our players aren't committing to actions at the outset that, when push comes to shove, they wouldn't actually take. In other words, we'd like to rule out incredible threats.

Suppose you've got a dollar and I've got a hand grenade. I want you to give me the dollar and you'd like to keep it, but we'd both prefer not to be blown up by a hand grenade. Your choice is simple – give me the dollar ("yes") or not ("no") – but I've got to devise a strategy that tells me whether and when to pull the pin. I can pull it only if you refuse to give me the dollar ("if no"), only if you give me the dollar ("if yes"), whether you give me the dollar or not ("always"), or under no circumstances ("never"). Strange as some of these seem, putting them all in front of us is useful for now, which we do in Figure 11.1, where I get 1 for any outcome in which I get the dollar and don't get blown up, 0 for not getting the dollar and not getting blown up, and -3 for getting blown up (whether or not you give me the dollar); your preferences are symmetrical with respect to the disposition of the dollar, and you'd also prefer not having the dollar to getting blown up. Thinking through our incentives informally, it should be clear that, if I'm ever given the choice of pulling the pin on a grenade once you've already refused to give me the dollar, I wouldn't carry out the threat, because in this game I'd rather be poor than dead ($0 > -3$). Sensible, right? As it happens, the rules of Nash Equilibrium don't agree.[33]

---

[32] Remember: descriptive realism isn't very useful for its own sake.

[33] The following discussion should tell you something about whether Jabba really needed to give in to (someone dressed like) Boushh demanding an exorbitant bounty for a Wookiee while brandishing a thermal detonator.

PROPOSITION 11.1 *The strategy profiles (if no; yes) and (never; no) are each a Nash Equilibrium.*

Proof First, for (if no; yes) to be a Nash Equilibrium, it must be the case that

$$u_{\text{me}}(\textit{if no}; \text{yes}) \geq \max\{u_{\text{me}}(\neg \textit{if no}; \text{yes})\}$$
$$\text{and } u_{\text{you}}(\text{if no}; \textit{yes}) \geq u_{\text{you}}(\text{if no}; \textit{no}).$$

The first inequality is satisfied because $1 \geq \max\{1, -3\}$, and the second is satisfied because $0 \geq -3$. No player has a profitable deviation, so (if no; yes) is a Nash Equilibrium. Second, for (never; no) to be a Nash Equilibrium, it must be the case that

$$u_{\text{me}}(\textit{never}; \text{no}) \geq \max\{u_{\text{me}}(\neg \textit{never}; \text{no})\}$$

and

$$u_{\text{you}}(\text{never}; \textit{yes}) \geq u_{\text{you}}(\text{never}; \textit{no}).$$

The first inequality is satisfied because $0 \geq -3$, and the second is satisfied because $1 \geq 0$. No player has a profitable deviation, so (never; no) is a Nash Equilibrium. $\square$

The game in Figure 11.1 has two Nash Equilibria. That's not surprising in itself, but the fact that a patently ridiculous equilibrium exists at (if no; yes) in which I threaten to blow us both up – against my own interests when I'm in control of the grenade – to get you to give me the dollar should give us pause. If you refuse to give me the dollar, I'm faced with a choice over living without it (getting 0) or pulling the pin on my grenade (-3). You (surely) know I wouldn't do that if faced with the choice. Yet Nash Equilibrium allows me to commit ahead of time to pulling the pin! The reasoning behind the equilibrium is simple: if pulling the pin is what I'm going to do, your best response is to give me the dollar, and if you're giving me the dollar, it makes perfect sense to make this threat, because it's never called in. But that's only in a world where precommitments are possible, and the situation we're modeling here, war termination, isn't much like that. Fortunately, a more reasonable equilibrium also exists at (never; no), where you'd reasonably reject any threat on my part to pull the pin and just keep the dollar for yourself, safe in the knowledge that I'd never detonate the grenade on the way to a payoff of -3.

Still, we've got no way, under the rules of Nash Equilibrium, to choose one equilibrium over the other, and coordination would be next to impossible given our conflicting interests. When we considered coordination issues in Chapter 10, multiple equilibria were more feature than bug, but in this case we've got a bigger problem; it seems to violate our idea that leaders are calculating and frugal, that they'd probably be able to see through patently incredible threats like promising to actively pursue one's own worst possible payoff by yanking the pin on a grenade over the paltry sum of a single dollar. We've taken care thus far to make sure that strategy profiles entail credible threats, but we're now at a point where it's worth thinking about what makes threats credible and how that influences the strategies that states choose in equilibrium: if states fight wars with an eye to their effect on subsequent peace settlements, then we need to make sure that the settlements we see in equilibrium are ones that could actually be chosen. In other words, we need a method of ruling out Nash Equilibria like (if no; yes) that rest on incredible threats, allowing us to focus to those like (never; no) that make more sense. Ruling out incredible threats, it's important to remember, isn't just a matter of what seems reasonable. If we saw an outcome that involved you giving me a dollar while I hold a grenade, we'd risk coming up with a terrible explanation if we didn't take into account the fact that I'd never use that grenade on both of us.

To solve this problem, we turn to a refinement of Nash Equilibrium, which helps us eliminate some equilibria from consideration (or, if you prefer, refining the set of equilibria), focusing on a subset that are better suited for the questions we ask of our models. It's clear that the issue with the dollar-grenade game is precommitment – i.e., my ability to choose a strategy in which I do something insensible because the bluff is never called. Nash Equilibrium doesn't accommodate the idea that some actions are taken in sequence, one after the other, and in full knowledge of what the other player has just done (but in fairness, it's not designed to). Sometimes, precommitment makes sense – when strategies are simple, taken simultaneously, implemented autonomously or with delay, or without knowledge of what the other side is choosing – but not at other times, like a face-to-face attempt to use a hand grenade to extort a dollar *or* when exchanging offers at the negotiating table during a war. In situations like this, we'd expect players to do the best they can *given what's already happened*, and we need a solution concept that lets us focus only on those threats or promises that players want to carry out when the opportunity arises. That solution concept is **Subgame Perfect Equilibrium** (or SPE).

DEFINITION 11.3   *At a **Subgame Perfect Equilibrium**, each player does the best it can do moving forward from any point, given the play of the game to that point.*

If that definition seems a bit technical, it's easiest to explain by introducing a new way of representing games that captures their dynamism, the

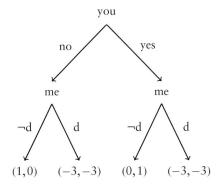

Figure 11.2 Extorting a dollar with a hand grenade (in the extensive form).

idea that players can know previous moves and make choices in response to those moves. Figure 11.2 converts the dollar-grenade game from the strategic form to the *extensive form*, which allows us to represent the sequentiality of actions using a game tree. Each available action is represented by a node, which leads either to branches with further choices (nodes) or to outcomes and payoffs at terminal nodes.[34] Looked at in this way, where my choice over using the grenade clearly happens after your decision over whether to yield the dollar, any strategy that entails me actually pulling the pin, which yields a payoff of -3 when I could clearly do better, should be a bit suspect. Subgame Perfect Equilibrium allows us to take this sequence of moves seriously, which we do by breaking extensive form games into subgames, where a subgame contains every move including and following a single choice node.

DEFINITION 11.4 *A **subgame** begins at a single choice node and contains all choice nodes that follow it.*

In Figure 11.2, there are three subgames: one beginning with my choice of detonating the grenade (d) or not ($\neg$d) after you give me the dollar, a similar choice following your refusal to give me the dollar, and a third subgame beginning with your initial choice and including all subsequent choices. We want to ensure that players choose best responses, or that they play Nash Equilibria, in every subgame; this is key to ruling out incredible threats that can be best responses if we look for Nash Equilibria only for the game as a whole. Once we've broken a game down into subgames, which represent relevant points at which players can choose based on previous choices – that is, dynamically – then finding best responses reduces to a process called backward induction, where we start at the game's last move,

---

[34] Oddly, though we call them trees, most expand either down or to the side – unlike most trees. But I suppose "game root system" doesn't sound quite as good.

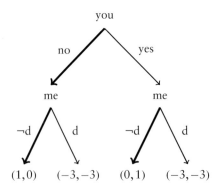

Figure 11.3 Backward induction in the dollar-grenade game.

see what players would actually do if faced with the opportunity, then work back to the beginning to discover a sequence of optimal choices that takes seriously the dynamic nature of the interactions we're interested in studying. This ensures that players can only promise to do things they'd want to do, allowing other players to expect them to behave that way as well. With *backward induction* completed, we're left with a strategy profile that's both a Nash Equilibrium *and* one that doesn't involve strategies in which I'd set off a grenade that I really, really don't want to set off.

Applying backward induction to the game in Figure 11.2 is straight-forward. Starting with my choice of pulling the pin after you give me the dollar, I'll clearly not detonate the grenade, because $1 > -3$. Next, if you don't give me the dollar, I'm faced with a payoff of -3 if I pull the pin and 0 if I don't, and the math makes it clear that I won't pull the pin. As trivial as that reasoning sounds, we've just used it to rule out as a best response any strategy in which I pull the pin on the grenade. Faced with that game-ending choice, I'd never do it, so we'd like to rule out equilibria in which I make such a threat and you're forced to act as if you believe me. That leaves us with only one strategy consistent with the idea that players choose optimally in every subgame: "never." Figure 11.3 demonstrates backward induction by highlighting best responses in bold, showing that the equilibrium we find is (no; ¬d, ¬d), which is equivalent to (never; no) in the strategic form. Correctly anticipating that I'll back down from any threat to pull the pin on the grenade – that any such threat would be cheap talk (Definition 5.6) – you play "no" and keep your dollar. Proposition 11.2 proves the existence of this equilibrium, and while we attack the problem from a slightly different angle, the logic of mutual best responses still determines equilibrium reasoning:

- **You:** "He'll never pull the pin, so I'm better off refusing to give him the dollar, which yields 1 as opposed to 0."

- **Me:** "No matter what she does with that dollar, I'm better off not pulling the pin on the grenade."

Neither of us has a profitable deviation, which ensures that our strategies are in equilibrium, and since neither of us is ever indifferent at any choice node, we know that this Subgame Perfect Equilibrium is also unique. Easy, right?

PROPOSITION 11.2 *The strategy profile (no; ¬d, ¬d) is a Subgame Perfect Equilibrium.*

Proof For (no; ¬d, ¬d) to be a Subgame Perfect Equilibrium, it must be the case that

$$u_{\text{me}}(\neg d | \text{no}) \geq u_{\text{me}}(d | \text{no}) \quad \text{and} \quad u_{\text{me}}(\neg d | \text{yes}) \geq u_{\text{me}}(d | \text{yes})$$

for me and

$$u_{\text{you}}(no | \neg d) \geq u_{\text{you}}(yes | \neg d).$$

The first two inequalities are satisfied because $0 \geq -3$ and $1 \geq -3$, respectively, and the third is satisfied because $1 > 0$. Both players choose optimally in every subgame, so (no; ¬d, ¬d) is a Subgame Perfect Equilibrium. □

If you work through the proof, you'll see more clearly the difference between Nash and Subgame Perfect Equilibrium. By allowing precommitments, the former means that I can adopt a strategy of "if no," forcing you to accept a consequence that I wouldn't impose on you if you were to call my bluff. And since my bluff is never called in a strategy profile of (if no; yes), my payoff for a strategy of "if no" is 1 and changing my strategy doesn't result in a different payoff. That works as a Nash Equilibrium, but not as a Subgame Perfect Equilibrium, because backward induction requires that we consider what I would do if ever given the choice of using the grenade; rather than consider strategies as a whole, we break them into their constituent choices, conditioning my decision to pull the pin on your prior choice and forcing us as analysts to consider, just as our players would, whether or not I do have a profitable deviation from detonating a hand grenade over a dollar. In games where sequencing is important, where the dynamics of action and reaction are essential for explaining outcomes, Subgame Perfect Equilibrium recovers our central premise that leaders are frugal, calculating players. That turns out to be essential next, when we use the logic of SPE to analyze how wars launched to solve commitment problems reach their ends.

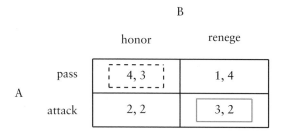

Figure 11.4 Incredible commitments and preventive war.

11.2.2 Commitment Problems and Subgame Perfection

Figure 11.4 reproduces Figure 2.5, which we used to illustrate in Chapter 2 how the inability of a rising state (B) to commit to the status quo as it grows stronger can encourage a declining state (A) to launch a preventive war. The unique Nash Equilibrium, highlighted with a solid line, sees A attack because it knows that, should it pass up a war today, B will use the time afforded to acquire new strength of which it can take advantage tomorrow. The logic of preventive war stipulates that A prefers fighting at today's relatively favorable distribution of power, but that's about as far as we got in Chapter 2, apart from noting that the goal of a preventive war is to arrest, end, or reverse the growth of a rising side's power in order to preserve commitments to the status quo (Definition 2.13). But short of the empirically rare instance of simply destroying a rising state or replacing its government with a puppet,[35] how exactly fighting can achieve that goal isn't entirely clear.[36] How does a contest in killing and destruction make commitments credible when they weren't before the shooting started? How can fighting make a strategy profile like (pass; honor), highlighted with a dashed line, an equilibrium rather than (attack; renege)? More concretely, how can fighting get us from a situation in which commitments aren't credible to one in which they are, where deals are self-enforcing once reached?

To answer this question, let's recall the basics of preventive war (Definition 2.13). First, in an international system ordered by de jure anarchy, nothing in principle can stop a state from using military strength to seek changes to the status quo by threatening or waging war. Second, states rise and fall in their military strength as their economies expand or contract, as they acquire and lose allies, as their institutions or leaders change, as they conquer or yield new territory, and as they build or give up military capabilities. When power is shifting, the rising state is happy to remain

---

[35] See Reiter (2009) and Wolford, Reiter, and Carrubba (2011).
[36] See Leventoglu and Slantchev (2007) for a treatment of this same question.

at peace, which allows it to grow stronger and in the future renegotiate today's settlement more to its liking. (Remember that this was precisely Russia's position in Chapter 4, where it planned to rearm in peace until the Hapsburgs put Serbia's fate in the balance.) But when power is shifting both substantially and quickly, the declining state may launch a war from today's position of strength – keeping in mind that "strength" here is relative – in order to avoid the consequences of declining power. But the story shouldn't stop there if war is an instrument of politics. The model in Chapter 2 assumes that war can solve a commitment problem, but that begs a pretty big question. Why should combat, a competition in killing and destruction, have anything to do with making today's distribution of power salvageable? How can fighting another country make its commitments credible?

For war to solve a commitment problem, fighting must alter the rising state's future ability or opportunity to renegotiate today's bargain. It could alter both, of course, but one is sufficient. In terms of the game in Figure 11.4, fighting would have to rearrange the rising side's incentives such that "renege" is no longer a best response to everything the declining side does.[37] We can imagine fighting doing that in several ways. At the extreme, eliminating the opportunity to renege could mean replacing the government, as the United States did to Iraq in 2003, or "crushing" the rising state and ending its independent political life, as Austria-Hungary hoped to do to Serbia in 1914. From a modeling perspective, we wouldn't need to change our initial model for these kinds of wars; they simply end when the process unleashed at the outbreak plays itself out. But more limited solutions can also work, such as forcing an opponent into an alliance as part of the settlement or securing control over its finances, both of which can give the declining state control over the other's foreign policy.[38] Japan tried to impose terms like these on China throughout the early twentieth century, sometimes with war and sometimes only in its shadow, precisely because it feared China's return to great power status.[39] Fighting can also alter the ability to renegotiate, by eliminating the sources of rising power, like Iraq's suspected weapons of mass destruction in 2003 or Russia's creeping completion of the Trans-Siberian Railway in 1904. Finally, fighting may make using newfound power unattractive for an opponent through the simple destruction of military capabilities and the very objects in dispute[40] or by moving a

---

[37] Recall from Proposition 2.4 that reneging is a dominant strategy when the commitment problem is at play.

[38] See Morrow (1991), Weitsman (2004), and Pressman (2008).

[39] See, inter alia, Paine (2012), Tooze (2014), and Xu (2017).

[40] See Leventoglu and Slantchev (2007).

mutual border to a location more defensible for the declining side.[41] Thus, fighting itself can solve commitment problems, eliminating the sources of shifting power, the attractiveness of using it, or the freedom of action to do so.

Our task now is to write down a dynamic game that captures what we think is important about the beginning and end of preventive war, especially when war doesn't simply disarm one side but allows a self-enforcing agreement after some period of fighting. First, we'd like to ensure that this new game shares as many features as possible with the static game in Figure 11.4; the fewer new moving parts we add, the easier it is to keep track of what premises are doing what in our new argument. It wouldn't do, for example, to write down a model in which war could occur for a reason other than commitment problems, because it would stand in the way of isolating the role of fighting in creating conditions for a new settlement. Second, we'd like similar interactions to occur over time, such as honoring and reneging on agreements, which tells us we'd like a repeated, or iterated, game. Imagine, for example, playing the dollar-grenade game multiple times in a row. Third, players should have the option of both "real" and "absolute" war, which allows us to say something about how the choice of real war can be influenced by the expected course of a fight to the finish. Let's turn to formalizing these ideas.

To satisfy our requirements, we can break our original model of preventive war into two distinct instances of crisis bargaining, one before and one after state B has a chance to rise in relative military strength, provided that rise isn't prevented by state A. Players receive a payoff for each play, or *iteration*, of the game, and we assume that they value receiving one dollar today a little more than waiting to receive the same dollar tomorrow – that is, they discount the future, and the more they discount it the less patient they are, the more willing they are to forgo a larger payoff tomorrow for a smaller one today. For example, if the dollar-grenade game were played twice and you received a dollar each time, then in the second iteration you'd receive 1, and the game would end. But in the first period, you receive 1 and expect to receive 1 in the second iteration, though looking into the future you'd weigh that second payoff with a discount factor δ, which is bound between 0 and 1, or $\delta \in (0, 1)$. Therefore, your payoff for a strategy profile that gives you 1 each period would be $1 + \delta 1$. And, given that I can't credibly threaten to light off a grenade to extort these two dollars, my payoff for the whole game, looking forward from the beginning, is $0 + \delta 0 = 0$.

---

[41] See Goemans (2000, p. 33).

B

	honor$_1$	renege$_1$
honor$_1$	4, 2	3, 1
renege$_1$	3, 1	3, 1

A

Original distribution of power, $t = 1$

Figure 11.5 Crisis bargaining and shifting power at $t = 1$.

These basics established, we can specify a simple two-period repeated game.[42] In each period, which we'll index by times $t = \{1,2\}$ to indicate the first and second period respectively, states A and B make simultaneous choices over honoring or reneging on the status quo. If both states honor the status quo, the settlement in place at the beginning of the game remains in place, but if at least one reneges, we'll assume that the players go straight into a war. As it has been in all of our models so far, war is wasteful, and if it's fought players will look back with regret on agreements not signed – or, in this case, a settlement not retained – that would've left them better off than having fought. By allowing fighting to occur in each period, we allow for the possibility of both total wars (war occurs in both periods, which we assume eliminates one side) and limited wars (players fight in only one period), which is key to our goal of explaining why fighting can occur but stop and end in settlement. Figure 11.5 presents players, actions, outcomes, and preferences for the first period ($t = 1$). A's best outcome is for both to honor the status quo settlement (4), and it receives 3 if either side reneges and it must fight a war to defend its position. B receives 2 at the status quo and 1 if there's a war. Payoffs are distributed before the second period, where the actions available to our players will be identical but where the payoffs will be different as a function of what happens in the first period.

Before continuing, it's worth looking at the first period in isolation. If we were to solve the game in Figure 11.5 as it stands, i.e., if this were simply a static game, then the Nash Equilibrium at (honor$_1$; honor$_1$) is pretty obvious (and unique): both will honor the standing settlement, since A has no reason to renege on its best outcome if B honors it as well ($4 \geq 3$), and B finds war even less attractive than honoring the settlement

---

[42] In some analyses of the commitment problem, games are repeated (potentially) infinitely (Fearon 2004; Leventoglu and Slantchev 2007; Powell 2006), but we're going for simple here.

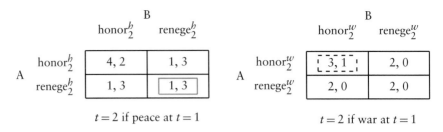

Figure 11.6 Crisis bargaining at $t = 2$ after shifted and preserved power.

$(2 \geq 1)$. That's useful, because we know that, unless we add something to the game, we can't use it to explain war. Absent shifting power, we should expect a peaceful equilibrium, and that's exactly what we see. In this chapter, we'll introduce shifting power between the first and second periods. The left panel in Figure 11.6 shows what the second period looks like if both players honor the settlement in the first: payoffs for honoring the original settlement are the same, but B's military strength has grown such that it now receives 3 for any outcome in which the states fight a war and A receives only 1. Critically, while A is still happiest when the settlement remains in place, B now prefers reneging on the agreement to honoring it, because it now thinks it can secure more for itself by fighting than at peace. If, on the other hand, a war occurs in the first period, A manages to prevent B's growth in power but at an across-the-board cost that shrinks the total pie to be divided (remember Figure 2.4). To keep things simple, we just subtract 1 from every payoff in the first period, such that the relative attractiveness of war and the settlement remains the same for both states. War in the first period preserves A's relative military position, but it now holds sway over a spoiled land, a ravaged city, or a morally compromised position in the global hierarchy, receiving 3 if the settlement is honored and 2 for war. B, its rise halted under the weight of A's attack, receives only 1 if the settlement is honored and 0 if the game ends in war.

This game satisfies our requirements of repetition and the possibility of real and absolute war (both of which are costly). It also introduces the two key elements we need from the preventive war story: shifting power and a war that can stop that power from shifting. The question for us is how A and B will play the game and whether it can tell us anything about how wars caused by commitment problems end short of one side disarming the other. Proposition 11.3 may look a little involved, but keep in mind that strategies are complete plans of action, outlining what players will do for contingencies that may not even be activated. After all, the equilibrium whose existence we're proving has a strategy profile of

$$(\text{renege}_1, \text{honor}_2^h, \text{honor}_2^w; \text{honor}_1, \text{renege}_2^h, \text{honor}_2^w),$$

but it tells a straightforward story about when war breaks out due to shifting power and how it ends, not with one side ground into the dust, but with both sides still standing and signing a new, self-enforcing settlement. To give the short answer, when the declining side is sufficiently patient (i.e., when it cares enough about the future), it launches a war, paying a cost to prevent power from shifting, then reaches a settlement with its once-rising opponent rather than keep on fighting when doing so offers no additional advantage.

PROPOSITION 11.3   *The strategy profile (renege$_1$, honor$_2^h$, honor$_2^w$; honor$_1$, renege$_2^h$, honor$_2^w$) is a Subgame Perfect Equilibrium when $\delta \geq 1/2$.*

Proof   For $(\text{renege}_1, \text{honor}_2^h, \text{honor}_2^w; \text{honor}_1, \text{renege}_2^h, \text{honor}_2^w)$ to be a Subgame Perfect Equilibrium, it must be the case that strategies constitute a Nash Equilibrium in every subgame. Beginning with the subgame at $t = 2$ following no war at $t = 1$, $(\text{honor}_2^h; \text{renege}_2^h)$ must be a Nash Equilibrium. Therefore, it must be the case that

$$u_\text{A}(honor_2^h, renege_2^h) \geq u_\text{A}(renege_2^h, renege_2^h)$$

and

$$u_\text{B}(renege_2^h, renege_2^h) \geq u_\text{B}(renege_2^h, honor_2^h).$$

The first inequality is satisfied because $1 \geq 1$, and the second is satisfied because $3 \geq 2$. No player has a profitable deviation, so $(\text{honor}_2^h; \text{renege}_2^h)$ is a Nash Equilibrium.

Next, in the subgame at $t = 2$ following a war at $t = 1$, $(\text{honor}2_w; \text{honor}_2^w)$ must be a Nash Equilibrium. Therefore, it must be the case that

$$u_\text{A}(honor_2^w, honor_2^w) \geq u_\text{A}(renege_2^w, honor_2^w)$$

and

$$u_\text{A}(honor_2^w, honor_2^w) \geq u_\text{A}(honor_2^w, renege_2^w).$$

The first inequality is satisfied because $3 \geq 2$, and the second is satisfied because $1 \geq 0$. No player has a profitable deviation, so $(\text{honor}_2^w; \text{honor}_2^w)$ is a Nash Equilibrium.

Finally, in the subgame at $t = 1$, it must be the case that, anticipating strategies at $t = 2$,

$$u_A(renege_1; honor_1) \geq u_A(honor_1; honor_1) \Leftrightarrow 3 + \delta 3 \geq 4 + \delta 1$$

and

$$u_B(renege_1; honor_1) \geq u_B(renege_1; renege_1) \Leftrightarrow 1 + \delta 1 \geq 1 + \delta 1.$$

The first inequality is satisfied only when $\delta \geq 1/2$, and the second is satisfied because $0 \geq 0$ (both sides of the inequality cancel out). No player has a profitable deviation in any subgame, so $(renege_1, honor_2^h, honor_2^w; honor_1, renege_2^h, honor_2^w)$ is a Subgame Perfect Equilibrium when $\delta \geq 1/2$. ☐

To see what we can learn from Proposition 11.3, we need to distinguish between equilibrium strategies and equilibrium outcomes. The former is simply a statement of the strategy profile, the contingencies that list what players *would* do if called upon. The latter is what, among the many possibilities covered in equilibrium strategies, would be the observable, behavioral implications of those strategies. The choices that get made (not the ones that get threatened) in a strategy profile constitute the **equilibrium path**, or the path of play, which in the SPE of the dollar-grenade game would be you refusing to give me the dollar and me not pulling the pin; me not pulling the pin after you gave me a dollar, on the other hand, would be *off* the equilibrium path, even though it's a necessary part of my strategy.

DEFINITION 11.5   *The **equilibrium path** is the set of threats and promises that are called in (i.e., observed) during play of the game.*

Strategies tell players what to do at any point so that they can judge the consequences of making any given choice, but only some choices are taken and thus observable by us, the analysts, at the equilibrium. In Chapter 3, for example, players engaged in a mutual naval buildup to avoid the possibility of the other's unilateral buildup. And in our preventive war equilibrium, A's goal is to avoid reaching the subgame in which B has gained exploitable strength. The consequences that would follow – B reneging on the status quo and forcing A to swallow its worst possible outcome – drive A's actions, but those consequences are never realized. Rather, A reneges in the first period despite B trying to honor the agreement, paying the costs of war to ensure that in the second period both states honor the original settlement, now diminished in value by costly fighting. In strategy profile terms, where the equilibrium path is in bold, we have

$$(\textbf{renege}_1, honor_2^h, \textbf{honor}_2^w; \textbf{honor}_1, renege_2^h, \textbf{honor}_2^w),$$

and in Figures 11.5 and 11.6, the equilibrium path gets solid lines, off-path (but still equilibrium) behavior dashed lines. If we're to use this equilibrium or one like it as a guide to examining the historical record we can state a simple guiding rule: the equilibrium path represents what we should see happening, and off-path behavior is what at least one character in our story should be trying to avoid.[43]

We can now return to this chapter's motivating puzzle: why do wars end short of one side's total defeat? In this model, A and B can in principle fight an "absolute" war; all it would take is one player choosing to renege in the second period after having fought in the first. Yet in the "real" war equilibrium of Proposition 11.3, they choose instead to honor the status quo in the second period, and the reasoning is simple: after a round of fighting that stabilizes the distribution of power, stalling or averting B's rise and A's concomitant decline, further fighting would be wasteful.[44] Even one round of fighting and subsequent settlement is wasteful compared to a strategy profile in which both honor the agreement in both periods, because $4 + \delta 4 > 3 + \delta 3$ for A and $2 + \delta 2 > 1 + \delta 3$ for B. This is a strategy profile, like (¬build; ¬build) in Chapter 3, that players would look back on with regret, creating the inefficiency puzzle of war that we posed in Chapter 2. And if either player were to renege in the second period ($t = 2$) subgame following war at $t = 1$, they'd get a payoff reflective of the status quo, but even more wasteful, only further diminished in value: (2, 0) as opposed to (3, 1). If, on the other hand, fighting hadn't stemmed B's rise sufficiently, then we'd see different war payoffs that wouldn't induce B to honor the status quo, and A would have to keep fighting. Since we want to show that war can end short of one side disarming the other, war's inherent destructiveness ensuring what simple diplomacy can't ensure with sufficient credibility, our simple model here assumes that one "period" of fighting is enough to do the trick. But just how long and intense that round of fighting is can range from a simple raid on weapons production facilities to an arduous, bloody slog from the border to an enemy capital.

Wars that begin due to commitment problems end when fighting renders commitments credible, but what does that say about how long such a conflict should last? The waste of war ensures that states fighting preventive wars have no incentive to drag them out any longer than necessary; once fighting has made the status quo tenable, the time has come to wrap things up. But just how long preventive wars need to be

---

[43] The latter part poses a big challenge, though, because it presumes that we'd have records of decision-makers talking extensively about something that they might all have thought so obvious as not worth talking about extensively. Weak countries, for example, probably avoid provoking stronger ones all the time, but the need to reaffirm in the official record that avoiding a predictable military catastrophe is the reason is probably close to nil.

[44] For a more complex analysis of this process, see Powell (2012).

depends on the specific problem being solved, who's got the problem, and who's doing the solving. If disarming the rising side turns out to be necessary, destroying an enemy state or toppling its government, we should expect preventive wars – especially those between powerful equals, like great powers – to be fairly long; the task is large, and resistance is likely to be intense.[45] There are exceptions, like the rapid conquest of Iraq in 2003, due in large part to a tremendous disparity in military strength and the invaders' strategy of maneuver,[46] but in general it may take a while to conquer an enemy state.[47] If the goal is to eliminate budding but undefended weapons programs (think Iraq in 1981, *not* contemporary Iran or North Korea) or power-projecting infrastructure (like railroads in the late nineteenth and early twentieth centuries), to forestall an enemy's fortification or conquest of strategically valuable territory, or to prevent an imminent realignment to a rival camp, we might expect the war to be shorter than a war of conquest. Russia, for example, made short work in 2008 of the prospects that Georgia might join NATO – which would shift power in the Caucasus decisively against the former imperial master – by occupying Georgian territory and recognizing the independence of local separatists, closing off at low cost the possibility of NATO accession in the near future.[48] Our story can also explain an otherwise puzzling case of a war lasting perhaps longer than we'd expect. After successfully ejecting Iraqi occupation forces from Kuwait in 1991, the American-led coalition pursued retreating mechanized formations north on the so-called Highway of Death, wreaking havoc on Iraqi armor in what looked to many observers like so much overkill. But our model suggests a rationale consistent with what coalition forces insisted about their goals at the time: destroying Iraqi capabilities to invade Kuwait or, much more concerning, threaten Saudi Arabia in the future. Thus, wars waged to solve commitment problems may be long or short, and the specifics of how and why power is shifting and prevented from shifting should tell us a lot about just how long it'll take for any given war to run its course. Whatever other bargaining problems may be operating, making commitments to a settlement credible is a necessary condition for the guns to fall silent.

---

[45] See Powell (2006), Wagner (2007), and Weisiger (2013).

[46] Bennett and Stam (2006).

[47] And a lot of troops to occupy it afterward, as the United States apparently had to relearn after 2003. On this topic, see Ricks (2006).

[48] A similar strategy seems to have worked in Ukraine as well. In 2014, Russia seized and annexed the Crimean Peninsula before Ukraine could reorient itself toward the Western great powers, which might have forfeited Russian access to the naval facilities at Sevastopol.

11.3 RESTRAINT IN THE TRENCHES

Though we can only sketch the logic here, dynamic, repeated games can also resolve some puzzling patterns of battlefield behavior in the Great War. Trench warfare isn't known for its tranquility, but once the Western Front stabilized in the fall of 1914, a curious system of "live and let live" held along at least parts of the front. In between major battles ordered from above, British and German soldiers often tolerated each other's movements within rifle range, allowing them time to mill about, to eat, to collect their dead from No-Man's Land, even to fraternize as they did in the famous "Christmas Truce" of December 1914. All this occurred despite the fact that their countries were locked in a bloody, destructive war for their survival as great powers and that the soldiers in the trenches were at this point no less nationalist than the folks at home.[49] Generals didn't like "live and let live," nor did civilian politicians have any special love for it, yet until the institution of a system of regular raids to sustain attritional pressure later in the war, the system seemed to hold. But why?

PUZZLE 11.2 *How could German and British troops manage a "live and let live" system when their primary aims were to kill each other?*

In a pathbreaking study of cooperation, Robert Axelrod shows that the key to understanding the live and let live system is to recognize it as a special kind of Prisoner's Dilemma: an iterated, or repeated, one.[50] Like the repeated game we wrote down in Figures 11.5 and 11.6, where players interact in similar situations multiple times, the lulls between battles on the Western Front looked like a repeated version of the Prisoner's Dilemma that we used to think about the Anglo-German naval race in Chapter 3. In this case, though, the potential endpoint of the interaction is unpredictable; soldiers in the line don't know when the next offensive will be ordered, so they never know when their everyday cross-trench interactions will end. In these lulls of indeterminate length, suppose that units on the front can either shoot to kill when they see another solider across the line or, short of keeping their own rifles silent, merely fire off some shots that keep up the appearance of holding the line but do no damage. Short of a major offensive, nothing's at stake except survival and the chance to pick off a few enemy troops. Each side would most like to shoot while the other doesn't, followed by neither side shooting at the other, then both sides shooting, then refusing to shoot back while the other shoots to kill. If we let "not shoot" be cooperation (or C) and "shoot" be defection (or D), then we've

---

[49] See Philpott (2014, chapter 4) and Watson (2014, chapters 2 and 4).
[50] See Axelrod (1984, chapter 4).

got a simple Prisoner's Dilemma, and if played once, we know the unique Nash Equilibrium: both sides shooting to kill.

But if two conditions are satisfied – (1) there's always a chance of future interactions, and (2) players can devise schemes whereby they punish one another for breaking the rules in previous periods – then a Subgame Perfect Equilibrium can emerge in which neither side shoots to kill on the equilibrium path.[51] We call these devices "punishment strategies," because they allow players to threaten dire consequences for taking certain actions. For example, players in a repeated Prisoners Dilemma might play Grim Trigger strategies: "play C until someone plays D, then play D ever after." This is the most severe possible threat, but it works: knowing that they'd forfeit cooperation (which is pretty valuable in the long run) forever, players can be induced to resist the temptation to take the short-run gains of playing D today. Subgame Perfect Equilibrium requires that these threats be credible, of course, and the Grim Trigger is easy in that regard: defection in the Prisoner's Dilemma is always a best response to defection, even in repeated settings. So, when players can threaten to pull the plug on future cooperation if the other defects, then both can be encouraged to cooperate on the equilibrium path.[52]

Axelrod identifies another strategy that's less grim but that can also sustain cooperation in the iterated PD: Tit-for-Tat. Tit-for-Tat has many variations, but it its simplest form its a story about reciprocity: "play C if the other player chose C in the previous period, but play D if the other player chose D in the previous period." If soldiers on the Western Front knew that shooting to kill while others went about their business during major lulls in the fighting would be met with a proportionate response, then they could resist the short term temptation to pick off whatever Brit happened to pop into view, saving their own skins until they had no choice to go "over the top" when their commanders ordered it. It wasn't until later in the war, when the times between major battles were filled with raids that ordered small detachments into enemy trenches – critical to pinning the enemy down in an attritional equilibrium (recall Chapter 8) – that the "live and let live" system could no longer work, because the periods during which mutual refusals to shoot could occur were too short; soldiers could no longer be sure that their restraint today would be met with restraint tomorrow if another enemy raid was in the

---

[51] For an accessible treatment of punishment strategies in repeated games, see Morrow (1994, chapter 9).

[52] Another popular punishment strategy is Penance, in which a player who defects today must pay a price, cooperating while the other defects against it for some period of time, before a return to cooperation. Consistent with its name, this strategy allows for forgiveness and a return to cooperation.

offing, so why not shoot that German before he could get you? Reciprocity on the battlefield can be a powerful force, and not just in between major battles. Morrow, for example, shows that it can account for the (relatively) humane treatment of prisoners of war on the Western Front during the First *and* Second World Wars; when armies believe that (1) their restraint will be matched by the other side and (2) any abuses will be matched by the other side, then they can treat their prisoners fairly well. But when governments prefer unrestrained battlefields, which happens when they want to discourage their own soldiers from surrendering, like the Soviet Union, Japan, and Germany (on the Eastern Front) in the Second World War, then reciprocity can't keep a lid on horrific violations of the laws of war.[53]

11.4 COMMITMENT PROBLEMS AND CIVIL WAR

Great power wars may be unique in their ability to threaten global stability – and, since the onset of Mutually Assured Destruction,[54] human survival – but civil war is an arguably older and generally more ubiquitous phenomenon. Controlling the state is valuable because it entails a monopoly on the use of organized violence within borders recognized by other states and all the prerogatives that come with that nominal sovereignty.[55] From separatist conflicts like the American (1861–1865), Second Sudanese (1983–2005), and Yugoslav (1991–1999) civil wars to contests for control of the central government like those in China (1911–1949), Spain (1936–1939), and Syria (since 2011), civil wars determine who controls the basic units of the international system: territorial states. Russia itself descended into civil war after the Bolshevik seizure of power in 1917, ensuring that it would turn inward and sign a separate peace, in one of the rare instances of great power civil war. Civil wars are no less deadly for both soldiers and civilians than interstate wars; their staggering economic, social, and public health consequences can linger long after the shooting stops;[56] they spread across international borders and provoke repression next door;[57] they sometimes expand into full-blown interstate

---

[53] See Morrow (2014, chapter 5). Other chapters show that threats of reciprocity can also sustain limits on aerial bombing of civilians, the use of chemical and biological weapons, and more.

[54] I hesitate to put the acronym "MAD" in the main text, because it's been used *too many times* for a pun that's, frankly, too clever by half.

[55] See Coggins (2011).

[56] See, inter alia, Cohen (2013); Ghobarah, Huth, and Russett (2003); Iqbal and Zorn (2010); Lai and Thyne (2007), and Plümper and Neumayer (2006).

[57] Danneman and Ritter (2014); Miller and Ritter (2014).

wars;[58] and belligerents in interstate wars, like Germany in the Great War,[59] often try to foment them in enemy states. The end of the Cold War and superpower support for otherwise fragile states saw an eruption of new civil wars, and ongoing civil wars have increased in number due not only to new outbreaks but also to accumulation, as civil wars tend to last longer than interstate wars.[60] But if civil wars are fought to create a new bargain or restore an old one over who controls the state (a constitution), and in that sense share underlying causes with interstate wars,[61] why should they last longer?

PUZZLE 11.3   *Why do civil wars tend to last longer than interstate wars?*

Our discussion of how fighting solves some commitment problems more easily or quickly than others suggests a ready answer. When states reach a war-ending settlement, both sides can generally withdraw their armies safely behind their own (possibly expanded, possibly diminished) frontiers, still able to threaten armed force in defense of the deal just signed – the essence of self-enforcement. Many civil wars, though, are over control of the state itself (center-seeking wars) or over the geographical extent of the state's authority (separatist wars), leaving room for one and only one organization to wield the monopoly on organized violence fundamental to modern statehood. This means, in practice, that any settlement involving, say, power-sharing, domestic reform, or regional autonomy – that is, a settlement short of "absolute" war – requires the side receiving such a concession (like a rebel group) to disarm.[62] But disarming eliminates whatever leverage the rebels used to force the concession in the first place, enabling the government to later renege on its promise with a military made relatively stronger simply by the disarmament of the rebels. When they're temporarily weak, governments are willing to make concessions to rebels to preserve peace, but once recovered they're more than happy to renege. It is this fundamental incredibility of commitments to compromise settlements that drives rebel groups to sustain the fight in hopes of an ultimate victory or, at minimum, an indefinite delay of the government's return to full strength.[63] The Syrian government, for example, made numerous offers of power-sharing and even limited democratization in the early years of its civil war, only to see rebel groups consistently reject them. But contrary to the government's attempts to paint those rejections as extreme, as the product of terrorism and zealotry, saying no made sense

[58] Gleditsch, Salehyan, and Schultz (2008); Schultz (2010).
[59] See Payne (2011, chapter 2) and Boghardt (2012, chapter 2).
[60] Cunningham and Lemke (2013).
[61] See Wagner (2007).
[62] For early, influential work on this topic, see Walter (1997, 2002).
[63] See Fearon (2004).

for a constellation of rebel groups that believed any promised concessions to be incredible.

Waging a successful civil war entails securing, preserving, or creating a local or national monopoly on the use of organized force. A monopoly, of course, means that only one firm provides the good in question. If the goal is controlling the state, or creating a new one, then civil wars will end with either one side left standing, via military victory or exhaustion, or after substantial destruction renders the exploitation of a disarmed side prohibitively difficult. There's no implication that civil wars should more often have "winners," but the process of solving the underlying commitment problem by victory, forced exhaustion, or destruction can be very long. It's also complicated by the fact that there are no borders to withdraw behind and preserve one's army for future use. The Chinese Communists nearly lost their long civil war for that very reason. Exhausted after the Nationalists' Fourth Encirclement Campaign in the mid-1930s and staring down the barrel of a Fifth after their Long March, they were saved by the timely escalation of Japan's war in China and the foreign-brokered United Front with the Nationalists; that's a far cry from withdrawing behind an international border and living to fight another day. Civil wars, then, are defined by a uniquely thorny commitment problem, where ending the war short of defeat, exhaustion, or destruction requires one side to allow a potentially disastrous shift in power. As a result, war aims are pushed toward totality, to demands for the whole pie, the capture of the state or the destruction of the opponent's military power. And that tends to take far longer than, say, the seizure of territory or the destruction of weapons programs entailed in interstate wars driven by commitment problems.

We've got a resolution to our puzzle, but we can also explain another fact about civil war that's frequently, if erroneously, put forward as a cause. It's not uncommon to hear that civil wars begin and last because each side's aims are fundamentally incompatible, especially in cases of clear ideological conflict like the Nationalist-Communist struggle of the historically bloody Chinese Civil War.[64] The conventional reasoning goes something like this: the Nationalists and Communists were simply too far apart in their aims, which excluded the other by ideological program, for a war not to occur *and* for that war to take an eternity to work itself out. But that reasoning runs into trouble when we consider the occasions on which both sides *did* cooperate, at least nominally, in the face of Japanese invasion beginning in the 1930s, as well as the many other examples of nationalists and communists in other countries managing *not* to kill each

---

[64] For a species of this explanation embedded in an otherwise excellent analysis of war in the region from 1911 to 1949, see Paine (2012).

other in large numbers. A more plausible story, implied by our analysis in this chapter, is that the commitment problem at the heart of civil war *explains* why belligerents would adopt extreme aims like the eradication of the enemy. It also explains why ideologically extreme factions end up fighting each other, for all intents and purposes, to the death: their extreme preferences are a clean, pragmatic match to the political imperatives of waging the "absolute" civil war demanded by the underlying commitment problem. In other words, extreme war aims can be a symptom, not a cause, of civil war.

11.5   CONCLUSION

We began this chapter by asking a question that our model in Chapter 2 couldn't answer: how war can solve commitment problems not by the empirically rare case of disarming an opponent through total military victory but by making a self-enforcing settlement possible well short of an "absolute" war. The answer comes down yet again to the simple fact that war is costly, which gives calculating and frugal players strong incentives not only to avoid it but also to end it once fighting becomes unnecessary. In the case of war caused by commitment problems, our focus in this chapter, fighting allows belligerents to reach a negotiated settlement that is, in contrast to the *status quo ante bellum*, self-enforcing once the rising side's ability or opportunity to renegotiate is eliminated. Total victory is one solution to the problem, but it's far from the only one. Fighting can destroy the sources of shifting power or the ability and attractiveness of using it through sheer destructiveness, and the difficulty of the task – say, total conquest or simply wrecking the other's offensive capabilities – determines how long commitment-driven wars endure before settlement becomes possible again. This intentional, instrumental move from peace to war to peace is what historian Geoffrey Blainey has in mind in the quote that opened this chapter: "A valid diagnosis of war will be reflected in a valid diagnosis of peace."[65]

Resolving our motivating puzzle required that we introduce dynamic games, both extensive form and repeated, and Subgame Perfect Equilibrium to write down a model that could provide insights unavailable from our initial forays into explaining war. Useful as these new tools are, we introduced them this late in the narrative for a very good reason: we simply haven't needed them yet. War, you'll note, occurs in this chapter for the very same reason it does in Chapter 2: the threat of shifting power and a rising side's inability to commit to maintaining the status quo forces

---

[65] Blainey (1988, p. 3).

the hand of a declining side, who launches a war it knows to be costly in order to arrest or prevent its loss of relative power. We needed dynamic games and Subgame Perfect Equilibrium, though, to think about how states choose to end their wars – which the static game in Chapter 2 assumed would happen. By ruling out incredible threats, Subgame Perfect Equilibrium allowed us to show that wars, even high-stakes preventive wars, need not be "absolute" when they've achieved their purpose and made a self-enforcing bargain possible that wasn't beforehand. In substantive terms, extending our analysis of war to a dynamic setting allowed us to show that the costliness of war is, as we noted in Chapter 1, fundamental to understanding its role and occurrence in the international system. That fighting is wasteful sets a high bar for explaining why calculating, frugal decision-makers knowingly bear those costs, but it also helps us explain why they choose to stop bearing them: to save the costs of what they know would be a bootlessly expensive "absolute" war. As we'll see in Chapter 12 as well, "absolute" war is the threat that typically stays off the equilibrium path, the outcome that even bitter enemies can agree on the value of avoiding, that nonetheless shapes who gets what, how much of it they get, and how much of others' shares they get to dictate, in international politics.

11.6 EXERCISES: INTERDEPENDENCE AND WAR

The war-fighting model spread across Figures 11.5 and 11.6 has a pretty involved solution, so in this section we'll get some extra practice with Subgame Perfect Equilibrium and backward induction, which should be useful before tackling that more complicated model. We'll focus in this section on a simpler setting, analyzing an extensive-form variant of the crisis bargaining game we introduced in Chapter 2. First, we'll show how commitment problems and shifting power can cause war in a dynamic setting. Then, in a second game we'll introduce the idea of trade interdependence, which can discourage war by creating opportunity costs of forgone economic exchange. We'll close by using these exercises to say something about a long-running debate about the First World War focused on whether or not extensive global economic interdependence had any impact on the outbreak of war in 1914.

Let's begin by translating the logic of the commitment problem to an extensive form game. Figure 11.7 shows one way in which we can do this, where country A chooses between attacking country B or passing in the first move; attacking leads to a war, while passing gives B the chance to honor the status quo or to renege on it from a position of strength. If A attacks, it can force the status quo to survive by defeating B, but if A passes,

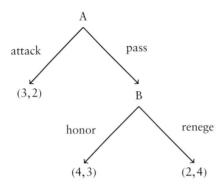

Figure 11.7 Commitment and war in the extensive form.

B grows militarily stronger and the status quo survives only if B chooses to honor it. B moves last, so it can't commit not to renege on the status quo – which pulls the distribution of benefits, like a border, in B's favor – if doing so will be in its interest. We'll assume for now that renegotiations happen peacefully, such that B gets its best outcome if it reneges (4), its next-best outcome if it honors the status quo (3), and its worst outcome if A attacks (2), denying B the opportunity to revise the status quo. For its part, A's best outcome is to pass and see B honor the status quo (4), keeping today's bargain intact while avoiding the costs of war, worst is to pass and allow B to renegotiate from a position of strength in the future (1), and in the middle is a war launched from today's position of relative strength (3), which locks in the status quo with a costly war. How will A and B play this game?

EXERCISE 11.1   *Prove the existence or nonexistence of a Subgame Perfect Equilibrium of the game in Figure 11.7 in which A passes and B honors.*

EXERCISE 11.2   *Prove the existence or nonexistence of a Subgame Perfect Equilibrium of the game in Figure 11.7 in which A attacks.*

With these exercises completed, let's think about another dimension of the First World War. We saw in Chapter 4 that shifting power, between Austria and Serbia on the one hand and between Germany and Russia on the other, offers a good account of how the war began. General war had been on the European mind for some time by the time Gavrilo Princip felled Franz Ferdinand, but some observers remained optimistic that war could be avoided because, by 1914, global economic interdependence had reached unprecedented levels. Trade in goods and services, financial flows, even the movements of people, across borders were at an all-time high, even between putative rivals like Britain and Germany. War would compromise these trading relationships, harming labor, capital, and (as

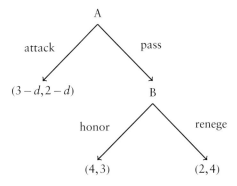

Figure 11.8 Trade and the opportunity costs of war.

a result) tax revenue. This forgone trade represents an **opportunity cost,** which is the cost associated with choosing one option over another. For example, the opportunity of going out on a Thursday night before a Friday exam is the drop in your grade relative to staying in and, if not studying, at least being well rested; the opportunity cost of signing an alliance with country X is now-damaged relationships with its enemies, who'd otherwise have no issue with you; and the opportunity cost of war is all the economic exchange that won't take place as firms avoid doing business in war zones, as blockades strangle an enemy's ports, as production priorities shift from goods for export to means of destruction, and as falling imports force consumers to pay higher prices for expensive domestic goods that could've otherwise been imported.

DEFINITION 11.6   *An **opportunity cost** is the loss of a potential benefit associated with choosing one action over another.*

The greater the flows of goods and services and capital and labor across borders, the greater the opportunity costs of war. In other words, as states become more economically interdependent, the more they rely on one another for their economic well-being, the more hesitant they should be to go to war and put at risk the gains from trade. This argument remains popular, especially as globalization has accelerated in the global recovery from the Second World War.[66]

Figure 11.8 offers us one way to think about opportunity costs and war by making one simple change to our extensive-form model of the commitment problem. Players, actions, and outcomes remain the same, but here we subtract from each country's war payoff a shared cost parameter ($d > 0$), representing the extent of economic interdependence between A and B. If A launches a preventive war, it locks in the territorial status quo

---

[66] See, inter alia, Keohane and Nye (1977) and Russett and Oneal (2001).

by arresting, ending, or reversing B's growth (Definition 2.13), but doing so comes at a cost not only of destroying part of the land but of reducing the value of trade that would continue at its higher, prewar levels if only A passes on the chance to attack. Remember that B gets to renegotiate from a position of strength if A passes, so trade continues unabated as long as A and B avoid war.

EXERCISE 11.3   *Prove the existence of a Subgame Perfect Equilibrium of the game in Figure 11.6 in which A attacks, then state the conditions under which it exists.*

EXERCISE 11.4   *Prove the existence of a Subgame Perfect Equilibrium of the game in Figure 11.6 in which A passes, then state the conditions under which it exists.*

Once you've completed these exercises, it's worth thinking about how equilibria – and, in this case, outcomes – differ once we introduce the opportunity costs of war. The game in Figure 11.7 has a single SPE, and it's a violent one. But we found two SPE for the game in Figure 11.8, one of which is peaceful; A passes, despite the certainty that B will go on to renege on the status quo, because it can be compensated for the costs of future weakness with continued access to trade. When states can get what they want more easily through trade than through conquest, war looks less attractive as a tool of statecraft, and this is precisely the sense in which economic interdependence has been argued to pacify international relations. It's also the reason that, since China's economic recovery from the early twentieth century began in earnest in the 1980s and 1990s, the United States has worked to integrate it into the global trading system – to increase both potential rivals' stakes in the survival of the current balance of power.

The link between economic interdependence and peace makes for a compelling argument, but it sits uncomfortably against the idea that in 1914, precisely when global economic integration had peaked, the great powers – prime drivers and beneficiaries of the global economic system – marched willingly to a cataclysmic war. In fact, this apparent problem for the argument has been cited as evidence against the thesis that economic interdependence can reduce the chances of war; surely, if economic integration promotes peace, it should've done so when cross-border flows were at a world-historical high.[67] But does this really constitute evidence against the claim? Recent work in political science suggests not, because

---

[67] See, e.g., Waltz (1979), Blainey (1988), and Mearsheimer (2001). But there are *plenty* of others.

economic integration and interdependence were hardly uniform.[68] The July Crisis, in fact, broke out in the part of Europe that was among the least interdependent – the Balkans – between countries without the extensive trade ties that characterized the wealthy triad of Britain, Germany, and France. If the War was to break out anywhere, the interdependence thesis would expect it to be in a less-integrated part of Europe, and that's precisely what happened. Furthermore, as you proved in the last two exercises, interdependence doesn't rule out war; it just raises the threshold of the stakes that would encourage interdependent countries to fight it.[69] This is arguably what we see as wealthier, more interdependent countries like Great Britain join the fray; as we saw in Chapter 6, the threat of a localized war on the Continent wasn't enough to draw Britain in immediately, but once the whole European balance of power was in play, not even extensive trade with Germany could discourage Britain, the world's richest maritime trading state, from leaping into the dark along with the other great powers.

---

[68] This line of reasoning is due to Gartzke and Lupu's (2012) excellent reassessment of the interdependence thesis as it applies to the First World War.

[69] That suggests an intriguing corollary: rising interdependence should discourage low-stakes wars, but the wars with stakes high enough to get over the threshold will be larger and more destructive. So, as interdependence increases, war may become less likely, but the wars that do occur will be bigger and more consequential.

12 The Theory of War IV: Information and War Termination

> *By seeing peace and war as alternatives, we can be neglectful of their mutual dependence.*
>
> Hew Strachan,
> *The Origins of the First World War*

Chapter 11 showed how fighting can solve commitment problems, allowing states to negotiate an end to war well before it becomes "absolute." Left open, though, is the question of how war can solve information problems. We'll answer this question by addressing an identical puzzle:

Why do most wars end in a compromise peace rather than total victory?

This chapter shares a puzzle with Chapter 11, but the answer is quite different. War can solve commitment problems by changing players' *payoffs*, but it solves information problems by changing players' *beliefs*, their subjective estimates about the state of the world. Commitment problems are solved by changing the facts on the ground, but information problems are solved by persuading an enemy of something that a state has every incentive to lie about: one side convinces the other that it deserves a better deal than what was initially on offer, because the other comes around to a new belief about what an absolute war would look like. In other words, war solves information problems by producing agreement on certain facts between states that may otherwise despise and distrust one another. Our task is to figure out how the waste, destruction, and spilled blood of combat can make enemies agree that a specific, limited settlement is better than the "absolute" settlement of a fight to the finish.

We'll introduce a solution concept, Perfect Bayesian Equilibrium (PBE), designed to help us analyze information problems in dynamic environments, where new information and updated beliefs turn out to be critical to explaining how fighting can reduce uncertainty about what a fight to the finish would look like, making settlement possible where it wasn't before. The result will be a working knowledge of how information problems figure into the duration and termination of war – as well as the sometimes frantic, sometimes unhurried, and often insincere diplomacy that accompanies it. We'll learn several new things along the way:

- how to identify Perfect Bayesian Equilibria in dynamic games;
- how fighting can reveal information that diplomacy can't;
- why war aims and bargaining positions change over the course of the war;
- how fighting creates settlements that don't reflect battlefield outcomes.

By viewing war as a more dynamic process than we did even in Chapter 11, where war aims didn't really change over time, we'll see the battlefield and the negotiating table become places where information is revealed, beliefs updated, and bargaining positions changed in response. This allows us to crack open the black box of war and look for the politics of what's sometimes called the most honest place on earth: the battlefield.[1] Once again, the cost of war will prove critical in explaining its features: over time, fighting screens out those unable to bear the costs by forcing them to cut deals before the war becomes too expensive, and the longer the war continues, the more convinced an uninformed side becomes that it's got to offer more generous terms to bring the conflict to an end. Beliefs converge through this process on the likely outcome of an "absolute" war, creating conditions of effectively complete information where, as we saw in Chapter 5, war won't occur (at least not because of information problems). After working through this logic in a pair of models, one that follows the dollar-grenade debacle of Chapter 11 and another that dives straight into the politics of war termination, we detail what our model implies for the duration of wars caused by information problems and establish some expectations about what to look for when we return to our narrative of the Great War.

Key Terms for Chapter 12

- Information Set
- History (in a game)
- Perfect Bayesian Equilibrium
- Out-of-Equilibrium Beliefs
- Semi-separating Equilibrium

---

[1] There may be honesty on the battlefield, but that doesn't mean everyone agrees on what he sees: for everyone who says that there are no atheists in foxholes, someone else says that there are *only* atheists in foxholes. I owe that point to Rick Morgan.

12.1   THE PUZZLE OF PERSUASION

When we posed our puzzle about war termination in Chapter 11, we noted that belligerents tend overwhelmingly to stop short of an "absolute" war in which the victor fully disarms the vanquished, not out of any sense of mercy but because going any further would be wasteful. Even if the most obvious way to solve commitment problems might be simply eliminating the state that can't make credible promises to abide by the status quo, fighting tends to persist only as long as necessary to get that job done: to eliminate either the sources of shifting power or the incentives to exploit it, and generally no more. But wars caused by information problems pose a rather different, ostensibly thornier problem. Information problems are solved not by rearranging an enemy's payoffs but by changing an enemy's mind, convincing it to offer a better deal – certainly not something that war might be viewed as all that useful in bringing about, with armies on the march and in the trenches, flag-draped coffins and wounded soldiers coming home, and populations whipped into a frenzy by wartime propaganda.[2] So we'll pose the same question we did previously:

PUZZLE 12.1   *Why do most wars end in compromise peace rather than total victory?*

Our colloquial understanding of war, with its victors and their parades and its losers and their indemnities, renders the rarity of Clausewitz's "absolute" wars puzzling. But the idea that war creates convergent beliefs, that it leads belligerents to agree on something as contentious as who's more likely to win an apocalyptic struggle for survival, may seem strange. Some approaches to understanding conflict, in fact, predict that fighting should lead not to a convergence of expectations but to increased, ostensibly "irrational" enmity. Theories of enduring rivalry, for example, posit that states tend to develop hostile, distrustful images of adversaries that are both hard to shake and exploitable by hawkish factions at home that can ride fear, hatred, and militarism to political power.[3] Pairs of rival states make up about 6 percent of the international system, yet they're involved in roughly half of its conflicts,[4] and this pattern is often attributed to these hidebound, ingrained hostile images that lead states to prize harming each other over any reasonable consideration of relative power or the costs of war.[5] National leaders are even punished politically, seeing reduced chances of retaining office, when they extend

---

[2] The latter takes many forms: I remember in fifth grade getting my hands on Operation Desert Storm trading cards. Looking back, that's a bit surreal.

[3] Colaresi (2005); Diehl and Goertz (2000); Vasquez (1993, 2009).

[4] See Diehl and Goertz (2000); Goertz and Diehl (1993).

[5] Colaresi, Rasler, and Thompson (2007).

olive branches that rival states refuse to grasp.[6] It's not in any sense, nor is it proposed to be, an environment conducive to the effective integration of new information about the distribution of power or an opponent's willingness to fight to the bitter end.

Yet rivals wage wars all the time without disarming one another. Russia and the Ottoman Empire, for example, fought numerous wars in the late nineteenth and early twentieth centuries, over both border territory *and* the long-standing Russian desire to dominate the Turkish Straits. Yet despite the implications for the balance of power, nontrivial levels of racial and religious enmity between the ruling classes, and one side's desire to *rename the other's capital after its own monarch*, neither Russian nor Ottoman troops ever solved the problem by conquering or sacking the other's capital.[7] In fact, two rivals could hardly be worthy of the name if one *did* manage to disarm the another, because the multiple disputes, crises, and wars by which we identify them simply wouldn't exist.[8] The concept of rivalry has done a lot of useful work for political science, especially in unpacking the domestic politics of long-run competition between hostile states and identifying the consequences,[9] but its focus on mistrust, enmity, and the craven demagoguery of office-seeking politicians would seem to overpredict the duration of war and the frequency of "absolute" outcomes between rivals. A theory that predicts states to focus on harming one another at all costs isn't compatible with a world in which most wars, even those between rivals, end in "real" as opposed to "absolute" outcomes. What's missing, as we'll see below, is an appreciation of the waste inherent in war – the destruction and dislocation that both reveals information about how long states can hold out against pain imposed by the other and encourages them to end wars as soon as possible, even in the face of seemingly insurmountable levels of national antagonism.

12.2   SOLVING INFORMATION PROBLEMS

We know from Chapters 4 and 6 that commitment problems informed several decisions to join the Great War. But the adoption of strategies of attrition ensured that there would be a significant informational component in the process of war termination: belligerents each had a better

---

[6] Colaresi (2004); Davies and Johns (2016).

[7] On the long Russo-Turkish rivalry, see Blainey (1988) and, for the latter part of that period, McMeekin (2015).

[8] To be fair, some rivalries are identified simply on the basis of leaders' *beliefs* about long-term threats (Thompson 2001; Thompson and Dreyer 2012).

[9] See, e.g., Colaresi (2004), Rider (2009, 2013), Owsiak and Rider (2013), and Rider and Owsiak (2015).

idea than their opponents of how long they could hold out, yet they had no incentive to admit just where they thought their own breaking points were. But if belligerents can reach agreement on who will be the last one standing, then they can reach a settlement that reflects these shared beliefs (in rough terms) but saves the costs of war. The question for us is how fighting can resolve that uncertainty, how it can convince one state making the other a miserly offer at the negotiating table to become a bit more generous and induce its enemy to settle. To answer it, we'll return to the world of dynamic games, capturing once again the sequencing that was important in Chapter 11. This time around, a player enters the game with private information over the attractiveness of fighting a war, which necessitates that we look for a Perfect Bayesian Equilibrium (PBE), i.e., the dynamic version of the Bayesian Nash Equilibria that we first introduced in Chapter 5. As we did before, though, we'll introduce this new solution concept in a decidedly different environment than the grinding industrial tragedy of the First World War.

12.2.1 Perfect Bayesian Equilibrium

Perfect Bayesian Equilibrium is a refinement of both Bayesian Nash Equilibrium and Subgame Perfect Equilibrium, and like them it's a method of eliminating some equilibria that don't make as much sense as others. We introduced SPE to help us think about the credibility of threats in dynamic settings, and that process was made easier because we assumed that players knew previous moves in the game – that is, they made choices, and could expect to make future choices, under complete information. That setting was just fine for analyzing how wars solved commitment problems; we were interested in how fighting could change commonly known payoffs, so introducing private information would've been a wasteful exercise. But if we're interested in whether and how fighting can change *beliefs*, then we need to work out a way to write down and solve games with the possibility of learning, games in which players can use Bayes' Rule to learn about previous moves in the game.

Figure 12.1 presents us with just such a problem.[10] Suppose that, sometime after my failed attempt to extort a dollar from you with a hand grenade, you've decided that you want to prevent me from showing up at happy hour with my colleagues. I suspect that you've got some kind of plan up your sleeve to ambush me, so I can either stay in my office and miss happy hour or, realizing that grenades are no way to get what I want, carry either a small or a big stick with me for self-defense. If I go to happy

---

[10] This game is drawn from McCarty and Meirowitz (2007, p. 208), but names, actions, and payoffs have been changed.

hour, you've got to decide whether to ambush me from behind some well-chosen bushes. My best outcome is to get to happy hour unmolested (5), and while I'd prefer to stay in the office than to deal with an ambush (0), I'd still rather throttle you with a big stick (−1) than a small one (−3). Your best outcome is for me to simply stay in my office and miss happy hour (5), though you'd rather not have to ambush me when I leave the office (0), and the bigger the stick I carry the more painful the ambush will be (−2 if I've got the small one, −5 if I've got the big one). Ideally, you'd like the threat of an ambush to ruin my afternoon, while I'd just like to avoid the hassle and enjoy a nice IPA.

But you've got a problem. In addition to the very reasonable desire to avoid getting clocked by a stick-wielding professor, you can only see from behind the bushes whether I leave the office – not the size of the stick I'm carrying. We represent this by a dotted line connecting two decision nodes at an **information set**, which collects moves that one player can't distinguish from one another.

DEFINITION 12.1   *An **information set** collects choice nodes that players can't distinguish from one another.*

If an information set contains only one node, like my first move, we call it a singleton, because players know where they are in the game at that point – a key element of complete information games. But when information sets contain multiple nodes, players can't distinguish the path that led them to their current choice from at least one other path. Thus, in Figure 12.1, you can't tell whether I've played big or small. Rather than being able to condition your choice on the size of the stick I'm carrying, you've really only got one choice – ambush or not – even when the payoffs for launching your attack differ based on the size of the stick I'm carrying. You'll recall that this is exactly how we thought about uncertainty over types in

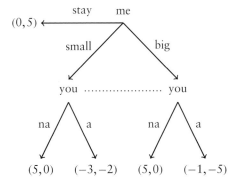

Figure 12.1 Ambushing a professor who just wants to get to happy hour.

Bayesian games (Chapter 5), where Nature assigns one player's type but doesn't inform the other player. It's a different context, but it's the same metaphor of one player being unable to distinguish some previous moves from others.

With the game specified, let's solve it. Following Chapter 11, we might first like to try backward induction. But it becomes clear pretty quickly that we can't. When you've got a choice over ambushing me or not, you don't know whether I've got the big or the small stick. You can't condition your choice on my previous choice, which means you don't know the consequences of choosing an ambush – that is, whether you'll receive a -2 or a -5. We can't write down a meaningful comparison where you consider ambushing or not based on my choice of carrying the small or the big stick. In a technical sense, we can't do backward induction here because your choices don't constitute proper subgames, which begin with singleton information sets (recall Definition 11.4). In fact, there's only one subgame – the whole game itself – which forces us for now back to the rules of Nash Equilibrium.[11] Finding Nash Equilibria in the extensive form really isn't that different from the normal form: we simply look for a strategy profile, take its final payoff as given, and then see whether any player has a profitable deviation. As you might've anticipated, that exercise produces something a little odd.

PROPOSITION 12.1   *The strategy profiles (stay; a), (small; na), and (big; na) are each a Nash Equilibrium.*

Proof   First, for (stay; a) to be a Nash Equilibrium, it must be the case that

$$u_{\text{me}}(stay; a) \geq u_{\text{me}}(small; a) \quad \text{and} \quad u_{\text{me}}(stay; a) \geq u_{\text{me}}(big; a)$$

for me and

$$u_{\text{you}}(stay; a) \geq u_{\text{you}}(stay; na)$$

for you. The first inequality is satisfied because $0 \geq -3$, the second because $0 \geq -1$, and the third because $5 \geq 5$. No player has a profitable deviation, so (stay; a) is a Nash Equilibrium. Second, for (small; na) to be a Nash Equilibrium, it must be the case that

$$u_{\text{me}}(small; na) \geq u_{\text{me}}(stay; na) \quad \text{and} \quad u_{\text{me}}(small; na) \geq u_{\text{me}}(big; na)$$

---

[11] It's worth noting, though, that whatever Nash Equilibria we find will also be Subgame Perfect Equilibria, because SPE simply requires that strategies entail Nash Equilibria in every subgame.

for me and

$$u_{\text{you}}(\text{small}; na) \geq u_{\text{you}}(\text{small}; a)$$

for you. The first inequality is satisfied because $5 \geq 0$, the second because $5 \geq 5$, and the third because $0 \geq -2$. No player has a profitable deviation, so (small; na) is a Nash Equilibrium. Finally, for (big; na) to be a Nash Equilibrium, it must be the case that

$$u_{\text{me}}(big;\text{na}) \geq u_{\text{me}}(stay;\text{na}) \quad \text{and} \quad u_{\text{me}}(big;\text{na}) \geq u_{\text{me}}(small;\text{na})$$

for me and

$$u_{\text{you}}(\text{big}; na) \geq u_{\text{big}}(\text{small}; a)$$

for you. The first inequality is satisfied because $5 \geq 0$, the second because $5 \geq 5$, and the third because $0 \geq -5$. No player has a profitable deviation, so (big; na) is a Nash Equilibrium. ☐

Proposition 12.1 states that the game in Figure 12.1 has three Nash Equilibria. But only two make sense. In strategy profiles (small; na) and (big; na), I carry a stick to happy hour and you choose not to ambush me. You can infer which stick I'm carrying because you know my strategy – even when you can't observe my move, the common conjecture would still tell you my strategy, just like it does in the static games we've analyzed where moves are effectively simultaneous. Remember that, even in dynamic settings, Nash Equilibrium allows players to precommit to their strategies; the trick for refinements like SPE and PBE is to rule out precommitments that don't make sense. So, when you know that I'm carrying a big stick or a small sick, you wisely choose not to get in between me and my afternoon pint, remaining in defilade and perhaps defusing the conflict that began with my ill-considered decision to brandish a hand grenade in Chapter 11. Sensible as those equilibria are, they exist alongside one that isn't quite so satisfying. At (stay; a), my best response to your strategy of ambush is to stay in my office (because 0 is better than getting ambushed), and your knowledge that I'll stay in (and guarantee you a payoff of 5) means that you're free to threaten an ambush. Note that your payoff given my strategy is 5, because your threat is never called in; if you deviate to na, your payoff is still 5, because we hold the other player's strategy constant when checking for profitable deviations. Just like the equilibrium in Chapter 11 at which you give me a dollar despite my incredible threat of pulling the pin on a grenade, your precommitment to ambush keeps me in my office and, of course, leaves you free to threaten the ambush. We can't rely on backward induction to rule out this incredible threat, but we can do something like it once we take care of that information set.

PBE's refinement starts with the idea of players' *beliefs* about the history of the game. Players have some subjective probability distribution over possible nodes of the game based on the paths of play (or **histories**) that got them to this point.

DEFINITION 12.2   *A **history** is a set of moves that leads to a given information set in a dynamic game.*

This allows players to choose actions that are *sequentially rational* – that is, actions that allow players to do the best they can looking forward from any point based on their beliefs about where they are in the game. Under the rules of Nash Equilibrium, the only way we can pin down an action for you in Figure 12.1 is to precommit you to a strategy, but that's not a terribly useful solution when it produces equilibria in which your strategy dictates that you do things we both know you'd never do. But if we allow our players to reason a little more – a little more realistically, even – about what's going on in the game they're playing, we can let them make choices that reflect what they can figure out about the history of play based on what they know about each other's strategies. In dynamic games, Nash Equilibrium constrains players not to use valuable information, even when it's right in front of them. Perfect Bayesian Equilibrium, by contrast, allows our players to use that information.

The final element of Perfect Bayesian Equilibrium is responsible for its namesake: on the equilibrium path – that is, when players choose as their strategies predict that they will – other players can update their beliefs about where they are in the game using Bayes' Rule. It's important to note, though we won't worry too much about it right now, that PBE does not require that beliefs that are off the equilibrium path be updated according to Bayes' Rule. Beliefs that follow an action *not* expected to be taken in equilibrium are *undefined*, because the denominator of Bayes' Rule for an event that occurs off the equilibrium path is zero. This would be the case in pooling equilibria (Definition 5.9), where all player-types are expected to choose a single action but where we still need to know what would happen in the event they deviated in order to work out the equilibrium. (See the exercises at the end of this chapter for more on pooling PBE and out-of-equilibrium beliefs.) Back to the equilibrium path, as we saw in Chapters 5 and 6, Bayes' Rule allows us to begin with statements about a player's prior beliefs and then use the rules of conditional probability to see how these beliefs can be updated to form *posterior beliefs* in light of new information provided by each other's strategies. Put very, very crudely, Perfect Bayesian Equilibrium is the imperfect-information version of Subgame Perfect Equilibrium: it imposes sequential rationality on our players and requires that their beliefs about previous moves in the game are consistent with each other's strategies.

DEFINITION 12.3   *At a **Perfect Bayesian Equilibrium** each player does the best it can do moving forward from any point, given its beliefs (updated by Bayes' Rule when possible) about the play of the game to that point.*

If we're to find PBE for the game in Figure 12.1, we need to find strategy profiles in which (1) players have chosen mutual best responses and (2) their beliefs about previous moves are based on each other's strategies. We know, thanks to our search for Nash Equilibria, that three strategy profiles entail mutual best responses, but PBE allows us to rule out one of them. If the problem with (stay; a) is that you'd committed yourself to an incredible threat of ambushing me as I left my office, let's see how giving our players consistent beliefs can eliminate that strategy profile. At (stay; a), the only reason that ambushing me makes sense as a best response is that you believe that I've not left the office, which guarantees you a payoff of 5; but if there's *any* chance that I've left the office, then a strategy of ambushing me stops making sense. To see how, suppose that you know I've left the office, but that you believe I'm carrying the small stick with probability s and the big one with probability $1-s$. That lets us write down an expected utility comparison, which states that your expected payoff for playing na is greater than for playing a when

$$EU_{\text{you}}(\text{na}) \geq EU_{\text{you}}(\text{a}) \Leftrightarrow s \times 0 + (1-s) \times 0 \geq s \times (-2) + (1-s) \times (-5).$$

Solving for s, we get

$$s \leq \frac{5}{3},$$

which states that for any possible belief you might hold that I've played small or big – because probabilities can only be in the (inclusive) range $[0, 1]$, you'd never find it sequentially rational to ambush me. For you, na is a dominant strategy, *provided that you're required to realize where you are in the game when you make the choice.*

Here's another way of thinking about it: if you're faced with the choice of mounting your ambush or not – that is, if you see me walk out of my office with a stick of indeterminate size – then you know that I've chosen not to stay in my office; otherwise, if I'd stayed in the office, you wouldn't be making a choice at all. Bayes' Rule confirms this intuition. If we let Pr(stay|a, na) be the probability that I've played "stay" given that your information set has been reached, that you're choosing between a and na,

$$\Pr(\text{stay}|a, \text{na}) = \frac{\Pr(\text{stay}) \times \Pr(a, \text{na}|\text{stay})}{\Pr(\text{stay}) \times \Pr(a, \text{na}|\text{stay}) + \Pr(\neg\text{stay}) \times \Pr(\neg\text{stay}|a, \text{na})}$$

$$= \frac{0 \times 0}{0 \times 0 + 1 \times 1} = 0,$$

then your belief that I've played stay – the only thing that would justify playing a – has to be zero. Therefore, no beliefs about the play of the game so far can justify your choice of anything other than na, which is always better than actually mounting the ambush. This tells us immediately that (stay; a) can't be a PBE, because you'd choose a strategy that would commit you to an action inconsistent with what would have to be true about the game when you'd be making the choice.

The remaining two Nash Equilibria, (small; na) and (big; na), however, *can* be Perfect Bayesian Equilibria as long as we specify beliefs for you that are consistent with my strategy – that is, as long as we don't allow you to believe something that supports a patently incredible threat.

PROPOSITION 12.2   *The strategy profiles (small; na), with beliefs* $\Pr(small) = 1$, *and (big: na), with beliefs* $\Pr(big) = 1$, *are each a Perfect Bayesian Equilibrium.*

Proof   For (small; na) to be a Perfect Bayesian Equilibrium, it must be the case that

$$u_{\text{me}}(small; \text{na}) \geq u_{\text{me}}(stay; \text{na}) \quad \text{and} \quad u_{\text{me}}(small; \text{na}) \geq u_{\text{me}}(big; \text{na})$$

for me and

$$u_{\text{you}}(\text{small}; na) \geq u_{\text{you}}(\text{small}; a)$$

for you. The first inequality is satisfied because $5 \geq 0$, the second because $5 \geq 5$, and the third because $0 \geq -2$, where the latter is supported by your belief that $\Pr(\text{small}) = 1$. Strategies are sequentially rational and consistent with beliefs updated according to Bayes' Rule where possible, so (small; na) is a Perfect Bayesian Equilibrium. Finally, for (big; na) to be a Perfect Bayesian Equilibrium, it must be the case that

$$u_{\text{me}}(big; \text{na}) \geq u_{\text{me}}(stay; \text{na}) \quad \text{and} \quad u_{\text{me}}(big; \text{na}) \geq u_{\text{me}}(small; \text{na})$$

for me and

$$u_{\text{you}}(\text{big}; na) \geq u_{\text{big}}(\text{small}; a)$$

for you. The first inequality is satisfied because $5 \geq 0$, the second because $5 \geq 5$, and the third because $0 \geq -5$, where the latter is supported by your belief that $\Pr(\text{big}) = 1$. Strategies are sequentially rational and consistent with beliefs updated according to Bayes' Rule where possible, so (big; na) is a Perfect Bayesian Equilibrium. $\square$

Proposition 12.2 leaves us with two PBE, both of which resolve the problem posed by the information set connecting your choices in Figure 12.1, because they allow you to reason that, if you see me leaving the office, your choice of mounting the ambush or not has an immediate impact on your payoffs – an impact that guarantees you'll never actually mount the ambush. It also allows me to reason that you won't mount the ambush, which frees me to leave the office and get to happy hour. Just to work it out explicitly, here's the reasoning for our two PBE:

- **Me:** "There's no way she'll actually ambush me, so I'm better off taking the big (small) stick and going to happy hour."
- **You:** "He's left his office, which means he's got the big (small) stick, so I won't mount this ambush."

In either the big or small stick strategy profile, neither of us has a profitable deviation, ensuring that our strategies are in equilibrium. But PBE also requires that your move be sequentially rational in that it doesn't commit you to an action you'd never take if given the chance. Equally important in sustaining the equilibrium, though, is the restriction that you hold reasonable beliefs about where you are in the game when you make your ultimate choice over retaliating against me for the dollar-grenade imbroglio.

If we didn't restrict our focus to Perfect Bayesian Equilibria in this game – that is, if we just found the Nash strategy profiles and called it a day – we'd produce two reasonable equilibria and one baffling one, and we'd have no way to arbitrate between them (without being, well, arbitrary). If multiple equilibria exist, then they've got the same logical status. Eliminating some from consideration requires either a compelling story about coordination on a focal solution (Chapter 10) or, if we're lucky, a refinement of Nash Equilibrium that can reasonably rule out some equilibria as candidates for coordination. That's what we've done here, by eliminating (stay; a) as an equilibrium that doesn't fit with our substantive premise that the people in our stories are calculating and frugal. There's still some indeterminacy in the game, but given your dominant strategy of not ambushing, we'd see a very similar outcome in either case: me leaving the office and arriving at happy hour without having to use whatever stick I leave with, and you shaking your fist in anger as I manage to slip away unpunished for threatening you with that grenade in Chapter 11. This example, like the one we used to introduce Subgame Perfect Equilibrium, may be trivial, but it reveals the important parts of PBE that we'll need to solve the much more complicated game in the following section, where we show how the process of fighting a war can lead states to update their beliefs about their opponent's preferences and, ultimately, reach a settlement short of a fight to the finish.

12.2.2   Information Problems and Bayesian Perfection

Chapter 5's strategic-form game of crisis bargaining under asymmetric information (Figure 5.4) gave us a simple and striking result: an uninformed side will risk war, making a demand that a resolute opponent will surely reject, when sufficiently optimistic that its opponent is irresolute. That static game helped us explain the outbreak of war, but it produced an additional result that we can build on in this chapter. If state A makes a demand that risks war, then by the end of the game A knows what it wishes it knew beforehand: that B is resolute and A would've been better off demanding only half the prize and saving the costs of war. But remember that A only learns this if it demands the whole pie; it learns nothing about B's type after a less aggressive demand that B accepts regardless of its type.[12] The violent equilibrium of that game is also a separating equilibrium (Definition 5.7), one that pretty starkly illustrates the tragedy of war: if only A knew beforehand what B couldn't credibly reveal, our belligerents could have cut a deal reflecting in rough terms the outcome of the war while saving them the blood, treasure, and destruction it ultimately took to reach a settlement. But war isn't a matter of putting the jukebox on shuffle and walking away. It's made up of battles, maneuvers, and campaigns, as well as peace overtures, demands, and negotiations that present constant opportunities to stop or continue the fighting.

That means we need a richer environment in which to think about bargaining while fighting, so Figure 12.2 presents a repeated, extensive-form crisis bargaining game that allows an uninformed side to make a demand to which the informed side can then respond. Before our belligerents move,

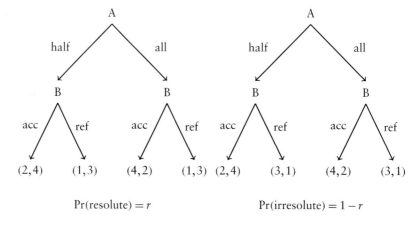

$$\Pr(\text{resolute}) = r \qquad\qquad \Pr(\text{irresolute}) = 1 - r$$

Figure 12.2 Information problems and war ($t = 1$ and $t = 2$ if no prior battle).

---

[12] A horrible, bloody example of "nothing ventured, nothing gained"?

however, a nonstrategic player called Nature chooses B's type according to a probability distribution, resolute (with probability r) or irresolute (with probability $1 - r$), and reveals that information only to B, leaving A uncertain over B's type. To give A some beliefs (and to measure its uncertainty), we assume that A knows the probabilities of Nature's random draw – i.e., that A knows how the coin is weighted – and this informs its prior beliefs over B's type. Getting a little more technical, if Nature is a player, then the weighting of the coin it flips to determine B's type is its strategy, which we assume is known to all other players. We do this, as you might have guessed following the previous section, because it allows us to say that A is uncertain over a previous move in the game (Nature's) and that A has a belief when it moves about what Nature's move might have been. This lets us solve the game with PBE and think about what A needs to believe in order to support the outcomes in equilibrium that we want to explain.

Begin with the first period, $t = 1$, where A is uncertain over B's type. When resolute, B prefers fighting to yielding the whole pie in a given period, while an irresolute B prefers to yield the whole pie rather than fight. As such, A does better in war against the latter than the former. A issues a demand for either half or all of the pie, then B responds to A's proposal by acceding ("acc") or refusing ("ref"). If B accedes, then the deal is implemented and payoffs are given out for that period, and if B refuses, the players fight a battle that not only yields an immediate war payoff but also shrinks the pie for the second period. If no war occurs in the first period – that is, if B accedes to A's demand – then the pie doesn't shrink and payoffs remain the same for the second period, when the same interaction occurs again. One way of thinking about the empirical record, where war is rare, is that states constantly renegotiate the status quo, more often than not tacitly retaining it; this makes the game's simple repetition both easy to analyze and conveniently realistic. If that seems odd, think about it this way: in an anarchic international system, states at peace can be thought of as playing a game like this every day (or even more frequently if some leaders have short attention spans), where the offer on the table is the status quo.

Payoffs reflect the basic crisis bargaining structure we've seen since Chapter 2. If there's been no war, either in the first period or in the second period following settlement in the first, A's best outcome is to secure the whole pie (4), followed by war against an irresolute B (3), securing half the pie (2), and finally war against a resolute B (1). B's payoffs for different divisions of the pie don't differ by type, as each most prefers to yield only half (4) and receives 2 for giving up the whole thing, but the resolute type prefers war (3) to yielding the whole pie and the irresolute type rates war as its worst possible outcome (1). If there has been a war, however,

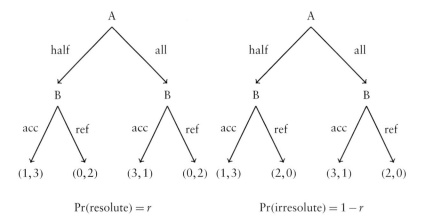

Figure 12.3 Information problems and war ($t = 2$ following a battle at $t = 1$).

second-period payoffs are reduced by 1 for both players, as shown in Figure 12.3, to account for war's waste and destruction. Fighting in the first period doesn't represent an entire war; it's a single battle or campaign in a potentially larger conflict, such as an attempt to capture a city, to seize border territory, to eject occupying forces from foreign land, or a daring, army-sized attempt to knock a great power out of an impending world war in a matter of weeks. This creates an opportunity for another battle in the second period, which we'll assume is decisive if it occurs: the loser of the second battle collapses militarily in an "absolute" war, its armies shattered, its capital conquered, its land blighted, its industry wrecked, etc. Finally, both players discount future payoffs by $\delta \in (0, 1)$, just as they did in the repeated game in Chapter 11. To round out the notation, we'll subscript A's belief that B is resolute by period, such that its belief is r_1 in the first period and r_2 in the second. This gives us a dynamic, repeated game in the extensive form that has the features we need to explain how information problems lead to war and how war can solve information problems, facilitating a settlement where one wasn't possible before.

This game is a bit more complicated than what we've encountered before, especially when it comes to finding an equilibrium. Just to pin down what our players will try to do in the first period, we need to analyze the second period in three different ways – as if A remains uncertain over B's type, as if A believes B to be resolute, and as if A believes B to be irresolute – and all that before deriving updated beliefs and figuring out strategies in the first period.[13] It's more work, but the logic behind our solutions hasn't

---

[13] Lest you think it insanely technical and a waste of time, it's what Clausewitz tried to do in the nineteenth century *without* the help of game theory. No wonder his magnum opus is still open to so much (mis)interpretation. On this latter point, see Wagner (2007) and Strachan (2007).

changed. The rules of mutual best response, sequential rationality, and beliefs updated according to Bayes' Rule are all the same. Equilibrium is still equilibrium: a set of expectations that make for a self-fulfilling prophecy. We'll use the same process in the same way that we've used it thus far, proposing an equilibrium that resembles the strategic process we want to explain, then seeing whether the assumptions we've written into our game can reproduce, and thus help us explain, the strategic process that puzzles us. Our goal in this section isn't to work out all the ways our game *could* be played. We simply want to show that it *can* be played in a certain way and under a set of conditions that resemble those under which the limited, "real" wars that dominate the historical record occur.

Before we solve the game, let's think about what features our equilibrium needs. First, the second period must end peacefully on the equilibrium path, with A making a demand to which B is willing to accede. This ensures that (1) we don't see an "absolute" war in equilibrium but (2) our belligerents must consider what one would look like when they choose not to fight to the finish. Second, if fighting is to solve the information problem, then something in the first period must lead A to update its beliefs about B's type. In other words, we need a separating equilibrium (Definition 5.7) in which each type of B takes a different action at $t = 1$, allowing A to update its beliefs heading into the second period. A's beliefs thus updated, players agree in the second period on just how much A can demand without provoking a war. A then demands just that amount, ending the conflict in a compromise peace that both sides prefer to further, wasteful fighting – fighting that would only produce a similar outcome at still greater, still more tragic, cost. If we can prove the existence of an equilibrium with these features, where only one type of B rejects A's first demands, A updates its beliefs over B's type as a result, and war stops short of a total outcome in the second period, we'll show that war can indeed solve information problems and open up space previously closed for a settlement.

Next, let's think about how the second period ($t = 2$) works once A has learned B's type. Suppose that A knows B to be resolute, which implies $r_2 = 1$. (Don't worry just yet about how we got here.) If A knows B's type, then we've got something resembling a crisis bargaining game under complete information, where the Subgame Perfect Equilibrium is by now obvious: A demands only as much as B is willing to yield without fighting, and B accedes. A will certainly take more if B will yield it, but it'll demand only half if it knows that demanding all leads to war; likewise, B won't go to war if A offers it good enough terms. If A *does* push B too far by demanding all, then war either continues (if it began in the first period) or breaks out (if war was avoided in the first period). The same is true if $r_2 = 0$, such that A knows B to be irresolute. Demanding all wins B's acquiescence (and A's best outcome), so there can't be an equilibrium in which A demands less, nor can there be one in which B refuses A's demands. So peace also obtains when A knows that it's facing an irresolute type. Therefore, as long as A knows B's type – which we can think of as both sides agreeing on, or having the same information about, what a fight to the finish would look like – then we'd expect a peaceful settlement. In each case, both parties agree that paying additional costs of war to produce an outcome substantially similar to what they could get in a settlement would be wasteful. A does worse against the resolute type than the irresolute type, to be sure, but a self-enforcing settlement reflecting that fact is better than war.

Our next question is how the outbreak of fighting in the first period can get our players to conditions resembling complete information in the second period, where they can end their war before crossing the "absolute" threshold. Proposition 12.3 outlines a screening process in which A can use its first demand to force a separation of types. Key to the story is that, while the irresolute type will accede to any demand in order to avoid a war, the resolute type accedes only to a demand for half, because it's got a higher war payoff than the irresolute type. The problem, as we saw in Chapter 5, is that B has no incentive to be honest about being irresolute, and that undermines its ability to credibly convey that it truly is resolute. To get types to separate, and thus to learn whether B is resolute or irresolute, A demands the entire pie; the irresolute type ends up yielding, "screening" itself out of the war by swallowing an unfavorable settlement that's still better than war for that type, leaving only the resolute type still fighting. The resolute B refuses to yield the entire pie, forcing an initial battle that reveals its type and forces A to lower its demands in order to secure a settlement that saves the costs of a total war. The question we must answer next is why this happens, or how a simple contest in killing and destruction that rearranges no player's preferences, as it did in Chapter 11, can produce a settlement that was impossible before the war began and people started dying.

PROPOSITION 12.3   *The following strategy profile and beliefs,*

- *A: Demand all at $t = 1$; believe $r_2 = 1$ and demand half at $t = 2$ if B refused at $t = 1$; believe $r_2 = 0$ and demand all at $t = 1$ if B acceded at $t = 1$; if $r_2 = r$, demand all at $t = 2$,*
- *B: When resolute, accede iff A demands half; when irresolute, accede whatever A demands,*

constitute a Perfect Bayesian Equilibrium when $r \leq 2/3$ and $\delta \leq 1/2$.

Proof Begin by establishing what Λ believes on the equilibrium path at $t = 2$, which depends on B's choice at $t = 1$. First, if B refuses A's demand for the whole pie at $t = 1$, A knows that only the resolute type would have done so. Therefore, letting R be the event that B is resolute, A's second period belief that B is resolute is

$$\Pr(R|\text{refuse}) = \frac{\Pr(R) \times \Pr(\text{refuse}|R)}{\Pr(R) \times \Pr(\text{refuse}|R) + \Pr(\neg R) \times \Pr(\text{refuse}|\neg R)}$$

$$= \frac{r_1 \times 1}{r_1 \times 1 + (1 - r_1) \times 0} = 1 = r_2.$$

Second, if B accedes to A's demand for all, then by a similar application of Bayes' Rule where $\Pr(\text{refuse}|R) = 0$, we know that $r_2 = 0$. These beliefs are consistent with B's strategy as stated in Proposition 12.2, so now it's left to verify that the proposed actions are sequentially rational.

First, though it occurs off the equilibrium path, we need to establish what happens if no separation of types happens in the first period; this ensures that A can calculate the consequences of not making an initial screening offer. So we must establish that (1) A demands all at $t = 2$ when $r_2 = r$, (2) the resolute B accedes iff A demands half, and (3) the irresolute B accedes to anything A demands. Begin with the resolute B, for which it must be true that

$$u_B(acc|\text{half}) \geq u_B(ref|\text{half}) \quad \text{and} \quad u_B(ref|\text{all}) \geq u_B(acc|\text{all}).$$

The first inequality is satisfied because $3 \geq 2$ following a battle and $2 \geq 1$ following no battle, and the second because $2 \geq 1$ following a battle and $1 \geq 0$ following no battle. For the irresolute B, it must be true that

$$u_B(acc|\text{half}) \geq u_B(ref|\text{half}) \quad \text{and} \quad u_B(acc|\text{all}) \geq u_B(ref|\text{all}).$$

The first inequality is satisfied because $3 \geq 0$ following a battle and $4 \geq 1$ following no battle, and the second because $1 \geq 0$ following a battle and $2 \geq 1$ following no battle. Next, following a battle, A demands all following a war when

$$\text{EU}_A(all) \geq \text{EU}_A(half) \Leftrightarrow r(0) + (1 - r)3 \geq r(1) + (1 - r)1,$$

which is true when $r \leq 2/3$. Finally, following no battle, A demands all when

$$\text{EU}_A(all) \geq \text{EU}_A(half) \Leftrightarrow r(1) + (1 - r)4 \geq r(2) + (1 - r)2,$$

which is true when $r \leq 2/3$.

Next, we consider the second period when $r_2 = 1$, which follows a battle at $t = 1$, where B has proven its resolve by refusing A's initial demand.

For (half; acc, ref) to be sequentially rational, it must be the case that

$$u_A(half; \text{acc}, \text{ref}) \geq u_A(all; \text{acc}, \text{ref})$$

for A and

$$u_B(\text{half}; acc, \text{ref}) \geq u_B(\text{half}; ref, \text{ref}) \quad \text{and}$$
$$u_B(\text{half}; \text{acc}, ref) \geq u_B(\text{half}; \text{acc}, acc)$$

for B. The first inequality is satisfied because $1 \geq 0$, the second because $3 \geq 2$, and the third because $2 \geq 1$. No player has a profitable deviation, and strategies are consistent with beliefs based on B's strategy at $t = 1$.

Now let $r_2 = 0$ in the second period, which follows a settlement at $t = 1$ – a settlement that only the irresolute type would've accepted, which leads A to believe that B is irresolute. For (all; acc, acc) to be sequentially rational, it must be the case that

$$u_A(all; \text{acc}, \text{acc}) \geq u_A(half; \text{acc}, \text{acc})$$

for A and

$$u_B(all; acc, \text{acc}) \geq u_B(all; ref, \text{acc}) \quad \text{and} \quad u_B(all; \text{acc}, acc) \geq u_B(all; \text{acc}, ref)$$

for B. The first inequality is satisfied because $4 \geq 2$, the second because $4 \geq 1$, and the third because $2 \geq 1$. No player has a profitable deviation, and strategies are consistent with beliefs based on B's strategy at $t = 1$.

Now, with the payoffs for screening (which occurs on the equilibrium path) and not screening (off the path) established, we can consider strategies at $t = 1$. Since A is uninformed over B's type ($r_1 = r$), we first verify that the proposed strategies are best responses for each player-type. Both types accede if A demands half (which fails to induce separation, leading to a second period where A retains its prior beliefs and demands all again), while resolute refuses and irresolute accedes if A demands all (inducing separation). First, the resolute B's strategy is sequentially rational when

$$u_B(acc|\text{half}) \geq u_B(ref|\text{half}) \Leftrightarrow 4 + \delta 3 \geq 3 + \delta 4,$$

and when

$$u_B(ref|\text{all}) \geq u_B(acc|\text{all}) \Leftrightarrow 3 + \delta 3 \geq 2 + \delta 3.$$

Both inequalities are satisfied for all values of $\delta \in (0, 1)$. The irresolute B's strategy is sequentially rational when

$$u_B(acc|\text{half}) \geq u_B(ref|\text{half}) \Leftrightarrow 4 + \delta 2 \geq 1 + \delta 3$$

and when

$$u_B(acc|\text{all}) \geq u_B(ref|\text{all}) \Leftrightarrow 2 + \delta 1 \geq 1 + \delta 3.$$

The first inequality is satisfied for all values of $\delta \in (0, 1)$, and the second is satisfied when $\delta \leq 1/2$. Finally, A demands all when

$$\text{EU}_A(\text{all}) \geq \text{EU}_A(\text{half})$$
$$r(1) + (1-r)4 + \delta\left(r(1) + (1-r)4\right) \geq 2 + \delta\left(r(1) + (1-r)4\right),$$

which is satisfied when $r \leq 2/3$. No player has a profitable deviation, and all strategies are consistent with beliefs updated according to Bayes' Rule where possible, so the proposed equilibrium exists when $\delta \leq 1/2$ and $r \leq 2/3$. □

We've proven the existence of a screening (i.e, separating) equilibrium, but what does it teach us? First, we can verify that war breaks out for the same reason it does in Chapter 5's static model: B's information problem. This reassures us that our more complex model captures the same underlying story. The uninformed side (A) faces a risk-return trade-off, in that demanding the entire pie produces not just one but two periods of A's preferred division of the pie *if* B turns out to be irresolute. But if A is wrong, such that B turns out to be resolute, B refuses the demand, touching off a costly war. In fact, war occurs for the same optimistic beliefs ($r \leq 2/3$) that it does in Chapter 5's static version of the game. In this repeated variant, however, A has a chance to benefit from the knowledge gained from observing B's refusal of its demands. A round of fighting occurs in which B proves that it deserves a better deal – i.e., one in which it yields only half the pie – than what A initially has on offer.

Why does B's initial rejection change A's beliefs? The costs of war are once again critical, because they discourage the irresolute type from mimicking the resolute type in oder to get a better deal. True, fighting for one period would convince A to offer better terms, but when war is sufficiently costly (or, as indicated by $\delta \leq 1/2$, when the irresolute type isn't patient enough to mimic a resolute type's willingness to endure pain), A can make a demand to which only the irresolute type is sure to accede. However B responds, A updates its beliefs about B's type, and in the case of refusal, its posterior belief (r_2) that B is resolute is

$$\begin{aligned} \Pr(R|\text{refuse}) &= \frac{\Pr(R) \times \Pr(\text{refuse}|R)}{\Pr(R) \times \Pr(\text{refuse}|R) + \Pr(\neg R) \times \Pr(\text{refuse}|\neg R)} \\ &= \frac{r_1 \times 1}{r_1 \times 1 + (1-r_1) \times 0} \\ &= 1. \end{aligned}$$

Once again, the action is in the denominator; if the probability that an irresolute type would refuse a demand for the whole pie is zero, then A knows that it's facing a resolute type if the demand is refused. War is costlier than diplomacy, shows of force, and the typical trappings of crisis bargaining, which makes it correspondingly harder for an irresolute type to bluff. If armies are sent into the field, an uninformed state's beliefs will change far more than it would if the opponent only *talked* about giving battle. This is what allows A, uncertain over B's resolve, to screen out irresolute types, with the promise of an extremely favorable deal (the whole pie) balancing out the risk of fighting a "real" war before settling on efficient terms with the resolute type. A second, "absolute," apocalyptic final battle is possible in principle, but if the initial battle reveals enough information, both parties have every incentive to cut a deal and avoid a costly, wasteful fight to the finish. The logic is straightforward, because it resembles crisis bargaining under complete information: if both sides agree on how the war would play out, why not cut a deal that reflects that but saves the costs of fighting? The terms of a self-enforcing bargain, in which neither gets less than it can expect to gain by fighting, are now known to both. Why not strike that very bargain?

Our equilibrium also identifies a few things we should observe in the historical record in wars that have significant informational components.[14] Consistent with our view of war as instrumental, we should see belligerents' war aims change over time in response to military and diplomatic events – like battles given, engagements won or lost, or peace overtures made and rejected. In this section's PBE, A makes a series of decreasing demands, from demanding all to demanding only half the pie, as it grows more pessimistic about B's type. Demanding all works if B turns out to be irresolute, but after fighting a battle that proves B is resolute, A proposes adequate settlement terms and brings the fighting to an end. This is only one instance of a more general trend in which belligerents raise and lower their war aims in response to information from the battlefield or the negotiating table.[15] After winning a string of engagements, a belligerent may realize it'll come out better in a total war than expected, and it'll require more at the negotiating table to call off the fighting, while a string of defeats tend to have the opposite effect. This process of learning and updating – sometimes quick, sometimes slow, always complicated by the fog of war – continues until beliefs converge on rough agreement over what a fight to the finish would produce for both sides.[16] Then, with that agreement reached, and assuming that there are no lingering commitment problems, we'd expect belligerents to strike a bargain to end the war.

[14] But see Wolford, Reiter, and Carrubba (2011) for a model showing that a lot of what we know about information problems and war termination changes when uncertainty interacts with shifting power.
[15] See, inter alia, Wittman (1979), Gartner (1997), Goemans (2000), and Reiter (2009).
[16] On this "principle of convergence," see Slantchev (2003).

12.3 FIGHTING, LEARNING, BARGAINING

Our model is simple – crude, even – when compared to more sophisticated models political scientists typically use to think about war as a costly process, but by capturing a few of the essentials it generates similar insights.[17] Fighting solves information problems, helping belligerents stop short of total war, because its wastefulness discourages irresolute states from mimicking resolute ones. We argued in Chapter 1 that war is the ultimate arbiter of who gets what in international politics, and states gauge their satisfaction with the status quo by making guesses about what would happen if they sought to renegotiate their share of benefits, or their place in the global hierarchy, by force. Just like they use crisis bargaining as a substitute for war, states use "real" war as a substitute for "absolute" war,[18] because wartime events can reveal information about the likely outcome of a fight to the finish.[19] Unlike wars that solve commitment problems, fighting doesn't actively change players' preferences. Rather, war changes their beliefs, creating agreement where none existed before about what settlements are mutually preferable to war.

Our model collapses many sources of uncertainty, many privately known factors that affect a state's war payoffs, into a single (fairly ambiguous) concept called *resolve*.[20] The simple act of refusing A's initial demand and fighting reveals something about B's war payoffs – i.e., that it's resolute – and many potential sources of private information can be revealed in just that way. Leaders typically know better than their enemies their own value for the stakes in dispute, their own personal sensitivity to the costs of war (whether material, moral, or psychological), their access to domestic and international sources of credit, the reliability of their allies, the support of critical parts of the public, and their ability to sustain a lengthy war effort without breaking either the economy or the political system. But, as we saw in Chapter 5, simply saying that any of these factors makes one willing to fight a war isn't believable, and it may take fighting, refusals to settle, or the outright (but temporary) rejection of negotiations to prove it. Finally, some private information can be revealed by both the act of fighting and battlefield outcomes.

---

[17] Recent examples, in addition to the Leventoglu and Slantchev (2007) piece cited above, include Goemans (2000), Filson and Werner (2002, 2004), Slantchev (2003), Powell (2004a), Langlois and Langlois (2009), and Wolford, Reiter, and Carrubba (2011).

[18] This analogy is due to Wagner (2000, p. 472).

[19] In more complicated models with more possible player-types, noisier battlefield events, and different sources of uncertainty (about which more a little later), a single battle may not reveal enough information to bring war to an end, but in most cases of wars driven by information problems, states end up settling well short of an "absolute" war.

[20] On the (too) many uses of the term in international relations scholarship, see Kertzer (2016).

From the effectiveness and survivability of weapon systems to the quality of leadership, training, and doctrine, the battlefield is a laboratory for inferring the likely course and outcome of an "absolute" war. To be sure, battles can produce ambiguous outcomes in the fog of war, and even victories and defeats can be discounted when the war effort isn't yet going at full tilt.[21] But to the extent that the battlefield sends clear messages about how armies perform in individual battles and campaigns,[22] which may indicate who's likely to win an "absolute" war, belligerents can use it to make judgments about the price at which they can purchase peace.

Even as the core strategic dynamic of fighting, learning, and bargaining remains the same, these different sources of uncertainty imply a variety of patterns that political scientists have uncovered in the historical record. First, when observable sources of military strength – like the size of the economy, the army, and the population from which reserves are drawn – are roughly equal, then unobservable information typically held private, like the quality of one's generals, troops, or war plans, play a bigger role in determining who'd win a fight to the finish, necessitating a possibly lengthy war to prove who deserves the better deal. Wars between observably unequal states, by contrast, are much shorter.[23] A string of consistent battle outcomes, which helps clarify the likely winner of an absolute war,[24] is also associated with quicker settlements, as are shocking battle outcomes, like a tide-turning reversal of fortune, that change beliefs dramatically about who's likely to disarm the other first.[25] Attritional contests like the First World War tend to be shorter when one side deploys a larger share of its population in the military (and to end pretty favorably for the same side).[26] But on the other hand, when substantial reserves have yet to be put into the field,[27] or when battles engage only limited numbers of troops and effort to produce ambiguous outcomes, less information is revealed, and wars drag on longer than those in which states are fully mobilized early on and when battles produce clear winners.

These empirical patterns are true on average, but a focus on the purely military aspect of war can still be misleading. Countries that get the better of the other on the battlefield don't always come out ahead in the negotiations that end the war. Shared beliefs about a hypothetical "absolute" war are what matter, and war outcomes are shaped by more than just battles won and territory held. The Russo-Japanese War is a notable (and,

---

[21] On this, see Philpott (2009, 2014).
[22] See Powell (2004a) and Werner and Yuen (2005), in particular.
[23] Bennett and Stam (1996); Slantchev (2004).
[24] Werner and Yuen (2005).
[25] Ramsay (2008).
[26] Langlois and Langlois (2009).
[27] Slantchev (2004).

as we saw in Chapter 4, a consequential) case in point. In the aftermath of China's Boxer Rebellion, Russia made a bid to climb the East Asian power hierarchy by consolidating its position in Manchuria and cutting a deal to build the Trans-Siberian Railway through Chinese territory on the way to securing access to Vladivostok, the "Lord of the East."[28] This looming consolidation of Tsarist power prompted Japan to launch a preventive war to secure its own foothold in Korea in 1904.[29] Hostilities began with a dramatic surprise attack on the Russian fleet at Port Arthur in northeastern China, and within months Russian forces were staggering backward across Manchuria under the weight of a Japanese onslaught whose ferocity surprised a Tsar previously "assured by his closest advisers that Japan would not in any circumstances fight."[30]

Japan won every major land engagement and smashed the Baltic Fleet (and Russian sea power in general) at the Battle of Tsushima Strait.[31] But as the *New York Times* would report after the war-ending Treaty of Portsmouth was signed in 1905, Russia,

> [a] nation hopelessly beaten in every battle of the war, one army captured and the other overwhelmingly routed, with a navy swept from the seas, dictated her own terms to the victory.[32]

Despite hurling the Tsar's army hundreds of miles back across Manchuria, securing the Liaodong Peninsula that housed Port Arthur, and ensuring its own political dominance in Korea, Japan got little else for its trouble: no presence in Manchuria (including Liaodong) and, especially galling to Japan's political class and public alike, no indemnity to cover the costs of a war that had very nearly broken the bank. But why, despite forcing the collapse of Russian power on that end of Eurasia, did Japan come out so poorly in the Treaty of Portsmouth?[33]

The answer, as it happens, turns out to be something that both Japan and Russia learned over the course of the war that had little to do with early battle outcomes: as long as its domestic political equilibrium held enough to keep armies in the field (see Chapter 5), Russia had access to far

---

[28] Vladivostok, then, is the Eastern equivalent of Tsargrad when it comes to aspirational names. For a military history of the conflict, see Connaughton (2003), and for a political scientist's view of the war not too dissimilar from the one presented here, see Streich and Levy (2016).

[29] See Paine (2017, pp. 50–54).

[30] See Connaughton (2003, pp. 23–24).

[31] Which led to the Tsar's caution in the naval war that we saw in Chapter 10, to say nothing of his determination to rearm and focus on the Balkans, which would set off fateful alarm bells in Berlin (Chapter 4).

[32] Quoted in Connaughton (2003, p. 344).

[33] Yes, that's in the United States, but the treaty is named not for Portsmouth, New Hampshire, but for the Portsmouth Naval Shipyard in Kittery, Maine.

more credit from the other great powers than Japan did (on war finance, see Chapter 13). With its manpower reserves and an ability to borrow that Japan couldn't match, the animating question for the belligerents was "Would Russia run out of popular public support before Japan ran out of funds to sustain the war?"[34] Once it became clear that Russia, despite its initial losses, would be able to leverage its deep manpower reserves and overland supply lines thanks to generous borrowing from the European great powers, beliefs on the likely outcome of an "absolute" war converged on something that gave Japan far less than it had in hand by the fall of 1905. It may have controlled parts of Manchuria, but the Treaty of Portsmouth ordered both Russian *and* Japanese forces out of the region – nominally Chinese but vulnerable as the Qing Empire grew steadily weaker – and denied Japan the indemnities typically understood to be a victor's privilege. Part of the reason, to be sure, was pressure from the other great powers, all of which wanted to prevent either Russian or Japanese predominance in China. But equally important was the realization in Tokyo that, if it walked away from the table in Portsmouth, it could do little better against an ineffectual yet better-funded Russian war machine. The Tsar could've thrown more troops into the maw, and Japan could've kept killing them in large numbers, but when the money ran out – and the coffers were nearly empty – Korea would've been a generous share of the pie indeed. Well before the Red Army made it manifest later in the century in both Europe and Asia, Russian quantity had a quality all its own.[35]

12.4 CONCLUSION

War – violent, nasty, uncivilized, and wasteful – is an extension of diplomacy. The costs of war did double duty in this chapter, explaining both why states have powerful incentives to end wars well before they become "absolute" and why fighting is able to reveal otherwise private information about players' war payoffs. If B is more likely when it's resolute than when irresolute to refuse A's demands – either beginning or staying in the war – then fighting takes on screening properties; A can set its demands such that B accedes when irresolute, giving A a favorable settlement, but fights when resolute, allowing A to adjust its bargaining posture again in what may end up being a sequence of proposals and counterproposals that change over time, reflecting updated beliefs about how a fight to the finish will ultimately play out. Once belligerents are in agreement on the

---

[34] Connaughton (2003, p. 342). See also Paine (2017, p. 69).
[35] As we'll see in Chapter 14, the Central Powers capitulated, yet they killed more soldiers and sank more ships than their enemies. They did, however, lose all the battles that matter in a war of attrition: the last ones.

likely outcome, once beliefs *converge*, the strategic setting approximates a static crisis bargaining game under complete information, and formerly warring parties can strike a deal in which neither expects to do better by returning to the field of battle. War reveals information relevant for reaching a settlement, and while it's based around changing an enemy's beliefs about the price of peace, it's not exactly a matter of peaceful deliberation; only because war is costly, painful, and destructive enough to discourage the levels of bluffing that are possible in simple diplomacy can it bring belligerents to agreement. It's a learning process, to be sure, but a violent one, where information is extracted painfully – but for that reason it's also an act of persuasion, of changing an enemy's mind. It's easy to overlook that learning process, so critical to explaining how wars end, when we also overlook the costs of war and the shared incentives it creates even for bitter enemies to avoid wasteful fighting. But when we view war as a costly way of doing business, not as an end in itself, just as much politics as elections and roll-call votes and cabinet formation, we can see that the onset and termination of war are bound up together, as Hew Strachan notes in this chapter's epigraph. And once again, it all comes down to recognizing that war, at its core, is costly.

Getting to these insights wasn't as easy as recognizing war's instrumental and costly nature, though. We introduced Perfect Bayesian Equilibrium, a refinement of the Bayesian Nash Equilibria introduced in Chapter 5 and the Subgame Perfect Equilibria of Chapter 11, that requires us to keep track of what players believe about unobservable, previous moves in the game. It's a remarkably flexible tool, allowing us to move from a model in which a strategic player's choice of carrying a big or a small stick is indistinguishable from the other to one in which a player's preferences are chosen by an imaginary player, Nature, in a move unobservable to the uninformed player. At the cost of a little more analytical effort, we were able to say something about how and when wars caused by information problems come to an end – no small feat, considering that more conventional ways of thinking about war assume, explicitly or not, that politics stops once the guns begin booming and bombs begin falling. Negotiation during war is common, even when it's tacit, brutal, and bloody, and even patently insincere extensions of the olive branch are revelatory precisely because a chance to offer more acceptable terms was turned down. But without the deductively clear, precise accounting of how beliefs change in response to wartime strategy offered by Perfect Bayesian Equilibrium, it's easy to overlook this fundamental feature of war. We won't use PBE explicitly again in later chapters, but the logic of fighting, bargaining, and learning will prove critical in understanding precisely how and when the war came to an end both when and how it did.

12.5 EXERCISES: COMMUNICATION AND BLUFFING

In Chapter 5, we introduced the idea of an information problem (Definition 5.5), where incentives to misrepresent one's preferences over the use of force – say, resolve – can undermine the sharing of war-averting information. We worked out the logic of incentives to bluff informally, with a little help from Bayes' Rule, but in this section we'll set up an exercise that demonstrates information problems a little more explicitly and digs a bit deeper into the ideas of pooling equilibria (Definition 5.9) and out-of-equilibrium beliefs that we discussed above. Figure 12.4 formalizes yet another crisis between A and B, where A (the informed side) chooses whether or not to make some kind of deterrent threat, like making a show of force near a disputed border, after which B (the uninformed side) decides whether or not to fight A. We've stripped some of the richness out of previous models of the crisis, but this stark setup allows us to focus more directly on what we're interested in: the challenges of communicating resolve in the presence of incentives to misrepresent.

Nature makes the game's first move, choosing A's type (resolute with probability r, irresolute with probability $1 - r$) and, as indicated by the information sets connecting B's choice nodes, revealing it only to A. After learning its type, A chooses whether or not to make a threat, and after observing A's action B chooses to fight (f) or not ($\neg$f). B's payoffs are simple, in that it gets 1 for fighting an irresolute A and 0 for fighting a resolute A,

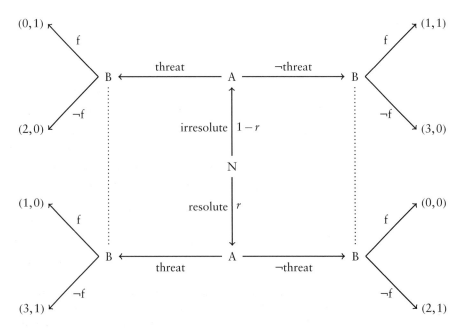

Figure 12.4 Threats and crisis communication.

but it gets 0 for failing to fight an irresolute A and 1 for avoiding a fight with a resolute A.[36] The problem, of course, is that B begins the game unsure of which type of A it faces. A's payoffs differ by type. If it's resolute, then it enjoys shows of military force, but whether it's made a threat or not, it prefers to avoid a war; its best outcome is to make a threat and avoid a fight (3), followed by no threat and no fight (2), followed in turn by a threat and a fight (1) and fighting after making no threat (0). The irresolute A, though, most prefers to avoid a fight without having to make a threat (3), followed by avoiding a fight after making a threat (2), fighting after no threat (1) and a fight that follows a threat (0). In essence, the resolute A has a taste for making military threats, and the irresolute type prefers to speak softly and avoid using a stick if it can.

First, let's demonstrate the existence of a pooling equilibrium (Definition 5.9), in which each player-type of A takes the same action, because it'll force us to think harder about off-path beliefs – that is, what we require our players to believe when something unexpected happens. In the pooling equilibrium we'll examine here, A makes a threat regardless of its type, so that's the only action for A that happens on the equilibrium path; B expects ¬threat to be played with probability zero. However, if both types of A are to know that playing threat is attractive, they need to know the consequences of playing ¬threat, and that means we need to know how B will respond to an unexpected event – which will be based on **out-of-equilibrium beliefs** (or OOE beliefs), also sometimes called "off-path" beliefs.

DEFINITION 12.4   *Out-of-equilibrium beliefs tell a player what to believe about prior moves if it reaches an unexpected (i.e., probability-zero) information set.*

Remember that Perfect Bayesian Equilibrium puts no restrictions on OOE beliefs, since the events that activate them occur with probability zero according to players' strategies. But while these beliefs are unrestricted, we'd still like to choose reasonable ones. Game theorists have worked out a number of ways to refine the set of plausible out-of-equilibrium beliefs in a given game, but we won't worry too much about that here; an example will suffice to show what we mean by "reasonable" beliefs. In what follows, we'll denote B's beliefs on the equilibrium path (which, you'll recall, must be updated via Bayes' Rule) as r' and out-of-equilibrium beliefs as r''. Proposition 12.4 characterizes a pooling equilibrium in which

---

[36] Yes, this follows pretty closely Morrow's (1994) treatment of the famous (and more entertaining) "beer-quiche game" (see his chapter 8), but as I've already written two examples in which I'm either wielding a grenade or fearing ambush by a student, I don't need to talk about choosing which of these items to eat for breakfast.

A makes a threat regardless of its type, and B plays ¬f if it sees a threat and f if no threat is made.

PROPOSITION 12.4   *The strategy profile (threat, threat; ¬f, f) and beliefs $r' = r$ and $r'' = 0$ constitute a Perfect Bayesian Equilibrium when $r \geq 1/2$.*

The exercises in this section are designed to help you build the proof on your own, so let's look at the nuts and bolts of this pooling equilibrium. We have a complete, contingent plan of action for each player, and the uninformed player has beliefs that tell it where it is in the game tree in the event that a threat is made ($r' = r$ such that it retains its prior beliefs) and that no threat is made ($r'' = 0$, which tells it that, if it sees ¬threat, it must've been an irresolute type that deviated from the pooling strategy). Before we set about proving the existence of this equilibrium, let's think about that particular OOE belief. Is it reasonable? B has to make some kind of guess here, and it's got to support the idea that whatever type deviates from the strategy of pooling on making a threat is worth fighting: that is, an irresolute type. We can immediately see that this makes a certain amount of sense: in the equilibrium, the resolute type gets its best outcome (3), so there's no way in which it could ever do better by deviating to ¬threat. There is, however, a logical possibility that the irresolute type could deviate and get its best payoff of not making a threat and avoiding a fight; it won't happen in this equilibrium, of course, but if any type is going to deviate from this pooling equilibrium, so B reasons, it's bound to be the type that has a built-in distaste for military threats. If, on the other hand, this equilibrium rested on B believing that a resolute type would give up its best payoff via a switch to ¬threat, we'd reject those OOE beliefs as unreasonable; generally, we want our players to believe that other players wouldn't do anything against type, or anything that's too perverse. So, in this case, an OOE belief of $r'' = 0$ seems reasonable.[37] Now, you can prove the existence of the proposed equilibrium.

EXERCISE 12.1   *Prove the existence of the PBE characterized in Proposition 12.2.*

In this equilibrium, the resolute A has an incentive to bluff, acting like a resolute type that enjoys making shows of force. This depends, however, on the knowledge that if it plays ¬threat, B will fight. This makes clear just how important OOE beliefs are, even though the eventualities they describe aren't supposed to happen in equilibrium. We chose $r'' = 0$,

[37] For more on refinements of OOE beliefs, see Cho and Kreps (1987), Fudenberg and Tirole (1991), and Morrow (1994).

which is consistent with the rules of PBE since OOE beliefs are undefined, but we could also derive the set of OOE beliefs that would support the equilibrium. We know that B fights if no threat is made, so we could simply write down an expected payoff comparison based on its OOE beliefs. For example, B fights when

$$r'' \times 0 + (1 - r'') \times 1 \geq r'' \times 1 + (1 - r'') \times 0.$$

With this comparison defined, the next exercise boils down to simple algebra.

EXERCISE 12.2 *For what out-of-equilibrium beliefs r'' are the strategies in Proposition 12.4 in equilibrium?*

It's also worth proving just how difficult communication is in this game. In the first step, your task is to prove that a separating equilibrium in which A makes a threat if resolute and no threat if irresolute, and in which B fights only if no threat is made, doesn't exist. What's the most efficient way to do so? (*Hint.* Remember the single deviation principle.)

EXERCISE 12.3 *Prove the nonexistence of a separating PBE with strategy profile (threat , ¬threat; ¬f, f).*

The solution to this exercise has probably gotten you thinking: how *could* a resolute type of A convey its resolve without giving an irresolute type the chance to bluff? (*Hint.* Remember that cheap talk is easy to dismiss, but other types of signals can make separation easier . . .)

EXERCISE 12.4 *Identify the simplest possible change you could make to the game in Figure 12.4 that would ensure the existence of a separating equilibrium.*

Your solution to this problem probably revolves around making military threats costly – say, making this a mobilization rather than a simple show of force – such that the resolute type is happy to pay some cost to separate itself, but the irresolute type finds the gains from bluffing not worth the cost. This, if you'll recall, is the costly signaling solution to the information problems we first identified in Chapter 5 and which, happily, can produce a separation of types short of an actual war, as happens in the main model of this chapter.

Finally, it's worth sketching out the logic of another type of equilibrium that might've come to mind as you thought about Exercise 12.4. We won't solve for this equilibrium, but it's not too far afield from what we've already seen; remember that the rules of PBE are the rules of PBE, no matter what game you apply them to. In a pure separating equilibrium (Definition 5.7), each player-type takes a unique action, and in a pooling equilibrium, all player-types take the same action (Definition 5.9). But in a **semiseparating equilibrium**, groups of player-types take the same action.

DEFINITION 12.5   *At a **semiseparating equilibrium**, groups of players take the same action, enabling only a partial revelation of private information.*

In the two-type world of the game in Figure 12.4, this means that the resolute A makes a threat while the irresolute A plays a mixed strategy, randomizing between threat and ¬threat. Thus, when B sees no threat, it learns that A is irresolute, but when B sees a threat, it knows only that A might be either type; it is, however, more sure than it was beforehand that A is a resolute type. Bayes' Rule is especially important here, as it allows us to calculate just how much more confident B is that A might be resolute. And since the only reason that players mix is indifference, Bayes' Rule also helps us calculate the probability with which B has to mix between fighting and not fighting upon seeing a threat to render the irresolute A indifferent enough to mix. If that sounds complicated, it is, but only in the calculation. In such a semiseparating equilibrium, B's probabilistic threat to fight ensures that A doesn't bluff too much when it's irresolute, while A's mixing strategy ensures that it's not always forced to swallow a fight when it's irresolute. Finally, as we first saw in our discussion of information problems and signaling in Chapter 5, sometimes the only way for a resolute type to persuade an enemy that it's more resolute than that enemy believes is to run a risk of war; if B doesn't fight with *some* probability in the semiseparating equilibrium, it can never keep A's incentive to bluff in check.

13 Too Proud to Fight? U-boats and American Neutrality

I wish with all my heart that I saw a way to …maintain a firm front in respect of what we demand of Germany and yet do nothing that might by any possibility involve us in the war.

Woodrow Wilson

This chapter explores one of the most significant turning points in the war, arguably the single most important event in creating what we now view as "The American Century."

> Why did the United States enter the Great War in 1917 after years of neutrality?

Long disdainful of European *realpolitik*, the United States would on April 6, 1917, declare war on Germany, joining the Entente as an "Associated," though not an "allied," power after years of nominal neutrality. Crossing this particular Rubicon would almost surely tip the attritional balance in favor of the Entente as mobilization limits were reached and morale threatened to collapse in the Entente and the Central Powers. Yet mere weeks before, in late January, American president Woodrow Wilson stood before the Senate and characterized his preferred outcome of the war as a "peace without victory," scandalizing London and Paris as he appeared to dig in his heels against widespread calls, at home and abroad, to join the war. Neutrality seemed to be going well for the United States, preserving its all-important freedom of the seas and retaining wide public support even as Germany got caught proposing an anti-American alliance to Mexico and Japan. So why did Wilson abandon a neutrality on which he campaigned for reelection in 1916? War with Germany tossed "peace without victory" unambiguously out the window, which makes the decision all the more puzzling: why help a side win a war that one hopes doesn't have a victor?[1] What happened to take American belligerence from anathema to inevitable by the spring of 1917? We'll see in this chapter that we can't solve this puzzle without solving a prior one: why Germany launched a campaign of unrestricted submarine warfare in 1917, rolling the iron dice in yet another audacious gamble that would almost certainly bring the United States into the war against it.

We'll analyze games that show how both the Central Powers and Entente internalized the prospects of American intervention, factoring it into their calculations and in the process helping to bring it about, Wilson's genuine reluctance to enter a global conflict too early notwithstanding. In the process, we'll also learn:

- how deterrence rests on credible threats of both force *and* restraint;
- why countries may limit their commitments to partners in war;
- how the means of paying for war shape its course and its outbreak;
- how individual leaders can shape international politics.

Expanding the insights of Chapters 11 and 12, we'll see in this chapter that the desire to influence the terms of the eventual peace settlement can implicate the behavior of both neutral states and belligerents, who try either to draw these neutrals in or keep them out of the war. Unless we account for Wilson's unique preferences over how the Great War should end *and* Entente and Central Powers beliefs about the fragility of American neutrality, we can't account for both the manner and the timing of American belligerence. We'll see that Wilson's decision to abandon neutrality reflected not a reversal but a course correction, a realization that his aims couldn't be achieved with a policy of neutrality – a realization brought about by belligerents half a world away whose actions he might've wished to control but that he manifestly couldn't. Entente indebtedness and German naval strategy were predicated on a shared belief in eventual American entry, creating in effect a self-fulfilling prophecy.[2] American intervention marked the beginning of the end of the old European-dominated balance of power, and Wilson's lofty rhetoric of fighting to secure a liberal, anti-imperial peace rooted in popular consent and self-determination, along with the promise of the liberal February Revolution in Russia, changed beliefs in belligerent and neutral countries alike about what was possible for the global order.[3] Still, Wilson's unique brand of idealism can't account on its own for American belligerence; he'd have preferred to dictate terms

---

[1] All the caveats from Chapters 11 and 12 we associate with the term *victory* are still active, of course. Victory and defeat are often the rhetoric of the war even when those terms are known to be far from the reality.

[2] I'm indebted to Tooze (2014) for this way of thinking about American entry, an argument in a book that has a deep strain of equilibrium reasoning built in. Go read this book.

[3] See Manela (2009).

to exhausted belligerents while American military and financial might remained unspoiled. We'll develop a solution to this puzzle by working out some ideas about how something as simple as deterrence rests on both resolve *and* restraint, how the means by which states pay for war shapes how (and whether) they fight it, and how individual leaders can shape the ostensibly impersonal forces of international politics.

13.1 DETERRENCE AND THE SUBMARINE WAR

When Woodrow Wilson asked Congress to acknowledge the existence of a state of war with Germany on April 2, 1917, he completed a process that saw the United States grow from a patchwork of former colonies clinging to the eastern edge of North America and tossed about on the currents of European imperialism to an active, if sometimes wary, participant in the global balance of power. 1823's Monroe Doctrine had claimed predominance in the Americas by proscribing the growth of European influence, and it seemed to have worked but for (1) threats of war staving off Britain's recognition of the rebellious Confederacy and (2) France's attempt to put a Hapsburg prince on the Mexican throne during the American Civil War.[4] A brief war that knocked Spain permanently out of the great power club and secured a maritime empire in 1898, but one whose "lackadaisical" effort didn't impress the great powers,[5] was one of the United States's only major power confrontations since the War of 1812. This convenient removal from the balance of power left Americans free to wage bloody wars of expansion against Native Peoples and to intervene with impunity in Mexico, the Caribbean, and Central America from atop the regional power hierarchy.[6] Thus, the rhetoric of neutrality in European affairs, enshrined in George Washington's famous (if misunderstood) farewell address, came easily. The great powers had come to blows only a few times in the century after Napoleon's final defeat in 1815, and the Crimean, Seven Weeks', Franco-Prussian, Sino-Japanese, and Russo-Japanese Wars barely tested American neutrality.[7] The American commitment to neutralism untested

---

[4] See Jones (2010). Really. You can't make this stuff up.

[5] See Herwig (2014, p. 309).

[6] The European powers cast a constant shadow over local American expansion; one of the reasons that the Mexican-American War was attractive in 1846 was a desire to gain territory in the West that could be denied to a Great Britain that the Americans didn't trust not to grab by pushing south from Western Canada. For an analysis of conflict in regional power hierarchies, see Lemke (2002).

[7] Which is all to say that we don't know whether the United States might've joined a global war before 1914. It did rather intentionally in 1812, and it's possible that the long dismissal of European power politics wasn't as sincere as a century of neutrality would suggest – especially if we compare this to the more seriously tested British commitment to Continental neutrality in the same period (recall Chapter 6).

for a century, by 1914 the impending collision between the Central Powers and the Entente posed an unprecedented dilemma.

A century of hindsight makes American belligerence on the side of the Entente in 1917 seem not so much puzzling as dilatory, coming only well after the war might've been tilted decisively against what look like natural enemies in the Central Powers. Security and economic cooperation with Western Europe, after all, has been a bedrock of American foreign policy for most of the ensuing decades, including the Anglo-American "Special Relationship." Furthermore, commitments to liberal governance,[8] shared (if far from healthy) racial attitudes,[9] free trade,[10] and the sanctity of international law are all associated with cooperative relationships between democratic countries,[11] up to and including supporting other members of the democratic community in war.[12] As a growing naval power both committed to free trade and mostly happy to let the Royal Navy enforce the freedom of the seas that supported it, the United States also shared an obvious preference with Britain for stifling Germany's bid for a European hegemony (recall Chapter 6). And its condescension toward European great powers notwithstanding, the United States didn't feel limited to throwing its weight around its own backyard. It forcibly (re)opened Japan to trade in the mid-nineteenth century; in 1899 scooped up Spanish possessions, including the Philippines, as colonies of its own (a deep and controversial irony); and participated in a multilateral intervention into the Boxer Rebellion against the Qing Empire in 1900. By 1914 the United States was a great power on the rise, no stranger to foreign adventures, and possessed of an ostensibly natural affinity for the Entente.

But hindsight is especially distorting here. A similarity of interests with the British and French over suppressing German power could as easily incentivize shifting the burden of fighting to the European powers (recall Chapter 7),[13] especially as the comparatively small American army spent 1916 tied down chasing Francisco "Pancho" Villa in Mexico.[14] Furthermore, Germany's first campaign of unrestricted submarine warfare, which saw its then-small contingent of U-boats sink merchant ships carrying Americans – 128 of which died on the *Lusitania*, the biggest such scandal in the United States – ended after the sinking of the *Sussex*, an act that claimed eighty lives and injured two Americans, thanks to an

---

[8] Russett and Oneal (2001).
[9] Vucetic (2011a).
[10] McDonald (2004).
[11] Gleditsch (2002).
[12] On military cooperation between democracies, see, inter alia, Leeds (1999, 2003a), Kadera, Crescenzi, and Shannon (2003), Gibler and Wolford (2006), and Mattes (2012).
[13] Otherwise known as "buck-passing" (Christensen and Snyder, 1990).
[14] See Gilderhus (1977) and Sandos (1981).

American threat to sever diplomatic relations. The American public had become pro-Entente if not pro-war,[15] and the "*Sussex* Pledge" allowed Germany to avert war with the United States at the cost of committing its submarines to outmoded "cruiser rules," which required giving adequate warning before sinking merchant ships.[16] This was obviously risky, since submarines lost their advantages of stealth if they had to surface and communicate with (increasingly armed) merchant ships, virtually eliminating the submarine as an effective weapon of war. But avoiding war with the United States made the pledge appear worthwhile, especially if it could be tied (as it was in the minds of the German leadership) to American pressure on the British to lift the blockade.[17] That hope would be disappointed, even as Great Britain knew that its blockade continued only at the pleasure of a United States on the path to greater naval power of its own, because the United States seemed to be getting what it wanted peacefully. The seas would remain free, and German bids for victory frustrated, without needing to join the war. And though American private lenders were happy to fund the Entente's war effort, the public was widely appalled by Britain's suppression of Ireland's Easter Rising in 1916, which in light of widespread coverage of German atrocities in Belgium only confirmed for many that the war had no "good guys" worth supporting.

In fact, by late 1916 the prospects of American intervention alongside the Entente looked dire. In November, the Federal Reserve's board honored Wilson's request to discourage American banks from lending to a nearly insolvent Britain and France.[18] Then, in January, Wilson gave his "peace without victory" speech, in which he not only drew moral equivalence between the Entente and the Central Powers but also expressed his view that one side's victory would lead only to the other's humiliation in a sure recipe for poisonous revanchism, dangerous militarism, and, so the argument went, yet another destructive war between Europe's great powers. The Old World, to Wilson's mind, had much to learn from the New. And the former Princeton professor surmised that German autocracy and British imperialism alike would learn the requisite lessons only once sufficiently humbled by American financial and military power. Wilson's speech followed his late-1916 push for mediation, in which he asked publicly for a statement of each side's war aims. Germany's peace note of December 1916, pushed by a Bethmann hoping for compromise but refusing to yield critical Germain gains in Belgium and Poland, was

---

[15] See Meyer (1916, p. 101).

[16] For a gripping history of the naval dimensions of the war, including debates over the legal status of submarines, see Sondhaus (2014).

[17] See Meyer (1916, p. 226).

[18] Tooze (2014, p. 50, and chapters 1 and 2 more generally).

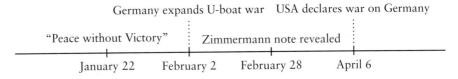

Figure 13.1 The end of American neutrality, 1917.

judged insincere in both Germany and the rest of the world,[19] and the Entente rejected Germany's terms out of hand.[20] With both sides refusing mediation and pushing ever harder for total victory over the other – in line with Chapter 11's model of preventive war – straining their populations, economies, and credit to the limit in what looked like a sure recipe for stalemate, awaiting their exhaustion looked not just feasible but prudent. When Wilson shocked the world in January 1917 (see Figure 13.1), it wasn't because he made anyone *more* optimistic that his country would join the war.

Through most of 1916, Germany's strategy had been to "pursue U-boat warfare to the maximum short of American belligerency,"[21] walking a windy tightrope between hoping that superior combat performance and the strategic defensive would allow it to outlast the Entente and avoid the likely catastrophe of millions of fresh American troops pouring into France.[22] In other words, Wilson's strategy of deterring Germany appeared to be working. But on February 1, 1917, with Russia stumbling for revolution and the Entente nearly insolvent (only the former of which was known in Germany),[23] Germany unleashed its U-boats, declaring a war zone (see Map 13.1) around the British Isles and threatening to sink any and all ships in the area in clear retaliation for the blockade that, though "distant," threatened to bring the German home front to its knees. The announcement forced Wilson to break diplomatic relations in February, only to be followed in March by the scandal of a leaked telegram from the German foreign minister Arthur Zimmermann proposing an alliance between Germany, Japan, and Mexico that promised the latter the return of territories lost in the Mexican-American War of 1846–1848. Mexico's military weakness and the understandably precautionary nature of the telegram, intended as insurance in case the Americans *did* enter the war, guaranteed that Zimmermann's telegram had less of an impact than

---

[19] Herwig (2014, p. 310).
[20] Stevenson's (1988) treatment of intrawar peace feelers is excellent.
[21] See Stevenson (2004, p. 212).
[22] On belligerents choosing their war aims to deter potential intervention, see Werner (2000) and Yuen (2009).
[23] On the anticipation of Russia's troubles, see Herwig (2014, p. 311).

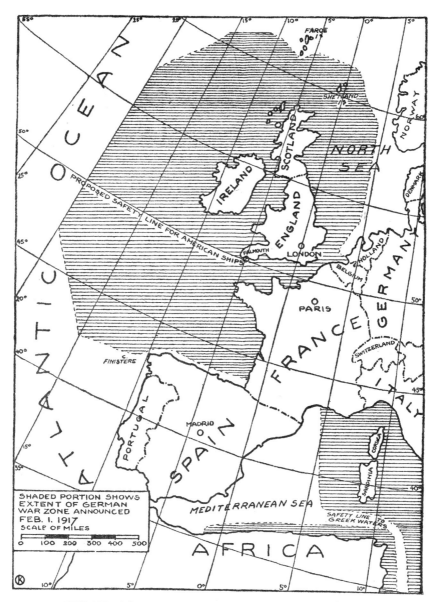

NEW GERMAN SUBMARINE WAR ZONE OF FEBRUARY 1, 1917

Map 13.1 Germany's declaration of unrestricted submarine warfare, 1917. From Reynolds, Churchill, and Miller (1916).

popular memory in the United States might lead us to expect.[24] But the announcement of unrestricted submarine warfare, so long held in check by the prospect of American intervention, marked a major escalation.

[24] For a staggeringly complete history of the telegram, from its origins to its interception and dissemination to its effects on the American public, see Boghardt (2012). His analysis

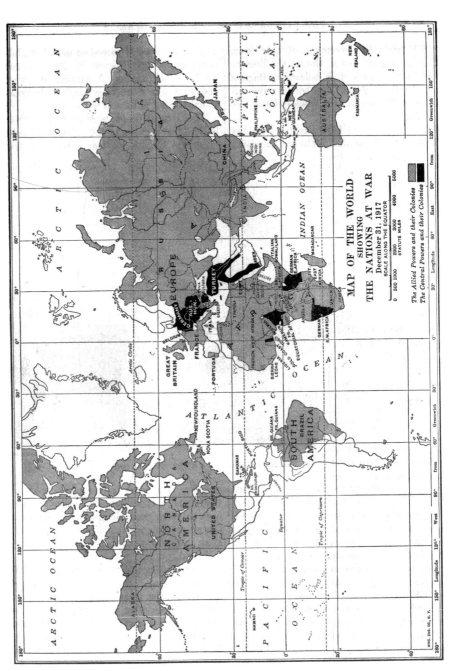

Map 13.2 The world at war, 1917. From McMurry (1919).

Germany's decision to unleash the U-boats against Entente shipping, which dismissed Wilson's remonstrations about freedom of the seas and improved Germany's chances against the Entente by leveling the playing field at sea, almost certainly led Wilson to accept that belligerence – not some variant of neutrality, whether principled or "armed," as he had it – was necessary.[25] Wilson had acknowledged on the campaign trail in 1916 that neutrality might become intolerable,[26] and yet he billed himself after the sinking of the *Lusitania* as "too proud to fight."[27] Committing American blood and treasure in 1917 that he'd studiously preserved since 1914 could only squander it ahead of assuming the role of powerful mediator he envisioned for the United States at the peace conference, especially since siding with the Entente could only undermine whatever gestures he'd made toward impartiality in the past. Why would a man so committed to being the arbiter of a new balance of power, so committed to the idea of making American power-political primacy manifest in the world, equally unwilling to criticize the Entente blockade and to save Britain and France from financial ruin, decide ultimately to declare war on Germany, bringing about the starkly pro-Entente picture of the world at war in Map 13.2? Part of the answer is easy: he'd threatened Germany, at least implicitly, with war if it didn't maintain restrictions on its U-boats. Presumably, Wilson viewed an expanded naval war as worth abandoning neutrality to resist, and if he wasn't bluffing – as Germany clearly didn't believe he was, given its lengthy fidelity to the *Sussex* Pledge – why decide that being deterred by the Americans was worse than courting war against them? Solving the puzzle of American intervention requires that we answer both questions: why was unrestricted submarine warfare enough to provoke Wilson, and why, knowing that, did Germany declare a war zone around the British Isles anyway?

---

of newspapers around the country shows that the revelation of the proposed German-Mexican-Japanese alliance spoke loudest to those already in favor of intervention, swaying few of those already opposed to it into the interventionist camp, in contrast to Tuchman's (1985) conclusion that the telegram had a decisive impact on Wilson's decision to enter the war.

[25] The historical consensus here is pretty strong; the wheels were in motion well before the Zimmermann Telegram confirmed the value of intervention for interventionists and of neutrality for neutralists. See, inter alia, Hamilton and Herwig (2004, p. 220), Stevenson (2004), Strachan (2013), and Tooze (2014).

[26] See Neiberg (2016, p. 207).

[27] Whatever you think of Wilson and neutrality, that's a strong rhetorical move, if one that implies an explanation for war that we'd reject in this text as both misguided and self-serving.

13.2   EXPLAINING AMERICAN INTERVENTION

American intervention has received less historiographical attention than the outbreak of the war, but it's seen more than its share of unsatisfying explanations. One possibility is that pressure from a hawkish public and rival politicians (like the ever-fighty Teddy Roosevelt) proved too much for Wilson to resist. But the president was doggedly independent in formulating policy, especially in matters of war and peace. Another popular argument, in this and any war since Lenin's famous contemporary polemic, is that "big business" wanted war as part of a search for markets. It appeared on the floor of the Senate after Wilson's war address, but the American business community, just like those in other belligerent nations, roundly hoped to avoid war.[28] True, the Entente was ruinously in debt to the United States by spring 1917, but on its own that predicts American intervention much sooner in order to minimize the risk attached to the investment. And if war *were* good for business, again, the United States would've entered sooner. Another plausible story has it that the German decision to relaunch unrestricted submarine warfare, in variable combination with the revelation of the Zimmermann Telegram, proved pivotal for the American public, Congress, and Wilson himself.[29] We have very little documentary evidence about the secretive Wilson's mindset in the months between the escalation of the U-boat campaign and his war address, but any account based on German provocations begs the question of why Germany would've taken these steps, *knowing* that they risked bringing the Americans into the war. Unrestricted submarine warfare was clearly important in Wilson's calculations, but we can't lay American intervention at the feet of the U-boat war without explaining *why* Germany took the decision in the first place. Explaining a strategy with a strategy is a non sequitur.[30]

PUZZLE 13.1   *Why did the United States enter the Great War in 1917 after years of neutrality?*

PUZZLE 13.2   *Why did Germany resume unrestricted submarine warfare when it would surely bring the United States into the war?*

Our challenge in this chapter is to explain why Germany believed that it had no choice but to unleash the U-boats in a decision eerily reminiscent of its decision to invade Belgium despite the risk that it would bring Britain

---

[28] See Hamilton and Herwig (2004, pp. 221–222). Upsetting as it might sound for those that like to blame its outbreak on profiteers, war is just bad for most businesses in belligerent countries.

[29] See Hamilton and Herwig (2004, pp. 213, 221–223).

[30] I'm indebted to Amanda Licht for the pithy statement that you can't explain a strategy with a strategy, dummy.

into the war (recall Chapter 6). To see why, despite losing few of its initial conquests, winning a swift and shattering victory over Romania, and sensing the impending fall of the Tsar, it unleashed its U-boats in 1917, we need to look not to the United States but to Germany's principal opponent in the war: the Entente. By late 1916, both the Entente and the Central Powers believed that American intervention on the side of the former was more or less inevitable, requiring only the slightest, unpredictable provocation. In this context, Wilson's desire to mediate, to oversee the end of European power and the beginning of a Pax Americana from a position of powerful neutrality, couldn't help but be frustrated.[31] That Wilson most wanted to take the lead after the other great powers had exhausted themselves was clear, but the objects of his plans had designs of their own – designs that, intentionally or not, made American intervention the very foregone conclusion that Germany and the Entente assumed it to be.

13.2.1 Solving the Puzzle

Figures 13.2 and 13.3 present two extensive-form games, both under complete information, that allow us to piece together a coherent strategic story about how the Entente and the Central Powers each take actions that both anticipate and precipitate American entry. The core of each model is Germany's choice over unrestricted and restricted submarine warfare and the subsequent American choice between joining the war on the side of the Entente and remaining neutral. But in the second model, Germany's decision is preceded by an Entente choice over how much debt to incur on Wall Street, over just how tightly to tie its financial fortunes to the apparently tepid support of Wilson's America. Germany knows that unleashing its U-boats in a desperate gamble to knock Britain out of the war is likely to provoke war with the United States, but the second model gives the Entente the chance to shape American decision-making by making it more difficult for Wilson to maintain his commitment to neutrality, ultimately undermining his ability to deter Germany from wreaking havoc in the North Atlantic. Whether Wilson can deter a widening of the naval war will come down not to the credibility of his threat to join the war, which sustained the *Sussex* pledge, but to the waning credibility of his corresponding promise *not* to join the fray if Germany keeps its U-boats on the leash.

---

[31] Wilson's vision of world order was certainly anti-European and partially anti-imperialist, but it was also unambiguously racist. He might've wanted to break the old European imperial hold on the globe, but he was equally adamant that it should still be in the hands of white people, especially when confronted with the rise of Japan to great power status in Asia. See Tooze (2014, chapters 2 and 4).

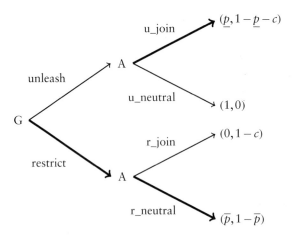

Figure 13.2 German strategy and American intervention.

American and German preferences over the eventual outcome of the war drive the game in Figure 13.2. First, Germany's elite believes that its days are numbered – politically and potentially mortally – unless the spoils of victory, including territorial gains very much like those laid out by the *Septemberprogramm* in September 1914 (recall Chapter 6), can cover the costs of a ruinous war.[32] In December 1916, Chief of the Admiralty Staff Henning von Holtzendorff submits a report arguing that unless something changes, Germany's best hope is a peace of exhaustion, which will be as disastrous for the German elite as an outright military defeat. He points an accusatory finger at the British "starvation blockade," which has tightened its grip as Germany faces its scarcity-induced "turnip winter" of 1916–1917.[33] Germany must knock Britain out of the war if there's to be any chance of survival, he reasons, but that can only be done by cutting Britain off from its primary sources of strength: its empire, its trade, and its major benefactor – the United States. Britain's power depends on its imperium, from which it draws soldiers and laborers, strategic position, and the financial potential to pay down what will be enormous postwar debts.[34] In principle, making Britain less great is an elegant and tempting solution. Without it, Germany's leaders must stare into a maw they can only escape by securing a clear military victory. For Germany's elite in 1917, it's victory or bust.

Across the Atlantic, the United States is also concerned by a possible German victory. Wilson's neutralism may be covered in a fine rhetorical veneer, resplendent with invocations of the rule of law and the rights of

---

[32] See, inter alia, Goemans (2000, esp. pp. 106–115), Herwig (2014, chapter 8), and Stevenson (2011, chapter 1).

[33] See Herwig (2014, p. 309).

[34] On the role of empires in the First World War, see Gerwarth and Manela (2015).

small nations in a world heretofore dominated by the strong, but it's instrumental, a means to achieving his preferred settlement at war's end. As early as 1915, Wilson confirms to Secretary of State Robert Lansing that he can see the value of belligerency if it means both defeating Germany and restraining the colonial powers of the Entente, the cornerstone of his vision for the postwar world.[35] Wilson's ideal endgame includes the prevention of a Continental hegemony under the Kaiser, but after that he parts ways with his eventual Entente partners:

> the world he wanted to create was one in which the exceptional position of America at the head of world civilization would be inscribed on the gravestone of European power.[36]

Wilson's often called an idealist, but that's mostly because his plans for postwar collective security through the League of Nations (about which more in Chapter 14) came to naught. As he tells Congress in January, his *ideal* outcome is a peace of exhaustion with no military victor, one that allows him *carte blanche* as leader of the only great power left standing to dictate the terms of a new global order sustained by American financial power. As we saw in Chapter 11, preventive wars often see their aims pushed toward totality. And German victory precludes such a role for Wilson, a fact of which his confidante Colonel Edward House has been reminding him since the war began.[37] True, he wields tremendous leverage over the Entente, with Britain and France deeply in debt to Wall Street and the former's blockade surviving mostly at his pleasure, but the one outcome over which he has no subsequent leverage is also the only outcome that Berlin's political class finds tolerable: a German victory. And while rising American military and economic power, buttressed by growing public sentiment that a German victory would be unacceptable,[38] ensure that Wilson's ability to guarantee a favorable outcome of the war is on the rise in early 1917, Germany's power to do the same for itself is on the wane, setting up what is by now an all-too-familiar strategic tension.

Figure 13.2 covers the period from the sinking of the *Sussex* through winter 1916–1917, in which Germany must choose between unrestricted (playing "unleash" in the model) and restricted submarine warfare, where the former declares a war zone around the entirety of the British Isles and targets any ship in the vicinity and the latter remains faithful to the *Sussex* Pledge. After observing Germany's choice, the United States chooses whether to join the war against Germany (u_join if Germany unleashes the

---

[35] Stevenson (2004, p. 255).
[36] Tooze (2014, p. 54).
[37] See Meyer (1916, p. 37). House, by the way, wasn't an actual colonel; in fact, he never served in the military.
[38] See Neiberg (2016, p. 212).

U-boats, r_join if Germany restrains them) or remain neutral (u_neutral, r_neutral respectively). We've restricted the American choice set, denying the United States the option to join the war against the Entente, but this is consistent with what we know about American interests and what other belligerents *believed* about American interests. Siding with the Central Powers was logically possible, but the relevant parties believed that it would always be less attractive for the United States than either neutrality or siding with the Entente. The common conjecture from 1914 onward didn't contain any credible idea that the United States would join the Central Powers, so we can leave it out of our story in this chapter and not worry that we're working from a bad metaphor.

In defining outcomes we'll take seriously Admiral Holtzendorff's prophecy of defeat at the hands of the British if the blockade can't in some way be broken, which is consistent with the total aims to which commitment problems can drive preventive wars. War outcomes arise probabilistically, in that players don't know the true state of the world when they make decisions. Either Germany or the Entente wins, but since the true state of the world is uncertain, we'll work with expected payoffs. First, suppose that if the U-boats are turned loose and Wilson preserves American neutrality (unrestricted; u_neutral), Germany secures victory by forcing a British capitulation. However, if the U-boats haven't been unleashed and the Americans join (restricted; r_join), bolstering the Entente's flagging war effort with fresh dollars, dreadnoughts, and doughboys, Germany is sure to lose the war. Between these extremes are two other outcomes. If the submarine war remains restricted but the Americans stay neutral (restricted; r_neutral), then Germany wins with probability $\bar{p}$ and loses with probability $1 - \bar{p}$.[39] If the United States intervenes in response to unrestricted submarine warfare (unrestricted; u_join), then Germany preserves a fighting chance of victory ($\underline{p}$) that's better than certain defeat but less than its chances under restricted warfare and American neutrality, such that $\underline{p} < \bar{p}$. Ranking Germany's chances of victory by outcomes in Figure 13.2, we have $1 > \bar{p} > \underline{p} > 0$. America's choice over joining the war, which Wilson has tied to Germany's continued observance of cruiser rules, shapes whether Germany can secure its best prospects, which includes a potentially Pyrrhic victory, or must risk its worst prospects, which may include exile, jail, or death for its political elite.[40]

To flesh out the payoffs, suppose that Germany receives 1 for victory and 0 for defeat. Likewise, since Wilson's worst outcome is a German

[39] Keep in mind that probabilities can range only from 0 to 1, so $p \in [0, 1]$, which means that p is an element of the set of numbers between 0 and 1, inclusively.

[40] On the personal risks posed to leaders who lose wars in moderately repressive, semiexclusionary political systems like Imperial Germany's, see Goemans (2000).

victory (the only outcome that excludes him as arbiter of the final settlement), the United States receives 0 for a German victory and 1 otherwise. Germany's already fighting a war, so we'll assume the associated costs are sunk; it's already straining its economy and population to the limit, so any diversion of effort to the submarine war simply shuffles around costs it's already paying. For the United States, though, joining the war entails substantial new costs, from sending its growing navy, laden with newly built dreadnoughts, into harm's way to raising an army beyond the paltry 100,000-strong force partially deployed in Mexico to diverting even more treasure away from productive investment. Therefore, we'll introduce a variable c that represents the costs the United States has to pay to join the war. Since it's a cost, we assume that $c > 0$. We've modeled war as costly in previous chapters, but we've represented it only as a simple shrinking of the total pie. But in this case it's useful to think about the upfront costs that the United States will have to pay to finally – and, as it happens, irrevocably – join the game of great power politics; for any outcome in which the United States joins the war, it pays c. These expected payoffs appear in Figure 13.2.

Proposition 13.1 describes the Subgame Perfect Equilibrium we need to exist (the moves are also highlighted bold in Figure 13.2) if we're to explain why Germany keeps its U-boats in port under pain of American intervention. At (restrict; u_join, r_neutral), Germany leashes its submarines at the cost of keeping perfidious Albion's blockade in place, while the Americans enter the war only if Germany abandons cruiser rules, staying neutral otherwise – however disingenuous that neutrality is to German eyes. The United States successfully deters Germany from unleashing the U-boats in this equilibrium, and while that rests in part on an American willingness to join the war in response, it also hinges on American willingness to stay out of the war if Germany plays by the rules of the *Sussex* Pledge. Deterrence rests on both resolve *and* restraint, not on unconditional or unpredictable commitments to fight. Once we establish the existence of this deterrence equilibrium, we can ask how Entente strategy contributes to the breakdown of deterrence.

PROPOSITION 13.1 *The strategy profile (restrict; u_join, r_neutral) is a Subgame Perfect Equilibrium when $\bar{p} \leq c \leq 1 - \underline{p}$ and $\bar{p} < 1 - \underline{p}$.*

Proof For (r; uj, rn) to be a Subgame Perfect Equilibrium, it must be the case that

$$u_A(uj) \geq u_A(un) \quad \text{and} \quad u_A(rn) \geq u_A(rj)$$

for A and $u_G(\text{r}) \geq u_G(\text{u})$ for G. The first inequality is satisfied when

$$1 - \underline{p} - c \geq 0 \Leftrightarrow c \leq 1 - \underline{p},$$

the second inequality when

$$1 - \overline{p} \geq 1 - c \Leftrightarrow c \geq \overline{p},$$

such that A can threaten to intervene only in the event of G choosing u when $\overline{p} \leq c \leq 1 - \underline{p}$. This inequality requires $\overline{p} < 1 - \underline{p}$ if it is to be possible to satisfy it. The third inequality is satisfied when $\overline{p} \geq \underline{p}$, which is true by definition. No player has a profitable deviation in any subgame, so (r; uj, rn) is a Subgame Perfect Equilibrium when $\overline{p} \leq c \leq 1 - \underline{p}$ and $\overline{p} < 1 - \underline{p}$. □

What sustains deterrence of unrestricted submarine warfare until 1917? The logic of Subgame Perfect Equilibrium, which forces us to think about the credibility of threats in dynamic games, provides the key. First, Germany must believe that it can keep the United States out of the war by honoring the *Sussex* Pledge, and it must believe that the current war of attrition under blockade offers it better prospects than unleashing the U-boats and drawing the Americans into the war. We know that the latter is true, because by 1916 belligerent exhaustion has ensured that the great powers of 1914 remain so in name only. If the Americans join the war, they can decide the outcome – but only if they get across the Atlantic in time and in sufficient numbers. If Germany can keep the Americans out of the war by restricting its U-boats to cruiser rules, it wins with probability $\overline{p}$, ensuring that it's better off than turning the U-boats loose, which in the face of American involvement implies a lower expected chance of victory, $\underline{p}$. Second, this willingness to keep the U-boats leashed depends on an American strategy of maintaining neutrality if U-boats honor cruiser rules. If Wilson can't promise to stay out of the war, then Germany has nothing to lose and everything to gain by trying to sever Entente supply lines. Our equilibrium shows that the United States can stay out of the war if submarine warfare remains restricted as long as Germany's chances of victory under restricted U-boat warfare ($\overline{p}$) aren't too high. Otherwise, the United States joins regardless of German strategy. Through much of 1916, that seems a safe bet, as the Entente's offensive on the River Somme helps force a German retirement at Verdun and as the Brusilov Offensive pushes the Central Powers back in the East. But middling German prospects aren't enough; American costs of joining the war must also be high enough to restrain Wilson when Germany observes cruiser rules yet low enough to force his hand if Germany unleashes the submarines and brings victory within reach, or

$$\overline{p} \leq c \leq 1 - \underline{p}.$$

In other words, the United States needs to be able to join if it must, but joining can't be so attractive that it'll enter the war no matter what Germany does. Germany can thus maintain U-boat restrictions, confident that its chances may not be great – the "rational pessimism"[41] that's carried it since 1914 means they weren't – but that those chances are much better if the Americans can be kept out of the war. But as 1916 turns into 1917, that proves a very big, very weighty, "if."

When we think about deterrence (as we did briefly in Chapter 4), we typically focus on a specific part of the calculation, i.e. the credibility of threats to fight.[42] Modern deterrence theory developed during the Cold War, when the dominant concern among scholars and policymakers was how to make credible threats to fight on behalf of others, especially when those others might be on different continents and when coming to their defense might mean the exchange of nuclear weapons.[43] Trading Seoul or London for Austin or Chicago was a difficult proposition, which made finding ways to increase the credibility of threats to risk a Third World War, from American troops in Europe to the interposition of American ships between Cuba and Soviet ships delivering nuclear weapons, all the more important. But in some cases, like Wilson's attempts to restrict German naval strategy, the threat to fight isn't in question: too many Americans dying after running afoul of German torpedoes would've clearly brought a reluctant Wilson into the war. What's important in 1917 is the promise *not* to fight as long as Germany obeys cruiser rules and, so insulting to German minds, tolerates an abominable British blockade. Absent some basic reassurance that compliance with an opponent's demands won't save it from punishment, the target of a deterrent threat might decide that there is nothing left to lose,[44] and then do the very thing that its opponent hopes that it won't do.[45]

As such, Figure 13.3 presents a game that incorporates the third major player in our story, the Entente, which must choose just how tightly to tie its prospects in the war to an eventual American intervention. As its peacetime armies disappear into Flanders fields and its coffers begin to run dry due to increasing arms production and conscription, the Entente has to look abroad for funding, a ready source of which is the generally pro-Entente business community in the United States. American wealth and agricultural production are critical to the British and French war efforts,

---

[41] See Harrison (2016, p. 140).

[42] For just a small sampling, see Russett (1963), Schelling (1966), George and Smoke (1974), Huth (1988, 1997), Nalebuff (1991), and Fearon (2002).

[43] See, again, Schelling (1966).

[44] I don't know for sure this is what Foo Fighters had in mind when titling their third record, but I like to think it is.

[45] On the use of threats and reassurance in coercion, see Kydd and McManus (2017).

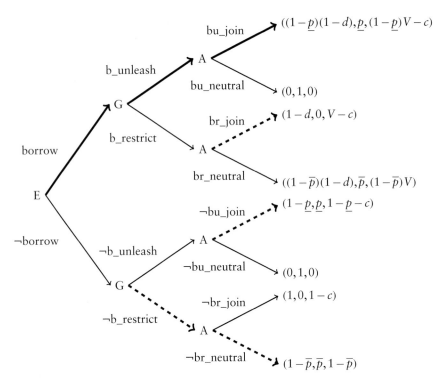

Figure 13.3 Entente borrowing, German strategy, and American intervention.

but the price of that dependence is escalating debt, which by December 1916 threatens insolvency. Entente borrowing has been a boon to the American economy, but Wilson is none too pleased, and he considers trying to curtail the Entente's ability to borrow on Wall Street. But by late 1916, enough American wealth is tied up in the survival of the Entente that British Prime Minister David Lloyd George believes "[t]he more that Britain borrowed in America and the more it purchased, the harder it would be for Wilson to detach his country from the fate of the Entente."[46] As Entente indebtedness increases, letting Britain and France go under becomes an increasingly risky proposition for an American president that has to care about the health of his own economy as much as his chances to reshape global politics. Furthermore, Entente indebtedness can't escape German notice; by the end of 1916, virtually all belligerents expect that transatlantic financial ties will be connected to any American decision over joining the war.

We can use these facts – Entente indebtedness and common knowledge of the same – to write down in Figure 13.3 a simple extension of our first model. The Entente, like the United States, wants to prevent a German

[46] Tooze (2014, p. 49).

victory, so it gets 0 if Germany wins and 1 otherwise. But before Germany makes a decision about how to use its submarines, the Entente chooses whether to borrow or not (¬borrow) from private lenders in the United States. If the Entente doesn't float loans on Wall Street, then the world looks much as it does in Figure 13.2, which doesn't take Entente strategy into account. But if E does borrow, it incurs debts, which we'll represent with $d > 0$, to finance its war effort and that it will only need to pay in the event that it wins the war.[47] The substantial sums borrowed – this *is* a world war, after all – also rearrange American incentives, introducing the damage to its economy that might follow from the default that might follow an Entente collapse (i.e., a German victory).

Notably, we're keeping military prospects the same whether or not the Entente borrows. That's a distortion of reality, to be sure, because every dollar put into the war effort should advance the cause of Entente victory, but we do it because we want to isolate the effect of Entente indebtedness on American actions. We're stacking the deck against Entente borrowing by stripping one of its effects out of our theory, and that's useful; if American entry happens in our model, it can only be because of Lloyd George's rationale of eventually forcing Wilson's hand to prevent German domination of Europe, and that can be the only rationale for borrowing. Listing the Entente's payoffs first, it receives 1 in the event of German defeat and 0 otherwise, but for any outcome after it borrows and doesn't lose the war we subtract d for its debt. Finally, if the Entente borrows, the United States no longer receives 1 for a German defeat but $V > 1$, such that preventing German victory is even more valuable because of the debts owed by the Entente. Not because Wilson changes his mind, and not even because the military balance might've changed, but because his claims to neutrality grow decreasingly credible as the Entente lashes its fate ever closer to the health of the ostensibly neutral American economy.[48] Especially as Germany has seen Wilson consistently demand of it fidelity to idiosyncratic – or, less charitably, strange and unprecedented – interpretations of the law of the sea even as he tolerates a British blockade of less than unassailable legality (recall Chapter 10).

Our extended game is a bit more complex, but keeping the logic of backward induction in mind, it's not much more of a challenge to solve. We first identify the set of choices we'd like to explain – Entente borrowing, unrestricted submarine warfare, and American intervention – then see whether and under what conditions an equilibrium with these actions can exist. Remember, though, that a strategy maps out an action for *all*

---

[47] Countries that suffer military defeat can, and often do, repudiate their war debts. See Slantchev (2012) and our related discussion later in this chapter.

[48] See Strachan (2013, p. 228) and Tooze (2014, p. 40).

contingencies in the game (Definition 2.5), so that players know what they're avoiding when they choose one action over another. Conveniently, the game with Germany and the United States is a proper subgame (Definition 11.4) of the larger game, so we know that if the Entente plays ¬borrow, the game between Germany and the United States plays out just as it does in Figure 13.2: with no extra incentive to save the Entente, Wilson can credibly threaten to intervene if Germany unleashes the U-boats and to remain neutral if the U-boat war stays limited. This implies that any Subgame Perfect Equilibrium of the three-player game in Figure 13.3 has to include the strategies (¬b_restrict; ¬bu_join, ¬br_neutral) in the no-borrowing subgame. With that established, it remains for us to state the rest of the equilibrium we'd like to find

(borrow; b_unleash, ¬b_restrict; bu_join, br_join, ¬bu_join, ¬br_neutral).

In words, the Entente borrows from the United States, Germany restricts the U-boats if the Entente doesn't borrow but unleashes them otherwise, and the United States can promise to stay out of the war if the U-boat war remains restricted if and only if the Entente doesn't borrow. But if the fate of the Entente is tied to the fate of the American economy through heavy borrowing, then the United States will join the war to save the Entente whether or not Germany unleashes the U-boats.

PROPOSITION 13.2   *The strategy profile (borrow; b_unleash, ¬b_restrict; bu_join, br_join, ¬bu_join, ¬br_neutral) is a Subgame Perfect Equilibrium when*

$$d \le 1 - \left(\frac{1-\overline{p}}{1-\underline{p}}\right),$$

$\overline{p} < 1 - \underline{p}$, and $\overline{p} \le c \le \min\{\overline{p}V, (1-\underline{p})\}$.

Proof For (b; bu, ¬br; buj, brj, ¬buj, ¬brn) to be a Subgame Perfect Equilibrium, it must be the case that $u_A(\neg buj) \ge u_A(\neg bun)$, $u_A(\neg brn) \ge u_A(\neg brj)$, and $u_G(\neg br) \ge u_G(\neg bu)$ in the subgame following E's choice of ¬b. Since this subgame is identical to the game in Figure 13.2, we can rely on the proof of Proposition 13.1 to say that these strategies are in equilibrium when $\overline{p} \le c \le 1 - \underline{p}$ and $\overline{p} > 1 - \overline{p}$.

Next, in the subgame following E's choice of b, it must be the case that

$$u_A(buj) \ge u_A(bun) \quad \text{and} \quad u_A(brj) \ge u_A(brn)$$

for A and $u_G(bu) \ge u_G(br)$ for G. The first inequality is satisfied when

$$(1-\underline{p})V - c \ge 0 \Leftrightarrow c \le (1-\underline{p})V$$

and the second inequality when

$$V - c \geq \left(1 - \overline{p}\right) V \Leftrightarrow c \leq \overline{p} V.$$

We know from the no-borrowing subgame that our equilibrium requires $\overline{p} < 1 - \underline{p}$, which means that $\overline{p}V < (1-\underline{p})V$ is also true. That allows us to say that $c \leq \overline{p}V$ is the more important of these two constraints, because it "binds" – that is, if c falls below $\overline{p}V$, it also falls below $(1-\underline{p})V$, so we only need to write down the binding constraint. Next, since $\overline{p}V > \underline{p}$ but may be greater or lesser than $1 - \underline{p}$, we can write the constraints on c as

$$\overline{p} \leq c \leq \min \left\{\overline{p} V, \left(1 - \underline{p}\right)\right\}.$$

Finally, the third inequality (which supports G's decision to play bu) is satisfied when $\underline{p} \geq 0$, which is sure to be true.

With the consequences of both borrowing and not borrowing established, we can say that E plays b when $u_E(\mathrm{b}) \geq u_E(\neg \mathrm{b})$. This inequality is satisfied when

$$\left(1 - \underline{p}\right) \left(1 - d\right) \geq 1 - \overline{p}, \Leftrightarrow d \leq 1 - \frac{1 - \overline{p}}{1 - \underline{p}}.$$

No player has a profitable deviation in any subgame, so (b; bu, ¬br; buj, brj, ¬buj, ¬brn) is a Subgame Perfect Equilibrium when $\overline{p} < 1 - \underline{p}$, $\overline{p} \leq c \leq \min \overline{p}V, (1-\underline{p})$, and $d \leq 1 - (1-\overline{p})/(1-\underline{p})$. $\square$

As before, bold lines indicate equilibrium strategies, where solid bold lines indicate the equilibrium path of play – the outcomes we expect to observe – and dashed bold lines indicate strategies that remain off the equilibrium path – the dogs (of war) that don't bark. Entente borrowing, unrestricted U-boat warfare, and American entry occur on the path of play, allowing us to answer the questions with which we began this chapter. First, why does the United States join the war, and, second, why does Germany take steps it knows will provoke American belligerence? Our model shows that deterrence breaks down because the United States can't credibly commit to *stay out* of the war if Germany's prospects improve. In contrast to our two-player game in Figure 13.2, the United States is bound to join the war against Germany regardless of the latter's actions, which undermines deterrence just as surely as any incredible commitment to fight if the proscribed action is taken. Indeed, by late 1916, Germany views the United States as a de facto member of the Entente.[49] With American intervention likely no matter what it does on the high seas, Germany's leaders declare a war zone around the British Isles, sinking any and all ships that might be delivering the war materiel that sustain Britain's war

[49] See Neiberg (2016).

effort – before, according to overly optimistic projections from Admiral Holtzendorff, American troops can land in sufficient numbers to turn the tide against the Central Powers.

If we look at the conditions supporting Germany's choice in our model, this gamble – for which Germany has come in for no small amount of postwar criticism – starts to make sense: if Wilson will join the war anyway, then allowing it to happen unanswered yields no chance of success (0), but if the U-boats can be turned loose and at least stem the American tide, Germany's elite retains a fighting chance (p, that is) of survival. With Entente strength on the rise thanks to a practically inevitable American intervention, Germany's leaders roll the dice because *not* doing so would lead to certain disaster. Just as it did in the face of already long but rapidly lengthening odds in the summer of 1914, Germany decides in 1917 to ward off looming calamity by courting potential disaster, yet another grim instance of the rational pessimism that can drive declining states to take actions that seem, in retrospect, to only bring about the catastrophe that their leaders wish to avoid. "I don't give a damn about America," Ludendorff says in early 1917, expressing his view that, consistent with Hindenburg's view of the inevitability of American intervention, a new bid for victory over Britain shouldn't wait, especially for the incredible promise of American restraint.[50] "Regardless of how dangerous the United States might be militarily" – and Germany's general staff didn't think it would be – "the submarines seemed the only way to save the Central Powers. Their unrestricted use was coming to seem not an option but … an inevitability."[51]

But why, in the winter of 1916–1917, is Entente power on the rise, even as morale begins to crack on both home- and battlefronts and as economies begin to overheat from the massive mobilizations of the previous year? The answer, as we can see in Proposition 13.2, turns on how the Entente funds its war effort once its own domestic borrowing capacity is under strain: borrowing from the United States. The Entente knows that Wilson would like nothing more than to come in only at the end (if at all), when it'll be cheaper and when American belligerence can have an outsized effect on the peace settlement. But for the Entente, waging a war of survival against another great power coalition, there's little incentive to wait for that outcome. As it borrows dollars and purchases American grain, it changes Wilson's view of the war's outcome – increasing the value of a German defeat from 1 to V – and renders him willing to join the war to save a potentially insolvent Entente, even if Germany maintains limits on its submarine strategy.

---

[50] See Herwig (2014, p. 311).
[51] See Meyer (1916, p. 152).

To see how, let's examine American strategy in the upper part of the game tree, where the Entente has borrowed. We know that Wilson will join the war after Germany unleashes the U-boats even if the Entente hasn't borrowed heavily from the United States, so what's critical is the American willingness to intervene if Germany continues to honor cruiser rules, to hew to the strictures of the *Sussex* Pledge. If the Entente doesn't borrow, the United States joins when $1 - c \geq 1 - \overline{p}$, but if the Entente borrows, Wilson joins when $V - c \geq (1 - \underline{p})V$. And if we solve these inequalities for c, we can see that the United States joins when $c \leq \overline{p}$ in the first case (no borrowing) and $c \leq \underline{p}V$ in the second (borrowing). It's possible that the second condition is true while the first isn't. Thus, Entente borrowing can undermine Wilson's promise to stay out of the war even if Germany obeys cruiser rules. Extensive borrowing gives the United States a reason to save the Entente sooner than it otherwise might, and since Germany can observe this increasing convergence of interests, one that even Wilson will be hard-pressed to ignore, American deterrent promises ring hollow; the doughboys are coming eventually and in overwhelming numbers, whatever happens to shipping around the British Isles. With Germany treating American entry on the side of the Entente as a given, Wilson comes by April to believe that only belligerence can achieve his aims; with both sides mobilizing (and borrowing) to full capacity in a push for victory or nothing, he can either allow the Entente to go under *or* let it win and lose his leverage at the peace conference.[52]

We'll return to the specifics of Wilson's calculations below, but completing our discussion of the equilibrium requires that we ask whether the conditions supporting Entente borrowing make sense when we look at the historical record. Debt must be paid down after the war, so it's not a trivial thing to mortgage one's future to an outside lender. However, Entente borrowing from the United States carries with it the added benefit of dragging the latter into the war by increasing its stake in German defeat. If the Entente doesn't borrow, it doesn't owe Wilson a thing, but its chances of defeating a Germany honoring cruiser rules are $1 - \overline{p}$. If it does borrow, its chances of winning – even in the face of unrestricted submarine warfare – increase to $1 - \underline{p}$, because borrowing guarantees American intervention. And as long as forcing Wilson's hand doesn't lead to a crushing level of debt, borrowing so heavily, even from a country led by a neutralist like Wilson, makes sense. By borrowing from the United States, the Entente manages to effect a prospective, indeed nearly decisive, shift in the distribution of power. But as we saw in Chapters 2, 4, and 6, the state in prospective decline can hardly be expected to stand idly by.

---

[52] See Stevenson (2004, pp. 255 and 261).

Borrowing so heavily from the wary United States might have been risky, but "[i]f London and Paris entwined America ever more into their war effort, Wilson's hand would be forced. But it was, in fact, only Germany's anticipation of that logic that made it real."[53] In effect, the debt-driven convergence of American and Entente interests, Wilson's predilection for aloofness notwithstanding, undermined American deterrence and forced Germany into the very step that Wilson hoped to deter: an all-out war on the seas that would force his hand and put one more nail in the coffin of the United States's comforting narrative of unspoiled isolation.

13.2.2 Why "Associated," Not "Allied"?

When the United States finally joined the war, it did so as an "Associated Power," refusing to become a member of the Entente by signing the Declaration of London, which committed its members not to sign separate peaces with the Central Powers.[54] And when, on April 6, 1917, the House of Representatives passed the declaration of war, which had passed the Senate on April 4, it named only Germany, not the other Central Powers. In fact, the United States wouldn't declare war on Austria-Hungary until December, even then only in response to the latter's severance of diplomatic relations, and it pointedly never declared war on the Ottoman Empire. On the military side, its generals arrived in Europe jealously guarding their independence from Entente authority, trying to avoid "amalgamation" under an Entente commander even as the Western Front bent to the point of nearly breaking under the weight of Germany's 1918 spring offensive.[55] But why? With the global balance of power at stake, French and British morale showing signs of collapse, German submarines roaming the seas, and revolutionary Russia teetering on the brink of chaos, would a country with a shared interest in preventing a German victory work so hard, and so conspicuously, to limit its commitments to the very countries it's trying to save?

Our story of American intervention, especially Wilson's preferences over the outcome of the war, can shed some light on this question. If Wilson's most preferred outcome of the war is one in which no side can impose a victor's peace on the other, and if both sides have proven themselves unwilling to pursue a compromise peace, then committing fully to the Entente means facilitating just such a harsh settlement. Germany might not win, but an outright Entente victory secured with

[53] See Tooze (2014, p. 58).
[54] Note that this is distinct from the Declaration of London concerned with honoring the law of the sea discussed in Chapter 10.
[55] See Stevenson (2011, p. 43).

the unconditional cooperation of American arms may prove to be just as undesirable. Germany can't be allowed to win, but neither can an Entente now emboldened by the promise of fresh American troops poised to flood into Europe – eventually at the rate of ten thousand per day. Wilson's solution to the problem relies on the same factor that drove his alignment choice in the game in Figure 13.3: substantial Entente dependence on American arms and financing. While it might've forced Wilson's hand in joining the war, it also allows him to distance himself from Entente war aims, and dramatically so in the case of his famous Fourteen Points address in 1918. The United States and only the United States can tip the balance in the war – the Entente is out of options – so Wilson can credibly maintain a free hand as he hopes to restrain his new partners in the imposition of a peace settlement.[56] Signing the Declaration of London, for example, would restrict Wilson's options to force a peace of his own making on Europe by going over Entente heads; and refusing to declare war on most other members of the Central Powers coalition limited the places to which American troops could be deployed. It was a bold strategy, focused chiefly on positioning the Americans for the postwar peace negotiations, and certainly not one designed to win the hearts and minds of his French, British, Italian, and Russian partners. But it preserved a chance to avoid Wilson's worst possible outcome of facilitating an Anglo-French victors' peace that would, to his mind, merely perpetuate the cycle of great power war he believed himself uniquely capable of stopping.[57]

Like many events in the Great War, the way in which the United States intervened is a special, if perhaps extreme, case of a more general pattern in international politics. Just as we saw in the discussion of Italy and the Triple Alliance in Chapter 9, states choose the terms of their commitments to one another carefully in hopes of limiting their exposure to risk. They may add escape clauses, exclusions, or commitments to consultations rather than direct action,[58] all in the hopes of preserving their ability to resort to force at times and places of their choosing – that is, their freedom of action in an international system where the ultimate arbiter of who gets what is one's ability to impose one's will by force of arms. Intervention wasn't Wilson's first-best outcome, but he tried to mitigate its costs with an artful structuring of the American commitment that could, at a minimum, give him ultimate leverage over the Entente with boots on the ground and purse strings in his hands. But as we'll see in Chapter 14, Wilson's solution to the dilemma of both saving and restraining the Entente was a gambit that didn't quite pay off.

---

[56] See Sondhaus (2011, p. 315).
[57] I never said Wilson was humble. He *was* an academic, after all.
[58] See, inter alia, Mattes (2012) and Chiba, Johnson, and Leeds (2015).

13.3   WAR FINANCE

When we talk about the cost and waste of war, especially a bloody attritional struggle like the First World War, it's easy to focus only on its human and material dimensions, from lives lost, bodies maimed, and minds traumatized to fields laden with landmines and villages reduced to rubble. But the costs don't stop there. Wars cost both blood *and* treasure; every dollar devoted to destruction is a dollar that doesn't go to productive investment and consumption. Soldiers need salaries, clothing, food, and arms if they're to stay in the line and fight, and workers bringing in the harvest or producing the guns, shells, aircraft, ships, uniforms, and boots that sustain the war effort must also be compensated. From start to finish – and often afterward – war is expensive, especially when the stakes are national survival or clinging to the imperial trappings of great power status. Belligerents can pay for war by taxation (voluntary or forced), borrowing (foreign or domestic), printing money, and even plunder.[59] And as we saw in Chapter 12's discussion of the Russo-Japanese War, the ability to pay for war is just as important as, and sometimes more important than, the ability to win battles. Financial ties determined not only when but on which side the United States joined the Great War, but they also shape preparations for war, as well as its outbreak, duration, and outcome.

Decisions over war funding often come down to a trade-off between taxation, which is unpopular today, and borrowing, which requires repayment with interest – and will thus be unpopular tomorrow.[60] Anticipating their own costs of borrowing, states without access to cheap credit find it difficult to go to war,[61] either making painful concessions to their opponents or forgoing chances to make demands of others, though they often try to shore up this weakness by signing alliances, which can boost their available military strength more cheaply than purchasing or producing arms directly.[62] Those with good credit, those better able to issue bonds in foreign markets, are relatively more likely to initiate military disputes.[63] If states arm on credit, borrowing to sustain their armies as they contemplate deterring or wresting concessions from their enemies, then the expected costs of debt service can lead to war, because fighting may prove the only way to capture what states need to pay off their creditors.[64] The exigencies of war-making led to the widespread creation of central banks in the nineteenth century, which helped countries reduce

---

[59] On the variety of means by which states pay for war, see Zielinski (2016).
[60] Since war became an industrial endeavor, plunder just isn't enough.
[61] Shea and Poast (2018).
[62] Allen and DiGiuseppe (2013).
[63] DiGiuseppe (2015).
[64] Slantchev (2012).

their costs of borrowing during wartime.[65] But even the promise of cheap credit can lead states to be targeted in preventive conflicts by opponents hoping to forestall their opponents' rise,[66] because the freedom to arm cheaply can render any commitments not to recover lost strength incredible. Both Serbia and Russia discovered this in 1914 as their ability to arm on cheap French credit in the preceding years stoked the preventive fears in Austria and Germany that led ultimately to the outbreak of the Great War (Chapter 4).[67]

How states finance wars also shapes their duration and outcome. Waging war on credit can dramatically increase a state's minimum demands for peace negotiations, making settlements more difficult to reach short of a total military outcome,[68] while on the other hand dwindling access to credit can lead some states (like Japan in 1905) to accept settlements they'd otherwise scoff at. In fact, by late 1916 and early 1917 when Wilson issued his instructions to Wall Street and talked of "peace without victory," Britain was nearly insolvent, though Germany was unaware,[69] and Lloyd George wondered whether his plan of tying the United States ever closer to the Entente would pay off or force him into humiliating peace terms with the Central Powers. Indeed, higher costs of borrowing are associated with poor war performance – that is, less favorable settlements at war's end – more broadly,[70] and one potential explanation for the high rate of modern democracies' success in war is their generally better terms of credit, supported by publics that can punish leaders for defaulting on debt and ruining the country's reputation for repayment.[71] Debt may be more attractive than taxation as a means of paying for war, especially when the public prefers wars that don't impact its fiscal bottom line, but the temptation to fight with borrowed money is not without its risks. Military buildups and wars funded by deficit spending have contributed to cycles of boom and bust in the American economy in the post–World War II era, most recently in the form the 2003 Iraq War, funded in large part through borrowing, and the subsequent financial crisis that began in the United States in 2008 and led to the worldwide Great Recession.[72]

---

[65] Poast (2015).

[66] Shea (2016) argues that military regimes are particularly prone to this problem.

[67] For a similar story that links a state's ability to fund rearmament through taxation to preventive war, see Chapman, McDonald, and Moser (2015).

[68] Slantchev (2012).

[69] See Meyer (1916, p. 166).

[70] Shea (2014).

[71] Schultz and Weingast (2003). However, democracies don't appear to fund their wars with debt to a greater degree than nondemocratic states (Carter and Palmer, 2016).

[72] See Oatley (2015). And for an account of how international institutions helped ensure that the Great Recession remained that – and not a new Great Depression – see Drezner (2014).

13.4 NATIONAL LEADERS AND INTERNATIONAL POLITICS

Far more so than other belligerents, where cabinets and kaisers, ministers and military men wrangled over decisions for war and peace, the United States's entry into the Great War depended on the preferences of a single individual: Woodrow Wilson. The American political system affords the president wide latitude in foreign policy, and Wilson was a singular figure, at odds with strict neutralists like William Jennings Bryan in his own cabinet and interventionists in the opposition like Teddy Roosevelt. He was also a solitary one, leaving only a sparse documentary record for us to figure out his personal motives during the war years. Had Wilson not been president, the United States might've entered the war sooner and on different terms – many interventionists were staunchly pro-Entente, after all – and it might've taken a very different approach at the Paris Peace Conference, especially with a more obviously pro-Entente president.[73] Compared even to Lloyd George and the Kaiser, Wilson seems to have had an outsized effect on his country's strategy throughout the war years. This raises an important question: to what extent do individual leaders, as opposed to their place in the international system or their domestic politics, shape national preferences, foreign policy, and patterns of war and peace? To put a finer point on it, does it matter who leads, or is America's (or China's or Congo's or Egypt's) foreign policy basically the same no matter who's steering the ship of state?

Leaders make decisions under systemic and institutional constraints, from the military power they can bring to bear against their rivals and their geographical location to the need to keep constituents happy and divided powers over declaring and waging war. These constraints encourage continuity in a country's foreign policy through successive changes in leadership, but ultimate decisions over war and peace often rest on the shoulders of a president, a prime minister, a general secretary, or a dictator.[74] Political scientists have found that individual leaders can have profound effects on their country's foreign policy, even when politics remains "normal" in the sense that leaders dismissive of or bent on destroying the political system aren't in power. Many of these advances come down to recognizing two things about national leaders. First, they generally try hard to stay in office, which creates a private interest that may conflict with the public interest. Second, they can differ pretty radically from their predecessors and successors in their willingness to use force – that is, in their preferences. Woodrow Wilson might've been a singular figure in shaping his

---

[73] See, in particular, Hamilton and Herwig (2004, chapter 11).

[74] For an assessment of leader influence as against political institutions and the distribution of power, see Horowitz, Stam, and Ellis (2015, chapter 3).

country's foreign policy, but he's far from unique in that; national leaders, through differences in their preferences and political prospects, play an important role in the ebb and flow of politics in an otherwise impersonal international system.

Most leaders work hard to stay in office, but they differ pretty widely in their prospects of staying and the consequences of leaving. Dictators that need to please only a few cronies or generals typically hold onto power longer than leaders in democracies, who must stand for reelection against credible competition, but democrats have the advantage of relatively cushy posttenure fates; the lecture circuit is a far cry from the exile, jail, or death that greets many autocrats upon losing office.[75] In general, leaders at risk of losing office are less willing to initiate conflicts and less likely to be targeted in international crises than more secure leaders.[76] These patterns hold unless insecure leaders happen also to fear for their safety after being deposed, which leads them to wage more[77] and longer[78] wars, hoping to capture sufficient spoils to buy off their opponents or simply to undermine them, than leaders that can expect a safe retirement. Leaders in precarious political positions are uniquely likely to build military coalitions for international disputes, but the same desire to secure the international win that demonstrates competence and cements their hold in power dampens their selectivity, producing fractious coalitions with troublesome partners that more secure leaders can safely avoid.[79] Politically insecure leaders are also less likely than secure leaders to be deterred by human rights treaties from repressing their populations at home.[80] Not all leaders are subject to the same pressures, however, as some may face term limits, while others aren't held responsible for the foreign policy messes they inherit, giving them the freedom to cut the country's losses and terminate losing or stalemated conflicts.[81]

Their political security aside, leaders also differ individually in their preferences, especially over the desirability and appropriateness of using military force. For example, whether American presidents believe foreign threats emerge from domestic political systems or the structure of the international system shapes whether they engage in comprehensive (i.e., regime-changing) or limited interventions.[82] Rebels that go on to lead their countries appear uniquely likely to resort to force, combat veterans

[75] See Goemans (2000, 2008).
[76] See Chiozza and Goemans (2003, 2004).
[77] Chiozza and Goemans (2011).
[78] Goemans (2000).
[79] Wolford and Ritter (2016).
[80] Conrad and Ritter (2013).
[81] Croco (2005).
[82] Saunders (2011).

appear less belligerent than those with military service that didn't see combat, and there appear to be no systematic differences between male and female heads of state, at least in the modern era, in their rate of conflict participation.[83] Whatever their background, though, leaders generally take office with private information over their resolve, creating a "turnover trap" in which the rise of a new leader creates incentives for her to cultivate a reputation for resolve and her opponents to test that reputation. This produces cycles in which new leaders are more likely to see their crises escalate to war than longer-serving leaders with firmer reputations.[84] New leaders are also uniquely prone to being targeted with economic sanctions[85] and to get involved in arms races.[86] Leadership turnover may herald reconfigured alliance commitments, though only when new leaders represent major new domestic coalitions coming to power,[87] but it can also restore good relations when leaders that defaulted on sovereign debt or harmed trading relationships are replaced by new leaders eager to restore the national reputation.[88] Finally, anticipated leadership turnover may create commitment problems, such that the impending rise of a hawkish leader can lead rivals to attack otherwise dovish incumbents, hoping to seize what they can in war before a less cooperative hawk takes office.[89]

Their freedom of action may not be absolute, but national leaders – as well as transitions from one leader to the next – have proven consequential in understanding several patterns of war, peace, and diplomacy in the international system. Wilson, the Kaiser, and Lenin all loom large in the story of the First World War, but they're not anomalies for it; political science has shown that who leads *does* matter, but it's also shown when and how leaders matter most. And as we'll see in the next chapter, Wilson's preferences in particular shaped the negotiations for a final peace treaty in Paris, though not in ways that he anticipated, much less desired, when he first stepped onto the docks at Brest in 1918 to the rapturous applause of a continent captivated by his vision of a new world order.

13.5 CONCLUSION

We began this chapter by asking why, after years of neutrality, the United States joined the First World War in April 1917. If it were a simple matter of sharing the Entente's goal of stifling German power, the United

[83] Horowitz, Stam, and Ellis (2015).
[84] See Wolford (2007) and Wu and Wolford (forthcoming).
[85] Spaniel and Smith (2015).
[86] Rider (2013).
[87] Leeds, Mattes, and Vogel (2009).
[88] See McGillivray and Smith (2008).
[89] See Wolford (2012, 2018).

States might've joined sooner. But Woodrow Wilson's desire to build a Pax Americana on his country's unparalleled financial power after the other great powers exhausted themselves proved unworkable because the very belligerents whose behavior he hoped to control were able to shape his own incentives to join the war. As this chapter's epigraph indicates, Wilson wanted nothing more than to preserve the functioning of an international system that guaranteed his own country's seaborne commerce. As the war raged on, that desire collided with Germany's desire to break out of the British naval blockade, which Wilson could no longer deter after late 1916. Little had changed for the United States since the *Sussex* Pledge, apart from growing naval power that should have in principle made deterrence easier. To resolve this puzzle, we analyzed a pair of extensive form games with the logic of Subgame Perfect Equilibrium to show that American deterrence broke down not because Germany doubted Wilson's willingness to fight but because Germany believed Wilson could no longer credibly promise *not* to fight as his country's financial ties to the Entente grew more extensive. Rather than wait for American intervention, Germany decided to unleash its U-boats quickly, before large numbers of American troops could arrive in Europe. It was a gamble, to be sure, ranking alongside the very roll of the dice that started the war, but one that Germany's leaders took on knowingly. On January 17, Hindenburg summed up the attitude of the German high command: "It has to be. We expect war with America and have made all preparations. Things cannot get worse."

We know now that Germany's gamble didn't pay off. Spectacular early successes in sinking Entente shipping weren't followed up, as the British adopted the convoy system and developed new antisubmarine tactics. And eventually two million American troops would land in Europe, aimed both at crushing German "militarism" and restraining the Entente from dancing on its grave. In early 1917, though, it wasn't clear that things would go so poorly for the Central Powers; the U-boats were sending ton after ton of enemy shipping to the bottom of the Atlantic, Russia teetered on the brink of revolution, and Germany still held a commanding position in Belgian and French territory. The Entente would launch a new round of offensives in 1917, hoping to break out of the attritional stalemate on the Western Front as the Eastern Front collapsed after the Bolshevik Revolution, which pulled Russia out of the war and gave Germany the Eastern imperium it coveted, and both sides talked of the war continuing at least into 1919 or 1920. But by the middle of 1918, Germany's strategic ascendancy was a thing of the past, its allies shattered and its own troops reeling under the weight of a rapid Entente advance that posed the first threat to German territory since Russia's first incursions in the early weeks of the war. By November 1918, Germany's gains in the East would be undone, and it would be forced to sign a humiliating peace at Versailles, its territory intact but its Kaiser exiled to the Netherlands and its military and economic potential in shackles. The next chapter will trace just how Germany could go from victory in the East to near-total defeat in the span of a few months – a mere blink of an eye in an otherwise interminable war.

14 The End of the Beginning: Victory, Defeat, and Peace

> *We should find ourselves under the hammer the minute we let it slip from our hands.*
>
> Paul von Hindenburg
Out of My Life, vol. 2
>
> *The fight must be to the finish – to a knockout.*
>
> David Lloyd George

Our final puzzle is one of the most important of the modern era:

> Why did the First World War end in November 1918?

The Great War ended not with the bang we'd expect based solely on its name but with a whimper.[1] After years of brutal fighting, desperate gambles, and escalating rhetoric about upending or replacing the old balance of power, we could be forgiven for expecting an "absolute" war. And yet Germany asked for an armistice on October 4, 1918, even as its armies stood victorious over now-Soviet Russia, its own territory remained unconquered, and the Dual Monarchy had finally crushed the Serbian threat that sparked the July Crisis. Its enemies, those countries most committed to ending not only Germany's bid for European hegemony but also its ability to make another, granted that armistice with the German army still standing and a united German polity unchallenged in the center of Europe. With a better strategic position in Europe than it had in 1914 – that is, with the underlying Serbian and Russian commitment problems from Chapter 4 solved – why did Germany wave the white flag? And, with German ambitions not eliminated but potentially magnified after its victory in the East, why did the Entente grant the fateful armistice of 1918?

Our solution to this puzzle, which relies as much on rivalries within military coalitions as rivalries between them, will teach us a few things:

---

[1] A world-historical whimper, but a whimper nonetheless.

- how ending war can require solving more bargaining problems than caused it;
- why the First World War wasn't as "absolute" as it could've been;
- how domestic political institutions shape foreign policy;
- why some peace settlements are durable, while others are fragile.

We'll see in this chapter that explaining how the First World War ended requires that we leverage both of our models of war termination (Chapters 11 and 12). A war that began over shifting power between first Serbia and Austria-Hungary and, second, Russia and Germany created commitment problems for other countries, Britain and France in particular. And the way it was fought, through the Hellish slow burn of attrition, the steady mobilization of societies, and the continual addition of new belligerents, generated information problems over which side would ultimately outlast the other. Ending the war thus required solving both information *and* commitment problems. This chapter's discussion will show us that the war ended, first, once combat revealed that Germany could no longer win a fight to the finish and, second, once Germany solved its own commitment problem by acceding to Wilson's demands for democratization and breaking the power of the Prussian military elite. The solution, we now know, wasn't perfect. But we'll see that the Entente in particular viewed granting an armistice in November as worth the risk in return for reaching a settlement before too many American troops were on the ground, which would give too much control over the final settlement to Woodrow Wilson. We'll close by discussing why, exactly, demands for political reform might be included in states' war aims and why crafting peace settlements, especially after multilateral wars, can prove so difficult even after apparently resounding military successes.

Key Term for Chapter 14

- Armistice

14.1 ENDING WITH A WHIMPER

Why did the Great War end in November 1918? Why not 1916, as many hoped, or 1920, as those same people probably feared? As usual, we can always come up with an answer that seems obvious on the surface. After Bulgaria, the Ottomans, and the Hapsburgs had already cut deals with the Entente, Germany asked for and was granted its own **armistice**, an end to the fighting typically intended to allow for the negotiation of a final peace treaty.[2]

---

[2] The Korean War, which ended only with an armistice in 1953, is one of the more famous examples of wars ending without a final treaty. On the Korean War, see Wada (2013) and Stueck (1995, 2004), and on the decline in peace treaties over time, see Fazal (2013).

Figure 14.1 Endgame, 1918.

DEFINITION 14.1   *An **armistice** is a formal agreement to stop hostilities, sometimes followed by a treaty that formally ends the war.*

Armistices fall conceptually somewhere in between ceasefires, which can be informal and even localized agreements on a pause in fighting, and peace treaties, which are formal agreements that both end the war and specify a new set of rules for politics after the war. Where armistices entail only an end to the fighting, peace treaties tackle the thornier questions of postwar politics and the balance of power.

But why would Germany put itself at the mercy of the Entente in the fall of 1918? Russia had been defeated in the spring, forced to sign the humiliating Treaty of Brest-Litovsk, which stripped it of lands and population and production now under the sway of the Central Powers. Map 14.1 describes the situation as of August 1918 as "uncertain," but there was little doubt in Berlin and St. Petersburg about what had happened; Germany had imposed a victor's peace on its old Slavic rival.[3] As a result, hundreds of thousands of German troops could now turn West. Serbia had been crushed and Romania overrun, securing both Teutonic dominance in the Balkans and the link to Constantinople, while the Dual Monarchy – with no small amount of German assistance – had shattered the Italian armies at the Battle of Caporetto. Both Germany and Austria had solved the commitment problems that drove them to war in 1914. Yet on November 11, German guns would fall silent in an armistice that its leaders requested despite their own lands remaining unconquered. And on June 28, 1919, five years to the day that Gavrilo Princip fired the shots that would set the whole war in motion, Germany would sign the Treaty of Versailles, ceding territory, agreeing to heavy reparations, and accepting the infamous war-guilt clause (recall Chapter 4). Ascendant in the East and unconquered in the West, the *Kaiserreich* chose a path that it knew would lead to a notoriously harsh peace treaty.[4] But why give it all away? Why not fight on, when the very things for which it went to war were not only within reach but finally, securely in Germany's grasp?

[3] With Russia out of the war, this map looked very, very different than Map 13.2 in the previous chapter.
[4] See Herwig (2014, p. 246).

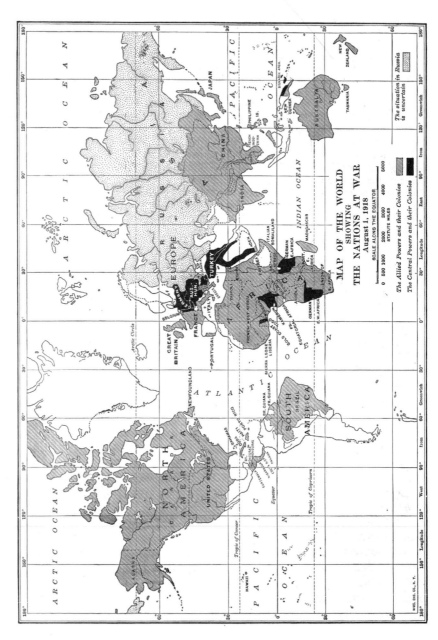

Map 14.1 The world at war, 1918. From McMurry (1919).

Map 14.2 The Western Front, 1915–1918. From Wells (1922).

Jumping back a few months (see Figure 14.1), Germany's massive spring offensive, the "Kasier's battle" or *Kaiserschlacht*, was bolstered by fifty-four divisions released from garrisoning the new Eastern empire. Ludendorff planned to abandon the defensive strategy dominant in the West since 1917, hurling as many divisions as he could against exhausted Entente troops in hopes of piercing the line and, depending on what opportunities emerged, either splitting the British and French armies at their joint in Belgium or driving on to Paris.[5] Beginning with Operation Michael in March, the fighting recalled the early weeks of the war. Map 14.2 shows that German heavy guns found themselves just within range of Paris, which once again faced the prospect of evacuation. Yet though the Entente bent under the pressure, its lines remained unbro-

---

[5] Ludendorff frequently built chances for improvisation into his plans, for which he's often criticized, as the habit seemed to focus on winning battles at the expense of winning the war. See, in particular, Stevenson (2011). But it's important to note that Moltke the Elder saw precisely this kind of planning as optimal, as the enemy's ability to respond and the vagaries of chance were sure to wreck any plan that tried to look too far into the future (Leonhard, 2018, chapter 2).

ken, just like Russian armies after their disastrous 1915 defeat in the Gorlice-Tarnów Offensive (recall Chapter 8). With maneuver restored, casualty rates were once again staggeringly high, outpacing in just two weeks the number killed in nine months at Verdun in 1916.[6] Ludendorff had gambled on breaking the attritional stalemate through a series of offensives aimed at searching for an exploitable breakthrough before his own reserves collapsed, and early successes created a sense of optimism in the army not felt since the early weeks of the war. But even a breakthrough large enough to keep Parisians up at night couldn't provide the decision he wanted, precisely because achieving that breakthrough chewed up so many of his reserves – a fact he could no longer hide from his troops.[7]

Ludendorff's last roll of the dice produced a decision; it just wasn't the one he wanted. British attrition and French *grignotage*, bolstered by 200,000 inexperienced but fresh-legged Americans debarking in France each month, eventually triumphed over German *materialschlacht*. With reserves drying up and morale collapsing in the face of a realization that the war wasn't as defensive as the government had portrayed it, the vaunted German war machine thew itself headlong into retreat. In its wake, the Entente and its American partner surged across Germany's last forward defenses – the vaunted Hindenburg Line – by October, restoring large swathes of French and Belgian territory. Beginning with the Second Battle of the Marne in July, which stopped the *Kaiserschlacht* in its tracks, through the "Hundred Days" battles of Amiens, Fifth Ypres, Second Somme, Meuse-Argonne, and Cambrai, and backed up by the naval blockade now bolstered by American dreadnoughts, the Entente's material and demographic advantages were finally and fully on display. American officers that would play crucial roles in the Second World War, like Douglas MacArthur, George Marshall, George Patton, and Harry Truman all saw action on the Western Front in the final months of the war, and their commander, General John Pershing, believed that victory – possibly entailing a march on Berlin – would take until at least 1919.[8] (That's probably easier to do, of course, if you've only just started fighting than if you've been at this already for several years.) Backed up with fresh American dreadnoughts, dollars, and doughboys, the Entente could now pose a serious threat to Germany itself.

But in fall 1918, with much of French but not Belgian territory restored (check out the November 11 line in Map 14.2), the threat of

---

[6] On this, see Stevenson (2011) and Kershaw (2015, chapter 2).
[7] On the soldiery's realization that the offensive war couldn't be won, as well as the government's inability to hide it from the army and the civilian population, see Goemans (2000, chapter 9).
[8] See Stevenson (2011, p. 43).

invasion – the first since Russian incursions into East Prussia in 1914[9] – was still just that: a threat. The German army might've been unable to wage an offensive war, but a defensive war on shorter lines and fought on and for home territory, premised on the idea of "rolling up like a hedgehog" and wearing down Entente forces increasingly far from their own homes, wasn't out of the question.[10] A defensive war would require fewer troops, and Brest-Litovsk established an Eastern European empire from which Germany might draw fresh resources. Poland and the Baltic states were to become become German vassals, and Ukraine was peeled off from Russia and granted a nominal independence under the guise of the national self-determination preached by both Wilson and (though they meant something quite different by it) the Bolsheviks.[11] The commitment problem of rising Russian strength that drew Germany into the war had thus been solved in resounding fashion. Father south, Serbia had been crushed, solving the commitment problem over which the Hapsburg armies had first marched; Italy no longer posed a serious threat to the Dual Monarchy's western flank; and the Ottomans could now rest easy knowing that the Russian threat to the Dardanelles would be dormant for some time.

But it wasn't all sunshine and light for the Central Powers. Germany's campaign of unrestricted submarine warfare hadn't lived up to the Navy's promises, faltering in the face of the convoy system, an unanticipated British ability to deal with agricultural scarcity, and the Americans' willingness to rush headlong into battle with borrowed French equipment and inadequate training.[12] Bulgaria's position north of the Greek port of Thessaloniki, where an Entente force had been encamped since 1915 in an attempt to influence Greek alignment, collapsed in September 1918, threatening the underbelly of the Hapsburg Empire – a soft underbelly made softer by the withdrawal of German troops to the now-active Western Front. Nonetheless, fighting through the Balkans promised to be slow for the Entente due to both the mountainous terrain and the now-shortening Hapsburg defensive lines.[13] For their part, the Ottomans started shedding territory as British forces, many contributed by the Government of India, advanced through Mesopotamia and the Levant. But advancing across the Arabian Desert and the riverine parts of the Cradle of Civilization with help from politically ambitious locals was a far cry from waging war in the Empire's Turkish heartland – a fact with which the Entente had become

---

[9] On this, especially its psychological impact on the German public, see Watson (2014).
[10] See Strachan (2013, p. 295).
[11] See Tooze (2014).
[12] See Sondhaus (2014) and Strachan (2013). And see Stevenson (2011) for the Americans' sometimes-baffling commitment to costly frontal assaults.
[13] See Stevenson (2011, pp. 142–148).

intimately familiar at Gallipoli.[14] Rapid Entente advances across open territory notwithstanding, defeating the Central Powers could be viewed reasonably as both distant in time and ruinously costly.

If Germany's request for an armistice looks puzzling, so was the Entente's willingness to grant it, if we take seriously the commitment problem that drove its remaining major partners, Britain and France, into war: the threat that Germany would dominate the Continent. We saw in Chapter 11 that some preventive wars can be difficult to solve short of waging an "absolute" war, and Entente leaders appeared quite aware of this fact. British Foreign Secretary Edward Grey, in discussions with Wilson's confidant and envoy Colonel Edward House, indicated that British war aims involved both the restoration of Belgium and an "end to militarism," which meant, in no uncertain terms, ending the reigns of the ruling houses of Hohenzollern and Hapsburg.[15] That a new balance of power would require Germany's full military defeat looked like a given, especially once the Entente could draw from the seemingly limitless well of American economic and military might. How else, apart from a war-winning drive into Germany that would at minimum disarm it and might even partition it, would the German question that had vexed Europe since at least the Thirty Years' War be given a satisfactory answer? If the Kaiser and his generals, who talked openly of a "Second Punic War" to follow the current one,[16] still ruled after the Great War, would they not try again to break out of their encirclement?[17] An armistice, especially one that might tempt a war-weary Europe into a hasty peace treaty while Germany's political class still stood, would surely promise only a temporary solution, one that might allow Germany the space to rest, recover, sow dissension in the Entente, and then resume the war on more favorable terms. Why even give the Kasier, Hindenburg, and Ludendorff – hardly the most trustworthy trio in the eyes of Paris, London, and Washington – the chance?

14.2   EXPLAINING WAR TERMINATION

In its pure form, our theory of war implies that belligerents stop the fighting once it's solved the bargaining problem, commitment (Chapter 11) or information (Chapter 12), that prevented settlement in the first place. But wars

---

[14] For more on the Gallipoli campaign, see Stevenson (2004), Strachan (2013), and McMeekin (2015).

[15] See Meyer (1916, p. 69).

[16] See Strachan (2013, chapters 8–10).

[17] As it happened, of course, the Kaiser and his generals weren't in charge when Germany tried again in 1939, but the generals had done plenty after the war to stoke public resentment at the outcome of the Great War.

are often chaotic and unpredictable, and some expand to include additional belligerents, issues, and bargaining problems. When fighting changes the facts on the ground, when governments fall and rise inside belligerent countries, when heretofore reliable partners drop (or are knocked) out of the war, and when new entrants choose sides and pursue their own ends, terminating a war may require solving more bargaining problems than were required to start it. The Korean War offers a useful example. It began in 1950 over control of a Korean peninsula divided along former Soviet and American occupation lines, but it soon drew in the United States under the aegis of the United Nations, followed by a Communist China fresh off securing victory in its own long civil war. Thus, the Korean War ended as a fight not just about Korea but about rankings in the regional power hierarchy. Solving the commitment problem between North and South, over which the war began, would've been insufficient by 1953, when ending the war required that the great power interveners resolve uncertainty about the likely course of further fighting and fears that each side might use a ceasefire to restart the war on more favorable terms.[18]

The Great War posed a similar set of problems for the countries that would end it. What started as a war about Serbian ambitions and Austrian decline in the Balkans expanded quickly into a war about the European, and then about the global, balance of power. Answering the Russian and Serbian questions simply wasn't enough to make a self-enforcing bargain possible between 1918's expanded set of belligerents. Therefore, if we're to explain why the First World War ended in the fall of 1918, we need to identify what bargaining problems remained active in the months leading up to Germany's request for an armistice and the Entente's decision to grant it.

PUZZLE 14.1   *Why did Germany request an armistice in 1918, and why did its enemies grant it?*

We'll show next that the end of the First World War came about by sequential solutions to, first, an information problem and, second, a commitment problem. The cumulative revelations of four years of fighting ultimately solved the information problem, just as our model in Chapter 12 leads us to expect, but once Germany's leaders expected almost certain defeat, they took steps to solve their own commitment problem before Entente and American arms could solve it for them. Finally accepting that victory was no longer possible, Germany's leadership decapitated itself, initiating a process of democratization that Wilson tied ever more closely over the course of October to his willingness to negotiate – and to trust any German

---

[18] On the end of the Korean War, see Reiter (2009).

commitment to stopping the fighting. Ultimately, beliefs about the sources of German ambitions and the attendant threat to the balance of power would shape the Entente's willingness to negotiate a peace short of an "absolute" war.[19]

14.2.1   Solving the Puzzle

The path to 1918's armistice begins with the resolution of an information problem rooted in a simple question: which coalition can outlast the other in a brutal war of attrition? But in the presence of commitment problems, agreement on the outcome of a fight to the finish may not be sufficient to end the war,[20] so once Germany comes to believe that ultimate victory isn't possible, we have to answer a second question: why did the Entente accept German promises to end the fighting in 1918? A straightforward application of Chapter 12's model can answer the first question, which saves us from writing down a fresh model, but the second requires one last game.

Let's start with the information problem. Neither side has an incentive to admit how long it thinks it can hold out, since doing so may reveal weakness to the other side, so it's left for fighting to reveal the true state of the world. The Central Powers have a smaller population and limited access to the sea, but they fight on interior lines and, through most of the war, German troops have killed more Entente troops than they've lost on their own. The Entente has the nominal advantages of population and wealth, but they depend on seaborne supply that'll only add to the logistical strain should their supply lines stretch into German territory. Attrition has minimized casualties relative to mobile warfare (recall Chapter 8), but it also reduces the information about the outcome of a fight to the finish provided by any given engagement. And as publics and armies grow weary of war, attrition increases the chances that the home front cracks before the battlefront.[21] If fighting can make obvious which side will ultimately win an "absolute" war, one hurdle to ending the conflict can be cleared, but the nature of attrition and the sudden increase in German combat power on the Western Front as of the spring means that more fighting will be required to prove one side's supremacy.

The slow working out of attrition has, by late 1918, hammered home some uncomfortable truths to the German high command. American

---

[19] For more on how causal beliefs about the origins of threats – politics inside states or the exigencies of surviving in an anarchic international system – see Saunders (2011).

[20] See Wolford, Reiter, and Carrubba (2011).

[21] Weisiger (2016) shows that intense fighting reveals far more information and allows for quicker settlements than the less-intense fighting that characterized attrition.

power has had an effect much sooner than expected, both because the submarine campaign can't sink enough ships and because the Americans jump into the line with French equipment and, compared to the original belligerents, appallingly little training. Germany's manpower reserves are nearly exhausted, sucked into the maw of the *Kaiserschlacht*, and its coalition has begun to crack, with Bulgaria signing an armistice on September 29,[22] effectively signing the death warrant of a Dual Monarchy increasingly dependent on Germany both militarily and politically.[23] The German army, finally convinced that victory is impossible – and that their own lives are likely to be spent in vain – has also lost its desire to fight. Reserves detraining to march into the progressively more desperate 1918 battles are jeered as "strikebreakers" by the disillusioned soldiers they replace, and when orders for a last, obviously suicidal sortie reach the naval base at Kiel, sailors mutiny, refusing to fight and calling for revolution. Likewise, street protests and industrial action paralyze urban centers as the truth of an unwinnable war spreads throughout Germany. Ludendorff can't help but acquiesce to this perfect storm of bad news, and he accepts the need for an armistice, which is requested in early October. The war looks very much like the second stage of our war termination model in Chapter 12; uncertainty about the ultimate outcome of the war is resolved, and if that's the only bargaining friction still operative, we should expect peace. But why would an Entente growing stronger by the day, with the threat of total war to conquer Germany ever more credible, accept it? For that, we'll need a model.

The game in Figure 14.2 presents the sequence of key moves that defines the end of the war, where the Entente and the Americans confront one final bargaining problem: Germany's questionable commitment not to try again to unhinge the European balance of power. We'll suppose that Germany will request an armistice but that it must choose the terms on which it does so. With the Entente braying about ending Prussian militarism and Wilson increasingly strident in the assertion that he'll only negotiate with a popular – as opposed to a military – government,[24] Germany's first move is a choice between democratizing (dem) and retaining the Hindenburg-Ludendorff military dictatorship that's effectively run the country since 1916 (¬dem). After observing Germany's choice, the Entente and the Americans (collectively labeled "E" to keep things simple) choose between fighting to the finish (d_fight, ¬d_fight) and granting the

---

[22] See Grayzel (2013, p. 164).

[23] This dependence, first noted in Chapter 7, would ultimately lead to scandalous Austrian peace feelers in 1917 and, as soon as the German shadow loomed a bit smaller, eagerness for an armistice.

[24] See, respectively, Meyer (1916, p. 69) and Goemans (2000, chapter 9).

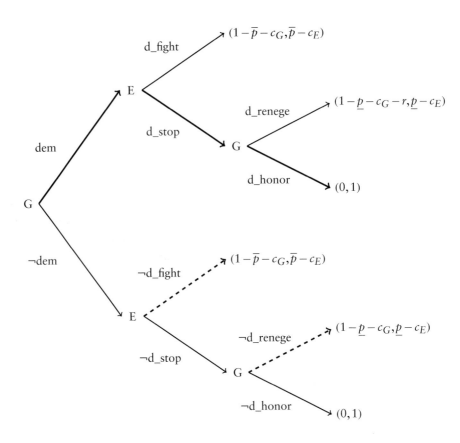

Figure 14.2 German political institutions and war termination.

armistice (d_stop, ¬d_stop). Fighting to the finish means an "absolute" war of the kind we considered in Chapters 11 and 12, but stopping gives Germany a chance to either honor the armistice (d_honor, ¬d_honor) or to renege (d_renege, ¬d_renege), taking advantage of an Entente pause to rest, recover, and restart the war on more favorable terms. Reneging means relaunching the war (and fighting to the finish) in the short term, and honoring the armistice means at least several years of peace. This extensive form allows us to capture a commitment problem in straightforward fashion. Germany has the last move, so as long as we choose the right solution concept, it can't promise ahead of time not to make the most advantageous choice if the Entente grants the armistice. But in contrast to our treatment of the commitment problem in Chapter 11, Germany has the option at the beginning of the game to tie its hands against the temptation to renege on an agreement, replacing a military government its enemies believe to be Hellbent on dominating Europe with a civilian government more eager to secure peace before Germany's politics, economy, and society plunge into the chaos of defeat by conquest.

Next, how do players rank outcomes? The game has six terminal nodes, but it can end in only three ways. First, the Entente can continue the war regardless of whether Germany democratizes, and we'll assume that E wins such a fight to the finish with probability $\bar{p} \in (0, 1)$, which yields its best outcome of 1, and loses, yielding 0, with probability $1 - \bar{p}$. Germany gets 0 for an Entente victory and 1 for an Entente defeat, but both sides pay a cost for continuing the war (c_E and c_G, respectively). Following our handling of expected utility in previous chapters, payoffs for G and E are $1 - \bar{p} - c_G$ and $\bar{p}_G$, respectively. If the war continues because Germany reneges on an armistice, then payoffs look similar but for two changes. First, the Entente's chances of achieving its best outcome – a prostrate Germany unwilling or unable to seek a European hegemony – are reduced, falling from $\bar{p}$ to $\underline{p}$, where $\underline{p} > \bar{p}$. Second, reneging is free if Germany refuses to democratize, but if it plays "dem," then reneging on the armistice entails an additional cost $r > 0$ that represents the difficulty of convincing the Reichstag, which contains pro-armistice democratic and social-democratic parties, to consent to a renewed war. Finally, Germany can honor the terms of the armistice, which divides the pie in a way that roughly approximates the likely outcome of an "absolute" war if the Entente simply continues the fight: G receives 0 and E receives 1. Both sides agree that the Entente can win with a certain probability, that it's less likely to win if it gives Germany a chance to breathe and renege on the armistice, and that bringing democratic parties into the political process will make it costlier (i.e., more difficult) for Germany to restart the war.

If we're to explain the end of the war, our solution to this model must account for several facts. First, Germany democratizes in its "revolution from above," first installing the civilian Prince Max von Baden as chancellor, then forcing the Kaiser's abdication and subordinating the military to Reichstag control. Second, the Entente must threaten to continue the war absent such assurances. Third, the Entente must follow through, granting an armistice upon German democratization yet refusing it if Hindenburg and Ludendorff remain in control. Proposition 14.1 describes just such an equilibrium, whose actions are again bolded (solid for actions taken on the equilibrium path, dashed for choices taken off the equilibrium path).

PROPOSITION 14.1   *The strategy profile (dem, d_honor, ¬d_renege; d_stop, ¬d_fight) is a Subgame Perfect Equilibrium when $\underline{p} \leq 1 - c_G \leq \bar{p}$ and $r \geq 1 - \underline{p} - c_G$.*

Proof   For (dem, d_honor, ¬d_renege; d_stop, ¬d_fight) to be a Subgame Perfect Equilibrium, it must be the case that $u_G(\text{dem}) \geq u_G(\neg\text{dem})$,

$$u_G(\text{d\_honor}) \geq u_G(\text{d\_renege}),$$

and

$$u_G(\neg\text{d\_renege}) \geq u_G(\neg\text{d\_honor})$$

for G, and

$$u_E(d\_stop) \geq u_E(d\_fight) \quad \text{and} \quad u_E(\neg d\_fight) \geq u_E(\neg d\_stop)$$

for E. For G, the first inequality is satisfied when

$$0 \geq 1 - \bar{p} - c_G \Leftrightarrow \bar{p} \geq 1 - c_G,$$

the second when

$$0 \geq 1 - \underline{p} - c_G - r \Leftrightarrow r \geq 1 - \underline{p} - c_G,$$

and the third when

$$1 - \underline{p} - c_G \geq 0 \Leftrightarrow \underline{p} \leq 1 - c_G.$$

For E, both inequalities are satisfied because both $1 \geq \bar{p} - c_E$ and $\bar{p} - c_E \geq \underline{p} - c_E$ are true by construction. No player has a profitable deviation, so (dem, d_honor, ¬d_renege; d_stop, ¬d_fight) is a Subgame Perfect Equilibrium when $\underline{p} \leq 1 - c_G \leq \bar{p}$ and $r \geq 1 - \underline{p} - c_G$. □

What reasoning supports this equilibrium? First, the Entente won't take seriously any German commitment to an armistice if the military remains in charge, so it'll keep up the fight rather than grant an armistice unless Germany democratizes. Allowing Germany to use a pause to regain military discipline and fortify the frontier is less attractive than simply fighting on while the Entente retains the advantage. Thus, refusing the armistice makes sense if Germany plays ¬dem. But a democratized Germany will honor the armistice, producing a settlement that reflects the Entente's crushing but slow-to-manifest battlefield superiority. Leaving a nearly sure thing on the table makes no sense when the alternative is still more costly, risky fighting. On the German side, democratization makes reneging on the armistice more difficult, and if it makes reneging difficult enough – that is, if $r \geq 1 - \underline{p} - c_G$ – then democratization can tie German hands against a temptation to renege that would with certainty provoke the Entente to pursue a fight to the finish. Therefore, in its first move of this SPE, Germany democratizes, committing itself to the settlement and taking 0 rather than risk swallowing its worst outcome of $0 - c_G$ in the event that the Entente wins the war. Proposition 14.1 shows that this SPE exists only when the Entente's chance of winning a prearmistice fight to the finish is high enough, or $\bar{p} \geq 1 - c_G$, which convinces Germany to cut its losses, and when the Entente's chances of winning would be sufficiently diminished if Germany gets a chance to rest ($\underline{p} \leq 1 - c_G$), which makes the threat to fight on credible if Germany doesn't democratize. Germany's inability to commit to an armistice if it retains a military government creates a commitment problem – one that the Entente will solve with a fight to the finish unless Germany solves the problem first by breaking the army's control over policy.

Keep in mind, though, that this equilibrium rests on both the fact of Entente superiority *and* agreement on that fact. Suppose, for example, that Germany retained some residual doubt about whether the Entente's demographic and financial superiority would be paired with the resolve required to turn those facts into a military advantage. In that case, democratization (which yields a pretty dire payoff of 0) looks less attractive than rolling the dice one more time in a bid to outlast the Entente in a defensive war after violating an armistice. Yet by late 1918, with Bulgaria's collapse and Austria's desire for a quick armistice of its own, any remaining illusions about the Entente's ability to win a fight to the finish have been rudely shattered. Solving the information problem, convincing Germany that victory is no longer in the cards no matter how favorable its kill ratios, is necessary to convince its leadership of the need to solve its own commitment problem in the fall of 1918.[25] This analysis works, however, only so long as we accept that the Entente agrees that democratization in Germany will restore a balance of power. Otherwise, the Entente may fight on. But why, after years of blood and toil, are the Entente powers okay with a settlement that leaves Germany united, its land unconquered, and its politics suffused with the idea that it hasn't *actually* been defeated? Why trust Germany, whose geographic position in the middle of Europe would pose the same strategic problems to dictatorships or democracies, to solve its own commitment problem when winning an absolute war is a very real, if still costly, possibility?

14.2.2 What Happened to the "Knockout"?

Lloyd George's epigraph opening this chapter is pretty unequivocal: "The fight must be to the finish – to a knockout."[26] Commitment problems can push the aims of preventive wars to absolutes, and the resolution of the question posed by Germany's 1871 unification – who would rule Europe? – looks very much like a case in point.[27] But as we saw above, and as German nationalists went to great lengths to emphasize in the interwar years, the war ended short of a fight to the finish. For all its destruction, for all the stress the Great War placed on politics, industry, and the very social fabric of the countries that waged it, the conflict ended (if just so)

---

[25] See Goemans (2000, pp. 284–290).

[26] See Meyer (1916, p. 153).

[27] On the commitment issue applied to Belgium in particular, see Reiter (2009), and on "absolute" war as a solution to commitment problems, see Wolford, Reiter, and Carrubba (2011).

short of Clausewitz's ideal of an "absolute" war. German territory was unconquered, and though its navy would be interned at Scapa Flow and strict limits placed on rearmament, Germany could still in principle defend itself. Germany wasn't fully disarmed, and as harsh as it was, especially in terms of reparations (about which more later), the Treaty of Versailles would also mark the first time that the other great powers recognized the legitimacy of a unified German state.[28] Not until 1945 would British, American, and Russian armies end a European war sitting atop a wrecked Germany, answering the German question with the simple, coarse decision of partition and disarmament. Why, especially as Foch mocked Versailles as an "armistice for twenty years,"[29] didn't the Entente just press on to Berlin?

This chapter's model focused on what united the Entente and their American associate in 1918: the willingness to accept Germany's "revolution from above" as sufficient insurance against reneging to grant an armistice. But leaving a sovereign German state in place, one that might freely return to the militarism that its enemies diagnosed as a cause of the war, wasn't a first-best solution to the commitment problem,[30] and it bears asking why Germany's enemies were willing to accept something short of full disarmament, of an ironclad assurance against revanchism.

PUZZLE 14.2   *Why didn't the victors of the Great War pursue a fight to the finish?*

Our story so far suggests two potential answers. First, following the logic of Chapter 11, an imperfect solution to the commitment problem can facilitate war termination when the costs of pursuing a more complete solution are prohibitive. But the German army disintegrated through a mix of surrender, retreat, and desertion as Entente and American armies rolled back its spring gains. The costs of war can be a powerful reason to accept a second-best solution to the commitment problem, but the costs of fighting an army increasingly unwilling to fight back likely weren't all that daunting in light of the possibility to putting paid to Germany's imperial ambitions. The war *could* have been taken into Germany, if not all the way to Berlin at least far enough to peel off independent Rhenish and Bavarian states and so reduce Prussia's hard-won dominance – and yet the Entente granted an armistice.

---

[28] See Tooze (2014, chapter 14).

[29] A prediction that would prove eerily accurate if one takes the 1939 Nazi-Soviet invasions of Poland as the end of the armistice. But given the fraught politics of the treaty, plenty of salty generals probably made skeptical predictions of its duration, and the odds that at least one of them would be right are probably pretty high. Foch was no prophet – just the beneficiary of a *very* dark coincidence.

[30] See, inter alia, Werner (1999) and Lo, Hashimoto, and Reiter (2008).

Second, and in line with previous chapters' stories about belligerents maneuvering themselves for advantage in eventual peace talks, whatever the net benefits of taking the war into Germany, doing so would dramatically reduce both French and British leverage in the final peace negotiations.[31] As more and more Americans landed in France, took on a larger share of the burden of rolling back the German army, and demanded a commensurately greater say in strategy, the Entente's war aims would be ever more firmly subordinated to Wilson's revolutionary vision for reshaping the balance of power – a vision that entailed stripping the victors of their empires and supplanting them in the global hierarchy with the newly unparalleled financial and military might of the United States.[32] Just as Britain contributed to France's defense in 1914 with an eye to guaranteeing its place at the peace talks (Chapter 7), Britain and France found themselves eager to bring the war to an end short of Lloyd George's prophesied knockout blow in order to make sure that they wouldn't be fully subordinated to the Americans when the time came to make peace.[33] If British and French forces on the Continent could remain intact, and if they could reasonably claim that they bore the lion's share of the effort to liberate Belgium and France, then they would stand a better chance of retaining their empires, their positions in the global hierarchy, and their shares in the spoils of war (read: reparations and imperial conquests) to which they felt entitled after humbling the Kaiser and his generals. But that meant forgoing the knockout blow that would've made the war "absolute," following Wilson in his willingness to accept democratization as a solution to the problem of German foreign policy ambitions, and (though they couldn't have foreseen it at the time) driving all the way into Germany when given another chance a generation later.[34]

14.3 DEMOCRACY AND WAR

When Wilson declared that he'd trust commitments made only by a democratic Germany, he invoked an idea that's animated both American foreign policy and research on the causes of war ever since. Following Immanuel Kant, Wilson subscribed to the notion that popular governments, those accountable through the ballot box to the very citizens that they'd ask to

[31] This is no small matter; remember from Chapter 7 that it kept the British in the line in 1914 when retreat was at its most tempting.
[32] Remember Wilson's ambitions in Chapter 13.
[33] See, inter alia, Goemans (2000) and Strachan (2013).
[34] On the Second World War in Europe, see Hastings (2010, 2012), Tooze (2006), and Kershaw (2012).

fight and die in war, make more credible commitments to peace than governments captive to the whims and jealousies of dictators or monarchs.[35] Democracies, so the story goes, should be more peaceful than autocracies in an era of mass mobilization when fighting wars requires popular support. Indeed, democracies have rarely made war on one another in the last two centuries,[36] even as they seem eminently willing to fight dictatorships, a pattern that Jack Levy famously dubbed "as close as anything we have to an empirical law in international relations."[37] Democracies also tend to win the wars they fight,[38] to do so cheaply as long as the war doesn't drag on too long,[39] and to honor their alliance obligations.[40] American Presidents Bill Clinton and George W. Bush both invoked this regularity as a rationale for the promotion of democracy abroad, the latter explicitly in the lead-up to the 2003 Iraq War. But while scholars agree on the existence of a "democratic peace," it has for a time been an empirical fact in search of an explanation.

Early explanations for the democratic peace followed a Wilsonian line, arguing that the externalization of norms of peaceful political competition that prevail inside democratic states makes for peace between them,[41] but this doesn't square with the willingness of powerful democracies to wage wars of conquest and subjugation against the weak when it suits them.[42] Other explanations focus on the working of democratic institutions. Some arguments hold that the difficulties of winning broad support in democratic systems make going to war prohibitively costly, if only in terms of delay,[43] but this predicts that democracies should be peaceful in general, not merely with one another.[44] A second set of institutional arguments focuses on the ease with which citizens can punish leaders at the ballot box for losing wars,[45] which explains why democracies tend to fight only those wars they can win *and* why they don't fight each other (because victory would be

---

[35] Kant, of course, believed that "perpetual peace" between a confederation of republics would arise only after centuries of warfare (see Wagner, 2007).

[36] The 1999 Kargil War between India and Pakistan is one of the few ambiguous cases of conflict between ostensible democracies (see Sarkees and Wayman, 2010).

[37] See Levy (1988, p. 662). For some early invocations of Kant to explain this pattern, see Doyle (1986), Russett and Oneal (2001), and Mitchell (2002).

[38] See Reiter and Stam (2002).

[39] See Bennett and Stam (1998).

[40] See Leeds (1999, 2003a).

[41] See, e.g., Dixon (1993) and Mitchell (2002).

[42] See Bueno de Mesquita et al. (1999, p. 792).

[43] See Maoz and Russett (1993).

[44] See Bueno de Mesquita et al. (1999, p. 792).

[45] See Fearon (1994), Schultz (1998), Reiter and Stam (2002), Bueno de Mesquita et al. (2003), and Debs and Goemans (2010).

prohibitively costly). In other words, the democratic peace relies on mutual deterrence. This explanation, however, can't account for the fact that the democratic peace as we know it is a post–World War I phenomenon; before 1919, pairs of democracies were actually more prone to military disputes than all other pairs of states.[46]

More recent work argues that the democratic peace has less to do with democracy itself and more to do with the hierarchical structure of the international system (recall Chapter 1). Coalitions led by democratic states won both world wars, after which they created new states, many of them democratic, and drew them into hierarchical security and economic relationships with democratic great powers like Great Britain and the United States. So aligned for fighting together in a potential future war, peace between these new democracies and their great power sponsors was a design feature of the new balance of power – often explicitly so, as organizations like NATO required its mostly democratic membership to settle outstanding territorial disputes when they joined the alliance. American allies, for example, tended to be (or to become) democratic,[47] to fight alongside one another in international conflicts, and *not* to fight one another, thanks to their shared subordination to a democratic great power.[48] In the language of statistics, the relationship between democracy and peace might be *spurious*: both democracy and peace share a common cause in the existence of an extensive hierarchy led by democratic great powers.[49] Democracy doesn't cause peace, nor does peace cause democracy; they're both caused by a third, underlying factor, in this case the creation of democratic zones of peace by the settlements of major wars. In the absence of American hegemony, then, there might have been little to prevent democratic states from going to war against one another in the twentieth century over the land, wealth, power, rights, and privileges that have traditionally driven rival states to war. After all, democracy in principle requires only that wars are popular – not that they're not waged against other democracies.[50]

---

[46] See McDonald (2015, p. 574).

[47] See Gibler and Wolford (2006).

[48] See McDonald (2015) for a compelling historical breakdown of the pattern of democratic peace and this particular alternative account rooted in hierarchical politics.

[49] In another argument for the spuriousness of democratic peace, Gibler (2012) argues that a link exists between peaceful borders and the survival of democracy, which is consistent with McDonald's (2015) story to the extent that the stability of some borders depends on great power guarantees or alliance commitments: NATO, for example, requires the settlement of outstanding territorial disputes as a condition of membership. It has no mechanisms to remove undemocratic states from the alliance, which means that NATO can't directly coerce states into becoming or remaining democratic (Reiter, 2001).

[50] See Wagner (2007, chapter 6).

The stakes in the debate over explaining the democratic peace aren't merely academic.[51] If democratic institutions on their own can promote peace between states, then spreading democracy, even by the sword (as the United States attempted with respect to Iraq in 2003), can only further the cause of peace. True, imposing democracy on Japan and (then-West) Germany after 1945 has seen those former militarist great powers make lasting peace with former enemies, but whether those examples translate to other contexts depends on *why* democratic states haven't fought one another since 1919. If both democracy and peace have been the product of democratic victories in and the reconstruction of the balance of power following the last two world wars, then we should be skeptical that the mere adoption of democratic politics in rival states will ensure that peace breaks out – especially as membership in the great power club shifts and changes over time. Rather, we should turn our eyes toward the maintenance of the current democratic-dominated global order and its continuation in the face of potential American decline.

14.4   THE POLITICS OF PEACE

The First World War offers a dramatic illustration of the challenges of negotiating and securing lasting peace. The war's expansion ensured that there were as many visions of a desirable settlement as there were claimants to shares of that settlement, even with the Russians distracted by their own civil war. Germany hoped that its "revolution from above" would spare it crushing reparations, especially as Wilson insisted that his quarrel wasn't with the German people but with their leaders. France hoped at minimum to recover Alsace-Lorraine and at maximum to seize the Rhineland and imperial rights in modern-day Syria and Lebanon. Britain sought the restoration of Belgium, the consolidation of its own position in the Middle East, and the continuation of its naval dominance. Italy wanted its due in the Trentino and Dalmatia (recall Chapter 9), especially the port city of Fiume, while Japan wanted recognition of its primacy in Shandong and a racial equality clause in the final treaty.[52] The United States, for its part, wanted lenient terms for Germany – that is, a reparation scheme that wouldn't cripple Continental Europe's most promising engine of growth – the breakup of Old Europe's empires, and the other great powers' assent to the construction of an international institution committed to the maintenance of peace: Woodrow Wilson's prized vision, the League of Nations.

---

[51] As if "academic" is somehow a bad thing. But I'll acknowledge the usefulness of the expression.

[52] On the rancor over Fiume and Shandong, see Neiberg (2017, chapter 4).

The League, which required its members to submit disputes to arbitration and to band together against military aggression, faltered early when the dominant postwar power, the United States, refused to join. The Senate's refusal to ratify the Treaty of Versailles is often identified as a cause of its failure in the face of Japanese, Italian, and German aggression through the 1930s. But this account confuses the symptom with the disease. By demanding that all states cooperate to oppose – and thus deter – aggression, the League was predicated on an almost insoluble collective action problem (Definition 7.1). Why jump to a victim's defense halfway around the world if no one else can be trusted to help pick up the slack? Congressional opposition to the League in the United States emerged from both a jealous, isolationist protection of American sovereignty, consistent with the incentive to free-ride on others' willingness to block aggression, and an idealistic disillusionment with the granting of Japanese rights in Shandong, which effectively traded Chinese territory for Japanese quiescence in a treaty nominally inspired by self-determination.[53] Yet even had the United States ratified Versailles, the collective action problem at the heart of Wilson's vision would've remained active, highlighting the twin challenges of making peace after war: dissatisfied former enemies must be deterred from returning to war, and former partners must also agree on how to deter challenges to the terms of their victory. In other words, stable peace after war requires the construction of self-enforcing bargains both across and within formerly warring sides, between former enemies and between the former partners that must share in and defend the new balance of power.

The last two decades have seen an explosion of political science research on the sources of durable peace.[54] First, costlier, longer-lasting, and more destructive wars produce longer spells of peace between both former enemies and former partners.[55] Peace between former enemies also lasts longer after the victors replace vanquished governments with more pliant regimes.[56] Yet peace is also more durable after unambiguous battlefield outcomes more generally, even when the war stops before a final military victory, because a consistent tide of battle reveals information about the likely outcome of a fight to the finish.[57] Third parties, be they great powers or peacekeeping missions, can ensure peace by guaranteeing settlements against opportunistic defections,[58] and great

---

[53] And recall that Japan had also just scooped up Germany's Pacific colonies, allowing it to menace American lines of communication with the Philippines.

[54] See Werner (1999) for the agenda-defining piece.

[55] See Werner (1999) and Wolford (2017).

[56] See Lo, Hashimoto, and Reiter (2008).

[57] See Werner and Yuen (2005).

[58] See Fortna (2003).

powers themselves can subsidize lasting peace by giving aid that can be withdrawn in the event of war.[59] On the other hand, wars that end due to third party pressure, especially when the fighting stops before it can reveal sufficient information about the likely outcome of a fight to the finish, are typically ripe for quick resumption.[60] Finally, settlements can also be fragile when winning coalitions fracture and fail to defend their gains against revanchist challengers, just as the Entente pretty famously failed to do in the face of Italian and German aggression in the 1930s. Winning coalitions themselves can also fall apart over their shares of the postwar pie, like Serbia and Bulgaria did in the Second Balkan War over who should control Macedonia, which they'd just captured from the Ottoman Empire in the First Balkan War.[61] Indeed, large winning coalitions, as well as those that must divide up freshly conquered territory, are uniquely prone to collapsing into intramural war after their victory, while those coalitions that can anchor themselves around great powers prove better at weathering small shifts in the distribution of power that would drive other coalitions to war.[62] Finally, when winning coalitions look fragile, unable to cooperate in defense of the settlement, their former enemies are more likely to go to war to overturn their defeats.[63]

What, then, can we say about the durability of the settlement produced by the First World War? The victors of course hoped to establish a new, durable balance of power (Definition 6.1), but such hopes proved illusory. It's easy to see the Versailles settlement breaking down in 1939 as German tanks raced into Poland under the cover of withering air support in an operation that prefigured the *blitzkrieg* that would conquer France in a mere five weeks in 1940.[64] But the Entente's attempt to reestablish the balance of power after its victory was much more fragile. Far from Foch's predicted "truce for twenty years," it didn't last two, as France fought a war against the Ottoman Empire in 1919 despite the latter signing an armistice in October 1918, and Russia and Poland fought a war to

---

[59] See Arena and Pechenkina (2016), who present compelling evidence that American aid to Israel and Egypt has served just such a function since the Camp David Accords, creating a substantial opportunity cost in forgone aid for the side that launches a war against the other.

[60] See Werner and Yuen (2005).

[61] See Glenny (2012, pp. 226, 243–248).

[62] On the effect of coalition size and great power anchors, see Wolford (2017), and on the effects of territorial redistribution, see Phillips and Wolford (n.d.). For the seminal statement on the fragility of large winning coalitions, see Riker (1962).

[63] See Wolford (n.d.), which shows that the risk of former enemies returning to war after coalition victories increases in the predicted risks that members of the winning coalition turn violently against each other.

[64] On the latter, see May (2000).

establish their new border in 1920.[65] At the other end of Eurasia, Japan would seize Manchuria in 1931, then invade China proper in 1937, the nominal solidarity of both declaring war against Germany during the Great War notwithstanding.[66] And if that weren't enough, Japan would also fight two wars against the Soviet Union in the late 1930s in another sign that the balance of power established at Versailles was hardly a stable one.[67] And Italy, dissatisfied with its own lot after the war, waged a brutal war of conquest in Abyssinia in the mid-1930s. Why was the settlement so fragile?

Setting aside 1919's Franco-Ottoman War, which we might think of as a continuation of the First World War since the Ottomans didn't sign a peace treaty until 1923 at Lausanne, the collapse of the Great War settlement reads like a failure of collective deterrence. The League failed to come to China's defense throughout the 1930s as Japan continued the process of establishing dominance begun in 1894, its members stood by while Italy waged a savage war of conquest in Abyssinia, and the Anglo-French coalition nominally opposed to German revanchism allowed the Nazi remilitarization of the Rhineland (forbidden by Versailles) and the annexations of Austria and Czechoslovakia. Losers *and* winners ran roughshod over the settlement that ended what had been to that point the most calamitous war in human history. Why did the Great War's winning coalition fail to follow up on its victory by building a more durable order, as they clearly hoped to do when they set about the business of making peace? Two answers suggest themselves. First, the United States ended the war as the most powerful state in history, but it refused to commit itself to the maintenance of the balance of power that its might helped create, hoping that financial influence alone might obviate the need for an American military commitment.[68] The winning coalition that would have to deter Germany, in other words, fell apart before the ink was dry on the war's final treaties. Congress demanded full repayment of Entente debt, which only encouraged Britain and France to press for the harsh reparations that undermined Germany's fragile postwar democracy, paving the way for Nazism and the politics of revenge and racial hatred to take the world even deeper into the uncivilized depths of world war. Finally, the balance of power created by Versailles, whatever its faults or merits, was incomplete, in that it proved difficult to accommodate the rise of Soviet Russia from the ashes of the Tsarist empire. Bent on recovering the old imperial domains under the guise of a workers' revolution and growing rapidly on the heels of forced industrialization,

---

[65] See Sarkees and Wayman (2010).

[66] On the link between the Sino-Japanese rivalry, the Chinese Civil War, and both world wars, see Paine (2012).

[67] See Goldman (2013, p. 17), who also shows that Japan also seriously considered a preventive war against Soviet Russia in 1932–1933.

[68] See Tooze (2014).

Stalin's Soviet Union was poised to rise even faster than Tsarist Russia after 1905, bringing Nazi fantasies of an Eastern European empire in line with the desire for yet another preventive war designed to break out of impending great power encirclement.[69] Had the United States used its leverage differently after the war, and had the Soviet Union been able (and allowed) to participate in crafting a new balance of power, then perhaps the Great War's victors would've built a more lasting settlement.

14.5   CONCLUSION

In 1918, Germany defeated Russia, turned west, and then capitulated in shockingly short order. We showed in this chapter that a puzzling request for an armistice in October, as well as the Entente's willingness to grant it, requires an appreciation of the twin bargaining problems sustaining the war by 1918: (1) residual, though waning, uncertainty about which side could outlast the other and (2) the questionable credibility of any commitment Germany's military leaders might make to abandon their dreams of a Continental hegemony. Germany rolled the dice in yet another life-or-death gamble with its spring offensive of 1918, which risked burning through its reserves and its will to fight, prompting German diplomat Kurt Riezler to quip that the Kaiser was poised to become "Wilhelm the Very Great or else Wilhelm the Last."[70] After the Entente, reinforced by a rising American tide barely stemmed by the U-boat campaign, proved it could outlast the Central Powers, Germany sued for peace. But with Germany's commitment to peace under military leadership in question, peace wasn't possible until the "revolution from above" gave Wilson and the Entente a civilian government with which they were finally willing to make peace. This eleventh-hour move toward democracy may have been an imperfect solution to the problem of German ambition, but it was enough to convince the Entente, increasingly wary of growing American influence, not to drive deeper into Germany.

The settlement embodied in Versailles and associated treaties – Trianon, Sèvres, Lausanne, Neuilly, and Saint-Germain – famously collapsed into a larger, bloodier, more savage war along (mostly) the same lines twenty years later. We know a few things about the sources of stable peace, but the story of the failure of the Versailles settlement is as rich in implications for the study of politics as the war itself. From Wilson's

---

[69] It's hard to understate the extent to which Hitler wanted to refight the First World War. On the other end of the political spectrum, Marx fantasized about refighting the Napoleonic Wars (Sperber, 2013), hoping like Hitler to finally destroy Russia. Turns out these two countries had a long animus that spans the political spectrum.
[70] Quoted in Herwig (2014, p. 312).

association with national self-determination, as sincere as it was designed to compete with the violent anti-imperial rhetoric of the Bolsheviks, to the survival and expansion of the French, British, and Japanese Empires, all of which would collide anew in the Second World War, to the war-guilt clause and harsh reparations that fed resentments and susceptibility to conspiracy theories among a humiliated German populace, the interwar period is awash in the same kind of hindsight that often distorts our view of the world-historical calamity that preceded it. Indeed, while the war ended in Western and Central Europe, it spawned violence that continued around the globe, from the violent dissolutions of the Russian, Hapsburg, and Ottoman Empires to calls for independence from the subject peoples of Entente metropoles in Africa and Asia.[71] Winston Churchill might've been right to call the Allied victory at the Second Battle of El Alamein in 1942 "the end of the beginning" of the Second World War, but there's an equally compelling argument to be made that the Great War represented only the end of the beginning of the modern era, characterized by a truly global balance of power that wrestles to this day with the terms on which the First World War and the Second that it spawned were brought to an end.

[71] See, inter alia, Gerwarth and Manela (2015) and Gerwarth (2016).

15 Conclusion: History and the Present

Everyone's a critic
looking back up the river.
Every boat is leaking in this town.

Eddie Vedder,
"Getaway" by Pearl Jam

There's nothing small about the Great War. Even the narrow slice of the war's politics covered here makes that clear, but our approach also clarifies the value of thinking carefully, clearly, and in "real time" when we try to understand politics. If this book has shown us anything, it's that the easy explanation isn't always the best one, especially when we're trying to learn something about the politics of war and peace, alliances and international law, diplomacy and military strategy. But if you've made it this far, you've also seen how the tools of game theory can help us slice through the sprawling, baffling complexity of the most consequential conflict in modern history and gain some real insight into how international politics works. We started with a few simple premises about the international system, describing its units and its organizing principles and its means of change, then leveraged the state of the art in political science to show how something even as apparently sui generis as the First World War can be understood as a collection of specific examples of more general political phenomena. Game theory was valuable not just for the rigor it imposed on our conclusions but because it forced us to put ourselves as much as possible inside the heads of the characters in our story, from French and German socialists deciding whether to support the war to mercurial Kaisers and ambitious generals letting slip the dogs of war to bookish presidents convinced that they, and they alone, were capable of making a lasting peace. Only by shedding the lens of hindsight were we able to identify useful solutions to some enduring puzzles about the war, in the process revealing that the world of 1914–1918 isn't all that different from our own and that, faced with similar incentives, we might make the very same decisions that popular memory condemns for throwing the world into chaos a century ago. Eddie Vedder says it well in this chapter's epigraph: it's easy to be a critic, but the facile, self-serving explanations we often invoke for the politics of war can blind us to the same processes playing out in our own time and in our own heads.

15.1 CONTEMPORARY INTERNATIONAL RELATIONS

Our final task is to see what we can learn about the international politics of our own time from our study of the First World War. Had we studied the war in isolation, without the disciplining device of game theory and the body of knowledge generated by political science, we'd likely struggle with poorly drawn analogies if we weren't deterred at the outset from trying to relate one of history's biggest outliers to the everyday politics of the international system. But as we've seen, a simple assertion that any war, great or small, is too unique for us to learn from doesn't wash.[1] The First World War was the product of a densely, strategically interconnected international system whose basic features have remained fairly consistent ever since: legally anarchic, de facto hierarchical, populated by territorial states (some of which have empires, most of which don't), and dominated in many ways by politics among the great powers. In 1914, as now, the world can look back on a long period of great power peace, even if the names and locations and sizes of those great powers have changed. As of this writing, more than seven decades have passed since the end of the last world war, an interval that's led to no small amount of hopeful triumphalism about war's obsolescence and/or humanity's ability to overcome it. But the First World War followed a century of great power peace, so the mere fact that 1945 was a long time ago shouldn't on its own offer much comfort. Rather than look at prevailing peace and hope that it continues, the story of the Great War tells us to look elsewhere, to recent and potential changes in the balance of power that's kept the great powers at (something like) peace since 1945.

The Austro-Serbian War grew into the First World War because it threatened to unhinge the European balance of power, implicating

---

[1] There's a genuine risk in focusing too much on what Cullen Hendrix calls the "charismatic megafauna" of international relations, the big flashy wars that grab our attention – just like the biggest animals in the zoo – but from which we can find it difficult to generalize if we're not careful. We'll have to stay mindful of that risk in this chapter's discussion, though it's mitigated by our approach of using the war as an example of more general political phenomena rather than as a basis for generalization. For Hendrix's excellent note of caution, see http://politicalviolenceataglance.org/2017/11/21/charismatic-megafauna-in-conflict-studies-or-why-wwii-is-the-giant-panda-of-the-conflict-security-field/.

Russian ambitions in the Balkans and Germany's desire to stifle Russia's post-1905 growth. The pre-1914 balance of power weathered numerous Russo-Ottoman wars, German unification, Japan's victory over Russia, and Austrian expansion in the Balkans, but Russia's "Grand Programme" of rearmament presaged such a shift in power that Germany might've been permanently encircled, and Chapter 4 showed how the July Crisis activated the preventive motives that drove first Russia and then Germany to war. The balance of power fell apart in 1914 because power was shifting between rival great power coalitions, with one poised to overtake the other to an unacceptable degree, and we can use that same logic to make guesses about today's balance of power. Some states may rise, like Tsarist Russia before 1914, others may fall, like Soviet Russia in 1991, altering the balance of coalitions even if memberships remain the same. But the balance of power, which rests on shared expectations about who'll side with whom in a general war, can also be upset by the rise of new great powers, especially when their alignments in future general wars are in question, like the United States in the early twentieth century and India in the twenty-first. In the early twenty-first century, just like the early twentieth, a rough balance of power sustains peace between a coalition committed to the status quo and one, less well-organized, dissatisfied with the current international order. Today's status quo coalition, led by the United States,[2] includes Great Britain and France, fellow victors in the Second World War, as well as Germany and Japan, former enemies in the same conflict. And though the latter two aren't as heavily armed as their other partners, that could change virtually overnight – a fact not lost on their most likely regional rivals in Russia and China, the two putative leaders of an anti-status quo coalition. Should American commitments to its allies falter, prompting Germany or Japan to rearm, should Russia or China once again see a collapse of central authority, should the latter dramatically increase military spending, or should a new great power of uncertain alignment climb into the ranks, we might see cracks begin to show in the contemporary balance of power.

As great powers rise and fall in the coming decades, they'll face many of the same dilemmas that confronted the decision-makers of 1914–1918. How can a superpower reassure fearful third parties that its aims aren't too aggressive, and how can other states make those judgments? International law and institutions, as we saw in Chapter 6, can shape both processes, not because international law has teeth but because it helps coordinate expectations. How can belligerents limit the scope and severity of their

---

[2] Provided, of course, that nothing happens between this writing and publication, and after 2016, that's no safe bet.

conflicts, and why do they stop the fighting short of the winner disarming the loser? Chapters 10, 11, and 12 showed that beliefs about the consequences of expanded or "absolute" wars affect both processes, and that the issues at stake and even the geographical location of the battlefield can shape the duration and scope of wars. How can great powers deter attacks on their friends and allies? Chapters 5 and 13 showed that deterrence rests on both credible threats to fight *and* credible promises not to fight if the target of a deterrent threat complies. What does it take to win a reluctant partner's military cooperation? Chapter 7 shows that coalitions work best together when their members have selfish incentives to provide collective goods, and Chapter 9 shows that a partner's willingness to join in the first place depends on both the quality and the credibility of the terms on offer. Finally, how long will wars last, and how can they be brought to an end? Chapters 11, 12, and 14 show how fighting can solve the bargaining problems that lead to war, and Chapter 8 explains why states consciously choose strategies of attrition that save lives in any one battle but serve chiefly to lengthen the war and convince soldiers and civilians alike that the strategy is futile – even when attrition offers the best hope of winning the war.

15.2 THE GREAT WAR AND POLITICAL SCIENCE

We're able to make these judgments thanks to this book's unique approach to studying the First World War, which treats it not as a singular event but as the product of political forces and strategic problems that continue to characterize international politics. It's often tempting to assume that one's own era is unique, that the past offers little insight into contemporary problems.[3] But if nothing else, we've seen that politics is politics, whenever it happens and whoever's involved. The course in introductory game theory onto which this narrative of the war has been grafted makes that clear. We dealt in mathematical abstraction, in simple metaphors and thought experiments that were both directly applicable to the history of the First World War and, if you look closely, very general. The tensions between de jure anarchy and de facto hierarchy, military coalitions and treaties of alliance, coordination, collective action, and the challenges of credible communication worked much the same in 1914 as they do today. There's nothing historically contingent about the models we analyzed in

---

[3] To wit: when people turn about twenty-four, they declare the musical genres they love "dead," not because those styles *are* dead but because people assume that nothing happened before they started listening to music and that nothing will happen once they lack the energy to find something new. "Smells Like Teen Spirit" didn't kill hair metal, as much as most of us wish it had.

the preceding chapters, and that's part of their strength; by stripping the politics of a particular, if consequential, war down to the essentials, we're able to frame it in the context of the rich body of knowledge generated by the game-theoretic analysis of politics.

The history of the First World War defines our present in two ways. First, its legacy continues to define the international system in which we live. American economic and military primacy were birthed, if not entirely acknowledged, in the aftermath of the war. The European empires whose death touched off civil conflict in Africa and Asia from the 1940s and Eastern Europe from the 1990s began their terminal decline in 1917. The postwar carve-up of the Ottoman Empire gave us the Balfour Declaration and decades of Arab-Israeli enmity, and the war stripped imperial Russia of lands that it retook in the Second World War, lost again in 1990, and whose independence it's tried to compromise in the twenty-first century. And the idea of an international institution that codifies the balance of power, however ineffective the League of Nations might've been, has survived to the present in the form of the United Nations – its Security Council in particular, which recreates the logic of a great power concert that kept the peace in Europe for a century after Napoleon's final defeat.[4] Wilson's Fourteen Points, elucidated on the heels of the Bolsheviks' still more radical (if ironically less sincere) repudiation of the old balance of power, electrified global public opinion by popularizing ideas about national self-determination that even Wilson himself would've found too extreme.[5] Finally, the war's demands on the publics that fought it can be credited with defining both modern liberal democracy in the West, including the idea of the modern democratic peace, and Chinese and Indian nationalism – two forces bound to grow in the future and demand their own accommodation in the balance of power.

The Great War also remains part of our present because we continue to learn from it. It's inspired decades of political science research on the causes of war, the nature and effectiveness of alliances, the waste and dangers of arms races, the implications of changing military technology, and the effectiveness of international law. It's large enough in scope to offer an example for any argument, as well as a counterexample for every contrarian. But the plural of *anecdote* is not *data*.[6] In this book, we leveraged the collected wisdom of subsequent decades of political science research, which allows us to see the First World War more clearly, as the

---

[4] On the Security Council and its role in preserving the balance of power, see Voeten (2001, 2005) and Chapman (2011).

[5] The guy was, in the final accounting, pretty racist.

[6] I first heard this in Micheal Giles's first-year research design seminar at Emory University. The provenance of the quote isn't easy to run down, just like the quote about allies we attributed to Churchill in Chapter 7, but it still rings true.

product of strategic dilemmas and political processes that animated and continue to animate international relations. The Great War's legacy may be bloody, but its lessons are illuminating, if only we're willing to learn from them, and that requires thinking about the protagonists in this great historical drama not as objects of praise or condemnation but as people to be understood, rationalized, and explained. Especially as the international system of the early twenty-first century enters a period of flux, we can learn from how we handled – or failed to handle – similar problems roughly a century in the past. The First World War may not be the most comfortable or satisfying analogy to the present, but it may yet prove the most apt.

Bibliography

Abbenhuis, Maartje. 2014. *An Age of Neutrals: Great Power Politics, 1815–1914*. Cambridge: Cambridge University Press.

Abramson, Scott F. and David B. Carter. 2016. "The Historical Origins of Territorial Disputes." *American Political Science Review* 110(4):675–698.

Allen, Michael A. and Matthew DiGiuseppe. 2013. "Tightening the Belt: Sovereign Debt and Alliance Formation." *International Studies Quarterly* 57(4):647–659.

Altfeld, Michael D. and Bruce Bueno de Mesquita. 1979. "Choosing Sides in Wars." *International Studies Quarterly* 23(1):87–112.

Antonenko, Oksana. 2008. "A War with No Winners." *Survival* 50(5):23–36.

Arena, Philip. 2015. "Crisis Bargaining, Domestic Opposition, and Tragic Wars." *Journal of Theoretical Politics* 27(1):108–131.

Arena, Philip and Anna Pechenkina. 2016. "External Subsidies and Lasting Peace." *Journal of Conflict Resolution* 60(7):1278–1311.

Atkinson, Rick. 1993. *Crusade: The Untold Story of the Persian Gulf War*. New York, NY: Houghton Mifflin.

Axelrod, Robert. 1984. *The Evolution of Cooperation*. New York, NY: Basic Books.

Barthas, Louis. 2014. *Poilu: The World War I Notebooks of Corporal Louis Barthas, Barrelmaker 1914–1918*. New Haven, CT: Yale University Press.

Bennett, D. Scott and Allan C. Stam. 1996. "The Duration of Interstate Wars, 1816–1985." *American Political Science Review* 90(2):239–257.

1998. "The Declining Advantages of Democracy: A Combined Model of War Outcomes and Duration." *Journal of Conflict Resolution* 42(3):344–366.

2006. "Predicting the Length of the 2003 US-Iraq War." *Foreign Policy Analysis* 2(2):101–116.

Benson, Brett V. 2012. *Constructing International Security: Alliances, Deterrence, and Moral Hazard*. Cambridge, UK: Cambridge University Press.

Blainey, Geoffrey. 1988. *The Causes of War*. New York, NY: Free Press.

Bobroff, Ronald P. 2014. "War Accepted but Unsought: Russia's Growing Militancy and the July Crisis, 1914." In *The Outbreak of the First World War: Structure, Politics, and Decision-Making*, ed. Jack S. Levy and John A. Vasquez. Cambridge, UK: Cambridge University Press, pp. 227–251.

Boghardt, Thomas. 2012. *The Zimmermann Telegram: Intelligence, Diplomacy, and America's Entry into World War I*. Annapolis, MD: Naval Institute Press.

Braumoeller, Bear F. 2012. *The Great Powers and the International System: Systemic Theory in Empirical Perspective.* New York, NY: Cambridge University Press.

Bueno de Mesquita, Bruce, James D. Morrow, Randolph M. Siverson, and Alastair Smith. 1999. "An Institutional Explanation for the Democratic Peace." *American Political Science Review* 93(4):791–807.

Bueno de Mesquita, Bruce, Alastair Smith, Randolph M. Siverson, and James D. Morrow. 2003. *The Logic of Political Survival.* Cambridge, MA: MIT Press.

Bull, Hedley. 1977. *The Anarchical Society: A Study of Order in World Politics.* New York, NY: Columbia University Press.

Bush, George H. W. and Brent Scowcroft. 1998. *A World Transformed.* New York, NY: Knopf.

Buttar, Prit. 2014. *Collision of Empires: The War on the Eastern Front in 1914.* New York, NY: Osprey.

Carr, Edward Hallett. 1964. *The Twenty Years' Crisis: An Introduction to the Study of International Relations.* 2nd ed. New York, NY: Harper Torchbooks.

Carter, David B. and H. E. Goemans. 2011. "The Making of the Territorial Order: New Borders and the Emergence of Interstate Conflict." *International Organization* 65(2):275–309.

Carter, Jeff and Glenn Palmer. 2016. "Regime Type and Interstate War Finance." *Foreign Policy Analysis* 12(4):695–719.

Chapman, Terrence L. 2011. *Securing Approval: Domestic Politics and Multilateral Authorization for War.* Chicago, IL: University of Chicago Press.

Chapman, Terrence L. and Dan Reiter. 2004. "The United Nations Security Council and the Rally 'Round the Flag Effect." *Journal of Conflict Resolution* 48(6):886–909.

Chapman, Terrence L., Patrick J. McDonald, and Scott Moser. 2015. "The Domestic Politics of Strategic Retrenchment, Power Shifts, and Preventive War." *International Studies Quarterly* 59(1):133–144.

Chiba, Daina, Jesse C. Johnson, and Brett Ashley Leeds. 2015. "Careful Commitments: Democratic States and Alliance Design." *Journal of Politics* 77(4):968–982.

Chiozza, Giacomo and Hein E. Goemans. 2003. "Peace through Insecurity: Tenure and International Conflict." *Journal of Conflict Resolution* 47(4):443–467.

2004. "International Conflict and the Tenure of Leaders: Is War Still *Ex Post* Inefficient?" *American Journal of Political Science* 48(3):604–619.

2011. *Leaders and International Conflict.* Cambridge, MA: Cambridge University Press.

Cho, In-Koo and David M. Kreps. 1987. "Signaling Games and Stable Equilibria." *Quarterly Journal of Economics* 102(2):179–221.

Christensen, Thomas J. and Jack Snyder. 1990. "Chain Gangs and Passed Bucks: Predicting Alliance Patterns in Multipolarity." *International Organization* 44(2):137–138.

Clark, Christopher. 2012. *The Sleepwalkers: How Europe Went to War in 1914.* New York, NY: HarperCollins.

Clark, Wesley K. 2001. *Waging Modern War.* New York, NY: PublicAffairs.

Clarke, Kevin A. and David M. Primo. 2012. *A Model Discipline: Political Science and the Logic of Representations*. New York, NY: Oxford University Press.

Clausewitz, Carl von. 1976. *On War*, ed. and trans. Peter Paret. Princeton, NJ: Princeton University Press.

Coe, Andrew J. and Jane Vaynman. 2015. "Collusion and the Nuclear Nonproliferation Regime." *Journal of Politics* 77(4):983–997.

Coggins, Bridget. 2011. "Friends in High Places: International Politics and the Emergence of States from Secessionism." *International Organization* 65(3):433–467.

Cohen, Dara Kay. 2013. "Explaining Rape during Civil War: Cross-National Evidence (1980–2009)." *American Political Science Review* 107(3):461–477.

Colaresi, Michael. 2004. "When Doves Cry: International Rivalry, Unreciprocated Cooperation, and Leadership Turnover." *American Journal of Political Science* 48(3):555–570.

2005. *Scare Tactics: The Politics of International Rivalry*. Syracuse, NY: Syracuse University Press.

Colaresi, Michael, Karen Rasler, and William R. Thompson. 2007. *Strategic Rivalries in World Politics: Position, Space, and Conflict Escalation*. New York, NY: Cambridge University Press.

Connaughton, Richard. 2003. *Rising Sun and Tumbling Bear: Russia's War with Japan*. London, UK: Cassell.

Conrad, Courtenay R. and Emily Hencken Ritter. 2013. "Treaties, Tenure, and Torture: The Conflicting Domestic Effects of International Law." *Journal of Politics* 75(2):397–409.

Copeland, Dale C. 2014. "International Relations Theory and the Three Great Puzzles of the First World War." In *The Outbreak of the First World War: Structure, Politics, and Decision-Making*, ed. Jack S. Levy and John A. Vasquez. Cambridge, UK: Cambridge University Press, pp. 167–198.

Croco, Sarah E. 2005. "The Decider's Dilemma: Leader Culpability, War Outcomes, and Domestic Punishment." *American Political Science Review* 3:457–477.

Cunningham, David E. and Douglas Lemke. 2013. "Combining Civil and Interstate Wars." *International Organization* 67(3):609–627.

Danneman, Nathan and Emily Hencken Ritter. 2014. "Contagious Rebellion and Preemptive Repression." *Journal of Conflict Resolution* 58(2):254–279.

Davenport, Christian. 2007. *State Repression and the Domestic Democratic Peace*. Cambridge, UK: Cambridge University Press.

Davies, Graeme A. M. and Robert Johns. 2016. "The Domestic Consequences of International Overcooperation: An Experimental Study of Microfoundations." *Conflict Management and Peace Science* 33(4):343–360.

Debs, Alexandre and H. E. Goemans. 2010. "Regime Type, the Fate of Leaders, and War." *American Political Science Review* 104(3):430–445.

Dennett, Daniel C. 1991. *Consciousness Explained*. New York, NY: Little, Brown.

Diehl, Paul F. and Gary Goertz. 2000. *War and Peace in International Rivalry*. Ann Arbor, MI: University of Michigan Press.

DiGiuseppe, Matthew. 2015. "The Fiscal Autonomy of Deciders: Creditworthiness and Conflict Initiation." *Foreign Policy Analysis* 11(3):317–338.

Dixon, William J. 1993. "Democracy and the Management of International Conflict." *Journal of Conflict Resolution* 37(1):42–68.

Downs, George W. and David M. Rocke. 1994. "Conflict, Agency, and Gambling for Resurrection: The Principal-Agent Problem Goes to War." *American Journal of Political Science* 38(2):362–380.

Doyle, Michael W. 1986. "Liberalism and World Politics." *American Political Science Review* 80(4):1151–1169.

Drezner, Daniel W. 2014. *The System Worked: How the World Stopped Another Great Depression*. New York, NY: Oxford University Press.

Easton, David. 1985. "Political Science in the United States: Past and Present." *International Political Science Review* 6(1):133–152.

Evans, Richard J. 2016. *The Pursuit of Power: Europe 1815–1914*. New York, NY: Viking.

Farrar, Lancelot L. 1973. *The Short-War Illusion: German Policy, Strategy and Domestic Affairs, August–December 1914*. Santa Barbara, CA: ABC-Clio.

Fazal, Tanisha M. 2007. *State Death: The Politics and Geography of Conquest, Annexation, and Occupation*. Princeton, NJ: Princeton University Press.

2012. "Why States No Longer Declare War." *Security Studies* 21(4):557–593.

2013. "The Demise of Peace Treaties in Interstate War." *International Organization* 67(4):695–724.

Fearon, James D. 1994. "Domestic Political Audiences and the Escalation of International Disputes." *American Political Science Review* 88(3):577–592.

1995. "Rationalist Explanations for War." *International Organization* 49(3):379–414.

1997. "Signaling Foreign Policy Interests: Tying Hands versus Sinking Costs." *Journal of Conflict Resolution* 41(1):68–90.

2002. "Selection Effects and Deterrence." *International Interactions* 28(1):5–29.

2004. "Why Do Some Civil Wars Last So Much Longer Than Others?" *Journal of Peace Research* 41(3):275–301.

Ferguson, Niall. 1999. *The Pity of War: Explaining World War I*. New York, NY: Basic Books.

Filson, Darren and Suzanne Werner. 2002. "A Bargaining Model of War and Peace: Anticipating the Onset, Duration, and Outcome of War." *American Journal of Political Science* 46(2):819–837.

2004. "Bargaining and Fighting: The Impact of Regime Type on War Onset, Duration, and Outcomes." *American Journal of Political Science* 48(2):296–313.

Fischer, Fritz. 1967. *Germany's Ams in the First World War*. New York, NY: W. W. Norton.

Fordham, Benjamin O. 2011. "Who Wants to be a Major Power?" *Journal of Peace Research* 48(5):587–603.

Fortna, Virginia Page. 2003. "Scraps of Paper? Agreements and the Durability of Peace." *International Organization* 57(2):337–372.

Frank, Richard B. 2001. *Downfall: The End of the Imperial Japanese Empire*. New York, NY: Penguin.

Freedman, Lawrence. 2005. *The Official History of the Falklands Campaign, Volume II: War and Diplomacy*. London, UK: Routledge.

Freedman, Lawrence and Efraim Karsh. 1991. "How Kuwait Was Won: Strategy in the Gulf War." *International Security* 16(2):5–41.

Fromkin, David. 2004. *Europe's Last Summer: Who Started the Great War in 1914?* New York, NY: Vintage.

Frum, David. 2015. "Requiem for American Exceptionalism." Available at www.theatlantic.com/politics/archive/2015/03/requiem-for-american-exceptionalism/388381/.

Fudenberg, Drew and Jean Tirole. 1991. *Game Theory*. Cambridge, MA: MIT Press.

Fuhrmann, Matthew and Yonatan Lupu. 2016. "Do Arms Control Treaties Work? Assessing the Effectivenes of the Nuclear Nonproliferation Treaty." *International Studies Quarterly* 60(3):530–539.

Fuhrmann, Matthew and Todd S. Sechser. 2014. "Signaling Alliance Commitments: Hand-Tying and Sunk Costs in Extended Nuclear Deterrence." *American Journal of Political Science* 58(4):919–935.

Gaddis, John Lewis. 1986. "The Long Peace: Elements of Stability in the Postwar International System." *International Security* 10(4):99–142.

Gamson, William A. 1961. "A Theory of Coalition Formation." *American Sociological Review* 26(3):373–382.

Gartner, Scott Sigmund. 1997. *Strategic Assessment in War*. New Haven, CT: Yale University Press.

Gartner, Scott Sigmund and Randolph M. Siverson. 1996. "War Expanson and War Outcome." *Journal of Conflict Resolution* 40(1):4–15.

Gartzke, Erik and Yonatan Lupu. 2012. "Trading on Preconceptions: Why World War I Was Not a Failure of Economic Interdependence." *International Security* 36(4):115–150.

George, Alexander L. and Richard Smoke. 1974. *Deterrence in American Foreign Policy: Theory and Practice*. New York, NY: Columbia University Press.

Gerwarth, Robert. 2016. *The Vanquished: Why the First World War Failed to End*. New York, NY: Farrar, Straus, and Giroux.

Gerwarth, Robert and Erez Manela, eds. 2015. *Empires at War: 1911–1923*. New York, NY: Oxford University Press.

Ghobarah, Hazem Adam, Paul Huth, and Bruce Russett. 2003. "Civil Wars Kill and Maim People – Long after the Shooting Stops." *American Political Science Review* 97(2):189–202.

Gibler, Douglas M. 2008. "The Costs of Reneging: Reputation and Alliance Formation." *Journal of Conflict Resolution* 52(3):426–454.
2012. *The Territorial Peace: Borders, State Development, and International Conflict*. Cambridge, UK: Cambridge University Press.

Gibler, Douglas M. and Scott Wolford. 2006. "Alliances, Then Democracy: An Examination of the Relationship between Regime Type and Alliance Formation." *Journal of Conflict Resolution* 50(1):129–153.

Gibler, Douglas M., Toby J. Rider, and Marc L. Hutchison. 2005. "Taking Arms against a Sea of Troubles: Conventional Arms Races during Periods of Rivalry." *Journal of Peace Research* 42(2):131–147.

Gilderhus, Mark T. 1977. *Diplomacy and Revolution: US–Mexican Relations under Wilson and Carranza*. Tucson, AZ: University of Arizona Press.

Gilpin, Robert. 1981. *War and Change in World Politics*. New York, NY: Cambridge University Press.

Gleditsch, Kristian Skrede. 2002. *All International Politics Is Local: The Diffusion of Conflict, Integration, and Democratization*. Ann Arbor, MI: University of Michigan Press.

Gleditsch, Kristian Skrede, Idean Salehyan, and Kenneth A. Schultz. 2008. "Fighting at Home, Fighting Abroad: How Civil Wars Lead to International Disputes." *Journal of Conflict Resolution* 52(4):479–506.

Glenny, Misha. 2012. *The Balkans: Nationalism, War, and the Great Powers 1804–2011*. New York, NY: Penguin.

Goemans, H. E. 2000. *War and Punishment: The Causes of War Termination and the First World War*. Princeton, NJ: Princeton University Press.

2008. "Which Way Out? The Manner and Consequences of Losing Office." *Journal of Conflict Resolution* 53(6):771–794.

Goertz, Gary and Paul F. Diehl. 1993. "Enduring Rivalries: Theoretical Constructs and Empirical Patterns." *International Studies Quarterly* 37(2):147–171.

Goldman, Stuart D. 2013. *Nomonhan, 1939: The Red Army's Victory That Shaped World War II*. Annapolis, MD: Naval Institute Press.

Grayzel, Susan R. 2013. *The First World War: A Brief History with Documents*. Boston, MA: Bedford/St. Martin's.

Gulick, Edward Vose. 1967. *Europe's Classical Balance of Power*. New York, NY: W. W. Norton.

Hall, Richard C. 2000. *The Balkan Wars, 1912–1913: Preude to the First World War*. London, UK: Routledge.

Hamilton, Richard F. and Holger H. Herwig. 2004. *Decisions for War, 1914–1917*. New York, NY: Cambridge University Press.

Hardin, Russell. 1982. *Collective Action*. Baltimore, MD: RFF Press.

Harrison, Mark. 2016. "Myths of the Great War." In *Economic History of Warfare and State Formation*, ed. Jari Eloranta, Eric Golson, Andrei Markevich, and Nikolaus Wolf. New York, NY: Springer, pp. 135–158.

Harsanyi, John C. 1967. "Games with Incomplete Information Played by Bayesian Players, I." *Management Science* 14(3):159–183.

Hastings, Max. 2010. *Winston's War: Churchill, 1940–1945*. New York, NY: Knopf.

2012. *Inferno: The World at War, 1939–1945*. New York, NY: Vintage.

2013. *Catastrophe 1914: Europe Goes to War*. New York, NY: Knopf.

Healy, Kieran. 2017. "Fuck Nuance." *Sociological Theory* 35(2):118–127.

Herwig, Holger H. 1990. "Disjointed Allies: Coalition Warfare in Berlin and Vienna, 1914." *Journal of Military History* 54(3):265–280.

2014. *The First World War: Germany and Austria-Hungary 1914–1918*. 2nd ed. New York, NY: Bloomsbury Academic.

Hindenburg, Paul von. 1921. *Out of My Life*. Vol. 2. New York, NY: Harper.

Horne, Charles F., ed. 1923. *Source Records of the Great War*. Vol. 4. New York, NY: National Alumni.

Horowitz, Michael C., Allan C. Stam, and Cali M. Ellis. 2015. *Why Leaders Fight*. New York, NY: Cambridge University Press.

Hotta, Eri. 2014. *Japan 1941: Countdown to Infamy*. New York, NY: Vintage.

Hughes, Daniel, ed. 1995. *Moltke on the Art of War: Selected Writings*. New York, NY: Presidio Press.

Hull, Isabel V. 2014. *A Scrap of Paper: Breaking and Making International Law during the Great War*. Ithaca, NY: Cornell University Press.

Huth, Paul K. 1988. *Extended Deterrence and the Prevention of War*. New Haven, CT: Yale University Press.

1997. "Reputations and Deterrence." *Security Studies* 7(1):72–99.

Iqbal, Zaryab and Christopher Zorn. 2010. "Violent Conflict and the Spread of HIV/AIDS in Africa." *Journal of Politics* 72(1):149–162.

Jeffery, Keith. 2016. *1916: A Global History*. New York, NY: Bloomsbury USA.

Jervis, Robert. 1970. *The Logic of Images in International Relations*. Princeton, NJ: Princeton University Press.

1978. "Cooperation under the Security Dilemma." *World Politics* 30(2): 167–214.

1997. *System Effects: Complexity in Political and Social Life*. Princeton, NJ: Princeton University Press.

Johnson, Jesse C. 2015. "The Cost of Security: Foreign Policy Concessions and Military Alliances." *Journal of Peace Research* 52(5):665–679.

Jones, Howard. 2010. *Blue and Gray Diplomacy: A History of Union and Confederate Foreign Relations*. Chapel Hill, NC: University of North Carolina Press.

Kadera, Kelly M., Mark J. C. Crescenzi, and Megan L. Shannon. 2003. "Democratic Survival, Peace, and War in the International System." *American Journal of Political Science* 47(2):234–247.

Kang, David C. 2010. *East Asia before the West: Five Centuries of Trade and Tribute*. New York, NY: Columbia University Press.

Keegan, John. 2000. *The First World War*. New York, NY: Vintage.

2005. *The Iraq War*. New York, NY: Vintage.

Kennan, George F. 1984. *American Diplomacy*. Expanded edition. Chicago, IL: University of Chicago Press.

Kennedy, Paul. 1980. *The Rise of Anglo-German Antagonism, 1860–1914*. London, UK: George Allen and Unwin.

Keohane, Robert O. 1984. *After Hegemony: Cooperation and Discord in the World Political Economy*. Princeton, NJ: Princeton University Press.

Keohane, Robert O. and Joseph S. Nye. 1977. *Power and Interdependence*. Boston, MA: Little, Brown.

Kershaw, Ian. 2012. *The End: The Defiance and Destruction of Hitler's Germany, 1944–1945*. New York, NY: Penguin.

2015. *To Hell and Back: Europe, 1914–1949*. New York, NY: Viking.

Kertzer, Joshua D. 2016. *Resolve in International Politics*. Princeton, NJ: Princeton University Press.

Knock, Thomas J. 1995. *To End All Wars: Woodrow Wilson and the Quest for a New World Order*. Princeton, NJ: Princeton University Press.

Kreps, David M. 1990. *A Course in Microeconomic Theory*. Princeton, NJ: Princeton University Press.

Kreps, Sarah E. 2011. *Coalitions of Convenience: United States Military Interventions after the Cold War*. New York, NY: Oxford University Press.

Kunz, Diane B. 1991. *The Economic Diplomacy of the Suez Crisis*. Chapel Hill, NC: University of North Carolina Press.

Kydd, Andrew H. 2000. "Arms Races and Arms Control: Modeling the Hawk Perspective." *American Journal of Political Science* 44(2):228–244.

2005. *Trust and Mistrust in International Relations*. Princeton, NJ: Princeton University Press.

Kydd, Andrew H. and Roseanne W. McManus. 2017. "Threats and Assurances in Crisis Bargaining." *Journal of Conflict Resolution* 61(2):325–348.

Lai, Brian and Clayton Thyne. 2007. "The Effect of Civil War on Education, 1980–97." *Journal of Peace Research* 44(3):277–292.

Lake, David A. 2009. *Hierarchy in International Relations*. Ithaca, NY: Cornell University Press.

Langlois, Catherine C. and Jean-Pierre P. Langlois. 2009. "Does Attrition Behavior Help Explain the Duration of Interstate Wars? A Game Theoretic and Empirical Analysis." *International Studies Quarterly* 53(4):1051–1073.

Lawrence, Mark Atwood. 2010. *The Vietnam War: A Concise International History*. New York, NY: Oxford University Press.

Leeds, Brett Ashley. 1999. "Domestic Political Institutions, Credible Commitments, and International Institutions." *American Journal of Political Science* 43(4):979–1002.

2003a. "Alliance Reliability in Times of War: Explaining State Decisions to Violate Treaties." *International Organization* 57(4):801–827.

2003b. "Do Alliances Deter Aggression? The Influence of Military Alliances on the Initiation of Militarized Interstate Disputes." *American Journal of Political Science* 47(3):427–439.

Leeds, Brett Ashley and Burcu Savun. 2007. "Terminating Alliances: Why Do States Abrogate Agreements?" *Journal of Politics* 69(4):1118–1132.

Leeds, Brett Ashley, Andrew G. Long, and Sara McLaughlin Mitchell. 2000. "Reevaluating Alliance Reliability: Specific Threats, Specific Promises." *Journal of Conflict Resolution* 44(5):686–699.

Leeds, Brett Ashley, Michaela Mattes, and Jeremy S. Vogel. 2009. "Interests, Institutions, and the Reliability of International Commitments." *American Journal of Political Science* 53(2):461–476.

Lemke, Douglas. 2002. *Regions of War and Peace*. Cambridge, MA: Cambridge University Press.

Leonhard, Jörn. 2018. *Pandora's Box: A History of the First World War*, trans. by Patrick Camiller. Cambridge, MA: The Belknap Press of Harvard University Press.

Leventoglu, Bahar and Branislav Slantchev. 2007. "The Armed Peace: A Punctuated Equilibrium Theory of War." *American Journal of Political Science* 51(4):755–771.

Levy, Jack S. 1988. "Domestic Politics and War." *Journal of Interdisciplinary History* 18(4):653–673.

1990–1991. "Preferences, Constraints, and Choices in July 1914." *International Security* 15(3):151–186.

2014. "The Sources of Preventive Logic in German Decision-Making in 1914." In *The Outbreak of the First World War: Structure, Politics, and Decision-*

Making, ed. Jack S. Levy and John A. Vasquez. Cambridge, UK: Cambridge University Press, pp. 139–166.

2015. "Correspondence: Everyone's Favored Year for War – or Not?" *International Security* 39(4):208–217.

Levy, Jack S. and William Mulligan. 2017. "Shifting Power, Preventive Logic, and the Response of the Target: Germany, Russia, and the First World War." *Journal of Strategic Studies* 40(5):731–769.

Lieber, Kier A. 2000. "Grasping the Technological Peace: The Offense-Defense Balance and International Security." *International Security* 25(1):71–104.

2007. "The New History of World War I and What It Means for International Relations Theory." *International Security* 32(2):155–191.

Lo, Nigel, Barry Hashimoto, and Dan Reiter. 2008. "Ensuring Peace: Foreign-Imposed Regime Change and Postwar Peace Duration, 1914–2001." *International Organization* 62(4):717–736.

Long, Andrew G. and Brett Ashley Leeds. 2006. "Trading for Security: Military Alliances and Economic Agreements." *Journal of Peace Research* 43(4):433–451.

Manela, Erez. 2009. *The Wilsonian Moment: Self-Determination and the Origins of Anticolonial Nationalism*. Oxford, UK: Oxford University Press.

Maoz, Zeev and Bruce M. Russett. 1993. "Normative and Structural Causes of the Democratic Peace." *American Political Science Review* 87(3):624–638.

Mattes, Michaela. 2012. "Democratic Reliabiity, Precommitment of Successor Governments, and the Choice of Alliance Commitment." *International Organization* 66(1):153–172.

May, Ernest R. 2000. *Strange Victory: Hitler's Conquest of France*. New York, NY: Hill and Wang.

McCarty, Nolan and Adam Meirowitz. 2007. *Political Game Theory: An Introduction*. New York, NY: Cambridge University Press.

McDonald, Patrick J. 2004. "Peace through Trade or Free Trade?" *Journal of Conflict Resolution* 48(4):547–572.

2009. *The Invisible Hand of Peace: Capitalism, the War Machine, and International Relations Theory*. New York, NY: Cambridge University Press.

2015. "Great Powers, Hierarchy, and Endogenous Regimes: Rethinking the Domestic Causes of Peace." *International Organization* 69(3):557–588.

McGillivray, Fiona and Alastair Smith. 2008. *Punishing the Prince: A Theory of Interstate Relations, Political Institutions, and Leader Change*. Princeton, NJ: Princeton University Press.

McMeekin, Sean. 2013. *July 1914: Countdown to War*. New York, NY: Basic Books.

2015. *The Ottoman Endgame: War, Revolution, and the Making of the Modern Middle East, 1908–1923*. New York, NY: Penguin.

McMillan, Margaret. 2014. *The War that Ended Peace: How Europe Abandoned Peace for the First World War*. London, UK: Profile Books.

McMurry, Frank M. 1919. *The Geography of the Great War*. New York, NY: Macmillan.

Mearsheimer, John J. 1983. *Conventional Deterrence*. Ithaca, NY: Cornell University Press.

1994–1995. "The False Promise of International Institutions." *International Security* 19(3):5–49.

2001. *The Tragedy of Great Power Politics*. New York, NY: W. W. Norton.

Meirowitz, Adam and Anne E. Sartori. 2008. "Strategic Uncertainty as a Cause of War." *Quarterly Journal of Political Science* 3(4):327–352.

Meyer, G. J. 1916. *The World Remade: America in World War I*. New York, NY: Bantam.

Miller, Gina Lei and Emily Hencken Ritter. 2014. "Emigrants and the Onset of Civil War." *Journal of Peace Research* 51(1):51–64.

Mitchell, David, Robert Webb, James Bachman, Mark Evans, and Toby Davies, writers. 2006. "That Mitchell and Webb Look." *That Mitchell and Webb Look*, season 1, episode 6. BBC Two. October 19.

Mitchell, Sara McLaughlin. 2002. "A Kantian System? Democracy and Third-Party Conflict Resolution." *American Journal of Political Science* 46(4): 749–759.

Mombauer, Annika. 2001. *Helmuth von Moltke and the Origins of the First World War*. Cambridge, UK: Cambridge University Press.

2013. *The Origins of the First World War: Diplomatic and Military Documents*. New York, NY: Manchester University Press.

Morey, Daniel S. 2016. "Military Coalitions and the Outcome of Interstate Wars." *Foreign Policy Analysis* 12(4):533–551.

Morgenthau, Hans Joachim. 1967. *Politics among Nations*. 4th ed. New York, NY: Knopf.

Morrow, James D. 1989. "A Twist of Truth: A Reexamination of the Effects of Arms Races on the Occurrence of War." *Journal of Conflict Resolution* 33(3):500–529.

1991. "Alliances and Asymmetry: An Alternative to the Capability Aggregation Model of Alliances." *American Journal of Political Science* 35(4):904–933.

1994. *Game Theory for Political Scientists*. Princeton, NJ: Princeton University Press.

2000. "Alliances: Why Write Them Down?" *Annual Review of Political Science* 3:63–83.

2014. *Order within Anarchy: The Laws of War as an International Institution*. New York, NY: Cambridge University Press.

Mulligan, William. 2014. "Restraints on Preventive War before 1914." In *The Outbreak of the First World War: Structure, Politics, and Decision-Making*, ed. Jack S. Levy and John A. Vasquez. Cambridge, UK: Cambridge University Press, pp. 115–138.

Myerson, Roger B. 1991. *Game Theory: Analysis of Conflict*. Cambridge, MA: Harvard University Press.

Nalebuff, Barry. 1991. "Rational Deterrence in an Imperfect World." *World Politics* 43(3):315–335.

Nash, John. 1950. "Equilibrium Points in *n*-Person Games." *Proceedings of the National Academy of Sciences* 36(1):48–49.

1951. "Non-cooperative Games." *The Annals of Mathematics* 54(2):286–295.

Neiberg, Michael S. 2016. *The Path to War: How the First World War Created Modern America*. New York, NY: Oxford University Press.

2017. *The Treaty of Versailles: A Concise History*. New York, NY: Oxford University Press.

Oatley, Thomas. 2015. *A Political Economy of American Hegemony: Buildups, Booms, and Busts*. New York, NY: Cambridge University Press.

Olson, Mancur. 1965. *The Logic of Collective Action: Public Goods and the Theory of Groups*. Cambridge, MA: Harvard University Press.

Olson, Mancur and Richard Zeckhauser. 1966. "An Economic Theory of Alliances." *Review of Economics and Statistics* 48(3):266–279.

Organski, A. F. K. and Jacek Kugler. 1980. *The War Ledger*. Chicago, IL: University of Chicago Press.

Orwell, George. 1953. *Such, Such Were the Joys*. New York, NY: Harcourt, Brace.

Ostrom, Elinor. 2015. *Governing the Commons: The Evolution of Institutions for Collective Action*. Canto classics ed. Cambridge, UK: Cambridge University Press.

Otte, T. G. 2014. "A 'Formidable Factor in European Politics': Views of Russia in 1914." In *The Outbreak of the First World War: Structure, Politics, and Decision-Making*, ed. Jack S. Levy and John A. Vasquez. Cambridge, UK: Cambridge University Press, pp. 87–113.

Owsiak, Andrew P. and Toby J. Rider. 2013. "Clearing the Hurdle: Border Settlement and Rivalry Termination." *Journal of Politics* 75(3):757–772.

Paine, S. C. M. 2003. *The Sino-Japanese War of 1894–1895: Perceptions, Power, and Primacy*. Cambridge, UK: Cambridge University Press.

2012. *The Wars for Asia, 1911–1949*. New York, NY: Cambridge University Press.

2017. *The Japanese Empire: Grand Strategy from the Meiji Restoration to the Pacific War*. Cambridge, UK: Cambridge University Press.

Palmer, Glenn, Vito D'Orazio, Michael Kenwick, and Matthew Lane. 2015. "The MID4 Dataset, 2002–2010: Procedures, Coding Rules and Description." *Conflict Management and Peace Science* 32(2):222–242.

Papayoanou, Paul A. 1997. "Intra-alliance Bargaining and US Bosnia Policy." *Journal of Conflict Resolution* 41(1):91–116.

Partem, Michael Greenfield. 1983. "The Buffer System in International Relations." *Journal of Conflict Resolution* 27(1):3–26.

Payne, Stanley G. 2011. *Civil War in Europe, 1905–1949*. New York, NY: Cambridge University Press.

Phillips, Julianne and Scott Wolford. N.d. "Intra-coalition Bargains and the Duration of Peace." Typescript, University of Texas at Austin.

Philpott, William. 1995. "Britain and France Go to War: Anglo-French Relations on the Western Front 1914–1918." *War in History* 2(1):43–64.

1996. *Anglo-French Relations and Strategy on the Western Front, 1914–1918*. London, UK: Palgrave Macmillan.

2009. *Three Armies on the Somme: The First Battle of the Twentieth Century*. New York, NY: Vintage.

2014. *War of Attrition: Fighting the First World War*. New York, NY: The Overlook Press.

Platt, Stephen R. 2012. *Autumn in the Heavenly Kingdom: China, The West, and the Epic Story of the Taiping Civil War*. New York, NY: Penguin Random House.

Plokhy, S. M. 2010. *Yalta: The Price of Peace*. New York, NY: Penguin.
  2014. *The Last Empire: The Final Days of the Soviet Union*. New York, NY: Basic Books.
Plümper, Thomas and Eric Neumayer. 2006. "The Unequal Burden of War: The Effect of Armed Conflict on the Gender Gap in Life Expectancy." *International Organization* 60(3):723–754.
Poast, Paul. 2012. "Does Issue Linkage Work? Evidence from European Alliance Negotiations, 1860 to 1945." *International Organization* 66(2):277–310.
  2015. "Central Banks at War." *International Organization* 69(1):63–95.
Powell, Robert. 1999. *In the Shadow of Power*. Princeton, NJ: Princeton University Press.
  2003. "Nuclear Deterrence Theory, Nuclear Proliferation, and National Missile Defense." *International Security* 27(4):86–118.
  2004a. "Bargaining and Learning While Fighting." *American Journal of Political Science* 48(2):344–361.
  2004b. "The Inefficient Use of Power: Costly Conflict with Complete Information." *American Political Science Review* 98(2):231–241.
  2006. "War as a Commitment Problem." *International Organization* 60(1):169–203.
  2012. "Persistent Fighting and Shifting Power." *American Journal of Political Science* 56(3):620–637.
Pressman, Jeremy. 2008. *Warring Friends: Alliance Restraint in International Politics*. Ithaca, NY: Cornell University Press.
Prost, Antoine. 2014. "The Dead." In *The Cambridge History of the First World War*, ed. Jay Winter. Vol. 3. Cambridge, UK: Cambridge University Press, pp. 561–591.
Ramsay, Kristopher W. 2008. "Settling in on the Field: Battlefield Events and War Termination." *Journal of Conflict Resolution* 52(6):850–879.
Rasler, Karen and William R. Thompson. 2014. "Strategic Rivalries and Complex Causality in 1914." In *The Outbreak of the First World War: Structure, Politics, and Decision-Making*, ed. Jack S. Levy and John A. Vasquez. Cambridge, UK: Cambridge University Press, pp. 65–86.
Razoux, Pierre. 2015. *The Iran-Iraq War*. Cambridge, MA: The Belknap Press of Harvard University Press.
Reed, William, David H. Clark, Timothy Nordstrom, and Wonjae Hwang. 2008. "War, Power, and Bargaining." *Journal of Politics* 70(4):1203–1216.
Reinhardt, Eric. 2001. "Adjudication without Enforcement in GATT Disputes." *Journal of Conflict Resolution* 45(2):174–195.
Reiter, Dan. 2001. "Why NATO Enlargement Does Not Spread Democracy." *International Security* 25(4):41–67.
  2009. *How Wars End*. Princeton, NJ: Princeton University Press.
Reiter, Dan and Allan C. Stam. 2002. *Democracies at War*. Princeton, NJ: Princeton University Press.
Renshon, Jonathan. 2017. *Fighting for Status: Hierarchy and Conflict in World Politics*. Princeton, NJ: Princeton University Press.
Reynolds, Francis J., Allen L. Churchill, and Francis Trevelyan Miller, eds. 1916. *The Story of the Great War: History of the European War from Official Sources*. 8 vols. New York, NY: P. F. Collier.

Ricks, Thomas E. 2006. *Fiasco: The American Military Adventure in Iraq.* New York, NY: Penguin.

Rider, Toby J. 2009. "Understanding Arms Race Onset: Rivalry, Threat, and Territorial Competition." *Journal of Politics* 71(2):693–703.

2013. "Uncertainty, Salient Stakes, and the Causes of Conventional Arms Races." *International Studies Quarterly* 57(3):580–591.

Rider, Toby J. and Andrew P. Owsiak. 2015. "Border Settlement, Commitment Problems, and the Causes of Contiguous Rivalry." *Journal of Peace Research* 52(4):508–521.

Rider, Toby J., Michael G. Findley, and Paul F. Diehl. 2011. "Just Part of the Game? Arms Races, Rivalry, and War." *Journal of Peace Research* 48(1):85–100.

Riker, William H. 1962. *The Theory of Political Coalitions.* New Haven, CT: Yale University Press.

Ritter, Emily Hencken. 2014. "Policy Disputes, Political Survival, and the Onset and Severity of State Repression." *Journal of Conflict Resolution* 58(2):254–279.

Rosecrance, Richard N. 2002. "War and Peace." *World Politics* 55(1):137–166.

Russell, Bertrand. 1996. *Power.* London, UK: Routledge Classics.

Russett, Bruce M. 1963. "The Calculus of Deterrence." *Journal of Conflict Resolution* 7(2):97–109.

Russett, Bruce M. and John Oneal. 2001. *Triangulating Peace.* New York, NY: W. W. Norton.

Saideman, Stephen M. and David P. Auerswald. 2014. *NATO in Afghanistan: Fighting Together, Fighting Alone.* Princeton, NJ: Princeton University Press.

Sandos, James A. 1981. "Pancho Villa and American Security: Woodrow Wilson's Mexican Diplomacy Reconsidered." *Journal of Latin American Studies* 13(2):293–311.

Sarkees, Meredith Reid and Frank Wayman. 2010. *Resort to War: 1816–2007.* Washington, DC: CQ Press.

Sarotte, Mary Elise. 2009. *1989: The Struggle to Create Post–Cold War Europe.* Princeton, NJ: Princeton University Press.

Saunders, Elizabeth N. 2011. *Leaders at War: How Presidents Shape Military Interventions.* Ithaca, NY: Cornell University Press.

Saunders, Elizabeth N. and Scott Wolford. N.d. "Elites, Voters, and Democracies at War." Typescript, Georgetown University and University of Texas at Austin.

Schelling, Thomas C. 1960. *The Strategy of Conflict.* Cambridge, MA: Harvard University Press.

1966. *Arms and Influence.* New Haven, CT: Yale University Press.

1978. *Micromotives and Macrobehavior.* New York, NY: W. W. Norton.

Schroeder, Paul W. 1989. "The Nineteenth Century System: Balance of Power or Political Equilribium?" *Review of International Studies* 15(2):135–153.

Schultz, Kenneth A. 1998. "Domestic Opposition and Signaling in International Crises." *American Political Science Review* 92(4):829–844.

2010. "The Enforcement Problem in Coercive Bargaining: Interstate Conflict over Rebel Support in Civil Wars." *International Organization* 64(2): 281–312.

Schultz, Kenneth A. and Barry R. Weingast. 2003. "The Democratic Advantage: Institutional Foundations of Financial Power and International Competition." *International Organization* 57(1):3–42.

Sechser, Todd S. and Matthew Fuhrmann. 2013. "Crisis Bargaining and Nuclear Blackmail." *International Organization* 67(1):173–195.

2017. *Nuclear Weapons and Coercive Diplomacy*. Cambridge, UK: Cambridge University Press.

Shea, Patrick. 2014. "Financing Victory: Credit, Democracy, and War Outcomes." *Journal of Conflict Resolution* 58(5):771–795.

2016. "Borrowing Trouble: Sovereign Credit, Military Regimes, and Conflict." *International Interactions* 42(3):401–428.

Shea, Patrick and Paul Poast. 2018. "War and Default." *Journal of Conflict Resolution* 62(9):1876–1904.

Slantchev, Branislav. 2003. "The Principle of Convergence in Wartime Negotiations." *American Political Science Review* 47(4):621–632.

2004. "How Initiators End Their Wars: The Duration of Warfare and the Terms of Peace." *American Journal of Political Science* 48(4): 813–829.

2005. "Military Coercion in Interstate Crises." *American Political Science Review* 99(4):533–547.

2012. "Borrowed Power: Debt Finance and the Resort to Arms." *American Political Science Review* 106(4):787–809.

Smith, Alastair. 1995. "Alliance Formation and War." *International Studies Quarterly* 39(4):405–425.

1996. "Diversionary Foreign Policy in Democratic Systems." *International Studies Quarterly* 40(1):133–153.

1998. "International Crises and Domestic Politics." *American Political Science Review* 92(3):623–638.

Snyder, Glenn H. 1984. "The Security Dilemma in Alliance Politics." *World Politics* 36(4):461–495.

1997. *Alliance Politics*. Ithaca, NY: Cornell University Press.

2014. "Better Now Than Later: The Paradox of 1914 as Everyone's Favored Year for War." *International Security* 39(1):79–104.

2015. "Correspondence: Everyone's Favored Year for War – or Not?" *International Security* 39(4):208–217.

Snyder, Jack and Kier A. Lieber. 2008. "Defensive Realism and the 'New' History of World War I." *International Security* 33(1):174–194.

Snyder, Timothy. 2010. *Bloodlands: Europe between Hitler and Stalin*. New York, NY: Basic Books.

Sondhaus, Lawrence. 2011. *World War One: The Global Revolution*. New York, NY: Cambridge University Press.

2014. *The Great War at Sea*. Cambridge, UK: Cambridge University Press.

Spaniel, Wiliam and Bradley C. Smith. 2015. "Sanctions, Uncertainty, and Leader Tenure." *International Studies Quarterly* 59(4):735–749.

Spence, Michael. 1973. "Job Market Signaling." *Quarterly Journal of Economics* 87(3):355–374.

Sperber, Jonathan. 2013. *Karl Marx: A Ninetheenth-Century Life*. New York, NY: Liverlight.

Starr, Harvey. 1972. *War Coalitions: The Distributions of Payoffs and Losses*. Lexington, MA: Lexington Books.

Steinberg, Jonathan. 1966. "The Copenhagen Complex." *Journal of Contemporary History* 1(3):23–46.

Stevenson, David. 1988. *The First World War and International Politics.* New York, NY: Oxford University Press.

1996. *Armaments and the Coming of War.* New York, NY: Oxford University Press.

1997. "Militarization and Diplomacy in Europe before 1914." *International Security* 22(1):125–161.

2004. *Cataclysm: The First World War as Political Tragedy.* New York, NY: Basic Books.

2011. *With Our Backs to the Wall: Victory and Defeat in 1918.* Cambridge, MA: The Belknap Press of Harvard University Press.

2012. "The First World War and European Integration." *The International History Review* 34(4):841–863.

Stoessinger, John G. 1993. *Why Nations Go to War.* 6th ed. New York, NY: St. Martin's Press.

Strachan, Hew. 2007. *Clausewitz's On War: A Biography.* New York, NY: Grove.

2013. *The First World War.* New York, NY: Penguin.

2014. "The Origins of the First World War." *International Affairs* 90(2):429–439.

Streich, Philip and Jack S. Levy. 2016. "Information, Commitment, and the Russo-Japanese War of 1904–1905." *Foreign Policy Analysis* 12(4):489–511.

Stueck, William. 1995. *The Korean War: An International History.* Princeton, NJ: Princeton University Press.

2004. *Rethinking the Korean War.* Princeton, NJ: Princeton University Press.

Tago, Atsushi. 2007. "Why Do States Join US-Led Military Coalitions? The Compulsion of the Coalition's Missions and Legitimacy." *International Relations of the Asia-Pacific* 7(2):179–202.

Tammen, Ronald L., Jacek Kugler, Douglas Lemke, Allan C. Slam, Carole Alsharabati, Mark Andrew Abdollahian, Brian Efird, and A. F. K. Organski. 2000. *Power Transitions: Strategies for the 21st Century.* New York, NY: Chatham House.

Tannenwald, Nina. 1999. "The Nuclear Taboo: The United States and the Normative Basis of Nuclear Non-use." *International Organization* 53(3):433–468.

2005. "Stigmatizing the Bomb: Origins of the Nuclear Taboo." *International Security* 29(4):5–49.

Tareke, Gebru. 2000. "The Ethiopia-Somalia War of 1977 Revisited." *The International Journal of African Historical Studies* 33(3):635–667.

Taylor, A. J. P. 1969. *War by Time-Table: How the First World War Began.* New York, NY: American Heritage.

Thompson, William R. 2001. "Identifying Rivals and Rivalries in World Politics." *International Studies Quarterly* 45(4):557–586.

Thompson, William R. and David R. Dreyer. 2012. *Handbook of International Rivalries: 1494–2010.* Washington, DC: Congressional Quarterly Press.

Tooze, Adam. 2006. *The Wages of Destruction: The Making and Breaking of the Nazi Economy.* New York, NY: Penguin.

2014. *The Deluge: The Great War, America, and the Remaking of the Global Order, 1916–1931.* New York, NY: Viking.

Tuchman, Barbara W. 1962. *The Guns of August*. New York, NY: Macmillan.
  1985. *The Zimmermann Telegram*. New York, NY: Random House.
Van Evera, Stephen. 1984. "The Cult of the Offensive and the Origins of the First World War." *International Security* 9(1):58–107.
  1998. "Offense, Defense, and the Causes of War." *International Security* 22(4):5–43.
Vasquez, John A. 1993. *The War Puzzle*. Cambridge, UK: Cambridge University Press.
  1999. *The Power of Power Politics: From Classical Realism to Neotraditionalism*. Cambridge, UK: Cambridge University Press.
  2009. *The War Puzzle Revisited*. Cambridge, UK: Cambridge University Press.
  2014. "Was the First World War a Preventive War? Concepts, Criteria, and Evidence." In *The Outbreak of the First World War: Structure, Politics, and Decision-Making*, ed. Jack S. Levy and John A. Vasquez. Cambridge, UK: Cambridge University Press, pp. 199–226.
Voeten, Erik. 2001. "Outside Options and the Logic of Security Council Action." *American Political Science Review* 95(4):845–858.
  2005. "The Political Origins of the UN Security Council's Ability to Legitimize the Use of Force." *International Organization* 59:527–557.
Vucetic, Srdjan. 2011a. *The Anglosphere: A Genealogy of Racialized Identity in International Relations*. Stanford, CA: Stanford University Press.
  2011b. "Bound to Follow? The Anglosphere and US-Led Coalitions of the Willing, 1950–2001." *European Journal of International Relations* 17(1): 27–49.
Wada, Haruki. 2013. *The Korean War: An International History*. New York, NY: Rowman and Littlefield.
Wagner, R. Harrison. 2000. "Bargaining and War." *American Journal of Political Science* 44(3):469–484.
  2001. "Who's Afraid of Rational Choice Theory?" Typescript, University of Texas at Austin.
  2007. *War and the State: The Theory of International Politics*. Ann Arbor, MI: The University of Michigan Press.
Walter, Barbara F. 1997. "The Critical Barrier to Civil War Settlement." *International Organization* 51(3):335–364.
  2002. *Committing to Peace: The Successful Settlement of Civil Wars*. Princeton, NJ: Princeton University Press.
Waltz, Kenneth. 1979. *Theory of International Politics*. Reading, MA: Addison-Wesley.
Ward, Michael D. 1982. *Research Gaps in Alliance Dynamics*. Vol. 19 of Monograph Series in World Affairs. Denver, CO: Graduate School of International Studies, University of Denver.
Watson, Alexander. 2014. *Ring of Steel: Germany and Austria-Hungary in World War I*. New York, NY: Basic Books.
Watson, Joel. 2013. *Strategy: An Introduction to Game Theory*. 3rd ed. New York, NY: W. W. Norton.
Weeks, Jessica L. 2008. "Autocratic Audience Costs: Regime Type and Signaling Resolve." *International Organization* 62(1):35–64.

Weisiger, Alex. 2013. *Logics of War: Explanations for Limited and Unlimited Conflicts.* Ithaca, NY: Cornell University Press.

2016. "Learning from the Battlefield: Information, Domestic Politics, and Interstate War Duration." *International Organization* 70(2):347–375.

Weitsman, Patricia A. 2003. "Alliance Cohesion and Coalition Warfare: The Central Powers and Triple Entente." *Security Studies* 12(3):79–113.

2004. *Dangerous Alliances: Proponents of Peace, Weapons of War.* Stanford, CA: Stanford University Press.

Wells, H. G. 1922. *The Outline of History: Being a Plain History of Life and Mankind.* Vol. 4. 4th ed. New York, NY: Macmillan.

Wendt, Alexander. 1992. "Anarchy Is What States Make of It: The Social Construction of Power Politics." *International Organization* 46(2):391–425.

Werner, Suzanne. 1999. "The Precarious Nature of Peace: Resolving the Issues, Enforcing the Settlement, and Renegotiating the Terms." *American Journal of Political Science* 43(3):912–934.

2000. "Deterring Intervention: The Stakes of War and Third-Party Involvement." *American Journal of Political Science* 44(4):720–732.

Werner, Suzanne and Amy Yuen. 2005. "Making and Keeping Peace." *International Organization* 59(2):261–292.

Wilkenfeld, Jonathan and Michael Brecher. 2010. *International Crisis Behavior Project.* Vol. 10. ICPSR Study #9286. Available at www.icb.umd.edu/data/icb %20version%2010%20release%20memo.pdf.

Williamson, Samuel R., Jr. 2014. "July 1914 Revisited and Revised: The Erosion of the German Paradigm." In *The Outbreak of the First World War: Structure, Politics, and Decision-Making*, ed. Jack S. Levy and John A. Vasquez. Cambridge, UK: Cambridge University Press, pp. 30–64.

Winter, Jay, ed. 2014. *The Cambridge History of the First World War.* Cambridge, UK: Cambridge University Press.

Wittman, Donald. 1979. "How a War Ends: A Rational Model Approach." *Journal of Conflict Resolution* 23(4):743–763.

Wolford, Scott. 2007. "The Turnover Trap: New Leaders, Reputation, and International Conflict." *American Journal of Political Science* 51(4):772–788.

2012. "Incumbents, Successors, and Crisis Bargaining: Leadership Turnover as a Commitment Problem." *Journal of Peace Research* 49(4):517–530.

2015. *The Politics of Military Coalitions.* New York, NY: Cambridge University Press.

2017. "The Problem of Shared Victory: War-Winning Coalitions and Postwar Peace." *Journal of Politics* 79(2):702–716.

2018. "Wars of Succession." *International Interactions* 44(1):173–187.

N.d. "Making Multilateral Peace." Typescript, University of Texas at Austin.

Wolford, Scott and Emily Hencken Ritter. 2016. "National Leaders, Political Security, and the Formation of Military Coalitions." *International Studies Quarterly* 60(3):540–551.

Wolford, Scott, Dan Reiter, and Clifford J. Carrubba. 2011. "Information, Commitment, and War." *Journal of Conflict Resolution* 55(4):556–579.

Wu, Cathy Xuanxuan and Scott Wolford. Forthcoming. "Leaders, States, and Reputations." *Journal of Conflict Resolution*.

Wylie, Neville, ed. 2002. *European Neutrals and Non-belligerents during the Second World War*. Cambridge, UK: Cambridge University Press.

Xu, Guoqi. 2017. *Asia and the Great War: A Shared History*. New York, NY: Oxford University Press.

Yuen, Amy. 2009. "Target Concessions in the Shadow of Intervention." *Journal of Conflict Resolution* 53(5):727–744.

Zagare, Frank C. 2011. *The Games of July: Explaining the Great War*. Ann Arbor, MI: University of Michigan Press.

Zielinski, Rosella Cappella. 2016. *How States Pay for Wars*. Ithaca, NY: Cornell University Press.

Zinnes, Dina A. 1980. "Three Puzzles in Search of a Researcher: Presidential Address." *International Studies Quarterly* 24(3):315–342.

Zuber, Terence. 1999. "The Schlieffen Plan Reconsidered." *War in History* 6(3):262–305.

Index